Soviet
Political
Dynamics

Soviet Political Dynamics

DEVELOPMENT OF THE FIRST LENINIST POLITY

Philip G. Roeder
University of California, San Diego

HARPER & ROW, PUBLISHERS, New York
Cambridge, Philadelphia, San Francisco, Washington,
London, Mexico City, São Paulo, Singapore, Sydney

Sponsoring Editors: Robert Miller/Lauren Silverman
Project Coordination: Michael Bass & Associates
Cover Design: Lucy Krikorian
Cover Photo: Philip Roeder
Text Art: Precision Graphics
Compositor: Modern Type & Design
Printer and Binder: R. R. Donnelley & Sons Company
Cover Printer: Lynn Art

Introduction and Part III photo from Sovfoto

Soviet Political Dynamics: Development of the First Leninist Polity

Library of Congress Cataloging-in-Publication Data

Roeder, Philip G.
    Soviet political dynamics.

    Includes index.
    1. Soviet Union--Politics and government--1917-
I. Title.
DK266.R593 1988   947.084'1   87-33437
ISBN 0-06-045555-1

87 88 89 90   9 8 7 6 5 4 3 2 1

Contents

Preface

Few political and social systems pose as many analytic puzzles for people in the West as the Soviet Union. For example, do the Soviet people really support their regime? Or is the Soviet system held together only by the terror of totalitarian autocracy? Have the Soviet leaders abandoned the practices of Stalin since 1953? If so, can we really use the Western term "pluralism" to describe the Soviet polity today? Have the Soviets been successful in their efforts to sustain economic growth and to engineer equality? Or will the faltering performance of the Soviet regime threaten its long-term stability?

These and other questions are important to the West, for the Soviet Union remains our most important competitor for power and influence around the world. Knowledge of its strengths and weaknesses is essential to our success in this competition. In addition, the Soviet Union has been a model for many other societies that might be labelled "Soviet-style" or Leninist polities; and our assessments of the Soviet record can help us to gauge the possibilities and limitations of these other polities. And in a still larger sense, as an alternative to the Western liberal-democratic model, the Soviet record helps us to understand our own political experience more clearly—what is unique, what is not—and to appreciate our very real successes and limitations.

Answering the important questions about the Soviet Union is a difficult problem, for information is often withheld from us. Nonetheless, Sovietology in the West has produced a community of resourceful scholars who have been able to peel away the layers of secrecy surrounding Soviet society. These scholars have not agreed in their answers to many of the most fundamental questions about the Soviet experience. Yet, their debates should be recognized as signs of the continued health of Western Sovietology.

This book grew from lectures that I gave over the past few years at the University of New Mexico. By their responses, my students—who have been a joy to teach—urged me to commit those lectures to paper. In the lectures I attempted to inspire in my students a love of scholarly inquiry—a desire to grapple with the puzzles of Sovietology. I have also attempted to impart to them a respect for scholarly disagreement and debate. These remain central objectives of this text.

In this text I have attempted to provide comprehensive coverage of the following topics: historical development and ideology; socialization, political culture, and participation; all-union and local policymaking institutions; a range of policy outputs, including economic, justice, nationalities, and national security policies; and speculation about the Soviet future. The presentation of topics is a conventional one in the study of comparative politics—first, historical and ideological background, and then "input" processes, policy making, and policy outputs. This presentation facilitates comparisons with other political systems and integration of this text into comparative courses. Yet, I have endeavored to divide chapters and subsections in such a way that the instructor preferring a different order of topics will find this text flexible and equally attractive.

In this text I have sought to provide some order and integration to the rich and diverse literature of Sovietology. The "classics" as well as the results of recent research in the field play an important role in this text. I have supplemented these with up-to-date material from my own research where appropriate. The approach in this test is analytical rather than simply descriptive, although there is also extensive description of institutions to provide students with a factual basis to evaluate analysis.

The analytic approach taken here is developmental. I argue vigorously in these pages that the Soviet Union has been a rapidly changing society that should be understood against the background of the problems of modernization and development. But I also have sought to give a "fair hearing" to the wide variety of views about the Soviet Union. In short, my purpose is not to "sell" a single point of view, but to acquaint students with the questions posed by the study of Soviet politics, the ways in which we have sought to answer those questions, and the richness in the diversity of our answers.

My debts in writing this book are many. Marianne J. Russell and Robert Miller of Harper & Row as well as Ellen Silge and Michael Bass of Michael Bass and Associates were instrumental in bringing this manuscript to print. My intellectual debts to the fine scholarship of many Sovietologists are acknowledged throughout this text. In particular, I owe many thanks to Darrell P. Hammer, Indiana University; David Williams, Ohio University; Rolf H. W. Theen, Purdue University; and Anthony T. Bouscaren, LeMoyne College, who reviewed this text for Harper & Row. An author could not ask for reviewers who were more knowledgeable, careful, and constructive.

Many students deserve much credit for helping to bring this text to completion. Robin A. Jones typed the manuscript and encouraged me with praise, even though she and I realized that the early draft of this manuscript was often less than inspired. Robert A. Brenden, Charles S. Bibbs, and Mark C. Petersen all read parts of this manuscript to offer a student's perspective; all three of these students, and Mark in particular, gave much of their time to offer constructive criticism and encouragement. George Rutherford provided several of the photographs reproduced in this book. And, of course, there are many other students—Donna, Gary, Gerald, Jon, Martha, Robin, Sandy, Tim, and dozens others—who have sustained me in the classroom and thus made this book possible. It is to these students that this book is dedicated.

Philip G. Roeder

Introduction: Why Study Soviet Politics?

Moscow, November 7, 1985

Although you are probably beginning to read this as an assignment in a college course, let me attempt to convince you that knowledge of Soviet domestic affairs is not simply a matter of academic significance. It has had and continues to have immense practical importance to Americans both as leaders and as citizens. The most dramatic cases of this are critical foreign policy decisions in which the United States must respond to Soviet action. Let us consider three examples of such decisions.

CUBAN MISSILE CRISIS
Washington, D.C., October 27, 1962

It is Saturday morning at the height of the Cuban Missile Crisis.[1] President John F. Kennedy has before him two very different messages from the Soviet Union, each responding to the U.S. blockade of Cuba announced on Monday. The first message arrived on Friday. Although it is officially a missive from the Soviet First Secretary and Chairman of the Council of Ministers Nikita S. Khrushchev, it is a personal letter that seems to be stamped with Khrushchev's own style. It is long, rambling, and even emotional at points. In this letter Khrushchev tells the President that the Soviet Union will remove its missiles from Cuba if the United States ends its blockade and pledges not to invade the island nation.

But the second letter has just arrived. Although it is also an official letter from the First Secretary, it is a far more formal document. It appears to have been approved by a large number of government officials before being dispatched by the Foreign Ministry.

In this second letter Khrushchev has upped the ante: For the Soviet Union to withdraw its missiles from Cuba, the United States must not only end the blockade and pledge not to invade Cuba, but also withdraw American missiles from Turkey.

The quandary that President Kennedy faces is this: To which of these two offers should he respond? What is the "true" Soviet position? And why has he received the two contradictory messages? The President's answers to these questions depend in part on which of two alternative explanations for the change in positions he accepts. One interpretation is that Khrushchev was overruled between Friday and Saturday—that the first letter reflects his personal position, but the second is a letter that his colleagues on the Politburo forced him to send. The problem with this interpretation is that many analysts believe Khrushchev is firmly in control and makes policy without having to clear it with his colleagues on the Politburo. A second interpretation is that Khrushchev simply changed his mind. This seems implausible, however, for Khrushchev has proven to be an artful negotiator up to this crisis; he must know that when he first offers a weak position and then "ups" his demands his adversaries will realize the weaker position is a compromise that may be acceptable to him. It is poor negotiating strategy to tip your hand in this way. For the President and the nation, the proper resolution to the quandary is essential. If he responds to the wrong memorandum, valuable time will be lost and the crisis may escalate beyond control.

THE DOWNING OF KAL-007
Washington, D.C., September 2, 1983

The National Security Council (NSC) is meeting to consider the American response to the news that on September 1, at about 5:08 A.M. Vladivostok time, a Korean airliner was shot down in Soviet airspace.[2] En route from New York to Seoul, the airliner, after having stopped in Alaska, strayed over Soviet territory. For about two and a half hours it traveled along a path that led first across the Sea of Okhotsk and then over Sakhalin Island. When it cleared Sakhalin and appeared to be bound for Vladivostok, a Soviet pilot shot it down, killing all 269 people on board.

The question facing Washington the next day is this: Why did the Soviet Union shoot down this commercial airliner? Four very different explanations are being offered, with very different implications for the United States and its policy response. The possibilities suggested are assassination, high-level foreign policy decisions, low-level regional reactions, and bureaucratic blunders. One explanation proferred is that the Soviets had only a narrow and immediate purpose: They wanted to kill someone on board KAL-007. Congressman McDonald of Georgia was a passenger on the airliner; as president of the John Birch Society he had been a prominent champion of anti-Soviet causes. Some in Washington are arguing that the Soviet action was designed to eliminate him. Yet, this is not an entirely satisfactory explanation, for if assassination was the Soviet objective, there would have been far simpler means to achieve it.

Another answer being offered in the capital is that the Soviet leadership was trying to send a message to the United States and other nations—perhaps to reaffirm the Soviet commitment to defend its borders in the Far East. Two countries challenge Soviet borders in the region: Japan claims four of the Kurile islands held by the Soviet Union and China claims major portions of the Soviet Far East purportedly seized unfairly by the Russian Empire in previous centuries. Or the Soviet Union may have been using the Korean airline incident to reinforce its commitment not in the Far East, but in Central Europe and the North Atlantic region. Having been frustrated in its efforts to forestall American missile deployments in Europe, the Soviet Union may have used this opportunity in the Far East to demonstrate that it could stand tough against the West and was beginning a new, more aggressive foreign policy.

Yet, explanations suggesting that the Soviet Union had some larger purpose in the downing of KAL-007 seem inadequate. Most importantly, the downing risked sacrifice of Andropov's recent foreign policy successes. Soviet Deputy Foreign Minister Mikhail Kapitsa had just been sent to China to reopen negotiations. A long-term agreement for grain purchases had just been signed with the United States. Andropov had even partially succeeded in distancing Western Europe from the United States by portraying the Soviet Union as a peace-loving, nonaggressive state. The airline incident could only jeopardize these gains.

In succeeding weeks, doubts about these explanations would grow in proportion to the maladroit handling of public relations by the Soviets. Andropov failed to comment on the incident for at least 28 days. Other official explanations were slow in coming and often inconsistent. By changing their story, the Soviet commentators made it appear that the leadership in Moscow did not initially know exactly what had happened in the Far East and had to change their rationalizations to cover themselves as more information became available.

Thus, some analysts suggest that the decision to shoot down KAL-007 was not a high-level policy choice but a local reaction initiated in Khabarovsk. In fact, Soviet Chief of Staff Marshal Nikolai V. Ogarkov claimed that the commander of the Far Eastern Military District, General Vladimir L. Govorov, had personally ordered the plane shot down. If so, why would General Govorov have made such a decision? He may simply have been following standard operating procedure—the general was under orders since a similar incident in 1978 to shoot down any such airliner in Soviet airspace that does not respond properly to Soviet instructions. Or the explanation may be found in the commander's personal motives. General Govorov, as the son of a hero of the defense of Leningrad, may have acted under the pressure to live up to the example of his father. Or Govorov may have been driven simply by a desire to save his own neck, knowing what had happened to the officers who had not reacted swiftly to the Korean airline incursion into Soviet airspace near Murmansk in 1978.

Yet explanations that focus on decisions made at the local level are not entirely convincing, since we are not at all certain that regional commanders make such decisions. Even though a 1978 Soviet law states that regional commanders have this authority, much evidence, such as the high level of centralization in decision making and recurring Soviet complaints about the unwillingness of military officers to take initiative, casts doubt on such explanations.

Lastly, another group of analysts is arguing that the answer lies somewhere other than the Politburo in Moscow or the commanding officer in Khabarovsk—that is, in either a failure of or the internal politics of the immense Soviet bureaucracy. For example, the decision to shoot the airliner, whether made by a high-level official or a regional commander, may have been based on the erroneous intelligence report that KAL-007 was not a commercial Boeing 747, but an RC-135 spy plane. Or the action may have been taken by military leaders intent on sabotaging Andropov's rapprochement with the West. These leaders may have believed that they could win more money for the military by sabotaging détente; the strategy had worked in 1960 and in 1964—why not in 1983?

The question of Soviet intentions is important to Washington and the American people, because the success of the National Security Council's response will in part depend on a proper "reading" of these purposes. If the reason for the airline disaster lies in something other than bureaucratic failings or individual reactions, our policy must address the issues. For example, if the downing of KAL-007 signals a shift to a more aggressive Soviet foreign policy, the NSC must be prepared to respond quickly.

THE SOVIET ATTITUDE TOWARD WAR

For well over two decades American strategic planners have struggled with a grisly question: Does the Soviet Union think it can fight and win a thermonuclear war? There is conflicting evidence from Soviet writings and public statements. Soviet Marshal Vasilii Sokolovskii, chief author of *Military Strategy,* wrote in the third edition:

> In its political and social essence, a new world war will be a decisive armed clash between two opposed world social systems. This war will naturally end in victory for the progressive Communist social-economic system over the reactionary capitalist social-economic system, which is historically doomed to destruction.[3]

Similarly, Marshal Nikolai I. Krylov, Commander-in-Chief of the Soviet Strategic Rocket Forces, wrote in the newspaper *Sovetskaia Rossiia:*

> Imperialist ideologues try to lull the vigilance of the peoples of the world, resorting to propagandistic deceptions to the effect that in a future thermonuclear war it would not be possible to be victorious. These lies are contradicted by the objective laws of history. . . . Victory in a war, if the imperialists dare to unleash it, would go to world socialism and all progressive humanity.[4]

While both of these military leaders make it quite clear that they believe victory is possible, Major General Nikolai Talenskii, in contrast, has written:

> In our day there is no more dangerous illusion than the idea that thermonuclear war can still serve as an instrument of politics, that it is possible to achieve political aims by using nuclear weapons and still survive.[5]

And in 1979, *Izvestiia's* commentator Aleksandr Bovin wrote:

> . . . the consequences of such a war would be a catastrophe for mankind, and in the current situation the one to risk making a first nuclear strike would inevitably be doomed to destruction by the forces available for a retaliatory strike.[6]

Their boss, General Secretary Leonid I. Brezhnev, seemed to endorse this view in 1974 when he said, "In recent years such a mass of weapons has been accumulated that it makes possible the destruction of all life several times over."[7] He was repeating the dogma introduced by Khrushchev that it would not be possible to build communism on radioactive rubble.

The puzzle that continues to haunt us in the West to this day is whom we should believe. What do the Soviets really think about the prospects of winning a thermonuclear war? One view, publicized widely by Harvard University historian Richard Pipes, is that the Soviets believe exactly what they say—that they can fight and win a nuclear war. Another posits the opposite position that the Soviets believe exactly what they say—that no one will win a thermonuclear war. Both sides support their respective interpretations by quoting public statements and writings of key Soviet officials and claiming that the contradictory evidence cited by their critics is either propaganda or pure bluff.

The outcome of the American debate over Soviet military policy will influence the way in which we seek to deter nuclear war. If the Soviets believe superpower nuclear war will bring mutual destruction, American strategic weapons procurements to deter such a war may need only to ensure that we have a survivable retaliatory capability to inflict unacceptable damage on the Soviet Union. If the Soviets believe such a war can be won, deterrence may well become the far more difficult task of convincing them that they actually will not be able to prevail militarily in a third world war.

SHAPING A RESPONSE TO SOVIET ACTIONS

In each of the three cases described, the problem is essentially the same: How do we reconcile contradictory evidence and signals from the Soviet Union? Specifically, how do we construct a coherent picture of Soviet intentions? And how do we respond? In these cases critical policy choices hinge on the answers to these questions: To which of the two Soviet memoranda on the Cuban missiles should we respond? How should we respond to the Korean airline incident? Should our efforts to deter superpower nuclear war seek to deny the Soviet Union the ability to prevail in such a conflict?

Answering questions such as these requires knowledge of the domestic policies and practices of the Soviet Union. Official Soviet ideology, for example, may contain clues to Soviet intentions or even to Soviet military and foreign policy aims. But knowledge of Soviet political culture may be even more important, for actual political beliefs and political activity, such as individual willingness to take initiative, may diverge from prescribed dogmas. The structure of Soviet institutions and the processes by which political actors come together to make policy may contain a key to unraveling Soviet "intentions," for we must first know who made a decision before we can begin to impute motives. And Soviet policies themselves—their successes and failures—give us an appreciation of the actual modes of Soviet behavior and the performance of the Soviet system.

These three topics—political culture and participation, institutions and policy processes, and policies and performance—occupy most of this text. Part 2 of this text addresses the first of these (socialization, political culture, and citizen involvement in politics); Part 3 addresses the second (Party, state, and political processes); and Part 4 the last (policy and performance). This ordering of materials corresponds to the most common paradigm in the study of comparative politics, which distinguishes political inputs, decision making, and outputs. While not forcing the analysis of Soviet politics into any one of the more rigorous models within this broad paradigm, this organization of materials should promote comparisons of the Soviet with other polities.

Analysis of these topics is inevitably filled with (and enlivened by) controversies. The frequent paucity of evidence as well as the emotion-charged nature of some issues has given rise to a healthy diversity of opinions in the field of Sovietology. The text presents not only significant recent research into these questions, but also the most important of the competing interpretations of Soviet affairs, permitting each a "fair hearing." The author's own views, when they are introduced, are clearly labeled as such.

Analysis of these topics is also historically contingent; that is, the answers to questions about the place of the citizen in Soviet politics, about policy-making processes, and about policy performance will differ significantly with the period analyzed. Indeed, a central theme of the following chapters is that one should consider the Soviet polity since 1917 as a rapidly developing political system, addressing many of the same problems confronted by less-developed countries (LDCs) of the Third World, and that the Soviet experiment should be analyzed as a deliberate attempt to formulate an alternative path of development to that taken by the industrialized societies of the North Atlantic region. To this end, the first part of this text discusses the society over which Vladimir I. Lenin and his Bolsheviks took power in 1917 and their views on the country's transformation and future. It also presents a chronology of the actual transformation of that society during 70 years of Soviet rule. The text's conclusion speculates about Russia's future.

NOTES

1. Robert F. Kennedy, *Thirteen Days* (New York: Norton, 1969), 85–99.
2. *New York Times,* 2 September 1983; Alexander Dallin, *Black Box: KAL 007 and the Superpowers* (Berkeley, Calif.: University of California Press, 1985); Seymour M. Hersh, *The Target Is Destroyed* (New York: Random House, 1986); Eric Anthony Jones, "Graham Allison's Conceptual Models and the 1983 Korean Airline Incident" (Paper presented at the Annual Meeting of the Western Political Science Association, Las Vegas, Nev., 28–30 March 1985).
3. Vasilii D. Sokolovskiy, *Soviet Military Strategy,* 3d ed., ed. Harriet Fast Scott (New York: Crane Russak & Company, 1975), 208–209.
4. Nikolai I. Krylov, "Pouchitel'nye uroki istorii," *Sovetskaia Rossiia,* 30 August 1969.
5. Quoted in Raymond L. Garthoff, "Mutual Deterrence, Parity and Strategic Arms Limitation in Soviet Policy," in *Soviet Military Thinking,* ed. Derek Leebaert (London: Allen & Unwin, 1981), 94.
6. Quoted in Garthoff, 96.
7. *Pravda,* 22 July 1974.

one

ROOTS OF THE CONTEMPORARY SOVIET REGIME

Vladimir Ilich Lenin (1870–1924)
Joseph Vissarionovich Stalin (1879–1953)
Nikita Sergeevich Khrushchev (1894–1971)

Leonid Ilich Brezhnev (1906–1982)   Konstantin Ustinovich Chernenko (1911–1985)
Iurii Vladimirovich Andropov (1914–1984)   Mikhail Sergeevich Gorbachev (1931–   )

Change has been central to the Soviet experience in its first 70 years. Created within a society that can be called the first *less-developed country (LDC)*, the Soviet regime has sought to transform that country and build the first socialist and communist societies. Thus, to understand the contemporary Soviet system it is necessary to have some acquaintance with its historical antecedents, the image of the future that the Soviet leaders have brought with them to the seats of power, and the history of development that has transformed the society they inherited.

Central to the dilemma of many LDCs like Russia before the October Revolution is the desire among significant parts of the population to enjoy the fruits of modernity without the many social ills experienced during modernization in the industrialized countries of the West. As Paul E. Sigmund observed over two decades ago,

> In their drive toward industrialization, the modernizing nationalists are not prepared to follow the model of the United States, the European nations, or Japan, each of which achieved economic development under private auspices. The nationalist leaders, [with some exceptions], are in agreement in rejecting the capitalist method of development as slow, inefficient, and unsuited to their conditions.[1]

The Bolshevik leaders of the Soviet Union were among the first leaders to reject the capitalist path. And in the subsequent seven decades of transforming their society by alternative means they created what has been called the Soviet model of development.

It is currently something of a verity in the United States that this Soviet model of development has lost its appeal in the world. Yet nothing could be further from the truth. At the beginning of 1987, at least 23 countries were ruled by regimes that

Table 1   RULING MARXIST-LENINIST REGIMES, 1987

	Europe	Asia	Africa	Americas
Autochthonous Regimes	USSR Yugoslavia Albania	China Vietnam Afghanistan Kampuchea Laos PDR Yemen	Angola Benin Congo Ethiopia Mozambique	Cuba
Imposed Regimes	Bulgaria Czechoslovakia German D. R. Hungary Poland Romania	Mongolia Korean DPR		
Marginal Regimes			Cape Verde Guinea-Bissau Madagascar Somalia*	Guyana Nicaragua Chile* Grenada*

*Historical cases: Chile, 1970–73, Grenada, 1979–83, and Somalia, 1969–77.

claimed to have adopted Marxism-Leninism as their official guide to revolutionary transformation.[2] (See Table 1.) (In another five countries, labeled "Marginal Regimes" in the table, the regimes have periodically, but not consistently, claimed to be led by Marxism-Leninism.) Only a minority of these regimes were initially imposed on their societies by Soviet arms; the majority claimed power through domestic revolutions, coups, or wars of national liberation. Moreover, among the 15 autochthonous Marxist-Leninist regimes, the majority have come to power since the mid-60s and over a third since the mid-70s. The Soviet Union, as the first of these Leninist polities, pioneered the developmental path upon which they have embarked. Although they may disagree with the current Soviet leadership about many specific policies, they share a common commitment to a developmental model that originated in the Soviet experience. Thus, for this reason, as well as for understanding the contemporary Soviet polity, familiarity with the Soviet model of development is important to us.

FOR FURTHER READING

For those students who wish to read further on the topics covered in the next three chapters, the following works may be particularly useful.

Besancon, Alain. 1976. *The Soviet Syndrome.* New York: Harcourt Brace Jovanovich.

Breslauer, George. 1982. *Khrushchev and Brezhnev as Leaders: Building Authority in Soviet Politics.* London: Allen & Unwin.

Carew Hunt, R. N. 1961. *The Theory and Practice of Communism.* New York: Macmillan.

Carr, E. H. 1950–1972. *A History of Soviet Russia,* 9 vols. New York: Macmillan.

Chamberlin, William H. 1952. *The Russian Revolution, 1917–1921,* 2 vols. New York: Macmillan.

Conquest, Robert. 1968. *The Great Terror: Stalin's Purge of the Thirties.* New York: Macmillan.

Crankshaw, Edward. 1966. *Khrushchev: A Career.* New York: Viking Press.

Daniels, Robert V. 1967. *Red October: The Bolshevik Revolution of 1917.* New York: Scribner.

Deutscher, Isaac. 1949. *Stalin: A Political Biography.* New York: Oxford University Press.

Dmytryshyn, Basil. 1978. *USSR: A Concise History,* 3d ed. New York: Scribner.

Domberg, John. 1974. *Brezhnev: The Masks of Power.* New York: Basic Books.

Fischer, Louis. 1964. *The Life of Lenin.* New York: Harper & Row.

Gilison, Jerome M. 1975. *The Soviet Image of Utopia.* Baltimore, Md.: Johns Hopkins University Press.

Haimson, Leopold H. 1965. *The Russian Marxists and the Origins of Bolshevism.* Cambridge, Mass.: Harvard University Press.

Hosking, Geoffrey. 1985. *The First Socialist Society: A History of the Soviet Union from Within.* Cambridge, Mass.: Harvard University Press.

Keep, J. L. H. 1963. *The Rise of Social Democracy in Russia.* New York: Oxford University Press.

Lewin, Moshe. 1968. *Russian Peasants and Soviet Power: A Study of Collectivization.* London: Allen & Unwin.

Medvedev, Roy and Zhores Medvedev. 1977. *Khrushchev: The Years in Power.* New York: Columbia University Press.

Meyer, Alfred G. 1957. *Leninism.* Cambridge, Mass.: Harvard University Press.

———. 1984. *Communism,* 4th ed. New York: Random House.

Nove, Alec. 1982. *An Economic History of the USSR.* New York: Penguin Books.

Pipes, Richard. 1974. *Russia Under the Old Regime.* New York: Scribner.

Riasanovsky, Nicholas V. 1984. *A History of Russia,* 4th ed. New York: Oxford University Press.

Scanlan, James P. 1985. *Marxism in the USSR: A Critical Survey of Current Soviet Thought.* Ithaca, N.Y.: Cornell University Press.

Schapiro, Leonard. 1955. *The Origins of the Communist Autocracy.* Cambridge, Mass.: Harvard University Press.

———. 1971. *The Communist Party of the Soviet Union,* 2d ed. New York: Random House.

Seroka, James and Maurice D. Simon, eds. 1982. *Developed Socialism in the Soviet Bloc: Political Theory and Political Reality.* Boulder, Colo.: Westview Press.

Tucker, Robert C. 1969. *The Marxian Revolutionary Idea.* New York: Norton.

Ulam, Adam B. 1965. *The Bolsheviks.* New York: Macmillan.

———. 1974. *Stalin: The Man and His Era.* New York: Viking Press.

Wolfe, Bertram D. 1964. *Three Who Made a Revolution,* 4th ed. New York: Dial Press.

NOTES

1. Paul E. Sigmund, *The Ideologies of the Developing Nations* (New York: Praeger, 1963), 12.
2. Philip G. Roeder, "CMEA and the New Marxist-Leninist States" (Paper presented at the Annual Meeting of the American Political Science Association, New Orleans, August 30–September 2, 1984).

chapter *1*

The First LDC:
The Road to Revolution

The day after the Bolsheviks stormed the Winter Palace and placed the remaining ministers of the Provisional Government under arrest, Vladimir I. Lenin, leader of the new regime, addressed the Second All-Russian Congress of Soviets. After the prolonged and stormy ovation that greeted him subsided, Lenin began his report on the Bolsheviks' plans for Russia. He opened with the simple commitment, "We shall now proceed to construct the socialist order."[1]

THE NATURE OF RUSSIAN SOCIETY IN 1917: CRISES OF DEVELOPMENT

It is one of the ironies of the Russian Revolution that the Bolsheviks came to power in 1917 with the objective of building a postindustrial society but quickly found that they confronted the task of simply dragging Russia into the twentieth century. The society they inherited from the previous rulers of Russia was hopelessly antiquated. The country was vast in its size and population and incredibly rich in its natural and human resources, but most of its wealth was untouched. The country was not a modern nation-state but a multiethnic empire. And the Russian social structure was still semifeudal. The economy was preindustrial in its productive methods and, as a result, kept much of its population in grinding poverty. The society they inherited had been ruled by antiquated political institutions. Since most of these had collapsed by late 1917, the Bolsheviks stepped into a near political vacuum.

Geography

Russian society in 1917 was a reflection in part of her geography.[2] The Russian Empire was the largest country in the world, occupying over two-fifths of the total land area of Europe and Asia and one-sixth of the world's land surface. This territory of over 8.6 million square miles was about two and a half times the size of the United States and its dependencies. In fact, it would have been possible to fit all of North America within the borders of the Russian Empire.

The Empire was not simply a vast, empty stretch of territory, however. It contained an incredible wealth of natural resources. Russia could be self-sufficient in the most important resources needed to support modern industry, but before the Revolution the natural resources were poorly developed. For example, the rivers of the Russian Empire could make the country self-sufficient in hydroelectric power. Yet, while total hydroelectric production today is about 70 percent that of the United States, before the Revolution it was less than 10 percent. At the time of the Revolution Russia possessed roughly half of the reserves of coking coal on the face of the earth—it is estimated that the Soviets today have enough coal reserves to sustain current production levels for 500 years into the future. Before 1917, however, those vast coal resources were little developed. In fact, in 1913 Russian coal production was less than one-tenth that of Britain. In addition to these energy resources, Russia had abundant supplies of metals essential to early industrialization. For example, the country possessed about half of the world's iron ore reserves and as much as 80 percent of such ferro-alloys as manganese. Yet Russia's pig iron and steel production before the Revolution was only half that of the United Kingdom.

The far-flung geography complicated the task of economic development. While nature had indeed bestowed immense wealth on the Russian Empire, it had played a cruel hoax by placing much of it beyond easy reach. The natural resources were often located in regions remote from population centers and in areas with harsh climates, increasing transportation, development, and production costs. The extraordinary effort needed to exploit these resources placed a special burden on any regime that ruled the Russian Empire and wanted to develop industrial self-sufficiency.

An additional, even more serious consequence of geography was what students of political development call a *crisis of penetration*—that is, extending "control to the more inaccessible parts of the national territory."[3] The immense size of the country threatened to overtax the administrative and control capabilities of any new regime, with the threat of either collapse at the center or piecemeal dismemberment at the periphery. The absence of defensible borders, particularly in the West, and the difficulty of defending regions remote from the capital, particularly in the Asian parts of the Empire, complicated the crisis of penetration by making it a crisis not only of domestic political development, but also of foreign policy.

Cultural Diversity

The Bolsheviks inherited with the vast land an unusually diverse population, which comprised over 100 different nationalities.[4] The Russians (sometimes called the "Great Russians") were a minority in their own country, constituting less than 45 percent of the total population. Other Slavs, ethnically related to the Russians (e.g., Ukrainians, Belorussians, Poles), made up another third of the population. The non-Slavs that accounted for the remaining quarter of the Empire's population came from diverse cultural, religious, and linguistic traditions.

The Empire was not an immigrant society. Its ethnic minorities were not hyphenated Russians. Most lived in their ancestral homelands; some had been conquered by the Tsarist government only recently. The Empire included most of its European regions and Siberia before 1800; the century before the revolution saw the addition of non-Russian territories and peoples on the periphery. The western borders were stabilized a century before the Revolution with the addition of Finland from Sweden (1809), Moldavia from the Ottoman Empire (1812), and the Polish Grand Duchy of Warsaw (1815). The border in the Caucasus was stabilized at about the same time with the annexation of the Kingdom of Georgia (1801) and later the Persian territories of Armenia and Azerbaidjan (1828); but consolidation of Russian control in the Caucasus came only after another four decades of warfare against local opposition that ended just a half century before the Revolution. The Central Asian peoples were added still later with the addition of Kazakhstan (1850) and then the conquest of the independent khanates in Tashkent (1865), Bukhara and Samarkand (1868), and Turkmenistan (1888). The control of these border regions remained tenuous, leading the Tsarist government (and the early Bolshevik regime that followed it) to accord special status to some people (e.g., Finland and the "protectorates" in Central Asia) that diluted their integration within the Empire.

As these peoples developed national consciousness, many came to resent Russian rule, wanting their own indigenous or independent governments.[5] National identity among the major European peoples had made a significant advance in the 1820s, as the Romantics' interest in their own languages and national histories fed a new cultural nationalism, often expressed in a rush of writings in the vernacular such as the Ukrainian poetry of Taras Shevchenko. The popular base of these incipient national movements was broadened as the Populists of the 1860s and 1870s made contact with the peasantry. And the movements began to take on organizational structure around 1900 with the establishment of political parties, such as the Revolutionary Ukrainian Party. Among the Asian populations the national awakening came somewhat later. For the Turks it began in the Crimea in the 1880s, with the first organized parties appearing only a decade before the October Revolution. The problem facing the Bolsheviks, or any successor to the Empire, was to keep these people from proclaiming their independence and setting up separate states.

The problem of holding the Empire together was aggravated by the fact that these people of diverse cultural traditions were at very different stages of development. The Latvians, for example, were more urbanized and industrialized. According to the 1897 census, 16 percent lived in cities, and only about 70 percent were engaged in agriculture and animal husbandry. At the opposite extreme, only 1 percent of the Kirgiz people of Central Asia lived in cities, and over 95 percent of them made their living from agriculture or animal husbandry, which was often nomadic.[6]

The difficulty of maintaining national unity was further complicated by the fact that most minorities resided in the peripheral regions of the Empire. The Russians occupied the Central Agricultural and Central Industrial regions around Moscow and Petrograd. The non-Russian Slavs, the Balts, and the Finns resided on the western border, the Caucasian peoples on the southern border with the Middle East, and most of the Turks in Central Asia. The non-Russians lived in the areas most remote from the centers of power, in areas over which Russian governments had the least control.

Thus, the ethnic divisions in the Empire aggravated the crisis of penetration by making the problem of "extending the power and authority of the administrative center" a problem of penetrating "into the compartmentalized, primordial structures of traditional society."[7] But more than this, the ethnic divisions confronted the Bolsheviks with a *crisis of identity*, a term defined in the context of political development as the urgent need to create feelings of a common nationhood or at least a sentiment for association across ethnic lines in a common political community.[8] For the new Soviet government, due as much to the aversion to "Great Russian Chauvinism" among the minority populations as to the ideological preferences of the Bolsheviks themselves, the resolution of the identity crisis could not come about simply by the inclusion of the minorities in the existing Russian nation. A new basis for community and unity—perhaps one other than organic nationhood—had to be found. Otherwise, how could the Bolsheviks hold together this society of over 100 nationalities?

Feudal Social Structure

The Bolsheviks inherited a social structure that was still semifeudal. As late as 1917, Russian social structure was, in many ways, like that of Europe centuries earlier—a society that was castelike, that supported great inequalities, and that lacked a substantial entrepreneurial class, or bourgeoisie.

Under the Tsars, Russia for many of its subjects—particularly its peasants—came close to being a caste society. Although modernity is supposed to bring a transition from a society of ascription-based status to one of achievement-based status, Russia had not yet completed this change. Russian subjects before the Revolution were born into what was called a civil estate, fixing them with a label (noble, merchant, burger, Cossack, or peasant) that most would carry throughout later life despite their accomplishments. One's civil status was important since rights and duties under Russian law were defined by this. There were even different laws, institutions, rights, and obligations for some civil estates. For example, peasants were required by law to render service to their villages, including taxes, manual labor to repair local roads, and participation in the harvest. Although the serfs were emancipated in 1861, for fiscal and administrative (or police) reasons, the emancipation act delegated responsibility for maintaining law and order and collecting taxes to the rural commune. No peasant was allowed to leave his commune without first obtaining the consent of his fellow citizens. Such consent was not readily given, because the departure of any peasant meant that the existing tax burden would be shared by fewer people. . . . The communes controlled the issuance of passports to peasants who took temporary work elsewhere and thus made sure that these workers would eventually have to return to pay their share of communal taxes.[9]

Even peasants who had moved to the city still bore obligations to the village and could be called back for the harvest or fixed with an exorbitant fee to buy out this obligation. In addition, there were separate laws and courts for some civil estates, particularly the peasants. (In western Europe, such practices had died out at least a century earlier; and in the United States, these had never existed.)

An illustration of the castelike nature of Russian society is the civil service—the *chinovniki*. Chinovniki in Russia were in many ways a microcosm of the larger Russian society. According to Richard Pipes, "the imperial bureaucracy displayed a distinct tendency to form a closed, hereditary caste." Until the last years of the Tsarist regime, individuals did not easily enter the civil service from outside this caste. And chinovniki "tended to associate only with their own kind." Within this caste there was high stratification, and relations were ones of fawning and bullying. To reinforce this hierarchy, there were distinctive symbols and titles for each of the 14 chinovnik ranks. Tsar Nicholas I introduced a code, running some 869 paragraphs, to spell out the rights and duties of each rank. For example, those in ranks 1 and 2 were entitled to be addressed "Your High Excellency." Those in ranks 9 through 14 were, by law, to be addressed simply "Your Honor." There were uniforms attached to each rank. Pipes reports, "Promotion from white to black trousers was an event of cataclysmic proportions in a chinovnik's life."[10]

This castelike social structure supported significant inequalities in society. The rights and duties of different castes were not only different; they were also unequal. For example, the duty of service to the village in the countryside was borne only by the peasants, not by other estates, which had largely shaken off their obligations in earlier centuries. Property and power were also distributed unequally in the Empire. Land was centrally important to this preindustrial society. And the average landholding of a noble in European Russia was about 15 times as large as that of a peasant. In some areas, such as the Baltic region, inequality was even more extreme, with the average noble-holding between 400 and 500 times the size of the average peasant-holding.[11]

The feudal structure of Russian society also meant the absence or weakness of industrial classes such as the proletariat and bourgeoisie. Although the proportion of the total population classified as peasants was falling rapidly in the two decades before the Revolution (from 86 percent in 1897 to 78 percent in 1913) peasants still constituted the vast majority of the population. Workers, artisans, and servants had grown only from 11.6 to 14.7 percent of the total. And until the decade preceding the Revolution, these classes did not begin to constitute a hereditary urban industrial proletariat, for until then the majority of the industrial workers remained in close contact with the countryside, working part time for industry and returning to their villages for the harvest. There was also no large-scale entrepreneurial class within Russian society. The earlier policies of the Imperial government had blocked the growth of a small merchant class, so that in the 1880s, when the Minister of Finance made a push for the industrialization and economic modernization of Russia, there was no indigenous entrepreneurial class to lead it. When industrialization took place, much of it was in the hands of the Imperial government or foreign investors. For example, coal and steel production in the Donets-Krivoy Rog region was largely financed and run by the English with the help of French and Belgian investors. The oil in the Caucasus was controlled by English and Swedish interests. Indeed, by 1914, over a third of all capital in private companies was owned by foreigners, including 100 percent in oil extraction, 90 percent in mining, 50 percent in the chemical industry, 42 percent in the metal goods industry, and 28 percent in textiles. Even the Tsarist government itself found foreign capital markets more responsive to its interest-bearing bonds, so that by 1914, almost half of the government debt was in foreign hands.[12] Because Russia never developed a large-scale middle class, it never developed what is purportedly the mainstay of a modern industrial democracy.

These social inequities contributed to a *crisis of distribution*, particularly, to demands for redistribution—demands that said, "Regardless of what may be the society's capability of producing more, *change* the bases upon which things valued are distributed among society's members!" According to political scientist Joseph LaPalombara of Yale University, it is this demand for redistribution that historically "has overtaxed elite capability and sometimes led to revolution and the destruction of existing political regimes."[13] There was no consensus among the social forces critical of the status quo on new distributive criteria, divided as they were between the achievement orientation of many of the entrepreneurial classes and the ascriptive orientation of the communal peasantry. This absence of value consensus deepened the crisis of distribution.

Preindustrial Economy

The Bolsheviks inherited an economy that was still preindustrial. Compared to Europe and North America, Russia was a far more agrarian society. In fact, just before the Revolution, 78 percent of the Russian population still lived in the countryside, while in the United States that figure was only about 50 percent and in England and Wales, it was under 22 percent.

During the two and a half decades before World War I, Russian had experienced substantial industrial growth (although it began from a narrow base). As Figure 1.1 shows, the decade before 1900 and the six years after 1907 saw annual growth rates in industrial output (manufacturing and mining value added) above 8 percent in the first period and above 6 percent in the second. Yet, while its sheer size made the Empire an international industrial power, on a per capita basis it remained a less-developed country. As Table 1.1 shows, the Tsarist government after 1860 was narrowing the gap on most indicators of industrialization that separated the Empire

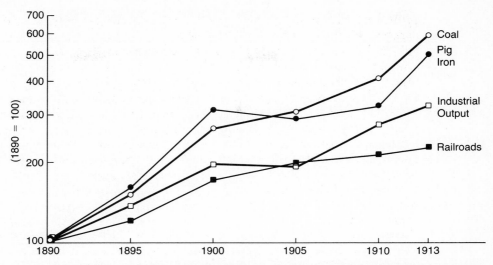

Figure 1.1 Russian Industrial Growth, 1890–1913 (semilogarithmic scale). Figures are index numbers for weight of coal and pig iron, value of industrial output, and total length of railways each year. (*Source:* P. I. Khromov, *Ekonomicheskoe razvitie Rossii v xix–xx vv.* [Moscow, 1950]; A. Nove, *An Economic History of the USSR* [New York: Penguin Books, 1982].)

from the rest of Europe and the United States. Nonetheless, it remained the least-developed European state before World War I, trailing behind even the relatively less-developed Mediterranean world in key industrial sectors.

The weak spot of the Russian economy was agriculture. The Russian peasant was not the heroic yeoman farmer with an ever-improving technology—the mainstay of the American agrarian myth. Russian peasant agriculture still used primitive productive techniques. A staple instrument in the hands of peasants was the *sokha*, a stick used as a plow. Among wealthier peasants this stick was affixed to a piece of metal to help break the soil; among poorer peasants it was simply a stick. Wealthier peasants harnessed the *sokha* to a horse; poorer peasants harnessed it to a wife or child. The three-field form of crop rotation, with strip-farming of divided and dispersed plots of land, was still the predominant crop cultivation technique among Russian peasants—a practice that had been prevalent in Europe during the Middle Ages but had largely died out there before the twentieth century.[14] As a consequence, Russian production remained low; yields of most crops were only a fraction of those found in the West (see Table 1.2).

Russian agriculture had not enjoyed the same rapid growth as the industrial sector. This was in part due to growing population pressure on the land—the rural population grew about 80 percent in the half century from the emancipation of the serfs to the beginning of World War I. And even though the frontier, particularly in Siberia, offered new lands for settlement, the restriction on peasant mobility that resulted from the commune's authority over its members prevented peasant resettlement; thus, a nearly static supply of land in the Central Agricultural Region was divided by an ever-growing number of peasants. The estimated annual growth in

Table 1.1   RELATIVE ECONOMIC STANDING OF WORLD POWERS, 1860–1910
(Index: Russia = 100*)

| | Industrial Sector | | | | | | | | | Agriculture | |
| | Cotton | | Pig Iron | | Railways | | Coal | Steam power | Agriculture | | |
	1860	1910	1860	1910	1860	1910	1910	1910	1860	1910
USA	1160	423	500	871	1900	508	1527	1125	300	382
UK	3020	660	2600	677	4400	288	1347	1500	267	214
Belgium	580	313	1380	806	3000	425	1090	—	147	164
Germany	280	227	280	645	2100	313	1063	813	140	227
Switzerland	1060	210	—	—	2800	367	—	1188	120	155
France	540	200	500	323	1800	363	483	—	193	155
Sweden	300	120	940	355	300	317	303	938	140	145
Spain	280	147	60	68	600	242	110	—	147	77
Italy	40	180	40	26	600	158	90	288	67	59
Russia	100	100	100	100	100	100	100	100	100	100

*Cotton, pig iron, and coal production figures are for weight per capita; railways show length relative to population and area; steam power is in terms of horsepower per capita; and agricultural output is figured as calories produced per male agricultural worker.

Source: Calculated from data in P. Bairoch, "Niveaux de développement économique au XIXe siecle," *Annales: Economies, Sociétés, Civilisations,* 20, 6 (November-December, 1965), 1091–1117.

Table 1.2   COMPARATIVE AGRICULTURAL YIELDS, 1911–1915
(Index: Russia = 100*)

	Wheat	Rye	Oats	Potatoes
Germany	324	222	244	184
England	324	—	229	207
France	191	126	160	117
USA	153	126	148	90
Russia	100	100	100	100

*Yield by weight.

Source: Russia. Glavnoe upravlenie zemleustroistva i zemledeliia. Otdel sel'skoi ekonomii i sel'skokhoziaistven-noi statistiki. *Sbornik statistikoekonomicheskikh svedenii po sel'skomu khoziaistvu Rossii i inostrannykh gosudarstv,* IX. Petrograd, 1916.

agricultural production of 1.7 percent between 1860 and 1914 was almost all eaten up by the growth in population.[15]

Commercial agriculture, particularly for industrial production and export, grew significantly in the last years before the Revolution, especially under the stimulus of the reforms of the Tsar's minister P. A. Stolypin. Removing some of the legal sanctions for the commune's control over individual peasant households, the Stolypin Reforms (1906–11) permitted peasant households to withdraw from the commune, claiming a portion of its lands as private property. Although this may have ultimately transformed Russian agriculture, the resistance of many communes to this change and the intervention of war and revolution less than a decade later left the reforms uncompleted. And if the long-term consequence of this transformation might have been a healthier agrarian sector, its short-term consequence was to hurt more peasant households than it helped, particularly with the apparent rise of landlessness among the poorer peasants who sold their holdings to more prosperous entrepreneurial farmers.

The sluggish performance of agriculture meant that the overall growth of the Russian economy did not keep pace with the more developed powers of the West. As S. N. Prokopovich's estimates of per capita national income show, during the two decades of most spectacular economic growth (1894–1913), Russia was actually falling further behind all other major European powers (see Table 1.3).

As a result of this premodern agrarian economy, most Russians were very poor. Per capita national income in European Russia in 1913 was the equivalent of about $600 (1985 U.S. dollars), about one-third of that of Germany at the time, less than a quarter of that of the United Kingdom, and under a sixth of that of the United States. Peasant household budget surveys conducted before the Revolution in order to estimate the monetary value of everything produced and consumed in peasant households estimated that the average peasant family in European Russia lived on the equivalent of $1000 per year (1985 U.S. dollars), or under $200 per capita. In some regions the average peasant household income was as low as $800, and in some villages only $450 per year. One consequence of this poverty was that many of the Russian people ate little and lived shorter lives. Russia at the time had the highest infant mortality and death rates in Europe; in European Russia, the rates for both were more than twice the rates in England and Wales.[16]

These economic problems would make rapid development a priority of any regime that succeeded the Tsarist government. World War I aggravated some of these problems. Conscription in the countryside, where the problem had been overpopulation, did not hurt agricultural production, but conscription of some 40 percent of the industrial labor force left the industrial sector hard pressed. The overtaxing of the limited transportation network and the collapse of the market under the pressure of rapid inflation led to food shortages and unrest in the cities. The economic problems confronting the successor regime were further aggravated by the loss of the more developed western portions of the Empire during the war and subsequent civil war; in 1912 these had accounted for almost a fifth of the Empire's total industrial output.[17]

Table 1.3 RUSSIAN PER CAPITA NATIONAL INCOME, 1894–1913
(as percentage of per capita income in other European states)

	1894	1913
United Kingdom	24.6%	21.8%
France	28.7	28.5
Germany	36.4	34.6
Italy	64.5	43.9
Austria-Hungary	52.6	44.4

Source: S. N. Prokopovich, *Opyt ischisleniia narodnogo dokhoda v Evropeiskoi Rossii* (Moscow, 1918).

Political Vacuum

The Bolsheviks also inherited a society in which there was a near total political vacuum. Ruled until March 1917 by the Tsar, the Russians possessed a government that by the standards of early twentieth-century Europe was a living antique. In Europe most states, even those that retained monarchs as chiefs of state, had developed complex, participatory political institutions that were characterized by functional differentiation and independence. The Tsarist government had begun this transformation belatedly and half-heartedly. For example, most European states had developed separate, independent institutions for judicial functions and for local government. In Russia, by contrast, independent provincial governments and an independent judiciary were established only in 1864. The provincial assemblies, or *zemstva*, which were to administer police functions, social services, and public health, were actually very limited in their powers. When intellectuals attempted to use the zemstva as a base for common political action, the power of these assemblies was restricted further, and each was placed under the direct control of a prefect (*zemskii nachal'nik* or land captain) appointed by the minister of interior from among the local landed nobility. Independent city governments were established only in 1870. The judicial reform of 1864, by introducing procedural guarantees such as trial by jury and by ensuring the competence and independence of judges, established model judicial principles that were as progressive as any in Europe. Yet, these courts were available only to a small minority of the population, with peasants being excluded in most instances. The courts lacked what is among the most fundamental requirements of modern justice—a published code of laws on which to decide cases. And the system of extraordinary courts established in 1881 removed the most sensitive cases from these guarantees.[18]

Europe had also developed constitutional limitations on the authority of its monarchs. Conversely, the first constitution of Russia was adopted only on April 23, 1906, barely 11 years before the Revolution. And in drafting this fundamental law, the Tsar kept to himself the "Supreme, Autocratic Power." The law reserved to the Tsar the sole power to initiate legislation. It gave him control over the executive branch, unrestricted control over foreign policy and the proclamation of war, and the power to dissolve the parliament (*Duma*), and to appoint one-half of its upper house with his sycophants. True, continued unrest in the Revolution of 1905 forced the Tsar to expand the formal role of the Duma, giving it the power to veto legislation and investigate actions of governmental officials. Yet, once revolutionary pressures began to subside, it became clear that the Tsar would dissolve the Duma if it showed true independence, as he did with the first two dumas elected in 1906 and 1907. And not content with this, he restricted and weighted the suffrage so as to ensure pliant bodies, which he gained in the Third and Fourth Dumas, elected in 1907 and 1912, respectively. Moreover, Duma control over governmental purse-strings promised in the heat of 1905 turned out not to prevent governmental spending without legislative authorization or even over a legislative veto.[19]

Europe had also developed participatory institutions. The suffrage, guaranteeing all male citizens an equal vote, was widespread in Germany, England, and most of Europe, but not in Russia. While in 1910 as much as 26.3 percent of the total

American population were enfranchised, as were 28.9 percent of the French population and 17.9 percent of the population of the United Kingdom, only 2.4 percent of the Russian Empire's people enjoyed this right. Moreover, votes were weighted by an elaborate scheme of representation by civil estate, so as to swamp peasant and worker representatives by those of the upper classes. In the election to the last dumas, the population was divided into four electoral colleges based on class, with one representative accorded to every 2000 landlord voters or 4000 urban voters, but only one for every 30,000 peasant voters or 90,000 worker voters. Similarly, the suffrage for the zemstva had been progressively restricted in the late nineteenth century, so that less than 1 percent of the population was entitled to vote. This restriction on participation was carried further by Tsarist attempts to suppress independent political activity. To quash mounting reformist and radical activism, censorship and control over the universities were tightened in the late nineteenth century, and zemstvo officials were denied the right to coordinate their activities or to petition central authorities directly. The Tsar's secret police, or Okhrana (literally, *okhrannoe otdelenie*, or security department), infiltrated, disrupted, and decapitated organizations that might have been the basis for independent political life. Formation of associations and trade unions was legalized only in March 1906, and even then the development of a free or autonomous associational life was hindered by such restrictions as the requirement that new organizations be approved by the Tsarist authorities, that they not hold meetings in hotels, restaurants, inns, or educational institutions, and that they not engage in political activities.[20]

By the end of the Tsarist regime, the Empire confronted a *crisis of legitimacy*—"a breakdown in the constitutional structure and performance of government that arises out of differences over the proper nature of authority for this system."[21] The loss of legitimacy of the old regime is attributed by Columbia University historian Marc Raeff at least in part to the growing distance between emperor and people. Symptomatic of, and perhaps contributing to, this alienation was the introduction of military parades under Nicholas I:

> Gone were the public balls, the fireworks displays, the triumphal entries, and the like, which had traditionally been occasions for the monarch to appear in public and take part in popular festivities. Military parades separated the monarch from the spectators. Regiment after regiment erected a moving wall of troops between the emperor and his people, and woe unto anyone who dared cross that forbidden barrier.[22]

At the same time, Tsars increasingly retreated into the privacy of their family lives and lost contact with their subjects.[23] Without institutions to incorporate independent political forces into the regime, the Tsarist government could not build loyalty to itself apart from loyalty to the person of the Tsar. Indeed, the Tsarist suppression of such forces led to their radicalization so that even professional associations joined with the revolutionary opponents of the regime.

These political institutions were shattered with the fall of Tsar Nicholas II in March 1917. The Provisional Government, which ruled between March and November of that year, was probably the last hope for democracy in Russia; but due to the demands of the war, it never developed legitimate participatory political institutions to fill the void. When that government also collapsed, the Bolsheviks faced a political vacuum.

In a sense, filling this vacuum with modern institutions could be part of the solution to all the developmental crises facing the Empire. Strong political institutions might force economic development. Modern political institutions would have the capacity to penetrate all corners of society, serving as the focus for a new political community and mobilizing its resources not only for development but also to resolve the distributive inequities in Tsarist society. Most importantly, only modern institutions would be able to address the *crisis of participation* unleashed by the revolutions of 1917. As the Harvard University political scientist Samuel P. Huntington has argued, "As political participation increases, the complexity, autonomy, adaptability, and coherence of the society's political institutions must also increase if political stability is to be maintained."[24]

In sum, the Bolsheviks came to power in 1917 thinking they would build socialism, but Russia, in a sense, frustrated those plans. The Bolsheviks found that they faced the formidable task of making Russia modern. They had to mobilize the unexploited resources of the country, bring together an ethnically diverse population into a single state, modernize a feudal social structure, industrialize an agrarian economy, and build a modern polity. Although their ideology had an important impact on the *way* they addressed these problems and the image of the future they hoped to build, much of the policy agenda itself was set by Russia and the multiple crises of development that confronted it.

THE ORIGINS OF THE BOLSHEVIK MOVEMENT

The Bolshevik movement that captured power in November of 1917 was in a very real sense the product of the Russian Empire's belated and uncertain effort to modernize. As in so many other developing societies, the early stages of modernization had produced an abundance of social groups critical of the old order. The number of students in higher education, for example, grew over 20-fold from the middle of the nineteenth century to the beginning of the First World War.[25] And with this expansion, universities and other institutions of higher education became ever more important centers of anti-Tsarist acitivity. The beginnings of industrialization, however, divided the Empire not only between proponents and opponents of modernization, but also among radically divergent prescriptions for change. The so-called Westernizers often advocated wholesale borrowing of capitalist and democratic institutions from the West. Many other Russians, seeing what modern industry had done to England, France, and Germany, did not want to re-create that experience. As is frequently the case among modernizers in less-developed countries, they wanted to avoid the social problems that Western Europe had experienced—to modernize without the pains of modernization. They sought to capture only the best of Western civilization and, in some cases, to preserve certain institutions or practices of the old order. This led to a number of political movements, each advocating a peculiar synthesis of Western and Russian ideals.

The Bolsheviks were the product of these political developments. They emerged toward the end of this period of industrialization under the Tsars, advocating one of a number of competing fusions of ideas. Specifically, the Bolshevik's ideology was the blend of two radical traditions: Western Marxism and Russian populism. From each of these the Bolsheviks borrowed ideals and tactics, bringing them together in a unique synthesis that distinguished the Bolsheviks from their opponents.

Populism and Marxism

Russian populism (*Narodnichestvo*) was a radical movement that came into its own in the 1860s and 1870s, focusing on the countryside and the peasantry. As one author has said about the Narodniki, "They idealized the peasant, they glorified his virtues, they decried his sorrows, and they fought for his material welfare."[26] *Narodniki* in the secret organization *Zemlia i Volia* (Land and Freedom), for example, planned a peasant uprising for the summer of 1863. A decade later, students, professionals, and even some nobility streamed to the countryside ("to the people" was their cry) to spread their message of enlightenment among the so-called "dark people" of the villages. There they were frequently met with silence or even hostility; some were arrested by the villagers and turned over to the Tsarist authorities. It was probably natural that this early radical movement would focus on the peasantry. If radicals were to transform this agrarian society or make a revolution, the countryside was a natural place to begin. Russia had a tradition of peasant unrest; the most violent and dramatic uprisings of Russian history had been in the countryside. If reformers were to find some weak link in Russian society that could bring about change in the Tsarist regime, it would be outside the urban areas.

The Narodniki, by translating the writings of Marx, were responsible for introducing these to the Russian readership. Yet they did not entirely believe Marx, giving his anticapitalist philosophy a peculiar twist. For the Narodniki, the lesson of Marx was to avoid industrialization entirely: If Russia avoided modern industrial society it would escape the evils that Marx described. Instead, the Narodniki's objective was to build an agrarian socialism. Many placed their faith in the peasant institutions of the countryside, particularly the village commune, or *mir*. The Narodniki saw these institutions of collective self-rule as the potential basis for a socialist cooperative society and an alternative to the evils of industrialization.

The Narodnik movement never achieved organizational unity, for the movement included within itself—over time and sometimes at the same time—a number of organizations with different programs of action, tactics, and strategies. One of these was the People's Will (*Narodnaia Volia*). Although People's Will had a very short history (established in 1879, it was crushed by 1881), it made an important contribution to the development of what ultimately became Bolshevism. People's Will advocated organizing a tightly disciplined conspiratorial party of professional revolutionaries that would engage in terror against the regime. People's Will argued that only if populists established small cells of professional revolutionaries that responded to a central chain of command could they make revolution. Thus, it sought to establish a network of secret organizations to infiltrate the government and army in order to prepare for an uprising against the Tsarist regime. People's Will also glorified terror, arguing that by dramatic acts against the regime revolutionaries could ignite the population and bring the downfall of the government. Ironically, the most dramatic terrorist act by members of People's Will was also its last action: In 1881 members assassinated Tsar Alexander II, and the Tsarist secret police immediately put an end to the organization.[27]

From the Populist tradition the Bolsheviks learned a number of lessons. One was the value of the peasantry; another was tactics. While the Bolsheviks never glorified terror, as Mikhail Bakunin and Sergei Nechaev had done, they were far more willing than other Russian Marxists to resort to violence (including terror) as a tactic for making revolution. A third lesson was organizational strategies.

The direct lineal ancestor of the Bolsheviks was not People's Will, but the group that, in 1879, broke with it over the issue of tactics. The Black Partition (*Chernyi Peredel'*) split with People's Will, denying that terror could be a primary instrument of revolution. It is the Black Partition, under the leadership of Georgi Plekhanov, that actually introduced Marxism to Russia. In 1883 the leadership of the Black Partition was forced to flee to Geneva, where they adopted the name Liberation of Labor (*Osvobozhdenie Truda*). Although this latter group adopted a program that was much like that of other Populists, calling for a democratic constitution, freedom of conscience, freedom of the press, freedom of assembly, and a socialized economy, they broke with much of the Populist movement over revolutionary strategy. They argued that Russia could not build socialism in the countryside but must build it in an industrialized society based on a proletariat and a class-conscious party. Thus, the immediate objective of the movement, they argued, should be to promote the industrialization of Russia and to build a proletarian party based on Marxism. In 1898, this group became the Russian Social Democratic Labor Party (RSDLP). From this Marxist tradition the Bolsheviks took the urban-centered strategy of proletarian revolution.[28]

The Bolshevik Synthesis

The Bolsheviks, alongside the Mensheviks (the more moderate Marxian socialists), emerged within the Russian Social Democratic Labor Party (RSDLP) as one of its two largest factions. As they developed, the Bolsheviks distinguished themselves from the rest of the Russian revolutionary movement by their unique synthesis of organization, revolutionary strategy, and tactics.

Organization   To the Bolsheviks, organization was essential. One of the early Narodnik proponents of tight party organization, Petr Tkachev, had written,

> The struggle can be conducted successfully only by combining the following conditions: centralization, severe discipline, swiftness, decisiveness, and unity of action. All concessions, all wavering, all compromises, multi-leaderism, and decentralization of the fighting forces weaken their energy, paralyze their activity, and deprive the struggle of all chances for victory.[29]

In 1902, Lenin echoed this view in his tract *What Is To Be Done?*. The party could not be a free association with open membership but, instead, must be composed of professional revolutionaries—individuals who make their living making revolution. In addition, this party must be tightly disciplined like a military unit, responding to a single chain of command. To support his view Lenin cited the experience of the Petersburg Union of Struggle for the Emancipation of Labor. In 1895, this organization had attempted to publish the newspaper *The Workers' Cause* (*Rabochee Delo*), but its relatively open membership permitted the organization to be infiltrated by the police, leading to the exile of many of its members.

Lenin repudiated what he called Economism, the strategy, adopted by the Labour Party in Britain and the Social Democrats in Germany, of giving trade unions a major say in the direction of the party. He argued that a revolutionary party that relies upon the spontaneous instincts of the trade union movement will soon become reformist and cease to be revolutionary. It will ask for incremental changes, like a shorter workday, a minimum wage, and social security, but it will not make revolution. In other words, left to its own devices, the trade union movement does not develop revolutionary consciousness. Instead, consciousness must be brought to the workers by a revolutionary party in the vanguard of the proletariat.[30]

Lenin's views on party organization would vary somewhat after the publication of *What Is To Be Done?*. At the core of the movement and party would always be the professional revolutionaries. Around but outside the party would be "the most diverse organizations of all kinds, ranks, and hues"[31] that would support the party and comprise the larger party-led movement. Some of these would have open mass membership. Between these were to be the part-time revolutionaries, such as "workers who distribute literature and lead oral agitation."[32] While Lenin consistently opposed indiscriminate inclusion of all members of the movement in the party, he wavered over time on the issue of whether part-time revolutionaries should be admitted to the party.

Lenin tried to press his views about party organization on the Russian Social Democratic Labor Party, and in the process helped to bring about the division of the RSDLP into separate Bolshevik and Menshevik organizations.[33] Formed in 1898, the Party held its first Congress in Minsk. (Actually, this first meeting included only nine delegates.) At this time Lenin began to press the RSDLP to assume the role that he would later prescribe in *What Is To Be Done?*. Using the newspaper *Iskra* (Spark), which he had established with Iulii Martov and Aleksandr Potresov and issued in collaboration with the Emancipation of Labor group, Lenin had already attempted to press his "orthodox" Marxist views against mounting revisionism among Marxists. He found that his views on organization were bringing about a division not only in the RSDLP but even in the editorial board of *Iskra* itself.

The Second Congress of the Russian Social Democratic Labor Party (1903) met in Brussels, since it was no longer safe to assemble in Russia. In a meeting of 43 voting delegates (some with multiple votes) and 14 nonvoting delegates, Lenin's skillful preparations netted the *Iskra* faction 33 of 51 votes, and it quickly asserted its control over the Congress. But when Lenin used the Second Congress to press his organizational views once again, the unity of the *Iskra* faction began to break down. Lenin initially lost at the Second Congress to those led by Martov, who advocated a more open, mass-membership party. Yet by organizational maneuvering within this Second Congress—getting both the Bundt, or Jewish faction, and the Economist

Lenin on Revolutionary Social Democracy

The following quotations from *What Is To Be Done?* present some of Lenin's views on party organization, strategy, and tactics.

The Party and the Working Class

[T]he *spontaneous* development of the working-class movement leads to its subordination to bourgeois ideology . . . for the spontaneous working-class movement is trade-unionism, . . . and trade-unionism means the ideological enslavement of the workers by the bourgeoisie.

Hence, our task, the task of Social-Democracy, is *to combat spontaneity, to divert* the working-class movement from this spontaneous, trade-unionist striving to come under the wing of the bourgeoisie, and to bring it under the wing of revolutionary Social-Democracy.

We must take up actively the political education of the working class and the development of its political consciousness.

We must "go among all classes of the population" as theoreticians, as propagandists, as agitators and as organizers.

Attributes of the Party

[T]he *role of vanguard fighter can be fulfilled only by a party that is guided by the most advanced theory.*

This struggle must be organized . . . by people who are professionally engaged in revolutionary activity.

We must have circles, trade unions, and organizations everywhere in as large a number as possible and with the widest variety of functions; but it would be absurd and harmful to confound them with the organization of revolutionaries, to efface the border-line between them, to make still more hazy the all too faint recognition of the fact that in order to "serve" the mass movement we must have people who will devote themselves exclusively to Social-Democratic activities, and that such people must train themselves patiently and steadfastly to be professional revolutionaries.

Centralization of the most secret functions in an organization of revolutionaries will not diminish, but rather increase the extent and enhance the quality of the activity of a large number of other organizations. . . .

[Within the Party] "freedom of criticism" [would mean] freedom for an opportunist trend in Social-Democracy, freedom to convert Social-Democracy into a democratic party of reform, freedom to introduce bourgeois ideas and bourgeois elements into socialism.

Give us an organization of revolutionaries, and we will overturn Russia!

The Program of Revolutionary Social Democracy

Revolutionary Social Democracy . . . subordinates the struggle for reforms, as the part to the whole, to the revolutionary struggle for freedom and for socialism. (376)

Social-Democracy leads the struggle of the working class, not only for better terms for the sale of labor-power, but for the abolition of the social system that compels the propertyless to sell themselves to the rich.

Source: V.I. Lenin, *Chto delat'? [What Is to be Done?]*, *Polnoe sobranie sochinenii*, 5th ed. 6. Moscow, 1960. (pp. 1–192).

faction to withdraw—Lenin temporarily emerged in control of the Congress. At this point he proclaimed his faction the majority—the Bolsheviks (distinguished from those who were temporarily the minority, the Mensheviks). Even though Lenin's Bolsheviks shortly thereafter lost on these issues of party organization and even lost control of *Iskra* to the Mensheviks, the labels stuck.

By 1905 the split within the RSDLP seemed to be complete. The Bolsheviks held their Third Congress in London; the Mensheviks held theirs in Geneva. Then, events back in Russia intervened to postpone a formal split. The Revolution of 1905, a massive uprising in the countryside and cities, produced a temporary reconciliation in the RSDLP and a "Unity" congress (the Fourth Congress, 1906) in Stockholm, in order to bring the factions back together again. Yet, even as the Unity Congress met, the Bolsheviks were slowly setting down roots in Russia as a separate organization, developing their own administrative apparatus and capturing control of local party organizations to place their supporters around Russia. By 1907, through successful maneuvering at the Fifth Congress in London, the Bolsheviks once again emerged as the majority within the RSDLP. There they repudiated the strategies of the Mensheviks, including cooperation with the Constitutional Democrats (Kadets), the party of moderate reform, and the idea of a large-scale mass party, which they rejected as "liquidationism." By 1912, Lenin and the Bolsheviks felt strong enough to formally break most ties with the Mensheviks, and so at their Sixth Congress in Prague (attended by only 14 voting delegates, including 2 Tsarist secret police agents) established the Bolshevik organization as a separate party, the Russian Social Democratic Labor Party (Bolsheviks). (It would actually be yet another year before the Bolsheviks ended their caucus or fractional association with the Mensheviks in the Duma and established a separate parliamentary group.)

Revolutionary Strategy   A second issue dividing the Bolsheviks from the Mensheviks was revolutionary strategy—specifically, their conception of how to make revolution. Most of the Social Democrats agreed that Marx's formulation seemed inappropriate to Russia; the Russian economy was still precapitalist, and so the Russian proletariat was weak. Yet the Bolsheviks and Mensheviks disagreed in their analyses of how to make revolution and build socialism in such a society.

The Mensheviks argued that socialism must await a long period of capitalist development. In the meantime, socialists would pave the way for bourgeois success by allying themselves with the middle-class parties, most notably the Constitutional Democrats, and attempting to build a modern constitutional democracy. Their tactics emphasized legal means, particularly parliamentary strategies like those developed by the Labour Party in Britain and the Social Democrats in Germany.

Although the Bolsheviks also began with the premise that Marx's formulation was not strictly appropriate to Russia in the early 1900s, they came to a different conclusion. Lenin argued that the proletariat must lead the revolution. Because the proletariat was a minority in Russia, it had to find allies to make revolution—but in the peasantry, not the bourgeoisie. The proletariat's revolution would proceed in two stages: Initially, a democratic revolution would establish the democratic dictatorship of the proletariat and the peasantry. (It would be democratic because it would represent a majority of the population, but also a dictatorship since any state is the rule of one class or alliance of classes over another.) This would pave the way for a second revolution, a socialist revolution that would establish the revolutionary dictatorship of the proletariat and the village poor. In this the proletariat would break its alliance with the rich peasantry and rely solely upon the proletarian elements in the countryside, in order to establish a dictatorship that could build socialism in Russia and move it toward communism.

Lenin's was an important synthesis. Marx had not developed a strategy for revolution that socialists could apply to preindustrial societies like Russia. Lenin brought together ideas from Russian Populism and from Marxism and combined them with the idea of the permanent revolution, which had come to him through Leon Trotsky and Parvus.[34] Although Lenin and the Bolsheviks never glorified the peasants or idealized them and were unwilling to place the peasant at the center stage of the revolution as the Narodniks had done, the Bolsheviks did come to understand from the Narodnik tradition that the peasantry was an essential ally in any effort to make revolution in an agrarian society. The idea of the permanent revolution meant that a party in a less-developed society, after beginning a revolution that was initially democratic, could then continue the revolutionary process after taking power, developing the revolution into socialism.

Tactics   A third issue that separated the Bolsheviks from the Mensheviks was their tactics. As noted earlier, the Bolsheviks were distinguished by their willingness to resort to violent means. In addition, the approach of the Bolsheviks to the major policy issues of the day separated them from the Mensheviks, particularly on the questions of what to do with the lands of the nobility and royal family and what to do about the non-Russian nationalities. The Bolsheviks came to distinguish themselves from other movements not only by their policy prescriptions, but also by the opportunistic manner in which they addressed these issues, subordinating issues of policy to the broader strategy of making revolution.

On the issue of land the Bolsheviks before 1905 were relatively indifferent. It was the 1905 Revolution that taught Lenin that he could not ignore this issue, for it was far too valuable to making revolution. Thus, in 1905, Lenin took the stand that all land should be nationalized as a means of production. Yet peasants did not want agricultural lands taken by the central government. And by mid-1917, submitting to the mounting revolutionary pressures among the peasants, Lenin had changed his position to the slogan "Land to the peasants!"—let the peasants confiscate it by whatever means. (Alternatively, the Mensheviks proposed municipalization; that is, local governing authorities such as each *mir* would take control of land, distributing the use-right to individual peasant households.) Once in power, Lenin changed his position again, once more advocating nationalization. Thus, Lenin distinguished himself from the Mensheviks not only by his stands, but by his willingness to switch positions tactically for the purpose of building a revolutionary coalition.[35]

We can see similar tactics in Lenin's handling of the issue of non-Russian nationalities. This issue was a double-edged sword for all the revolutionary parties. On the one hand, revolutionaries could use the issue against the Tsarist government, by mobilizing anti-Russian sentiment to subvert the Empire. On the other hand, if the revolutionaries came to power, what would be left of the Empire? If too successful at mobilizing nationalist sentiments, the revolutionaries might diminish their own success, by leading these peoples to declare their independence from the Empire.

The Mensheviks took the position that Russia could not be divided; with few exceptions, such as Finland, the Empire was one and indivisible. Lenin, on the other hand, looking for some way to combine the competing demands of undermining the Tsarist government but keeping the Empire intact, developed a unique solution. He advocated the principle of national self-determination and the right of all nationalities to secede, but added the caveat that each case of secession would be reviewed from the perspective of the interests of the proletariat and socialism. That is, if the secession of an individual republic, after a victorious socialist revolution in Russia, would empower a regressive feudal or capitalist leadership within that republic, Lenin and the Bolsheviks would oppose secession as a subversion of the Revolution.[36] In fact, once in power, the Bolsheviks fought a protracted civil war over four years trying to recapture many of the areas that had exercised their rights to secede during the Revolution.

On the issue of nationalities, the Bolsheviks' position set them apart from the other parties. The slogan of national self-determination excited many of the non-Russian nationalities. Those that argued that Russia was indivisible rapidly lost much of their non-Russian support. Yet it was also their tactical flexibility on this issue that distinguished the Bolsheviks.

THE COLLAPSE OF THE ANCIEN RÉGIME

Events in Petrograd from March through October of 1917 signalled the collapse of "the ancien regime."[37] Although the dissolution of the old order had begun decades earlier and would continue into the Soviet period, the abdication of Tsar Nicholas II and his brother, the Grand Duke Michael, on March 16, 1917, was an important turning point in that process. The events that immediately preceded the abdication began in Petrograd just over a week earlier (March 8), when a protest on International Women's Day against living conditions and food shortages widened into a general strike involving workers and students. The government's orders to fire on crowds three days later resulted not only in many deaths, but also in widespread revulsion against the government and even mutiny in the Petrograd garrison. From this point on, events quickly began to unwind. By the end of the week it had become apparent that armed force could not be used against the crowds; two task forces sent into Petrograd against the revolutionaries had simply melted away. The Tsar's advisors, including all the military officers he consulted, urged his abdication.

During that fateful week there arose two competing political centers that after the abdication would become the focal point for much of the political wrangling that characterized the eight months from March to November 1917. On March 12, in Petrograd's Taurida Palace, moderate and conservative leaders of the Duma, which the Tsar had just dissolved, established a Temporary Committee of the Duma in order to reestablish public order. And later that day in the same palace, leftist deputies and representatives of local labor groups established the Petrograd Soviet of Workers' and Soldiers' Deputies, on the model of a similar group established during the 1905 Revolution, in order to "struggle for the consolidation of the people's government in Russia." Four days later, with the abdication of the Tsar, the Temporary Committee of the Duma constituted itself the Provisional Government of Russia, headed by Prince Georgi E. Lvov as Premier. Although the Petrograd Soviet agreed to give conditional support to the new government, members of the Soviet, with the exception of the moderate Socialist Revolutionary Alexander Kerensky, obeyed the Soviet's ban on participation and initially refused to accept portfolios in the new cabinet. Setting the Soviet as watchdog over and increasingly in opposition to the Provisional Government, this fragile arrangement heralded in the period of dual power (*dvoevlastie*) that characterized the eight months before the Bolshevik seizure of power.

The Provisional Government proved to be of limited competence and highly unstable. Although it successfully adopted broad reforms guaranteeing many of the political rights of a liberal democracy, it was unable or unwilling to deal with the most pressing social problems of the day, including the food shortage in the cities, the land hunger in the countryside, and the pressures for greater independence among many of the non-Russian peoples. In particular, it continued to prosecute the war against Germany and Austria, even as this bled Russia and sparked protest against the government. Demonstrations that followed Foreign Minister Paul Miliukov's note reaffirming Russia's commitment to its allies brought his resignation on May 15 and a new coalition cabinet, including now 6 socialists, on May 18. The offensive begun on July 1 along the Galician front resulted in both a rout at the hands of the Austrian and German forces and growing resistance among Petrograd soldiers to being transferred to the front. This resistance led to two days of rioting in the streets under the banner "All Power to the Soviets" (July 16–18). The cumulative effect of these "July Days," the collapse of the Galician front, and a disagreement over domestic reforms was another cabinet crisis in which Kerensky replaced Lvov as Premier and socialists assumed 12 of the 16 cabinet posts.

The Provisional Government's movement to the left produced growing disaffection on the right. And on September 9, after demanding the imposition of martial law, resignation of the Provisional Government, and transfer of all authority to himself, the Commander-in-Chief of the armed forces, Lavr Kornilov, began a march on Petrograd that he thought would rally all God-fearing patriots to his cause and oust both the Provisional Government and Petrograd Soviet in a simple coup d'etat. But Kornilov had underestimated the opposition of the Petrograd garrison and workers, who sabotaged the railway movement and telegraph communications of his troops; nor had he counted on the ease with which the Petrograd garrison and workers could win over his own troops and turn them against him. By September 14, the coup attempt had failed. The "Kornilov Affair," however, produced yet another cabinet crisis, from which Kerensky only slowly patched together a new government. Moving still further to the left, Kerensky's government forced even more radical changes, including the proclamation of a republic (September 27) and dissolution of the Duma, in a bid to win popular support. At this late date, though, it seemed impossible to patch together legitimacy or authority with a broader constituency.

The chief beneficiaries of events during these eight months were the Bolsheviks. The collapse of the Tsarist regime in March had actually caught most of the Bolshevik leaders far from Petrograd—Lenin and Grigori E. Zinoviev in Switzerland, Joseph V. Stalin and Lev B. Kamenev in Siberia. The latter two returned to Petrograd on March 25, but Lenin arrived at the capital's Finland Station only on April 16, a month after the Tsarist abdication. Consequently, the Bolsheviks played only a minor role in the early days of the Revolution. Yet, from a membership of an estimated 23,600 in March, the Bolshevik organization grew rapidly to over 200,000 in August and perhaps as much as 350,000 in October.[38] This Bolshevik success can in part be attributed to the radicalization of public opinion in these months. Growing disillusionment and desertion in the armed forces, mounting worker militance expressed in strike activity that nearly trebled in the first four months of the Revolution, and fraying peasant patience with the dilatory land reform policies of the Provisional Government were reflected in growing support for the Bolsheviks. In addition, the participation of the other socialist parties in the Provisional Government and, therefore, their implication in its unsuccessful policies led many socialists to abandon these more moderate parties for the Bolsheviks. At the First All-Russian Congress of Soviets held in Petrograd on June 16, only a tenth (105) of the 1090 delegates claimed to be Bolsheviks, but less than five months later at the Second Congress (November 7) the Bolsheviks claimed about three-fifths (390) of approximately 650 delegates.[39] The Bolsheviks were also aided fortuitously by the events of late summer. Initially, the implication of the Bolsheviks in the "July Days" led the Provisional Government to attempt to suppress Lenin's party, imprisoning many leaders and forcing Lenin and others into hiding. But the Kornilov Affair led the Provisional Government to reverse itself, releasing Bolshevik leaders and arming Red Guards in order to turn back Kornilov's forces. On the basis of their role in the defense of the Revolution against Kornilov, the Bolsheviks moved quickly to assert their control over the Petrograd Soviet, securing adoption of their program and election of Leon Trotsky as the Soviet's "president" (Chairman of its Presidium), with a solid majority in its membership.

The collapse of the Kornilov coup, in Lenin's eyes, left the way open for a Bolshevik insurrection. In a letter sent in late September to the Bolshevik Central Committee from his place of hiding, Lenin argued that "having obtained a majority in the Soviets of Workers' and Soldiers' Deputies of both capitals [Petrograd and Moscow], the Bolsheviks can and must take state power into their own hands."[40] But the Central Committee at its October 6 meeting did not agree to immediate action and, after heated debate, decided only to call a Congress of Soviets for November 2 (later postponed to November 7), which might then serve as the occasion for a coup in its name. Outraged by the delay of armed insurrection, Lenin on October 20 slipped back into Petrograd, and by October 29 had convinced a 19-to-2 majority of the Central Committee (with 4 abstentions) to adopt his resolution committing the party to active preparations for a coup. (Kamenev and Zinoviev so opposed the idea of insurrection at this time that the former announced his resignation from the Central Committee and published in both men's names a disclaimer of insurrection, which made public, at least by implication, the "secret" Bolshevik decision to prepare a coup.[41]) With the assistance of the Petrograd Soviet under Trotsky's

The Tasks of the Proletariat in the Present Revolution ("The April Theses")

Upon his return to Petrograd from his exile in Switzerland, Lenin delivered the following program for action:

1. In our attitude towards the war, which under the new government of Lvov and Co., unquestionably remains on Russia's part a predatory imperialist war owing to the capitalist nature of that government, not the slightest concession to "revolutionary defencism" is permissible. The class-conscious proletariat can give its consent to a revolutionary war, which would really justify revolutionary defencism, only on condition: (a) that the power pass to the proletariat and the poorest sections of the peasants aligned with the proletariat; (b) that all annexations be renounced in deed and not in word; (c) that a complete break be effected in actual fact with all capitalist interests. . . .

2. The specific feature of the present situation in Russia is that the country is passing from the first stage of the revolution—which, owing to the insufficient class-consciousness and organization of the proletariat, placed power in the hands of the bourgeoisie—to its second stage, which must place power in the hands of the proletariat and the poorest sections of the peasants. This transition is characterized, on the one hand, by a maximum of legally recognized rights (Russia is now the freest of all the belligerent countries in the world); on the other, by the absence of violence towards the masses, and, finally, by their unreasoning trust in the government of capitalists, those worst enemies of peace and socialism. . . .

3. No support for the Provisional Government. . . .

4. Recognition of the fact that in most of the Soviets of Workers' Deputies our Party is in a minority, so far a small minority, as against a bloc of all the petty-bourgeois opportunist elements . . . who yielded to the influence of the bourgeoisie and spread that influence among the proletariat. The masses must be made to see that the Soviets of Workers' Deputies are the only possible form of revolutionary government. . . . As long as we are in the minority we carry on the work of criticizing and exposing the errors [in the masses' tactics] and at the same time we preach the necessity of transferring the entire state power to the Soviets of Workers' Deputies so that the people may overcome their mistakes by experience.

5. Not a parliamentary republic . . . but a Republic of Soviets of Workers', Agricultural Laborers', and Peasants' Deputies throughout the country, from top to bottom. Abolition of the police, the army and the bureaucracy. The salaries of all officials, all of whom are elective and displaceable at any time, not to exceed the average wage of a competent worker.

6. The weight of emphasis in the agrarian program to be shifted to the Soviets of Agricultural Laborers' Deputies. Confiscation of all landed estates. Nationalization of all lands in the country, the land to be disposed by the local Soviets of Agricultural Labourers' and Peasants' Deputies. The setting up of separate Soviets of Deputies of Poor Peasants. . . .

7. The immediate amalgamation of all banks in the country into a single national bank, and the institution of control over it by the Soviet of Workers' Deputies.

8. It is not our immediate task to "introduce" socialism, but only to bring social production and the distribution of products at once under the control of the Soviets of Workers' Deputies.

9. Party tasks: (a) Immediate convocation of a Party congress: (b) Alteration of the Party Program . . .; (c) Change of the Party's name [from Social Democratic to Communist].

10. A new International. We must take the initiative in creating a revolutionary International. . . .

Source: Vladimir I. Lenin, "O zadachakh proletariata v dannoi revoliutsii" [The Tasks of the Proletariat in the Present Revolution], *Polnoe sobranie sochinenii*, 5th ed., 31. Moscow, 1962. pp. 113–118.

leadership and particularly through the Soviet's Military Revolutionary Committee created on October 29, the Bolsheviks began to prepare for the armed strike with an estimated 20,000 Red Guards recruited in local factories, sailors of the Kronstadt and Baltic fleets, and sympathetic soldiers of the Petrograd garrison. By assigning commissars to individual military units in the capital and by giving them the power to veto orders to move the troops, the Military Revolutionary Committee neutralized the armed forces of the Provisional Government. At last, around midnight of November 6–7, the Bolsheviks under Lenin's leadership began their coup, meeting minimal resistance, and seized key points in the capital, including the central telephone and postal offices, the state bank and treasury, and the railway stations. Although later in the morning of November 7, Lenin would announce the overthrow of the Provisional Government, it was not until after midnight of the next day that his supporters took the Winter Palace. Having used only limited force, and having suffered only some 20 dead and a few wounded, Lenin's Bolsheviks could legitimately claim to hold, no matter how tenuously, the centers of power of the former Russian Empire. Now they faced the real task of transforming Russia.

THE LEGACIES OF EARLY BOLSHEVISM

Many of the lessons learned by the Bolsheviks early in their history have had a continuing, profound effect on Soviet politics. The organization and practices of the party and, in particular, its relationship to the larger society were shaped in the years before the Revolution.

The Bolshevik notion of the party as an elite of professional revolutionaries continues to be an important organizational principle in the Communist Party of the Soviet Union (CPSU). The Party continues to include only the most active members of society who are building communism.

The notion of a continuing revolution under the leadership of the party remains fundamental to the legitimacy of the CPSU. The Soviets see their history since 1917 as the movement forward of a revolution, initially building socialism and later building the foundations of communism. The party cannot leave society to its own spontaneous impulses; the revolution can move forward only under the direction of the class-conscious, ideologically inspired party.

The tactical flexibility of Bolshevism continues to be a prominent attribute of Soviet politics. Westerners often express surprise when the Soviets make dramatic changes in policies, criticizing such changes as a retreat from the ideals of the Revolution. The Soviets argue that tactical flexibility in the pursuit of the larger strategy of building socialism is necessary; it is pragmatism serving a higher purpose.

NOTES

1. Leon Trotsky, *The Russian Revolution*, ed. by F. W. Dupee (New York: Doubleday, 1959), 458.
2. This description relies heavily upon Paul E. Lydolph, *Geography of the U.S.S.R.* (Elkhart Lake, Wisc.: Misty Valley Publishing, 1979) and John C. Dewdney, *A Geography of the Soviet Union*, 2d ed. (New York: Pergamon Press, 1971).
3. Leonard Binder, "The Crises of Political Development," in Leonard Binder et al., eds., *Crises and Sequences in Political Development* (Princeton, N.J.: Princeton University Press, 1971), 63.
4. Russia, Tsentral'nyi statisticheskii komitet, *Pervaia vseobshchaia perepis' naseleniia Rossiiskoi Imperii, 1897 g.* (St. Petersburg, 1899–1904).
5. Richard Pipes, *The Formation of the U.S.S.R.*, rev. ed. (New York: Atheneum, 1968), 7–21.
6. *Pervaia vseobshchaia perepis'.*
7. Binder, "Crises of Political Development", 63.
8. Lucian W. Pye, "Identity and Political Culture," in Binder, *Crises and Sequences*, 110–111.
9. Marc Raeff, *Understanding Imperial Russia: State and Society in the Old Regime*, trans. by Arthur Goldhammer (New York: Columbia University Press, 1984), 181.
10. Richard Pipes, *Russia Under the Old Regime* (New York: Scribner, 1974), 286–287.
11. Russia, Tsentral'nyi statisticheskii komitet, *Statistika zemlevladeniia 1905 g.* St. Petersburg, 1907.
12. Basile Kerblay, *Modern Soviet Society* (New York: Pantheon Books, 1983), 212; Raeff, *Understanding Imperial Russia*, 213–214, 217; Peter I. Lyashchenko, *History of the National Economy of Russia to the 1917 Revolution*, trans. by L. M. Herman (New York: Macmillan, 1949).
13. Joseph LaPalombara, "Penetration: A Crisis of Government Capacity," in Binder, *Crises and Sequences*, 236.
14. For a fuller description of peasant farming see Geroid Tanquary Robinson, *Rural Russia Under the Old Regime* (Berkeley, Calif.: University of California Press, 1932).
15. Raymond W. Goldsmith, "The Economic Growth of Tsarist Russia, 1860–1913," *Economic Development and Cultural Change* 9 (April 1961), 441–475.
16. M. E. Falkus, "Russia's National Income, 1913: A Revaluation," *Economica* 35 (February 1969), 52–73; F. A. Shcherbina, *Krest'ianskie biudzhety* (Voronezh, 1900); L. Kritsman, *Materialy po istorii agrarnoi revoliutsii v Rossii* (Moscow, 1928).
17. Alec Nove, *An Economic History of the U.S.S.R.* (New York: Penguin Books, 1982), 16.
18. Raeff, 177–178, 186.
19. B. H. Sumner, *Survey of Russian History* (London: Duckworth, 1944), 67–68.
20. Stephen White, *Political Culture and Soviet Politics* (London: Macmillan Press, 1979), 28–29, 37.

21. Lucian Pye, "The Legitimacy Crisis," in Binder, *Crises and Sequences*, 136.

22. Raeff, 195–196.

23. Raeff, ibid.

24. Samuel P. Huntington, *Political Order in Changing Societies* (New Haven, Conn.: Yale University Press, 1968), 4, 79.

25. Pipes, 262–263.

26. Basil Dmytryshyn, *U.S.S.R.: A Concise History* (New York: Scribner, 1965), 25. On the origins of Bolshevism see Leopold H. Haimson, *The Russian Marxists and the Origins of Bolshevism* (Cambridge, Mass.: Harvard University Press, 1967); Adam B. Ulam, *The Bolsheviks* (New York: Macmillan, 1965).

27. Ulam, 70–95.

28. Haimson, passim.

29. Quoted in Dmytryshyn, 24.

30. V. I. Lenin, *Chto delat'? [What Is To Be Done?], Polnoe sobranie sochinenii*, 5th ed. (Moscow, 1960), 6:1–192.

31. V. I. Lenin, "Pis'mo k tovarishchu nashikh organizatsionnykh zadachakh" ["Letter to a Comrade about our Organizational Problems,"] *Polnoe sobranie sochinenii*, 5th ed. (Moscow, 1959), 7:1–32.

32. V. I. Lenin, "Shag vpered, dva shaga nazad" ["One Step Forward, Two Steps Back"], *Polnoe sobranie sochinenii*, 5th ed. (Moscow, 1959), 8:185–414.

33. Leonard Schapiro, *The Communist Party of the Soviet Union* (New York: Random House, 1960), Part I.

34. Ulam, 247–250.

35. Seweryn Bialer, "Leninism and the Peasantry in the Russian Revolution" (Paper presented at the SEADAG Rural Development Seminar, Savannah, Georgia, May 1974).

36. Ulam, 292–293.

37. Many works describe the events of the October Revolution in Petrograd. In particular, see William Henry Chamberlin, *The Russian Revolution 1917–1921* (New York: Macmillan, 1935) and Robert V. Daniels, *Red October* (New York: Scribner, 1967).

38. *Partiinaia zhizn'* No. 21 (November 1977), 20–21.

39. Chamberlin, I:159.

40. Chamberlin, I:203.

41. Daniels, 89–96.

chapter 2

The Soviet View of Development: Marxist-Leninist Ideology

The Bolsheviks sought not only to modernize the society they had inherited from the Tsarist and Provisional Governments, but also to build within the former Empire a society unlike any that had ever existed. Their image of this society was contained in their ideology; Soviet Marxism-Leninism, in an important sense, was the Bolshevik view of development.[1] It not only sketched the society the Bolsheviks sought to create, but also narrowed the means available to them in building it.

Although in the United States the term "ideology" is used quite widely to describe diverse belief systems, the following discussion of the ideology of the Soviet state will use the term in a narrower sense that is more appropriate to the role of ideology in the Soviet polity since 1917. Building on a definition originally offered by Zbigniew Brzezinski, we will say that the Soviet ideology is composed of both a doctrine and an action program. These two halves of Soviet ideology include general assertions about the inadequacy of the existing order (particularly of capitalism) as well as prescribed methods for change (class-based revolution) and some idealized goals for the future (communist society). The doctrinal component includes the philosophical foundations of the ideology, such as dialectical materialism and labor theory of value. These are the relatively unchanging principles of the ideology, many of which date from the times of Karl Marx (1818–1883) and Friedrich Engels (1829–1895). Derived from (and interrelated with) this doctrine is an action program, a more contingent set of dogmatic prescriptions for action. These dogmas, such as the inevitability of war between socialism and capitalism, change with time and circumstance.[2]

MARXIST-LENINIST DOCTRINE

Much of the doctrinal component of Soviet ideology is contained in the philosophy of Karl Marx, Friedrich Engels, and Vladimir Lenin.[3] Marxism-Leninism is a unique blend of Western European philosophy drawn from the Enlightenment tradition and Russian accretions largely untouched by modern liberalism. According to contemporary Soviet philosophers, Marxism makes three distinct intellectual contributions to Western thought and Soviet ideology: a philosophy, a system of political economy, and a sociopolitical theory. Leninism, in the modern Soviet formulation, is Marxism in the era of imperialism and proletarian revolution.[4] Lenin wrote under changed conditions not entirely foreseen by Marx. Thus, Lenin extended Marx's historical materialism to account for the rise of monopoly capitalism, imperialism, and the world socialist system. And Lenin added to Marx's sociopolitical theory the strategy and tactics of proletarian revolution in less-developed societies, a theory of the revolutionary party, and a theory of the socialist state and its administration.

The canon of Marxism-Leninism is voluminous. The current Soviet editions of the *Complete Collected Works* of V. I. Lenin and the *Collected Works* of Marx and Engels fill over 100 volumes. Marx and Engels's most important works are perhaps the *Manifesto of the Communist Party* (1848) and *Das Kapital* (1867–1893). Lenin's include *What Is To Be Done?* (1902), a tract on party organization; *Imperialism* (1916), a theory of international relations and foreign policy; and *State and Revolution* (1917), sketching his theory of the socialist state.

At the core of Marxism-Leninism is the belief that all existence is governed by objective laws and that natural and social science can reveal these to humankind. Engels wrote in *Anti-Duehring*,

> Active social forces work exactly like natural forces: blindly, forcibly, destructively, so long as we do not understand, and reckon with, them. But when once we understand them, when once we grasp their action, their direction, their effects, it depends only upon ourselves to subject them more and more to our own will, and by means of them to reach our own ends.[5]

The Soviet ideologist A. G. Spirkin asserts that Marxism-Leninism "proceeds from the fact that the world is knowable and that science penetrates ever more deeply into the laws of being. The possibilities for achieving knowledge of the world are boundless. . . ."[6] In particular, modern Marxism-Leninism seeks the laws of social development.

Philosophy of Dialectical and Historical Materialism

At the heart of Marx's philosophy is *dialectical materialism*, a theory of development that purports to be the foundation of all the specific natural and social sciences.[7] Dialectical materialism combines a theory of motion and development (dialectics) with the assertion that the sole basis of the world is matter (materialism). Central to the dialectic is the "law of the unity and conflict of opposites."[8] That is, in all realms of existence progress results from a process in which an initial unity is followed by a division into mutually exclusive opposites and then a new and higher synthesis. For example, Engels's explanation of the origins of solar systems stresses the differentiation of "previously chemically indifferent elements" in the primeval ooze and their subsequent combinations into new matter. This is followed by subsequent differentiation of chemicals and yet newer combinations.[9] This succession of thesis (initial unity), antithesis (differentiation and opposition), and synthesis (new unity) is the process of development in all natural and social realms. While these stages repeat, they do so at ever higher stages of development. Materialism asserts that matter is the "sole basis of the world." Thus, "dialectical materialism maintains that the world is *matter in motion*".[10] Importantly, if matter is the sole basis of the world, human consciousness does not exist independent from matter, but is preceded by and derived from it.

Dialectical materialism is the foundation of Marx's philosophy of history, which Soviet theorists present as the science of society called *historical materialism*. This theory views history as a developmental process involving a succession of socioeconomic formations—specifically, primitive communal society, slave-holding society, feudalism, capitalism, and communism. Each socioeconomic formation is "a qualitatively distinct society at a given stage of its development"; it is composed of a base and superstructure. The base includes "the material relations of production"—that is, the means by which humans produce goods. The superstructure is

the sum total of ideological, political, moral, and legal . . . relations as well as the organizations and institutions such as the state, the church, and the court system that are connected with them; and also various feelings, sentiments, views, ideas, and theories that taken together constitute the social psychology and ideology of a given society.[11]

In the relationship of the base to the superstructure, the productive forces of the former are the fundamental basis of human society.

As these productive forces develop (that is, as humankind comes to have greater control over nature), socioeconomic formations change. These changes bring changing social relations of production and, in particular, changing antagonistic class relations of dominance and subjection. Marx and Engels in the *Communist Manifesto* wrote that "the history of all past society has consisted in the development of class antagonisms, antagonisms that assumed different forms at different epochs. But whatever form they have taken, one fact is common to all past ages, that is, the exploitation of one part of society by the other".[12] In the capitalist order, for example, the proletariat ("workers") produces commodities with means of production that it does not own; the bourgeoisie ("capitalists") owns these means of production and through this ownership exploits the proletariat.

Class struggle (the differentiation of socioeconomic formations into classes and the opposition between classes) is the driving force in the dialectical development of society prior to socialism. And "social revolution is the normal means of transition from one socioeconomic formation to another in the progressive development of society."[13] But once the proletariat understands the laws of history as Marx explains them, it will end the process of class struggle by ending class structures. As Marx explained in a letter to J. Weydemeyer of New York,

> What I did that was new was to prove: 1) that the *existence of classes* is only bound up with *particular historical phases in the development of production*, 2) that the class struggle necessarily leads to the *dictatorship of the proletariat*, 3) that this dictatorship itself only constitutes the transition to the *abolition of all classes* and to a *classless society*.[14]

That is, the product of this developmental process will be communism.

Lenin extended Marxian historical analysis to the period of what he called "monopoly capitalism" or "imperialism," when the multiplicity of competing small-scale capitalist producers is replaced by large-scale monopolies associated with large banks. According to Lenin,

> Imperialism is capitalism in that stage of development in which the domination of monopoly and finance capital has taken shape; in which the export of capital has acquired pronounced importance; in which the division of the world by international trusts has begun; and in which the partition of all the territory of the earth by the greatest capitalist countries has been completed.[15]

With the replacement of small competitive firms by monopolies, capitalism enters its highest (and last) stage. In this stage, the accumulation of capital can continue and the proletariat in some capitalist countries can be bought off with higher standards of living through exploitation of colonies that provide protected markets and cheap raw materials. The stage of monopoly capitalism thus leads to predatory foreign policies and to wars among the capitalist states seeking ever-expanding markets and colonial empires. Imperialism also intensifies the law of uneven development among capitalist countries, for some of these countries profit from colonialism, while others do not. This uneven development is critical in the stage of imperialism for it can lead to proletarian revolution in the less-successful capitalist societies.

Lenin also expanded Marx's analysis of postcapitalist development—that is, the development of society after the proletariat seizes power. Marx, in the *Critique of the Gotha Program*, distinguished between a "first phase" and a "second phase" of communism, with the first representing a period of transition. Lenin, in *State and Revolution* and his later writings, associated these phases with the labels socialism and communism, respectively. This distinction became increasingly important to Lenin's thought and is now central to Soviet ideology, for it placed the path of Soviet development after 1917 in an historical context. At present, socialism and communism are treated as distinct "phases" of the same socioeconomic formation, with socialism including various stages, the last of which is presently called developed or mature socialism.

Political Economy

In addition to the concepts of dialectical and historical materialism, the doctrinal component of Marxist Leninist ideology includes an economic philosophy as well. The conceptual underpinnings of Marx's system of political economy are oftentimes called the *labor theory of value* and the *theory of surplus value.* Marx used these to explain capitalist economy in *Das Kapital.* The labor theory of value asserts that the value of a commodity is determined by the socially necessary labor expended in the making of it. That is, labor, either directly in the making of some commodity or indirectly through labor needed to create the tools used in the manufacturing process, is the only source of value in commodities.

The theory of surplus value declares that capitalists derive profits by expropriating some of the value provided by labor. Specifically, while the proletariat creates value, it is paid not for the full value of what it created, but only enough to maintain and replace the labor force. That is, labor power itself is treated as a commodity under capitalism and is paid only for the labor value necessary to provide it.[16] The difference between the subsistence wage paid the worker and the value of the commodities he produces is a measure of the exploitation of the worker by capitalists and the basis of the latter's profits.

Capitalists expand their profits through greater exploitation, either by lengthening the work day or by increasing worker productivity with machine production, so that workers produce more value but are paid no more for their labor. Capitalists can also expand profits by squeezing wages directly or reducing the labor force through layoffs. Marx predicted that with this expanding exploitation the development of capitalism naturally leads to growing accumulation (concentration) of capital in bourgeois hands and mounting misery of the proletariat as its poverty and unemployment grow.

Sociopolitical Theory

A third component of the Marxist-Leninist doctrine is a sociopolitical theory in which Marx described the nature of the state and the conditions for the revolutionary transformation of society. The state was defined as the consequence of irreconcilable class contradictions: "By means of the state, the economically dominant class imposes its political rule and suppresses the resistance of the oppressed classes. In antagonistic class society the state is in essence the instrument of violence by one class against another."[17]

The class nature of the state, as part of the superstructure, changes with the socioeconomic formation. Specifically, through revolution one class establishes its dictatorship over society. So, for example, the revolutions that attended the end of the feudal order and the rise of capitalism established the hegemony of the bourgeoisie. The proletariat in its revolution will put an end to bourgeois rule and establish "the revolutionary dictatorship of the proletariat."[18] But unlike earlier revolutions, the proletariat's will be the first in which the majority comes to rule. Moreover, this revolution will be different, for the proletariat, armed with Marxism, will ultimately put an end to classes, exploitation, and the state itself.

Lenin's addition to this sociopolitical theory, his theory of the strategy and tactics of revolution, addressed the unique problems facing revolutionaries in less-developed countries such as Russia: How should Marxists bring socialism to a preindustrial or early capitalist society? As noted in the previous chapter, Lenin agreed with the orthodox Marxist view that Russia was not yet ready for a pure proletarian revolution to build socialism and that Russia must first experience a democratic revolution, but he rejected the idea (common among the Mensheviks) of cooperation with the reformist bourgeoisie to build a parliamentary democracy. The bourgeoisie in Russia was not liberal and if it came to power would not set up a modern parliamentary republic. Lenin argued that, instead, the proletariat itself, in alliance with the peasantry, would have to establish a revolutionary democratic dictatorship of the proletariat and the peasantry. Under this dictatorship, the proletariat would use the period of industrialization to build the foundations for the socialist revolution that would lead to a pure dictatorship of the proletariat itself.[19] Thus, Lenin argued that proletarian and socialist parties have a central, not simply a supporting, role in making revolutions in preindustrial societies.

Lenin's theory of the party envisioned an instrument that could take power and build socialism in these early capitalist or even preindustrial societies. As noted in Chapter 1, this theory was forged in the Bolsheviks' struggle with the Mensheviks in the early Russian Social Democratic movement. The debate between these groups had focused on two questions: What should be the relationship of the party to the proletariat? And how should the party be organized internally? On the first issue the Mensheviks wanted to follow the West European model of a mass party open to broad membership and reflecting its members' interests. Lenin championed the concept of the vanguard party. He accused the Mensheviks of the error of tailism (*khvostizm*)—making the party subservient to the proletariat. He argued that the proletariat on its own is capable of developing only a trade union consciousness and cannot be relied upon to develop a revolutionary consciousness (*soznatel'nost'*) spontaneously. Instead, the party, as the repository of Marxist-Leninist ideology, must bring revolutionary consciousness to the working class, leading the proletariat rather than being led by it. On the question of internal party organization, Lenin argued for tight party discipline, expressed in the concept of *democratic centralism:* Specifically, minorities within the party must submit to the majority after all decisions; and the executive organs of the party must have the power to rid its membership of those who persist in opposing the decision of the party majority.[20]

Lenin's contribution to the Marxist theory of the state is rooted in his effort to reconcile two seemingly contradictory statements by Engels that had become fundamental to Marxist thought but had come to have potentially explosive implications for any new socialist regime. On the one hand, Engels had said that when the proletariat assumes power it would put an end to the state as a state. But on the other hand, Engels had said that under socialism the state would "wither away".[21] The first pronouncement suggests immediate consequences; the second suggests a long-term process. Lenin argued that both of these statements are true—that the state with coercive instruments would continue into socialism, but it would no longer be a state in the same sense it had been in class society. In *State and Revolution*, Lenin argued that the proletarian revolution would destroy the bourgeois state and replace it with

Lenin on the State

In *State and Revolution* Lenin offered the following observations on the state and administration after the proletarian revolution.

The Proletarian State

"The state is a special organization of force; it is the organization of violence for the suppression of some class. What class must the proletariat suppress? Naturally, the exploiting class only, *i.e.,* the bourgeoisie."

"The proletariat needs state power, the centralized organization of force, the organization of violence, both for the purpose of crushing the resistance of the exploiters and for the purpose of *guiding* the great mass of the population—the peasantry, the petty-bourgeoisie, the semi-proletarians—in the work of organizing Socialist economy."

"[D]uring the *transition* from capitalism to Communism, suppression is *still* necessary; but it is the suppression of the minority of exploiters by the majority of exploited. A special apparatus, special machinery for suppression, the 'state,' is *still* necessary, but this is now a transitional state, no longer a state in the usual sense, for the suppression of the minority of exploiters, by the majority of the wage slave *of yesterday,* is a matter comparatively so easy, simple and natural that it will cost far less bloodshed than the suppression of the rising of slaves, serfs or wage laborers, and will cost mankind far less."

". . . the organ of suppression is now the majority of the population, and not a minority, as was always the case under slavery, serfdom, and wage labor. And, once the majority of the people *itself* suppresses its oppressors, a 'special force' for suppression is *no longer necessary.* In this sense the state *begins to wither away*."

Administration in the Socialist State

"The specific 'commanding' methods of the state officials can and must begin to be replaced—immediately, within twenty-four hours—by the simple functions of 'managers' and bookkeepers, functions which are now already within the capacity of the average city dweller and can well be performed for 'workingmen's wages.' "

"Accounting and control—these are the *chief* things necessary for the organizing and correct functioning of the *first phase* of Communist society."

"The accounting and control necessary for this have been *simplified* by capitalism to the utmost, till they have become the extraordinarily simple operations of watching, recording and issuing receipts, within the reach of anybody who can read and write and knows the first four rules of arithmetic."

"Under Socialism, *all* will take a turn in management, and will soon become accustomed to the idea of no managers at all."

"Socialism will shorten the working day, raise the *masses* to a new life, create such conditions for the *majority* of the population as to enable *everybody,* without exception, to perform 'state functions,' and this will lead to a *complete withering away* of every state in general."

The 'Withering Away' of the State

". . . as to the 'withering away' or, more expressively and colorfully, as to the state 'becoming dormant,' Engels refers quite clearly and definitely to the period *after* 'the seizure of the means of production [by the state] in the name of society,' that is, *after* the Socialist revolution."

"We set ourselves the ultimate aim of destroying the state, *i.e.,* every organized and systematic violence, every use of violence against man in general. . . . [S]triving for Socialism, we are convinced that it will develop into Communism; [and] that, side by side with this, there will vanish all need for force, for the *subjection* of one man to another, and of one part of the population to another, since people will *grow accustomed* to observing the elementary conditions of social existence *without force and without subjection.*"

"Finally, only Communism renders the state absolutely unnecessary, for there is *no one* to be suppressed—'no one' in the sense of a *class,* in the sense of a systematic struggle with a definite section of the population. We are not Utopians, and we do not in the least deny the possibility and inevitability of excesses on the part of *individual persons,* nor the need to suppress *such* excesses. But, in the first place, no special machinery, no special apparatus of repression is needed for this; this will be done by the armed people itself, as simply and as readily as any crowd of civilized people, even in modern society, parts a pair of combatants or does not allow a woman to be outraged. And, secondly, we know that the fundamental social cause of excesses which consist in violating the rules of social life is the exploitation of the masses, their want and their poverty. With the removal of this chief cause, excesses will inevitably begin to 'wither away.' We do not know how quickly and in what succession, but we know that they will wither away. With their withering away, the state will also *wither away.*"

Source: V. I. Lenin, *Gosudarstvo i revoliutsiia [State and Revolution]* in *Polnoe sobranie sochinenii,* 5th ed., 33 (Moscow: Politicheskaia Literatura, 1962).

a new form of government. The dictatorship of the proletariat would be a democratic dictatorship of the majority over the minority, so that the state as a dictatorship by the minority would be abolished immediately.

> [Yet] the proletariat needs state power, the centralized organizations of force, the organization of violence, both for the purpose of crushing the resistance of the exploiters and for the purpose of guiding the great mass of the population—the peasantry, the petty-bourgeoisie, the semi-proletarians—in the work of organizing Socialist economy.[22]

And so, the state as a coercive instrument would continue, withering away only over the longer term. Not socialism, but "only Communism renders the state absolutely unnecessary, for there is no one to be suppressed."[23]

Lenin, lastly, introduced a theory of the administration of the Soviet state. To infuse the democratic dictatorship with proletarian content, he argued that the administration of the state must become popular. One of the accomplishments of capitalism had been to simplify the tasks of the state, particularly its administration, to what Lenin called "accounting and control"—"the extraordinarily simple operations of watching, recording, and issuing receipts, within the reach of anybody who can read and write and knows the first four rules of arithmetic."[24] He argued that those tasks could be performed by average proletarians:

Basic Concepts in Soviet Marxism-Leninism

- dialectical materialism—a theory of development that is the foundation of all specific natural and social sciences.
    dialectics
    materialism
    law of the unity and conflict of opposites
    thesis, antithesis, and synthesis
- historical materialism—a philosophy of history, applying dialectical materialism to the development of society.
    socio-economic formation
    base
    superstructure
    class struggle and social revolution
    imperialism (Lenin)
    socialism and communism as phases in a post-capitalist socio-economic formation
- labor theory of value—economic theory that asserts that the value of a commodity is determined by the socially necessary labor expended in the making of it.
- theory of surplus value—asserts that profits derive from the expropriation by non-producers of some of the value produced by labor.
    laws of capitalist accumulation and the concentration of capital
    law of increasing misery
- theory of the state—asserts that the state is an instrument of class domination.
    revolutionary dictatorship of the proletariat
    revolutionary democratic dictatorship of the proletariat and the peasantry (Lenin)
    theory of the vanguard party (Lenin)
    democratic centralism (Lenin)
    withering away of the state
    state administration as "accounting and control" (Lenin)

Under Socialism . . . for the first time in the history of civilized society, the mass of the population rises to independent participation, not only in voting and elections, but also in the everyday administration of affairs. Under Socialism, all will take a turn in management, and will soon become accustomed to the idea of no managers at all.[25]

In the first months after the Revolution the new Soviet regime actually began to bring average Soviets into the state administration. But four months after the Revolution, as the Soviet state began to grind to a halt under incompetent administration, Lenin increasingly spoke of the need to bring experts back into the state. He discovered that management of a complex state involves more than simply registering, filing, and checking.

Lenin's contributions to the doctrine addressed the problems of taking power and ruling a preindustrial society and provided the conceptual building blocks for a dictatorship of the central party organs over society. The dictatorship of the proletariat legitimated the rule of the proletariat over society. The vanguard party handed the power of the proletariat to the party itself as the organ that accurately perceives the interests of the proletariat, understands its ideology, and is the repository of orthodoxy. By democratic centralism the power of the proletarian dictatorship falls to the executive organs of the party.

CONTEMPORARY SOVIET IDEOLOGY

Contemporary Soviet ideology seeks an action program that is consonant with the philosophies of Marxist-Leninist doctrine. Once in power, as Lenin promised to the Second Congress of Soviets, the Bolsheviks began the task of building the socialist order. Nineteen years later, in 1936, Stalin declared that socialism "in the main" was finally victorious in the Soviet Union. The Soviet state had at last eliminated the last vestiges of capitalism and passed into the period of socialism. Since the time of Stalin, and particularly since 1959, the Soviet Union, in its official view, is a socio-economic formation in transition from socialism to communism. The precise location of the Soviet Union along that process, however, is affected by the shifting dogmas of the action program. In the period of optimism under Khrushchev the Party Program adopted by the 22nd Congress of the CPSU proclaimed that the Soviet Union had entered the period of "the full-scale construction of communism." With this announcement the prospect of achieving communism in the Soviet Union became very real. Since Khrushchev's fall, the Soviet authorities have avoided this formulation, and since 1967, have favored the phrase, "the stage of fully-developed [or mature] socialism."[26]

Marx and Engels had not provided explicit guidelines for building socialism, particularly for its later stages. Their writings provided some prescriptions for immediate action by a new socialist regime, and Lenin's response to the early problems of governing and transforming Soviet society have provided subsequent leaders with some dogmatic prescriptions for policy. But on most issues requiring action, the doctrinal component of Marxism-Leninsim has been silent. Thus, the Party has had to develop new dogmas that would explain the transition to communism. Soviet philosophers have engaged in considerable speculation, and at times even debate, in an attempt to define the Soviet Union's goals and the appropriate means to achieve these. Because the doctrine is silent on many of these issues, Soviet ideology since the Revolution has increasingly come to have a strongly teleological strain; that is, the socialist dogmas of the action program reflect the image of future communist society sketched by Marx, Engels, and the Communist Party, rather than the concrete prescriptions for action laid down by their doctrine. These policies, reflecting the changed and changing conditions facing the Soviet Union, have constituted the shifting dogmas of the contemporary Marxist-Leninist action program.

The shape of the communist future, it is worth noting, is an issue on which the writings of Marx, Engels, Lenin, and contemporary Soviet philosophers provide only a bare sketch with few concrete details. And Soviet philosophers have argued that it is unscientific, utopian, and therefore un-Marxist to attempt to construct an imagined future society. Nonetheless, the Party does provide a sense of where it believes the Soviet Union is headed as well as dogmatic prescriptions for what the Soviet Union must do to complete this transition. This contemporary Soviet ideology

The Nature of Socialism: The Official View

The Party Program adopted at the XXVII CPSU Congress offers the following definition of socialism.

The experience of the USSR and other socialist countries convincingly demonstrates the indisputable social, economic, political, ideological, and moral advantages of the new society [socialism] as a stage in the progress of mankind that is superior to capitalism, and it provides answers to questions that the bourgeois system is unable to resolve.

Socialism is a society on whose banner is imprinted "Everything in the name of man, everything for the good of man." It is a society in which:

- the means of production are in the hands of the people, and the exploitation of man by man, social oppression, the power of a privileged minority, poverty and the illiteracy of millions of people have been ended once and for all;

- the widest possible scope has been opened for the dynamic and systematic development of productive forces, and scientific and technical progress entails not the unemployment of millions but steady improvement in the well-being of the entire people;

- an equal right to work and its just remuneration in accordance with the principle "From each according to his ability, to each according to his work" are ensured, and the population enjoys such social benefits as free medical service and education and housing for a minimal payment;

- the indestructible alliance of the working class, the collective farm peasantry and the intelligentsia has been firmly established, women are granted genuinely equal rights with men, a reliable path to the future has been opened for the younger generation, and veteran workers are guaranteed social security;

- national inequalities have been eliminated, and the legal and practical equality, friendship, and brotherhood of all nations and nationalities have been established;

- genuine democracy—power that is exercised for the people and by the people themselves—has been established and is developing, and the ever-broader and equal participation of citizens in the administration of production, public and state affairs has been ensured;

- the ideas of freedom, human rights and the dignity of the individual have been filled with real and vital content, the unity of rights and duties is ensured, and one set of laws and moral norms and one discipline are in effect for everyone, creating favorable conditions for the all-round development of the individual;

- the truly humanistic Marxist-Leninist ideology prevails, the masses have access to all sources of knowledge, and an advanced socialist culture that incorporates all the best elements of world culture has been created;

- a socialist way of life has formed, based on social justice, collectivism, and comradely mutual assistance, a way of life that gives the workingman confidence in the future and elevates him spiritually and morally as the creator of new social relations and his own destiny.

Socialism is a society whose thoughts and actions in the international arena are aimed at supporting the aspirations of the peoples for independence and social progress and are subordinated to the main task—preserving and consolidating peace.

Source: *Pravda,* 7 March 1986.

comprises dogmas concerning the new communist man, new economic structures, changed social relations, and the transformation of political organization; and it includes some speculation about timetables for the future.

The New Communist Man

Fundamental to the Soviet view of the future is the claim that communist society will be populated by a new kind of human being—specifically, by a personality type called the "new communist man." Marxist philosophy stresses that human nature is not fixed, but, rather, is determined by changing historical conditions. That is, the succession of socioeconomic formations brings changes in prevailing notions of human needs, the role of the individual in society, and the pattern of relations among individuals. This premise is central to the view of the communist future, for without it that society would probably fail.

The new communist man will be a collectivist. Unlike men and women in earlier societies, the communist will reject egoism. The egoistic conception of material self-interest that is prevalent in class-based society and continues into socialist society, due to lags in consciousness, will be replaced during the transition to communism with an enlightened moral self-interest. For the first time, a citizen will come to recognize that what he or she has is the consequence of society. The individual will recognize that without society no one would have personal security, material well-being, or any of the other amenities of civilization such as language and culture. Thus, each will realize that one's self-interest is identical with society's interest.[27] For example, if society needs someone to perform an onerous task, say travel to the coldest wastes of Siberia to undertake back-breaking work, the new communist man would willingly assume this responsibility. The new communist man (and everyone else in society as well) would recognize that he or she is the logical person to perform the work and so would not even consider rejecting the task! The new communist man will even gain satisfaction from this work, knowing that he or she is acting on behalf of society. As the Soviet philosopher G. C. Grigor'ev has written, "For the conscious member of society, it will be sufficient to know of a decision taken by the collective . . . for him then and there to submit to that decision."[28] The new communist man would not conceive of an interest separate from that of society. "In communist society," according to Engels, "the interests of individuals are not opposed to one another but, on the contrary, coincide. . . ."[29]

The new communist man will develop a new appreciation of the value of labor. According to Lenin,

> Communist labor . . . is labor performed without expectation of reward, without reward as a condition, [but] labor performed because it has become a habit to work for the common good, and because of a conscious realization (which has become a habit) of the necessity of work for the common good—labor as the requirement of the healthy organism.[30]

The new communist man will find in labor an opportunity to fully develop his or her creative powers.

Communist Society: The Official View

The current Party Program describes communist society in the following terms.

The CPSU's ultimate goal is the building of communism in our country. Socialism and communism are two successive phases of the single communist formation. There is no sharp boundary between them: The development of socialism, the ever-fuller disclosure and implementation of its possibilities and advantages, and the strengthening of its inherent general communist principles, which has begun, signifies the actual movement of society toward communism.

Communism is a classless social system with a single form of public ownership of the means of production and full social equality for all members of society, where, together with the all-round development of people, productive forces will grow on the basis of constantly developing science and technology, all sources of public wealth will merge in a full stream, and the great principle "From each according to his ability, to each according to his needs" will be realized. Communism is a highly organized society of free and conscious toilers in which public self-government will be established, labor for the good of society will become the first vital requirement, as a recognized need, for everyone, and each person's abilities will be employed to the greatest benefit for the people.

The material and technical base of communism presupposes the creation of productive forces that open up opportunities for the complete satisfaction of the reasonable requirements of society and the individual. All productive activity under conditions of communism will be built on the employment of highly efficient technical means and technologies, and the harmonious interaction of man and nature will be ensured.

In the highest phase of the communist formation, the directly social nature of labor and production will be fully established. As a result of definitively overcoming the vestiges of the old division of labor and of related, substantive social differences, the process of the formation of a socially homogeneous society will be completed.

Communism signifies the transformation of the system of socialist self-government of the people and of socialist democracy into the highest form of the organization of society—communist public self-government. As the necessary social, economic, and ideological preconditions ripen and all citizens are enlisted in management, and given the appropriate international conditions, the socialist state, as Lenin foresaw, will become, to an increasing degree, "a transitional form from a state to a nonstate." The activity of state agencies will acquire a nonpolitical nature, and the need for the state as a special political institution will gradually disappear.

An inalienable feature of the communist way of life is a high level of consciousness, public activism, discipline, and self-discipline on the part of the members of society, under which the observance of uniform, generally accepted rules of life in a communist society will become an inner requirement and habit for each person.

Communism is a social system in which the free development of each person is a condition for the free development of all.

The CPSU does not set itself the goal of anticipating the features of full communism in every detail. As progress toward it is made and experience in communist construction is accumulated, scientific notions about the highest phase of the new society will be enriched and will take on concrete form.

Source: *Pravda,* 7 March 1986.

The new communist man will place a low value on the accumulation of material goods. As the Soviet philosopher G. Shakhnazarov has written, "Communism excludes those narrow-minded people for whom the highest goal is to acquire every possible luxurious object. . . . Communism assumes wise and enlightened members of society with a developed understanding of their goals."[31] The slavish pursuit of wealth and luxury is the consequence of class society and particularly of capitalist society; and with the transition to communism the individual will be freed of this.

The new communist man will be a well-rounded human being who will develop each potentiality to the fullest—a renaissance man. Engels wrote in *Principles of Communism* that "a communistically organized society will be able to provide its members with the opportunity to utilize their comprehensively developed abilities in a comprehensive way."[32] The Soviet philosopher S. G. Strumilin has written, "The purpose of [communism] is neither higher productive work, nor the shortest working day, nor complete abundance of material wealth and such . . . [but] the freedom of man from all external obstacles to the full development of all personal inclinations and abilities."[33] In other words, everyone will have the freedom to write poetry, to compose symphonies, to paint a portrait, and to run a marathon. Not everyone will be a great composer, painter, or runner, but each will have the opportunity to develop to the fullest, without artificial social limitations. The ideal of the renaissance man shows Marx and his Soviet disciples to be products of the Western Enlightenment tradition. Yet, unlike some Western philosophers such as John Stuart Mill, the Soviet view of the well-rounded individual appears to leave no room for the eccentric. Thus personal development, like all freedom in this future communist society, appears to be bound by the narrow limits of communist consciousness and collectivism.

In this society inhabited by new communist men there would be little problem with social deviance such as crime. In the Soviet view, crime is a failing of class society that persists into the transition stage of socialism only because consciousness lags behind the changes in the material conditions of society. But once communism is attained, almost all crime should disappear. According to Engels, "We eliminate the contradiction between the individual man and all others, we counterpose social peace to social war, we put the axe to the *root* of crime. . . ."[34] The minor violations that remain will be dealt with, not by the coercive instruments of the state, but by collective society, for collective disapproval will immediately bring most individuals guilty of small-scale deviance into line. More serious infractions may be dealt with by ad hoc investigative committees designated by society, but these will be rare.

The short-term policy implications of these notions about human psychological transformation are substantial. The centrality of this new communist man to the Soviet future has made socialization—the training, education, and moral upbringing of this personality—a primary concern of the Soviet regime. According to the Soviet ideologist G. M. Volkov,

The Party believes that the *key* to the successful fulfillment of the new economic and social plans lies *primarily* in further stimulating the creativity and initiative of the Soviet people and *in raising the level of their political awareness and labor productivity.* For this reason the intellectual and cultural development of the working people and their communist education become a prime consideration.[35]

Because, as Lenin noted, this consciousness will not develop spontaneously, the Party must assume the burden of accomplishing this end.

New Economic Structures

At the root of this harmonious society will be a changed economic structure—the material foundations of society. The shift to communism will witness a change in property relations. According to Engels in *The Principles of Communism*,

> the new social order will generally take the running of industry and all branches of production out of the hands of disjointed individuals competing among themselves and will instead run all these branches of production on behalf of society as a whole, i.e., according to a social plan and with the participation of all members of society. . . . Hence, private ownership will also have to be abolished, and in its stead there will be common use of all the instruments of production and the distribution of all products by common agreement, or a so-called community of goods.[36]

Under communism there will be only two types of property, all people's property and personal property, and the latter is likely to be limited to those objects that cannot be used by more than one person at a time (e.g., clothes, toothbrushes). One Soviet writer has gone so far as to say that perhaps even these personal items will simply be on permanent personal loan. Everything else, such as automobiles and homes, will be all people's property, owned by society but given on temporary loan to individuals for their personal use.[37] The private property basis of society will be eliminated.

The shift to the communist economy will also witness a change in the nature of work. Communism will eliminate the division of labor, and in particular, eliminate the differences between classes, between mental and physical labor, and between industrial and agricultural labor. Contemporary Soviet theorists argue that communism will also create the objective conditions for labor to become a source of pleasure for the working person. With the elimination of exploitation, labor will become a basis for expressing one's creativity. It is an interesting inconsistency in the Soviet view of labor that they also predict communism will produce a shortened workday. Engels argued,

> . . . human society has an abundance of productive forces at its disposal which only await a rational organization, an ordered distribution, in order to go into operation to the greatest benefit for all. . . . [G]iven this kind of organization, the present customary labor time of the individual will be reduced by half simply by making use of the labor which is either not used at all or used disadvantageously.[38]

If labor is so fulfilling and rewarding, why would anyone want to reduce the workday?

And this shift to the communist economy will produce a period of superabundance. By planned production, communist economics will be able to produce more than any previous society. Of course, since communist society is not consumption oriented, it will not have to produce as much to satisfy all social needs. Products will be distributed according to need, which, of course, will be moderate due to the enlightened sense of needs among new communist men. According to Marx in his *Critique of the Gotha Program*, communist "society [will] inscribe on its banners: From each according to his ability, to each according to his needs!"[39] Engels adds,

> Since we know how much, on the average, a person needs, it is easy to calculate how much is needed by a given number of individuals, and since production is no longer in the hands of private producers but in those of the community and its administrative bodies, it is a trifling matter *to regulate production according to needs.*[40]

In such a society, money will no longer be necessary, for money is the result of an economy of scarcity.

The transformation of the economic foundations of society implies certain policies in the short term that have been central to the Soviet model of development. The *Communist Manifesto* recommended that a newly successful proletarian revolution immediately adopt the following policies:

1. Abolition of property in land and application of all rents of land to public purposes.
2. A heavy progressive or graduated income tax.
3. Abolition of all right of inheritance.
4. Confiscation of the property of all emigrants and rebels.
5. Centralization of credit in the hands of the State, by means of a national bank with State capital and an exclusive monopoly.
6. Centralization of the means of communication and transport in the hands of the State.
7. Extension of factories and instruments of production owned by the State; the bringing into cultivation of wastelands, and the improvement of the soil generally in accordance with a common plan.
8. Equal liability of all to labor. Establishment of industrial armies, especially for agriculture.
9. Combination of agriculture with manufacturing industries; gradual abolition of the distinction between town and country by a more equable distribution of the population over the country.
10. Free education for all children in public schools. Abolition of children's factory labor in its present form. Combination of education with industrial production, etc., etc.[41]

In the early days, the Bolsheviks did indeed change the property relations in Soviet society and establish a planned, centrally managed economy. In more recent years, the Party has continued to emphasize that change in the economic base of society is at the root of the transition to communism. According to Volkov,

> The creation of the material and technical base of communism is . . . the decisive link in the chain of economic, social, political, and ideological objectives to be achieved in the construction of communism and is the essential prerequisite of success in reaching the final goal of social development—the formation of the fully developed individual.[42]

Central to building this "material and technical base of communism" is a "scientific and technological revolution" that will lead to the "comprehensive automation" of production.[43]

New Social Relations

The transformation of property relations during the transition to communism will bring the final elimination of classes. In the early days of the Soviet regime, according to the official view, nationalization of land and production eliminated the landowning class and the big bourgeoisie; later, collectivization eliminated the rich peasants. Today, only two classes survive in Soviet society, the working class and the peasantry. (The intelligentsia constitutes a separate stratum, but not a distinctive class.) In the Marxist view that classes are constituted by their relations to the means of production, the two classes are distinguished because the working class produces with publicly owned property, but the peasantry produces with collective-cooperative property. Unlike classes in capitalist society, however, these "are friendly classes united by common social aims and objectives. Under socialism there are not exploiters and exploited. . . ." To complete the transition to communism, the difference between these two forms of property must be eliminated. "The stage of developed socialism is the period during which these two forms of ownership are merged together."[44] Specifically, the collective farms must be transformed into state farms—into factories in the fields—so that the differences between labor in town and country will come to an end.

Communism will witness a change in basic human relations, not only in classes, but also in nations and the family. National differences, in the Marxist-Leninist view, are the product of capitalism. Moreover, "in capitalist society, based on private property and class antagonisms, exploitation of man by man is systematically augmented by the subjugation and plunder of some national groups by others so that relations among nationalities under capitalism inevitably assume the form of domination of some and subjugation of others.[45] While distinctions such as national languages survive under socialism, national relations are supposed to be more harmonious. In the Soviet Union, in particular, socialism is said to have "led to the emergence of a new historical community of men and women—the Soviet people."[46] And the consequence of socialism is purportedly the further "drawing together" of nationalities. Thus, even "the Soviet People is a transitional community of people on the way from class and national communities to the future worldwide, overall human community under communism."[47] Under communism, not only will national animosities disappear, but also national differences in culture and language will eventually wither away.

Not just large social forms like classes and nations, but also the smallest, the family, will be changed by communism. According to Engels in his *Principles of Communism*, communism will make the relations between the sexes a purely private affair which concerns only the persons involved, and calls for no interference by society. It is able to do this because it abolishes private property and educates children communally, destroying thereby the two foundation stones of hitherto existing marriage—the dependence of the wife upon her husband and of the children upon the parents conditioned on private property.[48]

The shift to communism will liberate families of many of their duties, such as cooking, cleaning, and laundering, for many of these will be provided by the collectivity. This will mean, at last, the liberation of women since many of these traditional tasks of the family have been their responsibility. And it will be the basis of unprecedented family harmony: Freed of the traditional sources of disharmony under class society, such as finances and household chores, "the marriage union under communism will be fuller, firmer and happier than it ever was in the past."[49] It will also free the citizen to become the public person that Western philosophers such as Jean Jacques Rousseau held out as the democratic ideal.

The shift to communism in the family will not, however, mean sexual promiscuity. According to Engels, "community of wives is a relationship belonging entirely to bourgeois society and existing today in perfect form as prostitution. Prostitution, however, is rooted in private property and falls with it."[50] The monogamous family will survive and will be stronger than ever as the basis of society, even though the formalities of marriage may wither away as a social institution rooted in class society. The place of children in this communist family is uncertain, however. Some Soviet philosophers argue that children should be cared for by the collectives as suggested by Engel's statement quoted in the previous paragraph; others, bowing to prevailing sentiment among contemporary Soviet parents, argue that the family itself will continue to care for them.[51]

Transformation of Political Organization

The shift to communism will also be marked by a significant transformation in the political organization of society. As Engels had said, the state will wither away. Yet there will still be a need for social organization to make decisions and to implement these.

With the elimination of classes and the inculcation of a communist consciousness, politics as we know it will come to an end. Politics as a contest for power and policy is rooted in a competition of narrow interests and will have no place in a communist society. Decision making in communist society will be based on scientific and technical foundations by decision makers presumably drawn from among the most able and qualified experts taking their turns in service to the community. As new communist men, they will not seek power, but will derive satisfaction from serving society.[52] The implementers of policy will be drawn from the broad population, for all will participate in the administration of society.

The institutional framework for communist self-administration is unclear. Soviet philosophers have not explained whether the soviets (officially, the state organs of collective self-rule) and public organizations will continue into communist society. It is clear from these writings, however, that there will be two areas in which centralized institutions will remain strong or become even stronger under communism: One is the economy; the other, the Party. Although the state will wither away, the centralization of the economy through the Plan will increase, and the Plan will actually become more comprehensive. But it will be a scientific plan, as enlightened planners make decisions on behalf of society's welfare that everyone will, of course, recognize as proper. The Party's role will also increase, particularly in the early stages of communism. With the withering away of the state, the Party will have to play a larger role in Soviet society, especially as building the consciousness of the new communist man becomes increasingly important. Soviet philosophers suggest that in later stages of communism, at a point they cannot yet foresee, the party itself may wither away as well.

The policy implications of this vision of future political organization are enormous. Nikita Khrushchev argued that the dictatorship of the proletariat was a state form appropriate to the transition from capitalism to socialism, but once antagonistic classes were eliminated there is no longer a need for this dictatorship. So Khrushchev dubbed the Soviet state the *all-people's state*—a new political "organization of the whole people led by the working class and its communist vanguard." It is itself yet another transitional stage on the way to communist self-management. To reach communism from the current stage of mature socialism the Soviet Union must improve Soviet socialist democracy. According to the Soviet philosopher E. Chekharin, this means

> increasing the social activity of all Soviet people, extending their participation in the administration of society, intensifying popular control over the work of the state apparatus, extending the terms of reference of public organizations and citizens' rights and freedoms, improving public discipline and strengthening the rule of law in every sphere of social and individual activity.[53]

Specifically, three major changes must be effected under the all-people's state to complete this transition. First of all, the state must be democratized by drawing the people to its administration. Particularly since Stalin's death, efforts have been made to expand the activities of local soviets and to bring larger portions of the population into the implementation and administration of policy. Yet, the withering of the state implies a declining role for its organs. So the second change is the transfer of state functions from the soviets to public organizations. And the third change in the transition to communism is the expansion of the party's role in society.[54]

Timetables for the Future

Soviet philosophers have disagreed among themselves and Party dogmas have changed over time on the matter of how long it will take for the Soviet Union to achieve communism. Stalin's announcement after 19 years of Soviet rule that socialism had been built "in the main" was followed 23 years later at the 21st CPSU Congress (1959) by the proclamation that the "complete and final victory of socialism" had been won in the Soviet Union. Following this, particularly in the late Khrushchev years, there was an optimistic sense that communism could be achieved within the lifetime of those who were living or at the longest within that of their grandchildren. The Program adopted at the 22nd Party Congress in 1961 described the current tasks of the Party as the full-scale construction of communism and predicted that the transition would be a 20-year process. The Program viewed the 1960s as a period in which the material bases of communism would be built, particularly by expanding production. The Soviet Union would surpass the United States in per capita production by 1970. The decade of the '70s, based on that material abundance, would complete the task of laying "the material-technical base of communism." While production would continue to increase, there would be a more important qualitative change in production as less attention would be paid to the immediate consumption needs of individuals and more would be paid to the collective needs of society. The Program predicted that after 1980 "the construction of communist society will be fully completed"; all that would remain would be for human psychology to catch up.[55] This optimism proved unwarranted.

The Party manifestly failed to achieve the goals of the 22nd Congress. The Soviet Union certainly did not surpass the United States in production per capita by 1970; it is nowhere near this goal even in the late 1980s! Since Khrushchev's removal timetables for the future have been far less exacting. In 1971, a decade after Khrushchev announced that the Soviet Union had entered the period of full-scale construction of communism, the 24th Party Congress announced that the country was, in fact, only in the period of "fully developed socialism." In December 1984, in an address to the Party Central Committee, Konstantin Chernenko warned that "before accomplishing the tasks directly linked to the construction of communism, it is necessary to pass through the historically lengthy stage of developed socialism."[56] The new Party Program adopted in March 1986 seems to confirm this view. And even though Mikhail Gorbachev's program for acceleration (*uskorenie*) of technological progress has placed a premium on speeding the transformation of the material and technical bases of society, there has been considerable caution not to tie this to the immediate achievement of communism. There is now little effort to develop time-tables to predict how long the building of communism will take.

DOES IDEOLOGY REALLY INFLUENCE SOVIET POLICIES?

There is significant disagreement in the West about the actual role of ideology in Soviet politics. Do Soviet leaders believe in Marxism-Leninism? Does this ideology guide their policies by influencing either their goals or choices of means? Broadly speaking, there are at least three major schools of thought on this issue, which can be arranged along a continuum from maximalist to minimalist positions.

At one extreme, the maximalist view sees Soviet ideology as a blueprint for action.

> Virtually all analysts would agree that in the years of struggle before the October Revolution the Bolsheviks took the theory which lay behind their movement in deadly earnest; there is also general agreement that in the 1920's the doctrine acted as a stimulus to the workers, who took pride in building up their country.[57]

Current Tasks in the Transition from Socialism to Communism

The current Party Program sketches the following program to further the building of communism.

The development of socialism into communism is determined by the objective laws of the development of society, which cannot be disregarded. As experience shows, any attempts to introduce communist principles without considering the level of the material and spiritual maturity of society, are doomed to failure and may bring both economic and political losses.

At the same time, the CPSU proceeds from the premise that sluggishness in carrying out transformations whose time has come and in accomplishing new tasks must not be permitted. The party believes that, in the development of the country in the 1970s and the early 1980s, along with achievements and undeniable successes, there were certain unfavorable tendencies and difficulties. To a significant extent, they were connected with the fact that changes in the economic situation and the need for thoroughgoing changes in all spheres of life were not given a timely or proper assessment, and the proper persistence in carrying out those changes was not shown. This impeded the fuller use of the potential and advantages of the socialist system and held back changes.

The CPSU believes that, in today's domestic and international conditions, the all-round progress of Soviet society and its progressive movement toward communism can be ensured by the acceleration of the country's social and economic development. This is the Party's strategic course, with the aim of a qualitative transformation of all aspects of the life of Soviet society: the fundamental renewal of its material and technical base on the basis of the achievements of the scientific and technological revolution; the improvement of social relations, first of all economic relations; thoroughgoing changes in the content and nature of labor and in people's material and spiritual living conditions; and the activation of the whole system of political, social, and ideological institutions.

The Party links the successful accomplishment of the projected tasks with the enhancement of the role of the human factor. Socialist society cannot function effectively if it does not find new paths for the development of the creative activity of the masses in all spheres of social life. The greater the scope of the historical goals, the more important it is that millions participate, with an interest in achieving them in a responsible, conscious, and active way.

On the basis of the acceleration of social and economic development, Soviet society must scale new heights, which means:

in the economic field: raising the national economy to a fundamentally new scientific, technical, organizational, and economic level and switching it onto the tracks of intensive development; achieving the world's highest level in the productivity of social labor, production quality, and productive efficiency; ensuring an optimal structure and balance for the country's unified national-economic complex; significantly raising the level of the socialization of labor and production; and bringing collective farm and cooperative ownership closer to public ownership, with the long-term prospect of merging them;

in the social field: ensuring a qualitatively new level of national well-being, with the consistent implementation of the socialist principle of distribution according to labor; creating a basically classless structure of society, and erasing the essential differences in social, economic, cultural, and living conditions between city and countryside; the increasingly organic combination of physical and mental labor in productive activity; the further cohesion of the Soviet people as a social and international community; and a high level of creative energy and initiative among the masses;

in the political field: developing socialist self-government of the people by means of the ever fuller enlistment of citizens in the administration of state and public affairs, perfecting the electoral system, improving the activity of the elected agencies of peoples power, enhancing the role of the trade unions, the Komsomol, and other mass organizations of the working people, and making effective use of all forms of representative and direct democracy;

in the field of spiritual life: the further consolidation of the socialist ideology in the consciousness of the Soviet people, the full establishment of the moral principles of socialism and the spirit of collectivism and comradely mutual assistance, providing access to scientific achievements and cultural values to the broadest masses, and the molding of comprehensively developed individuals.

The result of these transformations will be a qualitatively new state of Soviet society that will fully disclose the enormous advantages of socialism in all spheres of life. Thereby a historic step will be taken on the path to the highest phase of communism. The Party constantly correlates its policy, its economic and social strategy and the tasks of its organizational and ideological work with the communist future.

Source: *Pravda*, 7 March 1986.

This maximalist view, however, argues that Soviet leaders have continued to believe their ideology decades after the Revolution. Moreover, it argues that ideology has provided them with a framework through which they perceive the world, with concrete goals for its transformation and with an explicit guide for effective action. The British economist Peter Wiles, for example, argues, "the Communists are governed by their sacred texts." He characterizes Marxism-Leninism as "a secular religion and a dedicated way of life, . . . the Islam of the non-Islamic world." "Holy Russia" is led by "a full complement of well-educated cardinals and theologians whose great intellectual goal is Orthodoxy within the religion."[58] The British scholar R. N. Carew-Hunt asks, how else can one explain the inefficiencies of the Soviet system? For example, why did the Soviets collectivize agriculture and then refuse to reform this system even though it showed itself to be far less productive than the private plots? Hunt argues that an "index" of the importance of ideology can be found in the inefficiencies of the Soviet economy; the only explanation for their persistence is the leaders' belief in their ideology. He adds, "We should remind ourselves that no class or party ever finds it difficult to persuade itself of the soundness of the principles on which it bases its claims to rule."[59]

Contrary to the position of the maximalist school, however, there are pragmatic reasons for persisting with inefficient programs. Collectivized agriculture, for example, may not maximize short-term production, but it may be an efficient means to preserve the power of the leadership and to engineer the long-term transformation of the Soviet economy to modern industrialism. Moreover, ideology leaves the leadership considerable room to maneuver; one cannot find in it a clear guide to action for most policy questions facing the leadership. The ideology is far too contradictory and incomplete a guide.

Citing these criticisms of pragmatism and ideological flexibility, the minimalist position, at the other extreme of interpretation, argues that ideology is simply a vocabulary and an analytic framework for discourse. The Soviet leaders, whether they believe their ideology or not, cannot find in it a guide to goals or action; rather, they simply use the ideology to rationalize and legitimate policies made on pragmatic grounds. The University of Vermont historian Robert Daniels, for example, has argued that Soviet leaders manipulate ideology for self-serving reasons.

> The leader has had the power since Stalin's time to establish the meaning of ideology in an absolutely binding way. . . . There is no force to keep his interpretations honestly in conformity with the original meaning of the ideology; on the other hand there is every temptation to modify the meaning of the ideology, through reinterpretation, to make each new practical policy or expedient appear consistent with the original ideology. Thus, as the analysis of some recent Soviet policy shifts will show, ideology cannot determine or limit action except for some short-run rigidities; it is action, rather, that eventually supplies the up-to-date meaning of ideology.[60]

Samuel Sharp, considering the impact of ideology on foreign policy, argues that the major policy issues facing the Soviet leaders are short-term, practical questions that the ideology does not address.

> The point at issue is . . . whether the *ultimate* aims of the Communist creed are operative in policy determinations. In the present writer's view they are not; the fault of the opposing line of analysis is that . . . it tends to ignore the degree to which the pursuit of ultimate goals has been circumscribed in time and scope by considerations of *the feasible*.[61]

There is no opportunity to engineer ideological vision. In short, ideology does not influence policy.

Contrary to the arguments of the minimalist position, however, not all Soviet actions can be explained by pure pragmatism. This would assume a very naive notion of pragmatism. What means are "pragmatic" or "efficient" can be determined only when measured against goals, which in all likelihood are set by higher values. Moreover, leaders often must choose among several solutions to a problem, each of which is equally pragmatic in the sense that each entails an equal balance of benefits and liabilities. The measure of the importance of an ideology is not the extent of inefficiencies in a society, but rather which policy benefits that society considers most important, which inefficiencies or liabilities it will accept, and which it finds unacceptable. Ideology may even foreclose some options simply because they are unorthodox. In the longer term the ideology may evolve to accommodate these options, but in the short run of decision making they limit choice.

Intermediate between these two positions is the argument, favored by this author, that ideology provides Soviet leaders an analytic prism through which they view the world, but not a guide to action. The Harvard University political scientist Adam Ulam has argued that one cannot assume that Soviet officials who have been brought up in the faith of the Communist Party and who regularly proclaim its truth have remained unaffected by that ideology. The only way to succeed within the Party is through demonstrated orthodoxy.

> [Yet] gone in Soviet Russia today is the sense of the practical immediacy of the socialist doctrine which characterized the ten or fifteen years after the November Revolution. The reasons are manifold. One of them may be that . . . Marxian phrases and prescriptions simply have very little immediate relevance to the problems of the Soviet state and society of today.[62]

In particular, the ideology often provides contradictory policy prescriptions or is simply silent in many areas where action is required.

The role of ideology in Soviet policy has itself changed as Soviet society has been transformed by the Party that claims to be guided by that ideology. As a developmental philosophy, Marxism-Leninism primarily addresses the problems of early industrialization. Yet, as the Party armed with this doctrine succeeded in these early tasks, the doctrine has provided a less precise guide to action. As Ulam notes, "Paradoxically, the success of Marxism in Russia has meant its decline in importance, insofar as the original doctrine of Marx-Engels is concerned."[63] It continues to provide an idealized vision of the future, but it remains to the Party to create new dogmas to articulate an action program of means that will move the Soviet Union closer to that future. The continued legitimacy of the Party, rooted ultimately in its ideological orthodoxy, requires that the action program not be patently inconsistent with the doctrine of Marxism-Leninism. Nor can the Party change the action program too frequently in ways that manifestly contradict earlier dogmas. Yet, even according to the tenets of contemporary Marxist-Leninist orthodoxy, the action program is a set of *contingent* dogmas that the Party can propound authoritatively, rather than an independent, ossified limitation on Party action.

With this declining importance of ideology as a guide to action, its other functions have grown in relative significance. As a medium of communication, Marxism-Leninism provides members of Soviet society a conceptual framework for analysis and discourse. As an instrument of legitimation, Soviet ideology not only lends authority to the regime, but justifies many of its specific policies. In the socialization of Soviet citizens, the ideology defines the roles of citizens in a new and changing society. And as an instrument of integration, the ideology provides a basis for tying an ethnically diverse population to the Soviet regime in the absence of organic ties of nationality.[64]

NOTES

1. Robert C. Tucker, *The Marxian Revolutionary Idea* (New York: Norton, 1969), Chapter 4.
2. Zbigniew K. Brzezinski, *The Soviet Bloc: Unity and Conflict*, rev. ed. (Cambridge: Harvard University Press, 1969), 486; compare Willard A. Mullins, "On the Concept of Ideology in Political Science," *American Political Science Review* 66 (January 1972), 498–510. For one effort to draw out the unique characteristics of the Soviet ideology by contrasting it with the American belief system, see Zbigniew K. Brzezinski and Samuel P. Huntington, *Political Power: USA/USSR.* (New York: Viking Press, 1964), Chapter 1.
3. V. I. Lenin, "Perepiska Marksa s Engel'som" [The Correspondence Between Marx and Engels"], in *Polnoe sobranie sochinenii*, 5th ed. (Moscow: Politicheskaia Literatura, 1961), 24:264.

4. Joseph V. Stalin, *Foundations of Leninism* (New York: International, 1939), 10.

5. Friedrich Engels, *Anti-Duehring* (Moscow: Progress, 1969), 331.

6. A. G. Spirkin, "Dialekticheskii materializm," *Bol'shaia Sovetskaia Entsiklopediia*, 3d ed. (Moscow: Sovetskaia entsiklopediia, 1972), 8:231.

7. Spirkin, 233.

8. V. I. Lenin, "Karl Marks" ["Karl Marx"], in *Polnoe sobranie sochinenii* (1961), 26:53–55.

9. Friedrich Engels, "Introduction to *Dialectics of Nature*," in Karl Marx and Friedrich Engels, *Selected Works* (Moscow: Progress, 1969), 3:41–57.

10. Spirkin, 231; emphasis added.

11. V. Zh. Kelle and M. Ia. Koval'zon, "Istoricheskii materializm," *Bol'shaia Sovetskaia Entsiklopediia*, 3rd ed. (Moscow: Sovetskaia entsiklopediia, 1975), 10:571.

12. Karl Marx and Friedrich Engels, *Manifesto of the Communist Party*, in Marx and Engels, *Selected Works*, 1:125–126.

13. Kelle and Koval'zon, 571.

14. Karl Marx, Letter to J. Weydemeyer (March 5, 1852), in *Selected Works*, 1:528.

15. V. I. Lenin, *Imperializm, kak vysshaia stadiia kapitalizma [Imperialism: The Highest Stage of Capitalism]*, in *Polnoe sobranie sochinenii* (1962), 27:386.

16. Marx and Engels, *Manifesto*, 1:121.

17. Kelle and Koval'zon, 571.

18. Friedrich Engels, "Introduction to Karl Marx's *The Civil War in France*," in *Selected Works*, 2:188.

19. V. I. Lenin, "Otnoshenie sotsial-demokratii k krest'ianskomu dvizheniiu" ["Social-Democracy's Attitude toward the Peasant Movement"], in *Polnoe sobranie sochinenii* (1960), 11:221–222.

20. V. I. Lenin, *Chto delat'? [What Is To Be Done?]*, in *Polnoe sobranie sochinenii* (1960), 6:1–192.

21. Engels, *Anti-Duehring*, 332.

22. V. I. Lenin, *Gosudarstvo i revoliutsiia [State and Revolution]*, in *Polnoe sobranie sochinenii* (1962), 33:26.

23. Lenin, *Gosudarstvo i revoliutsiia*, 33:91.

24. Lenin, *Gosudarstvo i revoliutsiia*, 33:101; see also page 49.

25. Lenin, *Gosudarstvo i revoliutsiia*, 33:116.

26. For general discussions of contemporary Soviet ideology, see: Alfred B. Evans, Jr., "Developed Socialism in Soviet Ideology," *Soviet Studies* 29 (July 1977), 409–428; Ernst Kux, "Contradictions in Soviet Socialism," *Problems of Communism* 33 (November-December 1984), 1–27; Jim Seroka and Maurice D. Simon, eds., *Developed Socialism and the Soviet Bloc: Political Theory and Political Reality* (Boulder, Col.: Westview Press, 1982).

27. Karl Marx and Friedrich Engels, *The Holy Family* (Moscow: Foreign Language, 1956), 175–176.

28. Quoted in Jerome M. Gilison, *The Soviet Image of Utopia* (Baltimore, Md.: Johns Hopkins University Press, 1975), 172.

29. Friedrich Engels, "Speeches in Elderfeld," in Karl Marx and Friedrich Engels, *Collected Works* (London: Lawrence and Wishart, 1975), 4:246.

30. V. I. Lenin, "Ot razrusheniia vekovogo uklada k tvorchestvu novogo" ["From the Destruction of the Old Social Order to the Construction of the New"], in *Polnoe sobranie sochinenii* (1963), 40:315.

31. Quoted in Gilison, 173.

32. Friedrich Engels, "Principles of Communism," in *Selected Works*, 1:93.

33. Quoted in Gilison, 171.

34. Engels, "Speeches in Elderfeld," 4:248.
35. G. N. Volkov, *Osnovy Marksistsko-Leninskogo ucheniia* (Moscow: Politizdat, 1979), 249, 251.
36. Engels, "Principles of Communism," 1:88.
37. Gilison, 129–131.
38. Engels, "Speeches in Elderfeld," 4:251; Engels, "Principles of Communism," 1:92, 93.
39. Karl Marx, *Critique of the Gotha Programme*, in *Selected Works*, 3:19.
40. Engels, "Speeches in Elderfeld," 4:246; emphasis in original.
41. Marx and Engels, *Manifesto*, 1:126–127.
42. Volkov, 185–186.
43. Volkov, ibid.
44. Volkov, 205, 210.
45. A. M. Rumiantsev, *A Dictionary of Scientific Communism* (Moscow: Progress, 1984), 142.
46. V. A. Golikov, comp., *Sovetskii Soiuz: Politiko-ekonomicheskii spravochnik* (Moscow: Politizdat', 1975), 172.
47. Rumiantsev, 246, 248.
48. Engels, "Principles of Communism," 1:94.
49. Gilison, 107.
50. Engels, "Principles of Communism," 1:94
51. Gilison, 102–106.
52. Engels, "Speeches in Elderfeld," 4:248–249.
53. E. M. Chekharin, *Sovetskaia politicheskaia sistema v usloviiakh razvitogo sotsializma* (Moscow: Mysl', 1975), 218.
54. Chekharin, 215–224.
55. Nikita S. Khrushchev, *Report on the Program of the Communist Party of the Soviet Union*, October 17, 1961 (Moscow: 1961).
56. *Kommunist* (December 1984).
57. R. N. Carew-Hunt, "The Importance of Doctrine," *Problems of Communism* 7 (May-June 1958), 11.
58. Peter Wiles, "The General View, Especially from Moscow," in Peter Wiles, ed., *The New Communist Third World* (London: Croom Helm, 1982), 359.
59. Carew-Hunt, 12–13.
60. Robert V. Daniels, "Doctrine and Foreign Policy," *Survey* 57 (October 1965), 5.
61. Samuel L. Sharp, "National Interest: Key to Soviet Politics," *Problems of Communism* 7 (March-April 1958), 17–18.
62. Adam Ulam, "Soviet Ideology and Soviet Foreign Policy," *World Politics* 11 (January 1959), 155. Copyright © 1959 by Princeton University Press.
63. Ulam, 158.
64. Alfred G. Meyer, "The Functions of Ideology in the Soviet Political System," *Soviet Studies* 17 (January 1966), 273–285.

chapter 3

Development of the Soviet Polity

Although influenced by the character of the society the Bolsheviks sought to change and by the images of the future that they brought with them to power, the Soviet model of development did not spring whole from the October Revolution. This model, in fact, evolved after the October Revolution during episodic transformations over the next seven decades of Soviet rule. In the first of these transformations the Bolsheviks consolidated their control over the commanding heights of society. The second was marked by Stalin's "Revolution from Above." And in the third reformist experimentation, innovations under Khrushchev created the post-Stalinist welfare-state authoritarianism. Each of these episodes of rapid change was followed by retreat, reconstruction, or retrenchment—the first period, sometimes associated with the label "War Communism," was followed by the retreat of the New Economic Policy, the second by the Great Patriotic War and postwar reconstruction, and the third by the stagnation of the Brezhnev cartel. It appears that these cycles continue although there is nothing that makes these inevitable: The rise to power of a new generation of Soviet leaders in the second half of the 1980s has created the conditions for a fourth episode of change.

CONSOLIDATION OF SOVIET POWER

The Bolsheviks took power in Petrograd and a little over a dozen other major Russian cities during November 1917, but this did not give them control of the Empire. It remained for them to consolidate their power.[1] As shown by the elections to the Constituent Assembly held on November 25, the Bolsheviks did not command a majority among the masses, polling only 23.5 percent of the votes and coming in second behind the Socialist Revolutionary Party that commanded 41.0 percent.[2] Before the Constituent Assembly was disbanded by the Bolsheviks (after just one session on January 18–19, 1918), it underscored the tenuity of Bolshevik support by a 237-138 vote refusing to endorse the new government's enactments during its first two months in power. In fact, for the next four years the Bolsheviks found themselves fighting a combination of foreign and domestic foes in order to consolidate their control over what had been the Russian Empire.

Initially, the most pressing problem was the losing war with Germany, which Russia had been fighting since August 1914. Having diverted the attention of Russian governments from pressing domestic problems, the war had already claimed two regimes, the Tsarist and the Provisional governments, and it continued to bleed Russian society dry. If the Bolsheviks were to avoid the certain death that continued prosecution of the war would bring, they had to end it rapidly. Thus, they began negotiations with the Germans by the end of their first month in power. The negotiations dragged on for two and a half months; and in February 1918, the collapse of the talks brought a new German offensive and capture of many of the Empire's western borderlands. Yet March brought the Treaty of Brest-Litovsk, which effectively ended the war between Russia and Germany.

The Civil War

While the Brest-Litovsk Treaty ended the most immediate threat to the regime, it did not ensure Soviet control over all of Russia. For the next four years the Bolsheviks faced the triple threat of nationalist secession, White opposition, and foreign intervention.

Almost as soon as the Bolsheviks took power in Petrograd, they confronted the problem of secession by major parts of the Russian Empire as non-Russian nationalities began declaring their independence.[3] In the same month as the Revolution, the Estonians and Latvians declared their independence, and the Ukrainians declared that they would be autonomous within the Russian Empire. (After two months, the Ukrainians declared their independence.) In December the Lithuanians, Finns, and Belorussians all declared their independence. And in April the Transcaucasian republics of Armenia, Azerbaidjan, and Georgia proclaimed theirs. Moreover, within what remained of the Russian Empire, the Bashkirs, Crimean Tatars, Kazakhs, Kirgiz, and Turkmen each declared that they would be autonomous within any future Russian federation; and with time some of these nationalities too began to demand independence.

The Bolsheviks also faced growing domestic opposition from the anti-Bolshevik Russian armies known collectively as the Whites.[4] These forces began to organize as early as November and December of 1917. And within months of the Revolution, the Bolsheviks found themselves surrounded by hostile White Armies. (See Figure 3.1.)

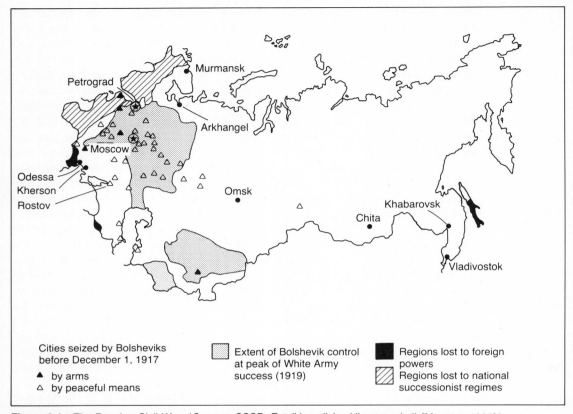

Figure 3.1   The Russian Civil War. (*Source: SSSR: Entsiklopedicheskii spravochnik* [Moscow, 1982].)

One of the first armies appeared in the South, at Rostov-on-Don, where former generals of the Tsarist army and former leaders of the Provisional Government organized the so-called Don Republic. Although this effort to establish a counter-government collapsed by the spring of 1918, the armies of Petr Krasnov, in alliance with the Germans, and Anton Denikin, with support from the Western allies, continued the fight to control the Don-Kuban region. In the Caucasus region Baron Petr Wrangel organized elements of the Russian Imperial Army against the Bolsheviks. By 1919, these armies in the South numbered about 160,000.

In northern Russia, at Arkhangelsk and Murmansk, the Tsarist General Eugene Miller organized an army of about seven to eight thousand. Farther to the west Nikolai Yudenich organized a force of 20,000 in Estonia.

The greatest threat to the Bolsheviks came from forces numbering some 125,000 organized in Siberia under the command of Admiral Alexander Kolchak. In September 1918, anti-Bolshevik forces formed a coalition government ("the Directory") at Omsk with the purpose of reestablishing a constituent assembly and building a democratic government; yet the Directory quickly split over internal plotting among factions. And in November 1918, Kolchak overthrew the Directory, proclaiming himself Supreme Ruler of all the Russias. By early 1919, the other anti-Bolshevik generals had recognized the Admiral as their leader.

Compounding these problems of nationalist secession and White opposition was the Allied Intervention by Russia's former wartime Allies—the United States, Britain, France, and Japan.[5] Initially the European and American actions had a narrow military purpose, seeking to force Russia back into the war against the Germans or at least to salvage the munitions that had been provided to the Provisional Government and were still stockpiled at Murmansk and Arkhangelsk. (Japanese ambitions were probably always greater, including the hope of carving out an empire in Siberia.) With time, however, the motivations changed and expanded and the Allied military operations continued after November 1918 and the defeat of Germany. Particularly for the Europeans, the hope of overthrowing the Bolshevik government and saving their investments in the Russian economy became more important. American motivations were more obscure: Some sought to check Japanese ambitions in Siberia, but many also hoped to establish democracy in Russia.

The British landed their first troops at Murmansk in March 1918, and then expanded this to Arkhangelsk. In April the Japanese landed at Vladivostok. By late 1918, the British had extended their control to the Caucasus oil fields, and the French had established control at Odessa and Kherson on the Black Sea. The French, British, and Japanese were joined by American Marines and contingents of Czechs, Serbs, and Italians.

Once in place, the Intervention forces began to work closely with the armies of the Whites. The British, for example, signed agreements with Miller that provided him supplies and safe refuge. Japan began cultivating local chieftains in Siberia, apparently as leaders of protectorates in an enlarged Japanese Empire.

Although the position of the Bolsheviks in the Civil War was at times desperate, the war slowly tipped in their favor. In the spring of 1919, Kolchak made a major thrust out of Siberia toward the Volga, but by June of that year the Reds had pushed him back into Siberia. During the summer and early fall of 1919, as the Bolsheviks were repulsing Kolchak's forces, the armies of Denikin, Wrangel, and Yudenich made a concerted attack from the south and west. Yudenich's armies pressed to within 30 miles of Petrograd; the armies of Denikin and Wrangel advanced from the south to within 250 miles of Moscow. By October 1919, however, the Red Army had successfully pushed these armies back into Estonia and the South. In January 1920, Kolchak abdicated as Supreme Ruler; and by April both Yudenich and Denikin had resigned, leaving Wrangel alone in the field.

The virtual collapse of the White cause in late 1919 dispirited the Allied governments, so that by the next January their Supreme Allied Council had ordered an end to the blockade of Russia and all Allied governments but Japan had withdrawn from Russia. (Japan did not withdraw until 1922.) The year 1920 saw one last White Army assault by Wrangel from out of the Crimea and one last foreign intervention from the new Polish state as it pressed into the Ukraine. Except for these insurgencies, the Bolsheviks by mid-1920 had rid Russia of most of the White Armies and Allied Intervention forces and could begin to face the problem of the secessionist governments.

In 1920 Bolshevik armies moved into Azerbaidjan and Armenia, and the next year into Georgia to establish control over most of the Caucasus. In 1920 Soviet armies moved into Central Asia, there to reclaim Bokhara, Khiva, and Turkestan. Following the 1922 withdrawal of the Japanese from Siberia, the Soviets took the rest of the Russian Empire's Asian holdings, so that by the end of that year, they controlled most of what had been the Russian Empire. The only losses were Finland; the Baltic states of Latvia, Lithuania, and Estonia; Poland; Bessarabia taken by the Rumanians; Kars and Ardahan taken by the Turks; and southern Sakhalin Island kept by the Japanese.

Why did the Bolsheviks Win?

How is it that, of the many who were contending, the Bolsheviks emerged as the ruling government of Russia? How is it that a small movement with barely 24,000 members at the time of the abdication of Tsar Nicholas II was able to take and maintain control of this vast Russian Empire? The reasons for the Bolsheviks' success may be found in a combination of the internal weaknesses of the opposition forces and the relatively perspicacious policies of the Bolsheviks.

The White cause suffered at least three major weaknesses.[6] The first was geography. The Whites operated on the periphery of Russia. While the Bolsheviks controlled most of the agricultural and industrial regions in the center of European Russia, the opposition forces were active in Siberia, in the South, and in the far north. As a consequence, the anti-Bolshevik forces operated in parts of Russia inhabited by non-Russians, many of whom actively opposed the cause of the Russian White generals. Being on the periphery also meant that the Whites operated in areas where the transportation network was sparse, as roads and railroads were less developed here than at the center; the local industrial base was inadequate to support the war effort of the Whites; and the White forces were geographically dispersed. Denikin's army in the South was isolated from Siberia by the Bolshevik-controlled Volga. Kolchak's armies were isolated from Miller by the great stretches of northern Siberia. Miller's forces in the North were isolated from Yudenich's by Bolshevik-controlled Petrograd. The White armies were never able to link their armies in a common military front to assault the Bolshevik center. Conversely, the Bolsheviks operated on a relatively compact territory that was inhabited mostly by Russians, that was criss-crossed by a dense transportation network for effective movement of troops, and that had the most highly developed industrial base.

A second weakness of the Whites was disunity among the leaders. The Directory in Omsk was, in a sense, a microcosm of this disunity. The Liberals and Social Revolutionaries faced a common Bolshevik enemy, and yet they fought among themselves until a strongman (Kolchak) usurped the power of the Directory. Similarly, even though the generals claimed to acknowledge Kolchak as their leader, they were seldom able to work with one another. Personal animosities and ambitions divided the opponents of the Bolsheviks.

And, last, the Whites were unable to mobilize popular support. Former Tsarist generals in Imperial uniforms did not ignite the popular imagination. They carried the stigma of close association with the old order; and by 1918, few Russians wanted a return of this. The Whites themselves aggravated their problems by failing to develop a program that would dispel the widespread belief that they represented conservative reaction. When Kolchak was asked about independence for Finland, he rejected it. When peasants demanded land reform, White leaders responded that such a program would have to await a constituent assembly after the Civil War was won.

The Bolsheviks, on the other hand, developed an effective response. Opposed to the disarray of the White Armies, the Bolsheviks developed the Red Army and a police apparatus that were unified and tightly disciplined. In contrast to the indecision of White political leaders, the Bolsheviks put forward a program for radical transformation of Russian society. Opposed to the dilatoriness of the Whites, who refused to take any action until victory or a constituent assembly, the Bolsheviks began, even during the Civil War, to build institutions to govern this future society.

The first of the Bolshevik successes was the work of the two men who developed the coercive arms of the Soviet state—Leon Trotsky and Felix Dzerzhinsky. The Russian army had disintegrated into a collection of individual units within four months of the Revolution.[7] Initially, the Bolsheviks did not want to reestablish a single centralized military, for on pragmatic grounds they did not think they could trust such an institution and for ideological reasons they thought that with the defeat of the old order a military would no longer be necessary. Thus, in the first months of the Revolution the organization and administration of Red Army units were left in the hands of local *soviets* (governing councils). But this arrangement proved inadequate to the task of fighting a civil war; and in the first months of 1918, as the Civil War began to heat up, the Bolsheviks came to recognize the need for a centralized, disciplined Red Army. By August 1919, this had grown to 300,000, and by January of the following year to over 5,000,000.

The task of fighting a civil war brought Leon Trotsky to the job of Peoples' Commisar [Minister] of War. In this position Trotsky addressed three major problems. First, he unified the local military units into a single Red Army, overseeing the establishment of a revolutionary War Council in September 1918 to centralize operations and a Council of Defense in November 1918 to mobilize all military, economic, social, and political forces to the Civil War. Second, Trotsky replaced the volunteer army with a conscript army, instituting universal military training in the spring of 1918 and conscription by June of that year. Third, he reestablished a hierarchical structure within the army through tight discipline and a central chain of command. In the summer of 1918, Trotsky eliminated the election of army officers, a democratic reform instituted in 1917, and reestablished the practice of appointing officers from above. He also began the practice of hiring skilled Tsarist officers, particularly from among the noncommis-

VLADIMIR ILICH LENIN

Born to a successful family in the city of Simbirsk (now Ulyanovsk) on April 22, 1870, Vladimir Ilich Ulyanov grew to one of the towering figures of the Twentieth Century. Although their father was a relatively well-placed educational administrator in the Volga region, all five Ulyanov children turned to revolutionary activity.) Vladimir's elder brother Alexander was arrested and hanged in 1887 for his part in the Populist plot to assassinate Tsar Alexander III.) While studying the law at the University of Kazan—he earned a degree with distinction in November 1891—Lenin was attracted to the writings of Karl Marx and the Russian Marxist Georgi Plekhanov and through the influence of these Lenin turned toward the formal theories of Marxism.

Maintaining a law practice as a public defender first in Samara and then in St. Petersburg, Lenin began to work closely with other Marxists in Russia. And in 1895, after travelling to western Europe to make contact with Plekhanov and other exiled socialist leaders, Lenin returned to St. Petersburg to help unify the Marxist groups in the Union of Struggle for the Liberation of Labor. For his work in the underground, Lenin was arrested in December 1895, jailed for fifteen months, and then exiled to Siberia. While at Shushenskoe along the Lena River (from which he later adopted the pseudonym Lenin), Vladimir Ilich, joined by his fiancee Nadezhda Krupskaya, continued his writing and contacts with revolutionaries around the Empire.

After his release from exile in January 1900, Lenin fled to the West. There with Plekhanov he issued the newspaper Iskra (The Spark) which was carried back to Russia and secretly distributed among revolutionary circles in the Empire, providing coordination to the otherwise atomized movement. With the brief exception of a short return to Russia in November 1905 (until 1907), Lenin remained in self-imposed exile in the West until 1917. During those years he sharpened his theories of party and revolution, published tracts on the current questions of the Russian Marxist movement, and engaged in the seemingly interminable factional disputes that led to the division of the movement between Bolsheviks and Mensheviks.

Following the collapse of the Tsarist regime in March 1917, the German offer of a sealed train permitted Lenin to return to Petrograd on April 16, 1917. After a tumultuous greeting at the Finland Station in the Russian capital, Lenin delivered his call for a proletarian revolution—his so-called "April Theses". Over the following months, he would continue to urge this course of action upon his Party and the Petrograd Soviet. The retaliation of the Kerensky Government for the "July Days" forced Lenin to flee the capital, but he was able to slip back into the city with the aid of a disguise around October 20. After heated debate within the Bolshevik Central Committee he won a majority over to his plan for an armed seizure of power in the capital.

As leader of the new Bolshevik regime, with the title "Chairman of the Council of Peoples' Commissars", Lenin presided over the conclusion of peace with Germany against strong Party opposition, the consolidation of Bolshevik control over the state against strong Party opposition, the consolidation of Bolshevik control over the state against opposition within and outside his Party, and the defeat of the White Armies and most of the national secessionist regimes. He rose to international leadership with the founding of the Communist International in March 1919.

In early 1922, the strain of governance—and perhaps the delayed effects of an assassin's bullet that had been lodged in his neck since August 1918—began to take its toll. Lenin fell ill and in May suffered a stroke that temporarily left him paralyzed and unable to speak. He partially recovered by the summer of that year and joined the Party debate over Soviet federalism and the structure of the new Union of Soviet Socialist Republics. But a second stroke in December left him paralyzed once again. Between December 23, 1922, and January 4, 1923, Lenin managed to dictate his "Testament", in which he sought to check the ambitions of individual heirs like Stalin and Trotsky and to ensure a collective leadership upon his death. Yet Lenin was forced to withdraw from political activity when a third stroke on March 10, 1923, deprived him of speech. Death came in Gorky on the evening of January 21, 1924, following a fourth stroke that morning.

sioned officers of the old order, to lead Red Army units. Because the Bolsheviks did not entirely trust these new officers, Trotsky instituted many of the checks on loyalty that have become a distinctive feature of the contemporary Soviet military, including the system of commissars and party cells within units.

At the same time that Trotsky was organizing the Red Army, Felix Dzerzhinsky was given the responsibility for organizing the police.[8] Just a month after the Revolution, the Bolshevik government established the All-Russian Extraordinary Commission for the Suppression of Counterrevolution, Sabotage, and Speculation. (It took its nickname from the words "Extraordinary Commission," *Chrezvychainaia komissiia*, Che-ke.) Initially the Cheka directed its terror against two targets—one, individuals actually engaged in activities against the Bolshevik regime, such as spies for the Whites and Allies, agitators inciting the population to anti-Bolshevik violence, organizers of local revolts, or buyers and sellers in arms; and the other, seemingly randomly selected representatives of those classes that the Bolsheviks thought were natural enemies of the regime, including former members of the nobility, landowners, and the clergy. The latter were selected for coercion, so as to terrorize the group as a whole and prevent them from opposing the Bolsheviks.

A second strength of the Bolsheviks was the early adoption of a program, called War Communism, that responded to the revolutionary temperament of society and permitted the Bolsheviks to mobilize its resources on behalf of the Revolution. War Communism was, first of all, a program to build a communist society. In March 1919, the Eighth Congress of the Russian Communist Party (Bolsheviks) adopted the second Party Program proclaiming, "The Bolshevik Revolution has begun to lay the foundation of a communist society." Reflecting the high optimism of the period, the program held out great hopes for the immediate future. For example, it would lead to the liberation of women, freeing them "from all the burdens of antiquated methods of housekeeping by replacing these with house communes, public kitchens, central laundries, nurseries, and the like." The program also committed the Party to establish a democratic government, to provide education for all Soviet citizens, to build a modern industrialized and planned economy, to raise the standard of living, and to create an egalitarian society in which national privilege was eliminated and Russians would not dominate other peoples. Even though most of the population at this time probably would not have considered itself Bolshevik, the popular sentiment had grown increasingly radical in a short time, demanding rapid and thoroughgoing reform. The Bolshevik program responded to this.

Equally important to the Bolsheviks, War Communism permitted the mobilization of Russia's productive resources. The program meant the near-total nationalization of the economy, permitting the regime to establish direct control over all production and distribution so as to employ these resources on behalf of the Bolshevik cause. In June 1918, the government issued a decree nationalizing all large-scale industry. In August it gave the Supreme Economic Council and the Commissariat of Agriculture the power to regulate and oversee the management of every enterprise; and to the Commissariat of Food it gave the responsibility for overseeing the distribution of all commodities. The Soviet government also established universal labor duty in this period. By tying laborers to their factories so they could not leave their jobs and by prohibiting strikes, the Soviets ensured that much of central Russia's labor-power was harnessed to winning the Civil War. And the government established a policy of forcible requisition of all agricultural surpluses. Peasants had to sell their surplus to the Commissariat of Food. The fixed low price for these surpluses and the actual size of each peasant's surplus were determined by administrative fiat and all too often by the caprice of local committees. In June 1918, to aid the Commissariat of Food in requisitioning surpluses, Committees of the Village Poor were organized. In August, because the committees did not seem to be squeezing enough food from the countryside, food requisition detachments were organized, each to be composed of at least 75 workers and peasants and issued two to three guns. This proved to be a more certain way to squeeze out a surplus.

A third strength of the Bolsheviks was their success at institutionalizing the Revolution. That is, the Bolsheviks transformed the Party from a conspiracy to a regime. (This is often a very difficult transition for revolutionary movements, and those that cannot make the transition from conspiracy to governance often fail to retain power.)

Until its Eighth Congress, Party delegates assembled periodically in a congress that made major decisions, handing over the responsibility for running the Party between congresses to its Central Committee. Much of the responsibility for administering the Party, such as keeping the records of membership, had been left to Yakov Sverdlov. When he died, the Bolsheviks discovered that they had virtually no records and no administrative apparatus at a time when the Party's tasks were rapidly becoming more complex. In a report to the Eighth Party Congress, one delegate complained, "Comrade Sverdlov had all the details concerning the Party activists of Russia in his head, wherever they might be. Now he is dead and no one knows where certain Party activists are."[9] Thus, the Party adopted a more complex organizational structure, in which new institutions—a Politburo a Secretariat, and an Orgburo—were assigned the responsibilities of leading and administering the Party between meetings of the Central Committee. (The Orgburo was subsequently eliminated, its responsibilities assumed by the Secretariat.)

This was an important transition in the Party, for it adapted the Party's institutions to the problems of governance.

The Bolsheviks also began to build alongside the Party a parallel, but separate state administrative framework that would permit the Communist Party to rule Soviet society.[10] The structure of these institutions emerged in a series of decrees of the new regime and was made formal in the first Soviet Constitution of July 10, 1918. A legislature, called the All-Russian Congress of Soviets, was to have supreme authority—at least on paper. It would elect out of its membership an interim legislature, the Central Executive Committee, which in turn would elect the cabinet or Council of Peoples' Commissars (*Sovnarkom*).

Congress of Soviets   ⟶   Central Executive Committee   ⟶   Council of Peoples' Commissars

To extend its governance beyond the capital, the Bolshevik regime replaced local institutions with a hierarchy of soviets directly elected at the lowest levels and composed of delegates from lower soviets at the intermediate and highest levels. Although dominated by the Communist Party, the state was a separate organizational apparatus, containing institutions that could incorporate the larger non-Party population into the Soviet regime. This separation of the state permitted the Party to preserve its revolutionary elan and elite status, while also overseeing the daily administration of a modernizing society.

Among the most significant institutional innovations was the nationality-based federalism designed to hold the non-Russian peoples within the Bolshevik state and to ease the reintegration of those that had already seceded. The minority enclaves within the Russian-dominated areas were designated autonomous republics and regions within a Russian Soviet Federative Socialist Republic (RSFSR). The Bolshevik reclamation of Asia did not bring the immediate annexation of all these areas into the RSFSR, but establishment of formally independent peoples' republics for the Far East, Bukhara, and Khiva. Similarly, the Transcaucasian, Ukrainian, and Belorussian peoples were organized in soviet socialist republics. Although increasing integration was forced on these nominally independent states in both foreign and domestic affairs, relations between the RSFSR and these peoples' republics and soviet socialist republics were formally governed by treaties. Only on December 30, 1922, did the RSFSR and the soviet socialist republics sign a treaty to establish the political federation called the Union of Soviet Socialist Republics. This was formalized in the second Soviet constitution, made public on July 6, 1923, and ratified on January 31, 1924.

The Legacies of Early Rule

Many of the policies developed by the Bolsheviks during the Civil War and under War Communism have continued to influence Soviet politics and policies to this day. Most importantly, the period of War Communism set the institutional foundations of the Soviet regime. The separation of Party and state, the federal structure of the state, the institutions that make and administer policies—all were developed in this period.

The coercive arms of the new regime were also established in this period. The decision to develop the Red Army as a centralized, disciplined hierarchy, although initially a response to the pressing problems of the Civil War, set the foundations of what has become one of the key institutions of Soviet society. More specifically, the organizational structure of the military and the methods by which the Party has attempted to ensure its control over the military continue in many ways to reflect Trotsky's initial design. Similarly, the development of the Soviet police apparatus is a legacy of the Civil War. Established as an extraordinary commission to respond to the unusual circumstances of the Civil War, the Cheka continued after that conflict and later expanded its activities, becoming the G.P.U., the N.K.V.D., and, more recently, the K.G.B.

The Civil War also led to the early establishment of a nationalized economy under Party direction. The rapid socialization of the economy was undertaken to mobilize the resources of the Soviet state on behalf of the Bolshevik cause during the Civil War. While the New Economic Policy (NEP) that followed was a partial retreat from the more onerous features of War Communism, it was in the Civil War that the Bolsheviks laid the foundations for the command economy.

And the period of War Communism left a legacy of antipathy and distrust between the peasantry and the regime. The effort to extract a surplus from the peasantry for the war effort produced hostility in the countryside toward the Bolsheviks. Armed uprisings were met with force. This turmoil and the more passive resistance of peasants to Bolshevik exactions led to a decline in cultivation by as much as 25 percent in the Caucasus, 50 percent in Siberia, and 80 percent in some areas of the Ukraine.

THE FIRST SUCCESSION: STALIN'S RISE TO POWER

On May 26, 1922, Vladimir I. Lenin, founder and unchallenged leader of Russian communism, suffered a paralytic stroke. While in office Lenin had been the undisputed leader of the Soviet regime; but with this first stroke, he lost his ability to speak and to move his right arm or leg and so relinquished many of his responsibilities to others in the leadership. On December 22 he suffered a second stroke; the following March, a third stroke; and on January 21, 1924, he died.

Soviet History (1917–1945): A Brief Chronology

1917.	Nv 7.	Bolshevik seizure of power in Petrograd.
1918.	Mr 3.	Brest-Litovsk Treaty; growing Civil War.
	Mr 11.	Soviet Government moves to Moscow.
	Je 28.	Decree nationalizing large-scale industry.
1919.	Mr 2-6.	First Congress of Communist International in Moscow.
	Mr18-23.	VIII Party Congress.
1920.	Ja-Fb.	Final defeat of Denikin in south, Kolchak in Siberia.
	Ap 27.	Polish offensive in Ukraine begins.
	Oc 12.	Peace with Poland.
	Nv 16.	Wrangel driven from Crimea.
1921.	Fb 25.	Soviets overthrow Menshevik Government in Georgia.
	Fb 23-Mr 17.	Suppression of Kronstadt sailors' rebellion.
	Mr 8-16.	X Party Congress: End of 'War Communism'.
1922.	Ap 4.	Stalin becomes General Secretary.
	Ap 26.	Lenin's first stroke.
	Dc 30.	Formation of USSR.
1923.	Mr 10.	Lenin's second stroke; formation of triumvirate.
1924.	Ja 21.	Lenin dies.
1925.	Dc 18-31.	XIV Party Congress
1926.	Jl-Oc.	Stalin's victory over Left Opposition.
1927.	Dc 2-9	XV Party Congress: Speedier industrialization.
1928.	Oc 1.	First Five-Year Plan begins.
1929.	Ja 31.	Trotsky deported from USSR.
	Nv 17.	Bukharin removed from Politburo; Collectivization.
1930.	Nv 27-Dc 7.	Trial of 'Industrial Party'.
1931.		
1932.	Dc 31.	First Five-Year Plan completed.
1933.	Spring	Famine in south.
1934.	Ja 26-Fb 10.	XVI Congress of Communist Party.
	Dc 1.	Assassination of Kirov: Beginning of Great Purge.
1935.	Jl 25-Ag 20.	VII Comintern Congress: Popular Front Policy.
1936.	Ag 25.	Trial of Zinoviev and Kamenev.
	Sp 26.	Yezhov appointed to NKVD: 'Yezhovshchina'.
	Dc 6.	Adoption of 'Stalin' Constitution.
1937.	Je 12.	Purge of armed forces.
1938.	Mr 2-15.	Trial of Bukharin and Rykov.
	Dc 30.	Beria replaces Yezhov in NKVD.
1939.	Ag 23.	Nazi-Soviet Pact.
	Sp 7.	Soviet attack and occupation of Eastern Poland.
	Nv 29.	Soviet attack on Finland: 'Winter War'.
1940.	Mr 12.	End of 'Winter War' with Finland.
	Je 28.	Bessarabia annexed from Rumania.
	Jl 21.	Latvia, Lithuania, Estonia added as Union Republics.
1941.	My 6.	Stalin assumes Chair, Council of Peoples Commissars.
	Je 22.	German attack on Russia.
1942.	Sp 23.	Beginning of Stalingrad counteroffensive.
1943.	Fb 2.	End of German resistance at Stalingrad.
1944.	Ag-Sp.	Soviet troops in Bucharest (Ag 31), Sofia (Sp 16).
1945.	Ja-Fb.	Soviet Troops in Warsaw (Ja 17), Budapest (Fb 17).
	Fb 7-12.	Yalta Conference.
	My 9.	End of War with Germany.
	Jl 17-Ag 2.	Potsdam Conference.

Quite naturally, the question that arose following his first stroke was, who would succeed Lenin? Who would be the next leader?[11]

At the time of Lenin's first stroke, there was no obvious heir, a fact that Lenin himself underscored in December 1922, as he dictated his Testament. In this document Lenin assessed his likely heirs and found them incapable of filling his position singlehandedly. Instead, he advocated a collective leadership.

In the absence of a designated heir or an obvious successor, Lenin's illness and death sparked an intense struggle for the succession among those people Lenin had assessed and found wanting. The struggle focused in the Party's Politburo, which, at the time of Lenin's death, included seven men:

Joseph V. Stalin (General Secretary)

Grigori E. Zinoviev (Leningrad Party Secretary)

Lev B. Kamenev (Moscow Party Secretary)

Leon D. Trotsky (Peoples' Commissar of War)

Nikolai I. Bukharin (editor, *Pravda,* and later, head of Comintern)

Alexei I. Rykov (Chairman of Sovnarkom)

Mikhail P. Tomsky (Head of Trade Unions)

Among these seven men, the individual with the greatest personal authority was Leon Trotsky, a highly visible leader of the Revolution, a gifted orator and writer, and an impressive intellect. Yet among these seven, the one who proved to be the ablest strategist and tactician in intraparty maneuvering was Joseph Stalin.

Stalin's strategy in the succession was to isolate the most powerful contender at each point, rallying the other members of the Politburo behind himself. When he had eliminated his opponent, securing the election of a Stalin loyalist to replace him on the Politburo, Stalin would then turn his fire on the next most powerful contenders—his previous allies.

Stalin's tactics were twofold, involving both organization and policy. Stalin's organizational tactic was to pack the membership of those organs to which the Politburo was formally accountable, the Central Committee and Party Congress. When a showdown came in the Politburo, Stalin could turn to these bodies to expel or isolate his opposition. Stalin's policy stands tended to be opportunistic. He used the key policy debates of the time to promote his power aspirations, making dramatic swings from one side of an issue to the other—often, it would appear, simply to serve his personal power needs.

The Isolation of Trotsky

The struggle for power began even before Lenin's death, for Stalin and Trotsky began to maneuver for the succession as early as 1923. Stalin initiated an organizational ploy to pack the Central Committee with his supporters: In April 1923, he se-

IOSIF VISSARIONOVICH STALIN

The man who was to become perhaps the single most powerful despot and the leader of the second more powerful state in the mid-Twentieth Century was born to a humble cobbler's family in the Caucasus. Born on December 21, 1879, in the Georgian village of Gori, Iosif Vissarionovich Dzhugashvili grew up in a pious household dominated by a father who often ruthlessly beat his son while drunk.

After a brief education at the church school in Gori, Stalin went on to the Tblisi Russian Orthodox Theological Seminary to study for the priesthood. But his study of Marxist texts and underground activity earned him expulsion from the latter in 1899. Remaining in Tblisi, Stalin joined the revolutionary underground in 1900, travelling around the Caucasus to foment labor unrest. For this activity between 1902 and 1913, Stalin was arrested eight times—often imprisoned and exiled to Siberia. Stalin was an early supporter of Lenin: When the Russian Social Democratic Labor Party split between Mensheviks and Bolsheviks, Stalin joined the latter. When the Bolsheviks established their first Central Committee in 1912, Lenin appointed Stalin to serve on that body.

The collapse of the Tsarist regime in March 1917 caught Stalin in exile in Siberia (since July 1913); but by March 25 of that year he managed to reach Petrograd. Assuming the editorship of Pravda, a position he had held before his last exile, Stalin joined Lenin in urging an armed seizure of power in the capital.

During the early years of Soviet power Stalin served on various fronts of the Civil War and held the posts of Peoples' Commissar for Nationality Questions and Peoples' Commissar for Workers' and Peasants' Inspection until 1923. More importantly, in 1922 he assumed the newly created post of General Secretary of the Party—the position that he would occupy until his death and from which he would build dictatorial powers. (Stalin did not again assume a post in the state apparatus until May 1941, when in anticipation of war he appointed himself Chairman of the Council of Peoples' Commissars.)

From 1924 until his death in 1953, Stalin's biography is the history of the Soviet Union. His victory over Trotsky and the Left and Right Oppositions in the Twenties permitted him to establish himself as autocrat and to initiate the revolutionary transformation of Soviet society in the Thirties. Stalin achieved true global stature—reflecting the rise of the Soviet Union to great power status—as one of the "Big Three" Allied wartime leaders and then as ruler of an empire in Eastern Europe.

Stalin's last years were marked by growing paranoia, by petrification of the Stalinist system, and apparently by plans to unleash a new purge of the leadership. But death on March 5, 1953, cut these last plans short.

The person and personality of Stalin have continued to be controversial even after his death. The ornate cult of personality that developed around Stalin was followed under Khrushchev by efforts to expunge his memory from society. His name was removed not only from streets and cities, but also from the pages of history; the many likenesses of him that had graced the Soviet Union were hidden from public view. Since Khrushchev, many policy shifts have been described as Stalinist; some political tendencies within the Party elite have been labelled neo-Stalinist; and many in the broader population are said to yearn for a strong leader of Stalin's ilk. Efforts to resurrect his memory, however, have apparently been aborted.

Stalin and Stalinism have been nearly as controversial in the West. In particular, many have asked whether Stalinism was the inevitable culmination of the Russian Revolution and Leninism. Robert C. Tucker (Stalin as Revolutionary, New York, 1973) has sought the origins of Stalin's tyrannic brutality, finding much of the answer in Stalin's personality. Stephen F. Cohen (Rethinking the Soviet Experience, New York, 1985) has argued that the Soviet Union could have, indeed, taken a different path in the Twenties (Bukharinism), if only Stalin had not overwhelmed his opponents in the post-Lenin succession.

cured approval of a reorganization plan, reinforcing the subordination of the Politburo to the Central Committee and enlarging the membership of both the Central Committee and the Central Control Commission. (Members of the Central Control Commission had the right to participate in Central Committee deliberations.) The new members were to be elected by the Party Congress, which was itself elected at regional Party meetings. Stalin knew that regional Party secretaries tended to be elected to the Party Congress and that many of these secretaries depended on him personally, as General Secretary of the Party, for their tenure in office. Stalin knew that he could count on the support of these secretaries in any Politburo dispute with Trotsky that was forced into the larger forum of the Central Committee for resolution.

Trotsky's response to this challenge was maladroit, making an assault on Stalin's plan for reorganization that only isolated Trotsky further. In October 1923, he addressed first the Politburo and then the Central Committee, attacking the growing dictatorship of the secretaries over the Party. The Central Committee was not sympathetic, for many of its members were themselves Party secretaries who had staked their careers on the development of Stalin's dictatorship of the Secretariat. Indeed, the Central Committee responded by formally criticizing Trotsky for a "grave political mistake" and "factionalism" and calling on him to cease all "anti-Party" activity. Trotsky was not deterred however; and in December 1923, he carried his case to the public with an article in *Pravda*. There he argued that the Party must reassert control over its own apparatus. But this brought condemnation the next month from a Party conference that branded Trotsky's views "petty-bourgeois deviations from Leninism," again accused him of factionalism, and warned him to cease this factionalism or lose his membership in the Party. Trotsky retreated and at the Thirteenth Party Congress in May 1924 formally recanted.

Then, in November 1924, the struggle between Trotsky and Stalin flared again, but this time over state policies. On the eve of the seventh anniversary of the October Revolution, Trotsky published a series of essays collected under the title *The Lessons of October,* in which he attacked NEP and called for continuation of the "permanent revolution."

The New Economic Policy or NEP had been a strategic retreat from the policy of War Communism.[12] Opposition to War Communism had produced not only a rural uprising, but mounting strike activity in the cities, culminating on March 2, 1921, in the rebellion of sailors at the Kronstadt naval base near Petrograd. Although the Bolsheviks crushed the revolt with force, it convinced the regime of the need to abandon War Communism. The retreat began in March 1921, with the replacement of forced sales of agricultural surpluses by a progressive tax-in-kind. Then new laws established the rights of peasants to use their land, to lease it, and to work it with hired labor. Although this retreat initially focused on the peasants, it began to have significant spillover effects for the rest of the economy. If the peasants were free to sell their after-tax surpluses, the Soviet authorities had to permit private markets in which to sell; and thus, private trade was legalized. If there was to be private trade, the regime had to reintroduce money, which had been eliminated under War Communism. With the devel-

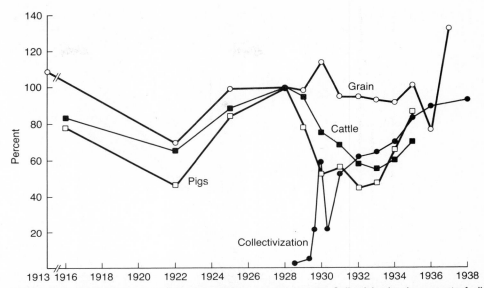

Figure 3.2 Collectivization and Agricultural Output, 1913–1938. Collectivization is percent of all households in collective farms; agricultural production is percent of 1928 level. (Source: From data in A. Nove, *An Economic History of the USSR* [New York: Penguin Books, 1982].)

opment of a private market based on a cash nexus, entrepreneurs or "Nepmen" began to emerge. In order to induce the peasants to produce for the market, the production of consumer goods had to be expanded. To encourage this, many manufacturing establishments were turned back to private management. And to encourage this private enterprise, the regime reestablished a free labor market in which workers could move from one factory to another and negotiate their own wages. NEP, in this way, resulted in the development of a significant private economy in which entrepreneurs once again owned or managed some factories and wealthy peasants accumulated power in the countryside. These reforms had the desired consequence. By 1925, Siberian agricultural output had reached over 92 percent of its previous peak (1916) and Ukrainian output reached over 96 percent of that level; industrial output doubled between 1920–1921 and 1922–1923, reaching over a third of its previous peacetime high (1913). (See Figures 3.2 and 3.3)

Trotsky attacked NEP as a retreat from the Revolution, abandoning planning, denationalizing small industry, and permitting a market to develop once again. But Trotsky had underestimated the popularity of NEP in late 1924, even within the Party. And, playing to this sentiment, Stalin defended NEP, arguing that it was the wrong time to begin rapid industrialization.

The second policy dispute concerned continuation of the "permanent revolution." It had been an article of faith among many Bolsheviks after the Revolution that Russia could not build socialism on its own and that if their Revolution was to succeed it would require the support of socialist revolutions in advanced industrialized countries. To encourage these, the new Soviet regime should expend

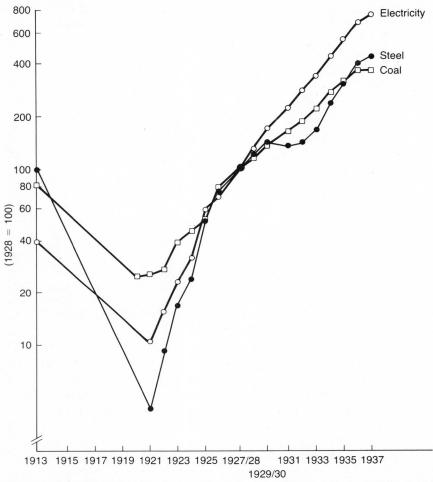

Figure 3.3 Industrial Output, 1913–1937. (Source: From data in A. Nove, An Economic History of the USSR [New York: Penguin Books, 1982].)

scarce energies in support of Communist insurrections in Europe. By 1923, however, particularly after the failure of Communist insurrections in Germany, much of the Party was less enthusiastic about the idea of permanent revolution. Many of the regional Party secretaries, in particular, favored attending to the immediate tasks of reconstruction at home and opposed wasting resources abroad. Trotsky attacked Stalin for his lack of revolutionary enthusiasm and called on the Russians to continue the permanent revolution. Stalin again defended the popular stance. As late as April 24, Stalin had reiterated his faith in the ideal of the permanent revolution; but in December of that year, just after Trotsky's criticism, Stalin came out strongly for the policy that would subsequently be labelled

"socialism in one country." In arguing that the Soviet Union could build socialism on its own and should not squander scarce resources on adventures in Europe, Stalin had accurately gauged opinion in the Party, and so further isolated
Trotsky.

Trotsky hurt his own cause with an important tactical blunder in 1924. He
not only attacked Stalin, but also Zinoviev and Kamenev, calling attention to
their questionable role in the October Revolution, when they opposed the plan
for a coup d'etat and then leaked the Bolsheviks' plans to the authorities. By re-
opening this wound, Trotsky forced Zinoviev and Kamenev to turn to Stalin for
support. Their dependence on him strengthened Stalin's ability to isolate Trotsky still further and after January 1925, Trotsky ceased to play a significant role
within the Politburo.

Triumph over the Left and Right Oppositions

Having isolated Trotsky, Stalin then turned against his fellow triumvirs, Zinoviev and Kamenev, but to do this, Stalin had to ally himself with Bukharin, Rykov, and Tomsky—all staunch defenders of NEP. Stalin appeased these leaders
on the right, with the introduction of policies to reinforce and expand NEP, specifically lowering the tax on peasants and easing restrictions on the hiring of
agricultural labor. By the Fourteenth Party Congress in December 1925, Stalin
apparently felt his alliance with the right was strong enough to permit an attack
on the Leningrad and Moscow Party secretaries. In preparation for this showdown Stalin had continued with organizational maneuvers, packing the Congress
with still more Party secretaries and Stalin loyalists. Stalin branded the position
of Zinoviev, Kamenev, and their allies as the "Left Opposition," condemning
their calls for rapid industrialization and for an assault on the *kulaks* (rich peasants) in the countryside.

Zinoviev and Kamenev imprudently turned to Trotsky for support. Since
Trotsky had already been discredited for his opposition, Stalin in the spring of
1926 could announce that he had discovered a "United Opposition," led by all
three men. In their public statements, the United Opposition restated Trotsky's
criticisms of Stalin's growing dictatorship over the Party, but also attacked NEP,
calling again for rapid industrialization and for liquidation of the kulaks. Yet
NEP was still popular with the Party, and Stalin countered with a defense of
that policy. By the end of 1927, he had won the expulsion of Zinoviev, Kamenev, and Trotsky from the Party, along with 75 of their followers.

Having eliminated Trotsky and his confreres from the Politburo, Stalin
replaced them with his own personal following (including Sergei M. Kirov, Via-
cheslav M. Molotov, Anastas I. Mikoyan, Lazar M. Kaganovich, and Jan E. Rud-
zutak). He now faced opposition only from the right. In 1928, just after ousting
the Left Opposition, Stalin himself began to espouse "leftist" policies, calling for
rapid industrialization under central planning, for elimination of the kulaks, and
for collectivization of agriculture. The result was the abandonment of NEP and
the initiation of the Five-Year Plans. This switch in position permitted Stalin to

take advantage of a significant shift in sentiment regarding NEP and to attack his former allies. In late 1927, NEP was beginning to break down; and in the eyes of many within the Party, the "scissors crisis," whereby peasants failed to deliver adequate produce to meet the demands of industry, required drastic action. In January 1929, Stalin announced that he had discovered a "Right Opposition," and through organizational maneuvers and policy appeals was able to isolate Bukharin, Rykov, and Tomsky, and he secured their removal from all Party and state posts by November 1929. By the end of 1929, Stalin was the sole member of Lenin's Politburo still in power.

THE STALINIST REVOLUTIONS

Much of what we now recognize as the Soviet pattern of development began not at the time of the October Revolution and not under Lenin, but over a decade after the Revolution under the rule of Joseph Stalin, in the second episode of change. The years of Stalin's rule can be divided into three separate periods: the revolutionary transformation of Soviet society (1928–39), the Second World War (1939–45), and the reconstruction and petrification of the Stalinist system after the war (1945–1953). The first of these witnessed a sweeping transformation in Soviet society, sometimes called the "Second Revolution," the "Stalinist Revolution," or as Stalin himself preferred, the "Revolution from Above."

In actuality the period of revolutionary transformation of Russia witnessed five closely related revolutions: an agricultural revolution that transformed the institutions of the Soviet countryside, setting the foundations for modern collectivized agriculture; an industrial revolution that set the structure of the command economy; a social revolution that transformed the structure of Russian society and created a new hierarchy of privilege; a cultural revolution that harnessed the arts to the task of transforming society; and a political revolution that gave the Party nearly monopolistic control over all institutions and made the General Secretary autocrat within the Party. These revolutions not only transformed the Soviet society, culture, polity, and economy, but also created many of the institutions that today distinguish the Soviet model of development.

The Agrarian Revolution

The transformation of Soviet society as a whole was most profound in the countryside.[13] A primary impetus for Stalin's agrarian revolution was the failure of the agrarian sector during NEP to deliver sufficient produce to the cities to feed a large urban population and to provide the raw materials needed to industrialize. In addition, the Soviet Union needed a surplus for export in order to buy material and machinery from the advanced economies of the West. This problem became acute as the Soviet Union began its First Five-Year Plan in 1928, calling for ambitious expansion of heavy industry.

The failure of the agrarian sector to deliver surplus during NEP was due, in part, to the changes brought about by the October Revolution: By permitting the dissolution of the large estates that had dominated the countryside under the Tsarist regime, it had eliminated the principal producers of the agricultural surplus sold to the cities and abroad. These estates had been replaced by a multiplicity of small peasant households unable to produce a marketable surplus. Before 1917, peasant households numbered 17 or 18 million, but by 1927, they had jumped to 25 million—most with small holdings, inadequate equipment for commercial farming, and a still-primitive productive technique. As a consequence of NEP, the agricultural sector had shown a significant upturn in production since the depths of the Civil War and War Communism (see Figure 3.2), but peasants had still not developed a commercial orientation. This was aggravated by imprudent government pricing and procurement policies that further discouraged market sales. In the last years of NEP, only about 13 to 21 percent of the harvest was sent to the cities; most was consumed in the countryside by the peasants themselves. Grain exports in 1925–1927 had fallen to about one-sixth of their 1913 level.[14]

The first signs of a break came in late 1927 and early 1928, when Stalin began to indicate that NEP might not continue in the countryside. But it was in December of 1929 that Stalin initiated his agrarian revolution, as he called for the elimination of kulaks as a class and sent Party, military, and police functionaries to the countryside to bring about the collectivization of agriculture.

The agricultural revolution replaced the 25 million household farms with four new rural institutions. The state farm (*sovkhoz*) was to operate like a factory in the field. Workers paid a wage would live in dormitories or urban settlements and tend the fields much like factory workers. More common was to be the collective farm (*kolkhoz*), a transitional stage on the way to state farms. Theoretically the collective farm was constituted from pooled land that would be operated in common by the households. Thus, peasants worked with one another in collective brigades; and their pay was not a wage but a portion of the production after payment of taxes. Alongside the kolkhoz was the Machine Tractor Station (MTS): Farm machinery was pooled in stations that conducted all heavy-machine operations on nearby collective farms. The MTS system not only made the most efficient use of the country's scarce machinery, but also provided a means to extract additional taxes, in the form of fees imposed on the farms, and a center for Party control over the surrounding countryside. Last was the private plot. In 1935, peasant households were granted the right to hold approximately one acre apiece to work for their own needs or for sale in the local markets.

These changes put an end to capitalist agriculture in the Soviet Union. In October 1929, only 4.1 percent of Russian peasant households had been in collective farms; but by January 1930, this number had jumped to 21 percent, and two months later to 58 percent. In succeeding years there were tactical retreats and then renewed efforts to collectivize, so by 1938, 93.5 percent of all Russian peasant households had been forced onto collective farms (see Figure 3.2). The agricultural revolution that replaced the 25 million peasant holdings with 242 thousand collective farms was a very brutal transition. The decision to eliminate the kulaks as a class provided disgruntled neighbors an opportunity to settle old scores.

An OGPU (secret police) report of February 28, 1930, provides a matter-of-fact description of occurrences in one locality:

> "Certain members of the workers' brigades and officials of lower echelons of the Party-Soviet apparatus" deprived members of kulak and middle peasant households of their clothing and warm underwear (directly from the body), "confiscated" head-wear from children's heads, and removed shoes from people's feet. The perpetrators divided the "confiscated" goods among themselves; the food they found was eaten on the spot; the alcohol they uncovered was consumed immediately, resulting in drunken orgies. In one case a worker tore a warm blouse off a woman's back, and put it on himself with the words, "You wore it long enough, now I will wear it." The slogan of many of the dekulakization brigades was: "Drink, eat, it's all ours."[15]

In the process an estimated 300,000 peasant households—that is, about one-and-a-half million individual peasants—were exiled. Approximately three-fifths of these were sent to work camps or special collective farms under close scrutiny.

The unintended consequences of the agricultural revolution were momentous. Following the collectivization program, Soviet agriculture took years to recover from the associated destruction of livestock and crops. Peasants who resisted collectivization destroyed their herds rather than permitting them to be confiscated. The Soviet author Mikhail A. Sholokhov recounts:

> Stock was slaughtered every night in Gremyachy Log. Dusk had hardly fallen when the muffled, short bleats of sheep, the death squeals of pigs, and the lowing of calves could be heard. Both those who had joined the kolkhoz as well as individual farmers killed their stock. Bulls, sheep, pigs, even cows were slaughtered, as well as cattle for breeding. The horned stock of Gremyachy was halved in two nights. The dogs began to drag entrails about the village; cellars and barns were filled with meat. . . . "Kill, it's not ours any more. . . . " "Kill, they'll take it for meat anyway. . . . " And they killed. They ate till they could eat no more.[16]

Comparison of livestock holdings in Russia at the beginning of the collectivization campaign (1928) with those that existed six years later reveals that by 1934 the number of horses had fallen by 57.3 percent, cattle had fallen by 40 percent, over half of the hogs had been destroyed, and the number of sheep and goats had fallen by 64.6 percent (see Figure 3.2). In the nomadic regions of Kazakhstan it is estimated that the number of sheep and goats had actually fallen as much as 86.5 percent. In addition, there was substantial loss of human life, much of it due to the famine of 1932–1933. The dislocations of collectivization and the forced delivery of produce to the cities left many in the countryside to starve. Comparisons of the 1937–1938 census with the estimated population in 1927–1928 suggest that between 3.5 and 10 million people died in those years.

And the collectivization program sparked a peasant rising in the countryside against the regime. Although they never achieved national or even regional unity, it is estimated that as many as 200 guerrilla bands operated in the Moscow region and 212 operated in the lower Volga region during these years.

The Industrial Revolution

The same problems that induced Stalin to collectivize agriculture also seem to have led him to begin the rapid industrialization of the Soviet Union.[17] Industrial production on the whole had recovered to its 1913 levels by 1926, with the value (in constant rubles) of total factory output in the latter year surpassing the pre-war high by eight percent. Yet growth beyond this level, particularly in light of the ambitious investment plans of Stalin, would require greater direction and harsh trade-offs.

In the period from 1928 through the beginning of World War II, the Soviet economy underwent a rapid and dramatic transformation—the building of modern industry. Steel output between 1928 and 1940 increased by 326 percent, coal extraction by 367 percent, and hydroelectric generation by 866 percent. Highest priority went to heavy industry, with agriculture, housing, and consumer goods taking a secondary position (see Figure 3.3). Growth was highest in the first eight years; but in 1937 growth began to slump due to a growing defense burden (which rose from 3.4 percent of the budget in 1933 to 16.1 percent in 1936 and 32.6 percent in 1940) and due to the mounting toll of the Purges.

The Stalinist modernization campaign was, first of all, industrialization according to a plan. Coordination of economic planning was concentrated in the hands of Gosplan, the state planning commission, under the Council of Peoples' Commissars. Managers of enterprises increasingly acted as the faithful executors of operational plans handed down from the commissariats in Moscow that specified production levels, supply allotments, delivery schedules, and prices.

The plans of these early years were not always realistic or rational and, perhaps by design, were seldom fulfilled. The initial successes of the First Five-Year Plan in 1928–1929 brought increases in production targets and the decision to complete the First Plan in four years. As a consequence, production goals for all industry were nearly doubled in 1930–1931; but actual output did not meet the plan targets. Stalin claimed that the First Five-Year Plan had been fulfilled by December 1932—a claim supported by dubious figures for the value of gross industrial production. Yet raw output figures showed that few industries achieved their goals, with electricity output falling 39.1 percent below its target, coal production 14.3 percent below, and steel production 43.3 percent below. The Second Five-Year Plan (1933–1937) was less ambitious than the First Plan and subject to fewer irrational revisions; but actual production again fell short of plans in many sectors.

The Stalinist Revolution was industrialization by mobilization. Mass campaigns were organized from the center to support the priorities of the Plan. Most prominent was *Stakhanovism,* a campaign for improved labor productivity. Alexei Stakhanov, a miner who in September 1935 had produced 14 times his quota, was held up as a model for emulation by all workers. In 1936 work norms were raised throughout the economy to encourage Stakhanovites in all sectors.

The Stalinist industrial revolution brought a retreat from the proletarian ideals of the Revolution. Worker discipline replaced what limited worker democ-

racy had existed under NEP. Trade unions lost their few representative functions and became instruments of control over workers. During the First Five-
Year Plan, "flitting" from job to job and absenteeism were made punishable by
denial of rights to factory housing or insurance benefits. As war approached,
these restrictions became more severe; decrees in 1940 declared absenteeism and
tardiness over 20 minutes to be crimes punishable by imprisonment or compulsory labor.

The Stalinist industrial revolution saw the emergence of the Soviet Union
as a major power. In 1931 Stalin had proclaimed:

> It is sometimes asked whether it is possible to slow down the tempo somewhat, to
> put a check on the movement. No, comrades, it is not possible. The tempo must
> not be reduced! On the contrary, we must increase it . . . .We are fifty or a hundred
> years behind the advanced countries. We must make good this distance in ten
> years. Either we do so, or we shall go under.[18]

As it slowly caught up with the economies of the West, the Soviet economy, by
its sheer size, supported claims to "great power" status. For example, Russian
steel production jumped from 6 percent of the world total in 1910 to 14 percent
in 1939. The Soviet economy became more self-sufficient as well: The percentage of machine tools that had to be imported fell from 78 percent in 1932 to less
than 10 percent in 1936 and 1937. Estimates of the power levels of individual
states made by Beckman suggest that Russia narrowed the gap with the United
States (from a 6.5 to 1 American advantage in 1910 to a 2.5 to 1 advantage in
1939) and with Germany (from a 3.5 to 1 to a 1.2 to 1 German advantage in
those years) and may actually have surpassed the United Kingdom.[19]

The Social Revolution

The Stalinist revolution also brought a transformation of other social patterns.
Most visible were the rapid demographic changes. The urban population nearly
doubled from 28.7 million at the beginning of 1929 to 56.1 million at the beginning of 1939, jumping from 18 percent of the total population to 33 percent. The
proportion of the population represented by workers and their families more
than doubled from 12.4 percent in 1938 to 33.7 percent in 1939. And educational attainment rose: Annual graduation of specialists from higher educational institutions rose 157 percent from 1928–1932 to 1938–1940 and that from
specialized secondary institutions jumped 210 percent.[20]

The Stalinist revolution, in an important sense, buried the egalitarian aspirations of the Leninist period and erected in its place a new hierarchy of prestige
and privilege with a steeply stratified scale of rewards. In June 1931, Stalin condemned wage equality as "petty-bourgeois egalitarianism," legitimating wage differentials in the period of socialism. This inequality was made even more
extreme with the introduction of closed shops and "authorizations" to purchase
scarce items that guaranteed supplies of necessities and a wider array of luxuries
for those who were important to the Stalinist revolution, such as managers of facto-

ries, Party apparatchiki (members of the Party's bureaucratic apparatus), or military officers.

The social revolution also meant the transformation of social institutions. Some traditional institutions were eliminated. A 1930 decree dissolved the peasant village-communities (*mir*) in areas that had been collectivized. The forced *sedentarization* (forced settlement) of many nomadic peoples, particularly in Central Asia, struck at the very basis of their traditional life-styles. The dissolution of private associations atomized the urban population. Among each of these populations the associational vacuum created by the demise of traditional institutions was filled by new organs created under the Party's tutelage.

Conversely, the role of a few traditional institutions, notably the family, was reinforced. Traditional family structure had been eroded in the 1920s with legislation depriving fathers of their authority within the family, attacking the traditional religious sanctions on marriage, and easing restrictions on divorce. Stalin sought a return to a more traditional family structure by assigning parents legal responsibility for their children, by making divorce more difficult and abortion illegal, and by encouraging women to bear children. For the latter purpose, those women who bore 5 to 6 children were awarded the Order of Motherhood; for 7 children they received the Order of Mothers' Glory; and for 10 children the Order of Mothers' Heroine.

The Cultural Revolution

To integrate this rapidly changing society, Stalin initiated a revolution to create a new Soviet culture.[21] Countering the centrifugal pressures of modernization in a multiethnic society, this cultural revolution emphasized developing a new Soviet patriotism that would transcend individual nationalisms. For all nationalities this patriotism meant not only loyalty to an expanded political community, but also to Stalin and the institutions he had erected. To an important extent the cultural revolution also meant making the Soviet people modern, inculcating attitudes appropriate to modern, urbanized, industrialized society such as labor discipline, conformity, work habits appropriate to group settings like factories, and public orderliness.

The educational system played a central role in modernizing the Soviet citizenry and socializing a new generation of Soviet citizens to be fiercely loyal to the rapidly changing Soviet society. To this end, the experimentation in education that was so widespread in the 1920s came to an end, and many traditional practices returned. For example, classroom discipline, grading, and uniforms were reintroduced.

The Stalinist revolution meant a new degree of control over culture and a new uniformity in arts and literature. In the 1920s there had been only limited Party interference in the arts. As late as 1925, a Central Committee decree proclaimed that there was no Party line in the area of culture. And until 1929, both Communist and non-Communist authors could publish with only some restriction. It was a time of unusual experimentation in various artistic forms. Under Stalin, however, Soviet culture was made to conform to the strictures of *socialist realism,* which meant that literature and the arts must conform to the party line (*partiinost'*), must be accessible to the masses by eschewing "formalism" such as experimentation and abstraction, and must be realistic. The last of these meant not that the arts should be representational, but should present an "historically truthful depiction" of a society in transition; the simile often used to illustrate this point was the painting of a building in progress, which should depict the completed edifice. In the hands of Party hacks, literature and the arts often degenerated into heroic depictions of a distorted history and sentimental romances of the boy-meets-tractor genre.

Harnessing culture to the task of building this new industrialized, collectivized Russia required the building of new institutions of control over the arts. Not content with the negative sanctions of censorship, Stalin erected organizations to harness the arts so that they actively promoted the messages of socialist realism. In 1932, the Party established the Union of Soviet Writers to control the literati, followed by unions for the other previously independent creative professions (e.g., artists and architects).

The Political Revolution

At the heart of the other transformations was a political revolution, producing a dramatic shift in the distribution of power within the Soviet Union. It led to a dictatorship of the Party over Soviet society and of one man over the Party—that is, a totalitarian autocracy. One of the consequences of this concentration of power was the atrophy of leading Party organs as Stalin increasingly ruled without them; Party congresses and Central Committe plena were held with less frequency, and the Politburo itself was often by-passed.

An indispensable means of this political revolution was terror.[22] During the period of the New Economic Policy the police (OGPU) had largely limited its coercion to enemies of the regime and had only slight impact on the broader population. During the period of collectivization, the terror expanded to include Nepmen, kulaks, and the intelligentsia. During the Stalinist revolutions, however, the terror grew to consume ever-larger portions of the Soviet population, ultimately consuming even many within the Party and leadership itself.

The spark that ignited the Great Purge was the assassination on December 1, 1934, of Sergei Kirov, the Party Secretary of Leningrad and member of the Politburo.[23] Stalin accused his former opponents—Zinoviev, Kamenev, and Trotsky—of the crime, but few in the West have accepted this view. A growing community of Western analysts has argued that Stalin himself plotted the crime. Specifically, Kirov led a push at an unreported session of the Congress and Central Committee to relax the pace of the Stalinist revolutions and to trim Stalin's power. Stalin struck back with a massive purge of Kirov's followers in the Leningrad Party organization and of the membership of the Party Congress and Central Committee that had sought to contain his power. He immediately ordered the arrest of hundreds of Leningraders and in January 1935, staged the trial of Zinoviev, Kamenev, and seventeen other Old Bolsheviks, sentencing them to 5 to 10 years. In the spring of 1935, thousands of Leningraders were sent to Siberia. But this was still a relatively relaxed period of the Great Purge, one associated with NKVD chief Genrikh Yagoda.

The brutality of the Great Purge grew immensely after September 1936, with the replacement of Yagoda by Nikolai Yezhov, who presided over the period of show trials, mass arrests, and executions sometimes called the *Yezhovshchina*. Yezhov's dominance lasted until December 1938, when he was replaced by Lavrentii Beria. The Purges at this time concentrated their terror on eight groups.[24] The Old Bolsheviks such as Bukharin, Zinoviev, Kamenev, and Rykov were accused of having murdered Kirov, of working with Trotsky, and of conspiring with Japan and Germany to overthrow the Soviet regime and restore capitalism. A second group of victims comprised those leading Party figures who had participated in the conspiracy to contain Stalin's power. These victims included 56 percent of the Party Congress, 70 percent of the Central Committee, 80 percent of the Sovnarkom, and over 80 percent of regional Party secretaries. Third, a majority of the senior officers of the Soviet military fell victim to the Purge, including not only such prominent figures as Marshal Mikhail N. Tukhachevsky, but also as many as 35,000 other military personnel. According to Khrushchev, the victims included 3 of 5 marshals, 13 of 15 army commanders, all admirals commanding fleets (and all of their initial replacements), 30 of 58 army corps commanders, and 311 of the 406 regimental commanders. Managers of Soviet industry constituted a fourth group to fall victim. Both Party and state leaders of the non-Russian republics also bore the brunt of the purges. Indeed, almost every one of these was accused of "bourgeois nationalism." A sixth group included the early leaders of the NKVD. When Yagoda was replaced as head of the NKVD in 1936, he and his followers then became victims of the secret police. A similar fate befell Yezhov and his followers in 1938. Those who had had contacts abroad, including diplomats, foreign trade officials, foreign communists, and veterans of the Spanish Civil War, were also purged. And lastly, those who through some misfortune were related to or had had ties with any of the previously listed individuals also fell victim. For example, because Commissar of Justice Prilenkov, a victim of the Purge, had been a mountain-climber, hundreds of alpinists also fell victim to the terror after his demise.

The outcome of the Great Purge was the elimination of all opposition to Stalin, permitting him to consolidate autocratic power. Of the 15 full and candidate members of the Politburo elected in February 1934, 4 were executed, 1 committed suicide under mysterious circumstances, 1 suffered a heart attack under mysterious circumstances, 1 was assassinated under circumstances that implicate Stalin, and another was removed but permitted to live. Only 7 survived on the Politburo until the Eighteenth Party Congress in 1939—Stalin and his loyalists Molotov, Kaganovich, Mikoyan, Andrei A. Andreev, Klementii E. Voroshilov, Mikhail I. Kalinin, to be joined by Andrei A. Zhdanov and Nikita S. Khrushchev. The Great Purges also led to large-scale imprisonment and death among the general population. Andrei Sakharov has estimated that hundreds of thousands died as a result of the high Purges, while the total number of victims, including arrests and deaths, reached as many as 12 to 15 million.

Yet, Stalin's political revolution was not simply destructive terror; it was also institution-building. The mobilization of Soviet society on behalf of the Stalinist revolutions was assisted by the new auxiliary organizations of the Party that enrolled much of the population. Centralized control over all institutions generated a new network of monitoring agencies. And the so-called Stalin Constitution of December 6, 1936, modified Soviet state institutions.[25]

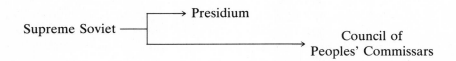

A bicameral Supreme Soviet meeting twice a year would now elect two bodies—a Presidium to serve as an interim legislature and corporate chief of state and a Council of Peoples' Commissars (after 1946, Council of Ministers) to serve as a cabinet.

War and Reconstruction

The pace of transformation slumped by the end of the 1930s. The institutionalization of the initial reforms made subsequent changes more difficult. And the approach of war diverted resources from these revolutions to military preparations.

Soviet participation in World War II was delayed by an accommodation with Germany. Stalin used this time to adjust his nation's western borders. The Nazi-Soviet (or Molotov-Ribbentrop) Pact of August 23, 1939, assigned to the Soviet Union much of the western borderland that had been lost in the Civil War. The Russo-Finnish or Winter War initiated against Finland on November 30, 1939, netted the Soviets territory near Leningrad, but full-scale military involvement in World War II did not begin until June 22, 1941. On that day the German forces initiated "Operation Barbarossa," with the objective of seizing the industrial regions around Moscow and Leningrad and the mineral and agricultural centers of the Ukraine and the Caucasus. Soviet accounts of the Great Patriotic War divide the subsequent history of Soviet involvement into three periods: The retreat beginning in June 1941 was followed by efforts to stop the German advance, leading to stabilization of the front at Leningrad, Moscow, Stalingrad, and the Caucasus. On November 19, 1942, with the counterattack at Stalingrad, the Soviets began the second stage during which they sought to seize the strategic initiative and reverse the war. Following victories at Stalingrad (January 1943) and Kursk (July 1943), the Soviet forces were on the offensive, so that in January 1944, Soviet troops initiated the final phase—that of clearing German troops from Soviet soil and participating in the final defeat of the Axis powers.[26]

The costs of the war were overwhelming. Soviet military casualties may

Soviet History (1946–1986): A Brief Chronology

1946.	Mr 15.	Peoples' Commissariats renamed Ministries.
1947.		Zhdanovshchina, launched.
1948.	Ag 31.	Zhdanov dies.
1949.	Ap.	Voznesensky dismissed.
1950.	Fb 14.	Treat of Friendship and Alliance with China.
1951.		
1952.	Oc 5–14.	XIX Congress of Communist Party.
1953.	Ja 31.	Discovery of 'Doctors' Plot'.
	Mr 5.	Death of Stalin: Khrushchev, Malenkov, Molotov.
1954.	Mr 7.	Virgin lands campaign launched.
1955.	Fb 8.	Malenkov resigns as Premier; Bulganin succeeds.
1956.	Fb 14–25.	XX Congress of CPSU: Khrushchev's 'Secret Speech'.
	Oc 23.	Soviet troops intervene in Hungary
1957.	My 7.	Economic reorganization: Sovnarkhozy created.
	Jn 22–29.	'Anti–Party Group' defeated.
1958.	Mr 27.	Bulganin resigns: Khrushchev, CM Chair
1959.	Ja 27–Fb 5.	XXI Congress of CPSU.
	Sp 15–27.	Khrushchev visit to USA and UN.
1960.	My I.	U–2 Incident; Paris summit conference breaks down.
	Nv.	Conference of Communist Parties: Rift with China.
1961.	Oc 17–31.	XXII Congress of CPSU: New Party Program.
1962.	Oc 22–Nv 20.	Cuban Missile Crisis.
	Nv.	Bifurcation of Communist Party.
1963.	Ag 5.	Agreement reached on Nuclear Test Ban Treaty.
1964.	Oc 14.	Khrushchev ousted: Brezhnev-Kosygin leadership.
	Nv 16.	Party industrial and agricultural organs reunified.
1965.	Mr 24–26.	Brezhnev agricultural reforms.
	Sp 27–29.	Sovnarkhozy abolished; ministries reestablished.
	Dc 9.	Podgorny appointed Chair, SS Presidium.
1966.	Fb 10–4.	Sinyavsky-Daniel trial.
	Mr 29–Ap 8.	XXIII CPSU Congress.
1967.		
1968.	Ap 30.	Appearance of Chronicle of Current Events.
	Ag 20–21.	Invasion of Czechoslovakia.
1969.	Mr 2–6.	Border clashes with Chinese.
1970.	Ag 12.	Agreements with Germany on borders.
1971.	Mr 30–Ap 9.	XXIV Congress of CPSU: detente decision.
1972.	My 22–30.	Visit by Nixon: sign ABM agreement.
1973.	Je 18–25.	Brezhnev visit to USA.
1974.	Je 27–Jl 3.	Moscow Summit: Arms control agreements.
1975.	Ag 1.	Final Act of ECSC (Helsinki Accords).
1976.	Fb 24–Mr 5.	XXV Congress of CPSU.
1977.	Je 16.	Brezhnev assumes Chair, SS Presidium.
	Oc 7.	New Soviet Constitution adopted.
1978.		
1979.	Je 18.	SALT II Agreement signed.
	Dc 25.	Soviet invasion of Afghanistan.
1980.	Oc 23.	Tikhonov replaces Kosygin as CM Chair.
1981.	Fb 23–Mr 3.	XXVI CPSU Congress.

1982.	Nv 12.	Andropov elected General Secretary.
1983.	Je 16.	Andropov assumes Chair, SS Presidium.
1984.	Fb 13.	Chernenko elected General Secretary.
1985.	Mr 11.	Gorbachev succeeds Chernenko.
1986.	Fb 25–Mr 6.	XXVII CPSU Congress.

have exceeded 7 million and civilian deaths may have been almost twice this number, for a total in excess of 20 million dead. Material losses included 1710 cities and 70,000 villages, including about half of all urban living space in the occupied territories, 32,000 factories, 98,000 collective farms (over one-third of the total number), and 1876 state farms. Livestock herds had been so devastated in the war zone that on January 1, 1946, the number of cows in the Soviet Union was 17.6 percent below the level exactly five years earlier, the number of horses fell by 49.0 percent, and that of pigs by 61.5 percent.

During the war Stalin intensified efforts to concentrate political power in his own hands and to hold Soviet society together with patriotic appeals. But for the sake of the war effort he was forced to make important tactical retreats in his revolutionary transformation of the Soviet Union. Many of these were symbolic, including the accommodation with the Russian Orthodox Church and the appeals to the traditional nationalism of both Russians and non-Russians. More substantial, however, was the suspension of the economic and social revolutions of the 1930s.

At the end of the war, Stalin committed the Soviet Union to reconstruct the system he had built earlier.[27] The Fourth Five-Year Plan (1946–1950) placed primary emphasis upon rebuilding heavy industry, with particular attention to those strategic sectors of the economy essential to Soviet military power. Conversely, the consumer sector received far less attention. Reconstruction also meant rebuilding the institutions of Stalinism. Where collective farms had been destroyed and peasants had seized their remaining assets for individual cultivation, collectivized agriculture was reimposed.

The reconstruction of the Stalinist system also brought intensified efforts to prevent any criticism and retreat from the Stalinist revolutions. Independent thinking in the late Stalin years was discouraged by new intellectual regimentation, which until 1948 was under the supervision of the Party Secretary Zhdanov. This period of the *Zhdanovshchina* not only glorified Soviet and Russian accomplishments (many real, but all too many simply fabrications), but also intensified attacks on the West. It touched not only politics, historiography, and literature, but all areas of intellectual endeavor, including music, linguistics, and the natural sciences. To preserve his revolutions, Stalin attempted to enshrine many of their practices in ideological dogmas. In his *Economic Problems of Socialism in the USSR* (1952), he anathematized proposals for reform, particularly for greater consumer goods production at the expense of growth in producers' goods or for slowing the transition from kolkhoz to sovkhoz.

Stalin's tight control over policy became more complete. The Politburo, which had been superseded by the State Defense Committee (GKO) during the war, never regained its institutional life in the late Stalin years. To dilute the power of the leading organs of the Party (and apparently to limit their constraints on his personal power), Stalin secured an organizational reform at the Nineteenth Party Congress (October 1952) that expanded the Politburo from 10 to 25 members and renamed it the Presidium, expanded the Secretariat to 10 members, and doubled the membership of the Central Committee. The revelation of the so-called "Doctors' Plot" in January 1953 accused Kremlin doctors purportedly allied with the United States of killing Zhdanov by administering the wrong medication. This seemed to implicate many in positions of power and to suggest that Stalin planned a new purge of the leadership.

Stalin sought to perpetuate his revolutions through control of the impending succession. At the end of the Great Patriotic War, Stalin was 65 years old and had to begin thinking about his own mortality and about the men who would succeed him. In particular, Stalin had to pick his heirs. Until 1948, Stalin appeared to favor Zhdanov, although he increasingly relied on the Party Secretary Georgi M. Malenkov as a counter-heir to check Zhdanov's power. Following Zhdanov's mysterious death in August 1948, Malenkov emerged as heir; and to check his growing power, Stalin in December 1949 brought Nikita S. Khrushchev from the Ukraine to serve as Secretary of the Moscow regional Party organization and as counter-heir.

POST-STALINIST POLITICS AND POLICY

On the night of March 1, 1953, Joseph Stalin suffered a brain hemorrhage and by March 5 was dead. The dictator's death did not end his influence on politics. The Stalin revolutions are, after the October Revolution itself, the most important legacy in post-Stalinist politics. They created many of the institutions and practices through which Soviet politics have continued to operate, helping to set the policy agenda for three decades. Ever since Stalin, a dominant concern in Soviet domestic politics has been Stalinism—to what extent it should be preserved and to what extent it should be dismantled.

Yet the death of Stalin did mark an important watershed in Soviet history. The pressures for reform of the most onerous practices of Stalin could not be quieted by leaders who lacked the authority of their predecessor and were unwilling to employ his terror. Without Stalin, continuation of these practices would become increasingly dysfunctional. Thus, the death of Stalin ushered in the third of the episodic transformations of Society society.

The Rise of Khrushchev

There was a short delay of about six hours in announcing Stalin's death, during which the new collective leadership parcelled his authority, in order to minimize the chances of instability upon the announcement. The new leaders established a

Party Presidium (Politburo) of 10 members, rather than 25, which was to be the institutional focus of a new collective leadership. This was to be led by a triumvirate that included Georgi M. Malenkov as Chairman of the Council of Ministers and Party Secretary, Lavrentii P. Beria as head of the secret police, and Vyacheslav M. Molotov as Minister of Foreign Affairs. In addition, the Politburo included (in order of precedence):

> Klementii E. Voroshilov (Chairman, Supreme Soviet Presidium)
>
> Nikita S. Khrushchev (a Party secretary)
>
> Nikolai A. Bulganin (Minister of Defense)
>
> Lazar M. Kaganovich (Deputy Chairman, Council of Ministers)
>
> Anastas I. Mikoyan (Minister of Foreign Trade)
>
> Maxim Z. Saburov (Chairman, Gosplan)
>
> Mikhail G. Pervukhin (Deputy Chairman, Council of Ministers)

It is from this group that the new leader would emerge.

In fact it was Nikita Khrushchev who finally emerged as heir to Stalin by 1957.[28] In his rise to power Khrushchev employed a strategy much like that of Stalin, at each turn isolating his principal opponents with Khrushchevian loyalists. Khrushchev's tactics were also much like Stalin's. Using policy in the pursuit of power, Khrushchev made a dramatic swing from left to right. He also artfully manipulated personnel through his control of the Party apparatus and engineered institutional changes that furthered the power of his followers and diluted that of his opponents.

The first victims of the succession struggle were, in fact, not Khrushchev's. The collective leadership, apparently in anticipatory self-defense, removed the Stalin guard, those who had been Stalin's closest protectors and advisors. Among these were Stalin's son Vasilii, his personal secretary Aleksandr N. Poskrebyshev, and the commandants of the Kremlin Guard, the City of Moscow, and the Moscow Military District.

The second victims were Beria and his associates in the police. Although initially one of the ruling triumvirate, Beria showed himself to be far too ambitious for the collective leadership. He secured the placement of his followers to leadership positions in the Transcaucasian republics and began to make appeals to these and other nationalities by championing greater autonomy for the non-Russian peoples. He populated the police with his own personal following and appeared ready to engineer a coup. Beria was arrested in June 1953, and executed in December—the last execution of a Politburo member in the Soviet Union. The collective leadership apparently felt that it would be unsafe to leave him in prison where his own police would be the guards. What would prevent him from using his personal ties to engineer a coup from his cell-block? After his arrest, the police organization was purged of Beria's followers.

Disarming Malenkov. The third victim of the succession struggle was Malenkov.[29] After Beria had been eliminated, the triumvirate was reconstituted to in-

NIKITA SERGEEVICH KHRUSHCHEV

The son of a Russian miner, Nikita S. Khrushchev was born on April 17, 1894, in the village of Kalinovka (Kursk province). Khrushchev joined the Party in 1918, serving with the Red Guards as a political activist during the Civil War. The end of the war offered Khrushchev the opportunity for a technical education at the Donets Industrial Institute; and there he also began his Party work as secretary of the Institute's party cell, followed by full-time Party work in the Ukraine. In 1929 Khrushchev moved to Moscow to study at the Industrial Academy, followed by a series of appointments to the apparatus in the capital, culminating in his election to the Central Committee in 1934. Stalin selected Khrushchev to serve as the first secretary of the Ukrainian Party apparatus in 1938—a post that brought candidate membership on the Politburo and then full membership the following year. In the Ukraine Khrushchev oversaw the local war-time effort and its post-war reconstruction. In December 1949 Stalin recalled Khrushchev to Moscow to serve on the Secretariat and perhaps to serve as counterweight to Stalin's heir-presumptive Georgi Malenkov.

Although not initially part of the triumvirate that succeeded Stalin, Khrushchev used the opportunity of Beria's execution and his position in the Party Secretariat (a post that would be dubbed First Secretary in the latter half of 1953) to defeat the other contenders in the succession. By March 1958, he had assumed the post of Chairman of the Council of Ministers as well.

Khrushchev's innovative policies and flamboyant style won him enemies within his own Politburo and by October 1964 a majority voted to remove him. In retirement at a country home just outside Moscow, Khrushchev and his wife Nina Petrovna remained in obscurity, seldom appearing in public. He died on September 11, 1971.

clude Malenkov, Molotov, and Khrushchev. As Stalin's heir designate, Malenkov was initially in the most powerful position, for as both Chairman of the Council of Ministers and a Party secretary, he alone held commanding administrative posts in both the state and the Party apparatuses.

Malenkov had also shown himself to be an ambitious man, and this had already cost him some of his power. On March 14, 1953, Malenkov was removed from one of his posts, that of Party secretary. This removal had a significant, but probably unintended, consequence: the competition that subsequently grew between Malenkov and Khrushchev increasingly became a competition between institutions—Party versus state.[30]

The economic policies of Stalinism became a central issue in this confrontation. Malenkov's strategy, relying on the personnel of the state apparatus, was to press for greater autonomy for state administrators and for policies that would reward them with increased access to consumer goods. In August 1953, Malenkov revealed his plan for a "New Course"—a significant redirection of the Stalinist economy that would place increasing emphasis on consumer-goods production at the expense of heavy industry. To accomplish this, defense expenditures would be cut in conjunction with a relaxation of the Cold War confrontation with the West.

Khrushchev relied upon the Party apparatus, as Stalin had done in the 1920s; and by September 1953, he emerged as the First Secretary, a position similar to Stalin's General Secretary. And, like Stalin, Khrushchev argued that consumer-goods production must not be expanded at the expense of capital goods, that heavy industry must retain its primacy in the economy, and that military expenditures must remain high to check the ever-predatory imperialist states. Khrushchev did, however, present himself as an agricultural innovator, proposing the Virgin Lands program in February 1954 to cultivate millions of acres in Central Asia and Siberia and introducing a "corn" program in January 1955 to produce fodder—all to ameliorate the sorry state of Stalinist agriculture.

These diverging strategies and policy prescriptions divided the Politburo. Khrushchev allied with its more conservative members, including Molotov, Kaganovich, Voroshilov, and Bulganin. Malenkov found support from Saburov and Pervukhin.

In late 1954, Khrushchev and the conservatives stepped up their attack. In December 1954 and January 1955, *Pravda* attacked the New Course, portraying it as un-Marxist and, therefore, ideologically unacceptable. At a Central Committee Plenum on January 25, 1955, Khrushchev branded proposals for giving priority to light industry as a new "right deviation." By February, Khrushchev and his allies were able to force Malenkov to resign the chairmanship of the Council of Ministers in favor of Bulganin. Ironically, in his official resignation Malenkov claimed that he lacked the experience necessary to fill the post. Although removed from his top state post, Malenkov remained on the Politburo for another two years.

Khrushchev's De-Stalinization Campaign   The next victims of the succession were Khrushchev's erstwhile conservative allies. Once Khrushchev successfully eliminated Malenkov as his chief contender for power, he began to distance himself from the conservatives, becoming a reformer himself by arguing for significant breaks with the Stalinist past.

Khrushchev called for relaxation of foreign policy tensions, in particular championing the cause of reconciliation with Tito's Yugoslavia. Since Molotov had been personally involved in Stalin's break with Tito in 1949 and opposed the rapprochement, Khrushchev's success in this matter discredited Molotov. Khrushchev also championed a détente with the West. In May 1955, the Soviet Union signed the Austrian State Treaty agreeing to end the joint occupation of Austria and to reunite it as a neutral state. This was followed by Soviet participation in the Geneva conferences, which helped extricate France from the Indo-China wars. And, significantly, Khrushchev began to renounce the doctrine of the inevitability of war between capitalism and socialism.

The capstone to this campaign came in February 1956, when Khrushchev delivered his now-famous Secret Speech to the 20th Party Congress, in which he dramatically revealed the extent of the Stalinist purges and the costs of Stalin's repression. From 1953 to 1955 the pace of de-Stalinization had been relatively moderate, but with this speech Khrushchev stepped up the pace of change. The de-Stalinization campaign was not simply a relaxation of Stalinist policies, but also a weapon in Khrushchev's struggle against his former conservative allies, for Khrushchev attempted to associate his opponents with the crimes of Stalin.

In this struggle, Khrushchev promoted his personal supporters to positions of power, including the cooptation of Mikhail A. Suslov and Alexei I. Kirichenko into the Party Presidium in 1955. He expanded the size of the Secretariat and at the 20th Party Congress secured expansion of the Central Committee, permitting him to bring in his loyalists from the regional and republican Party organizations. Moreover, institutional changes shook the bases of his opponents' power. In May 1957, Khrushchev secured passage of the *sovnarkhoz* reform, establishing regional economic councils to replace many of the Moscow-based ministries. This stripped power from the ministries in the state apparatus, where many of Khrushchev's opponents had their greatest strength, and transferred much of the responsibility for coordination of the economy to local Party secretaries, among whom Khrushchev had built his power base.

Khrushchev's policies in the struggle with the conservative opposition backfired in 1956, for his de-Stalinization campaign fed the East European unrest that culminated in revolts in Poland in October and in Hungary in November. The conservatives used the revolts as an occasion to press their demands for moderation of the de-Stalinization campaign and to curb Khrushchev's power.

The showdown came in June 1957: Khrushchev was confronted with a majority of the Party Presidium, led by Voroshilov, Malenkov, Molotov, and Kaganovich, that demanded his resignation.[31] Surprisingly, in the three-day meeting that followed, Khrushchev argued that he had not been elected by the Presidium, but by the Central Committee, and so only the latter body could remove him. Even though the Presidium vote was reportedly seven to four against him, Khrushchev successfully forced the question into the Central Committee, where he knew his support was strong. Khrushchev had prepared for exactly such a day by cultivating an alliance with the Minister of Defense, Marshal Georgi K. Zhukov. As Khrushchev called on the Presidium to turn this issue over to the Central Committee, Zhukov scrambled the Air Force to bring loyal Party secretaries from all over the Soviet Union to Moscow. When the Central Committee was convened (June 22–29, 1957) and the vote taken, who was voted out? Not Nikita Khrushchev, but his opponents! Branding them the "Anti-Party Group," Khrushchev succeeded not only in removing them from the Politburo, but in exiling them from Moscow—Molotov to Outer Mongolia as the Soviet Ambassador, Malenkov to Central Asia as director of a hydroelectric station, and Kaganovich to Sverdlovsk as director of a cement factory.

One of the last victims of the succession was Marshal Zhukov.[32] Reliance on the military in these power struggles had strengthened Zhukov's hand, giving Khrushchev cause to fear yet another challenge to his power or to Party predominance. Zhukov was demanding a high price—significant relaxation of Party control over the military. Thus, in October 1957, while on a state visit to Albania, Zhukov was recalled to Moscow, where he was informed that he had been relieved of his posts.

Having removed the men who came to power with him in 1953, Khrushchev was able to bring in a new generation of Party Presidium members, one more pliant to his will. Of the original post-Stalinist Presidium, only Khrushchev, Mikoyan, Bulganin (until 1958), and Voroshilov (until 1961) remained full members at the end of 1957; 11 new members, including Suslov, Kirichenko, Leonid I. Brezhnev, and Frol R. Kozlov, had been elevated since March 1953. At the culmination of this succession, Khrushchev held the most important Party and state positions. In addition to being a member of the Politburo and First Secretary of the Party, Khrushchev became Chairman of the Council of Ministers on March 27, 1958. Khrushchev had at last gained for himself the institutional bases to make a bid for the power previously held by Stalin.

Khrushchevian Policies

The Khrushchevian period was one of important experiments and innovations both in institutions and in policies, in the effort to find a post-Stalinist equilibrium. These changed much that had been inherited from the Stalin era, but in the end left far more intact. The succession struggle brought the replacement of the industrial ministries with the *sovnarkhozy*, a reform that changed the way in which the Soviet economy and society were administered. In 1958 the Machine Tractor Stations were eliminated. In 1962 the Party was divided into two parallel hierarchies with separate agricultural and industrial Party organizations below the republic level.

In addition to these institutional innovations, Khrushchev's policies abandoned some of the verities of the Stalinist era. De-Stalinization had begun during the succession struggle as an attack on the cult of the individual and as a return to collective leadership as Lenin had prescribed. But it grew to include a return to "socialist legality" with amnesty for many of the victims of Stalinist repression, the codification of law, and the development of procedural norms for the judicial process. Restrictions on literature and the arts were relaxed. The easing of artistic censorship had begun during the succession struggle with the publication of Ilya Ehrenburg's novel *The Thaw* and Vladimir Dudintsev's *Not by Bread Alone.* Yevgenii Yevtushenko began publishing his poetry openly. Following Khrushchev's victory over his opponents, there was a further blossoming of literature and the arts, much centered around the journal *Novyi Mir.* De-Stalinization also came to mean a moderation of Stalin's policies of Russification, with greater attention to the problems of the non-Russian nationalities. And it meant a shift in economic priorities. While Stalin had argued strongly for the preeminence of Group A (heavy) industries over Group B (light) industries, Khrushchev permitted increased emphasis on consumer-goods production. Even though he initially attacked the New Course, as he consolidated his power Khrushchev came to champion such programs as expanded construction of urban housing, increased meat and milk production, and new investments in the chemical industry for fertilizers and consumer goods.

Khrushchev's policies have sometimes been called "populist" in the West.[33] Educational reform in 1958 was designed to give peasants and workers greater access to higher education. Trade union organizations were given expanded authority in factory labor matters; and soviets were allowed more say in local policies. Comrade courts and volunteer police (*druzhinniki*) allowed expanded citizen participation in the administration of law. Party membership was opened to a larger percentage of the population; and mandatory "membership renewal" permitted more Party members to participate in high Party organs by requiring that one-third of the membership of these organs be replaced with each election.

Yet Khrushchevian policies were also frequently erratic. Khrushchev more than once announced a bold policy innovation from which he later retreated. For example, his dramatic reform of Soviet education in 1958 was repealed before he left power in 1964. And the sovnarkhoz reform of 1957 that was to decentralize the economy was already being abandoned to recentralization by 1959. In order to give direction to the local economic councils, Khrushchev found it necessary to establish republic-level sovnarkhozy and then a Supreme Economic Council in Moscow and to reestablish some of the centralized ministries that had previously been included in the Council of Ministers (e.g., the State Committee for Construction). And by 1963 the Central Committee had reduced the number of regional councils from the original 105 to 47.

Khrushchevian literary policy underwent swings between de-Stalinization and re-Stalinization. During the succession it vacillated through three periods: the initial thaw from mid-1953 to mid-1954, subsequent restriction on publication heralded by the removal of the editor of *Novyi Mir* (Aleksandr T. Tvardovsky), and then renewed thaw with Khrushchev's Secret Speech to the 20th Congress. In early 1957, following the explosions in Poland and Hungary, Khrushchev began a new campaign of tightened controls, banning Boris Pasternak's *Dr. Zhivago*. But in early 1959 he initiated a new easing with an address to the Writers' Congress. Late in 1959 Khrushchev again tightened control of the arts, but early in 1962 he relaxed these once again, permitting publication of Alexander Solzhenitsyn's *One Day in the Life of Ivan Denisovich* in November. Only a month later, however, he began a campaign against abstract art, but in July 1963 again loosened controls over literature.

The most costly inconsistencies were in economic policies, which seemed to be in constant flux. For example, the New Course of Malenkov held out the hope of a rapid expansion in consumers' goods; and in October 1953 Mikoyan promised that in two to three years' time Soviet industry would annually produce a million television sets, a half-million vacuum cleaners, and over three-hundred thousand refrigerators. Yet the Sixth Five-Year Plan (1956—1960) gave continued priority to the producers' goods sector. Moreover, even the Plan was frequently changed; at the end of the first year of the Sixth plan, its overly ambitious targets were revised and the Plan itself was replaced by a Seven-Year Plan (1959—1965). But even this was in essence abandoned in June 1963.

Shifts in policies were even more pronounced in the agricultural sector, producing a string of agricultural failures. After Stalin's death the new leadership had lowered the tax burden and delivery quotas for peasants, raised the procurement prices for grain, vegetables, meat, and dairy products, and granted the kolkhoz limited autonomy in planning its production. Succeeding years saw campaigns to expand production in the virgin lands, grow corn, and manufacture chemical fertilizers. Despite these initiatives and despite a massive campaign to send over 200 thousand workers to the countryside, the harvest of 1960 was disastrous, resulting among other things in the starvation of over nine million sheep.

This led to criticism of the organization and administration of agriculture, barnstorming tours of the countryside by Khrushchev, and purchases of grain overseas. By 1964, Khrushchev had committed the Soviet Union to a seven-year crash program of agricultural development that featured prominently the expansion of fertilizer production. Nonetheless, at the end of the Seven-Year Plan, agricultural production had risen only 14 percent over its 1958 level, falling almost a third below its target level.

Erratic policy shifts during the post-Stalin succession have been attributed to the power struggle, but the continuation of this changeable policy into the period of Khrushchev's ascendancy is not so easily explained. Indeed, it has given rise to speculation among Sovietologists about the extent of Khrushchev's power in this latter period.[34] Two very different explanations have been made for these swings in policy: Khrushchev's personality and the Khrushchevian policy process. The difference between these two views reflects the fundamentally diverging assumptions of two schools of Sovietologists.

Those who argue that the Soviet system tends to totalitarian autocracy often attribute the erratic policies to Khrushchev's personality. In this view, if Khrushchev had successfully consolidated autocratic control after 1957, then Soviet policy in this period must have reflected his personal predispositions. Curiously, Khrushchev's "style" of leadership is also the official Soviet explanation for these attributes of Khrushchevian policy. When removed in 1964, Khrushchev was criticized by his successors for "adventurism" and "hare-brained scheming," for if they did not fault Khrushchev personally, they would have to fault the Soviet system, possibly undermining its legitimacy.

Khrushchev's personal predispositions have also been used to explain the innovations of this period. Khrushchev has variously been called a populist, a reformer, and a liberal. He was responsible, in this view, for the great optimism of the early 60s that believed the Soviet Union would soon surpass the United States in production and that communism would be achieved in the lifetime of their grandchildren. Khrushchev's personal philosophy also might explain the attempts to eliminate some of the more restrictive Stalinist policies and to establish a broader participatory process.

Those who argue for a more competitive view of the Soviet system maintain that it was leadership politics that produced these shifts. This view contends that Khrushchev never fully consolidated power. Although he eliminated the Anti-Party Group in 1957 and 1958, he faced a whole new opposition that began to develop in late 1959. Kozlov and Suslov became the focus of a growing opposition within the Politburo that with time became the majority that removed Khrushchev in October 1964. This opposition was a coalition not only of those who rejected Khrushchevian policies, but more importantly of those who opposed his efforts to expand his power.

In this view, Khrushchev's failure to consolidate power completely and the growth of his opposition can account for both the erratic nature of Khrushchevian policy and the peculiar nature of the innovations in this period. Policy swung wildly when Khrushchev was overruled. After presenting a bold initiative as a trial balloon and seeing it shot down, Khrushchev was forced to retreat under fire and to try something new. Moreover, in order to keep his opponents off-balance, Khrushchev found it necessary to take initiatives that were unusually bold. Thus, the specific policies that Khrushchev advocated may not only have been expressions of Khrushchev's populism, but also ploys or political maneuvering to outdo his opponents. For example, Khrushchev as First Secretary of the Party used the sovnarkhoz reform in 1957 to attack those opponents who were concentrated in the state administrative apparatus of the Council of Ministers. How better to weaken their position in Moscow than to destroy the institutions on which they had built their power? By this reform, Khrushchev could also increase the power of the Party bureaucracy on which he had based his personal power, for the Party would play an expanded role in the central coordination of the economy. Similarly, the bifurcation of the Party in 1962, according to this argument, weakened Khrushchev's opponents within the Party. And the mandatory turnover of membership in Party organs would prevent any new opposition from emerging within those bodies. Even the de-Stalinization campaign itself may have been a power ploy. For example, in 1961 at the 22nd Party Congress, Stalin's body was removed from the Lenin mausoleum and planted along the Kremlin wall. His name was deleted from Party records. This campaign to denigrate the memory of Stalin provided Khrushchev the opportunity to weaken his opponents by attempting to label them Stalinists.

The Brezhnev Cartel

The ouster of Khrushchev on October 14, 1964, brought not only a shift in leadership personnel but also a change in the ways the leadership attempted to deal with the Stalinist legacy. The bold experimentation of the Khrushchev era would give way to a plodding and increasingly stagnating proceduralism. Khrushchev had been vacationing on the Black Sea when a telephone call from Brezhnev brought him back to Moscow. He was apparently kept under guard while on the airplane and was escorted to a meeting in which a nearly unanimous Presidium informed him of his retirement. At a meeting of the Central Committee this was made official.

Khrushchev was replaced by a collective leadership, which included at its head Brezhnev as General Secretary and Alexei N. Kosygin as Chairman of the Council of Ministers.[35] Some argue that collective leadership constituted a triumvirate that included Nikolai V. Podgorny, a Party Secretary and later Chairman of the Presidium of the Supreme Soviet; others argue that it actually constituted a quadrumvirate that also included the Party Secretary Suslov.

The new leadership confronted problems of declining economic growth rates and a stagnating agricultural sector. With a membership that was little changed from that of the late Khrushchev years (with the exception of Khrushchev himself) the leadership continued in many of the policies of the previous years, earning the early Brezhnev policies the label "Khrushchevism without Khrushchev." Significantly, much of the successors' criticism of Khrushchev faulted his style—specifically, the erratic and sometimes extreme nature of his pol-

LEONID ILICH BREZHNEV

A steelworker's son, Leonid I. Brezhnev was born on December 19, 1906, in the town of Kamenskoe (later Dneprodzerzhinsk). Too young to serve in the Revolution or the Civil War, Brezhnev first joined the Komsomol in 1923. After completing advanced training at the Kursk Technicum for Land Utilization and Reclamation in 1927, he served as a land utilization specialist in the early collectivization drive, rising to local administrative posts. From 1931 to 1935 Brezhnev studied evenings at the F. E. Dzerzhinskii Metallurgical Institute in his home town, while working as a fitter in a metallurgical plant. Joining the Party in 1931, he served as secretary of the Institute's Party committee and chairman of his factory's trade union committee. By 1937 he had been elected deputy chairman of the city soviet's executive committee

Brezhnev entered full-time Party work in 1938, moving to Dnepropetrovsk, where he rose to the post of secretary for propaganda in 1939 and secretary for defense industry in 1940. After service as a political officer (rising to the rank of major general) during the war, Brezhnev returned to the Ukraine to serve as first secretary initially of the Zaparozhe committee in 1946 and then the Dnepropetrovsk committee in 1947. By 1950 he had risen to the post of first secretary of the Moldavian republic. Although the 1952 enlargement of the Party Presidium (Politburo) brought Brezhnev an appointment to that body, he was not among those on the reconstituted Presidium after Stalin's death.

Brezhnev's rise in the Fifties was closely tied to Khrushchev's fortunes. In 1954, the latter sent Brezhnev to Kazakhstan to serve as second secretary and then first secretary of the republic and to oversee the implementation of the virgin lands program on which both staked their careers. He was rewarded in 1956 with posts in Moscow as Party secretary for heavy industry and in 1959 as secretary for defense industry. In 1957 he became a full member of the Party Presidium. In 1960, Brezhnev traded his Party secretaryship for the Chairmanship of the Supreme Soviet Presidium, but in 1963 returned to the Secretariat.

The removal of Khrushchev in October 1964 did not initially bring Brezhnev the authority of his predecessor. But his slow accumulation of power was marked by the growing authority of his statements in domestic and foreign affairs. This was capped in 1977 with his assumption of the post of Chairman of the Supreme Soviet Presidium. His last years, however, were marked by growing stagnation. The mounting infirmities of old age increasingly removed the General Secretary from public view, and on November 10, 1982, claimed his life.

---

icy innovations. And much of their remedial action focused on development of a new proceduralism, not only in administration but also in leadership politics and policy making.

One of the first reforms of the new leadership was to reverse some of Khrushchev's institutional changes. In November 1964, they reunited the local Party organizations, eliminating the bifurcation. (They also returned the name of the Party Presidium to that of Politburo in 1966). By October 1965, they had eliminated the sovnarkhozy and reestablished the ministries, returning many of the same people to lead the ministries who had staffed them seven years before! Institutionally, it appeared to be a return to pre-Khrushchevian patterns.

The new leadership was marked by a new style of politics. There appears to have been an implicit compact among the successors to maintain a collective leadership among them by adherence to four principles:[36] First, the leaders would keep the two top posts in separate hands. And a Central Committee decree made it explicit that one individual would not again be permitted to become both General Secretary and Chairman of the Council of Ministers. Second, the leadership agreed to reduce the opportunities for patronage. Indeed, in 1966 they eliminated the requirement that a third of the members of Party organs be changed with each election. Third, there appears to have been an agreement to distribute the seats in the Politburo, the Secretariat, and the Presidium of the Council of Ministers so as to avoid undue overlap in the membership of these bodies, blocking any one of those institutions from dominating the others—in particular, stopping the Secretariat from dominating the Politburo. And fourth, the leaders established a system of countervailing power among themselves, distributing the positions at the highest levels so that key leaders could maintain their autonomy and check the power of others.

In addition to these changes in the distribution of power within the leadership, there appears to have been a turn toward greater institutionalization of representation on the Politburo, development of consultative processes to include experts and interests in policy making, and the institutionalization of decision-making processes themselves.[37] It would appear that over half the membership of the Politburo had become institutionalized by the mid-70s, in that key state and Party positions as well as certain regional posts were almost automatically represented in the Politburo regardless of the incumbent. One of the most important steps in this direction was the decision in April 1973 to include among the members of the Politburo the ministers of Defense and Foreign Affairs and the Chairman of the KGB. At the same time, the new leadership saw a growth in consultation with experts during the policy-making process. The Party established scientific commissions to provide expert input into decision making. The Politburo came to consult regularly with experts from the Academy of Sciences, which was encouraged to develop institutes in policy areas. And the leadership appears to have developed procedures for regular consultation with affected interests and new techniques for polling public opinion. Third, the growth in proceduralism meant a growth in committee decision making. That is, those in narrow functional areas were permitted greater participation and given greater autonomy in policy making. The leadership divided responsibilities as a sort of political "cartel," resisting monopoly by any one leader of all policy arenas.

One of the consequences of this new collectivism was an apparent decline in the power struggle. This is not to say that there were no power struggles, nor to say that Brezhnev did not begin to accumulate growing authority, for beginning in 1968, the General Secretary appeared to grow markedly in stature. Yet as late as 1975 the British Sovietologist Archie Brown could write, "Though Brezhnev is more than a first among equals within the Politburo, he is much less than a Khrushchev. There is no doubt that the Politburo collectively is now more powerful than the general secretary individually."[38] And Darrell Hammer of Indiana University could remark, "Even more than Khrushchev, Brezhnev appears to function as the presiding officer of an oligarchy. . . . It would appear that Brezhnev is the representative of a broad consensus within the leadership—a consensus which says: Don't rock the boat."[39]

The first leadership confrontation appears to have involved Podgorny and his followers among the liberalizers who wanted further de-Stalinization. In 1965 these were slowly eased from their most important positions of power, a shuffle in which Podgorny was moved from the Party Secretariat to the Chairmanship of the Presidium of the Supreme Soviet. Yet even after his removal from the Secretariat, Podgorny remained on the Politburo until 1977. The second confrontation appears to have involved the *Shelepintsy*, or conservatives surrounding Alexander Shelepin. Beginning about 1967 the Shelepintsy were slowly eased from their power bases within the Komsomol (the Party's youth auxiliary), KGB, and Trade Union apparatus. In that year, Shelepin was removed from the Party Secretariat, although he remained on the Politburo. His allies were removed from the KGB in 1967 when Yuri V. Andropov was made head of that body in an effort to reassert Party control over the police.

The denouement of both of these confrontations came only a decade later, when Brezhnev began a second marked expansion of his power. In 1975 Shelepin was removed from the Politburo, and in 1977 Podgorny was removed both from the Chairmanship of the Supreme Soviet Presidium and from the Politburo. When Brezhnev himself assumed the Chairmanship of the Presidium, he had finally (after 13 years) added to his position as head of the Party a key (although largely ceremonial) post in the state. And by November 1978, following the removal of Kirill T. Mazurov, he had also succeeded in eliminating from the Politburo the principal checks on his power. The only independent powers in that body appear to have been Kosygin, who was aging and ailing, and Andrei P. Kirilenko and Suslov, both close allies of Brezhnev. To replace his deposed opponents, Brezhnev was able to promote Konstantin U. Chernenko and Nikolai A. Tikhonov, close associates of Brezhnev since his early years.

An opportunity for further expansion of Brezhnev's power came in October 1980, when Kosygin retired due to illness, and Tikhonov assumed his post as Chairman of the Council of Ministers. It appeared that Brezhnev would now be able to consolidate his position further and to become the power that Khrushchev had been. But ill health and leadership politics intervened. Brezhnev was by now seriously ill, reportedly suffering from arteriosclerosis, gout, leukemia, and emphysema. And in March 1982, he may have suffered a stroke, after which he temporarily disappeared from public view.

With the growing commitment to proceduralism came a slowed pace of social transformation. Columbia University political scientist Seweryn Bialer has observed that the Brezhnev cartel was marked by "the desire for a 'return to normalcy' through policies of institutional continuity, gradualism, accommodation, and reassurance of the elite."[40] Policies during the nearly two decades of the Brezhnev cartel, in fact, presented fewer significant institutional changes than in the previous one decade under Khrushchev. Aside from the restoration of the ministries and the reunification of the Party, the most important of these were the production associations and agroindustrial complexes—amalgamations to promote cooperation among ministries' chief administrations and among industrial enterprises and farms. More typical of the Brezhnev cartel than institutional transformation was the effort to make existing institutions perform more efficiently by modifying the incentive structures of subordinates.

Planned growth targets in these years were moderated. In contrast to what *Pravda* described as Khrushchev's "actions based on wishful thinking, boasting, and empty words," speeches by Soviet leaders in the Brezhnev era stressed the need for "realism" in planning. While the Seven-Year Plan in Khrushchev's last years projected annual growth rates in national income above seven percent, the Eighth and Ninth Plans of the Brezhnev period (1966–1970 and 1971–1975, respectively) projected rates below seven percent; and the Tenth Plan (1976–1980) even projected rates below five percent. Particular emphasis was given to the agricultural sector: "We understand," Brezhnev had said, "that an upsurge in agriculture is something that is vitally necessary to us for the successful construction of communism."[41] This meant, in particular, a commitment to mechanization in the countryside.

The consequence of this moderation and commitment to proceduralism was growing stagnation.[42] These problems continued to dog the Brezhnev cartel into the 1980s. The most visible manifestation of this stagnation was the decline in actual economic growth. By 1979 and 1980 it had ground down to an annual rate of perhaps one percent.

THE RISE OF GORBACHEV

Even before Brezhnev's death on November 10, 1982, a new shuffle for power had begun, involving the figures that would later attempt to succeed him. This initiated a succession that continued for at least four years, culminating it would appear in the growing consolidation of power in the hands of Mikhail S. Gorbachev.[43] The consequence of this succession is a change of political generations—the rise to power of the first leaders since the early '20s that have not served under Stalin. (Gorbachev, for example, turned 22 only three days before Stalin's death.) These leaders inherited from the Stalin generation the mounting problems of a stagnating economy and society, but fewer of its preconceived notions about the limitations on action. Thus, the rise of this generation may herald changes in policies as profound as those in the 1920s and 1950s. The Soviet Union may be about to enter another period of significant transformation as it begins the stage of advanced industrialism.

The succession struggle apparently began as those around Andropov attempted to discredit Brezhnev's closest allies. In the late winter and spring of 1982 there was a seemingly amusing affair involving circus performers: Between January and March, Boris Tsygan ("the Gypsy"), a millionaire Soviet circus performer, Anatoly Kolevatov, head of the Soviet circuses, and Boris Buryatin were arrested for black-market activity, including smuggling diamonds and foreign currency. These performers had been close friends of Brezhnev's daughter,

Galina Churbanova (Buryatin was allegedly her lover), so that the charges by the secret police appeared designed to embarrass Brezhnev for his tolerance of corruption, even in his own family, and to discredit his closest associates, including his heir-apparent, Chernenko. At about the same time as the first of these arrests a disagreement between Suslov, a partisan of Brezhnev, and S. K. Tsvigun—the second-in-command of the KGB, a participant in the black-market investigation, and a partisan of Andropov—apparently led Tsvigun to commit suicide. Brezhnev and Suslov, breaking with Soviet protocol, refused to sign the obituary for Tsvigun. (Suslov himself died six days later on January 26, 1982.)

In the two and a half years after Brezhnev's death, three leaders assumed the post of General Secretary: Andropov came to power on November 12, 1982, Chernenko on February 13, 1984, and Gorbachev on March 11, 1985. The speed and ease with which each transfer of power took place suggests that the process of succession was being institutionalized. Andropov's election by the Central Committee was announced just two days after Brezhnev's death; the elections of Chernenko and Gorbachev were announced in even shorter time. Indeed, with little fanfare the leadership had transferred to Gorbachev many of Chernenko's responsibilities, including chairing Politburo meetings, weeks or months before Chernenko's death, as a prolonged illness kept him from his office. The leadership appeared to continue to abide by its implicit compact of two decades earlier maintaining a balance among leading institutions, particularly in representation within the Politburo, and preventing the General Secretary from assuming the Chairmanship of the Council of Ministers even when the retirement of Tikhonov, on September 17, 1985, presented this opportunity. (Nikolai I. Ryzhkov was named Tikhonov's successor.) As if to underscore the commitment to collectivism and checks on power, the leadership did not make the appointment of the General Secretary to the Chairmanship of the Supreme Soviet Presidium routine. Andropov did not acquire the latter post until June 1983, seven months after his elevation to the Party leadership. And while Chernenko was given the Presidium post just two months after his accession to the Party leadership (April 1984), Gorbachev was not given this post initially. In fact, on July 2, 1985, it was given to Andrei A. Gromyko.

A consequence of the succession process itself was continued indecisiveness in policy. During Brezhnev's last year the Central Committee adopted a Food Program that committed the Party to extending the agroindustrial complexes and expanding investment in the rural infrastructure (e.g., storage and transportation). Andropov added a commitment to some decentralization of authority to the production associations, enterprises, and farms. Yet by early 1985 these reforms had been only partially implemented. The short tenure and failing health of the leaders and Chernenko's protection of vested bureaucratic interests against significant reforms led to immobilism.

Gorbachev may prove to be the man who is able to break this stagnation—to begin again the process of modernization in Soviet society. His relative youth (54 years of age when he became General Secretary, compared to 68 for Andropov and 72 for Chernenko) gives Gorbachev the opportunity for a relatively long tenure in office, during which he may be able to consolidate power and engi-

YURI VLADIMIROVICH ANDROPOV

Described variously as a cosmopolitan gentleman of liberal tastes and Russia's policeman who crushed the Hungarian Revolution in 1956 and Russian dissent in the Seventies—an enigma may well be the lasting judgment of Yuri V. Andropov. Although his statements following his assumption of the post of General Secretary on November 12, 1982, seemed to portend a break with the stagnating policies of his predecessor, Andropov's fifteen-month tenure as General Secretary (and Chairman of the Supreme Soviet Presidium after June 16, 1983) did not produce profound changes.

Born on June 15, 1914, in Nagutskaya (Stavropol krai) to a railway worker's family, Andropov began party work in the Komsomol in 1936, rising to first secretary of the youth organization in the Yaroslavl region in 1938 and in the Karelo-Finnish S.S.R. in 1940. Following the war, Andropov rose to be second secretary of the Party organization in the Karelian republic and in 1951 moved to Moscow to work in the Central Committee Apparatus. Serving in the Soviet embassy from 1952 to 1957, Andropov rose to the rank of ambassador in 1954 and played a central role in crushing the Hungarian Revolt two years later. Returning to Moscow in 1957, Andropov headed the Central Committee's Department for Liaison with Workers and Communist Parties of Socialist Countries for the next ten years. In 1967 he rose to chair the KGB and assume a candidate membership on the Politburo. (He was promoted to full membership in 1973.) In May 1982, apparently in anticipation of the coming succession, Andropov traded his chairmanship of the KGB for a post as Party Secretary responsible for appointments.

KONSTANTIN USTINOVICH CHERNENKO

Konstantin U. Chernenko and his thirteen month tenure as General Secretary (also Chairman of the Supreme Soviet Presidium after April 1984) are probably doomed to be forgotten as a footnote in history. Born to a peasant family in September 24, 1911, at Novoselov in Krasnoyarsk krai, Chernenko began party work in 1929, heading the local Komosomol agitation and propaganda organ and joining the Party two years later. His rise that began in the late Forties was closely tied to that of Brezhnev—serving as the head of Agitprop in Moldavia from 1948 to 1956 and then in Moscow as head of the Mass Agitation Work Department of the CPSU. Under Brezhnev's patronage, Chernenko became chief of staff to Brezhnev's Supreme Soviet Presidium in 1960 and then head of the General Department to his Secretariat in 1965. Eleven years later Chernenko was elevated to the Party Secretariat and then to the Politburo as a candidate in 1977 and a full member in 1978. Losing out to Andropov in the contest to succeed Brezhnev in 1982, Chernenko finally seemed to have achieved victory with Andropov's death on February 10, 1984, only to have that snatched from him by failing health that kept him from his duties for the last months of his tenure as General Secretary. On March 11, 1985, Chernenko died.

neer change. As someone who began his political career in the post-Stalin years, Gorbachev is not burdened by personal involvement in the Stalin legacy and potentially less burdened by its solutions to the problems of modernization. And as a graduate of Moscow University's Law Faculty, Gorbachev possesses the most ad-

MIKHAIL SERGEEVICH GORBACHEV

The place in history of Mikhail S. Gorbachev is still uncertain. Whether he will consolidate power and build the authority needed to change Soviet society, whether his political sympathies are with the post-Stalinist reformers—these are questions that remain to be answered. Born on March 2, 1921, to a peasant family in the village of Privolnoe in Stavropol krai, Gorbachev is the first Soviet leader to begin his Party career after Stalin's death. Entering Moscow State University in 1950, Gorbachev graduated from the law faculty in 1955. He joined the party in 1952, while at the University. After graduation, Gorbachev began Party work as leader of the Komsomol in Stavropol krai and entered full-time work in 1962. He rose rapidly in the Krai Party organization, becoming its first secretary in 1970. Close ties to members of the All-Union Secretariat, including Fedor Kulakov and apparently Mikhail Suslov, may have won him a post in Moscow in 1978 as Party Secretary responsible for agriculture. Candidate membership on the Politburo followed in 1979, and full membership in 1980. His close association with Andropov won him expanded responsibilities within the Secretariat for the whole economy and for Party appointments. Although passed over in 1984 to succeed Andropov, Gorbachev apparently assumed many of the responsibilities of General Secretary in the months before Chernenko's death. And only five hours after the announcement of the latter's death Gorbachev was appointed General Secretary. In his nominating speech, Andrei A. Gromyko told the Central Committee, "Comrades, this man has a nice smile, but he's got iron teeth." What should one expect from such a leader?

vanced formal education of any General Secretary to this time and possibly greater openness to new ideas.

Gorbachev moved quickly to consolidate his power.[44] By the end of the June 1987 Central Committee Plenum, 8 of the 13 voting members (other than Gorbachev himself) and 4 of the 6 candidate (nonvoting) members had been elevated since Gorbachev assumed office just twenty-seven months earlier. The removals or retirements from that body included the two men who were most likely to challenge Gorbachev's claim to the post of General Secretary—Viktor V. Grishin and Grigorii V. Romanov. The new appointments included several (e.g., Alexander N. Iakovlev) who were clearly allies of Gorbachev. In the Secretariat 10 of the 12 secretaries had been elevated since Gorbachev's assumption of the General Secretary's post. These key appointments and the appointment of Ryzhkov to the Chairmanship of the Council of Ministers seems to have broken the power of what remained of the old Brezhnev-Chernenko faction in the Party leadership and strengthened Gorbachev's hand. Turnover was also particularly high among members of the Council of Ministers, including such ministers and ministerial-level officials as the Chairman of Gosplan and the ministers of Defense, Finance, Foreign Affairs, and Internal Affairs.

The public statements of Gorbachev suggest that, if successful at consolidating power (particularly against the resistance of the entrenched bureaucracy of the Brezhnev years), the new leader's policies may produce profound change in Soviet society. The Soviet press has called for "new thinking" (*novoe myshlenie*)—new ways of approaching social, economic, and political problems. And the Gorbachev proposals certainly seem to be characterized by this.

In the area of economic reform, the watchwords of the Gorbachev program are acceleration (*uskorenie*), intensification (*intensifikatsiia*), and restructuring (*perestroika*). The economic plan for 1986–2000 holds out the hope of doubling the national income (accelerated growth), including consumer goods and services, by the end of the century. Much of this growth is to be accomplished through improvement in labor productivity by means of more efficient (or more intensive) use of existing resources and by means of a technological revolution. But, in addition, it will require structural reform. Ryzhkov, in his presentation of the long-term economic plan to the Party Congress, called for "profound restructuring of the Soviet economy." Gorbachev, while reassuring the Congress that he would not abandon the socialist or planned economy, called for greater autonomy for farms and industrial enterprises in production decisions and for greater flexibility and market realism in prices. He attacked "the inertness and stiffness of the forms and methods of administration" and "the escalation of bureaucracy" that "began to build up in the economy in the 1970s"—a none-too-well disguised attack on the Brezhnev years. Legislation in succeeding months seemed to permit restructuring primarily on the fringes of the economy, by encouraging individual economic initiative in selected areas of service delivery, such as small-scale cooperative fast-food operations. But the Central Committee Plenum of June 25–26, 1987, seemed to take an important step in the direction of structural change in the state-run sector of the economy: It endorsed reforms to begin decentralization of economic decision making to the enterprise level and to introduce some flexibility in wholesale and retail prices. Like Andropov before him, Gorbachev has also cited the corruption that grew during the Brezhnev regime as a source of its bureaucratic failure and has made "exactingness" and discipline (coupled with a campaign against alcoholism) major themes in his program. He has extended this to include an attack on the privileges of the elite.

Equally visible elements of Gorbachev's program for *novoe myshlenie* are the leader's proposals for democratization (*demokratizatsiia*) and his apparent commitment to openness and a freer flow of information (*glasnost'*). At the January 1987 Central Committee Plenum Gorbachev proposed the gradual introduction of competitive elections into the process of selecting both Party and state officials; and the June 1987 elections to local soviets experimented with contested seats in a few constituencies. Describing democratization as the means to unleash popular energies on behalf of *perestroika*, he told the Plenum, "We need democracy like air. If we fail to understand this, . . .our policies will fail and reconstruction will collapse, comrades."[45] *Glasnost'* was manifest in 1986 in the prompt news reports of the sinking of the Soviet liner Admiral Nakhimov, with the loss of some 400 lives, and the sinking of a Soviet nuclear submarine. Greater tolerance of diversity in the arts, the release of political prisoners, and the easing of restrictions on emigration all seem to signal a new direction in policy. The limits of *glasnost'*, however, are suggested by the continued arrest of dissidents (although at a much reduced rate in 1987) and the refusal to publish the speeches of his Central Committee critics alongside Gorbachev's call for democratization.

The accomplishments of the first two and a half years of Gorbachev's leadership are substantial, particularly when contrasted with the stagnation of the years immediately preceding. Nonetheless, much of the Gorbachev program remains a promise for the future rather than an accomplished fact. And the prognosis for its success appears closely tied to Gorbachev's success at maintaining and consolidating his power. It is unclear whether Gorbachev will be able to continue the pace of his early consolidation. One consequence of growing institutionalization of the powers of the General Secretary may be to speed the transfer of essential powers guaranteed to the post but to retard expansion of the power of the General Secretary much beyond this. Few of the Politburo members—and surprisingly few of the members of the new Central Committee—owe their political careers to Gorbachev, and most have an interest in preventing him from accumulating so much power that he could use it against them or their interests.

Gorbachev appears to have encountered resistance to some of his proposals for reform. Plans to impose a retirement age on officials and to introduce contested elections within the Party, plans that would have expanded Gorbachev's opportunities to make or influence new appointments, were rebuffed. Gorbachev himself has complained that resistance pervades the bureaucracies of many institutions. Egor Ligachev, the second-ranking Party leader, has frequently taken a more conservative position on issues of reform, for example cautioning audiences not to take *glasnost'* too far in reexamining history or testing the bounds of socialist realism. The strength of this sustained, but veiled, opposition to Gorbachev's reforms has led some Western analysts to question whether Gorbachev can succeed. Some have even argued that if he does not retreat from his reforms he risks "being removed á la Khrushchev within the next few years."[46] Conversely, if he prevails over the opponents of change and persists in his reformist program, Gorbachev's leadership may mark a significant break with the post-Stalinist period and usher in a fourth episode of transformation in Soviet development.

NOTES

1. Among the many works on the Russian Revolution, the best surveys are probably Edward H. Carr, *The Bolshevik Revolution, 1917–1923,* 3 vols. (New York: Macmillan, 1951–1953); William H. Chamberlin, *The Russian Revolution, 1917–1921,* 2 vols. (New York: Macmillan, 1935); and John L. Keep, *The Russian Revolution: A Study in Mass Mobilization* (New York: Norton, 1976).

2. Oliver H. Radkey, *The Elections to the Russian Constituent Assembly of 1917* (Cambridge, Mass.: Harvard University Press, 1950).

3. Richard Pipes, *The Formation of the Soviet Union: Communism and Nationalism, 1917–1923* (Cambridge, Mass.: Harvard University Press, 1954); John S. Reshetar, Jr., *The Ukrainian Revolution, 1917–1920* (Princeton, N.J.: Princeton University Press, 1952); Arthur E. Adams, *Bolsheviks in the Ukraine: The Second Campaign, 1918–1919* (New Haven, Conn.: Yale University Press, 1963); Firuz Kazemzadeh, *The Struggle for Transcaucasia, 1917–1921* (New York: Philosophical Library, 1951); and Alexander Park, *Bolshevism in Turkestan, 1917–1927* (New York: Columbia University Press, 1957).

4. On the White Armies, see: David Footman, *Civil War in Russia* (New York: Praeger, 1962); Russell E. Snow, *The Bolsheviks in Siberia, 1917–1918* (Madison: Far-

leigh Dickinson University Press, 1977); Anton Denikin, *The White Army* (London: Cape, 1930); Pyotr N. Wrangel, *The Memoirs of General Wrangel* (London: Williams and Norgate, 1929).

5. On the Intervention, see George F. Kennan, *The Decision to Intervene* (Princeton, N.J.: Princeton University Press, 1958); Robert D. Warth, *The Allies and the Russian Revolution* (Durham, N.C.: Duke University Press, 1954); John Bradley, *Allied Intervention in Russia* (New York: Basic Books, 1968); George A. Brinkley, *The Volunteer Army and Allied Intervention in South Russia, 1917–1921* (Notre Dame, Ind.: Notre Dame University Press, 1966); Richard Goldhurst, *The Midnight War: The American Intervention in Russia, 1918–1920* (New York: McGraw-Hill, 1978); James W. Morley, *The Japanese Thrust into Siberia, 1918* (New York: Columbia University Press, 1957); Canfield F. Smith, *Vladivostok under Red and White Rule: Revolution and Counterrevolution in the Russian Far East, 1920–1922* (Seattle, Wash.: University of Washington Press, 1976); Richard H. Ullman, *Anglo-Soviet Relations, 1917–1921: Intervention and the War* (Princeton, N.J.: Princeton University Press, 1961); Betty M. Unterberger, *America's Siberian Expedition, 1918–1920* (Durham, N.C.: Duke University Press, 1956); and John A. White, *The Siberian Intervention* (Princeton, N.J.: Princeton University Press, 1950).

6. Basil Dmytryshyn, *USSR: A Concise History* (New York: Scribner, 1965), 97.

7. On the early development of the Red Army, see D. Fedotoff-White, *The Growth of the Red Army* (Princeton, N.J.: Princeton University Press, 1944); and John Erickson, *The Soviet High Command, 1918–1941* (New York: St. Martin's Press, 1967).

8. On the origins of the Cheka, see George Leggett, "Lenin, Terror and the Political Police," *Survey* 21 (1975), 157–187; Boris Levytsky, *The Uses of Terror: The Soviet Secret Police, 1917–1920* (New York: Coward, McCann, and Geoghegan, 1972); George Leggett, *The Cheka: Lenin's Political Police* (New York: Oxford University Press, 1981); and Robert Conquest, *The Soviet Police System* (London: Bodley Head, 1968).

9. *Vos'moi S'ezd RKP(b), Mart 1919: Protokoly* (Moscow, 1959), 165. On early Party organization see Leonard Schapiro, *The Communist Party of the Soviet Union,* Part II (New York: Random House, 1960). See also Robert Service, *The Bolshevik Party in Revolution, 1917–1923* (New York: Barnes & Noble, 1979).

10. On the early Soviet constitutions see Aryeh L. Unger, *Constitutional Development in the USSR: A Guide to the Soviet Constitutions* (London: Methuen and Co., 1981). See also T. H. Rigby, *Lenin's Government: Sovnarkom 1917–1922* (Cambridge, England: Cambridge University Press, 1979).

11. On the succession issue see Myron Rush, *Political Succession in the USSR,* 2d ed. (New York: Columbia University Press, 1968). Many works have been written on the period of Stalin's rule and on Stalinism. Among the studies of Stalin the student may want to consult are Isaac Deutscher, *Stalin: A Political Biography* (New York: Oxford University Press, 1949); and Adam B. Ulam, *Stalin: The Man and His Era* (New York: Viking Press, 1973). Among the interpretations of Stalinism, the student may want to consult Robert C. Tucker, ed., *Stalinism: Essays in Historical Interpretation* (New York: Norton, 1977); Tariq Ali, ed., *The Stalinist Legacy: Its Impact on 20th Century World Politics* (New York: Penguin Books, 1984); G. R. Urban, ed., *Stalinism: Its Impact on Russia and the World* (Cambridge, Mass.: Harvard University Press, 1986); Robert C. Tucker, *Stalin as Revolutionary, 1879–1929: A Study in History and Personality* (New York: Norton, 1973); and Roy A. Medvedev, *Let History Judge: The Origins and Consequences of Stalinism* (New York: Knopf, 1972). Among the more provocative studies on the other principal figures in this period are Stephen Co-

hen, *Bukharin and the Bolshevik Revolution: A Political Biography, 1888–1938* (New York: Random House, 1974); Isaac Deutscher, *The Prophet Armed: Trotsky, 1879–1921* (New York: Oxford University Press, 1954): Isaac Deutscher, *The Prophet Unarmed: Trotsky, 1921–1929* (New York: Oxford University Press, 1959); and Isaac Deutscher, *The Prophet Outcast: Trotsky, 1929–1940* (New York: Oxford University Press, 1963).

12. On the NEP period see Edward H. Carr, *The Interregnum, 1923–1924* (New York: Macmillan, 1954); Edward H. Carr, *Socialism in One Country, 1924–1926* (New York: Macmillan, 1958); and A. Erlich, *The Soviet Industrialization Debate* (Cambridge, Mass.: Harvard University Press, 1967). See also Paul Avrich, *Kronstadt 1921* (Princeton, N.J.: Princeton University Press, 1970).

13. On collectivization see Moshe Lewin, *Russian Peasants and Soviet Power* (London: Allen & Unwin, 1968); R. W. Davies, *The Socialist Offensive, the Collectivization of Soviet Agriculture, 1929–1930* (London: Macmillan, 1980); D. Male, *Russian Peasant Organization before Collectivization* (Cambridge, England: Cambridge University Press, 1971); and Lazar Volin, *A Century of Russian Agriculture: From Alexander II to Khrushchev* (Cambridge, Mass.: Harvard University Press, 1970), 189–273.

14. Alec Nove, *An Economic History of the U.S.S.R.* (New York: Penguin Books, 1982), 111.

15. Merle Fainsod, *Smolensk under Soviet Rule* (Cambridge, Mass.: Harvard University Press, 1958), 245.

16. Nove, 174.

17. On the Stalinist industrialization campaign, see Nove, 188–268; Donald R. Hodgman, *Soviet Industrial Production, 1928–1951* (Cambridge, Mass.: Harvard University Press, 1954); Abram Bergson,*The Real National Income of Soviet Russia since 1928* (Cambridge, Mass.: Harvard University Press, 1961); Naum Jasny, *Soviet Industrialization 1928–1952* (Chicago: University of Chicago Press, 1961); and E. Zaleski, *Stalinist Planning and Economic Growth 1932–1952* (Chapel Hill, N.C.: University of North Carolina Press, 1980).

18. I. V. Stalin, "O. zadachakh khoziaistvennikov" ["The Tasks of the Business Executives"], *Voprosy Leninizma [Problems of Leninism],* 10th ed. (Moscow: Partizdat, 1936), 445.

19. Peter R. Beckman, *World Politics in the Twentieth Century* (Englewood Cliffs, N.J.: Prentice-Hall, 1984), 89, 169.

20. U.S.S.R., Tsentral'noe Statisticheskoe Upravlenie, *Narodnoe khoziaistvo SSSR v 1963 g.* (Moscow: Statistika, 1965), 7–8, 574.

21. On the cultural policies of Stalin see, for example, Harold Swayze, *Political Control of Literature in the USSR, 1946–1959* (Cambridge, Mass.: Harvard University Press, 1962).

22. On the Purges and the use of terror see Robert Conquest, *The Great Terror: Stalin's Purge of the Thirties* (New York: Macmillan, 1968); and Boris Levytsky, *The Stalinist Terror in the Thirties: Documentation from the Soviet Press* (Stanford, Calif.: Hoover Institution Press, 1974). Two important traditional interpretations of the Purges are Barrington Moore, Jr., *Terror and Progress, USSR* (Cambridge, Mass.: Harvard University Press, 1954); and Zbigniew K. Brzezinski, *The Permanent Purge: Politics of Soviet Totalitarianism* (Cambridge, Mass.: Harvard University Press, 1956). For a recent controversial study that disputes the prevailing interpretation of Stalinist politics and the Purges, see J. Arch Getty, *Origins of the Great Purges: The Soviet Communist Party Reconsidered, 1933–1938* (Cambridge, England: Cambridge University Press, 1985).

23. Medvedev, *Let History Judge,* 152–191; Ulam, *Stalin,* 375–388; Alec Nove, *Stalinism and After* (London: Allen & Unwin, 1975), 52–54.

24. Nove, *Stalinism and After,* 54–55.

25. On the Stalin Constitution see Julian Towster, *Political Power in the U.S.S.R., 1917–1947* (New York: Oxford University Press, 1948), and Unger.

26. P. A. Zhilin, "Velikaia Otechestvennaia Voina Sovetskogo Soiuza, 1941–1945," *Sovetskaia Voennaia Entsiklopediia* (Moscow: Voenizdat, 1976).

27. On post-war politics and reconstruction see Timothy Dunmoore, *Soviet Politics, 1945–53* Macmillan, 1984); Werner G. Hahn, *Postwar Soviet Politics: The Fall of Zhdanov and the Defeat of Moderation, 1946–53* (Ithaca, N.Y.: Cornell University Press, 1982). Data from *Narodnoe khoziaistvo SSSR v 1963 g.,* 311.

28. On Khrushchev and the Khrushchev era see George W. Breslauer, *Khrushchev and Brezhnev as Leaders: Building Authority in Soviet Politics* (London: Allen & Unwin, 1982); Robert Conquest, *Power and Policy in the USSR* (New York: St Martin's Press, 1961);Edward Crankshaw, *Khrushchev: A Career* (New York: Viking Press, 1966); Nikita S. Khrushchev, *Khrushchev Remembers* (Boston: Little, Brown and Company, 1970); Nikita S. Khrushchev, *Khrushchev Remembers: The Last Testament* (Boston: Little, Brown and Company, 1974); Carl A. Linden, *Khrushchev and the Soviet Leadership, 1957–1964* (Baltimore, Md.: Johns Hopkins University Press, 1966); Roy Medvedev and Zhores Medvedev, *Khrushchev: The Years in Power* (New York: Columbia University Press, 1977); and Roy Medvedev, *Khrushchev* (Oxford, England: Basil Blackwell, 1982).

29. On Malenkov see Martin Ebon, *Malenkov: Stalin's Successor* (New York: McGraw-Hill, 1953).

30. Rush, 60–63.

31. Roger W. Pethybridge, *A Key to Soviet Politics: The Crisis of the Anti-Party Group* (New York: Praeger, 1962).

32. Roman Kolkowicz, *The Soviet Military and the Communist Party* (Princeton, N.J.: Princeton University Press, 1967), 113–135; Timothy J. Colton, *Commissars, Commanders, and Civilian Authority: The Structure of Soviet Military Politics* (Cambridge, Mass.: Harvard University Press, 175–195.

33. Breslauer, *Khrushchev and Brezhnev,* 52.

34. Carl A. Linden et al., "Conflict and Authority: A Discussion," *Problems of Communism* 12 (September-October 1963), 27–46; 12 (November-December 1963), 56–65; Merle Fainsod et al., "The Coup and After," *Problems of Communism* 14 (January-February 1965), 1–31; 14 (May-June 1965), 37–45; 14 (July-August 1965), 72–76.

35. On Brezhnev and the Brezhnev era see Breslauer, *Khrushchev and Brezhnev,* Part III; John Dornberg, *Brezhnev: The Masks of Power* (New York: Basic Books, 1974); Paul J. Murphy, *Brezhnev: Soviet Politician* (Jefferson: McFarland and Co., 1981).

36. T. H. Rigby, "The Soviet Leadership: Towards a Self-Stabilizing Oligarchy?" *Soviet Studies* 22 (October 1970), 175.

37. Grey Hodnett, "The Pattern of Leadership Politics," in Seweryn Bialer, ed., *The Domestic Context of Soviet Foreign Policy* (Boulder, Colo.: Westview Press, 1981), 97–98; George W. Breslauer, "On the Adaptability of Soviet Welfare-State Authoritarianism," in Karl W. Ryavec, ed., *Soviet Society and the Communist Party* (Amherst, Mass.: University of Massachusetts Press, 1978), 8–9; and Jerry F. Hough, "The Brezhnev Era—The Man and the System," *Problems of Communism* 25 (March-April 1976), 11.

38. Archie Brown, "Political Developments: Some Conclusions and an Interpretation,"

in Archie Brown and Michael Kaser, eds., *The Soviet Union Since the Fall of Khrushchev* (New York: Free Press, 1975), 234.

39. Darrell P. Hammer, *U.S.S.R.: The Politics of Oligarchy* (New York: Praeger, 1974), 319, 320.

40. Seweryn Bialer, "The Soviet Political Elite and Internal Developments in the USSR," in William E. Griffith, ed., *The Soviet Empire: Expansion and Detente* (Lexington, Mass.: Lexington Books, 1976), 32.

41. Breslauer, 138.

42. Rigby, 190.

43. On the Brezhnev-to-Gorbachev succession see Martin Ebon, *The Andropov File* (New York: McGraw-Hill, 1983); Zhores Medvedev, *Andropov* (Oxford: Basil Blackwell, 1983); Vladimir Solovoy and Elena Klepikova, *Yuri Andropov: A Secret Passage into the Kremlin* (New York: Macmillan, 1983); Jonathan Steele and Eric Abraham, *Andropov in Power: From Komsomol to Kremlin* (Oxford, England: Martin Robertson, 1983); Jerry F. Hough, "Andropov's First Year," *Problems of Communism* 32 (November-December 1983), 49–64; and Marc D. Zlotnik, "Chernenko Succeeds," *Problems of Communism* 33 (March-April 1984), 17–31.

44. Among the growing number of works that describe Gorbachev's rise to power, the student may want to consult Dusko Doder, *Shadows and Whispers: Power Politics Inside the Kremlin from Brezhnev to Gorbachev* (New York: Random House, 1986). Other recent works of note on Gorbachev's rise include Zhores A. Medvedev, *Gorbachev* (New York: Norton, 1986); Richard Owen, *Comrade Chairman: Soviet Succession and the Rise of Gorbachov* (New York: Arbor House, 1987); and Christian Schmidt-Hauer, *Gorbachev: The Path to Power* (Toppsfield, Mass.: Salem House, 1986). On the policy problems facing Gorbachev, and his reform options, see Timothy Colton, *The Dilemma of Reform in the Soviet Union* (New York: Council on Foreign Relations, 1986); Marshall I. Goldman, *Gorbachev's Challenge: Economic Reform in the Age of High Technology* (New York: Norton, 1987); and Martin Walker, *The Waking Giant: Gorbachev's Russia* (New York: Pantheon Books, 1986).

45. *Pravda*, 30 January 1987.

46. Peter Reddaway, "Gorbachev the Bold," *The New York Review of Books* 34 (May 28, 1987), 25.

two

POLITICS AND THE
SOVIET CITIZEN

"In the unity of the party and people lies the strength of Soviet society"

War Memorial, Kiev

Workers' Monument, Moscow

"The policy of the CPSU is the policy of peace"
"We value the preservation of peace most of all"

Among the crises of development that confronted the Bolsheviks when they assumed power in 1917 and that have continued to trouble their regime over the past seven decades are those crises of citizenship requiring a change in the relationship of individuals to their polity. The crises of identity and legitimacy required new loyalties to an enlarged and rapidly changing political community and to young and sometimes fluid political institutions. The crisis of participation demanded that citizens be educated to new forms of political involvement.

Many of these problems of development and even many of the Soviet solutions to these problems are common to developing societies. For example, the Soviet industrialization campaign required a modern "cultural code of disciplined labor" similar to what is sometimes called the Protestant Ethic.[1] Yet, the Soviet response to these problems has not been identical to that in the West. The rejection of the capitalist path of development and the Soviet image of its future have provided many unique solutions to these problems—solutions that distinguish the Soviet model of development. The Soviet image of its future has given these problems an urgency that did not wane with early developmental successes. In particular, the centrality of new communist man to the success of this future makes the relationship of the individual to the polity an ever-present concern of the regime.

The next two chapters address these issues under the labels political culture, socialization, and participation. *Political culture* is the pattern of subjective orientations toward political objects found among the members of a society. Sidney Verba explains this concept by adding that political culture

> refers to the system of beliefs about patterns of political interaction and political institutions. It refers not to what is happening in the world of politics, but what people believe about those happenings. And these beliefs can be of several kinds: they can be empirical beliefs about what the actual state of political life is; they can be beliefs as to the goals or values that ought to be pursued in political life; and these beliefs may have an important expressive or emotional dimension.[2]

The process by which members of a society acquire these beliefs is *socialization*, a process that shapes and transmits a political culture.[3] Socialization can maintain existing patterns of political belief, preserving a political culture, or transform those patterns, changing or creating a political culture. The pattern of political *participation* in a society is an expression of its political culture—that is, the pattern of knowledge and feelings about the political system, about its institutions, and about the proper role of the individual in politics.

A society's political culture, socialization processes, and patterns of participation are vitally important, for they are essential ingredients in the long-term stability of a polity.[4] Specifically, stable Leninist political structures require a *congruent* political culture—that is, one that accords legitimacy to its policies, institutions, authoritarian processes, and Marxist-Leninist values. If citizens begin to doubt these, they may be moved to withdraw from active participation in public life or to oppose the regime outright. Either of these forms of "antisocial behavior," if widespread, is a threat to the Leninist regime.

Students familiar with the study of comparative politics will recognize that the two chapters in this part of the text are closely tied to those that follow. In David Easton's model of political systems, which has provided a paradigmatic organization to the study of political systems, the topics addressed in the next two chapters are commonly associated with input processes:"[5]

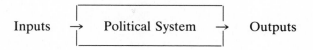

Inputs → Political System → Outputs

The third part of this text goes on to consider the decision-making processes within the political system, and the fourth addresses the outputs or policies and performance of the polity.

FOR FURTHER READING

For those students who wish to read further on the topics covered in the next two chapters, the following works may be particularly useful.

Alexeyeva, Ludmilla. 1985. *Soviet Dissent: Contemporary Movements for National, Religious, and Human Rights.* Middletown, Conn.: Wesleyan University Press.

Barghoorn, Frederick C. 1976. *Détente and the Democratic Movement in the USSR.* New York: Free Press.

Bronfenbrenner, Urie. 1970. *Two Worlds of Childhood: US and USSR.* New York: Simon and Schuster.

Brown, Archie, and Jack Gray, eds. 1979. *Political Culture and Political Change in Communist States.* London: Macmillan Press.

Friedgut, Theodore H. 1979. *Political Participation in the USSR.* Princeton, N.J.: Princeton University Press.

Geiger, H. K. 1968. *The Family in Soviet Russia.* Cambridge, Mass.: Harvard University Press.

Grant, Nigel. 1979. *Soviet Education,* 4th ed. New York: Penguin Books.

Hollander, Gayle Durham. 1972. *Soviet Political Indoctrination: Developments in Mass Media and Propaganda Since Stalin.* New York: Praeger.

Inkeles, Alex, and Raymond A. Bauer. 1961. *The Soviet Citizen: Daily Life in a Totalitarian Society.* Cambridge, Mass.: Harvard University Press.

Jacoby, Susan. 1974. *Inside Soviet Schools.* New York: Hill and Wang.

Kassof, Allen. 1965. *The Soviet Youth Program: Regimentation and Rebellion.* Cambridge, Mass.: Harvard University Press.

Matthews, Mervyn. 1982. *Education in the Soviet Union: Policies and Institutions Since Stalin.* London: Allen & Unwin.

Mickiewicz, Ellen Propper. 1967. *Soviet Political Schools: The Communist Party Adult Indoctrination System.* New Haven, Conn.: Yale University Press.

Powell, David E. 1975. *Anti-Religious Propaganda in the Soviet Union: A Study of Mass Persuasion.* Cambridge, Mass.: MIT Press.

Reddaway, Peter. 1972. *Uncensored Russia.* New York: American Heritage Press.

Rigby, T. H., and Ferenc Feher, eds. 1982. *Political Legitimation in Communist States.* New York: St. Martin's Press.

Rosen, Seymour. 1971. *Education and Modernization in the USSR*. Reading, Mass.: Addison-Wesley.

Rothberg, Abraham. 1972. *The Heirs of Stalin: Dissidence and the Soviet Regime, 1953–1970*. Ithaca, New York: Cornell University Press.

Ruble, Blair A. 1981. *Soviet Trade Unions: Their Development in the 1970s*. Cambridge, England: Cambridge University Press.

Schapiro, Leonard, ed. 1972. *Political Opposition in One-Party States*. New York: Wiley.

Shatz, Marshall S. 1980. *Soviet Dissent in Historical Perspective*. Cambridge, England: Cambridge University Press.

Spechler, Dina R. 1982. *Permitted Dissent in the USSR: Novy Mir and the Soviet Regime*. New York: Praeger.

Tokes, Rudolf L. 1975. *Dissent in the USSR: Politics, Ideology, and People*. Baltimore, Md.: Johns Hopkins University Press.

Tomiak, J. J., ed. 1983. *Soviet Education in the 1980s*. New York: St. Martin's Press.

Weaver, Kitty. 1981. *Russia's Future: The Communist Education of Soviet Youth*. New York: Praeger.

White, Stephen. 1979. *Political Culture and Soviet Politics*. London: Macmillan Press.

Zajda, Joseph I. 1980. *Education in the USSR*. New York: Pergamon Press.

NOTES

1. Timothy W. Luke, "The Proletarian Ethic and Soviet Industrialization," *American Political Science Review* 77 (September 1983), 595–596.
2. Sidney Verba, "Comparative Political Culture," in Lucian W. Pey and Sidney Verba, eds., *Political Culture and Political Development* (Princeton, N.J.: Princeton University Press, 1965), 7: also see Gabriel A. Almond, "Comparative Political Systems," *Journal of Politics* 18 (1956), 396.
3. Richard E. Dawson and Kenneth Prewitt, *Political Socialization* (Boston: Little, Brown and Company, 1969), 27.
4. Gabriel A. Almond and Sidney Verba, *The Civic Culture* (Boston: Little, Brown and Company, 1965), 20.
5. David Easton, "An Approach to the Analysis of Political Systems," *World Politics* 9 (April 1957), 383–400.

chapter 4

Creating Soviet Man: Socialization and Political Culture

Preserving a new Leninist regime and then building a socialist or communist society require a transformation of political culture. Thus, central to the Soviet model of development are extraordinary efforts to develop institutions of socialization that can envelop the citizen throughout his life.[1] In these efforts the Soviet regime has found that many agents of socialization that predated the October Revolution have offered stubborn resistance to its message. Those that were dispensable, such as the non-Bolshevik press and the Church, were eliminated or severely curtailed. Those that were indispensable, such as the schools and the family, were replaced with Soviet-controlled institutions or were subjected to pressures to control the content of their socialization. To supplement these, the regime also created new institutions, such as youth auxiliaries of the Party, to present its message. The resulting agents of childhood, adolescent, and adulthood socialization have played a central role, through the cultivation of a congruent political culture, in the survival of the Soviet regime and the transformation of Soviet society.

Much of what is distinctive about socialization in the Soviet model of development stems from the relationship between polity and society in a Leninist state—one that differs significantly from that in a polyarchy.[2] If one begins by imagining two polar opposite ideal-types, the *directive* polity directs society, seeking to remake it in the image of the polity's ideology. At the opposite extreme, in the *responsive* polity, politics is a reflection of society. The Soviet Union and other Leninist regimes tend toward the first extreme; western polyarchies, toward the second.

Due to this fundamental difference, while most of the *agents* of socialization are similar in form in Leninist polities and polyarchies, they differ in the extent of centralized control. Agents of socialization like the family, schools, and youth organizations are the institutions that teach citizens their orientations to political life. In a Leninist society these are more likely to be directly controlled by the Party or indirectly controlled by the Party through the state. In a polyarchy there is far more pluralism among the agents of socialization; local schools, the Boy Scouts, and the press, for instance, are autonomous institutions not directly controlled by national political leaders.

While many of the *objects* of socialization are similar under directive and responsive regimes, the extent to which those objects are undergoing dynamic change divides the two polities. The objects of socialization include the institutions, persons, and symbols toward which one develops cognitive, affective, and evaluative orientations. In Leninist societies these objects tend to be far more dynamic. That is, Leninist leaders typically seek to transform existing attitudes toward objects of socialization and to create new attitudes toward objects that have not previously existed. In creating the new communist man, the Soviets seek to change orientations to political life and to create new orientations necessary to life in the future communist society. In contrast, socialization in a polyarchy tends to be more static, reinforcing attachments to existing institutions—that is, to the status quo.

While the *processes* of socialization reveal many parallels in directive and responsive systems, they differ in the extent of their integration or homogeneity. The processes are the means by which individuals develop orientations toward political objects, including both explicit and implicit political learning. That is, not only is one taught overt knowledge and attitudes about politics, as in classroom instruction or adulthood indoctrination, but also one learns implicit lessons, particularly those defining political roles, through activities such as participation in youth groups. In a Leninist society the lessons tend to be far more homogenous: Soviet socialization processes are more likely to teach a single integrated set of values through all agents of socialization and to all members of society. By contrast, in a polyarchy the processes of socialization are more heterogeneous: One is taught many diverse and sometimes inconsistent political lessons; and individual citizens often differ in the lessons they learn.

SOCIALIZATION IN THE FAMILY

The most important socializing agent in Soviet society is probably the family. Until starting school, most young Soviets spend a majority of their time within this institution. And there the young Soviet learns not only the first, but also some of the most enduring lessons about authority and participation in decision making.

The importance of the family as an agent of socialization presents the Soviet system with a thorny problem: The Party seeks to direct the socialization process through the most important agents; yet, the family is probably the institution in Soviet society that is least responsive to control from the center. Moreover, the family tends to be not an engine of social change, but a conservator of past social patterns. (This should be qualified by the findings in studies of pre- and postrevolutionary child-rearing that suggest that Russian families did, in fact, respond to the Revolution with changes in values.[3]) This problem is aggravated when both the mother and father work, for the task of raising the children is often handed over to *babushki* (grandmothers), who are likely to be purveyors of attitudes that prevailed, not one, but two generations earlier. Thus, the Party confronts the problem that in attempting to create new communist man, the earliest and in some ways the most important socialization is in the hands of one of its most traditional elements—those who are likely to be least reflective of official attitudes about the communist future.

The lessons learned within the family are not entirely at variance with the needs of the present Soviet political system.[4] For example, in his comparison of Soviet and American child-rearing, the Cornell psychologist Urie Bronfenbrenner argues that a major consequence of Soviet child-rearing practices is submissiveness and conformity. Within the Soviet family, the relationship between parent and child is emotionally loaded; Soviet parents show far greater physical affection toward children and protective solicitousness for their welfare than do American parents. Discipline within the Soviet family is less likely to rely on physical punishment and more likely to use "withdrawal of affection." "By gesture, word, intonation, or eloquent silence the parent is quick to convey his emotional wound." This Soviet practice seems the antithesis of the practice common in America, where the parent assures the errant child of continued parental affection even as the parent physically punishes the child for bad behavior. The Soviet pattern of discipline has important behavioral consequences. Bronfenbrenner concludes that "a warm, constricting mother-child relationship maximizes dependency and produces a child who is readily socialized to adult standards." A population that is conformist, obedient, and orderly as a result of this family socialization is essential to the maintenance of an existing authoritarian polity. Yet, a directive polity that seeks to transform society also needs citizens who can be independent, self-confident, aggressive, and innovative—character attributes that the Soviet family seems to stifle.

Not satisfied with the results of the spontaneous socialization processes within the family, the Soviet authorities have attempted to develop alternatives. Most pervasive has been the effort to direct the content of socialization within the family through the publication of official child-rearing manuals for parents. Most of what is contained in these manuals is simply good advice on child hygiene, proper feeding, and the like. Yet, to an extent unknown in the West, Soviet child-rearing manuals also contain important political messages. For example, one manual published by the Academy of Pedagogical Sciences states that its purpose is to help "parents to bring up their children properly so that they can grow up to be worthy citizens of our socialist nation." A prominent theme in such manuals is the primacy of obedience and self-discipline. Lest the interconnectedness and political importance of these attributes escape the Soviet reader, one authority on child-rearing writes:

> Obedience in young children provides the basis for developing that most precious of qualities—self-discipline. . . . This is an important aspect of preparing young people for life in a Communist society. We shall be asked: what about developing independence in children? We shall answer: if a child does not obey and does not consider others, then his independence invariably takes ugly forms. Normally this gives rise to anarchistic behavior which can in no way be reconciled with laws of living in Soviet society. Where there is no obedience, there is no self-discipline; nor can there be normal development of independence.[5]

Aside from the frightening image of munchkins in black shirts that this quotation conjures, it points up that training in obedience and self-discipline is important not only for the present Soviet family and the existing Soviet society, but also for life in future communist society.

To enforce or reinforce this prescribed socialization within the family, the larger community, including neighbors, teachers, and co-workers, is encouraged to take a meddlesome interest in the internal affairs of individual families. Parents' Committees organized at each school, under instructions from the Ministry of Education, take an active interest in the home life of students to see that the family reinforces the lessons of schools. If this does not produce results, "it is possible for the parents' trade union or factory committee to take an interest, which is harder to resist than the disapproval of neighbors."[6] (In the early years after the Revolution, in order to check anti-Soviet parents, children were encouraged to denounce their parents. Even today Pavlik Morozov is heralded as a martyr for his death at the hands of fellow villagers after young Pavlik denounced his father as a collaborator with the kulaks and testified against his father in court for opposing collectivization.)

A second response to the problems of socialization in the family has been the development of alternative agents of socialization for preschool children. In recent years, the most intensive experiment with institutions that could isolate children from the influences of the family and more effectively create new communists was an experiment under Khrushchev with the boarding school (*shkola internat*).[7] As envisioned by the resolution of the 20th CPSU Congress (1956) that called these schools into being, the students would live at schools six days a week, returning to their families only on Sundays and school holidays. In the original conception these *internaty* were to become the predominant form of education throughout the Soviet Union and were to replace much of the socialization within the family. There was strong resistance to this, however, particularly from parents; and so, rather than isolating students from their families, the *internaty* have come to encourage regular involvement of parents in the schools and of students in the lives of their parents. Rather than becoming the predominant educational institution, the *internaty* have remained in the minority among schools.

For preschool children, the most common alternative or supplement to the family as an agent of socialization is the creche (*yasli*) and then the kindergarten (*detskiiy sad*).[8] In the Soviet Union this can begin as early as three months of age. Working families can leave children up to the age of three in child care, normally provided at the parents' place of employment for a nominal fee based on the parents' ability to pay. Working families can leave children between the ages of four and six at a kindergarten, also usually provided at the parents' place of employment. The dominant concerns in these institutions are, of course, simply caring for the children; teaching hygiene, safety, and basic social skills; and releasing the parents to work. They also, however, attempt to introduce the children to elementary political themes; and the older the age group, the more explicit these become. Even at an early age children learn about their community, the flag, national heroes like Lenin, and institutions like the Soviet Army, toward which the children are expected to develop reverence.

More common and more important in the political upbringing of preschool children are the lessons learned in these institutions through implicit socialization. Preschoolers learn social roles appropriate to Soviet society, particularly collectivism, at a very early age. For example, toddlers are commonly placed in playpens holding six to eight so that each begins to learn to live and work with others. Group games, complex toys, music, and other activities requiring cooperation and interpersonal coordination are used to develop social skills appropriate to life in a collectivist society. A motto often repeated among these children is *moe eto nashe, nashe moe* (what is mine is ours, what is ours is mine)—an essential attitude for the next generation of new communists.

SOVIET SCHOOLS AND SOCIALIZATION

At age six a child enters the first grade to begin what may be the most important socialization experience outside the family. Since 1917, Soviet schools have faced four major educational tasks essential to politics. First, the schools have been responsible for making Soviet citizens modern. It is the schools that can be credited with expanding literacy from 28 percent at the time of the Revolution to over 99 percent today. In a population that lived in a traditional, agrarian society until only recently, schools must teach rudimentary skills of an industrial society, such as the ability to live by the clock and to observe work discipline. Second, schools have had the task of uniting an ethnically diverse population. Third, they have had to create attachments to the Soviet system—to the Soviet Union as a political entity, to its state and party institutions, and to the symbols of the system. And last, Soviet schools have had to create loyalty to individual Soviet leaders.[9]

In this regard, the Soviet school is not unique. Nonetheless, the manner by which these socialization processes are conducted within Soviet schools is distinctive in many ways, particularly when compared to their American counterparts. Many of these distinguishing characteristics can be attributed to the centralized control of education in the Soviet Union. Direction of general education is in the hands of the Ministry of Education; college-level education is in the hands of the Ministry of Higher and Secondary Specialized Education. While corresponding ministries at the union-republic and autonomous republic levels can make minor changes in curriculum to meet local conditions, teachers conduct their classrooms with an amazing sameness from one end of the Soviet Union to the other. As the British scholar Nigel Grant notes: "With a few differences, children in, say, the fifth [grade] in an eight-year school in places as far apart as Moscow and Magnitogorsk, Tashkent and Tallinn, wear the same uniforms, observe the same rules of behavior, and study the same subjects from the same textbooks at the same pace."[10] As a consequence of this hierarchical control, the process of socialization in Soviet schools is far more homogeneous than in American schools. The curriculum teaches an integrated set of values to all Soviet youths. (The homogeneity of the process is heightened by the Soviet preference for comprehensive education—that is, a common curriculum for all students and the avoidance of "tracking" on the basis of ability.) The central control of education also makes the socialization process in schools strikingly responsive to the short-term political needs of the Party. For example, Allen Kassof noted during a visit in the initial period of de-Stalinization:

> In May 1956 a Pioneer Worker at a Moscow school told me that, until new books could be printed, she and her colleagues were under instructions to have the Pioneers pencil out references to Stalin in the old books and pamphlets and to substitute, wherever applicable, the phrase "the Soviet people." Thus, she explained, "Stalin's victory" in the Great Patriotic War would be changed to "the victory of the Soviet people." I was also told that the shift in the imagery concerning Stalin had profoundly upset and confused the children, for what they had learned only a short while before as an absolute and unalterable truth now was being held up to derision.[11]

Only hierarchically controlled, homogeneous process could make such a rapid transition in lessons.

The Soviet Curriculum

Soviet school children begin the 1st grade on the first of September following their 6th birthday. (Prior to 1986, Soviet students started the 1st grade after their 7th birthday.[12]) They are required to complete 9 grades (8 grades before 1986), although a complete secondary education runs through the 11th (previously, 10th) grade. The first 4 (3) years are designated elementary school (*nachal'naia shkola*), and the grades above this are designated secondary school (*sredniaia shkola*).

Upon completion of the 9th (8th) grade, the Soviet student must decide whether to continue with the last 2 years of secondary school, to enter a secondary specialized school offering a combination of academic and vocational education, to enter a professional-technical school offering principally vocational training, or to join the labor force, possibly continuing study through evening

Basic Guidelines for Reform in General-Education and Vocational Schools

(Approved by the Plenary Session of the Central Committee on April 10 and by the USSR Supreme Soviet on April 12, 1984.)

The demands made on the ideological-political upbringing of young people and the molding in them of a Marxist-Leninist world view and a feeling of responsibility, organization and discipline are growing. The Party sees growth in the ideological conviction, the amount of education and the vocational preparedness of new generations of Soviet people as an important prerequisite for the deepening of socialist democracy and the ever broader and more effective participation of the masses in the administration of production and of state and public affairs. In light of the sharp exacerbation of the international situation, it is necessary to heighten vigilance with respect to the intrigues of the aggressive forces of imperialism, which are conducting frenzied attacks against socialism and are counting on the political inexperience of young people.

Creating in pupils a Marxist-Leninist world view is the firm foundation of their communist upbringing. It is important that the teaching of both social-science and natural-science disciplines cultivate in pupils staunch materialist ideas, atheistic views, the ability to correctly explain natural and social phenomena and to act in accordance with our philosophical principles.

The teaching of subjects in the area of the social sciences and humanities must disclose, in a vivid and easy-to-understand form, the ways and means of the revolutionary renewal of the world, the basic principles and historical advantages of socialism and the reactionary, antipopular essence of capitalism; give—from class positions—convincing answers to questions of the present-day life of society that are of concern to young people; and show the inevitable victory of the ideas of communism. In lessons in history, social studies, literature and other subjects, it is necessary to consistently instill the ability to defend one's communist convictions and implacability toward philistinism, parasitism and a consumer mentality . . .

In ideological-political upbringing, overriding importance must be given to the molding of class-conscious citizens with firm communist convictions. All elements of the instructional and upbringing process and the school's entire public life should work to this end. [It is necessary] to rear young people on the ideas of Marxism-Leninism and on examples drawn from the lives and activities of K. Marx, F. Engels and V.I. Lenin and the historical experiences of the CPSU; to intensify the cultivation in pupils of a spirit of Soviet patriotism, socialist internationalism and the fraternal friendship of the USSR's people; to step up the activity of social and political clubs, museums, study groups and lecture centers; to regularly conduct excursions and hikes to places of revolutionary, labor and combat glory; to improve the organization of political information; to develop skills of political self-education; to broadly enlist Party workers, the best propagandists, Znanie Society lecturers and Party veterans in the social and political upbringing of pupils. The mass news media should be active and constant helpers of teachers, families and the public.

[It is necessary] to make fuller use in upbringing work of the symbols of the Soviet state . . . Everyone who enters adult life should know the USSR Constitution and the Constitution of his republic and be guided by them.

Moral and legal upbringing is extremely important in the molding of the new man . . . The school must develop the inner need to live and act according to the principles of communist morality and to unswervingly observe the rules of the socialist community and Soviet laws.

It is very important to instill from the early years collectivism, exactingness toward oneself and one another, honesty, truthfulness, kindness, devotion to principle, steadfastness and courage of character . . .

Socialist society has a vital interest in seeing to it that the younger generation grows up physically fit, healthy, cheerful and prepared for work and the defense of the homeland . . .

The military-patriotic upbringing of pupils must be based on their preparation for service in the ranks of the USSR Armed Forces, instilling love for the Soviet Army, and creating a lofty sense of pride in allegiance to the socialist fatherland and of constant readiness to defend it . . .

In the communist upbringing of pupils, a great deal depends on the young people's public organizations and on student self-government. It is necessary to resolutely enhance the prestige of Komsomol and Young Pioneer organizations and their role in the ideological-political upbringing of pupils and not to permit formalism, overorganization and petty tutelage in their guidance; to increase the responsibility and strengthen the solidarity of student collectives, supporting all their useful undertakings, initiatives and independent activities in every way, something to which N.K. Krupskaya, A.S. Makarenko and other outstanding figures in public education attached great importance.

Komsomol and Young Pioneer organizations should be a reliable support for teachers' collectives in improving the quality of studies, in molding class-conscious discipline and standards of behavior, in organizing socially useful labor and the meaningful use of leisure time, and in developing pupils' ability to look after themselves . . .

Source: *Pravda*, 14 April 1984.

or correspondence schools. After completion of secondary education, a student may apply, through competitive examination, to enter a higher educational institution (*vyshee uchebnoe zavedenie* or *vuz*).[13]

While in school, Soviet students are taught explicit political knowledge. In the first 11 years, students must take courses on history, government and law, and social studies (Marxism-Leninism). Under the curriculum in force prior to 1986, this grew from 4.3 percent of class time in grades 1 through 7 to 13.7 percent in the last 3 years. (In higher educational institutions, students must also give substantial attention to such courses. For example, Moscow State University's curriculum in Russian Language and Literature requires that a student spend about 12 percent of his or her lecture and practical training seminar hours in courses on Marxism-Leninism, political economy, and history of the CPSU.) While the actual number of hours in these courses may be less than in comparable schools in the United States, Soviet schools also attempt to infuse a political content or political theme into many courses that would seem unrelated to politics. Science, for example, can be a vehicle for explaining the materialist philosophy of Marx as well as the successes of Soviet research.[14]

Moral Education

Almost as important in Soviet schools as political indoctrination is the emphasis on moral upbringing or *vospitanie*, the inculcation of attitudes and habits appropriate to the developing communist society.

> The aim of moral teaching . . . is to produce a person who will be willing and able to put all the effort of which he is capable into work for the common good, building the new society under the guidance of the Communist Party and, furthermore, finding joy and fulfillment in the task.[15]

This moral upbringing seeks not only to reinforce the lessons of obedience and self-discipline urged upon the family, but also to develop "socialist patriotism and proletarian internationalism, a communist relationship to labor and to public property, [and] socialist humanism and collectivism."[16] The ideal of this communist morality is summarized in the Moral Code of the Builders of Communism, which prescribes not only "devotion to the pursuit of communism" and "love for the socialist homeland," but also "conscientious labor for the good of society," "high consciousness of social objectives," and collectivism.

Central to moral upbringing is the inculcation of what the Soviets call *kollektivnost'* or collective-mindedness; that is, the habit of thinking of oneself as a member of a collectivity. As the Soviet ideologist Georgii Smirnov has said, "The socialist system makes collectivism the fundamental principle of social relations, and enhancement of the role of the collective in the formation of the socialist personality becomes one of the characteristic features of socialism in its progress towards communism."[17] Thus, in schools children come into contact with an institution that will dog them throughout their lives—the *kollektiv*. Each *kollektiv* is one of a series of reference groups to which each person belongs. One belongs to many such collectivities throughout life and to many at each point in life—in school, in extracurricular groups, in living complexes, and in work places.

Many of the pedagogical techniques to instill *kollektivnost'* were developed by A. S. Makarenko, a Soviet pedagogist of the 1920s. Makarenko was confronted with the task of educating the "homeless waifs who, after the Revolution roamed the Soviet Union by the thousands, begging, stealing, and even killing to meet their needs."[18] The techniques of educating and socializing these problem children became a foundation for Soviet pedagogic practice. "As carried out in Soviet schools, his approach places major emphasis on work, group consciousness, and collective discipline."[19]

In school students are taught to think of themselves not in individualistic or egoistic terms, but as members of groups—a row, classroom, a school. The students are expected to participate in groups and to compete not as individuals, but as part of a group effort. Rewards are collective; individual rewards are discouraged. By this emphasis on collective reward (and collective deprivation of reward), students are taught to be responsible for their peers' behavior. What one person gets is by virtue of what the group gets, and so each becomes concerned about all the others in the group and begins to exert peer pressure for good behavior. Prescribed Soviet pedagogic technique encourages this. For example, a Soviet text for teachers contrasts two ways of dealing with children who are squirming in their chairs. The wrong way is to say, "Children, sit up straight!" for this encourages an individualistic response (each student attending only to his or her own behavior). The proper response is, "Let's see which row can sit the straightest." This creates an entirely different group dynamic. Suddenly each child realizes that he or she will be praised for good behavior, not only if he or she is good, but also only if everyone else in the row is good. Students then begin looking around to see who is letting the group down. At the same time, each child knows that if he or she does not sit straight, everyone else in the row is watching and will probably later chastise errant peers who do not uphold their part of the collective interest.[20]

Another aspect of *kollektivnost'* that the Soviet youngster encounters in the schools is stewardship or *shefstvo*. Stewardship, in a sense, is group adoption. Older classes in a school assume responsibility for younger grades, helping them with class projects, tutoring them when necessary. (Stewardship is not limited to the schools. Military units stationed within the Soviet Union often "adopt" a local collective farm or enterprise. The unit then is expected to help out during the harvest or peak production periods.)[21]

YOUTH ORGANIZATIONS

The political socialization within the school is reinforced by the youth organizations established by the Party. Almost every Soviet child from the age of 7 to 10 belongs to the Young Octobrists. The vast majority of children from ages 10 to 15 belongs to the Pioneers. And about half of the age group from 15 to 27 belongs to the Komsomol. These organizations do not operate independently of the schools, but play an intimate role in their socialization processes.

The Komsomol and Pioneer Organizations

The Komsomol (All-Union Leninist Communist League of Youth or VLKSM) was established within the first year of the Revolution, holding its inaugural congress in October 1918. Four years later the Komsomol established the Pioneer organization. While the early Komsomol showed signs of independence and internal diversity of opinion, these were soon restricted as the Party extended its control over the Komsomol first during the Civil War and later under Staliny. The Komsomol was founded as an elite revolutionary vanguard among youths that would provide the next generation of leaders, but increasing Party control under Staliny brought a change in its organizational mission. It ceased to be a training ground for future leaders and became primarily an agent of socialization among adolescents and young adults. Indeed, according to the preamble of its own charter, "the VLKSM helps the Party to bring up youth in the spirit of communism, to draw it into the practical construction of the new society, to prepare a new generation of well-rounded people who will live, work, and direct societal affairs under communism."[22]

The organization of the Komsomol parallels that of the Party and is under tight Party control. Its charter describes the Komsomol as "the active assistant and reserve of the Communist Party" that works under Party direction. The Komsomol's 41,944,000 members on January 1, 1985, belonged to 467,900 primary organizations in schools, places of employment, or residences, each of which works closely with a corresponding primary party organization.[23] The organization of the Komsomol closely resembles that of the Party. As in the Party, power within the Komsomol is concentrated in the secretaries, who tend to be full-time paid functionaries above the primary organization. These control the nomination and election of delegates and leading organs. Moreover, much of the actual direction of the Komsomol organization is in the hands not of Komsomol officials, but the secretaries of the Party organs that parallel the Komsomol at every level.

Individual Pioneers are organized in links, each of which is usually composed of 5 to 12 children in a classroom. Local Pioneer organizations operate under the joint direction of a local Komsomol organizer and adults employed at the school. The members of each link (*zveno*) join together to form a detachment (*otriad*) for the grade; and these in turn join together to form an all-school brigade (*druzhina*). Each link elects a leader (*vozhatyi*) and each detachment and brigade elects a small council of 3 to 5 students who in turn elect a leader for their unit. There is a less-formal Pioneer organization above the school, directed by the Central Council of the All-Union Pioneer Organization under the direction of the Komsomol. In 1980, this claimed a membership of about 20 million.[24]

The organization of the Young Octobrists is far less formal. Groups of Octobrists are organized by teachers to mobilize student assistance in classroom projects and to prepare students for membership in the Pioneers, but there is usually no formal organization at the school level.

Indoctrination and Moral Education

The Komsomol and Pioneers organize or coordinate a wide variety of extracurricular activities for youth, including clubs for arts and hobbies at school; clubs, libraries, youth orchestras, and drama groups at Pioneer Palaces; Young Naturalist Stations; sports competitions from the local to the all-union level; and summer camps. Throughout all these activities, the central purpose is the political and moral indoctrination of Soviet youth.

Pioneer and Komsomol organizations devote some of their energies to explicit indoctrination. For example, every Young Pioneer takes a pledge upon being admitted to membership:

> I, a Young Pioneer of the Soviet Union, in the presence of my comrades solemnly promise to love my Soviet motherland passionately, to live, learn, and struggle as the great Lenin willed and as the Communist Party teaches us.

The new member then promises to abide by the "Rules for Pioneers," which describe the Pioneer as one who "loves the motherland and the Communist Party of the Soviet Union."

Pioneer meetings become an occasion to discuss political issues. According to Kassof, three techniques are typically used to teach politically relevant themes: "informal indoctrination sessions in which teachers, leaders, and older Pioneers speak; simple stories assigned to the children, illustrating the traits of model Pioneers; and, most important, meetings held soon after initiation, devoted to the themes of friendship, comradeship, and collective life."[25] Pioneers are expected to read the organization's monthly *Pioner* and its twice-weekly newspaper *Pionerskaia Pravda*. Through the Pioneer and Komsomol organizations, youths are brought into the broader public life of Soviet society, including the parades and festivities to commemorate the October Revolution and celebrate May Day. Some Pioneers even participate in summer paramilitary exercises (*Zarnitsa*) providing premilitary training.[26]

In the Komsomol, explicit indoctrination becomes a more serious study of Marxism-Leninism and the current Party line. In addition to regular meetings of its membership, the Komsomol organizes compulsory extracurricular reading, lectures, seminars, and study groups. The Komsomol operates its own publishing house *Molodaia Gvardiia* (Young Guard), issuing books as well as the monthly *Molodoi Kommunist* (Young Communist) and the daily *Komsomolskaia Pravda*.

As important as this explicit socialization, these youth organizations reinforce the implicit socialization of the schools—in particular, strengthening *kollektivnost'*. Pioneer meetings become exercises in group problem-solving, and Pioneer organizations mobilize peer pressure to force conformity. The Komsomol is responsible for organizing collectives in dormitories, or in workplaces and military units for those who do not remain in school. At Moscow State University, for instance, every floor of a dormitory organizes a *kollektiv*. These not only maintain discipline and orderliness on their floor, but take an active interest in the students' entire existence. One former Komsomol member complained, "And then there's the unbearable interference with the intimate aspect of life . . . [When] someone was known for sleeping around, in the dormitory or even outside, in extreme form, well, someone would be called to account and put before the meeting."[27] *Komsomolskaia Pravda* regularly reports what the Komsomol holds out as exemplary activities by its *kollektivy*. For example, one *kollektiv* was heralded for its success in aiding a male member to reconcile with his wife and avoid a divorce. Another in Dnepropetrovsk was praised for organizing a raid on female dormitory rooms to ensure that wayward males were not present threatening the residents' morals and work discipline.[28]

The Komsomol is responsible not only for its own membership, but also for providing surveillance over, and uplifting guidance to, Soviet youths in general. Komsomol members are expected to act as models to be emulated by other youths. Komsomol patrols wearing red arm bands ensure that youth gatherings such as dances observe the organization's lofty standards of propriety. Generally, these target three groups of offenders within the larger youth population: The *bezdel'nik* or *tuneiadets* (idler or parasite) is a nonproductive member of soci-

Moral Upbringing of the Communist

Rules of the Octobrists

- Octobrists are future Pioneers.
- Octobrists are diligent, study well, like school, and respect grown-ups.
- Only those who like work are called Octobrists.
- Octobrists are honest and truthful children.
- Octobrists are good friends, read, draw, live happily.

Rules of the Pioneers

The Pioneer loves his motherland and the Communist Party of the Soviet Union. He prepares himself for membership in the Komsomol.

The Pioneer reveres the memory of those who have given their lives in the struggle for the freedom and the well-being of the Soviet motherland.

The Pioneer is friendly with the children of all the countries of the world.

The Pioneer studies diligently and is disciplined and courteous.

The Pioneer loves to work and to conserve the national wealth.

The Pioneer is a good comrade, who is solicitous of younger children and who helps older people.

The Pioneer grows up to be bold and does not fear difficulties.

The Pioneer tells the truth and guards the honor of his detachment.

The Pioneer strengthens himself and does physical exercise every day.

The Pioneer loves nature; he is a defender of planted areas, of useful birds and animals.

The Pioneer is an example for all children.

The Moral Code of the Builder of Communism

Devotion to the pursuit of Communism, love for the Socialist homeland, for the countries of Socialism;

Conscientious labor for the good of society; whoever does not work does not eat;

The concern of every one for the conservation and increase of social property;

A high consciousness of social obligation, an intolerance toward infringements of social interests;

Collectivism and comradely mutual aid; one for all and all for one;

A humane relationship and mutual respect among people; one person to another person—friend, comrade, and brother;

Integrity and truthfulness, moral purity, simplicity, and humility in social and personal life;

Mutual respect in family life, concern for the upbringing of children;

Implacable opposition to injustice, parasitism, dishonesty, careerism, greed;

The friendship and brotherhood of all the peoples of the USSR; intolerance toward nationalist and racist hostility;

Implacable opposition toward the enemies of Communism, the pursuit of peace, and the freedom of nations.

ety; he does not fulfill his obligations at school or work, but is instead often found drunk. The *stiliaga* (stylish) wears skirts that are too short or clothes that are too Western in appearance. The *khuligan* (hooligan) is a rowdy vandal. The Komsomol organization mobilizes peer pressure to force these youths to conform to the standards of the new socialist society.

In the youth organizations and schools, young Soviets are introduced to the institution of voluntary, socially useful work. Young Pioneers volunteer labor to clean the school, paint its walls, or tend its gardens. The Komsomol organizes more ambitious projects such as assistance with the harvest or with major community building projects. Indeed, Komsomol volunteers played a major role in the construction of Leningrad's Metro after World War II. This volunteer activity is often organized in national campaigns such as the *Subbotnik* (free Saturday), in which citizens across the country are urged to work without pay on a single day. This activity is not overtly coerced; the rewards or punishments are only weakly associated with participation or nonparticipation. (This presumably heightens the socializational impact of this activity. Psychological studies of cognitive dissonance suggest that if Soviet citizens participate only because they fear punishment for nonparticipation or expect immediate tangible rewards for participation, their attitudes would not be affected as acutely.[29]) The professed socializational objective is to inculcate communist attitudes toward labor.

SOCIALIZATION AMONG ADULTS

Socialization in the Soviet system continues into adulthood with a fervor that has no parallel in the West. While in Western polyarchies there tends to be a dramatic decline in the explicit socialization of individuals once they leave school, in the Soviet Union there is a concerted effort to continue this socialization at a very high level. In contrast to the more homogeneous experience of youths, however, among Soviet adults there is growing differentiation in the intensity of socialization and the sophistication of the message. Virtually all Soviet adults are exposed to the message of the press or mass media and most adult males have been subjected to the indoctrination that comes with obligatory military service. Far fewer participate in the explicit study of Marxism-Leninism offered by political schools.

Political Instruction

The most intensive overt socialization among civilian adults is conducted through the adult political education programs run by the Party. Actually the Party maintains two distinct programs. The first is the hierarchy of Party schools to recruit and train Party leaders for the socialization apparatus itself, to be opinion leaders in the media, education, and agitation. The highest of these schools is the Academy of Social Sciences of the Central Committee of the CPSU, which offers a three-year course of study to train theorists for the higher Party organs, editors and journalists, professors of Marxism-Leninism, and leading Party members in state and Party administration. Under the Academy are a number of union-republic and regional Party schools. These tend to be elite institutions, graduating only a few thousand students each year. The curriculum stresses formal study of Marxist-Leninist philosophy, political economy, and the history of the Soviet Union, CPSU, and international communist movement.

The second program is the more extensive network of schools to train Party members and non-Party *aktiv* from all segments of Soviet society. According to Ellen Mickiewicz of Emory University, the purpose of this system is "to provide for a lifelong study of Marxism-Leninism and the pronouncements of the party and government organs. All his adult life the student of the political instruction system is supposed to be actively and conscientiously studying in one of the branches of the system."[30] In 1985–1986, 21.2 million Soviets were receiving instruction through this system. Operating under the direction of the Central Committee's Propaganda Department, the local schools for part-time instruction are staffed and run by local Party organizations. Students usually begin with a five- to six-year program in the *politshkola* (political school), which teaches "the fundamentals of Marxism-Leninism." They can follow this with a six- to eight-year program in a more informal *circle* that provides lectures and discussions to reinforce independent study of "the classics of Marxism-Leninism, party documents, [and] political literature." At the highest levels, students may study in a local Evening University of Marxism-Leninism or participate in a more informal theoretical seminar to reinforce independent study. The curriculum at all levels stresses Marxist-Leninist philosophy, history of the CPSU, and theoretical economics, applying these where appropriate to current issues and Party polices.[31]

The Military

For most male citizens, however, the most intensive socialization experience is not voluntary political instruction but a two-year tour in the Soviet armed forces (three years for those inducted into the Soviet Navy). During those years the recruit is encapsulated in a total institution that isolates him from outside influences (leisure time is limited, leaves virtually unknown) and that structures almost every hour of his time. The Party uses this opportunity to cultivate attitudes.[32]

Since adoption of the USSR Law of Universal Military Service in 1967, even before formal induction, male students in the ninth and tenth grades must complete 140 hours (about two hours weekly over two years) of predraft military training in school or enterprise and must attend a seven- to eight-day summer camp. In this program, students receive instruction in military regulations, military discipline, and map reading; they practice drills and small-scale tactical exercises; and they become familiar with small arms. The program also provides intensive moral-patriotic education.

The armed forces themselves not only teach military skills, but also inculcate political values that the recruit will take back to civilian life. The political indoctrination of the troops within an individual military unit is the responsibility of an Assistant Commander for Political Affairs with the assistance of the unit's

Themes for Military-Political Instruction

In 1973, *Kommunist vooruzhennykh sil [Communist of the Armed Forces]* prescribed the following themes for political instruction within the military:

- the ideas of Marxism-Leninism;
- boundless devotion to the people, the homeland, the Communist Party, and the Soviet government;
- the invincible unity and fraternal friendship among the peoples of the USSR;
- proletarian internationalism and combat cooperation with the armies of the fraternal socialist countries;
- the moral code of the builders of communism;
- a spirit of high vigilance;
- class hatred for the imperialists and all enemies of communism;
- personal responsibility for the defense of the Soviet homeland;
- readiness to give one's life itself if necessary to achieve full victory;
- the domestic and foreign policy of the Communist Party;
- the revolutionary, combat, and labor traditions of the Party, the Soviet people, and its armed forces;
- the successes of building communism in the USSR and the building of socialism in the fraternal countries;
- the advantages of socialism over capitalism;
- pride in the homeland, its great achievements, and its noble victory.

Source: Herbert Goldhamer, *The Soviet Soldier: Soviet Military Management at the Troop Level* (New York: Crane, Russak, and Company, Inc., 1975), 70-72.

political section and its Party and Komsomol organizations. In formal lectures as well as daily agitation, these agents of socialization teach explicit political themes.[33] The political organs within the military unit also are responsible for maintaining morale, discipline, and solidarity among the troops. The military reflects and reinforces the socialization processes of the larger Soviet society, including mobilized peer pressure (e.g., *kollektivnost'*), socialist competition, stewardship (*shefstvo*—e.g., senior recruits assume responsibility for the training of younger ones), the *subbotnik* to occupy free time with socially useful labor, and a preference for moral over material rewards and punishment.

The Press and Mass Media

The form of socialization that Soviet adults are most likely to encounter is that conducted by the Soviet mass media on a daily basis. Media exposure within the Soviet population has reached extraordinary proportions. By 1984, the Soviet Union published 8327 different newspapers, ranging from the 31 All-Union dailies to numerous local weeklies. These published over 42 billion copies in 930,912 issues in 1984. (See Table 4.1.) Per capita circulation of the Soviet dailies is about two-fifths higher than for daily newspapers in the United States. In addition, in 1984, the Soviet Union published 5231 different journals and periodicals. By 1979, there were 594 radio receivers per 1000 population, guaranteeing reception by almost all households. And by 1981, 86 percent of the population also received television programs.[34]

The "primary mission" of the Soviet media, according to Mickiewicz, is socialization—to "change the ethical and moral outlook of the population" and to rouse "the population to participate in such a way as to contribute to the economic goals of the leadership."[35] These tasks shape the content of the Soviet media: The Soviet notion of newsworthiness does not give precedence to news of domestic natural disasters, accidents, or crime; nor does it have a place for human interest items like horoscopes; nor does it necessarily give preference to fast-breaking stories. (In recent years there appears to have been some relaxation in these practices, affording greater coverage to natural and man-made disasters within the Soviet Union and expanding human interest coverage, such as advice to lovelorn adolescents.) Instead, the press is expected to play an active roll in building communism. The means by which it is expected to achieve this are summarized in the "Basic Principles of the Soviet Press," which appear frequently in Soviet discussions of journalism:

1. Party-mindedness or loyalty to the Party (*Partiinost'*).
2. High ideological content (*Ideinost'*).
3. Patriotism (*Otechestvennost'*).
4. Truthfulness to Leninist theory (*Pravdivost'*).
5. A popular character (*Narodnost'*).
6. Accessibility to the masses (*Massovost'*).
7. Criticism and self-criticism (*Kritika i samokritika*).

The print media operate under the supervision of the State Committee for Publishing Houses, Printing Plants, and the Book Trade; the broadcast media are directly managed by the State Committee for Television and Radio Broadcasting; and the film industry is managed by the State Committee for Cinematography. (All of these committees are part of the Council of Ministers.) The media has also been controlled through the censorship system under the direction of the Chief Administration for Safeguarding State Secrets in the Press (sometimes known by its former acronym Glavlit), an agency attached to the Council of Ministers. As part of its censorship activities, Glavlit has maintained a lengthy list of items not to be published in the press. Glavlit has had the power to enforce these prohibitions through prior censorship of all printed materials in the Soviet Union. Yet with the rapid expansion of publishing in the Soviet Union, efficiency has required growing self-censorship by journalists and authors. University programs to train journalists, reinforced by postuniversity study in the Party's political education programs described above, are designed to ensure that journalists are steeped in the Basic Principles and understand their practical application. The Soviet journalist, in the words of *Pravda*, is expected to be "an ac-

Table 4.1   MAJOR SOVIET NEWSPAPERS, 1984

Newspaper (Publisher)	Circulation (in millions)
Trud (All-Union Council of Trade Unions)	15.4
Komsomolskaia Pravda (Komsomol)	11.3
Pravda (CPSU)	10.4
Pionerskaia Pravda (Pioneers)	9.7
Sel'skaia Zhizn' (CPSU)	9.5
Izvestiia (Council of Ministers)	6.4

Source: Ezhegodnik Bol'shoi Sovetskoi Entsiklopedii, 1985 (Moscow: Sovetskaia entsiklopediia, 1985).

tive fighter for the cause of the Party."[36] Moreover, Soviet journalists must belong to the USSR Union of Journalists, which sets performance standards and authorizes subject matter. Glavlit, the media, and journalists all operate under the close scrutiny of the Central Committee's Propaganda Department.

Agitation and Propaganda

In the earlier years of the Soviet regime, one of the most extensive networks of adult socialization was face-to-face propaganda and agitation, but in recent years, with the spread of literacy and the development of broadcast technology, this appears to have declined in importance. In the original system of Bolshevik agitation, all Party members were expected to be agitators among the population in all their daily contacts. This face-to-face agitation included speeches before mass meetings, group agitation with a few people, and individual agitation with one person.[37]

Today the unpaid Party volunteer specializing in agitation is perhaps more typical of the Party's agitational effort. Such volunteers fall under the direction of the local Party secretaries for propaganda and the Central Committee's Propaganda Department (still sometimes called by its former acronym, Agitprop). The Party maintains its control over the content of agitation through the training programs in the political schools described above and the weekly issues of *Bloknot Agitatora* (Agitator's Notebook). The latter identifies key themes for the agitator to address in talks and proven methods to heighten citizen enthusiasm for the Party and its policies. Agitation seems to peak during campaigns to fulfill economic plans or to bring in the harvest, during elections campaigns, and during major political events such as Party congresses. The number of agitators is variable, depending on the demands of the moment, and difficult to estimate. During an election campaign as much as 5 percent of the electorate—meaning 9 million citizens in the late 1980s—may serve as agitators.[38] These are supported by a network of agitation points (*agitpunkt*), Houses of Political Enlightenment, and over 100,000 Clubs and Houses of Culture.

The principal exception to this trend of declining importance of face-to-face agitation and propaganda is the continued importance of public lectures.

The Censors' List

The following was reported by *Washington Post* journalist Robert G. Kaiser:

In Moscow I obtained a partial list of the censor's forbidden topics from an unofficial but reliable source. This list speaks very well for itself . . .

- The itineraries . . . of members and candidate members of the Politburo.
- Information about the organs of Soviet censorship which discloses the character, organization and method of their work.
  Activities of the organs of state security and Soviet intelligence organs . . .
- . . . The amount of crime, the number of people engaged in criminal behavior, the number arrested, the number convicted . . .
- Information about the existence of correctional labor camps . . .
- Facts about the physical conditions, illnesses, and death rates of all prisoners in all localities.
- The number of illiterate people.
- Reports about the human victims of accidents, wrecks and fires . . .
- Information about the consequences of catastrophic earthquakes, tidal waves, floods and other natural calamities . . .
- Calculations of the relative purchasing power of the ruble and the hard currency for foreign states.
- The size of the total wage fund, or the amount of money which comprises the population's purchasing power, or the balance of income and expenditure of the population . . .
- Information about hostile actions by the population or responsible officials of foreign states against representatives of citizens of the USSR.
- The correlation between the cost of services for foreign tourists in the USSR and the selling price of tourist trips in the USSR.
- Information about export to foreign countries of arms, ammunition, military technology, military equipment . . .
- Information suggesting a low moral-political condition of the armed forces, unsatisfactory military discipline, abnormal relations among soldiers or between them and the population.
- The number of drug addicts . . .
- Information about occupational injuries.
- Information about the audibility of the radio stations of foreign states in the USSR.
- Information about the duration of all-union training sessions for athletes; information about the rates of pay for athletes; information about the money prizes for good results in sports competitions; information about the financing, maintenance, and staff of athletic teams . . .

Source: Robert G. Kaiser, *Russia: The Power and the People* (New York: Washington Square Press, 1984), 243-244.

The All-Union Society of Knowledge (*Znanie*), founded in 1947, shoulders much, although not all, of the responsibility for these lectures. With a 1985 membership of 2.7 million organized in 130,840 primary organizations, *Znanie* sponsored over 23 million lectures, with an attendance of over one billion. Often held in conjunction with cultural events such as a concert or dance (for which part of the price of admission is attendance at the lecture), these lectures can touch on issues as diverse as current events, science, or self-improvement.[39] (For example, in the late summer of 1985, *Znanie* in the Kuibyshev borough of Leningrad promised lectures on such topics as the international crisis in southern Africa, child-rearing under socialism, and family bliss under communism.)

SOVIET POLITICAL CULTURE

Have these extraordinary efforts to control the socialization of Soviet citizens actually produced the desired attitudes or political culture? This is not an easy question to answer, for the evidence is sparse. On balance, however, it would appear that the Soviet regime has succeeded in creating a population that is knowledgeable about the Soviet polity and loyal to it, if not all of its institutions and practices. It is not at all clear, however, whether socialization under the Soviet regime has created a popular commitment to its developmental goals that will sustain the continued transformation of Soviet society toward communism.

While much of the Soviet socialization process is open to public scrutiny, the consequences of that process—the attitudes of Soviet citizens or the political culture—are among the most tightly guarded secrets of the Soviet polity. To fill the informational void, Western analysts have had to rely on a variety of less-than-satisfactory sources in order to construct a picture of the Soviet political culture. Russian history is one of these sources. While noting the importance of Marxism, Adam Ulam attempts to find elements of "the political culture of the U.S.S.R." in "the history of the state and nation that trace their beginnings to the tenth century."[40] Russian culture is yet another source. Geoffrey Gorer hypothesizes, based on his study of the Russian practice of swaddling children, that Russians prefer external authority that is "firm and consistent, neither too tight nor too loose" and that they will tend to cycles of quiescent submission and orgiastic self-gratification.[41] Soviet ideology, of course, contains a body of beliefs to which citizens are supposed to subscribe. In the official writings and statements of Party leaders Nathan Leites finds (with the assistance of Freudian analytic concepts) an "operational code of the Politburo" containing "rules which Bolsheviks believe to be necessary for effective political conduct."[42] Observations by long-time Western residents in the Soviet Union, such as journalists, have provided yet a fourth source of information on attitudes among the Soviet citizenry.[43] Social scientists have supplemented this with systematic surveys of Russian emigrés. In the early 1950s Alex Inkeles and Raymond A. Bauer directed the Harvard Project on the Soviet Social System, which studied Soviet refugees who had fled to Western Europe and North America during or after World War II (329 by direct interview and 2718 by written responses to a questionnaire). The next wave of emigrés in the 1970s also led to a number of interview projects in North America, Western Europe, and Israel.[44] Lastly, the growth of Soviet sociology and public opinion polling has provided researchers with evidence of citizen attitudes toward politics and, particularly, toward the institutions of the socialization process itself.[45]

The available evidence suggests that the Soviet socialization system has substantially expanded citizens' political knowledge—what students of political culture sometimes call cognitions. Inquires shortly after the Revolution "found a generally favourable attitude towards the new regime but little conception of how it operated at all but the local level; and even members of the party were found to have a 'very weak grasp' of Communist theory and to be 'generally little interested in this question.' "[46] Conversely, recent interviews of ex-Soviet citizens in the West have found levels of political awareness and knowledge comparable to those in the advanced Western democracies. The success of the Soviet socialization program is underscored by Soviet studies; these have found that workers who attended political lectures or political education classes had a better knowledge of Communist philosophy and current Soviet policies than those who had not attended.[47] (It should be noted, however, that those who attended were more likely to be better informed and interested in sociopolitical questions even before attending.)

Yet, the success of the socialization process in spreading political knowledge among the citizenry should not be misread as a sign that Soviet socialization is characterized by superhuman efficiency and that all Soviet citizens possess encyclopedic familiarity with the dogmas of their leaders. "Investigations in Moscow and Tomsk . . . have found that at the end of a year of Marxist-Leninist study about a quarter of those polled were unable to define 'proletariat' or 'productive forces' [and] almost half were unable to define 'dictatorship of the proletariat.' "[48] One local Soviet survey of party propagandists found that they felt 41 percent of their students had not acquired a satisfactory level of knowledge in their political education classes.[49]

More difficult to gauge are the subjective attitudes of Soviet citizens. On balance, the political culture appears to support the expanded political community called the Soviet Union. The observations of long-time Western residents in the Soviet Union suggest a high level of patriotism among the Russians. *London Times* correspondent Michael Binyon writes,

> Patriotism in the Soviet Union knows no bounds. Russians are brought up from kindergarten to honor the motherland, to respect their leaders, to treat Lenin with religious reverence. They may—and do—joke about the Party, the leaders and the communist system. But they do not make fun of their country. . . . Young Russians, however unpolitical and materialist, are unashamedly chauvanistic.[50]

Even among the non-Russians there appears to be growing loyalty to the Soviet state. On this point, however, the evidence is ambiguous: The growth of fluency in the Russian language among these people, their growing "value integration" as they are Sovietized, and the growing social contact and intermarriage across ethnic lines all suggest growth in an expanded nationalism and the emergence of what the Central Committee has heralded as a "new historical collectivity of people—the Soviet people." Yet, there are chronic signs of strain in this new national or political identity. The persistence of cultural, economic, and power disparities between Russians and non-Russians and the evidence of higher levels of disaffection toward the Soviet system in the non-Russian regions than in the Russian-populated areas raises doubts about the Soviet success in building a larger community of loyalties. Moreover, some research findings suggest that modernization among the non-Russian nationalities may actually be bringing renewed national consciousness among the indigenous elites and, thus, may ultimately aggravate the centrifugal pressures.[51]

Not only does the political culture, however tenuously, appear to support the political unity of the Soviet Union, it would also appear to provide fairly widespread support for the basic institutions of the Soviet polity, economy, and society. Among many Soviets this support is rooted in a commitment to strong government. *New York Times'* correspondent Hedrick Smith, in arguing that support for authoritarianism is deep among the Russian people, reports that a surprising number are even nostalgic for the strong rule of a Stalin:

> . . . those who are nostalgic about the good old days under Stalin yearn most of all for his style of leadership. . . . As the leader who forged a modern state, who steeled a nation in wartime to emerge victorious, and then made the rest of the world tremble at Soviet might, Stalin embodies power. . . .
>
> This language of power is the language many Russians use when they recall Stalin, for they like a powerful leader.[52]

Perhaps for a larger part of the Soviet population, this commitment to a strong government, even if it does not include support for despotic techniques, does include an activist state. Even among Soviet emigrés who tend to reject such institutions as the secret police and collectivized agriculture, most have supported public ownership of the economy (particularly heavy industry and communications), extensive state planning of the economy, and comprehensive social welfare including job security and medical care. Also, while rejecting absolutism, terror, and injustice within the Soviet Union, these respondents attributed these not to inherent flaws of Soviet institutions but to specific leaders and their policies. Even though these emigrés typically criticized Soviet interference in personal affairs and voiced support for abstract civil rights, they tended to favor an activist (sometimes paternalistic) state and were often willing to sanction broad restrictions on the press, speech, and assembly.[53]

Inkeles and Bauer have summarized the Soviet political culture as follows:

> If we were to state in a single sentence the political forms and policies which the Soviet citizen, as represented by our refugee respondents, would favor, it would be this: A paternalistic state, with extremely wide powers which it vigorously exercised to guide and control the nation's destiny, but which yet served the interests of the citizen benignly, which respected his personal dignity and left him with a certain amount of individual freedom of desire and a feeling of security from arbitrary interference and punishment.[54]

Toward the political institutions of the Soviet regime and toward the Party's value system of Marxism-Leninism there appears to be less affection. Significant minorities appear indifferent to or disaffected from these. This lack of enthusiasm for the regime and its ideology is expressed, in part, through dissatisfaction with the political socialization system itself. Local Soviet surveys suggest that perhaps as much as two-fifths of those attending political education classes reported they did so simply because of "party discipline," "administrative pressure," or obligation. A local survey of propagandists revealed that only 8.9 percent thought their students had absorbed the class material as "firm personal convictions." The still-limited success at conversion to Marxism-Leninism is reflected in the persistence of religious belief among the Soviet people: Soviet scholars in the late 60s and early 70s estimated that between 15 and 30 percent of the Soviet population believed in God.[55]

On balance, the available evidence suggests significant congruence between the Soviet political culture and its authoritarian polity. If congruence is an ingredient of political stability, then the evidence suggests that the political culture should support the system into at least the near future. The directive Soviet polity, however, seeks to remake Soviet society, not simply to maintain it; and it is not at all clear that the political culture will continue to change at the same pace as Soviet institutions. The resulting gaps between political institutions and political consciousness (the Soviets themselves complain about "lags" in consciousness) may create points of vulnerability in the future. Moreover, the largely instrumental basis for Soviet legitimacy—that is, legitimacy based on approval of its accomplishments rather than on acceptance of more fundamental Marxist-Leninist values—may point to a further vulnerability of this congruence in the future. If the Soviet system fails to "deliver," it may find rapid decline in its popular support. And if, as studies of public opinion and electoral behavior in the Soviet Union suggest, dissatisfaction and disaffection toward the Soviet system increase with modernization, then the continued expansion of Soviet education—ironically, among the most important socialization mechanisms created by the Soviet regime—may lead to an erosion of this congruence and to instability.[56]

NOTES

1. See Peter Kenez, *The Birth of the Propaganda State: Soviet Methods of Mass Mobilization, 1917–1929* (Cambridge, England: Cambridge University Press, 1985); T. H. Rigby, Archie Brown, and Peter Reddaway, eds., *Authority, Power, and Policy in the USSR* (London: Macmillan Press, 1980).
2. Zbigniew K. Brzezinski and Samuel P. Huntington, *Political Power: USA/USSR* (New York: Viking Press, 1964), Chapter 2.
3. Alex Inkeles, *Social Change in Soviet Russia* (Cambridge, Mass.: Harvard University Press, 1968), 231–243; Alex Inkeles and Raymond A. Bauer, *The Soviet Citizen: Daily Life in a Totalitarian Society* (Cambridge Mass.: Harvard University Press, 1961), 219–228.

4. Gayle Durham Hollander, *Soviet Political Indoctrination: Developments in Mass Media and Propaganda Since Stalin* (New York: Praeger, 1972), 11; Urie Bronfenbrenner, *Two Worlds of Childhood: US and USSR* (New York: Simon and Schuster, 1972), 9–16, 70–74; H. Kent Geiger, *The Family in Soviet Russia* (Cambridge, Mass.: Harvard University Press, 1968).

5. Quoted in Bronfenbrenner, 12–13.

6. Nigel Grant, *Soviet Education*, 4th ed. (New York: Penguin Books, 1979), 71.

7. Jeremy Azrael, "The Soviet Union," in James S. Coleman, ed. *Education and Political Development* (Princeton, N.J.: Princeton University Press, 1965), 270–71, 257; Grant 104–109; John Dunstan, "Soviet Boarding Education: Its Rise and Progress," in Jenny Brine, Maureen Perrie, and Andrew Sutton, eds., *Home, School, and Leisure in the Soviet Union* (London: Allen & Unwin, 1980), 110–141.

8. Madeline Drake, "Soviet Child Care: Its Organization at the Local Level," in Brine, Perrie, and Sutton, 142–159; Grant, 84–88.

9. Alex Inkeles, *Becoming Modern: Individual Change in Six Developing Countries* (Cambridge, Mass.: Harvard University Press, 1974). See also Elizabeth Koutaissoff, "Secondary Education for All in a Forward-Looking Society," in Brine, Perrie, and Sutton, 73–91.

10. Grant, 38.

11. Allen Kassof, *The Soviet Youth Program: Regimentation and Rebellion* (Cambridge, Mass.: Harvard University Press, 1965), 90.

12. *Izvestiia* (14 April 1984 and 18 April 1984).

13. U.S.S.R., Tsentral'noe Statisticheskoe Upravlenie, *Narodnoe khoziaistvo SSSR v 1922–1982: Iubileinyi statisticheskii ezhegodnik* (Moscow: Finansy i statistika, 1982), 506, 509.

14. N. N. Shneidman, *Literature and Ideology in Soviet Education* (Lexington, Mass.: Lexington Books, 1973), 7–83, 117–118; Felicity O'Dell, "Socialization in the Literature Lesson," in Brine, Perrie, and Sutton, 92 –109; George Z. F. Bereday, William W. Brickman, and Gerald H. Read, eds., *The Changing Soviet School* (London: Constable, 1960). See also V. P. Eliutin, *Higher Education in a Country of Developed Socialism* (Moscow: Vyshaia Shkola, 1980), translated and serialized in *Soviet Education* 26–27 (July 1984-August 1985).

15. Grant, 58–59.

16. Shneidman, 4.

17. Georgi Smirnov, *Soviet Man: The Making of a Socialist Type of Personality* (Moscow: Progress Publishers, 1973), 164. See also S. M. Lepekhin, *Leninskie printsipy vospitaniia molodezhi* (Leningrad: Lenizdat, 1978); and Kitty Weaver, *Russia's Future: The Communist Education of Soviet Youth* (New York: Praeger, 1981).

18. Urie Bronfenbrenner, "Makarenko and the Collective Family", Introduction to A. S. Makarenko, *The Collective Family: A Handbook for Russian Parents* (New York: Doubleday, 1967).

19. Bronfenbrenner, *Two Worlds*, 49.

20. Bronfenbrenner, *Two Worlds*, 50–51.

21. Roman Kolkowicz, *The Soviet Military and the Communist Party* (Princeton, N.J.: Princeton University Press, 1967), 156.

22. Kassof, 14, 51.

23. *Ezhegodnik Bol'shoi Sovetskoi Entsiklopedii, 1985.* (Moscow: Sovetskaia entsiklopediia, 1985), 18.

24. *Bol'shaia Sovetskaia Entsiklopediia*, 3d ed. (Moscow: Sovetskaia entsiklopediia, 1971), 5:460, s.v. "Vsesoiuznaia Pionerskaia Organizatsiia" by T. A. Kutsenko and

S. A. Furin; *Bol'shaia Sovetskaia Entsiklopediia*, 3d ed. (Moscow: Sovetskaia entsiklopediia, 1975), 19:545, s.v. "Pioner" by V. I. Lebedinskii; A. M. Prokhorov, ed. *SSSR: Entsiklopedicheskii spravochnik* (Moscow: Sovetskaia entsiklopediia, 1982), 185.

25. Kassof, 82.

26. Herbert Goldhamer, *The Soviet Soldier: Soviet Military Management at the Troop Level* (New York: Crane, Russak, and Company, Inc., 1975), 70–72.

27. Kassof, 105.

28. Kassof, 134–135.

29. Daryl J. Bem, *Beliefs, Attitudes, and Human Affairs* (Belmont, Calif.: Brooks/Cole, 1970).

30. Ellen Propper Mickiewicz, *Soviet Political Schools: The Communist Party Adult Instruction System* (New Haven, Conn.: Yale University Press, 1967), 6–7.

31. Mickiewicz, 19–21; "KPSS v tsifrakh," *Partiinaia zhizn'* 14 (July 1986), 32.

32. Harriet Fast Scott and William F. Scott, *The Armed Forces of the USSR*, 2d ed. (Boulder, Colo.: Westview Press, 1981), Chapter 10; Andrew Cockburn, *The Threat: Inside the Soviet Military Machine* (New York: Random House, 1983), Chapter 3; William E. Odom, "The 'Militarization' of Soviet Society," *Problems of Communism* 25 (September-October 1976), 34–51.

33. Goldhamer, 90–104, 223–243.

34. *Ezhegodnik 1985*, 89–91.

35. Ellen Mickiewicz, "Political Communication and the Soviet Media System," in Joseph L. Nogee, *Soviet Politics: Russia after Brezhnev* (New York: Praeger, 1985), 35–36. See also Ellen Mickiewicz, "Policy Issues in the Soviet Media System," *Proceedings of the Academy of Political Science* 35 (1984), 113–123; and Thomas Remington, "The Mass Media and Public Communications in the USSR," *Journal of Politics* 43 (August 1981), 803–817.

36. *Pravda* (27 July 1965); Mickiewicz, "Political Communication," 41.

37. Alex Inkeles, *Public Opinion in Soviet Russia: A Study in Mass Persuasion* (Cambridge, Mass.: Harvard University Press, 1962), 67–68.

38. Theodore H. Friedgut, *Political Participation in the USSR* (Princeton, N.J.: Princeton University Press, 1979), 98-99.

39. Hollander, 149, 163; Mickiewicz, "Political Communication," 45; *Ezhegodnik 1985*, 22.

40. Adam B. Ulam, "The Russian Political System," in Samuel H. Beer, ed., *Patterns of Government* (New York: Random House, 1958), 452.

41. Geoffrey Gorer and John Rickman, *The People of Great Russia* (New York: Chanticleer Press, 1950). See also Margaret Mead, *Soviet Attitudes toward Authority* (New York: Morrow, 1955); and Dinko Tomasic, *The Impact of Russian Culture on Soviet Communism* (New York: Free Press, 1953).

42. Nathan Leites, *A Study of Bolshevism* (New York: Free Press, 1953); or Nathan Leites, *The Operational Code of the Politburo* (New York: McGraw-Hill, 1951).

43. Hedrick Smith, *The Russians*, rev. ed. (New York: Ballantine Books, 1984); Michael Binyon, *Life in Russia* (New York: Berkley Books, 1985); David K. Shipler, *Russia: Broken Idols, Solemn Dreams* (New York: Time Books, 1983); Elizabeth Pond, *From the Yaroslavsky Station: Russia Perceived* (New York: Universe Books, 1981); Robert G. Kaiser, *Russia: The Power and the People* (New York: Washington Square Press, 1984).

44. Inkeles and Bauer; Wayne DiFranceisco and Zvi Gitelman, "Soviet Political Culture

and 'Covert Participation' in Policy Implementation," *American Political Science Review* 78 (September 1984), 603–621.

45. Ellen Propper Mickiewicz, *Media and the Russian Public* (New York: Praeger, 1981); Hollander; Walter D. Connor, "Public Opinion in the Soviet Union," in Walter D. Connor and Zvi Y. Gitelman, eds., *Public Opinion in European Socialist Systems* (New York: Praeger, 1977), 104–131; Stephen White, *Political Culture and Soviet Politics* (London: Macmillan Press, 1979).

46. White, 69.

47. DiFranceisco and Gitelman, 607; White, 121, 127.

48. White, 129; see also Mickiewicz, "Political Communication," 47.

49. Stephen White, "The Effectiveness of Political Propaganda in the USSR," *Soviet Studies* 32 (July 1980), 323–348.

50. Binyon, 139.

51. White, *Political Culture*, 146–147, 149–150; Brian Silver, "Social Mobilization and the Russification of Soviet Nationalities," *American Political Science Review* 68 (March 1974), 45–66; Ellen Jones and Fred W. Grupp, "Modernization and Traditionality in a Multiethnic Society: The Soviet Case," *American Political Science Review* 79 (June 1985), 474–490; Theresa Rakowska-Harmstone, "The Dialectics of Nationalism in the USSR," *Problems of Communism* 23 (May-June 1974), 1–22; Philip G. Roeder, "Dissent and Electoral Avoidance in the Soviet Union" (Paper presented at the Annual Meeting of the American Political Science Association, New Orleans, Louisiana, 29 August–1 September 1985).

52. Smith, 330.

53. White, *Political Culture*, 95–112.

54. Inkeles and Bauer, 246–247.

55. White, *Political Culture*, 189; Stephen White, "The USSR: Patterns of Autocracy and Industrialism," in Archie Brown and Jack Gray, eds., *Political Culture and Political Change in Communist States*, 2d ed. (London: Macmillan Press, 1979), 46; Hollander, 67; David E. Powell, *Antireligious Propaganda in the Soviet Union: A Study of Mass Propaganda* (Cambridge, Mass.: MIT Press, 1975), 135–136.

56. Stephen White, "Economic Performance and Communist Legitimacy," *World Politics* 38 (April 1986), 462–482; Mickiewicz, *Media*, 133–137; Roeder, 29–32.

chapter 5

The Shadow Dance of Democracy: Citizen Participation

Central to the Bolsheviks' solution to Russia's crises of citizenship was the incorporation of the populace into the political process. Samuel P. Huntington has argued:

> Before the Bolshevik revolution no revolution was politically complete because no revolutionary leaders had formulated a theory explaining how to organize and to institutionalize the expansion of political participation which is the essence of the revolution. Lenin solved this problem, and in doing so made one of the most significant political innovations of the twentieth century. His followers elaborated the political theory and practice for mating the mobilization of new groups into politics to the creation and institutionalization of new political organizations.[1]

Many of these institutions mimic the mechanisms of democratic control, with campaigns and elections playing a central role in the continued mobilization of the population. But to harness popular energies to the task of transforming Soviet society, the regime has also developed new mobilizational techniques including auxiliary organizations, campaigns of popular discussion, and self-administration.

CAN THERE BE CITIZEN PARTICIPATION IN A LENINIST POLITY?

By the 1977 Soviet Constitution, the citizen is guaranteed rights that are essential to unfettered democratic participation in politics. According to this document, "all power in the USSR belongs to the people" (Article 2). Citizens are specifically guaranteed the right to participate in political processes, to submit proposals to the authorities, and to lodge complaints against the actions of the state (Articles 48–49, 58). Political guarantees support this right of participation, including the "freedom of speech, of the press, and of assembly, meetings, street processions and demonstrations" as well as "the right to associate in public organizations that promote [citizens'] political activity and initiative and satisfaction of their various interests" (Articles 50–51). These political rights are bolstered by guarantees of privacy as well as the inviolability of the citizen's person and home (Articles 54–56). The Constitution also guarantees a broad set of social rights, including "freedom of conscience," "freedom of scientific, technical, and artistic work," and rights to work, rest and leisure, housing, education, cultural benefits, and maintenance in old age, sickness, or disability (Articles 40–47, 52). The Constitution does make the enjoyment of these rights inseparable from the performance of a citizen's duties; and these duties form a substantial list, including observance of the laws, performance of socially useful work, protection of socialist property, defense of the Socialist Motherland, military service, respect for the rights of other citizens, particularly of other nationalities, concern for the upbringing of children, protection of nature and historical monuments, promotion of "friendship and cooperation with peoples of other lands," and support for the maintenance and strengthening of "world peace" (Articles 59–69). Nonetheless, on the face of it, the rights essential to democratic citizen participation are guaranteed by the Constitution.

This, it goes without saying, is not the underlying reality. The Soviet model of development has not duplicated the democratic practices found in Western industrialized societies. The forms of democratic participation mask a mobilizational regime. This fact has given rise to a debate among Western analysts of Soviet political affairs: It is indisputable that the Soviet Union is characterized by widespread citizen involvement in its public life, but can this involvement truly be called citizen participation? Can there be meaningful citizen participation in an authoritarian polity such as the Soviet Union, when the power to influence policy is limited to only a few individuals and groups?

Robert Sharlet of Union College has argued that citizen involvement in the public life of the Soviet Union cannot be labelled participation, for it lacks those essential attributes that define citizen participation in the West. He argues that participation must be voluntary, but "political involvement in Communist systems is rarely a matter of personal choice"; "effective withdrawal [from politics] is not an operative choice. . . . " Second, participation must result from a sense of "efficacy"—the individual's belief that involvement can affect "the decisional outcomes of government"—but in the Soviet Union there can be no such sense of efficacy. And participation produces meaningful and appropriate responses from the polity, which citizen involvement does not produce in the Soviet Union.[2]

Sharlet actually builds his case on a caricature of citizen involvement in the Soviet Union.[3] It is true that some of the most conspicuous forms of citizen involvement in Soviet public life are, in the main, mobilized activities. Yet, not all of this mobilized involvement is devoid of those essential attributes that he argues define participation in a polyarchy. Involvement is, in fact, voluntary, in that citizens can control the extent of their involvement by such choices as whether to join an organization, volunteer for a public commission, or run for office. (Jerry F. Hough has amassed a substantial body of evidence to show that higher levels of participation are closely associated with higher occupational and educational status, much as in Western polyarchies.[4]) Even in the most widespread forms of participation, such as voting, many citizens choose to abstain. Opportunities to influence political outcomes do exist (especially to gain individual benefits), suggesting that citizen involvement in the Soviet Union can be efficacious and that participants can be motivated by a sense of efficacy. But, more importantly, in addition to this mobilized activity, some citizen involvement in Soviet politics is actually spontaneous or autonomous, seeking individual or collective remedies from state authorities.

Nonetheless, citizen participation in the Soviet Union is decidedly different from that in a polyarchy. And the differences reflect the dichotomy between directive and responsive polities. Most importantly, the *balance* between participation as a means to mobilize and socialize a population, on the one hand, and participation as a means to gather information about citizen preferences, on the other, is different. The latter is far less important in the Soviet Union, the former far more so, than in a polyarchy. Secondly, the principal objectives of autonomous participation differ in each. In the Soviet Union, the most extensive autonomous participation focuses its energies on output processes to gain individual benefits rather than on input processes for collective goods through policies.

MOBILIZED PARTICIPATION

Why does a monopolistic party, like the Communist Party of the Soviet Union, go to such lengths to cultivate citizen participation when, in fact, this is unlikely to affect the composition of the leadership or the direction of their policies? The answer to this question can be found in the functions that citizen participation performs in the Soviet political system.[5] The first of these is socialization—imparting to citizens explicit information about the Soviet polity and continuing the implicit socialization in such habits as self-administration and conformity to the *kollektiv*. Second, participation legitimates the power held by the leaders of the Soviet system. Mass ratification of the policies and power of the Soviet authorities places a popular imprimatur on the Soviet system. For example, the electoral process "gives the average voter a sense of participation in the political process." And as the Princeton historian Cyril Black notes, "it may, in some subtle psychological fashion, commit him to sharing responsibility for the Party's directives."[6] Political participation is also a means of mobilizing the energies of the population on behalf of the policies of the state. In a relatively poor society such as the Soviet Union, many policies require large-scale citizen participation for successful implementation; that is, they substitute mass political participation for the scarce resources of an overtaxed state and Party administration. Finally, through the participatory process, the regime collects information about the needs and dissatisfactions of the population. Through citizen participation the regime learns what the citizenry believes must be done, what it thinks is done improperly, and what new issues might become serious problems in the future if left unaddressed in the present. Absent from this list of functions is, of course, the selection of rulers, for this is decidedly not a central function of the participatory process involving the average Soviet Citizen.

Voting

The most widespread form of participation in the Soviet system is voting. And it would appear from official reports that almost every Soviet citizen who has reached the age of 18 by election day votes. For example, in the election of deputies to soviets below the national level on 24 February 1985, 99.98 percent of the 185,321,639 eligible voters cast a ballot on election day; only 32,175 failed to show.[7] Voting is also, however, the least intense form of citizen participation, for the act of voting takes little effort and is of short duration.

Since the Soviet polity is organized like a parliamentary system, a citizen votes for deputies to legislative bodies, including the all-union Supreme Soviet and the union-republic Supreme Soviets as well as oblast, city, rural district, village, and city borough soviets. As in a parliamentary democracy, the citizen does not directly vote for the executive branch.

Elections are held every five years at the all-union level, every five years for union-republic and autonomous republic soviets, and every two and a half years for local soviets. Since the elections are staggered, three out of every five years are election years.

The voting itself takes place on a Sunday, a day most Soviets do not work. Polling stations are located in each precinct and are open from 6:00 A.M. to 10:00 P.M., making it easy to get to the polls. On election day, a voter takes his or her internal passport to the polling station, and upon showing it to the election officials is issued one ballot for each of the positions to be filled. The voter can then take the ballot(s) either to the voting booth or directly to the ballot box. Since each ballot has only one name—the official candidate—for a single position, the citizen can vote for the official list by simply folding the ballot and dropping it into the ballot box. To vote against the official candidate on any ballot requires entering the polling booth and striking the name of the candidate.[8]

In former years, it was assumed that anyone who entered the booth went there to vote against the official candidates, and officials with cameras were present to intimidate those who might consider entering the booths. As a consequence, few exercised this right. In recent years, however, one entering the booth is no longer suspect, for citizens now go in for a number of reasons other than voting against the official candidates. Apparently some enter the booth simply to affirm that they can vote against the official candidate, if they so choose. Others enter to write a request on the ballot for a special project of personal importance such as improvements in local public transportation. Still others use the opportunity to write patriotic slogans or even obscenities on the ballot. Nonetheless, only about three percent of the voters enter the booth. Thus, as in previ-

Election Day

Max E. Mote reconstructs the following "interview" on election day based on his discussions with residents in one Leningrad apartment house:

Q: Elections in the USSR impress Westerners. The overwhelming majority of Russians have come out to vote . . . .But still I wonder: Don't some people ever vote against the candidates?

A: Sometimes it does happen that people scratch the name off the ballot. It occurs more often out in the villages . . .

Q: Can persons step into the booth and write in the name of a candidate?

A: Of course a person can do this. But it also invalidates the ballot. You see, a candidate has to be nominated by an organization, approved in advance, and registered according to the statute.

Q: So a write-in would not be valid?

A: It would be meaningless. You can't elect anyone with a write-in vote.

Q: Perhaps this explains why few people make use of the voting booths with the curtains hanging in front of them. It looks like about one person in ten is getting into there.

A: More people go into them now than during the time of the cult of personality [the Stalin era]. In those days, someone was keeping track of the people who went into the booths. We don't do that any more.

Q: Don't some people stay away from the polls altogether? Aren't there any people who just refuse to vote? . . .

A: I heard of a case where some people decided they would not vote. They wanted to make a protest about their housing conditions . . . Several families were living in one of the older apartments. Last fall some workmen from the housing office came to fix the plumbing. Well, they cut a hole in the roof of one of the rooms used by all the residents, but when they finished the job they did not patch up the hole.

Q: It was thirty below last winter. What did they do about it?

A: The residents called the housing office and asked them to come and fix the roof. When this got no results, they called the Executive Committee of their city-[borough] soviet. No help. So they called up their deputy.

Q: Was he able to do anything?

A: No; the matter dragged on for months . . . .[It was] a minor job, but it became a matter of principle. Of course, they could have given the workmen a bottle or two of vodka and it would have been fixed before they left. But these people wanted to settle the matter honestly. Bribery is not a good thing.

Q: So on election day they decided they would not go to the polls?

A: No, they told the agitator who came to visit them that they were not going to vote unless the roof had been fixed by Saturday, the day before the election. This was an ultimatum.

Q: What could the agitator do?

A: First he had to get over his shock. It was an unusual experience for him.

But he called the housing office and told them to get a repairman over there right away.

Q: Did that do the job?

A: No, when Sunday morning came, the hole was still there.

Q: Did they vote?

A: Naturally they voted.

Q: Wasn't the atmosphere a bit tense when they showed up at the polls?

A: It may have been. I heard that the volunteer workers at the precinct gave them special attention when they came in, asking them with perhaps a bit of ambiguity how things were at home. The residents simply put it this way: Is a little hole in the roof any reason to be against the Soviet regime? Of course not.

Q: And so they all voted?

A: They voted, to a man. The roof is still not repaired.

Q: But what if they really had refused to come out to the polls, what would you do in a case like that?

A: I wouldn't do anything. But I would begin to think, now why is this person against the government? Yes, I'd want to investigate the matter.

Source: Max E. Mote. Soviet Local and Republic Elections. Stanford, CA: Hoover Institution, 1965. pp. 80-83

ous years, for most Soviet citizens voting is simply a matter of seeing that their names are checked off the voter rolls and voting for each official candidate by depositing each unmarked ballot in its box.[9]

In the June 21, 1987, elections to local soviets an important experiment with this voting arrangement was undertaken in about five percent of the villages, *raiony*, and cities—contested candidacies. In these localities, election districts were combined and more candidates nominated to stand for election than there were positions. On average, four candidates stood for three positions in these districts. Voters had to scratch out the names of all but the candidates they wished elected. The winners were the candidates with fewest negative votes. (The other candidates who were not disqualified by a majority of negative votes against them were reportedly to serve as reserve deputies who would replace winners who were later unable to hold office.) Whether this procedure will become commonplace as Gorbachev's speech to the January 1987 Plenum of the Central Committee seemed to suggest (that is, extended to all constituencies, to elections at the union-republic and all-union levels, and to elections within the Party) remains to be seen. If it does, it may not only change the formalities of balloting in the Soviet Union (such as requiring all voters to use the voting booth), but provide a mechanism by which voters can have at least a limited voice in the selection of their leaders.

As a consequence of the normal balloting procedure used today, however, almost all official candidates are elected to office in the main election. In 1984, all

1500 candidates for both chambers of the all-union Supreme Soviet received an absolute majority of votes in their respective constituencies; less than one percent of the electors voted against the official candidates. In 1985, all 10,188 candidates for the union-republic and autonomous republic Supreme Soviets received absolute majorities; and only 90 out of 2,304,703 candidates for local soviets failed to win a majority vote and so were defeated. All the defeated candidates were running for small village or rural district soviets, and in these constituencies new elections were scheduled to fill the posts.[10]

Should we believe the results of Soviet elections? In particular, should we believe that out of 185 million electors, less than 0.02 percent failed to vote? In the Turkmen SSR, for example, of 1,578,107 eligible voters in 1985, only 5 failed to vote. (This is a turnout that would put the best American political machine to shame.) In fact, quite surprisingly, the official figures may be fairly accurate or at least as accurate as election figures in Western democracies.

An important reason for the remarkably high turnout is the virtual absence of obstacles to voting. In contrast to some Western democracies where a major obstacle to voting is registration, in the Soviet Union it is difficult *not* to register. In fact, election agitators and members of electoral commissions will seek out citizens at their places of residence to ensure that all are registered. Further, on voting day, polling stations are everywhere. A station will be very near one's place of residence. The laws on elections also provide for balloting in a number of special circumstances: on board ships at sea, on long-distance trains, in railway stations and airports for passengers in transit on election day, in hospitals and medical treatment facilities, at military installations, at remote polar and meteorological stations, and at the sites of geological and scientific expeditions. For those who are bedridden, ballot boxes can be brought to their homes.[11] Under these circumstances, how could a registered voter fail to vote?

The obverse of the ease of voting in the Soviet Union is the difficulty of not voting.[12] The person responsible for ensuring that people participate is the local agitator, who is present at the polling place on election day and must remain on duty until everyone on the list of eligible voters has cast a ballot. Toward the end of the day, if not everyone has voted, the agitator and his assistants call on those whose names remain on the list of electors to encourage them to fulfill their civic duty.

The agitator's task is eased by a persistent element of fear among Soviet citizens. In an informal survey Theodore Friedgut asked citizens in Moscow why they voted. Many gave as one reason the fear that if they did not vote, some ill-defined retribution would be loosed upon them. Typically, these respondents reported that they did not know of anyone who had been punished for failure to vote, but nonetheless felt a gnawing fear that at some time failure to vote might cause them trouble. A citizen's internal passport is stamped when he or she has voted, so if one later has a run-in with the authorities, failure to vote might become just another cause for harassment.[13]

While the official electoral figures may be roughly accurate, nevertheless, it is likely that there is still some element of fraud in the figures—some overrepresentation of voter turnout. For instance, in some cases local agitators may collect the passports of citizens still on the list and vote for the delinquent, simply stuffing the ballots into the box for them. Another way to inflate the official figures is the Certificate of Right to Vote [in another place]. Unlike an absentee ballot, this permits a citizen to vote in any constituency in the country on election day. (It does not matter that the voter does not reside in the constituency in which he or she votes). The Certificate is a useful instrument for the harried agitator on election day, since no record is kept of whether an individual with such a certificate actually votes elsewhere. His or her name is taken off the list. As a consequence, local agitators may issue Certificates of Right to Vote in the names of anyone on the rolls that cannot be found on election day. After the names of most nonvoters have been removed from the list of eligible electors, the records will show that over 99 percent of these eligible electors in that precinct have met their civic obligation!

In fact, the official figures seem to hide a significant part of the Soviet citizenry who meet the legal requirements for enfranchisement, yet remain outside the electoral process entirely, appearing neither as registered electors nor as voters. The one figure the Soviet authorities never report is the percentage of the eligible citizenry that has actually registered to vote (as opposed to the percentage of registered electors who vote). In the 1985 election, for example, while 185.3 million people were registered electors, the population 18 years of age or older was about 198.0 million. That is, 12.7 million people (about 6.4 percent of the adult population) do not appear in the reported electoral results at all. (One estimate places the rate in Moscow as high as 20 percent.) And the number of these nonparticipants appears to be increasing each election at a steady rate. Soviet elections are less all-encompassing than the official figures might lead us to believe.[14]

If elections for the most part do not select the rulers of the Soviet Union, why bother with them at all? In part, the answer is that elections legitimate the system; they place a democratic-appearing imprimatur on the regime. (Also, it gives "democratically elected" posts to many, such as factory managers or local Party secretaries, who exercise real power, thereby legitimating that power.) The Soviet Union can report to the outside world that over 185 million people have ratified the leadership of the country. To the average Soviet citizen, if he or she harbors private doubts about the Soviet regime, Soviet elections (in the absence of independent means to test their results) warn that they will be isolated if they express dissent publically. Elections are also a part of adulthood socialization. They give the average citizen a sense of participation in politics. And, if psychological theories of cognitive dissonance are applicable to such situations, participation may convince the citizen that he or she is partially responsible for the regime and its policies. Conversely, the balloting is a very limited mobilization exercise, requiring little citizen effort. And elections probably play only a limited informational role for the authorities. Except for the epithets scrawled on the ballots and the figures for local participation rates that may signal local problems, little real information is collected from the balloting itself.

The Campaign Process

More important than the voting itself is the campaign that precedes the balloting, which usually lasts about two months and mobilizes over 20 million volunteers (about an eighth of the electorate) to help run the campaign and the elections. The campaign is a more intensive exercise than the balloting, although it involves a smaller number of citizens than the balloting on the final day.

The first step in any campaign in the Soviet Union is to organize electoral commissions for each soviet, for each constituency within that soviet, and for each precinct. The local commissions are responsible for updating the electoral rolls, supervising the balloting on election day, tallying the vote at the end of the day, and then reporting the results from the precinct. These are staffed by volunteers elected by local public organizations such as professional organizations and Party groups. In 1985, 959,087 such commissions were staffed by 8.8 million volunteers. The commissions usually involve the most active members of a community, drawing in not only Party members but the non-Party *aktiv* as well. At this point in the electoral process the Party's role is less visible, so that in 1985, for example, Party members made up only 41.1 percent of the commission volunteers. (Only about 36 percent, however, belonged to neither the Party nor the Komsomol.[15])

The second stage of the process is the nomination of candidates for the various offices. As in any one-party state, the nominations are the most important part of the elections; and it is in this phase that the role of the Party is critical. The process is a complex one, for in the mid-80s as many as 2,316,391 deputies acceptable to the Party must be nominated to soviets at all levels.

Apparently three types of nominations are made in this process. A number of people are nominated simply as an honor. For example, in the 1984 elections of deputies to the Supreme Soviet, Andropov received 39 nominations; Chernenko, 13, Tikhonov, 12; Gorbachev, 8; Romanov and Ustinov, 7; Aliyev and Gromyko, 6; and so on down the political pecking order. Each is eventually elected to only one seat. In addition to the honorary nominees are the *ex officio* nominees—individuals like the local Party secretary, manager of a large factory, or trade union secretary who are nominated automatically by virtue of the office they hold. At the oblast level perhaps a quarter of the deputies to the soviet are *ex officio* nominees. In the all-union Supreme Soviet this may reach as high as 86 percent of the deputies.[16]

The remaining nominees emerge from a quiet consultation process under the direction of the local Party organization with leaders of key institutions such as factories, collective farms, universities, and trade unions. The local *verkhushki* ("high ones") negotiate among themselves until they reach a consensus on a candidate whom they believe will be acceptable to the constituency. Following this, formal nomination meetings are held around the constituency in meetings of work collectives; and the citizenry is given an opportunity to discuss whom they will nominate. Miraculously, all the meetings in a constituency usually settle upon the same candidate after his or her name is put forward by a prominent member in each meeting. It is estimated, however, that in 1965, about 1 in

1000 of these nominees was rejected at the open meetings, compared with only about 1 in 25,000 nominees rejected at the polls. Thus, the nomination meeting can exercise some power. Smart local leaderships will anticipate any potential opposition to a candidate before these meetings and will select a nominee expected to encounter minimal or no resistance.[17] (The experiment with contested candidacies does not appear to have changed this nomination procedure significantly.)

Throughout the campaign, agitators maintain a fever pitch of propaganda, which is reinforced by the din of the press, radio, and television. The Party activates a series of agitation points (*agitpunkti*) and voters' clubs, which hold lectures for voters on the workings of the electoral system, the virtues of the Soviet polity, and the current policies of the regime. Each candidate must hold at least one meeting with his or her future constituents. Meetings for union-republic candidates are usually limited to formal speeches about the candidate and the Party's policies, followed by entertainment to bring out a larger audience. Meetings for candidates to lower-level soviets, however, can result in some real give-and-take, affording the audience opportunities to raise questions about local projects such as an overcrowded apartment building or personal concerns such as a delinquent pension check.[18] In the final days of the campaign, the agitator visits electors in their homes to explain the importance of the election and of Soviet democracy, to extoll the virtues of the candidate, and to exact a personal commitment to show at the polls on election day. (Agitators may also hear citizen complaints and forward them for remedial action.)

The campaign is designed to saturate the population—to make sure that everyone is contacted and hears the message of Soviet democracy. Based on figures from the 1969 campaign in the city of Kazan, it is estimated that there is one voters' club for every 2000 to 2500 voters and one agitation point for every 200 voters in rural areas or 1500 voters in urban areas. With so few constituents to serve, each club or agitation point can engage every citizen in the locality directly. In the mid-80s it appears that as many as 9 million agitators participate in all-union (national) elections. Each of these visits 30 to 40 voters in the course of an election, for a total of 270 to 360 million voters. Probably every one of the 185 million voters receives at least one visit.[19]

In the Soviet Union these election campaigns are an important part of adulthood socialization. Instruction in the workings of Soviet "democracy" reinforces the lessons learned earlier in life. For the volunteers staffing the commissions, the election is an exercise in collective responsibility, socially useful volunteer labor, and self-administration. For all citizens, the portrait of the candidate presented in the press provides a paragon for emulation. And, unlike the actual balloting, the election campaign is also a mechanism for gathering information, for it is during the campaign that the candidates and agitators must listen to individual voters and hear their complaints.

Membership in Public Organizations

Participation in public life through organizational membership also appears to involve virtually every Soviet citizen. Of course, membership in the Party is the

Finding the "Best Man" for the Job

Q: Precisely who is it that nominates the candidates?

A: Organizations nominate them. The election statutes require this.

Q: Would it be possible for a group of citizens, say the people who live in one neighborhood, to get together and decide to send "their" candidate to the local soviet . . .

A: No, this doesn't happen. An individual worker may get up in a meeting and recommend someone for candidacy, but this takes place in the meeting of some organization. People don't form groups for the purpose of nominating a man. Such a group would not be a registered organization, and therefore it would not have the right, according to law, to nominate anyone. I understand what you are thinking about, but this kind of thing does not occur in the Soviet Union.

Q: Within the organization, then, who chooses the man who will be nominated later on?

A: This is done by the party or union committee in the factory. The fact is that the party and union work closely on this . . . .There is a series of meetings. The first one is attended by a small number of people, and they go over the personnel files of the workers. Then there is another meeting, and more people are present. The number of persons attending the meetings grows as the process continues.

Q: Then by the time an open assembly nominates the candidate, there have been several meetings of the party and union groups to decide on who the candidate will be?

A: That is correct . . . .

Q: What kind of man is it that the selection committee chooses?

A: The best man. After all, we know the man's biography and have studied his characteristics. We don't choose someone who has just come to work for us.

Q: But what if you are mistaken in your choice?

A: We are seldom mistaken. Of course, it can happen that deep inside a man's character are traits which are difficult to see from his biography and which come to light only after the man is in office. But if such a thing happens, let's say a man drinks or steals, we can recall him. There is a new law on recall and it is easier to remove a man from office than it used to be.

Q: . . . .Now does it ever happen that people rise during these meetings and object to the nomination of a given candidate? Or is the nomination always automatic?

A: Not always. I have heard of cases out in the villages where some people objected to a candidate. But I never heard of it happening in Leningrad.

Q: Well, then, what happens if you choose a man for candidacy and the voters don't like him—will they reject the candidate on election day?

A: This happens very rarely. If a mistake has been made, there is recall.

Q: Exactly what qualities do you look for in a deputy?

A: First of all, a candidate has to have authority. He has to be a good worker. He should work conscientiously and when given a task carry it through to the end. And he should be well known, so that he commands the respect of people. We like people with experience in organizational work, people who have spent time doing things for others. This is the kind of a person who will make a good deputy.

Q: What about the candidates who were chosen today—do they have experience or other qualifications in administration?"

A: That is not necessary. We pick good people who have a sense of responsibility and who will carry out the tasks which are assigned to them.

Q: Another thing. You nominated four candidates at this meeting. One for each district. How did you know how many to nominate?

A: We got word from . . . the people in the party apparatus who organize the nominations. They let us know whom to nominate.

Q: How many candidates do you select?

A: We select one candidate for every opening. For example, in our city-[borough] there are 250 deputies to the city-[borough] soviet, so this means there will be 250 candidates.

Q: Doesn't it sometimes happen that you choose two candidates for one office?

A: I have heard that this sometimes happens out in the villages, but I have never seen it. You see, it would indicate a lack of confidence in the candidate if you were to nominate two men for the same post. It would mean you think one of them is not good enough for the office. We don't want to insult our candidates.

Q: Who arranges this so that it comes out even—one candidate for every office?

A: This is arranged by the party. It is their job to assign us the required number of candidates. They tell us how many.

Q: Another question in regard to this. Your factory, for example, has some shops located in other places in the city, yet the factory as a whole is nominating just one candidate to the Supreme Soviet of the RSFSR. There are different parts of your factory within election District 97. Isn't it possible that in the other parts of this factory, in other sections of town, the workers there will decide to choose a different candidate? Maybe you will, after all, end up with two candidates from the one district.

A: No, this will not happen. The man we are going to nominate has been settled on in advance, and so we will simultaneously nominate the same man in both parts of the factory.

Q: Who decided on this man?

A: This was decided on in the earlier meetings.

Source: Max E. Mote. *Soviet Local and Republic Elections.* Stanford, CA: Hoover Institution, 1965, pp. 25–30; 38–39.

most important. (Party membership is discussed in Chapter 7.) As mentioned in the previous chapter, the Young Octobrists, Pioneers, and Komsomol involve a majority of those below the age of Party membership.

One of the more important memberships for most Soviet adults is that in their trade union or professional organization. Trade union membership on January 1, 1985, stood at 136.3 million, in 764,000 primary and 597,000 shop organizations. These are grouped in 29 unions under the direction of the All-Union Central Trade Union Council. (There may also be two additional unions for workers in the missile-manufacturing and atomic energy fields.)[20] The Central Council, together with the less-powerful Trade Union Presidium, is elected by a Trade Union Congress that every five years brings together delegates from these 29 or 31 unions. Each union is organized on sectoral lines, so, for example, the Textile and Light Industry Workers Union includes all employees of the ministries in this sector, including administrators, line workers, and janitorial staff. The union organization in a factory falls under the jurisdiction of a regional committee of the sectoral union, which in turn falls under the dual jurisdiction of the all-union organization for that union and the oblast or republican council for all trade unions. While the chairmen and secretaries of trade union organizations are formally elected by their membership, they come under the tight control of superordinate trade union officials and the Party apparatus.

Trade unions provide their members with benefits that are difficult to acquire by other means. They provide pensions; administer social insurance for the sick or disabled and maternity-leave pay for expectant mothers; and provide a wealth of leisure-time activities through union clubhouses, sanitoria, and vacation resorts. Trade union organizations can seek solutions to workers' grievances, although usually only when they do not raise issues of larger policy. The union continues the work of adulthood socialization, organizing political lectures, concerting peer pressure to enforce desired behavior among co-workers, and mobilizing laborers for *subbotniki,* or drives to raise productivity and fulfill the factory's quota.[21]

For what might be called the independent professions, Soviet professional associations like the Association of Soviet Jurists and USSR Union of Journalists play roles similar to those of the trade unions. The separate unions of Architects, Artists, Cinema Workers, Composers, and Writers provide professional services and central control for the creative intelligentsia.

In addition to the trade unions, an elaborate network of extracurricular volunteer organizations under tight Party control permits the Soviet authorities to mobilize popular energies for more specific purposes. For example, the Union of Societies of the Red Cross and Red Crescent of the USSR, with a membership of about 100 million, prepares citizens for disaster relief in peacetime and civil defense in war. "Political" organizations like the Soviet Committee for the Defense of Peace, the Soviet Committee for European Security, the Student Council of the USSR, and the Union of Soviet Societies for Friendship and Cultural Relations with Foreign Countries (which oversees over 50 friendship societies for individual foreign countries) mobilize citizens to support the foreign propaganda of the regime and to act as "unofficial" liaisons with non-Soviet organizations and dignitaries overseas.[22]

Among the largest and most important of these organizations is the All-Union Voluntary Society for Assistance to the Army, Air Force, and Navy

(DOSAAF). Founded in 1927 as the Society of Friends of Defense and Aviation-Chemical Construction (OSOAVIAKHIM), DOSAAF has grown to an organization of over 107 million (1 January 1985) dues-paying members, organized in 358,000 primary organizations in schools and places of employment. The all-union organization that coordinates these primary organizations through a hierarchy of republic, oblast, municipal, and rural district committees engages in an ambitious program of publication for military preparedness, including the daily newspaper *Sovetskii Patriot,* three major magazines, and books and pamphlets that total several million copies annually (e.g., 25 million in 1984). Local DOSAAF organizations are required by the 1967 Law on Universal Military Service to help provide the preinduction military training of youths. DOSAAF has also played a major role in training civilians in military specialties, such as radio communications and transportation. DOSAAF naval clubs train citizens in skin-diving and sailing; aviation clubs train them not only in the theory of aviation but also in piloting and parachuting. (This program is partially a response to the problems of military preparedness in an economy of scarcity; for in the absence of these programs Soviet youths would not learn such skills as driving motorized vehicles, let alone working under the hood of a car, which are a normal part of adolescence in a more affluent society.) For its general membership DOSAAF also provides patriotic education and civil defense instruction.[23]

Thus, in addition to the continuation of adulthood socialization, an important function of organizational membership is mobilization of citizens to help carry out the policies of the Soviet regime, including industrial production and military preparedness. Some organizations, such as the foreign policy liaison groups, play a minor legitimation role, by orchestrating the voices of Soviet citizens on behalf of the policies of the Soviet regime. And still others, particularly the trade unions, play a minor information-gathering role, by keeping in touch with citizens' grievances. But the key function of these organizations appears to be socialization and mobilization.

Discussing Politics

The Soviets, from most indications, do not discuss politics freely with others or even among themselves. Spontaneous public debate of policy involving average citizens (as opposed to expert or elite debate) is virtually unheard of. Yet, open consideration of issues does take place through the odd Soviet ritual of orchestrated public discussions. On a routine basis, meetings are held near places of residence or employment under the leadership of a Party agitator. Apparently in some villages there are even meetings of the citizenry on a regular basis to discuss the internal affairs of the village.[24]

More peculiarly "Soviet", although less frequent, are massive campaigns of discussion that sweep the country. For example, in 1961, the Party orchestrated a public discussion of its new Program with meetings across the country in which 82 million people participated. Similar campaigns were held before the elimination of the machine-tractor stations in 1958, the adoption of the educational reform of 1958, and the issuance of the divorce edict of 1965. Before adoption of the 1977 Constitution, over 140 million people participated in public meetings during a four-month campaign. According to Leonid Brezhnev, these produced 400,000 proposed amendments, of which 150 were adopted by the Constitutional Commission.[25] But the purpose of these meetings is not, in the main, a free and open airing of opinions (information-gathering). Rather, they offer a forum to explain a policy to the citizenry and to demonstrate, through testimonials, the widespread support for it (socialization and legitimation).

Self-Administration

While in Western democracies there is typically only limited public participation in the implementation of policy (e.g., jury duty), in the Soviet Union this is widespread. Self-administration provides two important services for the Soviet polity: control and community service. Taken together these activities mobilize more than a quarter of the adult population—perhaps as many as 50 million Soviet citizens.

To control deviant behavior the Soviets have institutionalized adult peer pressure, continuing a pattern established in the schools and youth groups. The object of this, according to Theodore Friedgut, "is to make the regime your neighbor by having your neighbor represent the regime."[26] The most important of the peer pressure mechanisms are the *druzhiny* and comrade courts.

The *druzhiny,* organized in 1959, are volunteers, under the authority of the local soviet, who patrol the streets and housing complexes, maintaining order and enforcing the laws and the Party's notion of morality. (The *druzhiny* supervise and work closely with the Komsomol patrols described in the previous chapter.) Drawing together volunteers from the local Komsomol, trade union, and residence groups, the *druzhiny* number over 7 million in the 1980s. They apparently attract volunteers to serve a few hours every week or two through special honors and sometimes small privileges, through the satisfactions of contributing to community safety, and perhaps even through the perverse psychological pleasures of strutting about with a red armband monitoring one's neighbors. Individual detachments elect their own officers, although apparently under the watchful eye of the Party.

Comrade courts, also created in 1959, are official but informal tribunals below the regular hierarchy of courts organized in every residence or work place with over 50 people. The individuals who sit on these courts are elected by their neighbors and, for the most part, have no legal training. Some Soviet legal experts have questioned whether these courts dispense a form of "vigilante justice," ignoring the norms of "socialist legality." Appeal of an unjust outcome can be made from these courts to political institutions like the local soviet or factory trade union, but since the comrade courts are not part of the normal judicial hierarchy, there is usually no appeal to the regular People's Courts. Nonetheless, the comrade courts have the authority to hear cases and dispense punishment. The cases heard in a comrade court typically involve petty hooliganism or conflicts within or between families and are referred to the court by the *druzhiny.* For example, in a court in Moscow's Sverdlovsk district, most of the cases involved problems among families living in communal flats (apartments where several families share kitchen or bathroom facilities); six of the cases involved public drunkenness; three, minor theft of property; four, disputes within families; and four, problems of parasitism (people who refuse steady employment). By solving these problems among neighbors, the comrade courts relieve the caseload in the regular courts.

The control functions of *druzhiny* and comrade courts are reinforced by the all-inclusive network of residence committees. These are organized by neighborhood, block, street, or house (that is, a large apartment complex) for every 30 to 50 households and involve as much as 5 percent of the adult population in major cities in their activities. (The type of committee will depend on the residential pattern in the area.) Each of these, operating under the executive committee of the city or borough soviet, is responsible for supervising citizen behavior at home and plays a critical control function in maintaining the Soviet passport regime by keeping records of those living in the area and checking to ensure that the papers of all residents are in order.

Self-administration also provides important community services. The neighborhood, street, and house committees are responsible for mobilizing citizen energies to implement some of the policies of the local government, such as *Subbotniki* to clean and repair local facilities. Each also may organize a network of councils to provide libraries, child care centers, repair brigades, and other community services. By mobilizing volunteer energies, this citizen participation in implementation expands the capabilities of the overtaxed state and Party administrations. Soviet surveys suggest that on average a Soviet adult gives between two to four hours per month in such volunteer activity, amounting to about 18 million man-hours per day in volunteer labor for socially useful projects.[27] This participation also continues socialization in *kollektivnost'* as well as legitimating the polity through democratic-appearing involvement of citizens in output processes. Through the close daily contacts with citizens, these institutions of self-administration can also be lines for communicating information about local problems to higher authorities.

AUTONOMOUS PARTICIPATION

Not all citizen participation in the Soviet Union is mobilized through official channels. Some is spontaneous or autonomous, and not all of this is welcomed by the Soviet authorities. To explain the objectives of such autonomous participation, Columbia University's Seweryn Bialer suggests a distinction between "high politics" and "low politics" in the Soviet Union. "The former involves the principal political issues of society, the abstract ideas and language of politics, the decisions and actions of the societal leadership. The latter involves the decisions that directly touch the citizen's daily life, the communal matters, and the conditions of the workplace."[28] The average citizen, he argues, is indifferent to the former. Conversely, " 'low politics' constitute the very substance of the Soviet system of political participation." Although Soviet citizens do not consciously attempt to affect high politics, low politics may impinge on this. Of the two forms of participation considered in this section, the first, particularized contacts, involves low politics. The second, dissent, involves high politics. The different responses of the Soviet regime to these two forms of participation suggest an important operational principle of the Soviet polity: Autonomous participation is more likely to succeed if it is individual rather than collective and if it involves low politics rather than high.[29]

Particularized Contacts

A surprisingly large number of individual Soviet citizens contact local or national authorities with personal problems—they are actually encouraged to bring these to the appropriate individuals. If the complaint points up a larger social concern, it may highlight an impending problem to which the regime will want to attend. If it is a report of mismanagement by an individual bureaucrat or organization, it may draw the attention of higher officials to some administrator guilty of malfeasance or misfeasance. Most of the particularized contacts, however, are individual problems of no larger importance than a missing pension check or housing that needs repair.

Particularized contacts seem to be fairly common. The most frequent of these appear to be letters to the media. In 1984, for example, *Pravda* reported receiving 600,000 letters to the editor; the Central Television Authority 1.2 million letters; and all-union broadcasters 552,383 letters. A Soviet study of papers in Leningrad reveals that up to half of the letters received by a newspaper are simply expressions of gratitude for services or favors. Many are requests for information. But the remainder tend to be complaints, the bulk of which appear to address problems of housing, public transportation, services, and the retail trade. Most Soviet newspapers print a section of "Letters from Workers," in which selected letters appear. The letters selected for publication seem to be more representative of official than public concerns. And those addressing the most sensitive subjects are withheld from publication. Gayle Durham Hollander reports that in a sample of letters published in *Izvestia* and *Zaria Vostoka (Dawn of the East,* the Party paper for the Georgian SSR), almost three-quarters (73.6 percent) were negative in tone; only 8 percent were positive. Among the former, the most common topic was "economic management and bureaucracy" (26.4 percent of all letters), followed by the "technical development of society" and "public services" (each 10.3 percent), and then by "consumer products" and "cultural facilities" (6.9 percent each).[30]

The Party takes this source of information seriously. For example, a 1967 Central Committee Resolution ("On Improving the Work of Investigating Letters from Working People and Arranging Interviews for Them") required newspapers to take an active role in solving the problems that gave rise to the letters. Each newspaper appears to handle this responsibility a little differently. The letter department at *Pravda* employs about 45 people who not only prepare letters for publication, but also seek to facilitate contact between the citizens writing letters and the administrators who can help solve the problems. (A 1968 Presidium decision makes it mandatory that public agencies respond to letters from citizens forwarded by newspapers and that they resolve each problem within 15 days.) The administrators have an incentive to respond to these complaints, for failure to respond can bring a newspaper exposé or official investigation of wrongdoing. The staff of *Pravda* also compiles lists of complaints from letters and sends these to the staffs of the Central Committee Secretariat and Politburo in order to keep them informed of public concerns. Since it is easier to deal with problems mentioned in individual letters before they become sources of individual or collective disaffection, this primitive form of public opinion polling provides a useful safety valve as well as an independent check on the activities of lower-level bureaucrats.[31]

Citizens also contact public officials directly. A majority of these contacts too apparently concern individual pension and housing problems. A citizen's deputy to a local Soviet is often the first point of contact. The deputy can help the citizen make application to the appropriate administration or issue a certificate (*spravka*) attesting to the validity of the citizen's request, requiring an official or department to respond. Citizens may also go directly to individual administrators or to the executive committee of the local soviet. If the citizen feels the administrators have failed to resolve the problem, he or she can also approach the local Party authorities to request their intercession on the citizen's behalf or to the Procurator, who is charged with prosecuting malfeasance in office. Such citizen appeals to the authorities, and particularly to administrators, appear to be common. One oblast committee in 1959, for example, reported that it had received 7815 written complaints and 1561 office visits from its citizens in one year. In the Kirov district of Moscow, with a population of about a quarter million, the borough Soviet received applications in the first part of 1962 at an annual rate of 34,000.[32]

Wayne DiFranceisco and Zvi Gitelman of the University of Michigan, based on their interviews with 1161 ex-Soviet emigrés in the West, contend that this form of participation is prevalent in the Soviet Union. They argue "that the question of policy-making is a foregone conclusion to the great majority of Soviet people, and that the more important question to them is, 'How is policy *implemented?*'" The Soviet citizen does not expect laws to be applied equally to all citizens nor does he or she expect always to receive fair treatment from the Soviet authorities. But "he takes matters into his own hands when he is convinced that the routine workings of the system will not automatically confer upon him the benefits he desires." The less-educated citizens tend to favor bribery in the form of gifts to bureaucrats; the more-educated, to rely on pull (*blat*) and connections (*znakomstvo, protektsiia,* and *sviazy)*. All citizens tailor their strategies to the administration with which they must deal, relying more heavily on the strategies described above when dealing with administrations they perceive to be responsive to particularistic appeals (this excludes the military, for example) and with those dispensing scarce outputs (e.g., housing, university admissions). DiFranceisco and Gitelman describe this form of participation as "working the output side."[33]

The existence of this autonomous participation has profound implications for our understanding of the Soviet political culture. In Gabriel Almond and Sidney Verba's original study of the *Civic Culture,* they argue that the participatory modes in a society are an expression of its political culture. Frederick C. Barghoorn, using the nomenclature of Almond and Verba, describes the Soviet political culture as "subject-participatory." This "denotes the relationship among Soviet citizens of subordination to superiors in one or more bureaucratic chains of command and the obligation of all citizens to do their best to assure the performance by the collective to which they belong of its prescribed goals and objectives."[34] This interpretation is supported by studies of emigrés that reveal "a feeling of powerlessness in relation to the political authorities" (low political competence).[35] DiFranceisco and Gitelman, for example, found that less than 7 percent of the emigrés they interviewed felt it was possible to do something about an "unjust local law." Nonetheless, their study finds the Soviet citizen not to be a classic "subject" but what they call a "covert-participant." The Soviet citizen "participates in (or more precisely, attempts to manipulate) the implementation process in which institutions he can, utilizing a varied repertoire of assertive, creative, and illegal methods to secure his welfare from the extensive Soviet public sector." That is, as a consequence of the "covert-participant" political culture, Soviets do participate spontaneously, not through the official shadow dance of democracy, but by "working the output side" through particularized contacts.[36]

Much of this particularized contact by individual citizens has been denounced in official Soviet statements and in the writings of Soviet dissidents and Western journalists as corruption. If we use Joseph Nye's definition that "corruption is behavior which deviates from the formal duties of a public role because of private-regarding . . . pecuniary or status gains," then the Soviet administrator who succumbs to *blat* or *znakomstvo* in allocating scarce state outputs is corrupt. Yet, studies of corruption in developing societies have pointed out that this form of corruption may, in fact, be beneficial for an oligarchic regime facing democratic pressures. In particular, through its ability to respond to immediate, particularistic needs, the Soviet regime can enhance its legitimacy within a transitional population. Moreover, such responsiveness may also encourage Soviet citizens not to perceive their problems in collective terms requiring group political action.[37]

Dissent

The other major form of spontaneous participation with the intent of changing political outcomes is dissent. Rudolf L. Tokes, a political scientist at the University of Connecticut, has defined contemporary Soviet dissent as

a culturally conditioned political reform movement seeking to ameliorate and ultimately to eliminate the perceived illegitimacy of the post-totalitarian Communist-party leadership's authoritarian rule . . . through (1) structural, administrative, and political reforms; (2) ideological purification and cultural modernization; and (3) the replacement of scientifically unverifiable normative referents with empirical (nonideological) criteria as political guidelines and developmental success indicators.[38]

Dissent differs from particularized contacts because it does not seek individual material benefits, but collective nonmaterial benefits through social change—policies that are normally reserved to high politics. This difference in objective explains the very different response of the Soviet authorities.

The Soviets themselves distinguish dissent (*inakomyslie*), a term used by some Soviet authors to describe their own positions, from opposition (*oppozitsiia*), the "crime" of individuals like Leon Trotsky. The latter implies an aspiration to rule in place of the current leaders; the former does not. Dissent is the articulation of programs for reform. Soviet laws and punishments reflect this distinction: Articles 70 and 72 of the RSFSR Criminal Code address opposition (subversion, crimes against the state), prescribing severe punishment for this (imprisonment up to seven years and exile up to five). Article 190 addresses dissent, establishing less severe penalties (up to three years imprisonment or five years exile) for such acts as

> [possession or propagation of] deliberate fabrications [either written or oral], known to be false, which defame the Soviet regime and social system [or] the organization of, and likewise, the active participation in group actions which violate public order in a coarse manner or which are attended by clear disobedience of the legal demands of representatives of authority or which entail the violation of the work on transport of state and social institutions or enterprises.[39]

Although Soviet dissent is as old as the regime, the contemporary movement is the product of de-Stalinization. Until 1956, dissent was largely limited to conspiratorial underground circles among university students, the European non-Russian nationalities, religious sects, and prison camp inmates. Following Khrushchev's Secret Speech to the 20th Congress of the CPSU, however, dissent became increasingly open, creating a growing awareness of common purposes among previously isolated dissenters and drawing in an expanding circle of followers. From the mid-1950s until 1965, the most visible elements of this movement were writers who sought to distribute their works critical of past Soviet policies. The publication of Vladimir Dudintsev's novel *Not by Bread Alone* and Ilya Ehrenburg's *The Thaw* had an electrifying effect in the Soviet literary community and inspired an even more radical critique of Soviet policies in the works of Yosif Brodsky, Yuli Daniel, Andrei Sinyavsky, and Alexander Solzhenitsyn.

The movement underwent a dramatic change in 1965: As the Soviet authorities began to crack down on some prominent dissenters, the movement reacted with greater organization and activity and a growing commonality of purpose. The catalyst for this was the arrest in September of Sinyavsky and Daniel for arranging to have some of their works published in the West under the pseudonyms Abram Tertz and Nikolai Arzhak. In February 1966, they were tried under the articles of the RSFSR Criminal Code, triggering a wave of protest that began with a demonstration in Moscow's Pushkin Square on December 5, 1965, Constitution Day, under the slogan "Respect the Soviet Constitution!" The next years saw growing protest and demonstration activity as well as a flowering of underground publication, capped by the appearance in 1968 of the *Chroni-*

cle of Current Events. They also saw new organization in the movement, marked by the founding in 1969 of the Initiative Group To Defend Human Rights in the USSR and in 1970 of the Moscow Human Rights Committee.

The Soviet authorities have attempted to silence these dissidents or at least to dissolve their tenuous organizational ties and atomize the movement. And from 1970 to the mid-1980s, three waves of repressive measures successfully reduced dissident activity in the Soviet Union. In December 1971, the Politburo initiated the first of these campaigns, having apparently decided to close the *Chronicle of Current Events* and the affiliated *Ukrainian Herald.* The next year the KGB began a campaign of arrest and harassment, including surveillance and telephone taps, against those who had created and sustained the journals. For some there was expulsion: Valerii Chalidze of the Moscow Human Rights Committee was deprived of his Soviet citizenship while on a lecture tour of the United States in 1972, and Solzhenitsyn was arrested and deported in early 1974. The purpose of the attack on the *Chronicle* was apparently to break the growing coordination among groups that was made possible through this journal; but, instead, the attack produced vocal protest from Solzhenitsyn and Andrei Sakharov, an unexpected wave of demonstrations in the West, and pressure from the United States Congress. The KGB was forced to relax its pressure, and the *Chronicle* survived. Indeed, under the influence of the human rights provisions (Basket III) of the 1975 Helsinki Accords, the next years saw a rise in activity with the founding of the Moscow Helsinki Watch Group in 1976 (followed by similar groups in the Ukraine, Lithuania, Georgia, and Armenia), and a rise in protests and demonstrations.[40]

A second wave of repression was marked by the forced emigration of Andrei Amalrik and Vladimir Bukovsky in 1976. In December of that year, the KGB began arresting the founders of the Helsinki Watch groups. And in 1977, the Soviet authorities began to tighten the legal framework used against the dissenters, by strengthening laws on parasitism to be used against dissidents dismissed from their jobs, by expanding legal controls over printing and duplicating equipment, and by introducing new provisions for deprivation of citizenship. The hands of the Soviet authorities were stayed somewhat, however, by their continued concern to salvage a slowly unraveling détente relationship with the United States: Even though the arrests of such human rights activists as Yuri Orlov and Alexander Ginzburg were followed by heavy sentences, the Soviet regime showed increasing willingness to release imprisoned dissidents to the West.[41]

The third wave of repression began around the time of the Soviet invasion of Afghanistan in December 1979, the Western boycott of the 1980 Moscow Olympics, and the collapse of détente. The KGB focused its activity against the leadership of the dissident organizations so as to atomize the larger movement: Andrei Sakharov was removed from Moscow and exiled to Gorky in 1980. And the Moscow Helsinki Watch Group was eliminated in 1982. Punishment of dissenters increased so that there were about 200 known arrests per year, accompanied by increased physical violence against the arrested, lengthened sentences for the convicted, and expanded use of psychiatric facilities to isolate them. To break the ties of dissidents with the West, the authorities granted fewer requests for emi-

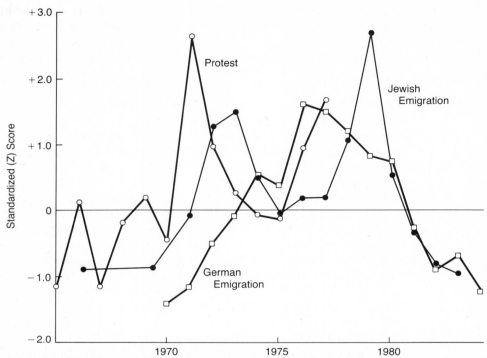

Figure 5.1 The Soviet Dissent Movement, 1965–1984. Figure charts fluctuation of protest activity in the Soviet Union, levels of Jewish emigration from the Soviet Union, and Soviet German emigrants to the Federal Republic of Germany. (Estimate of protest based on David Kowalewski, "Trends in the Human Rights Movement" in D.R. Kelley, ed. *Soviet Politics in the Brezhnev Era* [New York: Praeger, 1980], 150–181.)

gration, restricted overseas telephone circuits, and stepped up jamming of some foreign radio broadcasts. The cumulative effect of arrests, deportations, emigration, and a tightened legal regime was a decline in public dissent. By the mid-1980s, while the *Chronicle of Current Events* continued to appear sporadically, most of the organized groups had been broken or forced to go underground.[42]

The policy of openness (*glasnost'*) inaugurated by Gorbachev in the mid-1980s may signal a relaxation of this repression. Personnel changes in both the Ministry of Culture and the Central Committee's Culture Department have come as greater freedom of expression is tolerated in film and literature. Works released since 1986 have touched on such sensitive topics as Stalinism, collectivization, and drug addiction. Literary figures such as the poet Nikolai Gumilev have been rehabilitated, the abstract art of Vasily Kandinsky displayed publically, and the publication of Boris Pasternak's *Doctor Zhivago* promised. The release of Yuri Orlov to the West and the return of Andrei Sakharov to Moscow may be first steps in a return to the minimal levels of tolerance for dissident activity that had characterized the 1970s. By February 1987, over 140 political prisoners had been released, with a promise of further releases and a review of Article 70 of the RSFSR Criminal Code under which many had been arrested. (Restrictions on emigration also seem to have been eased with the publication in January 1987 of the previously secret emigration restrictions; and while only 914 exit visas were issued to Soviet Jews in all of 1986, over 600 were issued in the first three months of 1987 alone.) Still, it will require a wider official tolerance of spontaneous activity before the dissident movement regains its former vitality.

Despite the activism and high visibility of some within the movement, Soviet dissent throughout its history has remained fragmented organizationally and divided in its programs. Tokes identifies seven "issue areas" during the peak of activity between 1965 and 1971: (1) political democracy, (2) nationality rights, (3) human rights-socialist legality, (4) rationality [empirical rather than ideological approaches] in economics and research, (5) religious autonomy, (6) quality of life, and (7) artistic freedoms.[43] Not all constituent groups within the movement shared identical views on these issues.

Some of the earliest and most intense movements of dissent were those among non-Russian nationalities. Dating from the early years of de-Stalinization are the movements among the nationalities removed from their homelands during World War II and not permitted to return after Stalin's death—the Crimean Tatars, Volga Germans, and Meskhi of southern Georgia. In the 1960s, the Crimean Tatars reportedly collected petitions with over 3 million signatures, demanding their return to the Crimea. With continued denial of their petitions, all three nationalities turned to more active protest; and many of the Volga Germans and Meskhi upped their demands by seeking to emigrate to West Germany and Turkey, respectively. The national movement with the greatest visibility in the West has been that among Soviet Jews, many of whom, like the Volga Germans and Meskhi, have pressed for the right to emigrate.

Among the Soviet populations that reside within their traditional homelands, the national movements have been proportionately weaker (relative to their total populations). Reports of sporadic unrest in areas such as Yakutia, Turkmenistan, and Kazakhstan have reached the West in recent years. Yet, the strongest of the organized national movements appear to be found in the Ukraine and Lithuania. In the former, intellectual ferment among the Ukrainian intelligentsia has reflected the human rights movement in Moscow as well as expressing Ukrainian resentment of Russification. In Lithuania the national movement focuses on the Roman Catholic Church. Recurrent unrest has peaked in demonstrations and riots: In May, 1972, two days of riots in Kaunas followed the self-immolation by a student protesting religious and national persecution. And in October 1977, crowds in Vilnius turned a celebration of victory over a Russian soccer team into a demonstration, shouting "Freedom to Lithuania!" and "Russians, go home!" The Lithuanian movement is one of the few to survive the latest wave of repression.[44]

Religious dissenters have also been part of the movement, protesting the intrusion of the Soviet state into the affairs of their churches and official restrictions on religious practice. This protest has been most fully organized among the Lithuanian Catholics and the evangelical Christians. In 1965, Baptists, rejecting the leadership of the official All-Union Council of Evangelical Christian Baptists, created an independent Council of Churches of the Evangelical Christian Baptists and began an ambitious program of proselytizing, against the proscriptions of Soviet law. The less numerous Pentecostalists have also sought to organize independent congregations, but have focused much of their effort on appeals to emigrate to the West.[45]

The movements of dissent that are sometimes called "mainstream" dissent, because they do not represent the particularistic demands of an ethnic or religious group, actually represent a wide range of political positions. Peter Reddaway has distinguished three major intellectual tendencies: Neo-Leninists and Neo-Marxists, such as Roy Medvedev, seek to return the Party to true Leninism. Liberals and humanitarians (e.g., Sakharov) espouse a wide spectrum of views from liberal socialism or reformism to apolitical humanitarianism in defense of the persecuted. Liberal Russian nationalists (e.g., Solzhenitsyn), sometimes in the form of Slavophilism, advocate "moral regeneration of the Russian nation and the rebirth of Russian culture." These diverse movements coalesced in the 1970s into what has been broadly referred to as the "human rights movement."[46]

The means employed by dissenters are as diverse as their objectives. Statements by prominent individuals, such as Solzhenitsyn's 1967 letter to the USSR Union of Writers denouncing censorship, as well as collective petitions such as those circulated by the Crimean Tatars, have publicized the views of dissenters. Demonstrations, such as the protest in Red Square against the Soviet invasion of Czechoslovakia in 1968, and riots, such as the anti-Russian protests in Lithuania, have expressed collective outrage. More violent protesters have even turned to such means as hijackings by Jews seeking immediate emigration. A bombing in the Moscow subway in 1977 killed 7 and injured 37. Bombings and arson of public buildings and military depots in the Georgian SSR were designed to protest Russification and persecution of the Georgian Orthodox Church. And over a dozen self-immolations in Lithuania have protested persecution of the Catholic Church. [47]

The most common means of dissent has been the underground press, or *samizdat* (literally, "self-published"). The techniques of samizdat vary with the technology available to the dissenters. For many it has meant typing manuscripts with four or five carbons, distributing these to friends who read them and sometimes copy them again and then pass them along to other friends. In rare instances an author may have access to a duplicating machine in an office; and some of the more successful undertakings have even had small printing presses. (A police raid in the mid-1970s near Tsesis, Latvia turned up a Baptist "Christian Publishing House" that had printed 200,000 Bibles in various languages. The police reported finding 16 tons of paper along with the press![48]) In the early days of the contemporary movement, the technique of samizdat was used extensively by the Crimean Tatars, Lithuanians, and Baptists. The first samizdat journal appeared in 1959 and 1960 with Alexander Ginzburg's *Syntax,* which succeeded in publishing three issues of uncensored poetry and literature. As the technique of samizdat spread, it became increasingly politicized with essays on current events, memoirs of former prison camp inmates, as well as theoretical discussions of politics and economics. Reddaway summarizes the contents of the most successful samizdat journal, *Chronicle of Current Events:*

> the judicial or extra-judicial persecution of individuals for expression of their views; the severe conditions in the labor camps and mental hospitals used to imprison dissenters; the persecution of minority nationalities and religious believers; the activities of the censorship and a few other oppressive institutions; and reactions to the dissenter's situation in the outside world.[49]

The growing sophistication of samizdat spawned more advanced underground techniques, including *tamizdat,* works published overseas and smuggled back into the Soviet Union; *magnitizdat,* or underground tapes; *samefir,* or underground radio broadcasts; and *kinizdat,* or underground films. Nonetheless, *samizdat* has largely been a slow and inefficient mechanism for spreading dissenting views. For example, Roy Medvedev's monthly articles, published as the journal *A Political Diary,* were read regularly by only about 40 people.

Although samizdat has been the most important activity of the Soviet movement of dissent, not all dissent has been underground. At times the Soviet authorities have tolerated publication of moderately dissenting views. For example, Nikita Khrushchev permitted the publication of Alexander Solzhenitsyn's *One Day in the Life of Ivan Denisovich* in 1962. The longest record of this "permitted dissent" is the journal *Novyi Mir* (New World), published by the USSR Union of Writers. This journal printed essays, poems, and short novels that often criticized official policies, institutions, and values. *Novyi Mir* survived as a forum for dissent until 1970, both because its editors (particularly Alexander Tvardovsky) astutely excluded the most radical dissenters from its pages so as to avoid repression and because some members of the Party leadership, particularly Nikita Khrushchev, found the journal useful in internal leadership conflicts.[50]

The Soviet dissent that has been visible in the West draws its strength principally from the upper reaches of Soviet society. Its membership has been small: In 1975, Reddaway could write that the "mainstream" movement "has so far been supported at various times by only some 2000 people whose names we know"—that is, only about 1 in 100,000 Soviet adults. (The movements of religious and national dissent may be substantially larger; for example, a 1972 memorandum protesting religious persecution drew 17,000 signatures.) The "mainstream" dissenters have been drawn disproportionately from some of the most visible writers and scientists in the Soviet Union, giving them a political importance far beyond their numbers.[51]

Up to 1987, at least, the accomplishments of Soviet dissent, particularly in the area of policy, have been negligible. The exceptions to this have been few: One was the short-term success of the "permitted dissenters" around *Novyi Mir* in staying the hand of the early Brezhnev-Kosygin leadership (at least until 1970) and so preserving the relative independence of their journal. More recently, the Lithuanian Catholic movement has escaped the full force of the repressive wave of the 80s because the authorities fear its reaction. Another has been the success of over 250,000 Soviet Jews who have won the right to emigrate since 1965. Similarly, there have been individual successes in winning the release of imprisoned dissenters.[52] The successes of the Jews and imprisoned dissenters are instructive: *Policy* shifts (leading to significant increases in the volume of emigration) came only through external pressure from the West; in the absence of this, successes came only on an individual basis by citizens "working the output side" for individual rather than collective benefits. For the policy success of the dissent movement to grow, it is imperative that its membership grow and that their organizational ties become stronger. While incomplete evidence suggests the first is taking place with growing disillusionment within the scientific-technical elite, the waves of repressive measures against dissent have set back its growing organization. As will be discussed in the final chapter, even the Soviet dissenters themselves often argue that only a crisis in the Soviet system is likely to bring about significantly greater responsiveness to dissent by the authorities. In short, while the existence of dissent underscores the boundaries of the congruence of Soviet political culture with the institutions of the Bolshevik regime, the limited size of this dissent points up the success of that regime in addressing the crisis of participation that it inherited from the *ancien régime*.

NOTES

1. Samuel P. Huntington, *Political Order in Changing Societies* (New Haven, Conn.: Yale University Press, 1968), 335.
2. Robert S. Sharlet, "Concept Formation in Political Science and Communist Studies: Conceptualizing Political Participation," in Frederic J. Fleron, Jr., ed., *Communist Studies and the Social Sciences* (Chicago: Rand McNally, 1969), 244–253.
3. D. Richard Little, "Mass Political Participation in the U.S. and the U.S.S.R.: A Conceptual Analysis," *Comparative Political Studies* 8 (January 1976), 437–460. See also Theodore H. Friedgut, "Community Structure, Political Participation, and Soviet Local Government: The Case of Kutaisi," in Henry W. Morton and Rudolf L. Tokes, eds., *Soviet Politics and Society in the Seventies* (New York: Free Press, 1974), 261–296; Jerry F. Hough, "Political Participation in the Soviet Union," *Soviet Studies* 28 (January 1976), 3–20; Theodore H. Friedgut, "Citizens and Soviets: Can Ivan Ivanovich Fight City Hall?" *Comparative Politics* 10 (July 1978), 461–477; and Jan S. Adams, "Citizen Participation in Community Decisions in the USSR," in Peter J. Potichnyi and Jane Shapiro Zacek, eds., *Politics and Participation under Communist Rule* (New York: Praeger, 1983), 178–195.
4. Jerry F. Hough and Merle Fainsod, *How the Soviet Union Is Governed* (Cambridge, Mass: Harvard University Press, 1979), 305–314.
5. Howard R. Swearer, "The Function of Soviet Local Elections," *Midwestern Journal of Political Science* 5 (May 1961), 129–149; Howard Swearer, "Popular Participation: Myths and Realities," *Problems of Communism* 9 (September-October 1960), 42–51; Everett M. Jacobs, "What Soviet Elections Are, and What They Are Not," *Soviet Studies* 22 (July 1970), 61–76.
6. Cyril E. Black, "Soviet Political Life Today," *Foreign Affairs* 36 (July 1958), 575–576. See also Victor Zaslavsky and Robert J. Brym, "The Functions of Elections in the USSR," *Soviet Studies* 30 (July 1978), 362–371.
7. *Pravda,* 2 March 1985. Ronald J. Hill, "Continuity and Change in USSR Supreme Soviet Elections," *British Journal of Political Science* 2 (1972), 47–67.

8. *Komentarii k zakonu o vyborakh v Verkhovnyi Soviet SSSR* (Moscow, 1983); V. K. Grigor'ev and V. P. Zhdanov, *Vybory v Verkhovnye sovety soiuznykh, avtonomnykh respublik, v mestnykh sovety narodnykh deputatov i poriadok ikh provedeniia* (Moscow: Iuridicheskaia literatura, 1980); V. K. Grigor'ev and V. P. Zhdanov, *Vybory v mestnye sovety narodnykh deputatov i poriadok ikh provedeniia* (Moscow: Iuridicheskaia literatura, 1982).
9. Theodore H. Friedgut, *Political Participation in the USSR* (Princeton, N.J.: Princeton University Press, 1979), 111–113.
10. *Pravda,* 2 March 1985.
11. *Komentarii k zakonu,* 37, 86, 88–89.
12. Jerome Gilison, "Soviet Elections as a Measure of Dissent: The Missing One Per Cent," *American Political Science Review* 66 (September 1968), 817.
13. Friedgut, 114–115.
14. Friedgut, 116–130; Philip G. Roeder, "Dissent and Electoral Avoidance in the Soviet Union" (Paper presented at the Annual Meeting of the American Political Science Association, New Orleans, Louisiana, 29 August–1 September 1985).
15. *Pravda*, 2 March 1985.
16. Friedgut, 81–94; Alexander Rahr and Elizabeth Teague, "Supreme Soviet Nominations Indicate Kremlin Pecking Order," *Radio Liberty Research Bulletin* RL 72/84 (February 8, 1984). See also Ronald J. Hill, "Patterns of Deputy Selection to Local Soviets," *Soviet Studies* 25 (October 1973), 196–212.
17. Max E. Mote, *Soviet Local and Republican Elections* (Stanford, Calif.: Hoover Institution, 1965), 32–40.
18. Mote, 57, 63.
19. Friedgut, 95–108. See also Ronald J. Hill, "The CPSU in a Soviet Election Campaign," *Soviet Studies* 28 (October 1976), 590–598.
20. *Ezhegodnik Bol'shoi Sovetskoi Entsiklopedii, 1985* (Moscow: Sovetskaia Entsiklopediia, 1985), 17; U. S. Central Intelligence Agency, *Directory of Soviet Officials: National Organizations* (Washington, D.C.: Central Intelligence Agency, November 1984), 247–252; Hough and Fainsod, 399.
21. Blair A. Ruble, *Soviet Trade Unions: Their Development in the 1970s* (Cambridge, England: Cambridge University Press, 1981), 45–118; "The Educational Role of Soviet Trade Unions," *Soviet Education* 26 (December 1983).
22. U. S. Central Intelligence Agency, 257–261.
23. *Ezhegodnik Bol'shoi Sovetskoi Entsiklopedii, 1985* 23; William E. Odom, "The 'Militarization' of Soviet Society," *Problems of Communism* 25 (September-October 1976), 34–51. On Osoaviakhim, see William E. Odom, *The Soviet Volunteers: Modernization and Bureaucracy in a Public Mass Organization* (Princeton, N.J.: Princeton University Press, 1973). Herbert Goldhamer, *The Soviet Soldier: Soviet Military Management at the Troop Level* (New York: Crane, Russak and Company, 1975), 39–46.
24. Friedgut, 154.
25. Leonid I. Brezhnev, "On the Draft Constitution (Fundamental Law) of the Union of Soviet Socialist Republics and the Results of the Nationwide Discussion of the Draft" (Report and Closing Speech at the Seventh [Special] Session of the Supreme Soviet of the USSR, Ninth Convocation, 4–7 October 1977) (Moscow: Novosti Press Agency Publishing House, 1977).
26. Friedgut, 239. See also A. L. Unger, "Soviet Mass-Political Work in Residential Areas," *Soviet Studies* 22 (April 1971), 556–561.
27. Friedgut, 280.

28. Seweryn Bialer, *Stalin's Successors: Leadership, Stability, and Change in the Soviet Union* (Cambridge, England: Cambridge University Press, 1980), 166.

29. Bialer, 167.

30. CBS News, Inc., *60 Minutes* (Television broadcast of July 29, 1984); *Ezhegodnik Bol'shoi Sovetskoi Entsiklopedii, 1985,* 91; Ellen Mickiewicz, "Political Communication and the Soviet Media System," in Joseph L. Nogee, ed., *Soviet Politics: Russia after Brezhnev* (New York: Praeger, 1985), 45–46; Ellen Propper Mickiewicz, *Media and the Russian Public* (New York: Praeger, 1981), 7–8, 67–68; Mark Hopkins, *Mass Media in the Soviet Union* (New York: Pegasus, 1970), 304–305; Gayle Durham Hollander, *Soviet Political Indoctrination: Developments in Mass Media and Propaganda Since Stalin* (New York: Praeger, 1972), 46.

31. Hollander, 45; Hopkins, 303; Mickiewicz, *Media and the Russian Public,* 46.

32. Friedgut, 183, 225–229.

33. Wayne DiFranceisco and Zvi Gitelman, "Soviet Political Culture and 'Covert Participation' in Policy Implementation," *American Political Science Review* 78 (September 1984), 603, 611.

34. Frederick C. Barghoorn, *Politics in the USSR,* 2d ed. (Boston: Little, Brown and Company, 1972), 23; Gabriel Almond and Sidney Verba, *The Civic Culture* (Boston: Little, Brown and Company, 1965), 1–35.

35. Stephen White, *Political Culture and Soviet Politics* (London: Macmillan Press, 1979), 110.

36. Di Franceisco and Gitelman, 608, 619.

37. Joseph S. Nye, "Corruption and Political Development: A Cost-Benefit Analysis," *American Political Science Review* 61 (June 1967), 419; James C. Scott, *Comparative Political Corruption* (Englewood Cliffs, N.J.: Prentice-Hall, 1972), 145–157. Compare Konstantin M. Simis, *USSR: The Corrupt Society* (New York: Simon and Schuster, 1982); Hedrick Smith, *The Russians,* rev. ed. (New York: Ballantine Books, 1984), 106–134.

38. Rudolf L. Tokes, "Dissent: The Politics for Change in the USSR," in Morton and Tokes, 10. For other efforts to define this phenomenon, see Frederick C. Barghoorn, "Factional, Sectoral, and Subversive Opposition in Soviet Politics," in Robert A. Dahl, ed., *Regimes and Oppositions* (New Haven, Conn.: Yale University Press, 1972); and Peter Reddaway, ed., *Uncensored Russia: Protest and Dissent in the Soviet Union* (New York: American Heritage Press, 1972).

39. Quoted in Peter Reddaway, "The Development of Dissent and Opposition," in Archie Brown and Michael Kaser, eds., *The Soviet Union Since the Fall of Khrushchev* (New York: Free Press, 1975), 124: see also 122–124.

40. For a description of recent events, see Ludmilla Alexeyeva, *Soviet Dissent: Contemporary Movements for National, Religious, and Human Rights* (Middletown, Conn.: Wesleyan University Press, 1985). On the patterns of protest, see David Kowalewski, "Trends in the Human Rights Movement," in Donald R. Kelley, ed., *Soviet Politics in the Brezhnev Era* (New York: Praeger, 1980), 150–181.

41. Peter Reddaway, "Policy Towards Dissent Since Khrushchev," in T. H. Rigby, Archie Brown, and Peter Reddaway, eds., *Authority, Power, and Policy in the USSR* (London: Macmillan Press, 1980), 175.

42. Peter Reddaway, "Dissent in the Soviet Union," *Problems of Communism* 32 (November-December 1983), 10; Julia Wishnevsky, "Dissent Under Three Soviet Leaders: Suppression Continues, The Style Varies," *Radio Liberty Research Bulletin* RL 98/85 (March 21, 1985).

43. Tokes, 15–16.

44. Ann Sheehy, "Racial Disturbances in Yakutsk," *Radio Liberty Research Bulletin* RL 287/86 (July 25, 1986); Alexeyeva, 6, 68–70, 140–144.

45. Michael Bourdeaux, *Opium of the People: The Christian Religion in the U.S.S.R.* (London: Mowbrays, 1977); Gerhard Simon, *Church, State, and Opposition in the U.S.S.R.* (London: C. Hurst and Company, 1974)

46. Tokes, 18–20; Reddaway, "The Development of Dissent and Opposition", 128–131. See also Donald R. Kelley, *The Solzhenitsyn-Sakharov Dialogue: Politics, Society, and the Future* (Westport, Conn.: Greenwood Press, 1982).

47. Kowalewski, 157; Julia Wishnevsky,"A History of Recent Self-Immolations in the USSR," *Radio Liberty Research Bulletin* RL 74/77 (March 29, 1977); Ann Sheehy, "Three Executed for Moscow Metro Bombing," *Radio Liberty Research Bulletin* RL 44/79 (February 12, 1979); "Hijacker Stripped of Soviet Citizenship," *Radio Liberty Research Bulletin* RL 108/80 (March 10, 1980).

48. Kowalewski, 156.

49. Reddaway, "The Development of Dissent and Opposition", 127; Alexeyeva, 14.

50. Dina R. Spechler, *Permitted Dissent in the USSR: Novy Mir and the Soviet Regime* (New York: Praeger, 1982), xv–xvi, 248–258.

51. Reddaway, "The Development of Dissent and Opposition", 128; Barbara Wolfe Jancar, "Religious Dissent in the Soviet Union," in Rudolf L. Tokes, ed., *Dissent in the USSR: Politics, Ideology, and People* (Baltimore, Md.: Johns Hopkins University Press, 1975), 191.

52. Spechler, 248–264; Reddaway, "Dissent in the Soviet Union", 1–15; U.S. Senate. *Dangerous Stalemate: Superpower Relations in Autumn 1983* (Report of Study Mission led by Claiborne Pell) (Washington, D.C.: Government Printing Office, 1983), 44–45.

three

DECISION-MAKING
INSTITUTIONS
AND PROCESSES

N. I. Ryzhkov, Chairman of the USSR Council of Ministers, delivered a report to the 27th CPSU Congress on "The Guidelines of the Economic and Social Development of the USSR in 1986–1990 and for the Period up to 2000."

At the heart of the Soviet model of development is the institutionalization of politics in a participatory society. As Samuel P. Huntington has observed, "Not revolution and the destruction of established institutions, but organization and the creation of new political institutions are the peculiar contributions of communist movements to modern politics. The political function of communism is not to overthrow authority but to fill the vacuum of authority."[1] The new Bolshevik regime seized power in revolutionary circumstances in which new social forces had been recently mobilized into politics and the collapse of the old order had created a political vacuum. The Bolshevik response to this revolutionary situation constitutes the crux of the Soviet model of development: A revolutionary elite constituted as the Communist Party leads the larger population along its path of historic transformation through a structurally separate state. This elite incorporates a complex society into this state through elaborate institutions characterized by apparent diversity but practical uniformity.

The success of the Leninist polity is manifest in the stability of these political institutions, which have adapted to changing political generations and to changing political tasks. Despite the radical transformation of Soviet society, they have remained relatively unchanged in their broad outline. Thus, the Soviet Union has gained that rarest of political accomplishments—stable institutional structures in the face of changing political processes.

The next four chapters examine these structures and processes. The first two describe the all-union institutions of state and Party; the third, the institutions of subordinate levels of authority. In the last, we turn to the more problematic issue of the changing political processes within these institutions.

FOR FURTHER READING

For those students who wish to read further on the topics covered in the next four chapters, the following works may be particularly useful.

Brzezinski, Zbigniew K. 1962. *Ideology and Power in Soviet Politics.* New York: Praeger.

Brzezinski, Zbigniew K., and Samuel P. Huntington. 1964. *Political Power: USA/USSR.* New York: Viking Press.

Fainsod, Merle. 1967. *How Russia Is Ruled,* rev. ed. Cambridge, Mass.: Harvard University Press.

Friedrich, Carl J., and Zbigniew K. Brzezinski. 1965. *Totalitarian Dictatorship and Autocracy,* rev. ed. Cambridge, Mass.: Harvard University Press.

Hill, Ronald J., and Peter Frank. 1981. *The Soviet Communist Party.* London: Allen & Unwin.

Hough, Jerry F. 1969. *The Soviet Prefects.* Cambridge, Mass.: Harvard University Press.

Hough, Jerry F., and Merle Fainsod. 1979. *How the Soviet Union Is Governed.* Cambridge, Mass.: Harvard University Press.

Linden, Carl A. 1966. *Khrushchev and the Soviet Leadership, 1957–1964.* Baltimore, Md.: Johns Hopkins University Press.

Lowenhardt, John. 1983. *The Soviet Politburo.* Edinburgh: Canongate.

Rigby, T. H. 1968. *Communist Party Membership in the U.S.S.R., 1917–1967.* Princeton, N.J.: Princeton University Press.

Rush, Myron. 1968. *Political Succession in the USSR,* 2d ed. New York: Columbia University Press.

Skilling, H. Gordon, and Franklyn Griffiths, eds. 1971. *Interest Groups in Soviet Politics.* Princeton, N.J.: Princeton University Press.

Taubman, William. 1973. *Governing Soviet Cities: Bureaucratic Politics and Urban Development in the USSR.* New York: Praeger.

Unger, Aryeh L. 1981. *Constitutional Development in the USSR: A Guide to the Soviet Constitutions.* London: Methuen and Co.

Vanneman, Peter. 1977. *The Supreme Soviet: Politics and the Legislative Process in the Soviet Political System.* Durham, N.C.: Duke University Press.

NOTES

1. Samuel P. Huntington, *Political Order in Changing Societies* (New Haven, Conn.: Yale University Press, 1968), 335.

chapter 6

The Throne Before the Power: The Soviet State

Soviet political institutions resemble those of Western democracies. A constitution defines the powers of the state and limits these with guaranteed rights for the citizens. The institutions of the state are organized like those of a parliamentary democracy. Federalism divides powers between center and periphery. And the state and ruling party are structurally distinct.

In fact, the reality of Soviet politics is very different. While in all political systems there is a disparity and often a tension between constitutional prescription and actual practice, in the Soviet system this is extreme. When discussing the Soviet system, it is important to keep in mind that practice often diverges markedly from what is prescribed in the Constitution. In particular, behind all of the institutions described in this chapter, and reserving to itself the ultimate power to decide all issues it chooses, is the Communist Party of the Soviet Union. Nonetheless, the state institutions are not simply facades for the Party, for some do play an important role in the formulation and implementation of policy.

THE CONSTITUTION

The fundamental law of the Soviet Union, purportedly the basis for all other legislation, is the Constitution of the USSR. Sixty years after the Revolution, Brezhnev heralded "the adoption of the Soviet Union's new Constitution as one of the major events in the life of the Soviet people" and asserted that "the new Constitution is justly called the law of life of developed socialist society." Brezhnev went on to claim that Lenin himself had regarded the Soviet constitution as "a major political document."[1] In fact, contrary to Brezhnev's assertions, Soviet ideas about constitutionalism and the role of a constitution have undergone a profound metamorphosis since the October Revolution. Lenin himself changed from a contemptuous rejection of constitutions as artifacts of bourgeois democracy to a grudging acceptance of the need for such a document in the Soviet Union during the transitional period before the state withered away. It is revealing that Lenin accorded the constitution such limited significance that he did not even sit on the commission that drafted the first fundamental law, but delegated much of the Party's authority in this matter to Iakov Sverdlov and Joseph Stalin.

The present Constitution, adopted on October 7, 1977, at the Seventh (Special) Session of the Ninth Supreme Soviet, is the Soviet state's fourth. The first, the Constitution of the Russian Soviet Federated Socialist Republic adopted on July 10, 1918, was to be a temporary document for the transition period as classes were abolished and the state began to wither away. This fundamental law was drafted not as an independent limitation on the state, but simply as a record of the institutional accomplishments of the regime in its first eight months. Following the formation of the USSR in December 1922, this document was superseded by a new Constitution of the USSR, promulgated by the Second Congress of Soviets on January 31, 1924. While this second fundamental law maintained much of the strident rhetoric of revolutionary proletarian dictatorship contained in the first, it was also marked by a growing resignation to the permanence or at least longevity of the Soviet state with more thoughtful attention to institutions, particularly to the federal structure of the Soviet Union. On December 5, 1936, as the Great Purges were reaching their crescendo, the Soviet Union adopted a third Constitution, one that Stalin would describe as "the only thoroughly democratic constitution in the world." The officially announced occasion for the adoption of the new Constitution was the victory of socialism in the Soviet Union; but the actual motivation may have been to paper over the barbarity of the Purges and to mollify the Western democracies with whom the Soviet Union sought common cause against the growing aggressiveness of Germany and Japan. The document itself, sometimes called the "Stalin Constitution," was a more traditional constitution than its predecessors, bearing a strong resemblance in both style and content to the bourgeois constitutions that the Soviets had so maligned in previous years. In particular, it expanded the civil rights guaranteed citizens, eliminated certain class-based discriminations against the now-extinct bourgeoisie, the clergy, and the peasantry, and introduced universal, direct, and secret elections.[2]

Despite the rapid succession of constitutions, significant strands of continuity run throughout Soviet constitutional history. All Soviet constitutions fix Marxism-Leninism as the official ideology of the state. All proclaim popular sovereignty based on the working population and expressed through representative democracy as the foundation of the Soviet state. The Soviet constitutions reject separation of powers among the branches of government for a fusion of power under the supremacy of the soviets. All establish an elaborate federal structure reflecting the complex ethnic composition of the Soviet population. The Soviet constitutions establish "bills of rights," but subordinate these to the interests of a society building socialism and condition these on the duties of each citizen. And in all there is an absence of institutional remedies for unconstitutional or extraconstitutional actions by the state.

Constitutions normally perform three functions in political systems: They provide information about the political values and aspirations of a regime; they make explicit its institutional structure; and they define and limit the powers of each institution as well as the regime as a whole. The Soviet Constitution in no significant way performs the last of these functions. For example, when dissenters have argued that the Constitutional guarantees of free speech and assembly protect them against state prosecution, Soviet courts have refused to consider this argument. The Soviet Constitution does, however, sketch the institutional structure of the Soviet state (the second function); and even though the reality of Soviet politics deviates markedly from the principles of socialist democracy, the Constitution, if read properly, can give some clues to the true distribution of power in the Soviet polity. In particular, Article 6 of the Constitution makes it clear that the Party plays a "leading and guiding" role and is responsible for the direction of policy. The Constitution is most accurate when read as a normative document, propounding the official dogmas and aspirations of the regime.[3]

The Constitution of 1977, sometimes called the "Brezhnev Constitution," stretches for 174 articles, grouped in 21 chapters and 9 parts (see Table 6.1). The official normative foundations of the Soviet state are set out in the Preamble and Part I of the Constitution. The rights and duties of the Soviet citizen are detailed in Part II. At the heart of this document, Parts III to VIII describe Soviet governmental institutions and procedures; Part III sketches the federal structure of the Soviet state, Part IV sets down the system of popular representation through elected deputies to soviets at all levels of government, Part VI describes the all-union, or national-level, institutions of the Soviet state, Part VII describes these institutions at the lower levels of government, and Part VIII establishes the judicial institutions of the Soviet state.

Among the most curious characteristics of the Soviet Constitution of 1977 is its remarkably long gestation. Khrushchev first called for a new constitution at the 21st Congress of the Party in January 1959. In contrast to the 22 months it took to produce the Constitution of 1936, following a similar announcement by Stalin in February 1935, it took over 18 years to produce its replacement. Despite sporadic announcements that a draft constitution would be revealed shortly (made by Khrushchev in 1961 and 1962 and by Brezhnev in 1966 and 1972) the constitutional commission held only two publically announced meetings (1962 and 1964) before 1977. This delay, despite the promises of Soviet leaders, has led some Western Sovietologists to speculate that there must have been disagreement among leaders and legal experts over the extent of constitutional reform. The debate over substantive changes, part of which was published in the journals of the legal profession, appears to have centered on such issues as proposals for competitive (multicandidate) elections, extensions of sessions of the all-union Supreme Soviet to expand its legislative role, and the replacement of Soviet federalism by a more efficient territorial-administrative structure. These debates and the resulting delay in the Constitution should lead us to question why so much attention

Table 6.1   THE CONSTITUTION OF THE U.S.S.R. (Outline)

Preamble

I. *Fundamentals of the Social Order and Policy of the USSR*
    Chapter 1. The Political System (Articles 1–9)
    Chapter 2. The Economic System (Articles 10–18)
    Chapter 3. Social Development and Culture (Articles 19–27)
    Chapter 4. Foreign Policy (Articles 28–30)
    Chapter 5. Defense of the Socialist Motherland (Articles 31–32)

II. *The State and the Individual*
    Chapter 6. Citizenship of the USSR—Equality of Citizens (Articles 33–38)
    Chapter 7. The Fundamental Rights, Freedoms and Duties of Citizens
                (Articles 39–69)

III. *The National-State Structure of the USSR*
    Chapter 8. The USSR—A Federal State (Articles 70–75)
    Chapter 9. The Soviet Socialist Union Republic (Articles 76–81)
    Chapter 10. The Autonomous Soviet Socialist Republic (Articles 82–85)
    Chapter 11. The Autonomous Oblast and Autonomous Okrug (Articles 86–88)

IV. *Soviets of People's Deputies and Electoral Procedure*
    Chapter 12. The System and Principles of Activity of Soviets of People's
                 Deputies (Articles 89–94)
    Chapter 13. The Electoral System (Articles 95–102)
    Chapter 14. The People's Deputies (Articles 103–107)

V. *The Higher Organs of State Power and Administration of the USSR*
    Chapter 15. The Supreme Soviet of the USSR (Articles 108–127)
    Chapter 16. The Council of Ministers of the USSR (Articles 128–136)

VI. *Fundamentals of the Structure of Organs of State Power and Administration in
     the Union Republics*
    Chapter 17. The Higher Organs of State Power and Administration of a Union
                 Republic (Articles 137–142)
    Chapter 18. The Higher Organs of State Power and Administration of an
                 Autonomous Republic (Articles 143–144)
    Chapter 19. Local Organs of State Power and Administration (Articles 145–150)

VII. *Justice, Arbitration, and Procurator's Supervision*
    Chapter 20. The Courts and Arbitration (Articles 151–163)
    Chapter 21. The Procuracy (Articles 164–168)

VIII. *Emblem, Flag, Anthem, and Capital of the USSR*
     (Articles 169–172)

IX. *The Legal Force of the Constitution of the USSR and the Amending Procedure*
    (Articles 173–174)

is given by Soviet experts to the wording of the Soviet Constitution. Does this
mean the Constitution actually has some independent authority to limit political
practice? While this author is inclined to say that the available evidence argues
forcefully that it cannot, this anomaly should give us pause before analysts foreclose further investigation of this question.[4]

THE ALL-UNION STATE INSTITUTIONS

Despite Soviet derision of parliamentary democracy, the Soviet Constitution establishes a state structure that—particularly at its higher levels—closely resembles
parliamentary government. In the official Soviet view, the institution of the sovi-

ets is unique in that it rests on a fusion rather than a separation of legislative and executive powers.[5] In fact, however, the Soviet Constitution actually prescribes some division of legislative and executive responsibilities among bodies—under the supremacy of the soviets. Thus, the distinctions between the soviet system described in its Constitution and parliamentary government are more in the nature of minor institutional variants than fundamental differences, particularly when compared to governments that have developed the principle of parliamentary supremacy.

Because the Soviet state institutions resemble a parliamentary democracy, at least on paper, the structure of these institutions differs from those of a presidential system (e.g., the United States) in two very important ways.[6] First is the relationship between legislature and executive. Presidential systems are characterized by a separation of legislative and executive branches, in that each has a distinct set of powers and each is elected directly by the citizenry and independently of the other. In a parliamentary system, however, the executive is dependent upon the legislature, in that the executive does not have constitutionally separate powers from the legislature and it is the legislature, directly elected by the citizenry, that elects the prime minister.

The second difference is the organization of the executive itself. In a presidential system there is a unified executive, for the president plays two roles—head of government and chief of state. In a parliamentary system, however, these two roles are usually separated. In the United Kingdom, for example, the chief of state, the ceremonial and symbolic representative of the state, is the monarch; the head of government, the chief administrative officer of the state, is the Prime Minister.

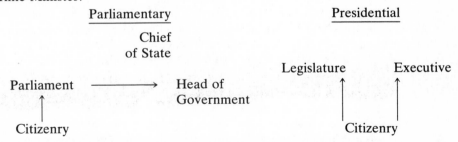

In the Soviet Union, at the all-union level Soviet citizens elect deputies to a legislature called the Supreme Soviet. The Supreme Soviet elects out of its membership a corporate chief of state, the Presidium. The Supreme Soviet also elects the head of government, the Chairman of the Council of Ministers, and his ministers.

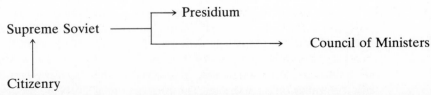

This is, of course, true only on paper: The formalities of elections mask an underlying reality in which the choice of personnel is made behind the scenes.

The Supreme Soviet

The all-union, or national-level, legislature of the Soviet Union is the Supreme Soviet. This body is purportedly the highest authority in the Soviet state: It is formally empowered to legislate on all matters within the jurisdiction of the Soviet Union. In reality, this is simply untrue. The Supreme Soviet's meetings are too infrequent and short. It discusses too few issues and passes laws that are often only vague statements of principle. And all its votes to date have been unanimous. These are not the signs of a vital law-making institution.

The system of soviets (councils) actually predates the Soviet regime. The original soviets of workers' delegates sprang up spontaneously during the Revolution of 1905. Following the February Revolution of 1917, the Soviet of Workers' and Soldiers' Deputies began activities in Petrograd (March 12, 1917), coming to see itself as an alternative to the Provisional Government. Similar councils were established throughout Russia, and a hierarchy of local, regional, and all-Russian congresses of soviets began to take form before October 1917. Lenin's Bolsheviks concentrated their efforts before taking power on controlling the soviets and, with the slogan "All Power to the Soviets," on challenging the Provisional Government in their name. Through the Constitution of 1918, the pyramid of soviets and congresses of soviets that had taken form in 1917 was made the formal foundation of the Soviet state. The All-Russian Congress of Soviets became the first Soviet legislature, the predecessor of the present Supreme Soviet. (Unlike the present Supreme Soviet, however, it was composed not of deputies from local constituencies but of delegates from the congresses below the national level.)

The modern Supreme Soviet is a bicameral legislature, reflecting the federal structure of the Soviet state. Each chamber, according to the 1977 Constitution, is to have equal numbers of deputies; and the total number of deputies has remained constant at 1500 since 1977. Deputies in both chambers represent single-member constituencies and serve five-year terms. One chamber, the Soviet of the Union, organized on the principle of equal representation based on population, is composed of 750 deputies, each representing a constituency of about 245,000 voters in 1985. The other, the Soviet of Nationalities, apportions its 750 seats among the nationality-based territorial units on the principle of representation proportionate to the unit's position in the federal hierarchy. That is, each union republic has 32 deputies, each autonomous soviet socialist republic has 11, each autonomous oblast has 5, and each autonomous okrug has one. Thus, all citizens are represented by at least two deputies, one in each chamber; and citizens residing in autonomous republics, autonomous oblasts, or autonomous okrugs have three representatives, one in the Soviet of the Union and two in the Soviet of Nationalities.

The deputies who compose the Supreme Soviet are not full-time legislators, but serve only a few days each year, taking leave from their normal employment. These deputies are drawn from a broad (albeit unrepresentative) cross-section of Soviet society. For example, 71.4 percent of the deputies elected in 1984 were Party members, a proportion that is over seven times that for the adult population as a whole. The proportion of Party members has fallen slowly, but consistently, since Stalin's death. There is further discussion of this decline in Chapter 8. Yet, Party members remain preponderant. Moreover, even among the non-Party deputies, many belong to the Party's youth auxiliary, so that as many as 86 percent of all deputies elected in 1984 were members of either the Party or the Komsomol. Similarly, the proportion of women among the deputies stood at 32.8 percent in 1984, representing a doubling in this proportion since 1937, but still only three-fifths of their proportion in the total adult population. The class status of deputies is also not a microcosm of Soviet society, for the 51.3 percent of deputies who were workers or collective farmers, according to official figures, were only about two-thirds of their proportion in the total adult population. Moreover, while some of these were exemplary workers, like Natalya V. Orlova, loom operator at the Dzerzhinsky Three Hills Cotton Combine, a disproportionate share of the workers and collective farmers were work brigade leaders and foreman.[7]

The formal powers of the Supreme Soviet, as listed in the Constitution, include:

(a) *Legislation.* Statues (*zakon*) of the Soviet Union must be enacted either by the Supreme Soviet or by a national referendum. Since the latter mechanism has never been used, such legislation would appear to be the sole prerogative of the Supreme Soviet. This body must also confirm all legislative actions taken by its Presidium between sessions of the Supreme Soviet. Despite extensive provisions for the introduction of legislation by state, Party, and public organs, legislative initiative actually appears to rest with the Party leadership; and, in fact, many legislative motions in Supreme Soviet sessions are made on behalf of the Party Central Committee or the Party groups within both chambers. To become law, legislation must be debated either in separate or joint sessions of the chambers and passed by majorities in both. If the chambers fail to reach agreement on a piece of legislation, which of course has never happened, the Constitution provides for conciliation procedures. In fact, the laws passed by the Supreme Soviet receive only the most cursory consideration in the formal sessions of the body. And the resulting legislation is cast in broad terms. Moreover, much of what would be classified as legislation in other countries appears in the Soviet Union not as formal actions by the Supreme Soviet but as the acts of other state, Party, and trade union organs.

(b) *Constitutional Amendment.* The power to adopt and amend the Constitution of the Soviet Union resides solely with the Supreme Soviet by a two-thirds vote of each chamber. No other approvals are required by the Constitution. Closely related is the power of the Supreme Soviet to change the federal structure of the Soviet Union by admitting new republics and forming new autonomous republics and regions. The Supreme Soviet, of course, does not actually initiate such actions and has not asserted independent authority in such decisions.

(c) *Fiscal Control.* Each year the Supreme Soviet must approve both the state plan and the state budget and must confirm reports on their execution. This is usually accompanied by a debate that lavishes praise on the plan as a whole, but may indirectly criticize details.

(d) *Election.* The Supreme Soviet formally elects the Presidium, Council of

Ministers, Committee of People's Control, Supreme Court, and Procurator-General. These elections take place during the first session of a newly elected Supreme Soviet. Replacements between sessions are made by the Supreme Soviet's Presidium and must be confirmed at the next legislative session. Nominations do not produce debate and are accepted unanimously.

(e) *Interpellation.* Deputies may address written or oral questions to the Council of Ministers, individual ministers, or the heads of other bodies formed by the Supreme Soviet. The officials are obliged to respond either orally or in writing within three days. The reply may be brought up for discussion in a joint meeting of the two chambers. In practice, this power is seldom used. And when employed, it is not equivalent to the question time in the British Parliament, but may actually be an arranged occasion for a major policy address by the responding official.

The Supreme Soviet and its respective chambers are also formally charged as the final authorities in their own affairs, with the power to certify the credentials of deputies, elect their own officers (a chairman and four vice-chairmen for each chamber), and elect standing committees.

The procedure of this bicameral legislature seems relatively simple. It is constitutionally required to meet twice a year, and it usually, although not always, does meet once during the second quarter of the year and once during the last quarter. As Table 6.2 shows, the first meeting each year usually results in the adoption of laws or general principles of legislation. In the second meeting each year, the Supreme Soviet discusses the state budget and plan for the coming year, passes these, and certifies that the previous year's plan and budget have been carried out. Each session usually lasts only two days, which are filled with reports, formal debates, and elections. The two chambers may meet jointly, which it normally does when it hears reports on the economy and budget and for formal election of All-Union officials. The chambers often meet separately to conduct debate and to vote on legislation.

The agenda, appointments to commissions, and the lists of candidates for key elections within each chamber of the Supreme Soviet appear to be under the control of its Council of Elders. The complex procedures for apportioning seats on each body, set down in the Regulations of the Supreme Soviet, result in two bodies of approximately 150 deputies each. Little is known of these, yet the remarkably smooth operation of the two-day sessions of the Supreme Soviet may be attributed to the thoroughness of their planning and control.[8]

The Supreme Soviet is something of a paradox. Although its plenary meetings are not active law-making sessions, the Supreme Soviet is composed of some of the most powerful people in the Soviet Union. For example, 74.1 percent of the voting members of the Party's Central Committee were elected as deputies to the Supreme Soviet in 1984.[9] Why bother to bring together some of the most powerful people of the Soviet Union into an institution that is otherwise not powerful? Part of the answer is probably to legitimate their power, for many are Party functionaries or industrial managers who do not hold other elective, national office. Legitimation, however, may not be the full answer.

Table 6.2 SESSIONS OF THE 10th AND 11th SUPREME SOVIETS

Session	Year	Dates	Length (days)	Legislation
10th Supreme Soviet				
First	1979	April 18–19	2	Regulations of Supreme Soviet
Second	1979	November 28–30	3	Plan and Budget Law on People's Control Law on Procuracy Law on State Arbitration Law on the Bar
Third	1980	June 24–25	2	Law on Local Soviets Law on Air Quality Law on Wildlife Protection
Fourth	1980	October 22–23	2	Plan and Budget Principles of Administrative Law Violations
Fifth	1981	June 23–24	2	Principles of Housing Legislation Law on Resident Aliens
Sixth	1981	November 17–19	3	Plan and Budget
Seventh	1982	November 23–24	2	Plan and Budget Law on State Borders
Eighth	1983	June 16–17	2	Law on Labor Collectives
Ninth	1983	December 28–29	2	Plan and Budget
11th Supreme Soviet				
First	1984	April 11–12	2	Guidelines on Education
Second	1984	November 27–28	2	Plan and Budget
Third	1985	July 2–3	2	Resolution on Environmental Protection Resolution on Procuracy
Fourth	1985	November 27–28	2	Plan and Budget
Fifth	1986	June 18–19	2	Five-Year Plan, 1986–1990
Sixth	1986	November 17–19	3	Plan and Budget Law on Individual Labor Resolution on People's Control
Seventh	1987	June 29–30	2	Law on State Enterprises Resolution on Restructuring of Economic Administration

Source: Pravda, 19–20 April 1979, 29–31 November 1979, 25–26 June 1980, 23–24 October 1980, 24–25 June 1981, 18–20 November 1981, 24–25 November 1982, 17–18 June 1983, 29–30 December 1983, 12–13 April 1984, 28–29 November 1984, 3–4 July 1985, 27–28 November 1985, 19–20 June 1986, 30 June–1 July 1987.

The paradox of the Supreme Soviet is more complex than this. It appears that there is some form of *ex officio* representation in the Supreme Soviet, for certain key offices in the Soviet Union are almost routinely represented in this body.[10] The composition of the Supreme Soviet elected in 1984 is typical. Over a third of the deputies are drawn from the key administrative organs of the Soviet state and the Party; that is, from the top six groups listed in Table 6.3. And these organs tend to enjoy secure representation in the Supreme Soviet.

With a few exceptions, the relative shares of these top six groups have remained fairly stable since the early 1960s. Representation of the Party apparatus has grown relative to the state apparatus in these two decades, but only slightly. More significant has been the shift in representation between center and periphery. All-Union officials (Party and state) have increased relative to regional officials in this period.

The practices of the Supreme Soviet suggest a prominent role for these *ex officio* representatives. Because they tend to enjoy secure seats in the Supreme Soviet, these deputies are more likely to acquire the skills essential to political influence in that body. Moreover, these *ex officio* representatives tend to play the most active and visible roles in Supreme Soviet sessions. The key speakers and key committee chairmen are usually drawn from among these deputies. For example, while 20.0 percent of the deputies elected in 1984 were members of the Central Committee, fully 56 percent of the committee chairmen were Central Committee members.[11] If the Supreme Soviet was purely democratic window-dressing for an authoritarian regime, there would be little reason to accord the "Who's Who Elite" this status. There would, in fact, be strong ideological reasons to feature workers and peasants prominently in the most visible positions.

Some evidence suggests that an important political process may, in fact, take place within the Supreme Soviet. It appears that the Supreme Soviet provides a forum for key regional and functional interests within the Soviet Union to press their views on the leadership and to bargain among themselves. (This would account for the *ex officio* representation.)

First, the speeches given in plenary sessions are a vehicle for expressing these views. For example, in the first three sessions of the 11th Convocation of the Supreme Soviet (1984-85), the number of speakers on any issue ranged from 7 in a joint session addressing the Basic Guidelines for Reform in General-Educational and Vocational Schools to 27 speakers in separate meetings of the two chambers addressing the 1985 State Budget. These speakers did not simply address the legislation before the Supreme Soviet at that moment. They often appeared to be intent on influencing the future direction of policy in the Soviet Union, particularly by adding issues to the policy agenda or pressing for pet projects in the speakers' home regions.[12]

Second, the commission structure of the Supreme Soviet may provide a forum for these interests to bargain among themselves behind the scenes. This is, of course, more speculative, since we know little of what is said in these commissions. Each of the two chambers has 16 standing commissions distinguished by policy area, plus a Credentials Committee (see Table 6.4). The duties of these commissions, according to the Regulations of the Supreme Soviet, include "preliminary consideration and preparation of questions within the jurisdiction of the USSR Supreme Soviet," assistance in the implementation of laws, and control (*kontrol'*) or oversight over the activities of state agencies and organizations.[13] Each of these commissions has 35 members (or 45 in the case of the Planning and Budget Commission) selected from among the deputies of the Supreme Soviet. (Those deputies who are officials of the all-union state organs are not eligible for membership on the standing commissions. This exclusion has led to

The "Minutes" of the First Session of the Eleventh Supreme Soviet

Day One: 11 April 1984

10 am.   First Meeting of Council of Nationalities
Session opened by oldest deputy of Council of Nationalities
    on motion of Council of Elders
Election of Chairman and four Vice-Chairmen of chamber
Confirmation of agenda and work procedures
Election of Credentials Committee (35 members)

12 pm.   First Meeting of Council of the Union
(Agenda identical to First Meeting of Council of
    Nationalities)

2 pm.   Second Meeting of Council of Nationalities
Chairman of chamber presiding
Report by Chairman of Credentials Committee
Adoption of Resolution recognizing credentials
    of all deputies
Adoption of Resolution establishing chamber's
    standing committees

3 pm.   Second Meeting of Council of the Union
(Agenda identical to Second Meeting of Council
of Nationalities)

5 pm.   First Joint Meeting of Supreme Soviet
Chairman of Council of the Union presiding
Election of Presidium of Supreme Soviet
    Motion by Gorbachev, on behalf of CPSU Central
        Committee, and seconded by Party group of Supreme Soviet
        and both chambers' Councils of Elders
    Unanimous election of Chernenko as Chairman of Presidium
    Unanimous election of Kuznetsov as First Vice-Chairman
        and of remaining members of Presidium
    Chernenko delivers acceptance address
Election of Council of Ministers
    Chairman of Council of Union reads resignation of
        Government
    Motion by Chernenko, on behalf of CPSU Central
        Committee, and seconded by Party group of Supreme
        Soviet and both chambers' Councils of Elders, to
        reappoint Tikhonov as Chairman of Council of Ministers
        and to instruct him to submit a proposal for the
        composition of Council of Ministers
    Adoption of resolution
Ratification of Presidium decrees
    Report by Secretary of Presidium
    Ratification of decrees and adoption of corresponding
        laws

Day Two: 12 April 1984

10 am.   Second Joint Meeting of Supreme Soviet
          Chairman of Council of Nationalities presiding
          Formation of Council of Ministers
              Tikhonov submits proposal, approved by the CPSU
                  Central Committee and Party group of Supreme Soviet
              Unanimous ratification of composition of Council
                  of Ministers
              Tikhonov addresses forthcoming activities of Council
          Report by Aliyev on Basic Guidelines for Reform in the
                  General-Education and Vocational Schools
              Discussion in which seven deputies address session
              Unanimous adoption of Resolution
          Motions, seconded by Party group of Supreme Soviet and
                  Councils of Elders of both Chambers, on composition
                  of People's Control Committee, Supreme Court, and
                  Procurator-General
              Discussion of proposals
              Formation of People's Control Committee
              Election of Supreme Court
              Appointment of Procurator-General
          Conclusion of session

speculation that these commissions were designed as a check by the central and regional Party secretaries on the work of the state apparatus.) The most important
of the Commissions are the budget and planning commissions; while most commissions meet only twice a year, the budget and planning commissions meet eight
times annually.

The standing commissions (which Roger Siegler characterizes as "conduits
for informational co-optation") may provide a forum for key interests and experts to influence policy. The membership of each commission is apparently organized so as to include deputies with the greatest expertise or interest in the
commission's subject matter. For example, the agricultural commission usually includes deputies with expertise on agriculture and from regions of the Soviet
Union with agricultural economies. If these commissions shape legislation, they
do so not through the initiation of legislation, but through the amendments, re-
wordings, and other details each adds to these bills.[14]

Attached to each commission are a number of preparatory groups that
meet even more frequently. The preparatory groups are formally charged with
drafting legislation and supervising implementation. There is some circumstantial
evidence (but only circumstantial) that these groups may also provide a forum
for key segments of Soviet society interested in a policy area to discuss policy
and supervise the administration of existing laws. Peter Vanneman of the University of Arkansas has even argued that "there is evidence that a significant
amount of the drafting of and deliberation over legislation takes place [here]."[15]

Table 6.3 OCCUPATIONS OF SUPREME SOVIET DEPUTIES, 1950, 1962, 1974 AND 1984 (percentages)

	1950	1962	1974	1984
Leading All-Union and Regional Officials				
All-Union Party official	1.1	1.9	1.7	2.5
Republic and local Party official	21.6	15.9	14.2	14.2
All-Union state official	1.4	3.8	6.7	7.3
Republic and local state official	20.3	12.4	7.3	4.9
Army and police officers	7.0	4.6	4.4	4.8
Trade union and Komsomol officials	2.1	1.2	1.2	1.2
Factory, Farm, and Production Association Personnel				
Directors and chairmen	15.2	9.4	8.1	7.3
Other employees	13.8	39.5	45.9	49.0
Other Occupations				
Cultural and ideological figures	3.9	3.2	3.2	3.5
Scientists and educators	10.5	6.3	6.0	4.3
Medical personnel	1.1	1.4	1.0	1.0
Other	2.0	0.4	0.3	0.0

Sources: 1984: *Pravda*, 7 March 1984, lists all deputies and their respective occupations. The classification is the author's. 1950, 1962, and 1974: Jerry F. Hough and Merle Fainsod, *How the Soviet Union Is Governed* (Cambridge, Mass.: Harvard University Press, 1979); some figures recalculated.

Table 6.4 PERMANENT COMMISSIONS OF THE SUPREME SOVIET

Each chamber has an identical set of 16 standing commissions:

Agro-Industrial Complex Commission
Budget and Planning Commission
Construction and Building Materials Industry Commission
Consumer Goods and Trade Commission
Education and Culture Commission
Energy Commission
Environmental Protection and Utilization of Natural Resources Commission
Foreign Affairs Commission
Housing and Municipal Services Commission
Industry Commission
Legislative Proposals Commission
Maternity, Child Development, and the Work and Life of Women Commission
Public Health and Social Security Commission
Science and Technology Commission
Transport and Communications Commission
Youth Affairs Commission

The conclusion that this circumstantial evidence points to a real, although circumscribed, political process within the Supreme Soviet is in no way universally held among Western Sovietologists. And the power of this body remains the subject of controversy in scholarly circles. The University of Wisconsin's John Armstrong, for example, describes Supreme Soviet sessions as "mere ceremonies of ratification, characterized by set speeches rather than debate." He ascribes only limited significance to its standing committees. And he concludes that "it is no exaggeration to describe the Supreme Soviet not as a real legislature, but as a rubber stamp."[16]

Vanneman, on the other hand, has argued that the Supreme Soviet serves as more than a rubber stamp, and that in the evolution of its role "it may gradually and incrementally be acquiring elements of decision-making." He contends that the Supreme Soviet plays a growing legislative role, with a shift of "a significant amount of the drafting and deliberation process from the Council of Ministers to the Supreme Soviet and its auxiliary bodies, especially its subcommissions." He adds that it has performed an expanding *kontrol'* function in its surveillance of the state apparatus and an investigative role that permits its subcommissions to gather technical information essential to its legislative functions.[17] Yet to say that these functions are expanding does not answer the question whether they have grown to the point that the Supreme Soviet is anything more than a peripheral forum in law making. This author would argue that they have not yet reached that point. At most, the evidence of infrequent, short, and often ritualistic meetings suggests that the Supreme Soviet can fine-tune policy proposals and hope to add items to the leadership's policy agenda, but it does not play an independent role as initiator or legislator of policy.

The Presidium of the Supreme Soviet

Formally a standing body of the Supreme Soviet and accountable to it, the Presidium of the Supreme Soviet serves as both an interim legislature and a collegial chief of state. Prior to the adoption of the Stalin Constitution, these functions were performed by the Central Executive Committee (CEC or *TsIK*) and its Presidium. Elected by the All-Russian Congress of Soviets, the bicameral CEC (composed of a Council of the Union and a Council of Nationalities) was to be the supreme organ of state power between sessions of the Congress. Yet its size, ranging from 200 at its origins to 751 at its peak, made it more like an interim Congress than an active decision-making body. As a consequence of this size, the unofficial Presidium of the CEC, a body that grew from 7 to 27 in these years, assumed many of the functions of the CEC itself.[18]

The modern Presidium is composed of 39 deputies of the Supreme Soviet, formally elected at a joint session of the two chambers of that organ. It includes a Chairman, a First Deputy Chairman, 15 Deputy Chairmen (who are the 15 chairmen of the presidia of the union republics), a Secretary, and 21 other members, who often are key regional Party secretaries or other functionaries from around the Soviet Union. For example, in the Presidium elected in 1984, the 21 regular members included 9 republic and regional Party first secretaries (Ukrainian SSR, Belorussian SSR, Kazakh SSR, Uzbek SSR, Bashkir ASSR, Tatar ASSR, Moscow City, Leningrad Oblast, Sverdlov Oblast) and 5 Chairmen or First Secretaries of all-union ideological propaganda auxiliaries of the Party (Komsomol, Trade Union Council, DOSAAF, Znanie Society, Committee of Women). (In July 1985, the Supreme Soviet relieved the Sverdlovsk Party First Secretary of his position on the Presidium, coincident with his election to the All-Union

Party Secretariat, and appointed the new General Secretary, Mikhail Gorbachev in his place.)

As an interim legislature and a standing body of the Supreme Soviet, the Presidium between sessions of the legislature can promulgate edicts (*ukaz*), issue decrees (*postanovlenie*), amend existing laws, change the borders of Union Republics, and change the composition of the Council of Ministers—all subject to the subsequent ratification of the Supreme Soviet.[19] The legislative significance of Presidium acts can be substantial. For example, in the first half of 1985, Presidium edicts expanded the pension system; imposed additional penalties for alcohol abuse, moonshining, and hooliganism; revised the legislation on military discipline; and streamlined the judicial procedures for hearing cases on hooliganism and child-support payments. The Presidium may also ratify and denounce treaties and nullify decisions of the Council of Ministers that do not conform to the law. It also coordinates the work of the Supreme Soviet's standing committees.

In its role as corporate chief of state, the Presidium formally calls the elections of deputies to the Supreme Soviet and convenes its sessions. It is responsible for instituting and issuing medals, honors, and ranks; granting pardons and amnesty; granting citizenship and asylum; receiving and sending ambassadors; and declaring martial law, mobilization, and war. Its Chairman often assumes the role of symbolic representative of the Soviet state on behalf of the Presidium and is, therefore, sometimes colloquially called the President, as a chief of state in a parliamentary system that has no monarch.

The Presidium, as a body, probably does not wield significant power. It appears to meet only about once every month or two; although meetings are not always reported. We do not even know if the Presidium actually meets as a whole on these occasions. In reality, its Chairman and Secretary may exercise the power of the Presidium in its name without a formal meeting of the entire body. One real power of the Presidium may be the *kontrol'* function that it exercises over the operations of the Council of Ministers, giving the Party secretaries who make up the Presidium a check on the state administration. To assist it in its work, the Presidium has a small apparatus, composed principally of a Secretariat and five departments (Awards, International Relations, Juridical, Problems of the Work of Soviets, and Publications).[20]

Chairman of the Presidium   Although it would appear that the position of Chairman of the Presidium (or earlier, Chairman of the Central Executive Committee) does not itself bestow major powers on its incumbent, it has recently been occupied by powerful individuals. The office apparently legitimates rather than confers power. The chairmen of the Presidium since 1960 have been among the most prominent Soviet leaders:

1917–1919	Yakov M. Sverdlov
1919–1946	Mikhail I. Kalinin
1946–1953	Nikolai M. Shvernik
1953–1960	Klimentii E. Voroshilov
1960–1964	Leonid I. Brezhnev

1964–1965	Anastas I. Mikoyan
1965–1977	Nikolai V. Podgorny
1977–1982	Leonid I. Brezhnev
1983–1984	Yuri V. Andropov
1984–1985	Konstantin U. Chernenko
1985–	Andrei A. Gromyko

Before 1964, Leonid Brezhnev, as heir-designate to Khrushchev, gave stature to this position. From 1965 to 1977, Chairman Nikolai Podgorny was a member of the triumvirate that succeeded Khrushchev, although with time he turned out to be the weakest of the three.

In 1977, Brezhnev assumed the position of Chairman for a second time and with this move combined his powerful positions in the Party with an important symbolic post in the state. He reportedly told the Presidium, following his appointment, that this decision "was by no means a formality." In particular, he explained that this combination of posts

> . . . reflected actual practice in our daily work, in which many members of the Politburo must deal with affairs of state, both at home and abroad. I myself, as General Secretary, have on many occasions . . . had to represent our country abroad at negotiations. . . . Now this practice will receive its logical formalization.[21]

While this may have added to Brezhnev's power by making official his position as the foreign policy representative of the Soviet Union and by giving him an independent institutional check on the Council of Ministers, it also signified that after a dozen years as General Secretary of the Party, Brezhnev was still not as powerful as Khrushchev had been: Brezhnev was unable to claim the more-powerful state position that Khrushchev had held—Chairman of the Council of Ministers.

When Brezhnev died, the position of Chairman of the Presidium was initially left vacant. Yuri Andropov became General Secretary of the Party in November 1982, but it was seven months before he became Chairman of the Presidium. Konstantin Chernenko, on the other hand, acquired the position only two months after assuming the position of General Secretary in February 1984. By that point it appeared as though it was becoming an institutionalized practice to make the head of the Party also the symbolic head of the state. And then, following the death of Chernenko, the Soviets broke this pattern: Rather than awarding Mikhail Gorbachev the position when he became General Secretary (March 1985), the Soviet leadership waited and in July 1985, bestowed it upon the Minister of Foreign Affairs, Andrei Gromyko. Gorbachev was simply made a member of the Presidium at that time.

Council of Defense More important than the Presidium itself is a body that, according to the Constitution, is formed by the Presidium, called the Council of Defense. This body is responsible for overseeing national security policy in its broadest sense, which in peacetime means setting national policies to man, outfit, and train the armed forces and to mobilize the Soviet economy in support of national defense.

Although the Constitution specifies that the Presidium "forms" the Defense Council and confirms its membership, it is undoubtedly the Party Politburo that actually appoints it. Though formally attached to the Presidium, it probably operates more like a subcommittee of the Politburo. From 1977 to 1985, the individual who occupied both the chairmanship of the Presidium and the position of General Secretary of the Party served as the Chairman of the Council of Defense. Then, with the separation of the first two positions, there was some doubt in the West who would act as Chairman of the Council of Defense. According to an announcement of August 1, 1985, General Secretary Mikhail Gorbachev, even though he is not Chairman of the Presidium, nonetheless currently occupies this position. (This reinforces our supposition about the Council's relationship to the Presidium and the Politburo.) The council also includes the Ministers of Defense and Foreign Affairs, the Chairman of the KGB, and probably leading Party secretaries and military officers.[22]

The Council of Ministers

The Council of Ministers, sometimes colloquially but not entirely accurately called the Cabinet, is the Government of the Soviet Union. The predecessor to this body, the Council of People's Commissars (*Sovnarkom*), was established in November 1917, and became the organ through which Lenin and the Bolsheviks directed the early Soviet state. (The original *Sovnarkom* included five members, with Lenin as Chairman, Trotsky as Commissar of Foreign Affairs, Rykov as Commissar of the Interior, Lunacharsky as Commissar of Education, and Stalin as Commissar for Nationalities.) The Council of People's Commissars was superseded between June 1941 and September 1945 by a State Defense Committee (GKO), a form of "war cabinet," but after World War II it was restored. By a 1946 reform its name was changed to the Council of Ministers.

The size of the Council has grown as the number of ministries has tended to rise over time. This has frequently been followed by reforms to reduce the number of ministries, after which it rises once again. For example, the number of ministries in 1947 stood at 59; in 1953 it was cut to 25, but by 1956 had risen again to 56; in 1958 Khrushchev reduced it to 19, but following his ouster, his successors set the number at 48 in 1966. By the late 1970s, the number exceeded 60.

The most ambitious experiment with an alternative to the ministerial structure of soviet administration began in May 1957, under the direction of Nikita Khrushchev, by which most ministries were abolished, turning over their management responsibilities to 105 regional economic councils (*sovnarkhoz*). The surviving ministries were limited to coordination within their respective sectors of the economy. This decentralization, however, hampered economic planning and coordination of the national economy, and thus was followed by a series of institutional changes after 1957 that led to recentralization of decision making and culminated in the elimination of the *sovnarkhozy* altogether and the restoration of the ministerial structure.

The contemporary Council of Ministers and its Chairman are formally elected by the two chambers of the Supreme Soviet sitting in joint session. Replacements between sessions of the Supreme Soviet, but subject to its subsequent ratification, can be made by the Supreme Soviet Presidium. Since the Soviet state is designed like a parliamentary democracy, the Council of Ministers is formally accountable to the Supreme Soviet (or between sessions of the Supreme Soviet, to its Presidium). The size of the Council is not fixed by the Constitution. In May 1986, it appeared to comprise 113 members, including its Chairman, who is sometimes called by Westerners the Prime Minister or Premier, 4 First Deputy Chairmen, 8 Deputy Chairmen, the 15 Chairmen of the union-republic Councils of Ministers, 59 ministers, 18 other chairmen of state committees (plus 3 of their first deputy chairmen holding ministerial rank), and 5 heads of other state agencies. (See Table 6.5.)

Formally the Council of Ministers is "empowered to deal with all matters of state administration within the jurisdiction of the Union of Soviet Socialist Republics insofar as, under the Constitution, they do not come within the competence of the Supreme Soviet of the USSR or the Presidium of the Supreme Soviet of the USSR" (Article 131). The formal purview of the Council, according to the Constitution and the Law on the USSR Council of Ministers, appears to touch all of Soviet society, including:

(a) *economics,* drafting and implementing the state plan, state budget, and measures regulating science, the environment, the monetary and credit system, and prices and wages;
(b) *sociocultural development*, providing public education, public housing, and social security, promoting public health and physical culture, and directing consumer and municipal services;
(c) *domestic order,* defending the interests of the state, protecting socialist property, maintaining public order, and protecting citizens' rights and freedoms; and
(d) *foreign relations,* directing Soviet diplomacy, foreign commerce, international cooperation, and the development of its armed forces.[23]

In reality, the Council of Ministers as a corporate body wields little power. Yet many of the ministries and state committees that are part of it may be individually powerful, and all are vitally important to the implementation of policy.

The Council of Ministers is empowered to exercise both legislative and executive powers. The Council performs legislative functions when it issues decrees (*postanovlenie*) and executive orders (*rasporiazhenie*), and when it ratifies or denounces international intergovernmental agreements. Many of the laws of the Soviet Union are, in fact, issued in the form of either decrees by the Council of Ministers or joint decrees by the Council of Ministers and the Central Committee of the Party. These decrees tend to be more technical and specific acts than the statutes of the Supreme Soviet or edicts of the Presidium. For example, to order the reconstruction of several key plants so as to improve steel production,

Table 6.5   COUNCIL OF MINISTERS: MINISTRIES AND STATE COMMITTEES (May 9, 1986)

All-Union Ministries
  Aviation Industry
  Automotive Industry
  Chemical Industry
  Chemical and Petroleum Machine Building
  Civil Aviation
  Communications Equipment Industry
  Construction of Petroleum and Gas Industry
    Enterprises
  Construction in the Far East and Trans-Baikal
    Region
  Defense
  Defense Industry
  Electrical Equipment Industry
  Electronics Industry
  Foreign Trade
  Gas Industry
  General Machine Building
  Heavy and Transport Engineering
  Instrument-Making, Automation Equipment, and
    Control Systems
  Machine Building
  Machine Building for Animal Husbandry and
    Fodder Production
  Machine Building for Construction, Road
    Building, and Municipal Services
  Machine Building for the Light and Food
    Industries and Household Appliances
  Machine Tool and Instrument-Making Industry
  Medical and Microbiological Industry
  Medium Machine Building
  Merchant Marine
  Petroleum Industry
  Power Machine Building
  Radio Industry
  Railways
  Shipbuilding Industry
  Tractor and Agricultural Machinery Industry
  Transport Construction

Union-Republic Ministries
  Coal Industry
  Communications
  Construction
  Construction of Heavy Industry Enterprises
  Construction Materials Industry
  Culture
  Education
  Ferrous Metallurgy
  Finance
  Fish Industry
  Foreign Affairs

  Geology
  Grain Products
  Health
  Higher and Secondary Specialized Education
  Industrial Construction
  Installation and Special Construction Work
  Internal Affairs
  Justice
  Land Reclamation and Water Resources
  Light Industry
  Mineral Fertilizer Production
  Nonferrous Metallurgy
  Petroleum-Refining and Petrochemical Industry
  Power and Electrification
  Timber, Pulp, and Paper and Wood Processing Industry
  Trade

State Committees
  Agroindustrial
  Cinematography
  Civil Construction and Architecture
  Computer Technology and Information Science
  Construction Affairs
  Foreign Economic Relations
  Foreign Tourism
  Forestry
  Hydrometeorology and Environmental Control
  Industrial Safety and the Supervision of Mines
  Inventions and Discoveries
  Labor and Social Affairs
  Material Reserves
  Material and Technical Supply
  Physical Culture and Sports
  Planning
  Prices
  Publishing Houses, Printing Plants, and Book Trade
  Safety in the Atomic Power Industry
  Science and Technology
  Standards
  State Security
  Supply of Petroleum Products
  Television and Radio Broadcasting
  Utilization of Atomic Energy
  Vocational and Technical Education

Other Agencies
  Administration of Affairs
  Administrative Board of the USSR State Bank
  Bureau for Machine Building
  Central Statistical Administration
  People's Control Committee
  State Board of Arbitration

Source: U.S. Central Intelligence Agency, *Directory of Soviet Officials: National Organizations* (Washington, D.C.: CIA, 1986).

the Central Committee and Council of Ministers issued a joint decree in March 1985, "On the Development and Technical Reequipping of Ferrous Metallurgy and Substantial Improvement of the Quality of Metal Output as a Most Important Structural Material." To improve accounting procedures the Council of Ministers issued a decree in October 1984, "On Transferring Intrafarm Land-Reclamation Systems from the Books of Collective Farms, State Farms, and Other Agricultural Enterprises to the Books of State Operated Water-Resources Organizations." The decision to issue a decree, it should be noted, is probably not made independently by the Council of Ministers.

The Council performs executive-administrative functions in its coordination and direction of ministries, state committees, and attached administrations. It is empowered to "organize the management of industrial, construction, and agricultural enterprises and amalgamations, transport and communications undertakings, banks, and other organizations and institutions of all-union subordination." It may also suspend decisions and decrees of the union-republic Councils of Ministers.

The Chairman and Presidium of the Council of Ministers   Unlike the chairmanship of the Presidium of the Supreme Soviet, the position of Chairman of the Council of Ministers may bestow significant powers upon its occupant, for this office places its holder in direct charge of the daily administration of many policies of the Soviet Union. The formal powers of the Chairman of the Council of Ministers are formidable:

(a) *appointments,* including the membership of the council of Ministers itself, which the Chairman submits to the Supreme Soviet or its Presidium between sessions for approval;
(b) *administration,* directing the work of the Council of Ministers and its Presidium;
(c) *diplomacy,* representing the USSR in international affairs; and
(d) *executive prerogative,* making decisions "in urgent cases" "on individual questions of state administration.[24]

A forceful Chairman may actually be able to exercise many of these powers, making him a power with whom a General Secretary must contend. It is, therefore, no accident that the list of the chairmen of the Council of Ministers (and Council of People's Commissars) includes some of the most powerful leaders in Soviet history:

1917–1924	Vladimir I. Lenin
1924–1930	Alexei I. Rykov
1930–1941	Vyacheslav M. Molotov
1941–1953	Joseph V. Stalin
1953–1955	Georgi M. Malenkov
1955–1958	Nikolai I. Bulganin
1958–1964	Nikita S. Khrushchev

1964–1980	Alexei N. Kosygin
1980–1985	Nikolai A. Tikhonov
1985–	Nikolai I. Ryzhkov

Lenin held this post until his death; Stalin held it after 1941; and from 1958, following the removal of the Anti-Party group and Nikolai Bulganin, Nikita Khrushchev assumed it. In 1964, the new collective leadership apparently agreed that the same person should not be both head of the Party and Chairman of the Council of Ministers, for this would have made the General Secretary too powerful and threatened the collective leadership. Alexei Kosygin, then, assumed the position of Chairman of the Council of Ministers in 1964, making him the second most-powerful figure in the collective leadership. He remained in this position until 1980, when ill health forced him to retire. Kosygin's replacement, Nikolai Tikhonov, broke with the previous pattern, for as the oldest member of the Politburo he proved not to be a strong political figure. This may have been part of a larger design, for after Kosygin's resignation Brezhnev may have wanted to ensure that the chairmanship was not assumed by a potential rival. Tikhonov finally retired in September 1985, relinquishing the position to Nikolai Ryzhkov, who had been a young protégé of Andropov and a close ally of Gorbachev. Ryzhkov's power is as yet untested.

The inner working group of the Council forms what is called the Presidium of the Council of Ministers. According to the Constitution, it includes the Chairman, First Deputy Chairmen, and Deputy Chairmen of the council of Ministers. While the Council of Ministers as a whole meets only once every three months, its Presidium apparently meets more frequently. This Presidium serves as an executive agency of the full Council, reviewing drafts of decrees and orders. (It may actually issue these in the name of the Council without its formal action.) More importantly, the Presidium is responsible for providing coordination of administration across the narrow sectors of the ministries and state committees. And to this end many of the First Deputy and Deputy Chairmen assume responsibility for several related ministries and state committees. The Presidium is empowered to issue day-to-day instructions to ministries and states committees to improve coordination. And it maintains permanent commissions to resolve disputes among them. In early 1986 commissions that could be identified included the Military Industrial Commission; Commission for Improvement of Management, Planning, and the Economic Mechanism; and Commission for Environmental Protection and Rational Use of Natural Resources.

Ministries and State Committees   The actual implementation of policy is in the hands of the ministries and state committees that compose the Council of Ministers. Soviet ministries resemble both the cabinet departments and the private corporations of Western societies, in that they provide public services (e.g., education, defense) and direct production in individual sectors of the economy (e.g., automobile production, grain production). The state committees for the most part are not production organizations, but are responsible for coordination across sectors of society (e.g., planning, prices, science and technology, state secu-

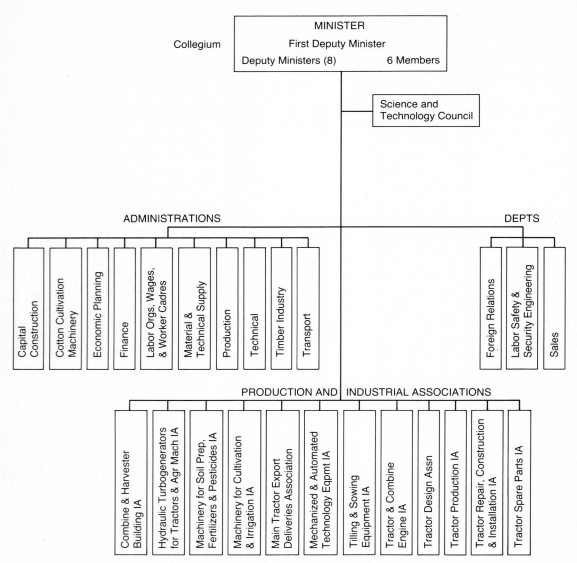

Figure 6.1 Organizational Structure of Ministry of Tractor and Agricultural Machine-Building. (*Source:* Drawn from data in U.S. Central Intelligence Agency, *Directory of Soviet Officials: National Organizations* [Washington, D.C.: CIA, 1986]).

rity). The Law on the USSR Council of Ministers describes their function as "inter-branch administration."[25]

Soviet ministers and state committee chairmen, unlike cabinet officers in many Western democracies, tend to be specialists in the field of their organization, having committed many years to service within it. Few have experience in other ministries or as policy generalists. And during the Brezhnev years, ministers and state committee chairmen tended to enjoy remarkably long tenure in their positions. For example, Hough notes that "of the sixty-eight members of the Council of Ministers (including deputy chairmen of the Council of Ministers) in 1966, only eighteen had retired or been removed by the spring of 1980—fourteen years later—despite the fact that the survivors then averaged seventy years of age."[26] Under Gorbachev these positions are apparently less permanent: In the first six months following his appointment to the post of General Secretary, 9 ministers and state committee chairmen were replaced, and in the first year this number was 18.

The minister or state committee chairman shares his decision-making authority with a *kollektiv,* the ministry's or state committee's collegium. The collegium usually directs over two dozen administrations, associations, and departments, employing in Moscow a staff of 1000 to 2000. The structure of the Ministry of Tractor and Agricultural Machine Building shown in Figure 6.1 may be fairly typical of all-union ministries engaged in production. The organization of state committees is similar to ministries, although state committees tend to be less-complex organizations. The chairmen of state committees have ministerial status.

Most ministries and state committees are elaborate hierarchies that stretch from Moscow down to the grassroots of Soviet society. They direct such institutions as the factories, farms, and educational and medical facilities throughout the Soviet Union. All-union ministries control these local institutions directly from Moscow. Union-republic ministries usually control the factories in the field indirectly, through corresponding ministries in the union-republic capitals and through local administrations in lower governments.

While the primary responsibility of these ministries and state committees is implementation of policies made at higher levels, they are not simply the unquestioning administrators of policy. They routinely influence policy through the many administrative decisions that fill in the details of broadly written policies. Moreover, many of these bureaucracies may constitute "interests" that seek to influence policy making in the leadership. But before we can discuss the issue of the realities of Soviet policy making, we need to examine the other principal institutions and actors in Soviet politics—the all-union Party organization and the union-republic and local governments, which we shall do in the following chapters.

NOTES

1. Leonid I. Brezhnev, "On the Draft Constitution (Fundamental Law) of the Union of Soviet Socialist Republics and the Results of the Nationwide Discussion of the Draft" (Report and Closing Speech at the Seventh [Special] Session of the Supreme Soviet of the USSR, Ninth Convocation, October 4–7, 1977) (Moscow: Novosti Press Agency Publishing House, 1977).
2. Aryeh L. Unger, *Constitutional Development in the USSR: A Guide to the Soviet Constitutions* (London: Methuen and Co., 1981), 9, 79, 273–274; Joseph V. Stalin, "On the Draft Constitution of the USSR" (Report Delivered at the Extraordinary Eighth Congress of Soviets of the USSR, 25 November 1936), in J. Stalin, *Problems of Leninism* (Moscow: Foreign Languages Publishing House, 1947), 540–568.

3. Unger, 1–5, 291; Robert Sharlet, "The New Soviet Constitution," *Problems of Communism* 26 (September-October 1977), 1–24. Compare Patrick O'Brien, "Constitutional Totalitarianism," *Survey* 23 (Summer 1978), 70–80.

4. Unger, 173–182, 221–222; Eberhard Schneider, "The Discussion of the New All-Union Constitution in the USSR," *Soviet Studies* 31 (October 1979), 523–541; Robert Sharlet, "De-Stalinization and Soviet Constitutionalism," in Stephen F. Cohen, Alexander Rabinowitz, and Robert Sharlet, eds., *The Soviet Union Since Stalin* (Bloomington, Ind.: Indiana University Press, 1980), 93–110; Jerome M. Gilison, "Khrushchev, Brezhnev, and Constitutional Reform," *Problems of Communism* 21 (September-October 1972), 69–78; Ronald J. Hill, "Soviet Literature on Electoral Reform: A Review," *Government and Opposition* 11 (Autumn 1976), 481–495; Grey Hodnett, "The Debate over Soviet Federalism," *Soviet Studies* 18 (April 1967), 458–481.

5. A. M. Rumiantsev, *A Dictionary of Scientific Communism* (Moscow: Progress Publishers, 1984), 249.

6. Douglas S. Verney, "Analysis of Political Systems," in Harry Eckstein and David E. Apter, eds., *Comparative Politics: A Reader* (New York: Free Press, 1963), 175–191.

7. A. I. Luk'ianov et al., *Sovety Narodnykh Deputatov: Spravochnik* (Moscow: Politicheskaia Literatura, 1984), 105. See also Ronald J. Hill, "Continuity and Change in USSR Supreme Soviet Elections," *British Journal of Political Science* 2 (1972), 47–67.

8. "Regulations of the Supreme Soviet of the Union of Soviet Socialist Republics," *Pravda* (April 20, 1979), articles 4–16.

9. Calculated from "Report of the Central Electoral Commission on the Results of the Elections to the 11th USSR Supreme Soviet on March 4, 1984," *Pravda,* 7 March 1984; and U.S. Central Intelligence Agency, *Directory of Soviet Officials: National Organizations* (Washington, D.C.: Central Intelligence Agency, 1984).

10. Jerry F. Hough and Merle Fainsod, *How the Soviet Union Is Governed* (Cambridge, Mass.: Harvard University Press, 1979), 367–370.

11. Calculated from "Report of the Central Electoral Commission on the Results of the Elections"; and Central Intelligence Agency.

12. Hough and Fainsod, 369–370.

13. "Regulations of the Supreme Soviet," Article 26.

14. Robert W. Siegler, *The Standing Commissions of the Supreme Soviet: Effective Co-Optation* (New York: Praeger, 1982), 44–104; Peter Vanneman, *The Supreme Soviet: Politics and the Legislative Process in the Soviet Political System* (Durham, N.C.: Duke University Press, 1977), 131.

15. Vanneman, 151–175.

16. John A. Armstrong, *Ideology, Politics, and Government in the Soviet Union,* 4th ed. (New York: Praeger, 1978), 164–165; John N. Hazard, *The Soviet System of Government,* 5th ed. (Chicago: University of Chicago Press, 1980), 105.

17. Vanneman, 151–175.

18. Julian Towster, *Political Power in the USSR* (New York: Oxford University Press, 1948).

19. D. Richard Little, "Legislative Authority in the Soviet Political System," *Slavic Review* 30 (March 1971), 57–73.

20. "Regulations of the Supreme Soviet," articles 17–25.

21. *Pravda*, 18 June 1977.

22. Matthew P. Gallagher and Karl F. Spielmann, Jr., *Soviet Decision-Making for Defense* (New York: Praeger, 1972), 18; Thomas W. Wolfe, *The SALT Experience* (Cambridge, Mass.: Ballinger, 1979), 57–58; Harriet Fast Scott and William F. Scott, *The Armed Forces of the USSR,* 2d ed. (Boulder, Colo.: Westview Press, 1981), 97–99.

23. "Law of the Union of Soviet Socialist Republics on the USSR Council of Ministers," *Pravda* (6 July 1978), articles 6–15.
24. "Law on the Council of Ministers," Article 29.
25. "Law on the Council of Ministers," Articles 21–22.
26. Jerry F. Hough, *Soviet Leadership in Transition* (Washington, D.C.: Brookings Institution, 1980), 67, 73.

chapter 7

The Instrument of Change:
The Communist Party

"Give us an organization of revolutionaries," Lenin proclaimed, "and we will overturn Russia!" The Party, in his conception, was to serve as the guiding force in the transition from capitalism to communism—not only to seize power, but also to transform society. In the official Soviet view, the Communist Party of the Soviet Union still plays the vanguard role that Lenin intended for it. Although institutionally separate from the state, it plays a guiding role within the state. In fact, the Party provides the nucleus of virtually all Soviet institutions. Thus, it is the Party that sets the general lines of policy and directs Soviet society in the building of communism.

The relationship between Party and society has not been unidirectional, however, for the Party has been affected by the changes that it has engineered.[1] The composition of the Party's membership has reflected the development of the Soviet economy and society. The institutional structure of the Party has grown with the tasks of the leadership. And the political processes within the Party and between the Party and other institutions have been transformed as the Soviet Union has developed from a presocialist society into mature socialism.

THE PARTY PROGRAM AND RULES

The official objectives and prescribed procedures of the CPSU are contained in the Party Program and the Party Rules. The CPSU has adopted three different Programs since the founding of the Russian Social-Democratic Labor Party, each marking an important turning point in the development of the Soviet Union and, hence, in the tasks of the Party. The First Program, adopted at the 2nd Congress in 1903, addressed the problems facing the Party as it sought to overthrow the Tsarist autocracy and the capitalist order. The Party adopted a Second Program at its 8th Congress in 1919, as it began to build the new socialist society. The Third Program, adopted at the 22nd Congress in 1961, marked the period of communist construction during which the Soviet Union, having completed the transition to socialism, would enter the stage of developed socialism and begin laying the foundations of communist society.

According to the new version of the Third Program, adopted at the 27th Congress in 1986, "the Third Program of the CPSU, in its present version, is a program of the systematic and all-round improvement of socialism and of the further progress of Soviet society toward communism on the basis of the acceleration of the country's social and economic development"[2]. The Program defines in Marxist-Leninist terms the environment in which the Soviet Union must act, recounting the development of the Soviet Union and describing its present international position (Part I). This is followed by concrete prescriptions for action in the body of the Program (parts II and III), which describes the policy line of the CPSU in domestic and international arenas. The conclusion of the Program reaffirms the centrality of the CPSU in Soviet society as it builds toward communism.

The Party Program describes the CPSU as the leading force of Soviet society, a role that "logically grows" under the current conditions of developed socialism and the international struggle against the forces of reaction. Preservation of this vanguard role, it claims, requires correct cadre and membership policies as well as proper Party decision-making procedures. Cadre policy is the Party's selection, supervision, and evaluation of personnel in key positions. Its membership policies bring into the Party "the most advanced representatives of the working class, the collective farm peasantry, and the State intelligentsia." The Party decision-making procedures must strengthen both intraparty democracy and Party discipline.

The Party Rules, which are adopted with appropriate revisions at each all-union Congress, set down the structure and procedures of the CPSU, serving as the Party's "constitution."[3] The Rules describe the rights and duties of both members and candidate members and describe the procedures for admission and expulsion (Parts I–II). They establish the structure and powers of the Party organs from the all-union level down to the primary party organizations, as well as the principles for Party elections, decision making, and leadership (Parts III–VI). And they describe the CPSU's relationship to government and public organizations, to the Komsomol, and to the armed forces (Parts VII–IX).

According to the Rules, the CPSU is organized along both production and territorial lines. That is, most primary party organizations (PPO), the basic membership groups, are organized in places of work, but Party organizations above this are organized along territorial lines. Lower levels of the Party are hypothetically "autonomous in deciding local questions, provided that these decisions are not at variance with Party policy." At each level of the Party hierarchy, the "highest leading organ" is the General Meeting, Conference, or Congress, which is composed of all members in the PPO or elected delegates at higher levels of the Party. Each of these "leading organs" elects a bureau or committee to serve as an executive body to direct "all current work of the Party organization." And, in turn, an apparatus is set up within each of these committees above the PPO "for current work with respect to organizing Party decisions and verifying their fulfillment and providing assistance to lower level organizations in their activity" (Articles 21–23).

The pillars of Party procedure, according to the Rules, are the three principles of democratic centralism, free and businesslike discussion, and collective leadership. Democratic centralism is described as "the guiding principle of the organizational structure and of the entire life and activity of the Party". It is defined by the Rules as:

(a) the election of all Party executive bodies, from bottom to top;
(b) periodic reporting by Party agencies to their Party organizations and to higher bodies;
(c) strict Party discipline and subordination of the minority to the majority;
(d) the unconditionally binding nature of the decisions of higher bodies on lower ones;
(e) *kollektivnost'* in the work of all organizations and leading organs of the Party and the personal accountability of every communist for the fulfillment of duties and Party assignments. [Article 19]

The second principle, free and businesslike discussion of Party policy, is described as "an important principle of intra-Party democracy." Nonetheless, while broad discussion "should be conducted in such a manner as to ensure the free expression of Party members' views", it must "exclude the possibility of attempts to form factional groupings destructive to Party unity or attempts to split the Party" (Article 26). Lastly, "the highest principle of Party leadership is collectivity of leadership." This the Rules describe as "a reliable guarantee against the adoption of voluntarist, subjectivist decisions, the development of a cult of personality, and the violation of Leninist norms of Party life" (Article 27).

Elections are supposed to be by secret ballot. (The only exceptions to this are some elections in primary party organizations with fewer than 15 members, where the procedure of open balloting can be adopted by the General Meeting.) Election in principle is by a majority vote of those Party members present and must permit Party members "the unrestricted right to challenge candidates and criticize them." Removal of an elected member of a committee is supposed to occur if he fails "to justify the high trust placed in him" or has "sullied his honor and dignity." The decision to remove him is made by a two-thirds vote of the committee itself. (Articles 24–25)

THE ALL-UNION PARTY INSTITUTIONS

Organizationally, the Party at the all union (national) level resembles the state. Paralleling the Supreme Soviet is a Party Congress. This nominally elects an interim legislature called the Central Committee to make policy between sessions of the Congress. The Central Committee, in turn, elects both the administrative arm of the Party called its Secretariat and the executive organ of the Party called the Politburo.

Actual power has gravitated with time toward the Secretariat and Politburo as the Congress and Central Committee have come to play less vital roles in the direction of the Party.

The Party Congress

The Party Congress, according to the Party Rules, is "the supreme body of the Communist Party of the Soviet Union" (Article 31). Specifically, its formal powers are:

(a) *Policy formation,* including approval and amendment of the Party Program and Rules and setting "the Party line on questions of domestic and foreign policy and . . . major questions of Party and state life and communist construction;

(b) *Election* of the Central Committee and Central Auditing Commission; and

(c) *Supervision* of these and other central Party organs by hearing and approving reports from them. [Article 33]

Unlike the Supreme Soviet, the Party Congress is a unicameral body, for the Party is not organized along federal lines.

Congresses are formally convened by the Central Committee. They now meet once every five years, the maximum interval set by the Party Rules. Extraordinary congresses between the regular sessions may be convened by the Central Committee or by one-third of the delegates to the preceding Congress; but none has been called since 1959. The size of each Congress (the "norms of representation") is not fixed by the Party Rules, but determined by the Central Committee. The 27th Congress in 1986 was composed of 5000 delegates (4993 actually attended) while the 26th five years earlier was composed of 4994. The delegates to the Congress are not chosen directly by the membership at large, but by the Party congresses and conferences immediately below the all-union level. Thus, except in the RSFSR, each union-republic Party Congress elects representatives to the all-union Party Congress. Since there is no union-republic Party organization for the RSFSR, delegates from that republic are elected directly by the oblast and some city organizations.

Congresses are held in the modern Palace of Congresses within the Kremlin. The occasion is a solemn celebration of the successes of the Party, attended not only by the elected delegates, but also by over 100 fraternal delegations from communist and workers' parties around the world—152 delegations from 113 countries in 1986.[4] All of this receives "gavel to gavel" live coverage on Soviet television and radio and in the newspapers. Congresses normally devote their first day to an address from the General Secretary, in the form of a Report of the Party's Central Committee. The General Secretary describes the domestic and global situation, assesses the accomplishments of the Party and Soviet Union in each arena, summarizes the major developments in Party organizational matters, and sets out the chief challenges and tasks confronting the Party that will call for future action. Frequently he will use the speech to highlight some major policy or programmatic issue. For example, at the 25th Congress in 1976, Brezhnev promised a new Soviet Constitution; at the 27th, one decade later, Gorbachev presented the new Party Program and the closely associated Plan for the economic development of the Soviet Union through the end of the century. The General Secretary's address is followed by reports on the Five-Year Plan (in recent years presented by the Chairman of the Council of Ministers) and on the Party's finances (from the Central Auditing Commission). These are followed by debates in which normally over 40 delegates address the Congress to praise the leadership, and then by a vote to endorse the reports and support the leadership. The Congress also formally elects the Central Committee to act as an interim Congress and the Central Auditing Committee to review Party finances.

Can the Party Congress Actually Influence Policy?

The Congress originally played an important role within the Party, featuring spirited debates over policy in its early years. An acrimonious disagreement over the Treaty of Brest-Litovsk ended in a split vote of 30 to 12 ratifying the peace settlement with the Germans. At the Eighth Congress the following year the so-called Military Opposition criticized the professionalization of the Red Army, including its use of former Tsarist officers, and mustered over 95 votes (against 174 for the majority) in a test vote. Since these early years, however, important procedural changes have diminished its power.

At the Tenth Congress in 1920, facing a determined "Workers' Opposition" advocating greater decentralization and expanded workers' control, Lenin secured passage of the resolution "On Party Unity." The resolution proclaimed,

> All class-conscious workers must clearly realize the perniciousness and impermissibility of fractionalism of any kind. . . . The Congress, therefore, hereby declares dissolved and orders the immediate dissolution of all groups without exception that have been formed on the basis of one platform or another (such as the Workers' Opposition group, the Democratic Centralism group, etc). Nonobservance of this decision of the Congress shall entail absolute and immediate expulsion from the Party.[5]

The Resolution marked a great watershed in Party history: No Party Congress since its adoption has been as lively. Opposition and debate did not cease immediately, however, and in the 1920s the Congress was one of the arenas of the great factional battles between Stalin and the Left and Right Oppositions. Yet the

Tenth Congress set down the principle by which opposition to the Party leader would in the future be identified with treason. And under Stalin, to quote the late Harvard Sovietologist Merle Fainsod, "congresses were transformed into rallies of Party and state functionaries who assembled to applaud and ratify the policies proclaimed by the Supreme Leader."[6]

In addition to the growing control of the Party leadership over dissent and factionalism in the Congress, the reasons for the body's declining role are not difficult to discern. First, the Congress was permitted to grow in size. (See Table 7.1) While a body of 104 delegates (the size of the 7th Party Congress in 1918) can actively debate and decide issues, one of 5000 finds this difficult. Second, congresses have become relatively infrequent. The statutory requirement has decreased from one convocation every year during the first two decades after the Revolution, to one every three years beginning in 1934, and then one every four years in 1952, and finally one every five years since 1965. And these increasingly lax requirements have been regularly violated in practice. Particularly under Stalin, the interval between congresses grew despite the statutory requirements: It was two and a half years between the 15th (1927) and 16th (1930) Congresses, another three and a half until the 17th (1934), then over five years until the 18th Congress (1939), and more than a decade until the 19th Congress (1952). Since Stalin's death, Party congresses have again become more frequent and regular, but regular congresses have still been held only once every 5 years since 1961. Third, the congresses have been brief, permitting the body little time to debate and decide policy. The 27th Party Congress in 1986, for example, lasted only nine days—simply not enough time for the Congress to set Party policy for the next five years. Fourth, and most important, the proceedings of these congresses have become formalistic. For example, all votes are unanimous. It is still safe to say, as Fainsod noted over two decades ago, that "the Party Congress remains a rally of the faithful, chiefly significant as a convenient platform from which the leadership proclaims new policies and goals, announces modifications in the rules and programs, and obtains formal approval of shifts in the top Party command."[7] Indeed, since the fall of Khrushchev, Party congresses have presented few surprises, becoming, in the words of the British Sovietologist Leonard Schapiro, as "bland, uneventful, colorless and smooth as a play being performed on the stage for the third year running."[8]

While the Party Congress is a quinquennial rally of the faithful, it is also a gathering of the Soviet elite. Some Western analysts have argued that these delegates may actually exert influence over the decisions of the Congress. Duke University's Jerry F. Hough, calculates that over a third of delegates to recent congresses are all-union, republic, or local officials, and almost a fifth are industrial or agricultural managers or military officers. Why bring together some of the most important figures in Soviet society for a Party Congress once every five years? Hough argues that influential members of the Party Congress, like those in the Supreme Soviet, help in a minor way to set the political agenda. In particular, many of the speeches delivered to each Congress by individual delegates draw attention to urgent concerns of the speaker. Although most of these are pleas for increased investment in local projects, some raise larger policy issues.

Table 7.1 GROWTH OF PARTY ORGANS, 1918–1986

Year	Congress	Date	Congress Delegates*		Central Committee Members*		Politburo Members*	
1918	VII	6–8 March	46	(58)	15	(8)	—	(—)
1919	VIII	18–23 March	301	(102)	19	(8)	5	(3)
1920	IX	29 March–5 April	554	(162)	19	(12)	5	(3)
1921	X	8–16 March	694	(296)	25	(15)	5	(3)
1922	XI	27 March–2 April	522	(165)	27	(19)	7	(3)
1923	XII	17–25 April	408	(417)	40	(17)	7	(2)
1924	XIII	23–31 May	748	(416)	53	(34)	7	(4)
1925	XIV	18–31 December	665	(641)	63	(43)	9	(5)
1927	XV	2–9 December	898	(771)	71	(50)	9	(8)
1930	XVI	26 June–13 July	1268	(891)	71	(67)	10	(5)
1934	XVII	26 Jan–10 Feb	1225	(736)	71	(68)	10	(5)
1939	XVIII	10–21 March	1569	(466)	71	(68)	9	(2)
1952	XIX	5–14 October	1192	(167)	125	(110)	10†	(4)
1956	XX	14–25 February	1349	(81)	133	(122)	11	(6)
1959	XXI	27 Jan–5 Feb	1269	(106)	‡		‡	
1961	XXII	17–31 October	4394	(405)	175	(155)	11	(5)
1966	XXIII	29 March–8 April	4619	(323)	195	(165)	11	(8)
1971	XXIV	30 March–9 April	4740	(223)	241	(155)	15	(6)
1976	XXV	24 Feb–5 March	4998	(0)	287	(139)	16	(6)
1981	XXVI	23 Feb–3 March	4994	(0)	319	(151)	14	(8)
1986	XXVII	25 Feb–7 March	5000	(0)	307	(170)	12	(7)

*Figures in parentheses are candidate members.

†At the end of the 19th Congress the Party Presidium was expanded to 25 members, but in March 1953, following Stalin's death, it was reduced in membership to 10.

‡Extraordinary Congress—no central Committee was elected.

In this way, CPSU congresses may provide an opportunity for public consultation with regional officials during the planning process, as national economic priorities are set.[9]

In addition, Hough argues, delegates to Party congresses may have some impact on the selection of the Central Committee. His evidence for this is tenuous. In the actual balloting for members of the Central Committee, the delegates to the Congress are presented a ballot and told to cross off the names of those candidates they find unacceptable. Yet, there are only as many candidates as there are positions for the Central Committee. (At the January 1987 Central Committee Plenum, Mikhail Gorbachev proposed multiple candidacies in Party elections—perhaps even at the all-union level. But this has not yet been adopted). It would appear that in the balloting itself the Congress currently exercises little influence over the composition of the Central Committee. Yet, according to Hough, the delegates may have some power in the matter before the final ballot is drawn up. At this stage, there is some consultation with the Congress delegates to ensure that the list will raise no objections.[10]

Hough presents his case as speculation with caution and caveats. It is undeniable that speeches before the Party Congress present slightly different views. Nonetheless, the importance of the Congress as a forum for the presentation of these views must be questioned, in view of the infrequency of its meetings. Most of these same "influentials" have far more frequent opportunities—at least twice a year in either the Supreme Soviet or the Central Committee—to present their views.

Central Committee

Since the Party Congress meets only infrequently, it elects a Central Committee to serve as an interim leading organ. According to the Party Rules, the Central Committee's powers include:

(a) *Interim Policy Formation*. Between Party congresses it "directs all the activity of the Party and of local Party agencies" and "creates various agencies, institutions and enterprises of the Party and directs their activity."

(b) *Leadership of State and Public Organs*. The Central Committee "directs the work of central state and public organizations of the working people" and carries out the Party's cadre policy.

(c) *Party Administration*. The Central Committee determines "the structure and staff of the Party apparatus," "appoints the editorial boards of the central newspapers and magazines under its control," and "distributes the funds in the Party budget and supervises its implementation."

(d) *Election*. The Central Committee elects the Politburo, Secretariat, and General Secretary and organizes the Party Control Committee.

(e) *Inter-Party Relations*. It represents "the CPSU in its relations with other parties."

In reality, it would appear that these powers are exercised in the name of the Central Committee by its Politburo and Secretariat [Articles 35–38].

The size of the Central Committee is not fixed in the Party Rules, but is determined at each Congress. The Central Committee elected in 1986 was composed of 307 full (voting) members and 170 candidate (nonvoting) members.[11] Candidate members are guaranteed the right to attend all plenary sessions and "the right to a consultative voice." Vacancies that open in the voting membership between sessions of the Party Congress are supposed to be filled from among the candidates.

Much of the membership in the Central Committee appears to be *ex officio*; in a sense, positions are elected to membership, rather than people. Robert Daniels, an historian at the University of Vermont, argues that since the early days of Stalin "a system of unwritten (or at least unannounced) rules . . . guarantee(s) Central Committee status to holders of elite-status bureaucratic office."[12] "It is therefore possible to view the Central Committee as a well-defined and quite stable set of leading job slots whose occupants enjoy the elite status conferred by Central Committee membership as long as and only as long as they occupy their respective offices."[13] Although this representation of "job slots" provides a certain stability to the institutional representation in the Central Committee, changes in the proportions have occurred (in recent years largely through expansion of the Central Committee), reflecting the changing policy concerns of the leadership.

Plenary sessions of the Central Committee must be held at least once every six months. We know little of what transpires in these meetings, for they are confidential, except for the final communiqué, decrees, and edited speeches published in the Soviet press. These plenary sessions are usually held either on the eve of a Supreme Soviet session or Party Congress, or on the occasion of a major policy announcement such as Gorbachev's program for scientific and technical progress, or during a grave domestic or international crisis (see Table 7.2). Given the brevity of its sessions and the gravity of the matters formally considered, one suspects that the formal meetings of the Central Committee are consumed in official announcements of policy, *pro forma* discussion, and ratifications of these policies.

Much of the important "legislation" in the Soviet Union is issued in the name of the Central Committee in the form of a Central Committee decree *(postanovlenie)*. Technically these decrees are not laws, but since they are binding on all Party members, among whom are the individuals who formally make the laws, they have the effect of legislation. Decrees of the Council of Ministers appear to have greater weight and urgency when issued as Joint Decrees of the Central Committee and Council of Ministers. These decisions are not all actually adopted by the Central Committee itself, however. Most are, in fact, issued and dated at times when the committee is not even in session. It would appear that only those relatively less-numerous decrees identified as acts of the plenary sessions of the Central Committee have actually been considered and adopted by the full body. The others were probably issued by the Politburo in its name.

The Elusive Power of the Central Committee

The power of the Central Committee is elusive. The institution predates the Bolshevik seizure of power in 1917, originating with the Russian Social Democratic Labor Party in 1898. During 1917, it was the Bolsheviks' Central Committee that decided Party policy and directed the activities of the Party organizations around Russia. Even after the Revolution, in the early days of the Soviet regime, the Central Committee initially continued to set Party policy and served as an arena for critical debates. It was, for example, in the Central Committee in November 1917, that Kamenev and Zinoviev fought for a coalition socialist government against Lenin's plan "for a homogeneous Bolshevik Government." The Central Committee continued into the late 1920's to be an arena for factional battles between Stalin and his opponents. But under Stalin it suffered much the same fate as the Party Congress.[14]

The reasons for the Central Committee's decline are much the same as those for the decline of the Congress. The usurpation of decision-making power by the Party leadership and the use of Party discipline to eliminate or silence any opposition within the Central Committee are among the most important.

Table 7.2   PLENARY SESSIONS OF THE CENTRAL COMMITTEE, 1981–1987

Year	Date(s)*	Principal Agenda Items
1981	3 March	Election of Politburo, Secretariat, and General Secretary
	16 November	Economic Plan and State Budget
1982	24 May	Food Program
	12 November	Election of General Secretary
1983	14–15 June	Ideology and Mass-Political Work
	26–27 December	Economic Plan and State Budget
1984	13 February	Election of General Secretary
	10 April	Reform of General Education and Vocational Schools
	23 October	Agriculture
	[19 November]†	
1985	11 March	Election of General Secretary
	23 April	Convocation of 27th Party Congress
	15 October	Agenda of 27th Party Congress (Party Program, Party Rules, and Plan)
		Economic Plan
1986‡	18 February	Political Report to 27th Party Congress
		Agenda of Party Congress (Program, Rules, and Plan)
	16 June	Economic Plan, 1986–1990
1987	27–28 January	Economic Administration Restructuring
		Party Cadre Policy
		[Democratization]
	25–26 June	Economic Administration Restructuring

*The pattern of meetings is slightly unusual in that during three of the years extraordinary sessions were called to elect a new General Secretary following the death of the incumbent.

†The plenary session scheduled for this date to consider the economic plan and state budget was cancelled at the last minute. Soviet officials explained that an earlier enlarged Politburo meeting that included regional Party secretaries considered these items. (*The Times of London*, 25 October 1984 and 23 November 1984).

‡No plenum was convened in late 1986. Reportedly disagreements within the leadership forced its postponement until January 1987.

Source: Pravda, 4 March 1981, 17 November 1981, 25 May 1982, 13 November 1982, 23 November 1983, 15–16 June 1983, 27–28 December 1983, 14 February 1984, 11 April 1984, 24 October 1984, 24 April 1985, 16 October 1985, 19 February 1986, 17 June 1986, 28–29 January 1987, 26–27 June 1987.

The size of the body has grown so that it is unable to decide policy quickly. (See Table 7.1.) The Central Committee on the eve of the October Revolution consisted of a dozen members, but by the end of Stalin's rule had reached 235 members; and it has continued to grow ever since, doubling again in size by 1981. The frequency and length of meetings have also blocked the Central Committee from exercising daily decision-making authority. According to a resolution adopted at the Eighth Party Congress in 1919, the Central Committee was to meet at least twice a month; and in the last quarter of 1920 it actually met weekly. Subsequently the statutory provision was changed so that meetings were required only once every two months beginning in 1922, once every four months in 1924, and only once every six months since 1952. Under Stalin, according to the revelations of Khrushchev's Secret Speech in 1956,

> Central Committee plenums were hardly ever called. It should be sufficient to mention that during all the years of the Patriotic War not a single Central Committee plenum took place. It is true that there was an attempt to call a Central Committee plenum in October 1941, when Central Committee members from the whole country were called to Moscow. They waited two days for the opening of the plenum, but in vain. Stalin did not even want to meet and to talk to the Central Committee members.[15]

Khrushchev's claims may be exaggerated. Nonetheless, the average number of meetings per year during the last two decades of Stalin's rule (1934–1953) was less than a tenth of what it had been during the first six years of Soviet power. Since Stalin's death, meetings have been held more frequently—at least twice a year, and in many years more often. Yet most sessions have convened for only one day since 1981, so that they are still not frequent and long enough to perform all the responsibilities assigned by the Party Rules.

To say that the Central Committee as a body normally exercises little power is not to say that the members of the Central Committee are powerless or that they cannot exercise power as a body under certain, perhaps extraordinary, conditions. The Central Committee contains the leading elite of Soviet society—the directors of the most important institutions and the holders of the highest expertise in Soviet society. (See Table 7.3.) Hough has labelled these the "Who's Who" elite of the Soviet Union; Ronald Hill has called them the Soviet Union's "incorporated experts".[16] Their positions and expertise give them considerable power not only as individuals, but sometimes as a collectivity, and potentially as a body.

Although it is clear that plenary sessions of the Central Committee do not make policy, Hough argues that the members of the Central Committee may actually participate in the discussion and making of policy. First, in the formal meetings of the Central Committee, the speeches delivered by members do actually debate policy. (Hough suggests that the decision not to publish stenographic reports of the Central Committee meetings after March 1965 has permitted debates to be frank.) Most of the speeches are apparently delivered by regional Party secretaries—most frequently by the Ukrainian, Belorussian, Kazakh, Uzbek, Moscow, and Leningrad Party secretaries. As in the case of speeches before the Supreme Soviet and Party Congress, these appear to focus on local needs, particularly for investment funds, but they can also touch on broader policy concerns. Yet, unlike speeches before the Supreme Soviet or the Party Congress, those in the Central Committee may be characterized on rare occasions by open controversy—such as debates in the late 60s over Soviet policy in the Middle East and toward Czechoslovakia and apparently debates in 1987 over democratization, *glasnost'*, and economic reform. The proposals and remarks may be taken into account when the Party leadership frames policy.

Second, outside the plenary sessions there may be a more informal, but more significant process of consultation that uses Central Committee members as "incorporated experts," who receive regular written briefings of Politburo meetings and the agenda of upcoming sessions. Some Central Committee members

Table 7.3   COMPOSITION OF THE CENTRAL COMMITTEE, MARCH 1986 (percentages)

	Full Members*	Candidate Members*	Total*
All-Union Party officials	8.8	5.9	7.8
Local Party officials	31.9	27.6	30.4
All-Union state officials	23.5	19.4	22.0
Local state officials	4.9	12.9	7.8
Foreign affairs officials	5.5	5.3	5.5
Military	7.5	7.6	7.5
Police	2.6	0.6	1.9
Culture-Propaganda officials	1.3	5.9	2.9
Scientific workers	3.6	4.1	3.8
Trade union officials	1.0	1.2	1.0
Managers-Workers	8.1	7.6	8.0
Other or unknown	1.3	1.8	1.5

*Columns may not sum to 100.0 due to rounding.

Sources: "CPSU Central Committee Full Members Elected by the Twenty-Seventh Party Congress in March, 1986," *Radio Liberty Research Bulletin* RL 145/86 (April 1, 1986); "CPSU Central Committee Candidate Members Elected by the Twenty-Seventh Party Congress in March 1986," *Radio Liberty Research Bulletin* RL 151/86 (April 9, 1986).

are brought into Politburo meetings to participate in the discussion of issues that concern them. Apparently they are even more frequently asked to submit memoranda of their views on major policy questions.[17]

The extraordinary occasions on which the Central Committee may directly exercise real power as a body are times of division within the top Party leadership. If Khrushchev's confrontation with the Anti-Party Group in 1957 is an operative precedent, the Central Committee may be able to play a decisive role in such critical showdowns. Even though Khrushchev was outvoted in the Politburo (then called the Presidium), he took the issue to the Central Committee, where a majority overturned the decision of the leadership. Even before that incident, Khrushchev turned to the Central Committee to win passage of his virgin-lands program in 1954, reconciliation with Tito in 1955, and the industrial reorganization of 1957.[18] It may well be that in future cases of significant disagreement within the Politburo, the Central Committee could again play a decisive role.

The Politburo

The leading policy-making and decision-making body within the CPSU is the Politburo. For such an important institution, the description of it in the Party Rules is decidedly brief: Specifically, the Politburo is elected by the Central Committee and is empowered "to direct the work of the Party between plenary sessions of the Central Committee." In reality, the Politburo has usurped much of the Central Committee's authority and normally directs the Party in its name. This makes the Politburo the principal decision-making body throughout Soviet society.

The Politburo (a contraction for Political Bureau) was created only after the Revolution (at the Eighth Party Congress in March 1919) as the Central Committee proved to be too cumbersome to direct the Bolshevik effort during the Civil War and Allied Intervention. (Actually, a political bureau had been created as early as October 1917, but this and other early efforts at organizational reform never resulted in a permanent institution.) During the 1920s, the Politburo rapidly assumed much of the decision-making authority within the Party, setting policy in virtually all spheres it chose to consider. In the latter half of the 1930s, however, the authority of the Politburo was eclipsed by Stalin's personal dictatorship, even though decisions continued to be made in its name. According to Khrushchev, Stalin used the threat of annihilation to intimidate many of its members. Indeed, apart from Stalin, only four of the other nine Politburo members in 1931 survived the Great Purge. Politburo meetings under Stalin "occurred only occasionally," and "many decisions were taken either by one person or in a round about fashion, without collective discussions."[19] Stalin, for example, would invite only those members whom he wanted, and in his last years divided them among informal subcommittees that met in place of the whole Politburo, leaving Stalin alone to provide coordination and leadership. Following the death of Stalin, the Politburo (called the Presidium from 1952 until 1966) resumed its regular meetings and much of its original power. In the mid-50s it once again became the forum for personal and perhaps "factional" battles among the leaders.

The size of the Politburo is not fixed by the Party Rules. Since 1965, it has averaged 20, including 13 full members and 7 candidate (nonvoting) members. It has ranged in size from 17 in 1965 to 23 in the mid-70s. (See Table 7.1.) Even though the Politburo has almost tripled in size since it was first created in 1919, it has remained small enough to discuss and set policy. In the past two decades there seems to have been growing institutionalization of membership in the Politburo. That is, as in the Central Committee, most positions in the Politburo during recent years appear to be assigned on an ex officio, or "job slot" basis. Throughout the history of the Politburo, the membership seems always to have included the General Secretary of the Party, at least one other CPSU secretary, the Chairman of the Party Control Committee, the Chairman of the Council of Ministers, and at least one First Deputy Chairman of the Council of Ministers.[20] Since Brezhnev's rise to power, the number of such ex officio memberships has grown. Seats are balanced among all-union Party secretaries, leaders of key all-union state institutions, and leaders of major regions. For example, the Politburo elected at the conclusion of the 27th Party Congress (March 6, 1986) included the General Secretary, three other secretaries from the Secretariat, and the Chairman of the Party Control Committee; eight state leaders, including the Chairman of the Council of Ministers and his First Deputy Chairman, the Chairman of the Supreme Soviet Presidium, the Ministers of Defense, Foreign Affairs, and Culture, and the chairmen of the KGB and Gosplan; and six key regional leaders, including the First Secretaries of the party organizations in Moscow, Leningrad oblast, the Ukraine, Belorussia, and Kazakhstan, as well as the Chairman of the Council of Ministers of the Russian SFSR.

The Politburo is formally elected by the Central Committee. Even before the Party Congress has adjourned, the newly elected Central Committee meets to elect the Politburo. After this, removals and new appointments are officially made at the Central Committee's plenary sessions. In actual practice, however, the Politburo appears to co-opt its own membership, and the Central Committee simply ratifies these decisions.

The Politburo in a sense functions something like a permanent "interdepartmental" committee with little formal organization. Its members are not formally salaried for their Politburo membership. The Politburo has no formal officers, although the General Secretary has been called the leader of the Politburo by the Soviet press. (The General Secretary apparently chairs most meetings of the Politburo. This may not have been true prior to Khrushchev's consolidation of power, for the best evidence available suggests that Stalin seldom chaired its meetings.) The Politburo does not have its own staff, but relies on that of the Secretariat (particularly its General Department) and the personal staff of the General Secretary to prepare its paper work.

The Politburo meets about once a week, usually for three to four hours on Thursdays, beginning at three in the afternoon. (The reports of the General Secretary to the Party congresses since 1976 indicate that the Politburo misses about five to ten weekly meetings each year, probably many during vacations and overseas trips by key leaders.) In these meetings, the members are apparently free to discuss the most important policy issues confronting the Soviet Union. That is, there are no formal limits on the power of the Politburo, and members apparently can involve themselves in the most minute details of policy if they choose. Yet, given the limits of their time, energy, and expertise, the Politburo probably spends most of its time setting priorities, allocating resources, and defining broad policies. Under Andropov, the Politburo began to report the general topics of discussion at each meeting on the front page of the next day's *Pravda*. Although these reports appear to be incomplete, particularly in the area of foreign policy, most meetings apparently discuss both foreign and domestic issues. The Plan frequently receives close attention. For example, the report on the meeting held January 6, 1987 stated that the Politburo considered improvements in the education of specialists, the results of Ryzhkov's meeting with the Premier of Hungary, and "several other questions" of domestic life and foreign policy.[21]

The proceedings of the Politburo, according to the limited evidence available to us, appear to be characterized by collective leadership, broad consultation, and consensual decision making. The Politburo seems to reach its decisions collectively. For example, during the five days of the Brezhnev-Nixon summit in May 1972, the Politburo met four times. In the process of the negotiations, the Soviets seemed to make important decisions regarding their negotiating stance at these Politburo meetings. As powerful as Brezhnev had become in the field of foreign affairs, he still had to secure the agreement of other members of the Politburo before he could make major changes in the Soviet position. Second, Politburo decision making apparently involves wide consultation with members of the Central Committee, the state apparatus, the Academy of Sciences, as well as other experts and affected parties. These participate in Politburo meetings at least to present expert reports and perhaps even to participate in the discussion of policy. Third, Politburo decision making stresses consensus among the leaders. The Soviet leaders have told us that the members of the Politburo rarely vote on major issues, but talk until a consensus is reached. The reason for this procedure is not entirely clear. It may be that by avoiding a show of hands on divisive issues the Politburo preserves collegiality. (It may also be, however, that the procedure only preserves the myth of collective leadership even as it permits inequality of power within the body, for rather than giving each an equal vote in policy decisions, this procedure permits some leaders' opinions to carry more weight than others'.)

Beyond this we know distressingly little about the inner workings of the Politburo. For example, we do not even know whether all members, including the candidate members, participate in the weekly meetings. It is unknown whether heated debate and disagreements occur regularly among these members. According to one Party historian, writing toward the end of Khrushchev's tenure, "Differences of opinion are frequently aired at meetings of the Presidium. This is an expression of the desire of the members of the Presidium to study the issue in question from all sides and in the greatest possible depth."[22] The limited evidence provided by the public statements of Politburo members during the Brezhnev years suggest that this may still be true.[23] Most importantly, the role of the General Secretary in these meetings is unclear: Does the Politburo usually ratify (or acquiesce in) his decisions, or must the General Secretary build a new consensus on each issue? The opinions of Western analysts regarding these issues are the bases of some of our most important disagreements about the Soviet political process—a topic to which we will turn in Chapter 9.

The Secretariat and Central Committee Apparatus

The Secretariat and the Central Committee apparatus that it supervises constitute the administrative arm of the Party. According to the Party Rules, the Central Committee elects the Secretariat "to direct current work, principally in selecting cadres and organizing the verification of fulfillment" (Article 38). The Central Committee apparatus contains the administrative departments of the Party that perform many of these functions. While structurally distinct, the Secretariat actually assumes direct responsibility for the apparatus. Taken together, these institutions resemble and function somewhat like a miniature Party council of ministers.

The Party Secretariat, like the Politburo, was created at the 8th Party Congress in March 1919, but was not initially the central institution that it was to become under Stalin. The powers that were later united in the Secretariat were originally divided between an Orgburo (Organizational Bureau), which was "to direct all organizational work of the Party," and a Secretariat with ill-defined authority. One year after its creation, the authority of the Secretariat was defined more carefully as "current questions" of administration, but it did not immediately become a center of power. This began to change, however, in 1921, as Stalin began to dominate the Orgburo and to direct the Secretariat. Then the power of these institutions burgeoned. On April 4, 1922, Stalin was appointed to the newly created post of General Secretary, the first among three secretaries in the Secretariat; and with the assistance of the other secretaries (Molotov and Kuibyshev) and with his control of the Orgburo, Stalin came to control the Party organization. (Although the Orgburo survived as a separate institution until the 19th Party Congress in 1952, it became increasingly difficult after 1922 to distinguish its work from that of the Secretariat.)

Stalin's control of the Secretariat and Orgburo gave him control of Party appointments and local Party activities. Stalin used the Orgburo to exercise control over appointments at the highest levels. He used the Party's Records and Assignment Department (*Uchraspred*) to make binding "recommendations" before the election of local Party officials. Then he extended this power to positions outside the Party as well. Through the Organization-Instruction Department (later, the Organization-Assignment Department—*Orgraspred*), Stalin sent instructors to supervise and "advise" local Party organizations, to report to the Secretariat on their activities, and to overturn local decisions when necessary. Stalin rounded out his control of Party activities through such Secretariat-Orgburo departments as those for women, villages, and, most importantly, Agitation and Propaganda (*Agitprop*).[24]

Almost since the time of its creation in 1922, the office of General (or First) Secretary has been the single most powerful position in the Soviet Union. The office has had only six incumbents:

1922–1953	Joseph V. Stalin
1953–1964	Nikita S. Khrushchev
1964–1982	Leonid I. Brezhnev
1982–1984	Yuri V. Andropov
1984–1985	Konstantin U. Chernenko
1985–	Mikhail S. Gorbachev

Stalin, during his rise to power, built this position to its full potential as the commanding height of the CPSU and Soviet society. Although this post was not initially filled following Stalin's death, leading to the speculation that it would be eliminated, Khrushchev was given the title "First Secretary of the Central Committee" in September 1953, and this proved to be the successor to Stalin's position. The conspirators who ousted Khrushchev in 1964 apparently had agreed among themselves even before Khrushchev's removal that Brezhnev would assume this post, and in 1966 returned to it the original title of General Secretary. The post-Brezhnev successions have all focused first of all on the question of selecting a new General Secretary.

The General Secretaries have never had to depend solely upon the Secretariat as a position of power. All have been members of the Politburo at the time of their appointments to the General Secretaryship; and all have continued to sit on the Politburo (and with time to lead it) after their appointments. Both Stalin and Khrushchev in their later years (1941–1953 and 1958–1964, respectively) served as Chairman of the Council of Ministers. Brezhnev in his last years (1977–1982), Andropov during his last 8 months, and Chernenko for 11 months all served as Chairman of the Presidium of the Supreme Soviet.

The size of the present-day Secretariat is not fixed in the Party Rules. Since 1965, it has averaged 10 secretaries, ranging between 9 and 12 members. The secretaries are formally elected by the Central Committee; and removals and appointments are made formally at its plenary sessions. But in practice, the Secretariat appears to coöpt its own membership. The Secretariat apparently meets once each Wednesday. It is empowered to issue Instructions to the lower levels of the Party apparatus.

Under the general direction of the General Secretary, the other CPSU secretaries appear to specialize in their responsibilities. The pattern that emerged under Brezhnev, and that appears to have continued through the 1980s, has two secretaries assume broad coordinating responsibilities—one for the economy and agriculture; the other for foreign affairs, ideology, and culture. The second of these positions seems to have been used from 1982 to 1984 to cultivate the heirs to the General Secretary. In the last months of Brezhnev's leadership, Andropov assumed this position; and then it was held by Chernenko under Andropov and by Gorbachev under Chernenko. Under Gorbachev, it appears to be held by Egor Ligachev.[25] Whether this is still the post for heirs apparent is unclear. Under the coordination of these two secretaries, the remaining secretaries apparently assume responsibility for narrower spheres such as agriculture. industry, foreign affairs, or ideology; and they supervise the Central Committee Apparatus.

Table 7.4 charts the interlocking nature of the top administration, showing the Politburo and Secretariat with changes through the October 1987 Central Committee Plenum. The four righthand columns show other key posts held by members of the Politburo and Secretariat.

The Central Committee Apparatus The Central Committee apparatus is composed of some 21 departments. Most of these (15 departments in 1986) are organized on sectoral lines and primarily supervise ministries, state committees, and public organizations.[26] (See Table 7.5.) The other departments principally administer the Party itself. (Some of these, however, also supervise non-Party agencies as part of their responsibilities.) The most important of all departments is the Organization-Party Work Department, which is responsible for appointments and personnel within the Party itself and in the Komsomol and trade unions. (The Party Control Committee, which oversees discipline among Party members, actually functions somewhat like a department of the apparatus. This body, formally elected by the Central Committee, investigates cases of improper conduct among Party members and serves as an appellate body for members expelled from their primary party organizations.) In addition to these departments, the Secretariat maintains a general business office, known as the Administration of Affairs Department, which is responsible for the "housekeeping" needs of the Secretariat, such as its finances, health facilities, and capital construction. The Gen-

Table 7.4 THE SOVIET LEADERSHIP: THE INTERLOCKING DIRECTORATE OF POST-REVOLUTIONARY ADMINISTRATION (22 October 1987)

	CPSU		STATE		
Politburo	Secretariat	Regional First Secretaries	Council of Ministers	Presidium of Supreme Soviet	Other Key Posts
M. S. Gorbachev	Gorbachev			X	
V. I. Vorotnikov			(ex officio)		Chairman, RSFSR CM
A. A. Gromyko				X (Chairman)	
L. N. Zaikov	Zaikov			X	
E. K. Ligachev	Ligachev				
V. P. Nikonov	Nikonov				
N. I. Ryzhkov			Chairman		
N. N. Sliunkov	Sliunkov				
M. S. Solomentsev					Chairman, Party Control Committee
V. M. Chebrikov			KGB		
E. A. Shevardnadze			Foreign Affairs		
V. V. Shcherbitskii		Ukraine		X	
A. N. Iakovlev	Iakovlev				
P. N. Demichev*				X (First Deputy Chairman)	
V. I. Dolgikh*	Dolgikh				
B. N. Yel'tsin*		Moscow			
Iu. F. Solov'ev*		Leningrad Oblast			
N. V. Talyzin*			Gosplan		
D. T. Iazov*			Defense		
	A. P. Biriukova				
	A. F. Dobrynin				
	A. I. Lukianov				
	V. A. Medvedev				
	G. P. Razumovskii				

*Candidate members of Politburo.

Table 7.5   CENTRAL COMMITTEE DEPARTMENTS (May 9, 1986)

Sectoral Departments	Principal Agencies It Supervises
Administrative Organs	Legal organs (e.g., Courts, Procuracy), police (e.g., KGB, Internal Affairs)
Agricultural Machinery	Tractor-production ministries
Agriculture & Food Industry	Agricultural ministries
Chemical Industry	Chemical industry ministries
Construction	Construction ministries and committees
Culture	Cultural ministry and professional unions
Defense Industry	Defense industry ministries
Economic	Financial agencies and planning committees
Heavy Industry & Power Engineering	Natural resource extraction and metallurgical industry ministries
Light & Consumer Goods Industry	Consumer goods ministries
Machine-Building Industry	Machinery ministries
Main Political Administration	Armed forces
Science & Education	Education ministries and Academy of Sciences
Trade & Domestic Services	Trade, consumer services, and utility ministries
Transportation & Communications	Communication and transport ministries
Functional Departments	**Responsibilities**
Cadres Abroad	Soviet personnel serving abroad
General	Housekeeping for Secretariat and Apparatus
International	Relations with nonruling communist parties
Organizational-Party Work	Local party organs, membership records, Komsomol, trade unions
Propaganda	Party agitation-propaganda (also supervises mass media)
Liaison with Workers and Communist Parties of Socialist Countries	Relations with ruling communist parties

Source: U.S. Central Intelligence Agency. *CPSU Central Committee Executive and Administrative Apparatus.* CR 86-13074.

eral Secretary also maintains a personal staff. Although we know little about this staff, it apparently grew in importance under Brezhnev.

The structure of the apparatus has not been constant.[27] The rapid expansion of Party responsibilities with the transformation of Soviet society has led to a number of reorganizations of the departments under the Secretariat's control. In 1934, the initial functional division of departments in which each (e.g., Organization-Assignment) performed a single function across all sectors of the Soviet economy and society was replaced by an industrial-branch or sectoral organization in which each department (e.g., Agriculture, Transport) performed all functions such as cadre assignment within a single sector. This reorganization permitted greater Party control over each sector but made greater demands on manpower. Thus, the apparatus grew both in size and power during this period. The Great Purge left the Party apparatus with too few experienced apparatchiki to staff the sectoral organization, and so the Secretariat returned to the earlier functional organization in 1939. Nine years later, however, the Party once again turned to a sectoral structure. Although there have been frequent changes in the number and names of departments within the apparatus, this sectoral organization has been maintained ever since. The one major, albeit temporary, reform was Khrushchev's series of reorganizations beginning in 1955 that resulted in two parallel sets of sectoral departments—one for the RSFSR, the other for the other union republics. The former reported to a Bureau for the RSFSR directed by Khrushchev. His successors eliminated this bureau and the duplicate departments in 1966.

Most of the present-day departments of the Central Committee resemble ministries or state committees. Each is directed by an appointed functionary called a head or chief (*zaveduiushchii*) who shares his decision-making authority within the department with a small collegium composed of his first deputy chief and one to seven deputy chiefs. Each department is divided into sections (*sektor*), which frequently parallel the ministries that the department supervises. The departments are staffed by Party employees known as instructors (*instruktor*) or, for special assignments, inspectors (*inspektor*). A department may also maintain a Consultants Group of in-house experts to conduct longer-term research. The size of these staffs in Moscow is a closely guarded secret. Western estimates range from under 1000 to almost 10,000, although most place the number of "responsible" officials between 900 and 1500, with perhaps another 2400 technical and clerical staff members.[28] These numbers are not large enough for the apparatus to assume the responsibility of directly administering the Soviet Union on a daily basis; instead, they are apparently limited to administering the Party and only supervising non-Party elements of society.

The Functions of the Secretariat and Apparatus.   According to the Party Rules, the Secretariat performs two essential functions: "selection of cadres" and "organizing the verification of fulfillment" (Article 38). It is probably also the case, although we do not have as much evidence of this, that the Secretariat and apparatus prepare materials for Politburo decisions and may even act as the principal policy-drafting agency for the leadership.

In implementing the Party's cadre policy, exercising what is called its *nomenklatura* power, the Secretariat verifies, approves, or makes key appointments at every level of society. (The closely related power to make "recommendations" for elective offices is sometimes called the power of *rekomendatsiia* but often is simply subsumed under the rubric nomenklatura.) According to former Party Secretary I. V. Kapitonov, "Cadre policy was and remains the key link of Party leadership, and a powerful lever through which the Party influences all affairs in society."[29]

The nomenklatura is actually a list of positions and appointments over which the Party exercises or can exercise control. These lists cover all sectors of Soviet society, including key appointments in the Party, the state, the military, trade unions, the press, industry, science, education, and even the arts. This power is exercised by the Party secretaries at all levels of the Party. The nomenklatura of the Party Secretariat at the all-union level apparently includes all Party and state positions at the all-union and union-republic levels, key oblast positions, and even some positions below that (e.g., industrial management positions that are considered vital to Soviet security). The union-republic secretaries control positions below the all-union nomenklatura; the oblast secretaries control positions below that; and so forth. Western estimates of the number of positions covered by the Party nomenklatura vary widely. For example, Rolf Theen estimates that in the mid-1970s the number of positions covered by the all-union, union-republic, and oblast nomenklatura lists was around 600,000, half within the nomenklatura of the all-union secretariat and over a third within that of the union-republic apparatus. Other estimates place the total number of positions on all Party nomenklatura lists as high as two or three million.[30] The *nomenklatury* ensure that the most important and powerful positions in the Soviet Union are held by individuals who, even if they are not Party members, are loyal to and support the Communist Party.

Nomenklatura is of at least two types: basic and registration. The former includes appointments that must be approved and confirmed by Party secretaries. (In actual fact, the Party can take the initiative in filling these positions.) Registration nomenklatura includes positions for which prior approval is not required; but in these appointments the Party must be kept informed. The various Western descriptions of nomenklatura actually disagree over the details of control. For example, some argue that there are three types of Party control: one in which the Party actually makes the appointments, a second in which the Party must approve appointments made by others, and a third in which the Party reserves the right to veto appointments made by others but does not usually intervene in such decisions. (Within the Soviet Union the term *nomenklatura* has acquired the colloquial meaning of "the Soviet elite," since these positions are roughly coextensive with the elite of Soviet society. This term has travelled with ex-Soviet emigrés to the West, so that the term has also been used recently in the West with its colloquial connotation.[31])

The second function of the Secretariat is officially called "the verification of fulfillment." That is, the Secretariat supervises the key institutions of society—Party, state, and public organizations—to ensure that they are, in fact, fulfilling the Plans and directives of the leadership. Verification of fulfillment by non-Party institutions is made possible by the extensive hierarchy of secretaries in lower Party organizations who exercise their right of supervision (*pravo kontrolia*) over management. Verification of fulfillment by these lower Party organizations is ensured by the Party "instructors" that each level of the Party apparatus can send to subordinate Party organizations. In addition, the apparatus can organize investigative commissions to examine the practices of a local Party organization, leaders of the local soviet administration, or managers of industrial or agricultural undertakings.[32]

The third function of the Secretariat and Central Committee apparatus, and the one about which we know the least, is the preparation of memoranda and draft decisions for the Politburo—specifically drafts of decrees to be issued in the name of the Central Committee. In preparing these memoranda and policy drafts, the Secretariat apparently consults widely with experts and affected parties. One of the great uncertainties, and thus the beginning point for an important debate within Sovietology, is the extent to which the Secretariat initiates policy proposals or responds to initiatives originating outside the apparatus. This is a debate to which we will return in Chapter 9.

THE PARTY MEMBERS

Critical to the Party's leading role in all institutions of Soviet society is its ubiquitous membership. For the Party, members provide the links with the larger Soviet society.

According to the Party Rules, membership is open to the most conscious and active members of Soviet society.

> Any citizen of the Soviet Union who accepts the Party Program and Rules, actively participates in the construction of communism, works in one of the Party organizations, carries out Party decisions and pays membership dues may be a member of the CPSU. [Article 1]

The admission procedures of the Party are, in fact, far more selective than these rules suggest. In practice, individuals do not freely join the local Party organization; they must be invited in, or "co-opted," by the local Party leaders.

The Party Rules set the minimum age for Party membership at 18 years, but those under the age of 25 can enter only from the Komsomol (Article 4). (Party Rules adopted before 1986 had set the latter age at 23.) Before admission to full membership, aspiring communists must pass through a candidate stage of one-year duration. To demonstrate worthiness, the candidates are expected to be exemplars of the qualities of the good communist—participating actively in Party meetings and its public activities, raising their political consciousness through individual and group study of Marxism-Leninism and Party documents, and exhibiting in their private and public lives those attributes of a "communist attitude toward labor" and "communist morality" demanded by the Party. Needless to say, the period of candidacy can be a nervous one! The candidates enjoy all rights and must shoulder all responsibilities of full membership, except they cannot cast a vote in Party meetings nor may they stand for election within the Party.

Admission to candidate status and then admission to full membership is conducted at the lowest level, in the primary party organization. At both stages each aspirant must present recommendations from three CPSU members who have belonged to the Party for at least five years and have known the aspiring member for at least one, working with him or her either on the job or in public activity. (There are two exceptions to this; the aspirant joining from the Komsomol must include a recommendation from his or her raion or city Komsomol committee as one of these three; and Party members who sit on the All-Union Central Committee as either full or candidate members may not make recommendations

THE RIGHTS AND DUTIES OF THE PARTY MEMBER

The Party Rules adopted at the XXVII CPSU Congress list the following duties and rights of the Party members.

It is the duty of the Party member:
- to firmly and steadfastly carry out the Party's general lines and directives, to explain the CPSU's domestic and foreign policy to the masses, to organize the working people for its implementation, and to facilitate the strengthening and expansion of the Party's ties with the people;
- to set an example in labor and to safeguard and increase socialist property; to persistently strive for an increase in productive efficiency, steady growth in labor productivity, improvement in the quality of production, and introduction in the national economy of the achievements of contemporary science, technology, and advanced experience; to improve his qualifications and to actively advocate all that is new and progressive and will have the maximum effect on accelerating the socio-economic development of the country;
- to actively participate in the political life of the country and in the administration of state and public affairs, to set an example in the performance of civic duty, and to actively facilitate the ever fuller implementation of socialist self-government of the people;
- to master Marxist-Leninist theory, to expand his political and cultural horizons, and to promote in every way an increase in the Soviet people's consciousness and their ideological-moral growth; to wage a resolute struggle against all manifestations of bourgeois ideology, private-property mentality, religious prejudices, and other views and customs that are alien to the socialist way of life;
- to strictly observe the norms of communist morality, to affirm the principle of social justice that is inherent in socialism, to place public interests above personal ones, to show modesty and decency, sensitivity and attention toward people, to respond promptly to the needs of the working people, and to be truthful and honest with the Party and the people;
- to consistently propagate the ideas of proletarian, socialist internationalism and Soviet patriotism among the masses of the working people, to wage a struggle against manifestations of nationalism and chauvinism, to actively promote the strengthening of friendship among the peoples of the USSR and fraternal ties with the socialist countries and with the proletarians and working people of the whole world;
- to promote in every way the strengthening of the defensive might of the USSR, and to wage a tireless struggle for peace and friendship among peoples;
- to strengthen the ideological and organizational unity of the Party, to safeguard the Party against the infiltration into its ranks of people unworthy of the lofty title of Communist, to display vigilance, and to keep Party and state secrets;
- to develop criticism and self-criticism, to boldly disclose shortcomings and strive for their removal, to combat ostentation, conceit, complacency, and hoodwinking, to administer a resolute rebuff to all attempts to suppress criticism, to oppose bureaucratism, parochialism, departmentalism, and all actions detrimental to the Party and the state and to report them to Party bodies, up to and including the CPSU Central Committee;
- to steadfastly carry out the Party line in the selection of cadres according to

their political, business and moral qualities and to be uncompromising in all cases in which the Leninist principles of the selection and up-bringing of cadres are violated;

- to observe Party and state discipline, which is equally binding on all Party members. The Party has one discipline and one law for all Communists, regardless of their services or the posts they hold.

The Party member has the right:

- to elect and be elected to Party bodies;
- to freely discuss questions of Party policy and practical activity at Party meetings, conferences, and Congresses, to submit proposals, and to openly express and uphold his opinion until the organization has adopted a decision;
- to criticize any Communist, regardless of the positions he holds, at Party meetings, conferences, and Congresses and at plenary meetings of the committee of any Party body. Persons guilty of suppressing criticism or persecuting anyone for criticism are to be held to strict Party accountability, up to and including expulsion from the ranks of the CPSU;
- to personally participate in Party meetings and in bureau and committee meetings when the question of his activity or conduct is under discussion;
- to address questions, statements, or proposals to Party bodies at any level, up to and including the CPSU Central Committee, and to demand an answer on the substance of his address.

Source: *Pravda,* 7 March 1986

for membership.) At both stages, the question of admission to candidacy or to full membership is decided by the General Meeting of members in the PPO. Little is known of the dynamics of decision making within the PPO on membership questions, but it appears that an investigation by the organization's secretary and a vote by its bureau recommending acceptance or rejection may be determinative in these matters. The General Meeting affords members the right to question the aspirant and, curiously, since it is normally an open public meeting, it permits even nonmembers from the community to participate. (Although we do not know the extent of participation in such meetings, the latter provision hypothetically permits the larger citizenry some say in the composition of Soviet society's vanguard.) At both stages admission is by a two-thirds vote of the members attending the local General Meeting, which must then be confirmed by the Party committee at the next-higher level (raion or city) (Articles 4, 14–18).

Membership obliges one to meet the demands of the Party for active participation, diligent study, and an exemplary personal life. Thus, the member commits himself to sacrifice much of his leisure time and even a part of his private, family life to the public demands of the Party. The primary instrument for this is the so-called party assignment (*partiinoe poruchenie*), a task given to an individual member by the PPO, its bureau, or its secretary.[33] This can be selection for an elective office (e.g., deputy to a local soviet or chair of a local trade union), volunteer work (e.g., the *druzhina*, or director of a youth group), or short-term duties (e.g., delivering a speech at a public gathering). Rejection of such an assignment is a violation of Party discipline, at least in theory. In addition to these duties, the Party member must pay monthly dues fixed by the Party Rules on a sliding scale, ranging from 10 kopeks for those with incomes under 70 rubles a month or 1.0 percent of incomes between 101 and 150 rubles monthly up to 3.0 percent of incomes over 300 rubles.

If Party membership was simply duties and obligations, few would join, but, in fact, it also promises important benefits.[34] The formal rights of membership include participation in the election of Party officials, discussion of Party policy, criticism of any communist, and submission of proposals to higher Party organs. While these are probably formalistic, they may accord many Party members a slightly larger voice in decision making through inclusion in the informal consultation processes that actually shape policy and select officials. For many Party members, the principal benefits of membership are those purposive rewards of participating in the implementation of the Party's policies and perhaps even the construction of communist society. Many also find in it that solidaristic sense of camaraderie that ties members of an elite together. (The Party reinforces this by social activities following Party meetings.) All too often, however, members join for purely self-regarding, frequently material, reasons. Party membership gives one status in the community that can set one above neighbors and co-workers. It can open doors to career advancement: The Party seeks out those who are the achievers in each segment of Soviet society; in turn, Party membership, although it is not an absolute requirement for advancement, increases the probability of further promotion. And Party membership opens up the possibility of a position in the Party apparatus itself, one of the most important career ladders in Soviet society.

Since not all Party candidates and members live up to the expectations of the Party, some, particularly those "careerists" who lack ideological conviction, are punished or expelled (articles 8–13). Members who have failed to pay their dues for three months "without valid reason" and have "effectively lost contact with the Party organization" are "considered to have dropped from Party membership." Members or candidates who fail to perform their Party duties or commit criminal offenses are subject to Party action in addition to any criminal proceedings initiated by the state authorities. The Party Rules prescribe four increasingly severe punishments for the wayward: admonition, reprimand, reprimand to be entered in the member's permanent record, and expulsion. Members can be "called to Party account" by their own primary party organization or a higher Party organization. Members are supposed to have the right to a full hearing of their case in a meeting at which they are present. Expulsion of members, according to the Party Rules, is decided by a two-thirds vote of the General Meeting of the PPO and must then be ratified by the raion or city Party committee. (Members who have been elected to the committees of higher Party conferences or congresses are guaranteed a special procedure; this apparently isolates the Party leadership from any grassroots actions against them—no matter how unlikely that may be —and it gives the leadership a freer hand in the removal of such members.) Party members, including expelled members, retain the right to appeal all penalties within two months to higher Party organs, all the way up to the all-union organs in the case of expulsion. We do not know, however, to what ex-

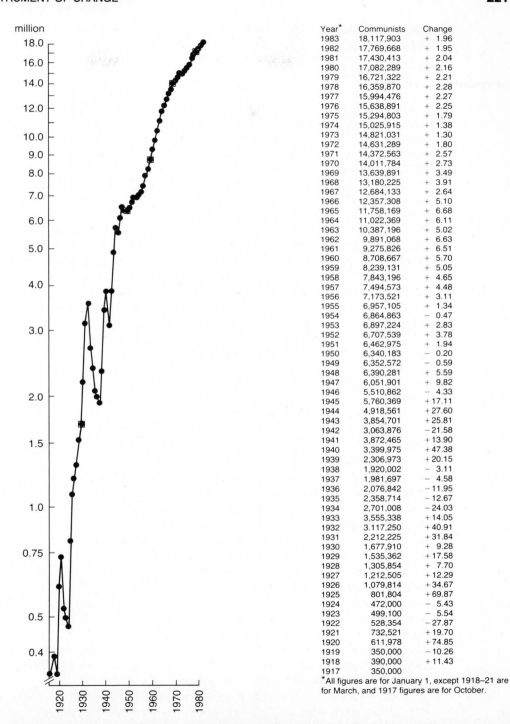

Year*	Communists	Change
1983	18,117,903	+ 1.96
1982	17,769,668	+ 1.95
1981	17,430,413	+ 2.04
1980	17,082,289	+ 2.16
1979	16,721,322	+ 2.21
1978	16,359,870	+ 2.28
1977	15,994,476	+ 2.27
1976	15,638,891	+ 2.25
1975	15,294,803	+ 1.79
1974	15,025,915	+ 1.38
1973	14,821,031	+ 1.30
1972	14,631,289	+ 1.80
1971	14,372,563	+ 2.57
1970	14,011,784	+ 2.73
1969	13,639,891	+ 3.49
1968	13,180,225	+ 3.91
1967	12,684,133	+ 2.64
1966	12,357,308	+ 5.10
1965	11,758,169	+ 6.68
1964	11,022,369	+ 6.11
1963	10,387,196	+ 5.02
1962	9,891,068	+ 6.63
1961	9,275,826	+ 6.51
1960	8,708,667	+ 5.70
1959	8,239,131	+ 5.05
1958	7,843,196	+ 4.65
1957	7,494,573	+ 4.48
1956	7,173,521	+ 3.11
1955	6,957,105	+ 1.34
1954	6,864,863	− 0.47
1953	6,897,224	+ 2.83
1952	6,707,539	+ 3.78
1951	6,462,975	+ 1.94
1950	6,340,183	− 0.20
1949	6,352,572	− 0.59
1948	6,390,281	+ 5.59
1947	6,051,901	+ 9.82
1946	5,510,862	− 4.33
1945	5,760,369	+17.11
1944	4,918,561	+27.60
1943	3,854,701	+25.81
1942	3,063,876	−21.58
1941	3,872,465	+13.90
1940	3,399,975	+47.38
1939	2,306,973	+20.15
1938	1,920,002	− 3.11
1937	1,981,697	− 4.58
1936	2,076,842	−11.95
1935	2,358,714	−12.67
1934	2,701,008	−24.03
1933	3,555,338	+14.05
1932	3.117,250	+40.91
1931	2,212,225	+31.84
1930	1,677,910	+ 9.28
1929	1,535,362	+17.58
1928	1,305,854	+ 7.70
1927	1,212,505	+12.29
1926	1,079,814	+34.67
1925	801,804	+69.87
1924	472,000	− 5.43
1923	499,100	− 5.54
1922	528,354	−27.87
1921	732,521	+19.70
1920	611,978	+74.85
1919	350,000	−10.26
1918	390,000	+11.43
1917	350,000	

*All figures are for January 1, except 1918–21 are for March, and 1917 figures are for October.

Figure 7.1 Growth of Communist Party Membership, 1917–1983. (*Source: Partiinaia zhizn',* 15 [August 1983].) Semilogarithmic scale shows growth rates over time.

tent these procedural guarantees are actually observed, for the inner workings of the Party organization on such matters are closely guarded secrets.

Party Growth, 1917 to 1987

Growth patterns in Party membership during the 70 years since 1917 reflect varying goals of the leadership. With tight control over admissions and expulsions (and with more Soviet citizens seeking admission than the Party is willing to accept), the Party leadership has been able to exercise considerable discretion in the size and composition of its membership. The size of the CPSU is, in the first instance, a result of the policy choices made by the Party leadership. Shifts in these membership policies have served to reinforce the leadership's short and long-term policy objectives over time.

The Party has grown to over 50 times its size when it seized power in 1917, but, as Figure 7.1 makes clear, this growth has not always been steady.[35] The Party experienced four periods of substantial growth after coming to power. During the Civil War years (1919–1920) it sought to expand its base of popular support. With the "Lenin enrollments" of 1924 and 1925, the Party began a campaign to "proletarianize" its membership, which soon became a drive during the First Five-Year Plan to bring the new workers, collective farmers, and managers into its ranks. Following the Great Purges, in an effort to replenish its membership and bring the new elite of socialism into the Party, membership again began to rise in 1938. The first year of the Soviet involvement in the World War II brought a dramatic fall in Party membership, but the next years saw a renewed drive to expand Party membership, as soldiers and other heroes of the war effort were encouraged to join.

Each of these periods of rapid growth was followed by a purge of the Party rolls that brought a decline in overall membership. (The Russian word used to describe this process—*chistka*, or purge—literally means a cleansing.) In 1921, Lenin ordered a purge of careerists and the unorthodox, particularly oppositionists like the Worker's Opposition, who had joined during the Civil War. The surge in membership during the First Five-Year Plan was followed by a Central Committee decision on December 10, 1932, to suspend all admission to the Party and to purge the careerist, disloyal, or less vigilant members who had flocked to the Party during the initial industrialization and collectivization drives. While the most substantial purges preceded Kirov's assassination, the elimination of Party membership continued into the period of the Great Purge with less numerous, but more dramatic, removals. In 1941, Party membership fell by 21.6 percent, due both to the many deaths in Party ranks during the first year of the war, and to the purge of members cut off from Moscow in the regions occupied by the Germans. And the rapid expansion during World War II was followed by a small-scale purge in 1945, notably among the candidate members who had been admitted from the Red Army.

Since the death of Stalin, Party growth has been far more consistent, with an overall trend toward declining growth rates, particularly as the growth in the Soviet adult population itself has fallen and as the Party approaches what its leaders appear to see as an optimal level. Stalin's last years had seen an erratic pattern of rapid growth in 1946 and 1947, followed by a decline in 1948 and 1949, and then renewed growth in 1950, 1951, and 1952. Under Khrushchev beginning in 1956, and into the first year of the Brezhnev period (1965), Party growth sustained high levels, proceeding at an average of 5.6 percent annually. The Brezhnev era brought a much slower growth rate; and this has continued since his death. Thus, between 1966 and 1986, Party membership grew only 2.1 percent annually.[36]

The Dilemmas of Party Membership

According to the British academic John H. Miller, the Party seeks to include within its membership two groups:

(1) All (or virtually all) persons who take, or interpret, decisions at any level in society, plus those who might be needed to replace them, and a substantial proportion of those who influence or communicate decisions. . . .

(2) A second, much larger group whose function is to permeate all walks of ordinary, non-party life, to gather and report information, to mobilize local opinion and lead local activity, and to verify performance.[37]

The guiding role of the Communist Party in Soviet society is institutionalized through its membership policies, ensuring that the individuals in leading positions throughout society are members of the Party. This includes not only the power-wielders of Soviet society, but also the more numerous "opinion-leaders" in each institution, who mediate communications between leaders and the citizenry. The former group, according to Miller's estimates, makes up about a seventh of the Party membership, and the latter group makes up the remainder.

To include these two groups within the Party, its membership has continued to expand. Yet the Party still seeks to maintain its "vanguard" status in Soviet society and rejects the role of a mass party. Thus, the leadership faces what Darrell P. Hammer of Indiana University has called "the dilemma of party growth"—to balance these contradictory pressures for representativeness and a continuing leadership role.[38] The Party has, in fact, grown since Stalin's death not only in absolute, but also in relative terms, thus potentially threatening its vanguard status. The percentage of adults who belong to the Party has nearly doubled from 5.7 percent in 1956 to 10.0 percent in 1986. The most rapid expansion took place during Khrushchev's years. The consequence was greater representativeness among groups previously excluded or "underrepresented" by the Party (e.g., workers, minority nationalities, technically trained workers). But if the rate for the early 60s had continued into the Brezhnev years, the Party would have reached 40 million members, or over one in five Soviet adults, by the mid-80s. Decisions taken in 1965 and 1966 slowed the growth trend. And since then, policy has emphasized "quality" in admissions, slowing growth relative to the adult population to only a fraction of its former rate.

Closely associated with the dilemma of Party growth is the dilemma of

Party composition. As a proletarian party, the legitimacy of the CPSU requires that workers be featured prominently among its members. Yet as the vanguard of Soviet society, the efficiency of the CPSU requires that white-collar leaders of all-union, union-republic, and local institutions play a major role. In part, this dilemma has been obscured by the ideological rationalization that all strata in Soviet society have come over to the political position of the proletariat. But this has not resolved the dilemma facing the Party's leadership.

White-collar members ensure that the levers of power in each institution are controlled by the Party. In Soviet society, the more important a position, the more likely it is held by a Communist Party member. As an illustration of this principle, Party membership rates among deputies elected to soviets rises with the level of the soviet in the territorial-administrative hierarchy: In 1985, only 42.8 percent of the deputies in local soviets were Party members, but at the union-republic level, the percentage was 67.1, and at the all-union level it was 71.4. Similarly, in the armed forces, the higher one's rank, the more likely that individual is a Communist Party member. Herbert Goldhamer estimates that, while only two-fifths of Soviet ensigns and warrant officers are members, fully three-quarters of all commissioned officers belong to the Party. Thus, the personal attributes that are highly correlated with power in Soviet society are also highly correlated with membership in the Communist Party: The higher one's education the more likely he or she is to be a CPSU member; men are more likely to be members than women; urban residents are more likely than rural residents; and so forth. And this is the source of the dilemma of Party composition.[39]

Although workers have constituted the largest social group in the CPSU's membership, they have, nonetheless, never constituted a majority of its members. And those of working-class *background* (that is, holding working-class occupations at the time they entered the Party) constituted a majority only in the early years of the Party. During the "Lenin enrollments" of 1924 and 1925 and the First Five-Year Plan, the membership drive to "proletarianize" the Party resulted in an expansion in worker membership, but the purges of Party membership in the 1930s hit these members particularly hard. And the membership drives of the pre- and postwar years emphasized those in white-collar occupations. Since Stalin's death, however, this trend has been reversed, and the proportion of members from working-class backgrounds has grown steadily. According to the Party's own figures, members of working-class background where 45.0 percent of the total Party membership in 1986.[40] (These figures overstate the proportion of members who hold working-class jobs, for many who entered the Party as workers and maintain that class designation have risen rapidly in their careers.)

Peasants also have been underrepresented in the Party. Even though peasants constituted a majority of the population at the time of the Revolution, Party members of peasant origins constituted only 7.5 percent of the total in 1917. This proportion rose in the 1920s but began to decline after that, initially due to the Stalin purges, which hit peasant members much as they did the worker members, and, since World War II, due to the declining proportion of the peasantry in the labor force.

The proportion of Party members listed as white-collar employees at the time of admission to the Party has shown a pattern just the reverse of that for workers. Declining from 32.2 percent at the time of the Revolution to 7.9 percent in 1932, the proportion of members of white-collar "origins" began to rise in the mid-30s under Stalin, reaching a majority of the Party membership (50.7 percent) by 1957. Since Khrushchev's consolidation of power, this pattern has been reversed: This proportion has fallen steadily, reaching 43.2 percent by 1986.[41]

Although members of working-class origins now constitute the largest social stratum in the CPSU, this does not mean that a worker's chance to join the Party is equal to that of someone in a white-collar occupation. For example, while workers and white-collar employees made up equal shares of the Party membership (43.7 percent) in 1982, workers outnumbered white-collar employees nearly 2.4 to 1 in the total population. The Australian Sovietologist T. H. Rigby has attempted to estimate the percentage of each occupation that holds Party membership, a statistic for which he coined the term "the party saturation rate"— essentially the probability of holding Party membership if one holds a given occupation. At the upper limits this rate is 99 to 100 percent of key state officials such as all-union and republic ministers and their deputy ministers, chairmen of oblast, city, and raion soviets, and heads of administrations of oblast governments. This is followed closely by the proportion among university presidents, directors of significant plants, collective farm chairmen, and senior officers of the armed forces. Based on such statistics, we estimate that the chances of being a Party member for a white-collar employee may be 2 to 3 times higher than for a worker, and it may be as much as 14 times higher for a factory director than for his workers.[42]

Even though the emphasis of Party policies has shifted over time between recruitment of workers and recruitment of white-collar employees, the Party admissions policy has been consistent in its efforts to draw the "best" representatives from each class. This has been reflected in the steady rise in the educational level of Party members, as Figure 7.2 shows. Today, the likelihood of Party membership is closely correlated with one's educational attainment. In the Ukrainian SSR, 78 percent of scientific workers with the doctor of science degree and 52 percent with a candidate of science degree were Party members in 1984. In 1981, 51 percent of those with a candidate of science degree (Ph.D.) or higher were Party members, followed by 29 percent of those with a complete higher education and 9 percent of those with a complete secondary education (including those with an incomplete higher education).[43] Thus, a Soviet adult with a higher education is over two and a half times as likely to be a Party member as someone with only a secondary education; an adult with the equivalent of a Ph.D. is four to five times as likely to be a member as the secondary school graduate.

One consequence of its emphasis upon the "best" representatives is that the Party membership has been unrepresentative (in the statistical sense) of the major ascriptive distinctions in the population—sex and nationality.[44] For example, men are about three times as likely as women to be Party members. (Chapter 12 examines these questions of equity at greater length.)

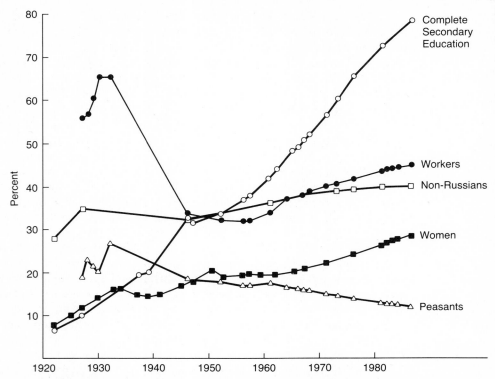

Figure 7.2 Composition of CPSU Membership, 1922–1986. (*Source*: Drawn from data in P. S. Shoup, *The East European and Soviet Data Handbook* [New York: Columbia University Press, 1981]; "KPSS v tsifrakh," *Partiinaia zhizn'* [July 1986].)

THE PRIMARY PARTY ORGANIZATION

All Party members must belong to a primary party organization (called a cell until 1939), which is usually organized in his or her place of work. PPOs exist within virtually all Soviet institutions that employ adults (and have at least three communists among these employees), including factories, retail shops, hotels, collective farms, universities, schools, military regiments, local soviet administrations, ministries, and embassies abroad. (In a few cases [18.4 percent of the total in 1986] these organizations are established on a territorial, rather than a production, basis in places of residence.) By the beginning of 1986, there were 440,363 primary party organizations.[45]

The PPO plays a critical role in the activities of the Party, for it is at this point that the Party comes into direct contact with most of its members and with the larger Soviet society. According to the Party Rules, the functions of the PPO include:

    (a) admission (and expulsion) of members;

    (b) political instruction of Communists;

    (c) agitation and propaganda among the working people;

    (d) mobilization of the working people to accomplish "the tasks of economic and social development";

    (e) implementation of the Party's personnel policy; and

    (f) supervision of management and workers to combat "manifestations of red tape, parochialism and departmentalism, . . . violations of state, labor and production discipline, . . . attempts to deceive the state, . . . [and] laxity, mismanagement, and waste . . . " [Article 58]

Importantly, the PPO serves as the representative of the Party "on the spot." In virtually every institution in Soviet society the PPO implements the Party's control over society through its right of supervision (*pravo kontrolia*) over managers and executives, its involvement in personnel appointments at the lowest levels, and its direct work with non-Party citizens in the institution and its neighborhood (Article 59).

    Although we sometimes talk of the PPOs as though they were a homogeneous set of organizations from one end of the Soviet Union to the other, they actually display a confusing variety of structures (Articles 52–57) (see Figure 7.3.). In the smallest and simplest PPOs, those between 3 and 15 members and candidates, the general meeting of members convenes once a month and periodically elects a part-time secretary and deputy secretary as well as delegates to the Party conference of the next higher Party organization. This "simple" structure, however, is uncommon.

    First, PPOs differ in the extent to which they have developed a hierarchy of subordinate organizations and groups within the PPO itself. Small PPOs (under 50 members) within complex institutions (e.g., a large factory with separate shops) may establish a subordinate party *group* in each shop, sector, or department with an unsalaried party group organizer (*partgruporg*) to lead it. Larger PPOs (over 50 members) may establish a subordinate Party *organization* in each shop, sector, or department and below these a party *group* in each work brigade. In this last example the Party organizations at each level (PPO and shop) must hold meetings once every two months, so that members attend an average of one meeting per month. In very large PPOs with over 300 communists, the general meeting of the whole PPO meets only infrequently; and the monthly meetings of members are held in the subordinate party organizations.

    Second, PPOs differ in the complexity of their executive organs. In small organizations with 15 to 300 members and candidates, the general meeting elects a bureau for a term of two or three years. This includes the secretary and deputy secretaries of the organization. In large institutions with over 300 Party members and candidates (or under certain special production conditions) the PPO may establish a committee that then elects the bureau and secretaries. In the largest organizations, with over 500 communists, the subordinate shop Party organizations can establish such committees.

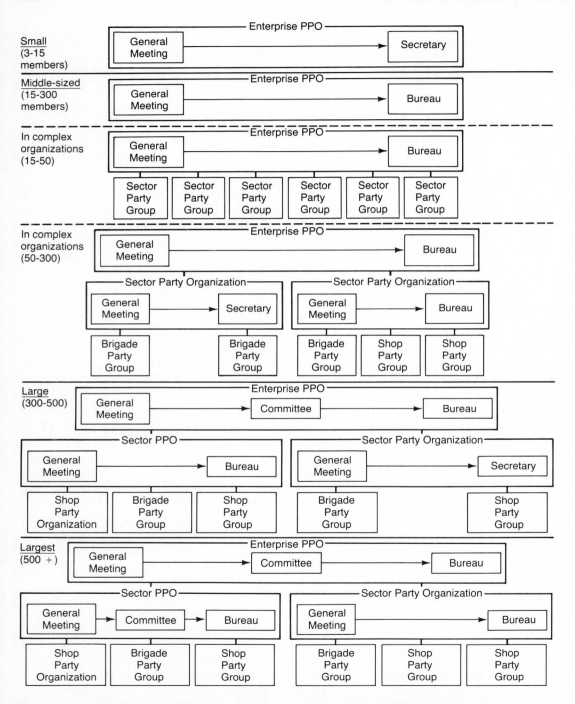

Figure 7.3 Alternative structures of Primary Party Organizations (distinguished by size of PPO and complexity of institution within which it is organized).

Third, PPOs are divided between those with "officials released from their regular work" to assume full-time responsibilities as Party *apparatchiki* and those without full-time officials. Only PPOs with 150 or more members can have full-time officials.

And last, PPOs differ in their status and that of their subordinate organizations. In the larger institutions with over 300 communists in which the Party organization has established a committee, the subordinate shop organizations may be given the rights of PPOs on membership matters. In still larger institutions with over 500 communists in which committees have been established at the level of the institution and each shop organization, the sector organizations subordinate to the shop organizations may be given the rights of PPOs on membership matters. And in the largest Party organizations with over 1000 Communists, the enterprise-level committee can be given the rights of a raion Party committee on membership matters.

The Party secretaries of the primary party organizations can play an important role in the life of the organization and of the institution within which it is located. Secretaries must have been Party members for at least one year before their election. They are normally elected for a term of two or three years, depending on the size of their organization. In the more important organizations the election of the secretary is frequently determined by a "recommendation" from higher Party committees. Some of the work of the secretary and his or her staff is simply bureaucratic, including collecting monthly membership dues and maintaining the organization's records. Yet the secretary who can use the position's powers effectively—particularly its power to make recommendations in membership matters, its determination of the Party assignments of members, its control over personnel appointments, and its right of supervision over management— can wield substantial power. The organization's position of secretary is also the lowest rung in the elaborate hierarchical Party apparatus that stretches all the way to Moscow. His loyalty to these higher Party officials is ensured by their control over his original appointment and subsequent promotion or removal, by continued supervision of him through visits by Party "instructors" sent by higher organizations, by the "veto" and "ratification" powers they exercise over many decisions at the lowest level, as well as through a continuous flow of directives and incessant telephone calls.

THE ROLE OF THE CPSU

In the West there is a tendency to portray the Communist Party of the Soviet Union as an institution apart from, and sometimes opposed to, Soviet society. Nothing could be further from the truth. Communists are very often one's parents, relatives, neighbors, or co-workers. Only by this presence throughout Soviet society and this daily, face-to-face contact with virtually all Soviet citizens can the Party continue to lead the transformation of Soviet society.

The role (or functions) of the Communist Party in Soviet society has been central to the transformation of that society.[46] As the ultimate authority on Marxism-Leninism, the Party propounds the dogmas that legitimate the policies of the Soviet regime and define its objectives (*ideological* function). Through its control over the education, "upbringing," and indoctrination of Soviet citizens, the Party has created a political culture that continues to support its rapidly changing socioeconomic and political institutions (*socialization* function). Continued success in this will be required if the Party is to create the new communist man of the future.

Party direction of the transformation process has required control of the key institutions of Soviet society so as to mobilize human energies on behalf of the Party's tasks. It is the Party that sets the general outlines of policy for the Soviet state and public organizations (*policy-making* function). Through its control of the "selection, training, and placement of cadres," the Party ensures that the commanding positions in these institutions are held by individuals who share the Party's vision of the future and its means of achieving its objectives (*staffing and leadership recruitment* function). And its supervision of implementation ensures that these institutions do, indeed, carry out the policies set down by the Party (*monitoring* function).

Lastly, as Ronald Hill argues, the CPSU performs a *system integration* function: "bringing unity and coherence to a political system that might otherwise lack those qualities."[47] It provides not only a unified apparatus to link periphery to center, but also a unifying myth to bind together citizens from very different cultural traditions and at markedly unequal levels of development. Holding together a society as diverse as the Soviet Union in geographical and human terms, particularly as that society has undergone revolutionary change, has been one of the most important accomplishments of the Party.

NOTES

1. See Ronald J. Hill, "The U.S.S.R.: Social Change and Party Adaptability," *Comparative Politics* 17 (July 1985), 453–471.
2. "Programma Kommunisticheskoi Partii Sovetskogo Soiuza," *Pravda*, (March 7, 1986), Preamble.
3. "Ustav Kommunisticheskoi Partii Sovetskogo Soiuza," *Pravda*, 7 March 1986.
4. *Pravda*, 26 February 1986.
5. V. I. Lenin, "Pervonachal'nyi Proekt Rezoliutsii X S"ezda RKP o Edinstva Partii" [Preliminary Draft Resolution of the Tenth Congress of the RKP on Party Unity], *Polnoe sobranie sochinenii*, 5th ed. (Moscow: Politicheskaia Literatura, 1963), 43:89–92.
6. Merle Fainsod, *How Russia Is Ruled* (Cambridge, Mass.: Harvard University Press, 1967), 142, 145, 217.
7. Fainsod, 217–218.
8. Leonard Schapiro, "Keynote—Compromise," *Problems of Communism* 20 (July-August 1971), 2.
9. Jerry F. Hough and Merle Fainsod, *How the Soviet Union Is Governed* (Cambridge, Mass.: Harvard University Press, 1979), 362; Howard L. Biddulph, "Local Interest Articulation at CPSU Congresses," *World Politics* 36 (October 1983), 28–52; Hough and Fainsod, 450.
10. Hough and Fainsod, 451–453.
11. *Pravda*, 7 March 1986.

12. Robert V. Daniels, "Office Holding and Elite Status: The Central Committee of the CPSU," in Paul Cocks, Robert V. Daniels, and Nancy Whittier Heer, *The Dynamics of Soviet Politics* (Cambridge, Mass.: Harvard University Press, 1976), 78.

13. Daniels, 78, see also Hough and Fainsod, 456–457.

14. John Lowenhardt, *The Soviet Politburo* (Edinburgh: Canongate, 1983), 15; Fainsod, 133, 146.

15. *Sovetskaia Istoricheskaia Entsiklopediia* (Moscow: Sovetskaia Entsiklopediia, 1965), 8: 274–275, "Kul't lichnosti Stalina"; Lowenhardt, *The Soviet Politburo*, 14, 16.

16. Ronald J. Hill and Peter Frank, *The Soviet Communist Party* (London: Allen & Unwin, 1981), 64.

17. Hough and Fainsod, 462–465.

18. Fainsod, 219–220.

19. Fainsod, 322–323.

20. Lowenhardt, 78.

21. Lowenhardt, 89–90; *Pravda,* 25 February 1976 and 24 February 1981; Hill and Frank, 67; *Pravda,* 7 January 1987.

22. G. I. Shitarev, *Voprosy Istorii KPSS,* No. 7 (1964), 37.

23. Philip D. Stewart, James W. Warhola, and Roger A. Blough, "Issue Salience and Foreign Policy Role: Specialization in the Soviet Politburo of the 1970s," *American Journal of Political Science* 28 (February 1984), 1–22.

24. On the history of the Party apparatus, see Fainsod, 176–208.

25. Alexander Rahr, "A New Chief Ideologist in the Kremlin," *Radio Liberty Research Bulletin* RL 183/85 (June 5, 1985).

26. U.S. Central Intelligence Agency, *Directory of Soviet Officials: National Organizations* (Washington, D.C.: Central Intelligence Agency, 1986), 13–18.

27. Fainsod, 176–208.

28. Hough and Fainsod, 423–424; Lowenhardt, *The Soviet Politburo,* 86; A. Pravdin, "Inside the CPSU Central Committee" (An Interview with Mervyn Matthews), *Survey* 20 (Autumn 1974), 95.

29. Bohdan Harasymiw, "Nomenklatura: The Soviet Communist Party's Leadership Recruitment System," *Canadian Journal of Political Science* 2 (November 1969), 493–512; Jerry F. Hough, *The Soviet Prefects* (Cambridge, Mass.: Harvard University Press, 1969), 114–116, 150–170.

30. Harasymiw, "Nomenklatura", 512; Rolf H. W. Theen, "Party and Bureaucracy," in Gordon B. Smith, ed., *Public Policy and Administration in the Soviet Union* (New York: Praeger, 1980), 41–44; John H. Miller, "The Communist Party: Trends and Problems," in Archie Brown and Michael Kaser, eds., *Soviet Policy for the 1980s* (Bloomington, Ind.: Indiana University Press, 1982), 21.

31. Michael Voslensky, *Nomenklatura: The Soviet Ruling Class* (New York: Doubleday, 1984).

32. Hill and Frank, 94–97.

33. M. I. Khaldeev and G. I. Krivoshein, eds., *Pervichnaia partiinaia organizatsiia: opyt, formy, i metody raboty* (Moscow: Politizdat, 1979), 254.

34. James Q. Wilson, *Political Organizations* (New York: Basic Books, 1974).

35. The most complete study of Party membership is T. H. Rigby, *Communist Party Membership in the U.S.S.R., 1917–1967* (Princeton, N.J.: Princeton University Press, 1968).

36. "KPSS v tsifrakh," *Partiinaia zhizn',* No. 14 (July 1981), 13; "KPSS v tsifrakh," *Partiinaia zhizn',* No. 14 (July 1986), 19; M. S. Gorbachev, "Politicheskii doklad Tsentral'nogo Komiteta KPSS XXVII S"ezdu Kommunisticheskoi Partii Sovetskogo Soiuza," *Pravda,* (February 26, 1986), 9. For an informative debate over the member-

ship policies under Brezhnev see T. H. Rigby, "Soviet Communist Party Membership Under Brezhnev," *Soviet Studies* 28 (July 1976), 317–337; Aryeh L. Unger, "Soviet Communist Party Membership Under Brezhnev: A Comment," *Soviet Studies* 29 (April 1977), 306–316; T. H. Rigby, "Soviet Communist Party Membership Under Brezhnev: A Rejoinder," *Soviet Studies* 29 (July 1977), 452–453.

37. Miller, 3–4.
38. Darrell P. Hammer, "The Dilemma of Party Growth," *Problems of Communism* 20 (July-August 1970), 16; Miller, 6; Gorbachev, "Politicheskii doklad", 9; "KPSS v tsifrakh" (1981), 13; United Nations Office of International Economic and Social Affairs, *Demographic Indicators of Countries: Estimates and Projections as Assessed in 1980* (New York: United Nations, 1982), 437.
39. *Pravda,* 2 March 1985; Herbert Goldhamer, *The Soviet Soldier: Soviet Military Management at the Troop Level* (New York: Crane, Russak and Co., 1975), 262–263.
40. Rigby, 412–453; "KPSS v tsifrakh" (1986), 22.
41. Rigby, 412–453; *Ezhegodnik Bol'shoi Sovetskoi Entsiklopedii,* 12; "KPSS v tsifrakh" (1986), 22.
42. U.S.S.R. Tsentral'noe Statisticheskoe Upravlenie, *Narodnoe Khoziaistvo SSSR, 1922-1982: Iubileinyi statisticheskii ezhegodnik* (Moscow: Finansy i Statistika, 1982), 30, 48; Hough and Fainsod, 347–351.
43. *Narodnoe Khoziaistvo SSSR, 1922-1982,* 42, 125; "KPSS v tsifrakh" (1981), 17–18; *Pravda Ukrainy,* 27 September 1984.
44. Rigby, 359–363; *Ezhegodnik Bol'shoi Sovetskoi Entsiklopedii,* 12; "KPSS v tsifrakh" (1981), 16, 18.
45. "KPSS v tsifrakh" (1986), 26.
46. Michael P. Gehlen, *The Communist Party of the Soviet Union: A Functional Analysis* (Bloomington, Ind.: Indiana University Press, 1969); Hill and Frank, 74–103; Juan Linz, "Totalitarian and Authoritarian Regimes," in Fred I. Greenstein and Nelson W. Polsby, eds., *Macropolitical Theory* (Reading, Mass.: Addison-Wesley, 1975), 208.
47. Hill and Frank, 102.

chapter 8

Politics at the Periphery: Republic and Local Institutions

The involvement of average citizens in the political life of the Soviet Union, the production of commodities by state-run factories and farms, and the provision of services by state administrations take place for the most part in institutions remote from Moscow. That is, much of the participatory and administrative, as distinct from the decision-making, activity of the Soviet Union takes place below the all-union level. Thus, a consideration of Soviet politics that looks only at the all-union institutions in Moscow would be incomplete.

TERRITORIAL-ADMINISTRATIVE STRUCTURE

The Soviet citizen must contend with a multiplicity of Party and state institutions, for the Soviet political system maintains roughly four layers of state and Party institutions below those in Moscow, distinguished one from the other by their territorial jurisdiction. Whereas political institutions in the United States are divided among only three levels of government (federal, state, and county or city), in the Soviet Union they are divided among all-union, union-republic, *oblast'*, *raion* or city, and village. Moreover, this division represents only the most common pattern of institutions; local practices actually present a mind-boggling number of deviations from this.[1]

The union republic is the sole territorial jurisdiction immediately below the all-union institutions, for the USSR is juridically the union of the soviet socialist republics. The 15 union-republic governments administer territories that range in

```
                        All-Union
                            |
                     Union-Republic
                            |
                         Oblast'
                            |
                    ┌───────┴───────┐
                  Raion            City
                    |
                  Village
```

size from the Russian Soviet Federative Socialist Republic, or RSFSR—about
the size of all 48 contiguous U.S. states plus Canada—to the Armenian Soviet Socialist Republic (SSR)—about the size of Maryland. These range in population
from the RSFSR with over 140 million people to the Estonian SSR with only
about 1.5 million. (See Table 8.1.)

In eight union republics the principal administrative subdivision immediately below the union republic is the *oblast'*. (Six of these oblasts carry the name
krai.) Five of the union republics are no bigger than oblasts themselves and thus
have no oblast-level administrative subdivisions. The remaining two have a few
oblast-level administrative subdivisions, but are not completely divided among
these. An oblast is usually about the size of an American state, ranging between
the size of New Hampshire and Indiana. At the extreme, however, Krasnoyarsk
krai in Siberia is larger than Alaska and Texas combined. These range in population from 6.5 million (Moscow oblast, excluding the city of Moscow) to under
300,000.

Below the oblast (or immediately below the union republic if there are no oblasts) are the city and rural district (*raion*) governments. (An exception to this
are the 85 largest cities in union republics with oblasts: These are directly subordinate to their respective union-republic governments.) The rural districts (roughly
equivalent to a county) are divided into villages and village settlements; and the
larger cities are divided into boroughs, each of which is also called a *raion*.

In actual practice, the Soviet administrative hierarchy is not as simple or uniform as this discussion suggests. As Figure 8.1 makes clear, there may be many exceptions to the patterns described above. For example, autonomous oblasts may
be contained within either a union republic or a krai. A few smaller cities are subordinate to other cities and, in a few cases, to urban raions of larger cities. In the autonomous okrugs (nationality-based raions), there may even be a sixth level of
soviets and administration. The combinations, while not limitless, are nonetheless many.

Soviet Federalism

Formally, the Soviet Union is a federal state. Yet, in its design it is a unique
form of federalism, differing from that found in the West: According to the description found in its Constitution, Soviet differs from American federalism in three sig-

Table 8.1   THE UNION REPUBLICS OF THE USSR, 1986

Union Republics	Territory (in 1000 km²)	Population (in hundred thousands)	Titular Nationality (percent)*	Russian (percent)*
RSFSR	17,075.4	144.1	82.6	—
Ukrainian	603.7	51.0	73.6	21.1
Belorussian	207.6	10.0	79.4	11.9
Uzbek	447.4	18.5	68.7	10.8
Kazakh	2,717.3	16.0	36.0	40.8
Georgian	69.7	5.2	68.8	7.4
Azerbaidjan	86.6	6.7	78.1	7.9
Lithuanian	65.2	3.6	80.0	8.9
Moldavian	33.7	4.1	63.9	12.8
Latvian	63.7	2.6	53.7	32.8
Kirgiz	198.5	4.1	47.9	25.9
Tadjik	143.1	4.6	58.8	10.4
Armenian	29.8	3.4	89.7	2.3
Turkmen	488.1	3.3	68.4	12.6
Estonian	45.1	1.5	64.7	27.9

*Figures for national composition are from 1979 census.

Source: Russia, Tsentral'noe Statisticheskoe Upravlenie, *Chislennost' i sostav naseleniia SSSR.* Moscow: Finansy i statistiki, 1985; Russia, Tsentral'noe Statisticheskoe Upravlenie, *Narodnoe khoziaistvo SSSR, 1985.* Moscow: Finansy i statistiki, 1986.

nificant ways. First, Soviet federalism is based on nationality, in that each federal unit is distinguished from the others (or at least they were so distinguished at the time it was originally established) by its predominant nationality (Article 70). Second, Soviet federalism provides not a single federal link (e.g., federal-state), but a more complex hierarchy of rights (Articles 76–88). That is, there is a federal link between the all-union and the union-republic governments; but below the union republics there are also three smaller territorial units (autonomous republics, autonomous oblasts, and autonomous okrugs) defined by nationality, each of which has some federal rights. Third, in the balance of power between center and locality, Soviet federalism tends to far greater centralism than American federalism. The Soviet system makes many more of the important decisions at the center, often relegating to the lower levels of government, whether guaranteed federal prerogatives or not, the task of simply implementing these. Absent from the Soviet system is the drama of conflict between state and federal governments that we take for granted in the United States. Yet, Soviet federalism is not simply a hollow shell; it is a more complex mechanism than that. And understanding Soviet federalism and the territorial-administrative structure of the Soviet state is important to understanding the institutions and some of the political processes and policy issues within the Soviet Union.

Union Republic   The highest nationality-based units are the union republics. Why is a nationality accorded the dignity of a union republic? The official Soviet

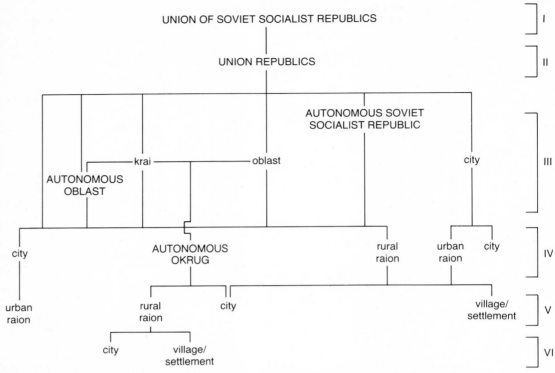

Figure 8.1 Territorial-Administrative Structure. (Territorial units in capitals are nationality based with "federality" rights.

explanation is threefold. First, each of these nationalities has an ancestral homeland within the Soviet Union in which that nationality has (or had) numerical preponderance. In 13 of the union republics the titular nationality (that for which the republic is named) still held a majority in 1979; and in all but 1 (Kazakh SSR) it was the largest nationality. Second, these nationalities are among those with the largest populations; each numbers over a million. And third, each of their homelands is on one of the international borders rather than deep within the territory of the Soviet Union, so that it can exercise its right to secede from the Soviet Union.

The Constitution of the Soviet Union guarantees the union republics four major prerogatives (Articles 72, 76–81). They are sovereign; they can conduct their own foreign relations; they have the right to secede; and they are represented within all branches of the all-union state institutions. In short, according to the Soviet constitutional myth, the union republics, having freely joined the Soviet Union, reserve to themselves the ultimate prerogative to determine their own destinies.

With the exception of all-union representation, however, these are hollow guarantees. For example, one would assume that an important element of sovereignty is territorial integrity. In fact, Article 78 of the Constitution guarantees that "the territory of a Union Republic may not be altered without its consent. The boundaries between Union Republics may be altered by mutual agreement of the Republics concerned, subject to ratification by the Union of Soviet Socialist Republics." Yet, in 1956, when the Soviets decided that the 16th union republic (the Karelo-Finnish SSR) was no longer useful, Moscow simply eliminated it as a union republic, demoting it to the status of an autonomous republic. Apparently the guarantee of sovereignty ensures very little—not even territorial integrity.

While union republics have the right to conduct their own foreign relations, none has conducted an independent foreign policy. Article 80 of the Constitution guarantees: "A Union Republic has the right to enter into relations with other states, conclude treaties with them, exchange diplomatic and consular representatives, and take part in the work of international organizations." Each of the union republics does in fact maintain its own ministry of foreign affairs, and the Belorussian SSR and Ukrainian SSR are even members of the United Nations. Yet, none of the republics actually engages in an independent foreign policy. Their ministries of foreign affairs are only administrative extensions of the all-union Ministry and are under the hierarchical control of Moscow. The Byelorussian and Ukrainian delegates to the United Nations have always voted with Moscow, even when Eastern European states have deviated from the leadership of the Soviet Union. (In the 1936 Constitution, union republics were also guaranteed the right to maintain their own armed forces, but the new Constitution makes no mention of this.)

And according to Article 72, union republics have the right to secede from the Soviet Union. But, Moscow made it clear during the Civil War that each demand for independence would be assessed from a proletarian perspective. If secession would not promote proletarian revolution, it would not be allowed. Needless to say, no union republic has yet seceded.

The union-republic governments are actually accorded representation at the all-union level—the one major prerogative that appears to be observed. Each union republic not only has 32 representatives in the second house of the all-union Supreme Soviet, but also representation in the executive and administrative organs of the all-union government: The Chairman of the Presidium of each union republic serves as a Deputy Chairman of the all-union Presidium, and the Chairman of the Council of Ministers of each union republic serves as a Deputy Chairman of the all-union Council of Ministers.

Most of the powers reserved to union republics are residual powers. Article 76 of the Soviet Constitution, paragraph 2, states: "Outside of the spheres listed in Article 73 of the Constitution of the U.S.S.R., a Union Republic exercises independent authority on its territory." That sounds impressive until one reads Article 73, which lists the powers of the all-union government, which include dominant authority in matters of republic and local organization and legislation; economic planning, budgeting, taxation, and monetary policy; social, scientific, and resource policies; and administration. After all the powers of the all-union government are subtracted, there is little residual power left.[2]

Autonomous Republic, Oblast, and Okrug   Below the union republics are 20 autonomous soviet socialist republics (ASSR). Why would a nationality be accorded the status of an autonomous republic rather than a union republic? According to the official explanation, one reason is simply a smaller population—most number under a million, but over a half-million (Table 8.2). Yet, a nationality with a population large enough to qualify for union-republic status may be accorded ASSR status if its national homeland is an enclave deep within the Soviet Union. For example, there are six million Tatars in the Soviet Union, but since their homeland is not on an international boundary they have only an autonomous republic. The official rationale is that these enclaves would not be able to exercise the sovereign prerogatives of the union republics—particularly, the right to secede![3]

The Soviet Constitution assigns the ASSR only residual powers—independent authority outside the jurisdiction of the Soviet Union and the union republic within which it is located (Article 82). As one might imagine, if the union republic has few powers left over after the powers of the all-union level are subtracted, there are even fewer left to the ASSR. Administratively an autonomous republic functions much like an oblast. It is subject to the union republic within which it is located, and, in most senses, simply administers policy handed down from above. An autonomous republic, however, is guaranteed representation at the all-union and union-republic levels (Article 83). The Soviet of Nationalities in the all-union Supreme Soviet includes 11 representatives from each autonomous soviet socialist republic. The autonomous republic also has guaranteed representation at the union-republic level, just as each union republic is guaranteed representation at the all-union level (Article 110).

At the oblast level there are eight autonomous oblasts. These are based on the homelands of nationalities with still smaller populations—most of these nationalities number close to 100,000. (A principal exception is the Jewish Autonomous Oblast in the Soviet Far East, the only Soviet "homeland" for the 1.8 million Soviet Jews.) The Soviet Constitution accords the autonomous oblast no specific powers (Article 86). Each does, however, send five deputies to the all-union Soviet of Nationalities (Article 110).

At the raion level there are 10 autonomous *okrugs*. These are reserved for nationalities with the smallest populations—most number under 50,000. Again, the Constitution assigns the autonomous okrug no specific rights except the right of representation in the all-union Supreme Soviet (one deputy each) (Articles 88, 110).

In sum, Soviet federalism is based on 15 union republics, each located in the territorial homeland of a major nationality. In addition, however, there are 20 autonomous republics and 8 autonomous oblasts for the homelands of nationalities, which exist alongside the 128 oblasts and krais without any federal rights. And alongside the raions are 10 autonomous okrugs.

Table 8.2   THE AUTONOMOUS REPUBLICS, OBLASTS, AND OKRUGS, 1986

	Territory (In 1000 km²)	Population (in hundred thousands)	Titular Nationality (percent)*	Russian (percent)*
Autonomous Republics				
Bashkir	143.6	3,870	24.3	40.3
Buryat	351.3	1,014	23.0	72.0
Dagestan	50.3	1,753	77.8	11.6
Kabardino-Balkar	12.5	724	54.5	35.1
Kalmyk	75.9	325	41.5	42.6
Karelian	172.4	787	11.1	71.3
Komi	415.9	1,228	25.4	56.7
Mari	23.2	731	43.5	47.5
Mordvinian	26.2	964	34.2	59.7
North Osetian	8.0	616	50.5	33.9
Tatar	68.0	3,537	47.6	44.0
Tuvinian	170.5	284	60.5	36.2
Udmurt	42.1	1,571	32.1	58.3
Chechen-Ingush	19.3	1,225	64.6	29.1
Chuvash	18.3	1,320	68.4	26.0
Yakut	3103.2	1,009	36.9	50.4
Karakalpak	164.9	1,108	31.1	2.4
Abkhaz	8.6	530	17.1	16.4
Adzhar	3.0	382	80.1	9.8
Nakhichevan	5.5	272	95.6	1.6
Autonomous Oblasts				
Gorno-Altai	92.6	179	29.2	63.2
Adygei	7.6	423	21.4	70.6
Khakass	61.9	547	11.5	79.4
Karachai-Cherkess	14.1	396	39.1	45.1
Jewish	36.0	211	5.4	84.1
South Osetian	3.9	99	66.4	2.1
Nagorno-Karabakh	4.4	177	75.9	0.8
Gorno-Badakhshan	63.7	149	90.4	1.4
Autonomous Okrugs				
Taimyr	862.1	54	16.5	68.2
Evenki	767.6	21	20.3	65.1
Nenets	176.7	53	12.8	65.8
Ust-Ordyn Buryat	22.4	129	34.4	58.1
Koryak	301.5	39	22.6	64.5
Chukchi	737.7	155	9.0	68.9
Komi-Permyak	32.9	162	61.4	34.7
Khanti-Mansi	523.1	1,047	3.2	74.3
Yamalo-Nenets	750.3	383	16.0	59.0
Agyn-Buryat	19.0	77	52.0	42.1

*Figures for national composition from 1979 census.

Source: Same as Table 8.1.

Why a Federal State?

The Soviet federal structure has been a controversial institution within the Soviet Union since its very inception. The expedient adopted during the Civil War proved to be an inadequate institutional basis for peacetime reconstruction: The RSFSR was tied to the nominally independent soviet socialist republics of the Ukraine, Belorussia, and the Transcaucasus through a tight system of bilateral treaties. Even though these treaties provided for a military alliance and economic union with common legislation and fused administrative agencies (e.g., commissariats of War and Navy, People's Economy, Foreign Trade, Finance, Labor, Transport, and Posts and Telegraphs), even though delegates from the ostensibly independent republics sat in the All-Russian Congress of Soviets and on its Central Executive Committee beginning in December 1921, and even though the Party of Bolsheviks maintained a tightly unified chain of command throughout all republics, still the Soviet leaders maintained the legal fiction that the republics were independent until the end of 1922. Only on December 30 of that year did the Union of Soviet Socialist Republics formally come into existence.

The shape of this union remained the subject of controversy even after the treaty of union was adopted; and it was resolved initially only with the approval of the Constitution of the USSR on July 6, 1923, and its ratification on January 31, 1924. Opinion within the Party during the early 1920s divided among three views, with Lenin and the Party Politboro adopting a middle ground between centralizers and decentralizers. The opponents of federalism pressed for a unitary state structure without institutional accommodation to the ethnic diversity of the Soviet Union. In particular, they opposed the formation of a second legislative chamber based on representation of nationalities. The proponents of decentralized federalism, who had their strongest bases of support in the Ukrainian and Georgian parties, argued for a degree of real autonomy for the republics, including more extensive decentralization of administration and a limitation on the RSFSR's domination of the all-union institutions. A compromise established new all-union institutions above those of the RSFSR, including a bicameral legislature with a second chamber for explicit representation of the nationality-based units, and permitted some decentralization of administration through separate people's commissariats in the union republics. The resulting Constitution preserved the legal fiction that soviet socialist republics were sovereign states that freely joined in a union.[4] (The autonomous soviet socialist republics, for the most part, had developed separately, by administrative action within the RSFSR, and therefore were not treated in the same way as the soviet socialist republics.)

The debate over Soviet federalism arose again over half a century later, as the drafting of the 1977 Constitution moved forward. Many of the proposals for reform advocated elimination of institutions that had been the foundation of Soviet federalism. In speaking to the Supreme Soviet on the draft Constitution, Brezhnev summarized some of these proposals that were rejected by the Constitution Commission:

> Some comrades . . . propose introducing in the Constitution the concept of an inte-
> gral Soviet nation, eliminating the Union and Autonomous Republics or drastically
> curtailing the sovereignty of the Union Republics, depriving them of the right to se-
> cede from the USSR and of the right to maintain external relations. The proposals
> to do away with the Soviet of Nationalities and to set up a unicameral Supreme So-
> viet are along the same lines. I think that the erroneousness of these proposals is
> quite clear.[5]

A participant in early discussions of the 1977 Constitution who subsequently emi-
grated to the West reports that its earlier drafts had actually accepted at least
one of these proposals—elimination of the union-republic's right to secede.
"Nevertheless, it somehow unexpectedly reappeared in the final draft . . . "[6]
Not all of the proposals for reform, however, argued for abandonment of federalism and further centralization: The pressure for a "bill of rights" for the republics within the new Constitution appears to have sought an expansion of republic
autonomy.[7]

As noted above, the territorial subdivisions of the Soviet Union have few actual rights or independent powers at their disposal. Why then have the Soviets de-
vised this elaborate federal structure? What purposes does it serve?

First, the nationality-based units ensure that local government can be
conducted in the language of the local nationality. On the one hand, this means
that non-Russians can address the state at the local level without the obstacle of linguistic discrimination. On the other hand, it permits Moscow to address its message to the Soviet citizenry in tongues it readily understands.

Second, these units ensure that the most visible local officials of the Soviet
state are drawn from the local nationality and that representatives of that nationality will be on the scene in Moscow. In almost all political systems—authoritarian
as well as democratic—power is more legitimate, or at least seems less onerous,
when it is wielded by individuals of one's own ethnic background.

Third, the institutions of these nationality-based units provide the basis for
accommodating diverse cultures in a single state. Within the strict limits of
centrally-imposed policies, the government of each unit can develop schools, newspapers, and such cultural institutions as performing troupes that in minor ways reflect peculiarities of the local culture.

And fourth, this structure has proven to be a flexible device to accommodate new nationalities as the Soviet Union has expanded. For example, the Moldavian, Lithuanian, Latvian, and Estonian republics were integrated within the
Soviet system after World War II with minimum disruption to Soviet institutions.

Behind the federalism of the Soviet state, however, is a unitary Party.
While the Party Rules guarantee all Party organizations autonomy "in the decision of local questions, unless their decisions conflict with Party policy," they
make clear that Party organizations lower on the territorial hierarchy must submit to decisions made by those higher on this hierarchy, and ultimately all are
bound by decisions made by the all-union organs.[8] While Party organizations

exist alongside each of the republican and local governments (except at the village level), none of these Party organizations (even those in the union republics or autonomous republics) is guaranteed any unique federal or reserved rights that would distinguish them from other local Party organizations. That is, federalism does not exist within the Party, even in principle.

UNION-REPUBLIC INSTITUTIONS

The union-republic governments resemble those at the all-union level. Each has a unicameral Supreme Soviet, ranging in size from 975 deputies in the RSFSR to 285 deputies in the Estonian SSR. (See Table 8.3 and Figure 8.2.) As in the all-union Supreme Soviet, these deputies are elected for five-year terms and must meet twice a year in regular sessions. The agenda and procedures of these sessions closely resemble those of the all-union body. The union republic's Supreme Soviet is purportedly "the highest body of state authority" and is "empowered to deal with all matters within the jurisdiction of the Republic under the Constitutions of the USSR and the Republic" (Article 137). Among the legislative acts of these bodies are the legal codes (*kodeks zakonov*) that regulate much of Soviet life, including such codes as criminal law, civil law, labor law, land law, and family law.[9] Although each Supreme Soviet adopts a separate set of codes for its union republic, these codes are remarkably uniform, following the guiding principles of legislation adopted by the all-union Supreme Soviet and the model codes drafted in Moscow. Each of these Supreme Soviets technically elects its own standing committees and a Presidium of from 13 to 37 deputies, including a Chairman of the Presidium who serves as ceremonial President of the union republic.

The Supreme Soviet in each union republic also elects a Council of Ministers, including a Chairman who serves as the chief executive officer of the union republic. The Councils of Ministers at the beginning of 1985 included from 23 to 34 ministers and 10 to 17 chairmen of state committees.[10] Union-republic ministries and state committees come under the direct control of the corresponding ministry in Moscow; republican ministries and state committees are supposed to be the highest authorities within their respective fields of competence (Article 135). These Councils of Ministers are empowered to issue decrees and executive orders and to suspend the decrees and executive orders of the executive bodies of territories immediately subordinate to the union republic. The independent decision-making power of these councils, however, is small.

Just as at the all-union level, in union republics (except the RSFSR) Party organs parallel the state institutions. These work under the tight leadership of the CPSU; the Party Rules prescribe that these republic organizations (as well as all local organizations below the union republic) must be "guided in their activities by the Program and Rules of the CPSU," conduct "all their work by implementing Party policy," and "organize the fulfillment of directives of the Central Committee of the CPSU" (Article 41). The "basic duties" of the republic (and local) Party organizations include:

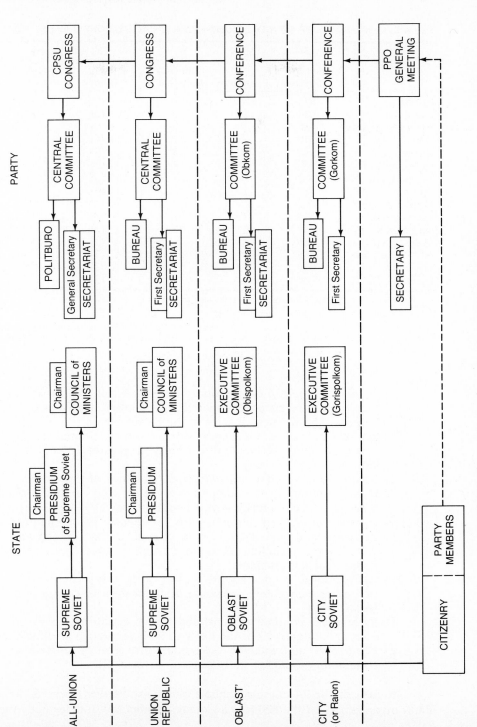

Figure 8.2 Structure of Soviet State and CPSU Hierarchies.

Table 8.3   MEMBERSHIP OF KEY UNION-REPUBLIC INSTITUTIONS, (July 31, 1985)

	State			Party		
	Supreme Soviet	Presidium	Council of Ministers*	Bureau	Secre-tariat	Depts*
RSFSR	975	39	55	— (—)†	—	—
Ukrainian SSR	650	25	62	11 (6)	7	17
Belorussian SSR	485	19	56	16 (0)	6	18
Uzbek SSR	510	21	52	11 (5)	6	16
Kazakh SSR	510	20	53	11 (0)	6	16
Georgian SSR	440	18	58	14 (5)	5	18
Azerbaidjan SSR	450	20	55	13 (5)	6	17
Lithuanian SSR	350	17	51	11 (4)	5	15
Moldavian SSR	380	19	52	11 (3)	5	15
Latvian SSR	325	13	47	10 (3)	5	15
Kirgiz SSR	350	15	46	12 (2)	5	14
Tadjik SSR	350	15	49	9 (3)	5	16
Armenian SSR	338	19	55	11 (7)	6	14
Turkmen SSR	330	15	51	12 (2)	5	16
Estonian SSR	285	13	44	11 (2)	5	15

*Figures for Council of Ministers and Party Departments are for January 1, 1985.

†Numbers in parentheses are candidate members.

Source: *Ezhegodnik Bol'shoi Sovetskoi Entsiklopedii, 1985* (Moscow: Sovetskaia Entsiklopediia, 1985), 97–182; U.S. Central Intelligence Agency, *Directory of Soviet Officials: Republic Organizations* (Washington, D.C., 1985).

(a) *popular mobilization:* "political and organizational work among the masses" for the purpose of mobilizing them to fulfill the economic, socio-cultural, and political policies of the Soviet Union;

(b) *popular education:* ideological work to raise communist consciousness among workers, including direct Party propaganda and guidance of the local mass media;

(c) *leadership of non-Party institutions:* "guidance of the soviets, trade unions, Komsomol, the cooperatives, and other public organizations through the communists working within them";

(d) *supervision of Party and non-Party institutions:* enforcement of Leninist principles and methods of leadership in all sectors of Party and state administration, including the strengthening of labor and state discipline, order, and self-discipline;

(e) *cadre control:* conducting the Party's cadre policy (that is, the selection of leading personnel), including the education of cadres in communist ideals;

(f) *Party administration:* organization and direction of the various institutions and enterprises of the Party in their respective localities; and

(g) *hierarchical accountability:* systematic provision of information and accountability to higher Party organs. (Article 42)

In each of the 14 union-republic Communist Parties (there is no separate Party organization for the RSFSR) a Congress composed of delegates from subordinate party organizations (e.g., oblasts) meets once every five years, just prior to the all-union Congress. According to the Party Rules, these meetings are to be devoted to hearing reports from the union-republic Central Committee, discussing other issues at its discretion, and electing a Central Committee, an auditing commission, and delegates to the all-union Congress (Article 44). In reality, the agendas, reports, discussions, and elections during sessions of these congresses are tightly orchestrated from Moscow through the Party apparatus, and as a consequence they are remarkably uniform from one union republic to the next. The Central Committee of each republic Party organization is empowered to exercise the highest Party decision-making authority within the union republic in the interval between meetings of the Congress. For the discussion of particularly weighty matters at the union-republic level, this Central Committee may call an extraordinary Congress or a Party Conference. Each republic Central Committee is empowered to direct the Party organizations in the territorial subdivisions of the union republic. To this end, it inspects their work and hears regular reports from their committees. The Central Committee must confirm chairmen of Party commissions, heads of the departments of the apparatus, and editors of the union republic's Party newspapers and journals. And it nominally elects a Bureau and sets up a Secretariat for the union-republic Party organization. Since the Central Committee is required to meet only once every four months, these last two bodies tend to act in the name of the Central Committee.

The union-republic Bureaus at the beginning of 1985 ranged in size from 11 to 19 members, of whom 10 to 18 were full (or voting) members. In a deviation from all-union practice, the Party Rules prescribe that these Bureaus must include the republic Party secretaries in their membership. With Party secretaries holding between two-fifths and one-half of all voting positions on most republic Bureaus, the Party apparatus can have determinative power in their deliberations.[11]

The Secretariats established by the union-republic Central Committees usually contain either five or six secretaries, one of whom is designated First Secretary and another as Second Secretary. In mid-1987, all but one of the former were drawn from the titular nationality of the union republic, while the second secretaries were all Slavs, usually Great Russians. These second secretaries, it has been surmised, represent Moscow's "man on the scene" to check indigenous first secretaries who might otherwise be tempted to be overzealous in their defense of the local nationality. (The decision to appoint an ethnic Russian as first secretary in the Kazakh Republic sparked riots in the streets of the republic's capital on the night of December 17, 1986.) The Secretariats are empowerered by the Party Rules to consider "current questions" and to verify the execution of decisions. As a practical matter, they supervise the 14 to 18 departments of their respective Central Committees. About three-fourths of these departments (e.g., Agriculture and Food Industry Department, Science and Educational Institutions Department) are engaged primarily in supervision of various sectors of local society; and the remainder (e.g., General Department, Organizational Party Works Department) are engaged primarily although not exclusively in the management of the Party as a complex organization.

LOCAL INSTITUTIONS

The over 50,000 local governments (52,007 in early 1985) at the oblast, city and raion, and village levels are critical in the Soviet administrative hierarchy.[12] According to Soviet descriptions, their responsibilities include:

(a) supervising fulfillment of the economic plan in the locality;
(b) directing construction outfits, retailing firms, and industrial enterprises under local subordination (particularly those associated with consumer goods production);
(c) providing housing;
(d) protecting public health, including the provision of medical services to individuals;
(e) providing education and cultural activities for residents; and
(f) maintaining municipal services such as roads, public transportation, traffic control, police protection, parks, water, and sanitation.[13]

In particular, these governments provide municipal and consumer services and oversee the production of many goods to meet the needs of average citizen-consumers.

In each local government there is a soviet of people's deputies, which is technically elected by the local population from single-member districts for terms of two and a half years.* While the Constitution (Article 146) empowers local soviets to "deal with all matters of local significance," it makes clear that they are to operate as part of a hierarchy: Local decisions must be "in accordance with the interests of the whole state" as well as local residents. And the local soviet must "implement decisions of higher bodies of state authority" as well as "guide the work of lower Soviets." The largest local soviets can be found in Moscow and Leningrad, with 1000 and 600 deputies, respectively. Most local soviets, however, range between 150 to 500 at the oblast level and 25 to 75 at the village level. Meetings of the full soviet, according to law, must take place at least four times a year, with the exception of village soviets in the Russian, Kazakh, Azerbaidjan, and Moldavian republics, which must meet at least six times annually.[14] Each meeting usually lasts only one day. Thus, the full soviets have little opportunity to direct local affairs.

Much of the actual administration of local affairs falls under the direction of the soviet's executive committee (*ispolkom*), which is formally a standing body of the soviet elected from among its members. By law, the ispolkom ranges in size between 5 to 13 at the oblast level and 2 to 7 at the village level. An ispolkom will frequently include the local Party committee's First Secretary and heads of such local administrations and departments as the local planning committee, the internal affairs administration (police), the People's Control Committee, and one or more economic administrations. These administrators often

*The institutions of an autonomous soviet socialist republic resemble those of the union republics. A Supreme Soviet, ranging between 110 and 280 deputies, elects a Presidium and Council of Ministers. In practice, however, these operate like the soviets and executive committees of the oblasts.

serve as an unofficial inner collegium directing the work of the whole ispolkom, sometimes making decisions in its name. While the full ispolkom appears to meet only twice a month, this inner group usually meets more frequently. Each ispolkom has a chairman, one or more deputy chairmen, and a secretary. Except for ispolkomy at the village level, they coordinate the activities of administrations, departments, and standing committees that provide many of the municipal services and direct the economy of the region. (See Figure 8.3.) The number of departments and administrations may be as few as a half dozen in a small raion, or over a dozen in a large oblast. For a "typical" oblast executive committee (*obispolkom*), these usually include the divisions shown in Table 8.4.

A typical larger city executive committee (*gorispolkom*) resembles that shown in Table 8.4. although it may lack either an agricultural or a food industry administration. At the upper extreme, however, the Moscow City executive committee, directing the largest local government in the Soviet Union, in 1975 supervised 18 main administrations, 29 independent administrations, 9 departments, and a number of commissions, inspectorates, and other services. At the other extreme, a rural raion government typically will be a much abbreviated version of the oblast or city.[15]

The Local Deputy

As noted in Chapter 5, over 2.3 million people are elected at all levels as deputies to soviets—the most common form of office-holding in the Soviet Union. These local deputies, while not a representative cross-section of Soviet society, are far more representative of the characteristics of the broader population than are the deputies to the all-union Supreme Soviet.[16] Party membership, as Figure 8.4 shows, is less prevalent among local deputies than among Supreme Soviet deputies. The rate of Party membership among these deputies has shown the same slow, but steady, decline as among all-union deputies; it is still, however, about four times the rate among Soviet adults. (The proportion of deputies who were members of neither the Party nor the Komsomol stood at just over one-third.) The rise in the proportion of local deputies who are women has brought this percentage close to the proportion in the adult population, so that by 1985 women deputies actually held a slight majority (50.3 percent). Similarly, the proportion of local deputies officially listed as workers or collective farmers is about a third higher than among all-union deputies. (Local deputies also appear to be younger than their all-union counterparts, in part because local office-holding is a training and testing ground for those early in their careers who may later be honored with an all-union seat.)

The Soviet deputy is what Theodore Friedgut has called the "man in the middle," for he serves at a critical juncture in the Soviet system—that between average citizens and the elaborate bureaucracy of local government. The deputy serves both as representative of his constituents to the local administration and as representative of that administration to his constituents.[17]

As representative of his constituents the deputy plays three roles: auditor,

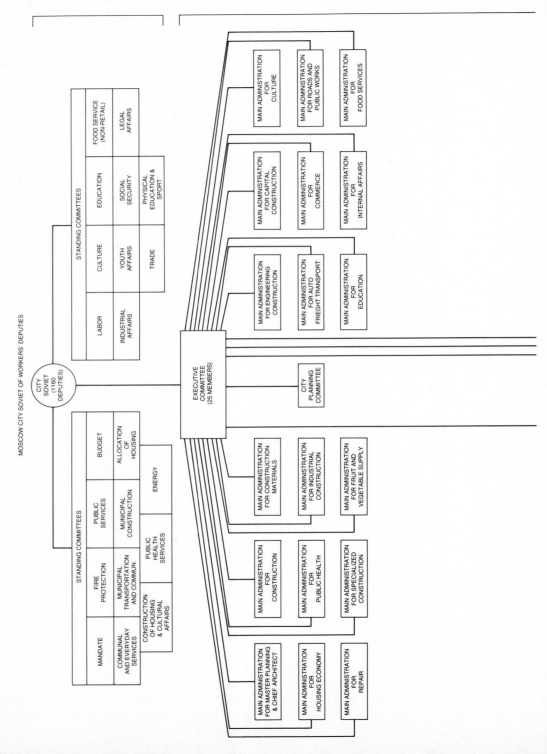

MOSCOW CITY SOVIET OF WORKERS' DEPUTIES

CITY SOVIET (1160 DEPUTIES)

STANDING COMMITTEES

MANDATE
COMMUNAL AND EVERYDAY SERVICES
FIRE PROTECTION
MUNICIPAL TRANSPORTATION AND COMMUN.
CONSTRUCTION OF HOUSING & CULTURAL AFFAIRS
PUBLIC SERVICES
MUNICIPAL CONSTRUCTION
PUBLIC HEALTH SERVICES
BUDGET
ALLOCATION OF HOUSING
ENERGY

STANDING COMMITTEES

LABOR
INDUSTRIAL AFFAIRS
CULTURE
YOUTH AFFAIRS
TRADE
EDUCATION
SOCIAL SECURITY
PHYSICAL EDUCATION & SPORT
FOOD SERVICE (NON-RETAIL)
LEGAL AFFAIRS

EXECUTIVE COMMITTEE (25 MEMBERS)

CITY PLANNING COMMITTEE

MAIN ADMINISTRATION FOR MASTER PLANNING & CHIEF ARCHITECT
MAIN ADMINISTRATION FOR HOUSING ECONOMY
MAIN ADMINISTRATION FOR REPAIR

MAIN ADMINISTRATION FOR CONSTRUCTION
MAIN ADMINISTRATION FOR PUBLIC HEALTH
MAIN ADMINISTRATION FOR SPECIALIZED CONSTRUCTION

MAIN ADMINISTRATION FOR CONSTRUCTION MATERIALS
MAIN ADMINISTRATION FOR INDUSTRIAL CONSTRUCTION
MAIN ADMINISTRATION FOR FRUIT AND VEGETABLE SUPPLY

MAIN ADMINISTRATION FOR ENGINEERING CONSTRUCTION
MAIN ADMINISTRATION FOR AUTO FRIEGHT TRANSPORT
MAIN ADMINISTRATION FOR EDUCATION

MAIN ADMINISTRATION FOR CAPITAL CONSTRUCTION
MAIN ADMINISTRATION FOR COMMERCE
MAIN ADMINISTRATION FOR INTERNAL AFFAIRS

MAIN ADMINISTRATION FOR CULTURE
MAIN ADMINISTRATION FOR ROADS AND PUBLIC WORKS
MAIN ADMINISTRATION FOR FOOD SERVICES

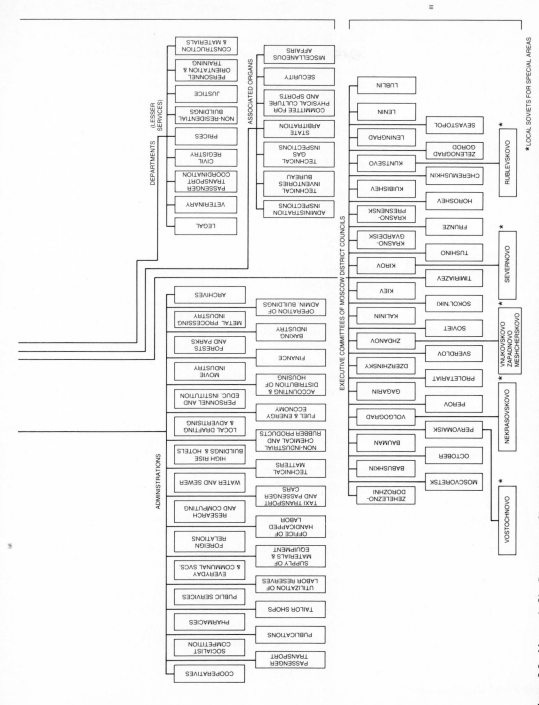

Figure 8.3 Moscow's City Government. Chart shows city soviet (*gorsovet*) and its standing committees (I), city executive committee (*gorispolkom*) and administrative agencies (II), and the subordinate city-borough executive committees (*raispolkom*) (III). (*Source: From Moscow's City Government* by E. S. Savas and J. A. Kaiser. Copyright (c) 1986 by Praeger Publishers. Reprinted by permission of Praeger Publishers.

*LOCAL SOVIETS FOR SPECIAL AREAS

DEPARTMENTS (LESSER SERVICES)

CONSTRUCTION & MATERIALS
PERSONNEL ORIENTATION & TRAINING
JUSTICE
NON-RESIDENTIAL BUILDINGS
PRICES
CIVIL REGISTRY
PASSENGER TRANSPORT COORDINATION
VETERINARY
LEGAL

ASSOCIATED ORGANS

MISCELLANEOUS AFFAIRS
SECURITY
COMMITTEE FOR PHYSICAL CULTURE AND SPORTS
STATE ARBITRATION
TECHNICAL GAS INSPECTIONS
TECHNICAL INVENTORIES BUREAU
ADMINISTRATION INSPECTIONS

ADMINISTRATIONS

ARCHIVES
METAL PROCESSING INDUSTRY
FORESTS AND PARKS
MOVIE INDUSTRY
PERSONNEL AND EDUC. INSTITUTION
LOCAL DRAFTING & ADVERTISING
HIGH RISE BUILDINGS & HOTELS
WATER AND SEWER
RESEARCH AND COMPUTING
FOREIGN RELATIONS
EVERYDAY & COMMUNAL SVCS.
PUBLIC SERVICES
PHARMACIES
SOCIALIST COMPETITION
COOPERATIVES

OPERATION OF ADMIN. BUILDINGS
BAKING INDUSTRY
FINANCE
ACCOUNTING & DISTRIBUTION OF HOUSING
FUEL & ENERGY ECONOMY
NON-INDUSTRIAL CHEMICAL AND RUBBER PRODUCTS
TECHNICAL MATTERS
TAXI TRANSPORT AND PASSENGER CARS
OFFICE OF HANDICAPPED LABOR
SUPPLY OF MATERIALS & EQUIPMENT
UTILIZATION OF LABOR RESERVES
TAILOR SHOPS
PUBLICATIONS
PASSENGER TRANSPORT

EXECUTIVE COMMITTEES OF MOSCOW DISTRICT COUNCILS

LUBLIN
LENIN
LENINGRAD
KUNTSEVO
KUIBISHEV
KRASNO-PRESNENSK
KRASNO-GVARDEISK
KIROV
KIEV
KALININ
ZHDANOV
DZERZHINSKY
GAGARIN
VOLGOGRAD
BAUMAN
BABUSHKIN
ZHELEZNO-DOROZHNI

SEVASTOPOL
ZELENOGRAD GOROD
CHEREMUSHKIN
HOROSHEV
FRUNZE
TUSHINO
TIMIRIAZEV
SOKOL'NIKI
SOVIET
SVERDLOV
PROLETARIAT
PEROV
PERVOMAISK
OCTOBER
MOSCOVORETSK

RUBLEVSKOVO *
SEVERNOVO *
VNUKOVSKOVO ZAPADNOVO MESHCHERSKOVO *
NEKRASOVSKOVO *
MOSCOVORETSK *
VOSTOCHNOVO *

supplicant, and ombudsman. In the first role, the deputy is responsible for supervising the administration to ensure that individual bureaucrats act within the law—the so-called *kontrol* function. As a supplicant, he is often the person who appeals to the administration on behalf of his constituents for a local project. For example, he may ask that the roads in his constituency be repaved, the sewers upgraded, or some apartments repaired. As ombudsman, it is often the deputy who intervenes within the administration on behalf of individual citizens who have been treated unfairly (e.g., a delayed pension check). The deputy's power to issue a certificate (*spravka*), requesting that an administrator redress a citizen's grievance, can give greater weight to these individual citizen requests.

As a representative of the ispolkom, the deputy plays the role of educator, consultant, and adjunct. In the first role, he presents the policies of the city and of the Soviet state to his constituents. He is required, by law, to hold public meetings at least twice a year in order to explain these. In his role as consultant the deputy is often responsible for providing expert advice to the local administration. Some deputies possess expertise of value to local administrators; but equally important is the deputy's role in the recruitment and co-optation of experts into the citizens' volunteer *aktiv* of the soviet. On the request of the ispolkom, deputies may even undertake surveys of community needs and citizen opinion. Lastly, the deputy is also an adjunct to the ispolkom in that he helps the administration carry out local policies. In particular, he is responsible for mobilizing his constituents through various self-help groups. "He helps rally the residents of streets and blocks to do Sunday work, whether to fulfill a voters' mandate [request for action], extend aid to a kolkhoz at harvest time, or refurbish a school that needs repair. . . ."[18]

Deputies perform many of their duties through the standing committees of their respective soviets and through their deputies' groups. These parallel and work closely with the administrations of the ispolkom and the citizens' residence and self-help groups. Many of the standing committees are organized along sectoral lines like the standing committees of the all-union Supreme Soviet. The deputies' groups differ from the standing committees in that they are organized territorially, not functionally; they exist only within the lowest units of representation (e.g., village, urban raion); and they bring together deputies not just from one soviet but often all the deputies who represent that locality in all soviets from the lowest up to the all-union. These groups facilitate direct contact between deputies and constituents; for example, some groups maintain duty rosters whereby four to five deputies sit each Saturday afternoon to receive citizens' complaints. The major part of the work of both the standing committees and deputies' groups, however, is not the representation of citizens to the executive committee, but the facilitation of the educator, consultant, and adjunct roles of the deputies.[19]

The Local Party Organization

At the oblast, city, and raion levels, but not at the village level, are found local Party organizations. In each, the highest authority is technically the Party confer-

Table 8.4   AGENCIES OF OBISPOLKOM

	Departments	Administrations
Planning Commission	Health	Consumer Services
	Education	Housing & Communal Services
	Construction	Local Industry
	Social Security	Food Industry
	Finance	Internal Affairs (Police)
	Justice	Culture
		Agriculture

ence. At the oblast level (including autonomous republics, autonomous oblasts, krais, and larger cities) these are composed of delegates from the subordinate city and raion organizations; and at the city and raion level (including the autonomous okrugs), of delegates from the primary party organizations. These are required by the Party Rules to meet in regular session once every two to three years—that is, once just before the union-republic and all-union congresses and another time midway between these congresses. These sessions may last only one day at the raion level or as much as three days in a larger oblast. Raion-level conferences tend to be devoid of real political activity—characterized by two British Sovietologists as political rallies "at which well-known local political leaders affirm the appropriate line, taking their cue from the . . . first secretary, under the watchful eyes of a representative of higher authority." At the oblast-level, however, "more weighty matters are debated . . . relating to the success of the area's economy, and sometimes giving local representatives a chance to voice dissatisfaction. . . ."[20] Each Conference elects a Committee to exercise the authority of the Conference between its sessions. (In 1986, these committees averaged around 185 voting and candidate members at the oblast' and union-republic levels and 90 at the city and raion level.[21]) Outside the RSFSR, conferences in territorial units subordinate to the union republic (e.g., oblasts in some republics, raions in republics without oblasts) elect delegates to the republic Congress; in the RSFSR, these elect delegates directly to the all-union Congress. Conferences of party organizations subordinate to an oblast-level organization elect delegates to that oblast-level Conference.

The oblast-level Committee (*obkom* or *kraikom*), is required by the Party Rules to meet at least once every four months; the city- or raion-level Committee (*gorkom*, *raikom*, or *okruzhkom*), at least once every three months. In fact, they often meet more frequently. As in the Central Committees at higher levels, the most important members of the local committees tend to be drawn from among the key Party and state officials (including officers of the military and police) in the locality, leaders of the local Komsomol and trade union organizations, directors of educational and scientific institutions, leaders of subordinate Party organizations and local governments, and key managers of industrial enterprises and farms. The obkom or kraikom elects a Bureau of between 7 and 17 mem-

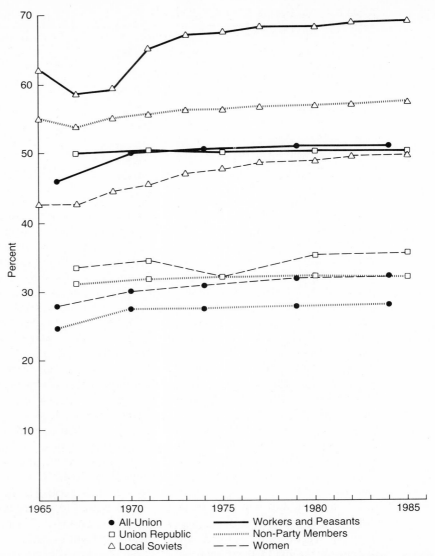

Figure 8.4 Characteristics of Soviet Deputies, 1965–1985. (*Source: Pravda*, 28 March 1965, 26 March 1967, 22 March 1969, 17 June 1970, 20 June 1971, 23 June 1973, 19 June 1974, 21 June 1975, 25 June 1977, 7 March 1979, 1 March 1980, 23 June 1982, 7 March 1984, 2 March 1985.)

bers, which must include the Party secretaries; and it forms a Secretariat. The gorkom, raikom, and okruzhkom each elects a Bureau, including the Party secretaries, but is not empowered to form a Secretariat.[22]

The first and second secretaries of a local Party organization normally divide the responsibility of general supervision of the local economy and general direction of intra-Party administration. The Party secretaries, whether joined in a formal Secretariat or not, play the critical role of directing the local Party apparatus. The larger obkom may have over a dozen departments, closely paralleling those of the union-republic Party, under the supervision of five or six secretaries. (The Moscow Gorkom, for example, the largest oblast-level Party organization, had 18 departments at the beginning of 1985, under the supervision of six secretaries.) Smaller committees will have fewer departments and secretaries, so that a small raikom may have as few as 4 departments, supervised by three secretaries. Like higher-level committees, the small raikom maintains a General Department to conduct the paper work of the raikom, an Organizational (Party Work) Department to supervise the lower levels of the Party by maintaining party records of all members and by controlling the staffing of the lower levels of the apparatus, and a Propaganda and Agitation Department to oversee the ideological instruction of Party members and the broader public. In place of the many departments for different sectors of the local economy found in the oblast-level Party organizations, the small raikom or gorkom may have a single Industry and Transportation Department in urbanized areas or an Agriculture Department in rural areas. As these differences in apparatus structure suggest, while all local Party organizations are actively engaged in the management of internal Party affairs, the lower levels of the Party play a smaller role in the management of the local economy and society. Each department at the raion level normally includes a head, sometimes a deputy head, and a few full-time employees called instructors, for a total of about a half-dozen cadres or apparatchiki per department.[23] (These are frequently assisted by volunteer "nonstaff instructors.")

The secretaries, department heads, and instructors (excluding nonstaff instructors) constitute the full-time staff of the local party, linked in the hierarchy of the Party apparatus. All tend to be well-trained specialists in fields appropriate to their respective positions. Estimates of the number of such Party employees below the all-union level range from 100,000 to about twice that number.[24]

This local Party organization has remained relatively stable in recent decades, except during the last two years of Khrushchev's leadership when he experimented with the bifurcation of Party organs below the union republic. In these years the Party organizations at the oblast level and below were divided between two parallel hierarchies for agriculture and industry. Primary party organizations within collective farms and state farms were subordinate to rural committees; PPOs within industrial enterprises were subordinate to urban or industrial-zone committees. At the oblast level, Party organizations were divided into separate agricultural and industrial organizations. Thus, at both the oblast and raion levels there were two parallel conferences, committees, and hierarchies of the apparatus. The union-republic Party organization, which was not divided, provided coordination for these two hierarchies. Khrushschev's reform failed to produce the anticipated rise in economic product on with increased specialization in Party administration and actually led to an inefficient duplication of effort. Just one month after Khrushchev's ouster, the new Party leadership eliminated this bifurcation of the lower Party apparatus and reestablished the institutions of two years earlier.[25]

PARTY CONTROL OF REPUBLIC AND LOCAL INSTITUTIONS

To maintain its control over the organs of republic and local government the Party uses many of the same mechanisms as it does at the all-union level. Control over the personnel in elected and appointed positions is maintained both through Party manipulation of the nomination process and through its nomenklatura powers. (In practice, the most important local positions fall within the nomenklatura of higher levels of the Party, so that the local Party organization may be limited to appointments at still lower levels—e.g., school principals and chief agronomists.)

The apparatus of the local Party committee plays a major role in Party supervision (*kontrol'*) over the local state administration. As at the all-union level, the departmental structure of the local Party apparatus parallels the sectoral organization of the local state administrations to facilitate the Party's monitoring of these. This organization also permits the Party to coordinate the activities of the various independent agencies in a locality and to resolve disputes among them. Thus, in a city, the Party organization and its first secretary, in the words of William Taubman, may even serve as "a sort of supermayor."[26]

The Party's leading role within local state institutions is not simply a matter of the local Party committee issuing directives that the local state institutions then execute, although this apparently does occur regularly. It also involves the institutionalized involvement of local Party leaders and of Party members in the daily activities of local government. A Party group is organized within each republic and local soviet. These usually meet prior to each session; and under the direction of the local or higher Party committee, they decide their positions on candidacies and policies. These positions are, of course, binding on members of the Party group, due to the principle of Party discipline. Since a Party group also tends to dominate the ispolkoms at each level (the chairmen, vice-chairmen, and secretaries of soviets are usually Party members), the Party exercises decisive control over almost all activities of the soviets.[27]

More-centralized Party control is provided by the Party secretaries from higher Party committees, who periodically participate in the deliberations of the lower soviets. For example, an obkom secretary might actively participate in the meeting of a raion soviet, "suggesting" a candidate for Chairman of the ispolkom.[28]

THE POWER OF LOCAL INSTITUTIONS AND INTERGOVERNMENTAL POLITICS

A question that continues to spark controversy among Western Sovietologists is whether local governments below the all-union level actually play an independent political role.[29] The Soviet system is highly centralized in principle as well as in practice. The principle that legitimates this is democratic centralism, which, according to the Soviet Constitution and the Party Rules, is the guiding tenet of state as well as Party organization. (The official definition of democratic centralism appears in Chapter 7.) Democratic centralism rests on the official fiction that the leading Party and state organs are elected by their respective representative bodies. That is, in the Party, the congresses and conferences from the all-union down to the raion Party organizations elect their respective Central Committees and committees; and the General Meetings of the primary party organizations elect their Bureaus. In the state, the soviets elect their Presidia and Councils of Ministers or ispolkoms. In actual practice, however, the candidates who appear on ballots have been selected by the leading Party organs at that level or above. That is, elections are actually a process of co-optation and selection from above.[30]

The second principle of democratic centralism is sometimes called "dual subordination," for leading organs are responsible not only to the representative bodies that "elected" them, but also to higher leading organs. For instance, the union-republic Central Committees are accountable not only to their respective Party congresses, but also to the Central Committee at the all-union level; the Secretariats, both to their union-republic Central Committees and to the all-union Secretariat. In the state, the principle of dual subordination means that soviets, committees, and administrations are accountable not only to those who formally elected them (soviets to electors, committees to soviets, and administrations to committees), but also to the soviets, committees, and administrations at higher levels. Thus, a gorispolkom in a small city is subject to the authority of the obispolkom, and its education department is subject to the education department of the obispolkom; and so on up the hierarchy.

Third, the minority must submit to the majority. Yet, there is seldom an open discussion of policy within the state or Party to permit the majority's voice to be heard. The British Sovietologist Leonard Schapiro has argued that "there have been few occasions . . . when the Party leaders have been unable . . . to keep discussion of policy within the limits which they considered desirable . . . "[31] Once a decision has been made by the leadership, deputies and Party members must cease all factional activity that might question or overturn that decision. This gives the leadership power to block dissent, for anyone who questions a decision may be characterized as a minority opposing the will of the "majority."

Lastly, decisions of higher organs are absolutely binding on lower organs. According to Fainsod, this clause contains "the essence of 'democratic centralism' ".[32] It establishes centralized decision making.

Behind the principle and practice of democratic centralism are many specific practices that result in significant centralization of authority and decision making. The legislative power of the all-union government, as prescribed in the Constitution (Article 73), includes "ensurance of uniformity of legislative norms throughout the USSR," which it does by issuing fundamental principles of legislation in each policy field. This results in adoption of virtually identical laws by each of the union republics.

Also important to this centralization of authority is the Unified State Budget of the USSR adopted each year by the Supreme Soviet. Critical to the independence of local governments in countries such as the United States is the independent taxing and spending authority of those localities. Such localized authority does not exist in the Soviet Union.[33] While all soviets at every level technically adopt their own budgets, in reality soviets below the all-union level only propose a budget to the authorities in the government immediately above them, and these budgets are then legislated by inclusion in the budgets of the superior governments. Importantly, only the all-union budget can levy taxes, and it determines the apportionment of these taxes between the all-union government and individual union republics. The 1986 State Budget, for example, authorized revenues of 414.5 billion rubles and expenditures of 414.3 billion rubles, with 183.8 billion rubles of each (44 percent) apportioned to the union republics' budgets. The budget established each union republic's total revenues and expenditures, within 1000 rubles. It specified the proportion (to within one-tenth of a percentage point) of the taxes collected in each republic that was to be retained by its government, and a ruble subsidy from the all-union budget to the budgets of some of the less-developed union republics.[34] It would be difficult to imagine greater budgetary centralization.

To compound this centralization, money is not given to regional or local governments in block grants, but rather goes directly to administrations within the local governments. Moreover, money is often given to local administrations with many restrictions on its use based on strict formulas determined in Moscow. So, for example, a local education administration receives a wage package from the education ministry, which tells it how many teachers it may hire and how much the teachers are to be paid.

Centralization of power also results from the independence from local control enjoyed by enterprises and institutions of all-union subordination. The local soviet's power to oversee the local economy is significantly diminished when the most important producers are enterprises directly controlled by all-union ministries. Such noncity agencies can disrupt local plans by independent building programs that place demands on the local soviet for housing and community services. Or they can begin their own municipal services altogether, working at odds to planned growth patterns for the locality developed in its soviet. In extreme instances, some localities come to resemble company towns with the key decisions affecting community life being made at "corporate" headquarters—the ministry in Moscow.[35]

Nevertheless, republic and local institutions are not simply extensions of the central institutions in Moscow, and this gives rise to a form of intergovernmental politics. According to Duke University's Jerry F. Hough, there are three recurring issues that are the most common focus of politics between the center and periphery in the Soviet Union: funding, autonomy, and nationality.[36]

One concern is the petitioning for funds. While most funds are issued to the localities by formula, the local governments may still petition for additional funds when the formula funds have proven inadequate. Moreover, regional and local governments may also petition for special projects such as a new factory outside the formula. This activity can have broad policy implications and may bring different regions or localities into conflict. For instance, the Ukrainian Party and state apparatus have pushed the all-union leadership in Moscow to expand coal extraction in the Ukraine. The Russian Republic government, at the same time, has argued that the Soviet Union should concentrate not on development of Ukrainian coal, but on development of the oil in the western basin of Siberia. For the local authorities, the "right" decision by the all-union authorities will mean local industrial development; for the Soviet Union as a whole it means a decision about energy policy.

A second recurring issue in these politics is autonomy. Local officials are often in the position of asking for greater discretion in such matters as personnel or the allocation of funds. One such disagreement is the debate over the control of housing funds. Ministries have often allocated housing funds directly to the factories subordinate to them, permitting the factories to construct housing in ways that disrupt local soviets' plans. City administrations have sought greater control over these funds. Such disagreements between the center and the periphery may also have broad policy implications, for they can become part of larger debates over decentralization.

A third issue involves nationality questions. The nationality-based governments have disagreed with Moscow over language policy, particularly the use of non-Russian languages in the schools. Students in the non-Russian regions of the Soviet Union may attend either a local-language school or a Russian-language school. Those enrolling in the latter have usually been required to study the indigenous language as a second language. Giving in to parental pressures, Moscow has at various times ruled that Russians need not study the local languages. One such decision led to a heated exchange between Moscow and the Azerbaidjani First Secretary, to the dismissal of the First Secretary, and to a retreat by Moscow on the language reform.

In short, republic and local government in the Soviet Union is not simply (or at least not always) the plodding implementation by faceless grey bureaucrats of decisions made in Moscow. In fact, as will be discussed in the next chapter, the bureaucratic politics between center and periphery may be one of the most important political processes in the Soviet Union.

NOTES

1. U.S.S.R., Prezidium Verkhovnogo Soveta, *SSSR: Administrativno-Territorial'noe Delenie Soiuznykh Respublik* (Moscow, 1984).

2. A. Shtromas, "The Legal Position of Soviet Nationalities and Their Territorial Units According to the 1977 Constitution of the USSR," *Russian Review* 37 (July 1978), 269–270; Jerry F. Hough and Merle Fainsod, *How the Soviet Union Is Governed* (Cambridge, Mass.: Harvard University Press, 1979), 483. On the international status of union republics see Henn-Juri Uibopuu, "International Legal Personality of Union Republics of USSR," *International and Comparative Law Quarterly* 24 (October 1975), 811–845.

3. E. M. Chekharin, *Sovetskaia politicheskaia sistema v usloviiakh razvitogo sotsializma* (Moscow: Mysl', 1975), 146–172.

4. Richard Pipes, *The Formation of the Soviet Union: Communism and Nationalism, 1917–1923* (Cambridge, Mass.: Harvard University Press, 1964), chapter 6.

5. Leonid I. Brezhnev, "On the Draft Constitution (Fundamental Law) of the Union of Soviet Socialist Republics and the Results of the Nationwide Discussion of the Draft"

(Report and Closing Speech at the Seventh [Special] Session of the Supreme Soviet of the USSR, Ninth Convocation, October 4–7, 1977) (Moscow: Novosti Press Agency, 1977).

6. Shtromas, "The Legal Position of Soviet Nationalities", 267.

7. Grey Hodnett, "The Debate over Soviet Federalism," *Soviet Studies* 18 (April 1967), 477–479.

8. "Ustav Kommunisticheskoi Partii Sovetskogo Soiuza," *Pravda* (March 7, 1986), Article 21.

9. A. I. Luk'ianov et al., *Sovety Narodnykh Deputatov* (Moscow: Politicheskaia Literatura, 1984), 144.

10. U.S. Central Intelligence Agency, *Directory of Soviet Officials: Republic Organizations* (Washington, D.C.: Central Intelligence Agency, 1985).

11. Figures calculated from U.S. Central Intelligence Agency.

12. *Pravda,* 2 March 1985.

13. Luk'ianov, *Sovety Narodnykh Deputatov,* 210– 362; "Law of the Union of Soviet Socialist Republics on the Basic Powers of the Krai and Oblast' Soviets of Peoples Deputies and the Autonomous Oblast' and Autonomous Okrug Soviets of Peoples Deputies", *Pravda,* (June 26, 1980), articles 9–26.

14. Luk'ianov, *Sovety Narodnykh Deputatov,* 99, 164.

15. Hough and Fainsod, *How the Soviet Union Is Governed,* 489–490; E. S. Savas and J. A. Kaiser, *Moscow's City Government* (New York: Praeger, 1985), 28–44; Everett M. Jacobs, "The Organizational Framework of Soviet Local Government", in Everett M. Jacobs, ed., *Soviet Local Politics and Government* (London: Allen & Unwin, 1983), 14.

16. See also Everett M. Jacobs, "Norms of Representation and the Composition of Local Soviets," in Jacobs, 78–94.

17. Theodore H. Friedgut, "Community Structure, Political Participation, and Soviet Local Government: The Case of Kutaisi," in Henry W. Morton and Rudolf L. Tokes, eds., *Soviet Politics and Society in the 1970s* (New York: Free Press, 1974), 261–296; Michael E. Urban, "Information and Participation in Soviet Local Government," *Journal of Politics* 44 (February 1982), 64–85. For an official view of the role of deputies see "Law of the Union of Soviet Socialist Republics on the Status of Deputies to Soviets in the U.S.S.R.", *Pravda,* 22 September 1972.

18. Theodore H. Friedgut, *Political Participation in the USSR* (Princeton, N.J.: Princeton University Press, 1979), 185.

19. Luk'ianov, *Sovety Narodnykh Deputatov,* 172; Friedgut, 204.

20. Ronald J. Hill and Peter Frank, *The Soviet Communist Party* (London: Allen & Unwin, 1981), 55.

21. "KPSS v tsifrakh," *Partiinaia zhizn'* No. 14 (July 1986), 28.

22. Hill and Frank, 60; "Ustav Kommunisticheskoi Partii", articles 43–51; Ronald J. Hill, *Soviet Political Elites: The Case of Tiraspol* (London: Martin Robertson, 1977).

23. U.S. Central Intelligence Agency, 35–37; Hough and Fainsod, 492–501.

24. Hough and Fainsod, 495–496; Robert H. McNeal, "Paying for the Party," *Survey* 22 (Spring 1976), 64.

25. Merle Fainsod, *How Russia Is Ruled,* rev. ed. (Cambridge, Mass.: Harvard University Press, 1967), 203–205.

26. William Taubman, *Governing Soviet Cities: Bureaucratic Politics and Urban Development in the USSR* (New York: Praeger, 1973), 47–48.

27. Bohdan Harasymiw, "Party 'Leadership' of the Local Soviets," in Jacobs, 99–104, 106–107.

28. Hough and Fainsod, 501–510.
29. See, for example, Joel C. Moses, *Regional Party Leadership and Policy-Making in the USSR* (New York: Praeger, 1974).
30. Fainsod, 210.
31. Leonard Schapiro, *The Government and Politics of the Soviet Union,* rev. ed. (New York: Random House, 1978), 143.
32. Fainsod, 210.
33. Raymond Hutchings, *The Soviet Budget* (Albany, N.Y.: State University of New York Press, 1983), 29–30.
34. Savas and Kaiser, 60–84; Carol W. Lewis, "The Economic Functions of Local Soviets," in Jacobs, 48–66; *Pravda,* 28 November 1985.
35. Taubman, 54–72; Carol W. Lewis and Stephen Sternheimer, *Soviet Urban Management* (New York: Praeger, 1979), 34.
36. Hough and Fainsod, 510–517.

chapter *9*

The Political Process

The question addressed in this chapter is deceptively simple: How are policies made in the Soviet Union? In actual fact, however, this is one of the most contentious issues in the study of modern Soviet politics. Western analysts have divided among at least four major schools of thought over this seemingly simple question—divisions that grow from their diverging answers to two still more fundamental questions about Soviet politics. The first concerns elite conflict within the Soviet Union: Is there a high level of conflict among participants in the Soviet policy process? The second question concerns the participation of political interests: Do interests outside the central leadership participate in the making of policy?

Each school of thought actually emerged from a description of the Soviet political process at a different stage in the transformation of Soviet society. During Stalin's leadership, the prevailing view was summarized in the theory of totalitarianism, which argues that policy making tends to be autocratic, characterized by consolidation of power in the hands of the General Secretary with little or no participation by interests outside the central leadership and little or no conflict within it. During the 1950s, however, particularly with the rise of the succession struggle following Stalin's death, Western analysts began to question whether Khrushchev would ever be able to consolidate the autocratic control that Stalin had held. Many argued that conflict within the Soviet leadership—specifically, within the Politburo and Secretariat—had become a central attribute of policy making. This argument gave rise to the conflict school of thought. In the 1960s, Western analysts debated the extent of participation in the Soviet policy-making process by elites outside this leadership. The political interests model of Soviet politics emerged from the argument that there is wide participation by such interests as industrial managers, military officers, and legal experts. And in the 1970s and 1980s, analysts criticized the assumption of group and leadership conflict that is central to the political interests model as inappropriate to the stable politics of the late Brezhnev era. The apparent incorporation of interest elites into the political process led some Sovietologists to adapt the model of corporatist politics to the analysis of the Soviet Union.

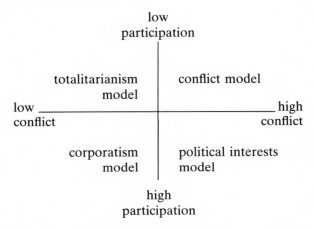

The succession of decision-making regimes that is at the heart of this debate among schools of thought has been closely tied to the transformation of Soviet society. The totalitarian autocracy of Stalin permitted the revolutionary transformation to socialism, but also created conditions that made the continuation of that mode of policy making increasingly dysfunctional. The leadership conflict model describes periods of transition that may recur when the transfer of power from one leadership to another is protracted, but which historically is most applicable to the transition from the autocratic rule of Stalin to the stable oligarchy of the Brezhnev years and after. The growing institutionalization of this stable oligarchy, with its routinized consultation of interest elites, has come as the forced-draft modernization of Soviet society retreats into history and as the complexity of policy problems under mature socialism demands inclusion of specialist-experts in policy making.

THE THEORY OF TOTALITARIANISM

The totalitarian model is not simply a theory of politics, but also a theory of the relationship of politics to the larger society. It is an effort to explain what seems to be a phenomenon peculiar to the 20th century—the rise to power of mass mobilizational movements that have sought to control and remake society totally. It initially emerged from the efforts to develop a conceptual model to explain Stalin's communism and Hitler's Naziism in the work of Hannah Arendt and William Kornhauser, but continued to develop in the area of Soviet studies through the efforts of Merle Fainsod, Carl Friedrich, and Zbigniew Brzezinski.[1]

According to Brzezinski and Friedrich, in their work entitled *Totalitarian Dictatorship and Autocracy,* totalitarian societies are characterized by seven attributes. Sometimes called the totalitarian syndrome, these may appear individually in other societies, but occur together only in totalitarian systems. They include an official ideology, a single party, terroristic police control, a monopoly of the means of communication, a monopoly of the means of armed coercion, a centrally directed economy, and revolutionary expansionism.[2]

It is the last of these that provoked the greatest concern in the West— *revolutionary expansionism.* The theory of totalitarianism argues that this is intrinsic to totalitarianism both as an expression of its revolutionary ideology and its domestic needs for regime maintenance. In the words of Friedrich and Brzezinski, "without an outward projection against a real or imaginary enemy, these regimes could not marshal the fanatical devotion the system requires for survival."[3] And the urge to expand will continue as long as the Soviet Union is totalitarian.

The totalitarian *ideology* that drives this expansionism is an official body of dogmas, containing a chiliastic vision of the future—a belief that one can build a perfect society on earth, remaking and perfecting humankind. It is all-encompassing in its scope, for it attempts to account for all aspects of the human experience.

This ideology is institutionalized in a *monopolistic party,* such as Germany's National Socialist (Nazi) Party or the Communist Party of the Soviet Union. The party is the instrument for implementing the ideology, and, like its ideology, seeks to be total. It takes responsibility for every aspect of the individual's life and seeks to politicize all of society and eliminate all private life. Within the party a single person usually emerges as the leader, be it Hitler as the Fuehrer or Stalin as the *vozhd'.* Just as the party comes to dominate all society, so the leader comes to dominate the party. Thus, the totalitarian state is typically an autocracy, and "the party constitutes the mainstay of [this] totalitarian dictatorship."[4]

Terroristic police control is used both by the party to eliminate its enemies within society and by the leader to eliminate his enemies within the party and is thus the basis of totalitarian autocracy. Terror, in a definition offered by Alexander Dallin and George Breslauer, is "the arbitrary use by organs of the political authority of severe coercion against individuals or groups, the credible threat of such use, or the arbitrary extermination of such individuals or groups."[5] Terror is not simply coercion, although the arbitrary application of coercion is an essential element. It includes

> police acting unrestrained by any outside controls, concentration camps and torture, imprisonment and executions without proof of guilt, repressive measures against whole categories of people, the absence of public trial and even any opportunity for defense, the imposition of penalties totally out of proportion to the actions of the accused, all on a scale without precedence in recent history.[6]

Terror rests on deterrence by creating fear. One of its purposes is to atomize society by creating distrust and suspicion, breaking society into its smallest constituent units (individuals). This creates an institutional or organizational vacuum in society, since individuals are afraid to associate with others, knowing that anyone to whom they talk might be an informant—even one's own children. The authoritarian party then fills this vacuum with its own set of auxiliary organizations. Totalitarianism, according to Hannah Arendt, is "a form of government whose essence is terror. . . . "[7]

Through this terroristic weapon the party and its leader are able to control all aspects of society just as the ideology dictates. The party establishes *near monopolistic control over the means of communication.* Radio and television are under tight central control. There may be many newspapers and periodicals in a totalitarian society, but there is only one editorial policy. Unofficial publications are suppressed as illegal dissent. The totalitarian party establishes a *monopoly over the means of armed combat.* The military, militia, and local police are under the tight control and close scrutiny of the party. And a totalitarian state maintains *central control over the economy.* In a Soviet-style system, all the key sectors of the economy are owned by the state. Even if property is left in private hands, its use is under the direction of a central plan.

The Totalitarian Polity

Zbigniew Brzezinski and Samuel Huntington, in one of the finest statements of the totalitarian view of Soviet society, *Political Power: USA/USSR,* draw out the distinguishing attributes of a totalitarian polity by comparing it with a polyarchical political system (the United States).[8] They begin their analysis with three questions, as shown in Table 9.1. First, who has the power to influence policy in each system? That is, how widespread is participation in decision making? Second, what is the nature of the decision-making process in each? And third, what are the attributes of policy in each? The answers to these questions point up the diametric opposition of the totalitarian and polyarchical models.

These two political systems differ in the availability of resources that empower participants in decision making. In a totalitarian polity these are few, the most important of which is control of the party organization. In fact, individuals and institutions outside the Politburo exercise little autonomous control over resources that can be used to influence policy, and so very few of these participate in totalitarian policy making. And at the extreme, when a leader has established autocratic control, he alone makes policy. In a polyarchical system, on the other hand, there are a diffuse set of political resources, such as votes, money, prestige, media, and productive facilities, widely available to participants both inside and outside the leadership. Hence, a broad spectrum of individuals and interests participates in policy making.

What are the consequences of this distribution of power for the political process? To answer this, Huntington and Brzezinski focus on four phases of the policy-making process: initiation of policy, persuasion, decision making, and execution. Initiation is "the first response to a new need or problem and the first formulation of a proposal to deal with it."[9] While in a democratic system new proposals

Table 9.1   POWER AND POLICY

Participation $\longrightarrow$	Process $\longrightarrow$	Policy
Who has power to influence policy?	How are policies made?	What are attributes of policy?
—Resources	—Initiation	—Choice
	—Persuasion	—Integration
	—Decision	—Innovation
	—Execution	

Source: Based on Samuel P. Huntington and Zbigniew K. Brzezinski, *Political Power: USA/USSR* (New York: Viking Press, 1964), chapter 4.

for policy bubble up from below (for example, from private groups or lower levels of the executive bureaucracy), in a totalitarian system they trickle down from above (from the party secretaries).

The processes of persuading others to support new policy proposals in each system also differ: In a democratic system one must build a broad consensus behind new ideas in order to gain their adoption. And in the process of gaining support from independent interests through compromises, the initial proposal is amended. In a totalitarian system, once a proposal has been initiated by a member of the leadership, he must convince at most a dozen men to support it. Once the leadership has adopted the proposal, it is a foregone conclusion that it will become policy; and so, in the persuasion stage, the leadership simply mobilizes broader support from interests outside the leadership.

During the decision phase in a democratic system there are numerous veto points, such as interest groups, Congress, and the Executive agencies, that must all be passed before a policy is adopted. In a totalitarian polity, on the other hand, the proposal that was modified during the persuasion phase "is either approved or vetoed by those who have the effective and legitimate authority to do so." Specifically, in the Soviet system the decision phase is the "brief and unitary" approval of the leadership's initiative by the Central Committee apparatus.[10]

During the execution phase, a polyarchical system still affords a chance for amendment and sabotage of a policy by those who have the responsibility for implementing it. In a totalitarian system faithful execution of the decision, under the close scrutiny of the party apparatus, is expected.

These differences in policy-making processes affect the attributes of each system's policy outputs. Because decision making in polyarchies involves many divergent interests, which can delay and amend decisions, policies in democracies are characterized by muddling-through and incrementalism, and they are seldom integrated across divergent policy areas. A totalitarian system, however, by virtue of its unity in decision making, is able to address clear-cut policy issues. Policies are more likely to offer an integrated response to problems that cut across issue areas. Totalitarian policy can also be boldly innovative rather than simply incremental.[11]

Totalitarian Autocracy

The theory of totalitarianism asserts that these polities tend to be autocratic. In the words of Friedrich and Brzezinski: "The documentary evidence clearly shows that Stalin, Hitler, and Mussolini were the actual rulers of their countries. Their views were decisive and the power they wielded was 'absolute' in a degree perhaps more complete than ever before. . . . [T]he totalitarian dictator is both ruler and high priest."[12] Totalitarian theory claims that the Soviet Union naturally tends towards one-man rule, because communist government leads to a dictatorship of the party over society and to a dictatorship of the leader over the party.

How is the General Secretary able to establish this autocratic rule within the Soviet Union? To answer this question, the theory of totalitarianism has addressed two narrower questions: How does the General Secretary come to dominate the Party? And how does the Party come to dominate society? Part of the answer is contained in the concept of terror. Yet the application of the totalitarian model to Soviet politics has provided a number of more specific answers to each of these questions as well.

The answer to the first is summarized in the concepts of *democratic centralism* (see Chapters 7 and 8), the *tyranny of the apparat,* and the *circular flow of power.* Leon Trotsky, in his struggle with Stalin, was one of the first to warn of the tyranny of the apparat, when he called for the subordination of the apparatus to the Party. With the bureaucratization of the Party after the Revolution, the apparatus came to dominate Party affairs. At all levels of the Party, the authority and power of the congresses or conferences were usurped first by the committees that they nominally elected and then by the Party secretaries "who ostensibly executed their will."[13] At the same time, the principle of democratic centralism—and more specifically, dual subordination—has placed this apparatus hierarchy under the control of the all-union Secretariat. Thus, by the General Secretary's control over these secretaries together with their control over their respective organizations, the General Secretary can determine Party affairs at all levels.

The circular flow of power (a term coined by the University of Vermont historian Robert V. Daniels) is a closely related concept. The General Secretary controls appointments to this apparatus, particularly to republic and regional secretaries, and uses this control over appointments as the institutional basis of his power.[14] The General Secretary, of course, attempts to appoint individuals who will support him, while at the same time Party secretaries already in these positions and wishing to retain them will attempt to demonstrate their loyalty to the General Secretary by supporting him against opponents. In particular, these Party secretaries will use their control over the composition of delegations to the all-union congresses to ensure the election of delegates loyal to the General Secretary, often securing their own election. Similarly, the delegates elected to the all-union congresses will elect a Central Committee that supports the General Secretary. If an opposition to the General Secretary should attempt to organize within the Party, the "loyalists," holding a majority in both the Congress and Central Committee, will isolate the opposition, brand it an illegal "faction," and demand that it submit to Party discipline under the rules of democratic central-ism.[15]

This technique was used by Stalin in his rise to power after his appointment as General Secretary in 1922. Stalin packed the Party Congress with his followers among the Party *apparatchiki,* so that Party officials represented 55.1 percent of the voting delegates at the 12th Party Congress in 1922, jumping from just 24.8 percent at the l0th Congress only two years earlier. Stalin used this control to isolate and eliminate Trotsky within the Congress and Central Committee.

Khrushchev used a similar ploy. Between 1953 and the 20th Party Congress in 1956, Khrushchev replaced 7 of the 14 union-republic secretaries and 41 of the 69 RSFSR oblast-level first secretaries. Three of the new union-republic secretaries and 6 of the new oblast secretaries had served with Khrushchev in the Ukraine in earlier years. With their help he packed the Party Congress and Central Committee with delegates he could trust. In his showdown with the Anti-Party Group, this support was decisive.[16]

To answer the second question—how the Party and its leader control Soviet society—the theory of totalitarianism points up three additional practices: the *leading role of the Communist Party* (see Chapter 8), *nomenklatura* (see Chapter 7), and the *institutionalization of mutual suspicion.* Addressing the last of these, Merle Fainsod argued that the Party leadership maintains its control over Soviet society by institutionalizing surveillance and creating mutual suspicion among individuals in parallel hierarchies.[17] Specifically, the leadership brackets every key institution in society with parallel institutions that have, as one of their responsibilities, the duty to keep watch over the institution in question. This practice touches all sectors of Soviet society including the military, the economy, and the arts. The logic behind this practice is simple—if everyone is watching everyone else, no one will be willing to sabotage the dictates of Moscow.

By way of illustration, the Soviet military is, first of all, a centralized chain of command, in which subordinates report to superior officers from the lowest squad all the way up to Moscow. In addition, however, the Party has used the parallel hierarchies of political commissars, Party, Komsomol, Procuracy, and police to penetrate and check the command. During the Civil War, the Party appointed political commissars within each unit to watch over the military. And with time, these political officers became institutionalized in a parallel hierarchy now called the Main Political Administration (MPA). (The political commissar in each unit is now called the Assistant or Deputy Commander for Political Affairs, or *zampolit.*) The zampolit is responsible, in part, for conducting the political education of the troops. In addition, he is part of a separate, parallel chain of command, responsible for surveillance over the troops.[18] The MPA hierarchy reports jointly to departments within the Defense Ministry and the Secretariat of the Party.

Working closely with the MPA is the parallel hierarchy of Party organizations within the military. A primary party organization is established in each unit for the Party members within it. The PPO secretary through the right of supervision in the unit plays an active role in surveillance over the regiment.[19] PPO meetings maintain Party discipline and watch the officers, in particular through the practice of *kritika-samokritika* (criticism–self-criticism) employed in all PPOs: An officer who is a Party member must assess and criticize the political performance of the unit and confess any personal shortcomings before the Party membership. In a meeting in which the officer is at least in theory on an equal footing with all other Party members, the officer's performance is opened to the scrutiny and criticism of the whole membership. These findings can be reported by the Party Secretary to a higher Party organ.

Under the direction of the PPO secretary is the Komsomol's primary organization in the unit. Since many in the military, particularly the conscripts, are too young to be Party members, the Komsomol organizations play a vital role in imposing Party discipline on the military. These organizations also scrutinize the reliability of the unit and report on their findings.

Alongside the Party and Komosomol is the local civilian Party organization. The Party Rules (Article 69) state that "the Party organizations and political agencies of the Armed Forces maintain close connections with local Party committees and regularly provide them with information about political work in the military units." The civilian Party secretaries are expected to take an active interest in the political life and health of the local units, participating in Party meetings and related political activities. In this way, they can report independently to the Party leadership on their findings.

Yet another parallel hierarchy of monitors is the civilian Procuracy (roughly equivalent to a public prosecutor's office), which is charged with investigating illegality within the military and prosecuting crimes. The Procuracy is assisted by the KGB, which maintains special sections within the military to keep dossiers on members of the armed forces.[20]

With the military chain of command watched by each of these parallel hierarchies, officers will not dare violate the wishes of the Party leadership. Of course, it is not just the military chain of command that is watched; each of these parallel hierarchies of monitors watches the others. Roman Kolkowicz, the UCLA-Rand specialist on Soviet military affairs, speculates that "the Party favors a certain degree of mutual distrust among [all of] them, for their competitiveness not only prohibits collusion, but permits the Party to play off one against the other and, in effect, to control the controllers."[21]

Critiques of Totalitarianism

The totalitarian view of Soviet politics has been increasingly criticized in recent years. For example, Amos Perlmutter of American University has written, "Arendt's existential thesis that totalitarianism is an effort to change the nature of man and the nature of nature is not very useful . . . any more than is Brzezinski's concept of the 'permanent purge' for explaining Soviet politics from Lenin to Brezhnev." He notes that "the political, institutional, and structural behavior of so-called totalitarian regimes does not exhibit [a] preeminent role of the ultimate ideology." He adds that "totalitarianism does not explain the dynamics of either its structures or its systems." Perlmutter proposes the term "modern authoritarianism" as an alternative to "totalitarianism," pointing up the many parallels rather than the sharp break with traditional authoritarian regimes.[22]

In addition, scholars have made more specific criticisms of the application of the totalitarian model to the analysis of contemporary Soviet politics, by asking whether the mechanisms that ensured Stalin's autocratic control over the Communist Party and Soviet society still operate as they did before 1953. For example, many have asked whether the terror that was an essential element of the totalitarian syndrome has survived de-Stalinization.

Still others have questioned whether the circular flow of power still operates as it did under Stalin and Khrushchev. Jerry F. Hough argues that General Secretaries since Khrushchev have not exercised the degree of control over appointments assumed by this theory. Specifically, upon assuming the position of General Secretary, Brezhnev announced a policy of "respect for personnel," which meant he would not remove officials as freely as Khrushchev had done before him. As a consequence, Brezhnev did not engineer the extensive turnover of republic and oblast secretaries that had been essential to the workings of the circular flow of power in the rise of Stalin and Khrushchev. (Under Gorbachev turnover seems to have risen once again: While from 1966 to 1981 at least four-fifths of the living members of the Central Committee were reelected at each Congress, in 1986 only 49.8 percent were reelected. Although only 1 union-republic first secretary was removed before the 1986 Party Congress [and Shevardnadze was actually promoted to the post of Foreign Minister], as many as 14 oblast-level first secretaries in the RSFSR were replaced.)[23]

Similarly, the extent to which the Party actively intervenes in appointments has been questioned. Although few would deny that the Party holds the ultimate power to make appointments, it may no longer exercise this power on a day-to-day basis in the manner described in the totalitarian view of nomenklatura. Appointments, it would appear, increasingly involve elaborate negotiation and consensus-building among interests outside the Party apparat. And promotions within institutions have become increasingly routinized.[24] Although nomenklatura still ensures the loyalty of all key appointees to the Party, it may be a less effective device of direction and control by the apparatus over the activities of other institutions.

The totalitarian theory of the institutionalization of mutual suspicion has also been criticized. Recent studies have raised questions about the relationship between monitor (e.g., MPA, Party) and monitored (e.g., military officer, industrial manager), finding that this relationship is often not antagonistic, but cooperative.

To be effective, a monitoring agency must be independent of the operating agency. It has been argued by Anthony Downs and by University of Toronto Sovietologist Timothy Colton that this means "there must be no exchange of personnel between the monitoring and operating agencies."[25] In the Soviet system, however, just the opposite is often true: the monitor and the monitored share similar training and parallel, intertwined careers. For example, Party secretaries who scrutinize industrial managers may have been trained in the same schools and steeped in the same standards as the managers they are supposed to watch. In fact, in many cases the Party secretaries were recently industrial managers themselves before becoming Party secretaries. They understand the problems facing the manager and may even have sympathy for the plight of the manager. Moreover, they may again be part of the industrial apparatus in the future, since careers take individuals back and forth between Party and state as they wind their way to the top.[26] Thus, Party secretaries often do not have a distinctive "Party perspective" that divides them from those they monitor; and so they are often not particularly effective monitors in the institutionalization of mutual suspicion.

Moreover, the monitor and monitored may have complementary career incentives, since promotion for both is frequently based on the same criteria. For example, both the industrial manager and the Party secretary in a factory depend upon fulfillment of the plan for career success. Since meeting or exceeding quotas is the measure of success for both of them, they share an interest in maximizing the resources allocated to the factory and minimizing the quotas imposed on it. They may even come to have a shared interest in covering for each other's violations of the plan if it will help the factory fulfill its quotas. As a result, at the local level, the monitor and monitored often are allies.[27] If Party secretaries are actually allies of the local people they are supposed to watch, they are not very successful at creating suspicion.

The ability of a monitor to create suspicion is further diminished because in a face-off between an administrator and the monitor, the latter is frequently not the more powerful figure. For example, a commanding officer usually outranks the zampolit in his unit. The officer is usually older and more experienced, often has a longer service record, and may even have been a Party member for more years than the zampolit.

These criticisms of the institutionalization of mutual suspicion have led some analysts to suggest that the relationship between monitor and monitored is actually a complementary division of labor, in which the local Party official often finds himself in the role of adjunct to the director of the operating agency. The Party officials specialize in reinforcing discipline, mobilizing enthusiasm, and encouraging technical competence among subordinates such as workers and soldiers, thus supporting and reinforcing the work of managers and officers rather than creating suspicion among them.

Such criticisms of the totalitarian model have led many Sovietologists to suspect that a more complex political process than totalitarian autocracy has developed within the Soviet Union. The first to challenge the totalitarian interpretation was the conflict school of thought.

CONFLICT: LEADERSHIP AND SUCCESSION

The proponents of the conflict school criticize what they see as totalitarian theory's assumption of harmony in the Soviet leadership.[28] British Sovietologist Robert Conquest wrote in 1962, "To assume that harmony now prevails among the Soviet leadership would be to assume that a very extraordinary change had taken place in the system."[29]

A central assertion of the conflict school is that the power to influence policy is dispersed among the Soviet leaders—that the polity is oligarchic rather than autocratic. Carl Linden focuses his analysis on "the narrow circle of a few dozen figures at the level of the Party [Politburo] and Secretariat." He argues that in the period of his case study (1957–1964),

> those around Khrushchev are seen not as non-entities or mere toadies, but men of power who represented real political and organizational interests. At no point do they appear as wholly malleable to the leader's purposes and, while opportunistic and skilled tacticians, they also are seen as men who more often than not possessed political identities which placed them to one side or the other in the political spectrum of the party.[30]

The conflict school recognizes that the leadership cannot be totally isolated from pressures of groupings within the broader Soviet elite, and that these can influence leadership politics. And the level of this involvement will grow with the level of disunity among the leaders.[31] Yet, unlike the political interests approach, the focus of the conflict school is not on this influence from outside the narrow leadership group, but on the factionalism within it.

A second key assertion of the conflict school is the indeterminacy of power in the Soviet leadership. It criticizes what it sees as the totalitarian school's assumption that the "formal positions [of the leader], virtually by definition, provide him with all the levers of power necessary to insure his dominance in the leadership and put him beyond the reach of effective challenge."[32] Instead, the conflict school emphasizes that the power of the General Secretary does not derive from constitutional or statutory powers nor does it inhere in his post. The division of powers among the leading organs of Party and state is ambiguous, leading to considerable overlap of responsibilities. In particular, the relationship of the General Secretary to the Politburo "remains equivocal." For example:

> Khrushchev's political power is viewed as being at no time a definite quantum but rather an unstable mixture of his native political skills, his accumulated prestige, his control over and influence in the political organization he headed, the assets and liabilities his leadership acquired through policy successes and failures, and finally the balance of forces in the political environment with which he had to deal.[33]

To compound this indeterminacy of the General Secretary's and other leaders' power, none enjoys a guaranteed term of office.

A third assertion of the conflict school, and the one from which its name derives, is that conflict is "a *continuous* and *critical* fact of Soviet political life." The reasons for this conflict include the indeterminacy of power: According to Linden, "The logic of Soviet politics inclines the leader to seek absolute power over the leading group, but the same logic also impels them to strive to inhibit or prevent the prime leader from acquiring it."[34] (Some analysts have recently argued that even under Stalin some forms of leadership politics took place.[35]) In addition, the ideology of Marxism-Leninism itself adds to the potential for conflict.[36] The vagueness of the ideology *permits* diverging interpretations and thus conflict over policy prescriptions. But more than this, the ideology may actually *create* such conflict. According to Linden, the Marxist-Leninist view of politics "as a life and death struggle between irreconcilable forces" and its "insistence on political monolithism" reduce the chances for pragmatic compromise within the leadership and reinforce the probability of conflict.[37]

The struggle for power is intimately intertwined with debate over policy. Linden asserts that policy is "the twin, not the pawn, of power; thus, the focus [of conflict theory] is on the nexus of power and policy, and on the combustion produced by their interaction."[38] These debates reflect policy stands by individual members of the leadership that are "consistent" across issues and that give rise to persistent divisions that can be labelled left and right, orthodox and innovative, or conservative and reformist. Drawing upon the distinctions made by Conquest and Linden, these two policy positions appear to divide as shown in Table 9.2. Linden stresses that despite their differences on these issues, left and right "remain dedicated to the preservation of the domination by the party over society at large." This keeps their struggle within bounds that will not threaten that domination.[39]

Among the most controversial features of the conflict school is its use of evidence.[40] An important part of the case made by these theorists are deductive propositions derived from the axiom that "conflict over power and policy animates the political process everywhere and Soviet politics are no exception."[41] But much of the evidence is also empirical. Ploss cites five types of such evidence:

1. Soviet "statements which tend to legitimate political argument" point to the existence of friction within the leadership.
2. Leaders' "rebukes of anonymous personalities for dissidence . . . [are] intended to discredit and isolate the chiefs of splinter groups . . . without having the conflict brought out into the streets."
3. "Shadings of textual emphasis," as in quotations from Lenin, are used to legitimate diverging positions.
4. "Modification of standard terminology" is used similarly.
5. "A leader's reticence about some question which his associates have commented on," may indicate opposition to that proposal.

This "language of conflict," according to Ploss, "points to the existence of debate in the leadership, helps to clarify active political issues, and suggests the positions of individual leaders."[42] Yet, this language of conflict in the words of Linden, is frequently characterized by "indirection, ambiguous allusion, and subtle manipulation of ideological and policy formulas."[43] Thus, one must posit (without firm evidence one way or the other in most specific instances) that the "esoteric debates" are the visible signs of a more profound struggle.

The conflict school has also been criticized for its tendency to fall into the trap of Kremlinology—to see every move at the top as "shot through with the struggle for protocol, prestige, and power . . . Every move is seen as a carefully plotted, conspiratorially conceived, predetermined plan whose every consequence is anticipated; every move has a secret meaning which detailed charting

Table 9.2   DIVISIONS IN POLICY POSITIONS

Left (Orthodox or Conservatives)	Right (Innovators or Reformers)
"External" orientation that stresses "necessities of the world struggle and the dangers from the outside enemy"	"Internal" orientation that stresses "prospects for a relatively stable international environment"
Concern with achievement of Communist society hence, "crash programs"	Concern with management of immediate problems hence, slower tempo of transformation
Ideological solutions to problems	Pragmatism
Doctrinal continuity	Theoretical innovation
Centralization of economy	Expanded local initiative
Investment priority to heavy industry and defense	Concessions to consumers
Rigid control over intellectuals	Tolerance for limited intellectual diversity
Forward policy in foreign affairs	"Less dangerous forms of struggle with the adversary abroad"

of protocol and word counting can uncover."[44] While recognizing the roots of their approach in the writings of such Kremlinologists as Franz Borkenau and Boris Nicolaevsky, the conflict theorists, and particularly Linden, go to some lengths to distinguish their approach by moving "beyond the initial Kremlinological tendency to play down the policy dimension of Soviet politics. . . ."[45] There is, nonetheless, particularly in Conquest's analysis, a tendency to write as though individual leaders adhere to few if any principles of policy, develop no institutional loyalties, and decide all issues on short-term, opportunistic grounds. Although he proposes the term "dynastics" for his approach, his particular use of the conflict model is very close to traditional Kremlinology.[46]

The Succession Problem

The struggle among Soviet leaders has been most acute during successions, when they must select a new leader or leaders. All political systems must sometimes select new leaders; and this becomes a particularly thorny problem for any system when a leader dies in office. In a constitutional order, the succession is institutionalized. Rules describe how an heir is to be found and how the transition is to take place. The procedure becomes institutionalized further when it is reinforced by practice and tradition that make the rules a reality. But in a political system like the Soviet Union's where power is weakly institutionalized, the transfer of power is indeterminant. Power does not inhere in specific positions either by constitutional prescription or long tradition. Nor are there explicit rules for the selection of new incumbents. As a consequence, the transfer of power in a system like the Soviet Union's is more likely to produce what Myron Rush has called a "succession crisis," a potential turning point in the political system at the time of the transfer.[47] A succession is the point of greatest plasticity in the Soviet political system, when institutions and their powers have the greatest potential for change. A succession is also the point of greatest vulnerability of the political system, when it is most vulnerable to pressures from the broader Soviet society for an expansion of participation.[48] A crisis may simply end with a continuation of the status quo, but it can also end in a dramatic transformation of the system.

Totalitarian theorists as well as the conflict school recognize the intensity of leadership conflict in a succession crisis. Yet the former tend to see this as a transitional stage in a succession-crisis–personal-dictatorship cycle of leadership: "Once a leader emerges victorious in the struggle a phase of dictatorial rule begins and stability is restored to the leadership."[49] Rush, the leading student of the succession problem, argues that succession normally proceeds through three distinct phases: "In the first phase, the preceding ruler's power is assumed by others so that government may continue; in the second, power is redistributed in more stable and lasting form; finally, there may be a third phase of consolidation."[50] At the center of the succession is the personal rivalry among "the most ambitious of the former ruler's heirs." While the succession continues, "contenders for the succession rely upon informal groupings of peers and followers who are like-minded or share common political or personal interests." The longer the struggle, the greater the likelihood that more interests outside the leadership will be brought into the decision-making process, at least during the duration of the crisis, as "auxiliaries of the protagonists." Before the new leader consolidates the powers of his predecessor, "the functions normally performed by the ruler go undone"; in particular, many policy issues are left unresolved and authoritative statements of ideology are not made.[51]

Overcoming the recurring succession crises is no simple matter. It is unlikely that Soviet leaders such as members of the Politburo would willingly assent to the formal institutionalization of the powers of a premier leadership position (e.g., the General Secretaryship), creating a post with powers that could be turned against them.[52] Nor is it likely that the premier leader would acquiesce in the institutionalized limitation of the potential powers of his position, even though that is a prerequisite to the institutionalization of procedures to pass those powers on to a successor. Short of the creation of a leadership post with guaranteed and limited powers and a formal procedure to pass those powers on to a successor, the leader has a number of options to try to manage the succession in order to attempt to avoid the crisis that will be occasioned by his death. None of these options, however, does more than attempt to reduce the indeterminacy of a specific succession, without resolving the longer-term problem of the inevitability of the crises themselves.

The first option for the leader is to designate an heir and then resign. This however, might not solve the succession problem, for the leader cannot guarantee that the other members of the Politburo will accede to his decision. Having stepped down from power, the former leader can no longer affect the succession, and his former associates may feel free to reverse his decision. Moreover, even if the leader could determine the outcome of the succession in this way, it is unlikely that any Soviet leader will find this an attractive option. The leader who hands his power to an heir and steps down may see many of his policies undone. His heir may not only reverse his policies, but also eliminate his friends and even turn on the former leader himself for fear that even as a private citizen the former General Secretary can serve as a rallying point for the new leader's opponents.

Another possibility for the leader is to designate an heir, cultivating his power and prestige in the hope that this chosen heir will succeed when the leader dies. This however, does not guarantee that the leader can determine the outcome of the succession and avoid a crisis. In particular, by appointing an heir the leader may drive the other members of the leadership to rally against the designated individual in order to prevent the rise of a new leader or even to protect their own opportunities to contend for that position. Rather than determine the outcome of the succession, this might increase the probability of a crisis. Moreover, an incumbent leader might find this option unattractive, for the heir may become overly ambitious and attempt to step into his patron's shoes before the incumbent is ready to retire. With the power given him by his patron, the heir may carry out this coup if he can convince his associates of the inevitability or desirability of his leadership and induce them to transfer their loyalties from the incumbent leader.

A third option open to the leader is to cultivate an heir, but check his power with a counter-heir. Any attempt by the heir-designate to seize power prematurely is checked by the ambitions and associates of the counter-heir. Stalin and Khrushchev, in fact, used this technique. Nonetheless, it does not appear to have resolved the problem of the succession crisis; and by creating rival powers it may actually have intensified the struggle for power upon Stalin's death. Moreover, by checking the power of his heir-designate, the incumbent leader may actually relinquish what little power he has to determine the outcome of the succession. In fact, it would appear that in the Stalin-Khrushchev succession it was the counter-heir (Khrushchev) rather than the leader's heir-designate (Malenkov) who ultimately won out.

Are succession crises still inevitable in the Soviet Union? Since 1917, the Soviet polity has weathered four succession-consolidation cycles: the Lenin-Stalin succession in the 1920s, the Stalin-Khrushchev succession in the 1950s, the Khrushchev-Brezhnev succession in the mid-1960s, and that from Brezhnev to Gorbachev in the 1980s. The surprising absence of public drama surrounding the last two of these suggests that successions are now less critical than in previous years. The reasons for this may be the development (and perhaps institutionalization) of procedures within the Politburo for filling the position of General Secretary and an emerging consensus among the leaders on the extent of his legitimate powers. It may also reflect a growing dispersal of power among the leaders as the periods between successions have become less autocratic and more oligarchic. To quote Rush, "If the ruler has great power . . . its transfer is likely to be difficult; but if he shares power with others in an oligarchy . . . the problem is appreciably eased."[53]

The Transformation of Leadership Politics

Although leadership conflict may represent a permanent feature of Soviet politics, as the conflict school contends, its intensity and forms have changed as the leadership itself has changed. Specifically, the transformation of Soviet society and the Soviet polity has brought with it significant shifts in the composition of this leadership. According to Dutch Sovietologist John Lowenhardt, between 1917 and 1980, four successive generations of leaders dominated the Politburo.[54] The first, the "revolutionary generation" from 1917 to 1924, "were urbanites, intellectuals who had spent some considerable time in the West, and were frequently at loggerheads with each other." This generation brought revolution to Russia and laid the foundations of the Leninist regime. The first Stalinist generation that succeeded it (1924–1934) was created by Stalin, principally from among the apparatchiki. It comprised "men who had risen by virtue of organizational work within the Party, unimaginative men usually of low social origins, without much education or much interest in theoretical disputes." These oversaw the initial, often brutal stages of Stalin's revolutions, including collectivization and industrialization. The second Stalinist generation (1934–1952) came to power with the purge of the first Stalinists. They tended to have higher levels of education than the original Stalinists and broader experience in the management of the new Stalinist economic machine (or other branches of the expanded state bureaucracy). They were, in a sense, the products of the revolutions engineered by the first Stalinist generation, and they brought into the Politburo itself the sophistication and expertise demanded by the increasingly complex institutions created in those revolutions. The fourth ("post-Stalinist") generation (1953–1985) was the product of Khrushchev and Brezhnev—a Politburo composed of men with still higher levels of education, who, unlike their predecessors, had risen through the republic and regional Party apparatus in their political careers. They were a generation of politician-generalists who were needed to coordinate the still more complex machinery of the Soviet economy and society. Finally, the rise of Gorbachev to General Secretary may signal the beginning of the triumph of a fifth generation, those who began their political careers after Stalin and rose to prominence under Brezhnev. These still tend to be politician-generalists who worked their way up through the Party apparatus. In the Politburo elected at the end of the 27th Congress (1986), for example, 9 of the 12 full members had previously served as first secretaries of a union republic, oblast, or city of union-republic subordination before their appointments; and 2 of the remaining 3 had served as all-union secretaries. Only Andrei Gromyko had not served as a party apparatchik.

These changes in the leadership have been accompanied by, and probably have contributed to, changes in leadership politics.[55] The intellectual gifts and relatively independent status of individual members of the leadership, such as Trotsky, Zinoviev, and Bukharin, gave rise to the spirited debate and oligarchic politics during the first years of Soviet power. The replacement of these "Old Bolsheviks" with a dependent leadership that was created by and served at the pleasure of Stalin permitted the leader to establish autocratic rule. The death of

Stalin brought a new oligarchic style to decision making during the succession. The effort by Khrushchev to impose his rule on a leadership that was not as dependent on him as their predecessors had been upon Stalin brought not a return to autocracy but the conflict-ridden leadership of which Linden writes. The collective leadership under Brezhnev and Kosygin was in a sense the creation of the Politburo itself, which chose this leadership rather than simply submitting to the victor in its ranks. "Respect for personnel" under this new leadership meant that Brezhnev did not attempt to create a Politburo of dependent leaders as Khrushchev had attempted and Stalin had succeeded in doing. The new leadership seemed to transform its strife-torn oligarchic style into a more stable cartel of authority with reduced conflict and a division of decision-making responsibilities (perhaps by subcommittees). In this arrangement, each member of the leadership participated in the decisions of his specialties and in decisions to resolve disputes between issue areas, but increasingly abstained from intervention and deferred to his colleagues in other issue areas. The rise of the fifth generation may inaugurate still greater pragmatism, lowering the stakes in political controversies and thus reducing the levels of conflict.

Leadership Politics and Policy

As suggested by the model of Brzezinski and Huntington introduced earlier in this chapter, changes in policy-making processes such as these should be reflected in the policies of the Soviet Union. In fact, each of the attributes of policy identified by Brzezinski and Huntington (choice, integration, and innovation) is affected by the level of conflict within the leadership and by the extent of consolidation or dispersal of decision-making authority within it.[56] Specifically, heightened conflict within the leadership diminishes the ability of the leadership to pursue policies that are consistent over time or coherent across issue areas. So, for example, the conflict school attributes the erratic nature of policy during the Stalin-Khrushchev succession and the last years of Khrushchev's leadership to the higher levels of leadership conflict at these times.[57] Dispersal of decision-making authority within the leadership reduces the capacity of the leadership to innovate. Thus, the tendency toward greater incrementalism in the Brezhnev era and fewer "hare-brained schemes" may have been the result of the greater "cartelization" of authority after 1965.

Leadership politics at the time of successions may have a very special effect on policy. The nature of that effect, however, is problematic and the object of heated debate in the West. University of California political scientist George Breslauer, surveying the Stalin-Khrushchev and Khrushchev-Brezhnev successions, argues that it is

> possible to discern two stages in each succession. The first stage . . . was characterized by rival programs for significant change in policy and structure, by zigzags in policy, and by polarization of positions as policy disputes fed into the power struggle. . . . The second stage . . . was characterized by the ascendancy of the party leader, by the forging and presentation of a comprehensive program for struc-

tural reform and budgetary redistribution at home, and by Soviet initiatives to improve the prospects for US-Soviet collaboration abroad.[58]

Valerie Bunce has argued that new general secretaries tend "to pump up public consumption in the period immediately following a succession" and then "to move toward less popular policies, once the succession has been resolved." This tendency leads to a policy "cycle of mass and then elite-oriented priorities" in the succession and postsuccession periods, respectively. Bunce accounts for this by arguing that Soviet leaders use the mass-oriented policies during succession periods in order to placate the masses and so avoid mass unrest that might occur during these periods of heightened leadership vulnerability.[59] The present author, however, has challenged this "succession-connection thesis," arguing that the heightened conflict that usually attends successions reduces the ability of a General Secretary to innovate with an upsurge in public consumption. Moreover, the effort to build support among his fellow leaders and interest elites gives a General Secretary the incentive to satisfy elite rather than mass interests.[60]

The balance of power between conservatives and reformers within the leadership may also affect policy. The conflict school emphasizes, for example, that the fate of Malenkov's "New Course" depended on the relative power of Malenkov's reformers and Khrushchev's conservatives. Similarly, a decade later, according to Linden, "Khrushchev's overthrow had been the result of a marriage of convenience between party conservatives and the more cautious reformers disturbed by Khrushchevian radicalism. . . . The policy measures Khrushchev's successors have come up with so far are hybrids reflecting compromise arrangements."[61] That is, the absence of bold innovation in Brezhnevian policy may be attributed not only to the cartelization of authority, but also to the unique balance of power between conservatives and reformers.

THE "POLITICAL INTERESTS" SCHOOL

Sovietologists are divided not only in their assessments of the extent of conflict within the Soviet leadership, but also on the issue of whether the power to influence policy is limited to the top leadership or extends to interests outside the Politburo. In contrast to both the totalitarian and conflict schools, the political interests school of thought argues that there is significant participation in decision making by interests outside the Politburo leadership. For example, H. Gordon Skilling of the University of Toronto, one of the fathers of this approach, argues that since Stalin's death Soviet politics have been

characterized among other things by the increased activity of political interest groups and the presence of conflict. Although decision-making in its final stage still remains in the hands of a relatively small group of leaders at the top of the party hierarchy, there has been, it is assumed, a broadening of group participation in the crucial preliminary stages of policy deliberation and in the subsequent phase of implementation.[62]

The origins of the political interests approach can be traced to growing dissatisfaction with both the totalitarian and conflict models. The former, they argue, ignores the inputs to policy from outside the Party. It assumes that the Party is completely autonomous of the larger society and that society is devoid of conflicts among rival groups or struggles over issues and interests. The changes in Soviet politics that followed Stalin's death made this an increasingly less useful assumption for analysis. The conflict school, while noting the existence of rivalry that might draw political interests into the political process, nonetheless, tends "to treat such groups as mere objects of manipulation by the top leaders and factions, and to discount the possibility of autonomous action by them." Moreover, the conflict school ignores all but a few interests, such as the state bureaucracy or Party apparatus, and assumes these to be unified or homogeneous interests, when they are in fact divided internally in their interests and opinions.[63]

A fundamental conceptual controversy that divides the political interests school itself into alternative theories and analytic approaches, is the definition of the interests that participate in the political process. Darrell P. Hammer of Indiana University, in advancing a model of "bureaucratic pluralism," defines these as "conflicting bureaucratic interests, with the ministries and the party apparatus acting as the chief interest groups."[64] Thus, Hammer minimizes the role of interests outside the administrative organs. Jerry F. Hough broadens this definition of the politically significant interests in his model of "institutional pluralism."[65] He argues that institutions such as trade unions and the Academy of Sciences as well as the ministries and Party departments are increasingly responsive to broader societal forces and are playing an ever-larger role in the political process. Skilling expands it still further, including "inchoate groupings" along with these formal institutions in his definition of "political interest groups." Skilling estimates that in the early 1970s these interest groups involved a little over a million Soviet adults (less than one percent of the total adult population), including, but not limited to, apparatchiki, managers of heavy industry, military officers, security police, lawyers, economists, and writers.[66] The British Sovietologist David Lane, in the presentation of his theory of the "group process of [Soviet] politics," expands this still further, stretching Skilling's definition of interest groups to include amorphous social groupings such as nationalities and estranged groups such as dissident writers.[67]

The Argument for the Political Interests Approach

It is important to note that much of the formal presentation of the political interests model has been cautious and even tentative. Skilling, for example, adds the caveat to his analysis that he does not assume

> that political interest groups are the principal feature of Soviet politics, or that these groups are the dominant factors in the political process. They are, however, an important element, the neglect of which makes the picture of Soviet politics incomplete and distorted, and the inclusion of which renders it richer and more authentic.[68]

Hough includes a similar cautionary note in his judgment that the Soviet system is only in the process of developing toward institutional pluralism, rather than having completed that transition.

Central to the political interests school is the assertion that particularistic interests press coherent views upon the leadership in order to shape policy. Skilling, for example, stresses that a political interest group is defined by "a common attitude, associated with, but not identical to, a common characteristic, [that] leads to an expressed common claim."[69] Yet the political interests school has been limited, because it is difficult to identify such groups on more than an ad hoc basis. For instance, Roman Kolkowicz has argued that on some issues the military exhibits high solidarity, yet on others divides along service or functional lines, between generations, or among cliques based on prior service.[70] This inconsistency is duplicated in other groupings such as the apparatchiki or economists. Moreover, an interest group on a specific issue may represent a temporary alliance among opinion groups from different occupations. Identifying recurring patterns in the composition of interest groups and the lines of division among them for the purposes of theory- or model-building remains a highly problematic undertaking.

The growing importance of interest elites has been variously attributed to the modernization of Soviet society, the decline of terror, the replacement of Stalin's autocratic rule with a collective and conflict-ridden oligarchy, and the conscious decision of Soviet leaders to consult with experts and affected interests.[71] Milton Lodge, in assessing the "participatory attitudes" among specialized elites, finds that these elites not only increasingly describe themselves as participants in the political process, but also express a growing expectation that they *should* participate.[72] The growth of interest elite participation in the policy process has been institutionalized through the co-optation of these elites into the decision-making process.[73] Frederic J. Fleron argues that through co-optation of specialized elites into the Party Congress, Central Committee, and Politburo, "the Soviet political elite can share responsibility for decisions with the specialized elites, have greater access to the specialized elites through their formal representatives, and probably maintain the legitimacy of the political elite in issuing directives to the specialized elites."[74] The political elite runs the risk, however, that these interest elites may actually threaten their monopoly of political power.

Ellen Jones of the Defense Intelligence Agency argues that this interest participation actually inheres in the structure of Soviet institutions—that "Soviet Party and governmental institutions are premised on the existence of conflicting organizational interests." In particular, the widespread use of advisory, management and decision-making committees throughout the Soviet polity at all levels, from all-union to local, institutionalizes this organizational representation. Both in theory and practice, she argues, "committee procedures are deliberately designed to routinize and systematize the interaction of organizational representatives. They reflect the high value that is placed on organizational participation in Soviet public policy formation."[75]

If studies of decision making in American politics are relevant, then this expansion of participants in the political process should affect both the policy process and policy outputs. Students of American politics have argued that a consequence of greater autonomy and competition among policy elites is policy making that tends to be slow due to competition and consensus-building, leaderless due to the diffusion of power and responsibility, and indecisive due to efforts to avoid conflict. This leads to an increased possibility of no policy due to stalemate, compromised policy, unstable policy with shifting ad hoc compromises, contradictory policy, paper policy that is officially promulgated but never fully implemented, and outmoded policy that continues without regard to changing circumstances.[76] Indeed, in the Soviet Union a consequence of the growing role of interests may have been exactly this. The policy-making process has come to involve more extensive consultation and even bargaining and compromise.[77] Due to this changed policy process, policy itself has become "highly political, reflecting conflicting forces and interests within the structure of the single party [and] of the national communist society. . . . "[78] Seweryn Bialer has found that the pattern of decision making in the post-Khrushchev leadership

> . . . puts a premium on compromise and is ill-suited to accommodate innovative ambitions which stray much beyond the existing consensus and to mobilize support for them. The increased security of all leaders, the greater diffusion of their everyday influence, the stability of the position of the top leader himself are paid for by narrowing the range of acceptable alternative solutions in internal policies, by stressing the managerial as counterposed to the political dimensions of decisions (i.e., the question of "how" rather than "what" to do), and by increasing the making of "nondecisions."[79]

Debate over the Political Interests School

The political interests school has been severely criticized by those who believe the Soviet system to be more monolithic than pluralistic.[80] Critics point up that traditional Russian antipathy to particularism and official Soviet proscription of factionalism conspire to stifle group activity. The current prohibition on autonomous organizing or associational activity prevents interests from developing an identity and from becoming a group. And interests that develop within bureaucracies cannot act autonomously due to the hierarchical control within and over these. The tight control, if not monopoly, over the means of communication enjoyed by the Party limits the articulation of independent, or unofficial, views. And the use of terms such as "interest group" and "pluralism" evoke parallels to Western polyarchies that are simply untenable.[81]

The political interests approach makes a strong, but less than conclusive, defense against these criticisms through a growing literature of case studies. One genre in this literature is represented by studies of specific interests and institutions, including the Party apparatchiki, the legal profession, industrial managers, and the police.[82] Probably the most widely studied of such institutions, aside from the Communist Party itself, is the Soviet military. Diverging interests between the military and the Party, according to Roman Kolkowicz, have given rise to disagreements over policy. Tension between the two results from the Party's deep ideological rejection of a standing army. The Party came to power with the belief that a standing military is an institution limited to class society, and thus with no place in a socialist or communist order. Even though the Party subsequently reconciled itself to the need for such an institution under socialism, this dogma still colors its relations with the armed forces. Secondly, the values of the military—including elitism, professional autonomy, and heroic symbolism—clash with the professed values of the Party. Thus, for instance, the military's desire for professional autonomy has led it to resist the controls the Party has attempted to impose on all institutions in Soviet society. And lastly, because the military possesses such immense power through its coercive instruments, the Party fears what it sees as the military's natural tendency toward "Bonapartism," the rise of a military leader to kill the Revolution. These differences lie at the heart of the clash of interests and conflict over policies that Kolkowicz sees in the history of Party-military relations.[83]

A second genre has been case studies of individual decisions that examine the role of interests outside the leadership in placing an issue on the agenda and influencing the outcome of a policy debate. One of the earliest of these was Joel Schwartz and William Keech's study of the adoption of the Educational Reform Act of 1958.[84] This case is significant for it came at a time when Khrushchev had presumably consolidated his control over the Party. Nonetheless, the study suggests that Khrushchev proposed a dramatic reform in education and lost—was forced to retreat from or to change his original proposal. In April 1958, in an address to the Komsomol Congress, Khrushchev proposed that the Soviet Union reform education, arguing that the existing system was leading youths to disparage the value of labor and that the higher education system in particular was giving preference to the children of wealthy Soviets over those from peasant and worker families. In September, he made specific proposals to the Party Central Committee in his "Theses on Education": Instead of completing a 10-year education without interruption, Soviet youths would initially complete 7 to 8 years of primary education, and then enter the labor force. Those wanting to continue their education and prepare for entrance to a university would take night or correspondence courses. (The best students would receive two to three days' release time each week to devote to their studies.) Only after completing 1 or 2 years of labor would students be permitted to enter an institution of higher education; and then during the first 2 to 3 years the students would study part-time while continuing to work. After hearing Khrushchev's Theses, the Central Committee appears to have broken with its normal procedures: No resolution endorsing these was adopted at the conclusion of the Plenum. Apparently there was inadequate support for Khrushchev's proposals; indeed, Khrushchev may actually have been overruled in the meeting.

In the next months there followed a relatively open debate over Khrushchev's proposal for "production education." Opposition to the proposal appears to have come from four identifiable groups. The educational establishment of teachers and administrators opposed the new policy as bad pedagogy that would degrade the quality of education of students in the 15- to 17-year age group. University administrators and scientists argued that the quality of their incoming students would fall, for after two years out of school, a student would be unprepared for university-level work. Factory managers did not want to be baby-sitters, fearing that 15- to 17-year-olds would be underqualified and undisciplined, disrupting factory production schedules. And parents flooded newspapers with letters objecting to the removal of their children from school in order to work in factories.

The law that was finally adopted in December 1958 represented a compromise. The new law preserved the secondary school system, but required students to take a few extra hours each week of polytechnical training ("shop"). This would not be labor in a work place, but education at school in industrial techniques. To compensate for the hours devoted to polytechnical education, secondary schooling would be extended an extra year, so that a complete education would require 11 rather than 10 years. Significantly, the new law preserved the division of education into two tracks—full-time and part-time education. Khrushchev had drawn particular attention to this division as a practice that discriminated against the children of peasants and workers, who tended to be enrolled only part-time. The new law also did not require labor as a precondition for admission to higher education. Instead, as a compromise with Khrushchev's proposal, students in their first year of higher education would be required to work part-time. (There would be exemptions for those who were involved in theoretical rather than applied studies, and for those in fields unrelated to production, such as the social sciences or humanities.) Essentially, the law established a mandatory "work co-op" program for those studying engineering.

Schwartz and Keech conclude that Khrushchev was overruled. Between the time that he committed his prestige to the initial reform proposals, and the time that the law was finally adopted, Khrushchev was forced to retreat. They surmise that there must have been a division at the top that provided an opportunity for the interest groups to present their views and obtain a modification in the reform.

This case study also illustrates the great gaps present in any examination of Soviet interest group behavior. The available evidence includes Khrushchev's initial proposal; Khrushchev's restatement of that position, suggesting he had not changed his mind; and the law that resulted shortly thereafter and that was different in principle as well as in detail from what Khrushchev had proposed. In addition, there are a series of statements by interest elites that appear to criticize the reform, although only by indirection. The case for interest group influence must fill some significant gaps in evidence, for we do not know what occurred in the Central Committee itself nor how Khrushchev's own position on this issue might have changed. Moreover, the political interests approach assumes that the often esoteric debates found in the Soviet press represent the positions of larger interests engaged in a conflict over policy.[84] (These problems are, of course, not unique to the political interests school and actually arise in any theory of Soviet politics, including the totalitarian model. For example, to ignore the diverging positions printed in the Soviet press because one postulates that interests cannot participate in policy making, as the totalitarian model is inclined to do, requires an intellectual leap of gargantuan proportions.)

A conceptual difficulty that runs throughout the political interests approach is its treatment of the role of the Party in Soviet politics and its relationship to interest groups. Rejecting the image of the CPSU as a dominating monolith, the political interests school has not come forward with a single alternative. In some analyses there is a tendency to treat the Party as just another, albeit more powerful, interest in Soviet society. Hough, alternatively, has suggested that the Party is evolving toward the role of a power broker. In his definition of pluralism, "political leaders serve essentially as mediators or brokers in the political process, their 'most universal function' being to bring 'men together in masses on some middle ground where they can combine to carry out a common policy'."[85] More common is the image of the Party as a political arena. For example, according to Vernon Aspaturian, the Party is "an arena in which the various Soviet elites make known their demands on one another, articulate their special interests, and try to impose their desires as the unified will of society as a whole."[86] In a recent variant of this image, Amos Perlmutter and William LeoGrande have proposed that analysis begin from the notion of a "dual-role elite"; all Soviet interest elites are also Party members, owing their highest loyalty to the Party, not their non-Party institution.

> The implications of the dual-elite arrangement for conflict resolution are profound. Serious conflicts, whether personal, ideological, or bureaucratic in genesis, are resolved within the party, not between the party and nonparty institutions or nonparty elites. The dual-role elites carry conflicts into the party, making every important conflict an inner-party conflict. The dual-role elites then carry the resolution of the conflict back to nonparty institutions, which must adhere to the position defined by the party. . . . On issues of consequence, bureaucratic structures do not face off with one another; they petition the party for a redress of grievances.[87]

This last view, however, when clarified, may lead to a still more amorphous conception of the Party.

Another conceptual difficulty is the political interests school's assumption of conflict among interests as an inescapable concomitant of their participation in policy making. Some argue that political intersts are likely to participate in the policy process only when conflict in the leadership leads its members "to broaden the scope of conflict by involving policy groups who might shift the balance."[88] Even among those who do not see sharp leadership conflict as a precondition for participation by interests there is a tendency to see that participation expressed through overt group conflict. A central assumption of Skilling and Griffiths' pioneering volume on Soviet interest groups is that Soviet politics are characterized by "the presence of group conflict." In the model of pluralism, according to Hough, "the political process revolves around conflict among a complex set of crosscutting and shifting alliances of persons with divergent interests."[89] Yet, with the rise of the Brezhnev leadership, overt conflicts among interests have been less common even as the consultative role of interests and their routine involvement in decision making seem to have grown.

Stressing the inapplicability of this assumption of group conflict to the Brezhnev era and the inability of the traditional pluralist model to explain the role of an activist state or Party, Valerie Bunce and John M. Echols, III, have proposed an adaptation of the Western model of corporatism to explain the Brezhnev period: " . . . a corporatist system places a premium on cooperation among politically important groups and institutions, the incorporation of functional interest groups and specialists into the policy process, and, simultaneously, a dominant role for an activist state." Thus, the state is not simply a forum, power broker, or interest, but an active, leading element in decision making. "Groups do not compete with one another through the state to obtain more for themselves. Instead, they are brought together by the state in active cooperation to achieve more for all; harmony is the watchword of a corporatist regime." Such a system, Bunce and Echols add, affects policy: It places major emphasis upon rational planning and social welfare policies to buy off the masses.[90]

A TWO-TIER MODEL OF OLIGARCHIC POLICY MAKING

The alternative models of the Soviet political process are all useful for specific purposes. The totalitarian model describes with abstraction and simplification the Stalinist period and by setting up an ideal type draws out the differences between the contemporary Soviet system and Western polyarchies. The conflict, political interests, and corporatist models describe Soviet politics during specific periods since Stalin's death and highlight differences between the contemporary Soviet system and the Stalinist past. Each, however, also suffers significant limitations to its utility or applicability. Most importantly, the totalitarian model blinds us to change in the Soviet polity since 1953, while the political interests and corporatist models tend to belittle the sharp contrasts between Leninist and non-Leninist politics. In all schools there has been a tendency to absolutist thinking—to insist that the phenomenon that serves as the focus of the school (e.g., conflict) is a central and ever-present attribute of Soviet politics rather than a variable. Each has found a body of undeniable evidence to support its contentions, but each resembles a blind man's description of an elephant that misses a larger reality. Indeed, the tendency to absolutist thinking has led each to ignore many of the insights of the other schools and thus, has hindered the synthesis of findings in the field.

Although there is no consensus in the field of Sovietology, the insights of recent case studies do suggest (perhaps only to this author) a useful model of Soviet decision making. This organizing model identifies key variables and suggests some interconnectedness among them.[91] It also includes a few hypotheses to suggest the specific ways in which these variables interact. As should be true of all models, this is a simplification of reality and as much an agenda for further research as a synthesis of what is already known.

The Structure of Policy Making

The politics of policy formation in the Soviet Union is best conceptualized as a two-tier process within the Party, bringing together leaders on the upper tier struggling among themselves for power and dual-role interest elites on the second tier shuffling for scarce resources. The leaders need supporters among the interest elites to promote their careers or maintain their positions; and the interest elites need patrons at the top to support their specific program requests.[92] In this view, Soviet politics is a process of actors within these two groups setting up alliances that cut across the two tiers. Policy emerges from the bargaining that results from the formation and maintenance of coalitions across these two tiers.

The decision process proceeds from initiation and persuasion to decision and then implementation along what Graham Allison has called "action-channels—a regularized means of taking governmental action on a specific kind of issue."[93] In the Soviet weapons acquisition process as described by Arthur Alexander, for example, "there is a standard sequence of steps in the design process that takes a concept from initial proposal to operational aircraft." Initiation of a proposal typically comes from a customer-ministry or a design bureau within a production- ministry. Following a decision by the Council of Ministers to begin development, a scientific-technical commission composed of representatives from the customer-ministries and production-ministries makes decisions on the technical specifications of the project at each stage. Under the commission's guidance the design bureaus (sometimes in competition with one another) move from preproject specifications to mock-up development and prototype construction and send the final prototypes to testing institutes. After a decision to begin production, probably at the Politburo level for all significant weapon systems, the action moves to a series production plant subordinate to the relevant production-ministry.[94] Such action-channels are important since, as Allison notes, they "structure the game by preselecting the major players, determining their usual points of entrance into the game, and distributing particular advantages and disadvantages for each game."[95]

The Participants

Who makes policy? (Can we adduce systematic propositions about who can participate in the decision-making process?)

It is something of an oversimplification, but useful nonetheless, to distinguish two types of participants in the policy-making process: individuals in the leadership seeking personal power (e.g., Khrushchev and Malenkov, Brezhnev and Podgornyi, Andropov, Chernenko, and Gorbachev) and interests seeking programs (e.g., military officers, industrial managers, apparatchiki). The structure of the action-channel will determine which leaders and interests participate in a decision. Hough, using a different image, argues that "one can speak of 'complexes' . . . and of 'whirlpools' . . . of specialized party, state, 'public,' and scientific personnel working within the respective policy areas. . . . In particular, policymaking power informally comes to be delegated to these complexes."[96] Since interests not "hooked on" to an action-channel normally may not spontaneously participate in such decisions, action-channels typically, but not always, narrow participation in specific decisions to relevant specialists.[97]

Although struggle for power among members of the leadership is constant, the intensity of this conflict, we can hypothesize, peaks during periods of succession and reaches its lowest levels when one among them has established autocratic rule (Hypothesis 1). Although interests are always in competition with one another for scarce resources, this conflict, by way of hypothesis, tends to remain latent when leadership conflict is low. In these circumstances, even though interests press proposals that conflict with those pressed by other interests, they do not directly confront one another. As the intensity of leadership struggle increases, however, this conflict is more likely to be manifest in direct confrontations among interests over the allocation of resources (Hypothesis 2).[98]

The manner in which an interest participates will be affected by its structure (Hypothesis 3)—a topic on which systematic research is needed in order to develop empirical categories to classify Soviet interests. Some interests, for example, are coextensive with single institutions, while others are interinstitutional. Interests such as the military are more hierarchical than interests like writers. And while many will be only ad hoc interests, some will be perennial or recurring single-issue interests, and still others will be recurring or permanent multi-issue interests.

Power

What gives participants power to influence policy? (Can we adduce systematic propositions about the intrinsic characteristics and extrinsic circumstances that increase a participant's power?)

Participants in the power struggle of the first tier, according to Myron Rush, rely upon "four chief sources of political power":

1. "The institutions of dictatorship," including most importantly the Party apparatus, but also governmental agencies (e.g., military, police) and public organizations (e.g., trade unions and intellectuals' organizations).
2. "Territorial bases of power," such as union-republic Party-state organizations.
3. "Professional groups," such as economic managers in productive enterprises.
4. "Personal influence."[99]

Interests that seek to influence policy have slightly different sources of power. One of these is expertise. Expert information is power in any system, but this is especially important in the Soviet Union because information is not freely available and there is a tendency toward departmentalization of information that hides it from others. For example, an interest with a monopoly of expertise on an issue can help shape policies in that area by defining the problems and formulating the options. The importance of departmentalism was pointed out to the United States during the negotiations over SALT I, when the American representative began to discourse in detail about Soviet strategic weapons. Colonel-General Nikolai Ogarkov of the Soviet General Staff took the American delegate aside to ask that he not discuss such matters in front of the representatives from the Soviet Ministry of Foreign Affairs, for apparently they had not been cleared to receive such information.[100]

The importance of expertise is illustrated by the development of government tort liability legislation. In December 1961, the Supreme Soviet adopted Principles of Civil Legislation that established in Article 89 state liability for damage to private citizens due to improper acts of officials. The law was passed only after five years of argumentation by legal scholars, who initially made their case before law school audiences. They subsequently argued their case in public conferences in the pages of such professional journals as, *Sovetskoe gosudarstvo i pravo* [Soviet State and Law], and before the Supreme Soviet itself. They even won their case against the opposition of the Ministry of Justice. The principal power the lawyers possessed was information or expertise.[101]

A second source of power is organizational resources. Interests that are interest *groups* are more powerful than those that are not.[102] This is particularly important in Soviet policy making, for organization is not a freely available resource. As a consequence, powerful interests tend to develop within existing institutions although they are not limited to them. More specifically, the structure of an interest will affect its power: For example, the power of an interest, we can hypothesize, will grow with the extent to which it is hierarchical, permanent, and a multi-issue interest (Hypotheses 4–6).

An example of the importance of organization is the debate in the 1960s "whether dirigibles should be constructed as an economical means of heavy air transport. . . . "[103] The "dirigible-enthusiasts," as they came to be known, proposed a fleet of blimps that would assist in transporting resources in remote areas of the Soviet Union. The Ministry of Aviation Production (MAP), which produces aircraft, opposed the idea. The proponents of the plan were scattered among a number of institutions, including the Academy of Sciences, city and local planning agencies, state committees, and ministries. Recognizing their disadvantage in confronting the unified bureaucracy of the MAP, the dirigible-enthusiasts made as one of their first recommendations the establishment of a state committee for dirigible-building. But MAP outmaneuvered the dirigible-enthusiasts and blocked this.

A third source of power for interests is access to the press and to public meetings. Interests that can place an issue on the public agenda and build a constituency by publicizing their views are more powerful than those that cannot. Once again, these resources are not freely available in the Soviet Union. In the previously cited case for example, the dirigible-enthusiasts were at a serious disadvantage because the professional journals and scientific conferences on air transport were controlled by the Ministry of Aviation Production, which denied them the opportunity to present their case. The dirigible-enthusiasts finally found patrons for a conference among the city fathers of Novosibirsk, who called the First All-Union Conference of Enthusiasts of Dirigible Building, in which they were able to present and distribute papers. They also found patrons among the editors of *Izvestiia* and *Literaturnaia Gazeta,* the newspaper for the Union of Writers. These permitted the dirigible-enthusiasts to publicize their views. Reflecting their frustration at MAP's monopoly over communication in the field of aviation, one of the dirigible-enthusiasts, T. Alekseeva, wrote in an article entitled, "We Throw Down the Gauntlet . . . ": "Once again, we throw down to the opponents of dirigibles the gauntlet of open discussion. Is it possible they will again keep silent?"[104]

Expertise, organization, and access to the media are not the only sources of power for interests. Access to top policy-making institutions (most importantly the Politburo, but more commonly the Central Committee) will permit an interest to express its views directly to the leadership.[105] Control of instruments of coercion may not be used to affect policy outcomes under normal conditions, but may contribute to others' perceptions of the interest's (potential) power and may be used in extraordinary situations such as a succession showdown (e.g., Anti-Party Group incident).[106] More intangible is the power that an interest may gain from its indispensability to the leadership, making leaders reluctant to alienate or remove its insistent members, and from its access to natural allies, which may incline the leadership to give its proposals special consideration.

The power of a leader or interest is a variable that depends in part on the possession of these power resources, each of which is itself a variable. In addition, the power of interests will vary with the level of conflict in the leadership, reaching its peak during succession crises (Hypothesis 7). The power of participants will also vary with the movement of a decision along its action-channel: An interest's power, we can hypothesize, is greatest at the initiation stage and lowest at the point of decision (Hypothesis 8).[107] And the power of interests will vary with the nature of the issue to be decided; the more complex an issue and the more specialized information needed, the greater the power of interests possessing relevant expertise (Hypothesis 9). Conversely, the more an issue touches upon or threatens the institutional predominance of the leadership, the less interests will be able to affect its outcome (Hypothesis 10).[108]

Positions

What policy positions are participants likely to take? (Can we adduce systematic propositions about the recurring stands of participants?)

A participant who can influence policy in the Soviet Union is likely to take positions that reflect his position within the system. Don Price, in observing American bureaucratic behavior, offered the aphorism "Where you stand depends on where you sit."[109] That is, the positions of a participant on policy issues can often be predicted from that person's position within the bureaucracy.

Power seekers and interests see different aspects of an issue. Everyone of course, argues, and probably each believes, that the problem he sees and the solution he proposes serve the best interest of the Soviet Union and the Party. The question that divides them of course, is *how* best to serve that interest. Power seekers tend to act as though they see that interest through the prism of personal power—as though they ask of a policy, "What can it do for my power aspirations?" (Hypothesis 11). Of course, leaders come to their positions with individual value preferences, but the indeterminacy of power in the Soviet polity, due to the weak institutionalization of power, forces all leaders to attend to their personal power. And the pressure of this context in which positions must be taken shapes the positions themselves. Interests tend to act as though they see the interest of the Soviet Union through the prism of organizational mission, as though they ask of a policy, "How can it help my institution fulfill its mission?" (Hypothesis 12).

The "personalistic perspective" of power seekers is most evident during succession struggles. Stalin, for example, moved from a moderate position to a rightist position and then to a leftist position as the needs of his personal power changed. Khrushchev made the shift from the conservative to the reformist position during the post-Stalin succession as his career needs changed.[110]

The issue itself often determines the types of interests that emerge in the second tier. Interests may divide and ally on bureaucratic, regional, educational, or generational lines.[111] For example, on the issue of investment priorities one can fairly safely predict that the military will line up with the defense industry to defend the privileged position of investment in heavy industry (Group A) and that the food industry and consumer-goods ministries will line up to urge greater attention to the consumer sector (Group B). Other issues will cut across these bureaucratic lines. For example in 1960, when Khrushchev proposed that the Soviet military go nuclear and cut the traditional armed forces, predictably, the military itself divided on the issue; the Strategic Rocket Forces and nuclear Air Defense Forces (PVO) were in favor of the idea, while the Army, the surface Navy, and the traditional PVO were opposed.[112] An area where further research is greatly needed is in the development of hypotheses to identify which issues are associated with different divisions and alliances of interest.[113]

It is not just the issue, however, that affects the shape of interests, for the same issue at different points along the action-channel will, in a predictable way, produce shifting divisions and alliances. So, for example, in the process of negotiated planning (to be described more fully in the next chapter), the stand that a participant takes on a proposed one- or five-year plan depends on whether at that moment a participant is a superior or a subordinate in the negotiations. Ministry officials will argue with "superiors" in Gosplan for higher supply allotments and lower production quotas, but then turn around to demand higher production with fewer supplies from subordinate factory managers.[114]

Ploys

How do participants attempt to influence policy? (Can we adduce systematic propositions about the tactics used by participants?)

Participants in the first tier use a number of ploys to influence policy, including:

1. Placement of supporters in strategic positions.
2. Reorganization of posts entirely so as to strengthen their supporters.
3. Appeals through the press to rally interests elite opinion.
4. Material incentives to interests who would support them.

For example, Khrushchev used all these ploys in 1953 to ensure that his Virgin Lands Policy would succeed and by this, promote his career. Malenkov opposed much of Khrushchev's program to grow wheat in Siberia and Central Asia and so, sought to scuttle it by placing his supporters in those state positions responsible for implementing the program—specifically, the Ministries of State Farms (A. I. Kozlov) and of Agriculture and Procurement (I. A. Benediktov). Khrushchev countered by pushing through a plan to reorganize the Ministry of Agriculture and Procurement, breaking it into two and securing the appointment of his own supporter (L. R. Korniyets) to Minister of Agricultural Procurement, the administrator who would now bear principal responsibility for carrying out the Virgin Lands Policy. Khrushchev also used his alliance with the editor of *Pravda*, D. T. Shepilov, to initiate a press campaign to extoll the successes in Central Asia. And Khrushchev appealed for support in the agricultural community by promising kolkhoz managers increased investment and greater autonomy.[115]

To affect policy, interests tend to rely on three different ploys that change with the movement of a decision along its action-channel: partisan analysis on the input side, sabotage on the output side, and colonization at the center. For the most part, interests rely on persuasion by means of partisan analysis, "showing the proximate policy maker how a policy desired by the interest group squares with the policy maker's philosophy, values, or principles."[116] In the Soviet system, partisan analysis may take some peculiar forms. One of these is competitive ideological appeals to demonstrate that one's policy prescription is "more orthodox" than the alternatives. For example, in a disagreement over the structure of the Academy of Sciences during the late 1950s and early 1960s, pure scientists sought to expel engineers or applied scientists, removing them to scientific institutions and laboratories under the control of economic institutions. To do so, they had to confront the Marxist dogma that practice and theory must go hand in hand. Nikolai Semenov, a physical chemist and spokesperson for the pure scientists, argued that in the contemporary era pure science had become a dynamic and creative force on its own and that it no longer needed to be tied to practice or production to sustain innovation. Ivan Bardin, a metallurgical engineer and spokesperson for the applied scientists in the Academy, argued that the old Marxist dogma was still valid.

A closely related ploy in these debates are competitive appeals to authority. For example, Semenov sought to rally interest-elite and leadership opinion on behalf of the proposed Academy reform by reminding them that the reform was consistent with Khrushchev's "splendid analysis of the role of science and new technology in the building of Communism."[117]

A third ploy is partisan analysis through historical reconstruction. Partisan analysis can reinterpret the lessons of history in order to show that these demonstrate the validity of a policy proposal. In the late 1950s, the military sought to wrest control over military doctrine from the Party ideologues, because they felt that control by ideologues without military expertise had led Soviet military strategy to lag behind developments in the West. Military historians argued their position, in part, by citing the lessons of early World War II, which they claimed showed that the initial reverses at the hands of the Nazi armies were due to excessive Party control and that these might have been avoided if military commanders had been given greater discretion.[118]

Finally, an interest may turn to outright manipulation and falsification of expertise. The Ministry of Timber, Pulp, and Woodworking, for example, turned to such ploys in order to secure approval for its operations near Lake Baikal. Baikal is the deepest and possibly the oldest lake in the world, with some of the purest fresh water and a unique flora and fauna. Environmentalists had tried to stop industrial pollution there. Near the lake however, are good stands of timber, which the Ministry saw as an opportunity to turn a quick ruble, meeting its production quota at minimum expense by building a pulp mill on the edges of Lake Baikal or one of its tributaries. The head of the Ministry's Cellulose, Paper, and Carton Administration argued, "We too are for the preservation of the lake, but we are also opposed to underutilizing its huge wealth, its water, and timber." To achieve this end, the Ministry had to convince the leadership that its operations would not pollute the lake or that the risk of pollution was justified by national needs. To make its case, the Ministry, it appears, deliberately underestimated the construction costs of the plant by $22 million, or one-third of the total. Moreover, the Ministry claimed that the purpose of the plant was to produce super-super-cellulose cord, which was purportedly essential to the tires of modern military aircraft. (It turned out, however, that Canada had already replaced super-super-cellulose with superior nylon cord and that the Soviet Union would probably follow suit.) In the end, the plant actually produced heavy cartons, which in no way required the pure waters of Lake Baikal. To meet the demanding pollution standards set by law, the Ministry "shopped around" to find a sanitary inspector to certify its compliance before operations could begin. When the Chief Sanitary Inspector of the Ministry of Land Reclamation and Water Management actually refused to certify the plant, the Ministry had to find a second, and finally a third, inspector before one would certify the plant for operation. Later, when the Ministry had to submit pollution reports in order to continue the plant's operations, it found an analyst to certify that the plant's production met state pollution standards by paying an annual fee of 100,000 rubles to his laboratory, under the guise of retaining the analyst as a consultant.[119]

Interests that cannot persuade may sabotage the implementation of policy. In the early 1960s, when Khrushchev attempted to impose tighter MPA control over the military, the armed forces met this "with various forms of resistance by letting discipline deteriorate drastically; by obstructing political appointees in commanding positions in the performance of their duties; by neglecting political indoctrination; and by openly questioning the skills, wisdom, and authority of the nonprofessional political functionaries in the officer corps and the political organs.''[120] Similarly, in 1964, the KGB apparently showed its dissatisfaction toward Khrushchev's rapprochement with West Germany, by initiating a campaign of harassment against West German officials that culminated on September 12, 1964, in a nearly fatal mustard gas attack against an employee of the West German Embassy visiting the Zagorsk Monastery.[121]

And lastly, interests that take a longer-term perspective on policy can attempt to build their influence over policy by colonization of the Politburo with leaders sympathetic to their policy positions. Interests may seek to have their leaders co-opted into the Politburo, for these co-opted elites may ensure direct say in decisions. In the most dramatic cases interests may seek to influence the outcome of successions so as to ensure that the General Secretary is sympathetic to their cause.[122]

The selection of ploys by an interest will reflect the power resources available to that interest (Hypothesis 13). It will also reflect, we can surmise, the structure of that interest (Hypothesis 14). For example, hierarchical interests such as the military will be less likely to engage in spontaneous, multifaceted articulation of interest than a less-hierarchical interest such as writers. The selection of ploys will also vary with the level of leadership conflict. By way of hypothesis: Interests with coercive capabilities are less likely to use these during periods of consolidated leadership (Hypothesis 15).[123] Also, the participation of interests in decision making is more likely to be autonomous during periods of intense leadership conflict and more likely to be co-opted or mobilized at other times (Hypothesis 16).

Policy

How will changes in the policy process affect policy outputs and outcomes? (Can we adduce systematic propositions about the relationship of the attributes of policy to changes in the policy process?)

Allison distinguishes between rational choice in which "the rational actor selects the alternative whose consequences rank highest in terms of his goals and objectives" and a political resultant—"resultants in the sense that what happens is not chosen as a solution to a problem but rather results from compromise, conflict, and confusion of officials with diverse interests and unequal influence."[124] The extent to which Soviet policy outputs and outcomes resemble political resultants rather than rational choice, we can hypothesize, grows with both the level of conflict among leaders and the extent of participation by diverse interests. Conversely, the consolidation of autocratic power will lead to policy that has the attributes of value-optimizing choice (Hypothesis 17).

More specifically, this diffusion of power among leaders and interests will increase the prospects of no policy, paper policy, and outmoded policy (Hypotheses 18–20). It will also increase the extent to which policy is unstable and contradictory (Hypotheses 21–22). It will favor incrementalistic responses over bold innovation (Hypothesis 23).[125]

In sum, this two-tier model treats Soviet policy as the output of a constrained bargaining process that is neither the unified choice described by the totalitarian model nor the open contest implied by the model of pluralism. More fundamentally, it treats that process as a variable and so the attributes of policy as variables too. It presents a set of variables and hypotheses that describes the interconnectedness of policy to the political process and of the political process to the distribution of power within the Soviet polity. It recognizes the insights of the conflict and political interests schools—that the diffusion of power has meant that Soviet policy may no longer be analyzed as if it were the monopoly of a single leader. But it also recognizes the sharp power disparities between leaders and interests and among interests themselves. The frequency and impact of participation in policy making fall rapidly the further one moves from the Politburo, making the term political pluralism inappropriate when analyzing Soviet politics.

NOTES

1. Hannah Arendt, *The Origins of Totalitarianism* (New York: Harcourt Brace Jovanovich, 1966); William Kornhauser, *The Politics of Mass Society* (New York: Free Press, 1959); Merle Fainsod, *How Russia Is Ruled*, rev ed. (Cambridge, Mass.: Harvard University Press, 1967); Carl J. Friedrich and Zbigniew K. Brzezinski, *Totalitarian Dictatorship and Autocracy*, 2d ed. (Cambridge, Mass.: Harvard University Press, 1965).
2. For alternative views of the defining attributes of totalitarian societies, see Carl J. Friedrich, "The Evolving Theory and Practice of Totalitarian Regimes," in Carl J. Friedrich, Michael Curtis, and Benjamin R. Barber, eds., *Totalitarianism in Perspective: Three Views* (New York: Praeger, 1969), 126; Zbigniew K. Brzezinski, *Ideology and Power in Soviet Politics* (New York: Praeger, 1962); Franz Neumann, *The Democratic and Authoritarian State* (New York: Free Press, 1957), 233–256; and Juan J. Linz, "Totalitarian and Authoritarian Regimes," in Fred I. Greenstein and Nelson W. Polsby, eds., *Macropolitical Theory* (Reading, Mass.: Addison-Wesley, 1975), 188–189, 191.
3. Friedrich and Brzezinski, 353.
4. Friedrich and Brzezinski, 59.
5. Alexander Dallin and George W. Breslauer, *Political Terror in Communist Systems* (Stanford, Calif.: Stanford University Press, 1970), 7.
6. Linz, 217.
7. Arendt, 474.
8. Zbigniew K. Brzezinski and Samuel P. Huntington, *Political Power: USA/USSR* (New York: Viking Press, 1964), Chapter 4.
9. Brzezinski and Huntington, 202.
10. Brzezinski and Huntington, 216–217.
11. Brzezinski and Huntington, 224–232.
12. Friedrich and Brzezinski, 31, 33.
13. Fainsod, 181.
14. Friedrich and Brzezinski, 35.
15. Robert V. Daniels, "Soviet Politics Since Khrushchev," in John W. Strong, ed., *The Soviet Union Under Brezhnev and Kosygin* (New York: Van Nostrand-Reinhold, 1971), 20.
16. Jerry F. Hough and Merle Fainsod, *How the Soviet Union Is Governed* (Cambridge, Mass.: Harvard University Press, 1979), 144–146, 213, 260–261.

17. Fainsod, 386–420.

18. Fainsod, 491. See also Michael J. Deane, *Political Control of the Soviet Armed Forces* (New York: Crane, Russak and Co., 1977).

19. "Ustav Kommunisticheskoi Partii Sovetskogo Soiuza", *Pravda*, 7 March 1986.

20. Jeffrey T. Richelson, *Sword and Shield: Soviet Intelligence and Security Apparatus* (Cambridge, Mass.: Ballinger, 1986), 231–236.

21. Roman Kolkowicz, *The Soviet Military and the Communist Party* (Princeton, N.J.: Princeton University Press, 1967), 87.

22. Amos Perlmutter, *Modern Authoritarianism: A Comparative Institutional Analysis* (New Haven, Conn.: Yale University Press, 1984), 63, 66–67.

23. Hough and Fainsod, 261. See, for example, Alexander Rahr, "Personnel Changes Since Gorbachev Came to Power," *Radio Liberty Research Bulletin* RL 243/85 (30 July 1985).

24. See Robert E. Blackwell, Jr., "Cadres Policy in the Brezhnev Era," *Problems of Communism* 18 (March-April 1979), 29–42.

25. Timothy J. Colton, *Commissars, Commanders, and Civilian Authority: The Structure of Soviet Military Politics* (Cambridge, Mass.: Harvard University Press, 1979), 85–112.

26. Jerry F. Hough, "The Party *Apparatchiki*," in H. Gordon Skilling and Franklyn Griffiths, eds., *Interest Groups in Soviet Politics* (Princeton, N.J.: Princeton University Press, 1971), 53.

27. Hough, 61.

28. Carl A. Linden, *Khrushchev and the Soviet Leadership, 1957–1964* (Baltimore, Md.: Johns Hopkins Press, 1966), 2.

29. Robert Conquest, *Power and Policy in the U.S.S.R.: The Study of Soviet Dynastics* (London: Macmillan, 1962), 12.

30. Linden, 7–8.

31. Conquest, 47.

32. Linden, 5.

33. Linden 7, 12–15.

34. Linden, 3, 12, 14. See also Conquest, 11.

35. See Gavriel D. Ra'anan, *International Policy Formation in the USSR: Factional "Debates" During the Zhdanovshchina* (Hamden, Conn.: Archon Books, 1983); and Werner G. Hahn, *Postwar Soviet Politics: The Fall of Zhdanov and the Defeat of Moderation, 1946–1953* (Ithaca, N.Y.: Cornell University Press, 1982).

36. Sidney Ploss, *Conflict and Decision-Making in Soviet Russia: A Case Study of Agricultural Policy, 1953–1963* (Princeton, N.J.: Princeton University Press, 1965), 1.

37. Linden, 11–12. See also Conquest, 19.

38. Linden, 7.

39. Linden, 18–19; Conquest, 26–27. See also Alexander Dallin, "Soviet Foreign Policy and Domestic Politics: A Framework for Analysis," *Journal of International Affairs* 23 (1969), 250–265; and Thomas H. Rigby, "The Limits and Extent of Authority," *Problems of Communism* 12 (September-October 1963), 36–41.

40. See the debates in Carl A. Linden et al., "Conflict and Authority: A Discussion," *Problems of Communism* 12 (September-October 1963), 27–46; 12 (November-December 1963), 56–65; and Merle Fainsod et al., "The Coup and After," *Problems of Communism* 14 (January-February 1965), 1–31; 14 (May-June 1965), 37–45; 14 (July-August 1965), 72–76. See also George W. Breslauer, *Khrushchev and Brezhnev as Leaders: Building Authority in Soviet Politics* (London: Allen & Unwin, 1982), 8–10; and the essays in Sidney I. Ploss, ed., *The Soviet Political Process: Aims, Techniques, and Examples of Analysis* (Lexington, Mass.: Ginn, 1971).

41. Linden, 10.
42. Ploss, 10–18.
43. Linden, 10.
44. Daniel Bell, "Ten Theories in Search of Reality: The Prediction of Soviet Behavior in the Social Sciences," *World Politics* 10 (April 1958), 351, 356. See the debate about Kremlinology among Arthur E. Adams, Robert Conquest, and Alec Nove in Walter Laqueur, ed., *The State of Soviet Studies* (Cambridge, Mass.: MIT Press, 1965), 115–143; and see Erik P. Hoffmann, "Methodological Problems of Kremlinology," in Frederic J. Fleron, *Communist Studies and the Social Sciences* (Chicago: Rand-McNally, 1969), 129–149.
45. Linden, *6*.
46. Conquest, 11, 13, 16, 23.
47. Myron Rush, *Political Succession in the USSR*, 2d ed. (New York: Columbia University Press, 1968), 72–73.
48. See Grey Hodnett, "Succession Contingencies in the Soviet Union," *Problems of Communism* 24 (March-April 1975), 1–21.
49. Linden, 3.
50. Rush, 1, 74.
51. Rush, 78–81, 84, 86–87.
52. Rush, 75.
53. Rush, 4.
54. John Lowenhardt, *The Soviet Politburo* (Edinburgh: Canongate, 1982), 64–73; Frederic J. Fleron, "Cooptation as a Mechanism of Adaptation to Change," *Polity* 2 (Winter 1969), 177.
55. See Grey Hodnett, "The Pattern of Leadership Politics," in Seweryn Bialer, ed., *The Domestic Context of Soviet Foreign Policy* (Boulder, Colo.: Westview Press, 1981), 87–118.
56. Philip G. Roeder, "Soviet Policies and Kremlin Politics," *International Studies Quarterly* 28 (June 1984), 171–193.
57. Linden, 206–207.
58. George W. Breslauer, "Political Succession and the Soviet Policy Agenda," *Problems of Communism* 29 (May-June 1980), 58.
59. Valerie Bunce, "The Succession Connection: Policy Cycles and Political Change in the Soviet Union and Eastern Europe," *American Political Science Review* 74 (December 1980), 966–977.
60. Philip G. Roeder, "Do New Soviet Leaders Really Make a Difference?" *American Political Science Review* 79 (December 1985), 958–976; Valerie Bunce and Philip G. Roeder, "The Effects of Leadership Succession in the Soviet Union," *American Political Science Review* 80 (March 1986), 215–224.
61. Linden, 228.
62. H. Gordon Skilling, "Groups in Soviet Politics: Some Hypotheses," in Skilling and Griffiths, *Interest Groups*, 19.
63. Skilling, 20.
64. Darrell P. Hammer, *U.S.S.R.: The Politics of Oligarchy* (New York, Praeger, 1974), 223–254.
65. Jerry F. Hough, "The Soviet System: Petrification or Pluralism?" *Problems of Communism* 21 (March-April 1972), 27–28.
66. Skilling, 24; H. Gordon Skilling, "Group Conflict in Soviet Politics: Some Conclusions," in Skilling and Griffiths, 379–380.
67. David Lane, *Politics and Society in the USSR,* 2d ed. (London: Martin Robertson, 1978), 233–261.

68. Skilling, "Group Conflict in Soviet Politics", 413.

69. Skilling, "Groups in Soviet Politics", 29.

70. Roman Kolkowicz, "The Military," in Skilling and Griffiths, 145–153.

71. Skilling, "Group Conflict in Soviet Politics", 399, 403–404.

72. Milton Lodge, "Soviet Elite Participatory Attitudes in the Post-Stalin Period," *American Political Science Review* 62 (September 1968), 839.

73. Erik Hoffmann, "Information Processing in the Party: Recent Theory and Experience," in Karl W. Ryavec, ed., *Soviet Society and the Communist Party* (Amherst, Mass.: University of Massachusetts Press, 1978), 73–74.

74. Fleron, 191.

75. Ellen Jones, "Committee Decision-Making in the Soviet Union," *World Politics* 36 (January 1984), 167, 170.

76. Warner R. Schilling, Paul Y. Hammond, and Glenn H. Snyder, *Strategy, Politics, and Defense Budgets* (New York: Columbia University Press, 1962), 24–26.

77. Alexander Dallin, "Domestic Factors Influencing Soviet Foreign Policy," in Michael Confino and Shimon Shamir, eds., *The U.S.S.R. and the Middle East* (New York: Wiley 1973), 33.

78. H. Gordon Skilling, "Interest Groups and Communist Politics," in Skilling and Griffiths, 17.

79. Seweryn Bialer, "The Soviet Political Elite and Internal Developments in the USSR," in William E. Griffith, ed., *The Soviet Empire: Expansion and Detente* (Lexington, Mass.: Lexington Books, 1976), 32. See also Jerry F. Hough, "The Bureaucratic Model and the Nature of the Soviet System," *Journal of Comparative Administration* 5 (August 1973), 13–67.

80. William Odom, "A Dissenting View on the Group Approach to Soviet Politics," World Politics 28 (July 1976), 542–567; Andrew Janos et al., "Pluralism in Communist Societies: Is the Emperor Naked?" *Studies in Comparative Communism* 12 (Spring 1979), 3–28; Archie Brown, *Soviet Politics and Political Science* (London: Macmillan, 1974), Chapter 3; David E. Powell, "In Pursuit of Interest Groups in the USSR," *Soviet Union* 6 (1979), 99–124. See the response in H. Gordon Skilling, "Pluralism in Communist Societies: Straw Men and Red Herrings," *Studies in Comparative Communism* 13 (Spring 1980), 82–88; and H. Gordon Skilling, "Interest Groups and Communist Politics Revisited," *World Politics* 36 (October 1983), 1–27.

81. Alexander J. Groth, "USSR: Pluralist Monolith?" *British Journal of Political Science* 9 (October 1979), 445–464; Sarah M. Terry in Janos et al., 5.

82. See the case studies in Skilling and Griffiths. Also see, for example, Peter H. Solomon, *Soviet Criminologists and Criminal Policy: Specialists in Policy Making* (New York: Columbia University Press, 1978); Karl F. Spielmann, "Defense Industrialists in the USSR," *Problems of Communism* 25 (September-October 1976), 52–69; and John McDonnell, "The Soviet Defense Industry as a Pressure Group," in Michael MccGwire, Ken Booth, and John McDonnell, eds., *Soviet Naval Policy: Objectives and Constraints* (New York: Praeger, 1975), 87–122.

83. Kolkowicz, 11–35.

84. Joel J. Schwartz and William R. Keech, "Group Influence and the Policy Process in the Soviet Union,"*American Political Science Review* 62 (September 1968), 840–851. Compare Philip D. Stewart, "Soviet Interest Groups and the Policy Process: The Repeal of Production Education," *World Politics* 22 (October 1969), 29–50. Other illustrations of this genre include Richard M. Mills, "The Formation of the Virgin Lands Policy," *Slavic Review* 29 (March 1970, 58–69; and Matthew P. Gallagher, "Military Manpower: A Case Study," *Problems of Communism* 13 (May-June 1964), 53–62.

85. Hough, "Soviet System: Petrification or Pluralism?", 29; Skilling, "Interest Groups and Communist Politics," 17.

86. Quoted in Skilling, "Interest Groups and Communist Politics," 16.

87. Amos Perlmutter and William LeoGrande, "The Party in Uniform: Toward a Theory of Civil-Military Relations in Communist Political Systems," *American Political Science Review* 76 (December 1982), 779.

88. Schwartz and Keech, 847–848.

89. Hough, "Soviet System: Petrification or Pluralism", 28.

90. Valerie Bunce and John M. Echols, III, "Soviet Politics in the Brezhnev Era: 'Pluralism' or 'Corporatism'?" in Donald R. Kelley, ed., *Soviet Politics in the Brezhnev Era* (New York: Praeger, 1980), 5, 8. See also Jerry F. Hough, "Pluralism, Corporatism, and the Soviet Union," in Susan Gross Solomon, ed., *Pluralism in the Soviet Union* (London: Macmillan, 1983), 37–60; Morris A. McCain, Jr., "Soviet Jurists Divided: A Case for Corporatism in the U.S.S.R.?" *Comparative Politics* 15 (July 1983), 443–460; and Charles E. Ziegler, "Issue Creation and Interest Groups in Soviet Environmental Policy: The Applicability of the State Corporatist Model," *Comparative Politics* 18 (January 1986), 171–192.

91. Karl W. Deutsch, *The Nerves of Government: Models of Political Communication and Control* (New York: Free Press, 1966), 8–10. For an alternative effort to formulate a model of decision-making, see John Lowenhardt, *Decision-Making in Soviet Politics* (London: Macmillan, 1981). See also the review of the literature in Arnold L. Horelick, A Ross Johnson, and John D. Steinbruner, *The Study of Soviet Foreign Policy: A Review of Decision-Theory-Related Approaches* R-1334 (Santa Monica, Calif.: Rand Corporation, 1973).

92. On the role of coalition-formation in Soviet politics, see Barbara Ann Chotiner, *Khrushchev's Party Reform: Coalition Building and Institutional Innovation* (Westport, Conn.: Greenwood Press, 1984); and Jiri Valenta, "The Bureaucratic Politics Paradigm and the Soviet Invasion of Czechoslovakia," *Political Science Quarterly* 94 (Spring 1979), 55–76.

93. Graham T. Allison, *Essence of Decision: Explaining the Cuban Missile Crisis* (Boston: Little, Brown, 1971). 169.

94. Arthur J. Alexander, *R&D in Soviet Aviation* R-589-PR (Santa Monica, Calif.: Rand Corporation, 1970), 7–20.

95. Allison, 170.

96. Jerry F. Hough, "The Brezhnev Era: The Man and the System," *Problems of Communism* 25 (March-April 1976), 14.

97. On the importance of points of access, see Solomon, chapter 8.

98. Schwartz and Keech, 848.

99. Rush, 84–86.

100. John Newhouse, *Cold Dawn: The Story of SALT* (New York: Holt, Rinehart, and Winston, 1973), 192.

101. Donald D. Barry, "The Specialist in Soviet Policy-Making: the Adoption of a Law," *Soviet Studies* 16 (October 1964), 152–165. See also Solomon, 131–132.

102. See Theodore H. Friedgut, "Interests and Groups in Soviet Policy-Making: The MTS Reform," *Soviet Studies* 28 (October 1976), 524–547; and Ziegler. Compare Donald R. Kelley, "Environmental Policy-Making in the USSR: The Role of Industrial and Environmental Interest Groups," *Soviet Studies* 28 (October 1976), 570–589.

103. Heather Campbell, *Controversy in Soviet R&D: The Airship Controversy* R-1001-PR (Santa Monica, Calif.: Rand Corporation, 1972), 1.

104. Campbell, 23.

105. Solomon, 132–133; Friedgut, 524–547.
106. Skilling, "Group Conflict in Soviet Politics", 389–390.
107. Jones, 186; Lowenhardt, 90–108.
108. Donald R. Kelley, "Interest Groups in the USSR: The Impact of Political Sensitivity on Group Influence," *Journal of Politics* 34 (August 1972), 860–888.
109. Dallin, 34; Valenta, 60–62.
110. Rush, 25–30, 58–71.
111. See Kolkowicz, 146–153.
112. Kolkowicz, 146–148.
113. See McCain. On generational divisions, see Mark R. Beissinger, "In Search of Generations in Soviet Politics," *World Politics* 38 (January 1986), 288–314; and George Breslauer, "Is There a Generation Gap in the Soviet Political Establishment?: Demand Articulation by RSFSR Provincial Party First Secretaries," *Soviet Studies* 36 (January 1984) 1–25.
114. See Joseph S. Berliner, *Factory and Manager in the USSR* (Cambridge, Mass.: Harvard University, 1957), 17–20, 225–226.
115. Ploss, 59–112.
116. Charles E. Lindblom, *The Policy-Making Process* (Englewood Cliffs, N.J.: Prentice-Hall, 1968), 65.
117. Loren R. Graham, "Reorganization of the U.S.S.R. Academy of Sciences," in Peter H. Juvelier and Henry W. Morton, eds., *Soviet Policy-Making: Studies in Communism in Transition* (New York: Praeger, 1967), 139.
118. Kolkowicz, 117–119.
119. Marshall I. Goldman, *The Spoils of Progress: Environmental Pollution in the Soviet Union* (Cambridge, Mass.: MIT Press, 1972), 178–209.
120. Kolkowicz, 165–166.
121. Frederick C. Barghoorn, "The Security Police" in Skilling and Griffiths, 114–115. See also Kelley, 580–585.
122. Kolkowicz, 289–300.
123. Skilling, "Group Conflict in Soviet Politics", 389–390.
124. Allison, 33, 162.
125. Roeder, 180–181. Jones, 187.

four

SOVIET POLICIES AND PERFORMANCE

Peasant woman
near Tula, 1985

Moscow skyline, 1985

The Soviet model of development is predicated on a future in which many of the traditional policy dilemmas of states will simply cease to exist, ensuring higher orders of material well-being, security, liberty, justice, and equality. But until classes have been extinguished and the state has withered away, the socialist state must confront many of the same policy challenges that confronted previous socioeconomic formations.

No functions are more fundamental to the modern state than ensuring the physical safety of its population (particularly against foreign attack), providing for the improvement of their material well-being, guaranteeing the observance of procedural justice in legal relations and distributive justice in social relations, and protecting the freedom of the individual to develop personal talents to the fullest. In each of these policy functions the Soviet model purports to be a more certain path to securing these ends than the path of capitalist development. As the current Party Program proclaims:

> The experience of the USSR and other socialist countries convincingly demonstrates the indisputable social, economic, political, ideological and moral advantages of the new society as a stage in the progress of mankind that is superior to capitalism, and it provides answers to questions that the bourgeois system is unable to resolve.[1]

It is the actual performance of the Soviet polity, measured against four of these fundamental policy objectives—material well-being, justice, equality, and national security—that occupies the final four chapters of this text. Is the Soviet command economy a more efficient means to improve the material well-being of the citizen? Is socialist legality just? Has socialism truly removed privilege and preference among classes and among the principal ascriptive groupings of society? And has the foreign policy of the Soviet regime effectively defended and promoted the interests of the Soviet people in international affairs?

NOTES

1. *Pravda*, 7 March 1986.

FOR FURTHER READING

For those students who wish to read further on the topics covered in the next four chapters, the following works may be particularly useful.

Azrael, Jeremy. 1966. *Managerial Power and Soviet Politics*. Cambridge, Mass.: Harvard University Press.

Azrael, Jeremy, ed. 1978. *Soviet Nationality Policies and Practices*. New York: Holt, Rinehart, and Winston.

Barry, Donald D., William E. Butler, and George Ginsburgs, eds. 1974. *Contemporary Soviet Law*. The Hague: Martinus Nijhoff.

Barry, Donald D., F. J. M. Feldbrugge, George Ginsburgs, and Peter Maggs, eds. 1977–1979. *Soviet Law After Stalin*, 3 vols. Alphen aan den Rijn, Netherlands: Sijthoff and Noordhoff.

Bergson, Abram, and Herbert S. Levine, eds. 1983. *The Soviet Economy: Toward the Year 2000*. London: Allen & Unwin.

Berliner, Joseph. 1957. *Factory and Manager in the USSR*. Cambridge, Mass.: Harvard University Press.

Berman, Harold J. 1963. *Justice in the U.S.S.R.: An Interpretation of Soviet Law,* rev. ed. New York: Vintage Books.

Berman, Harold J., and James W. Spindler. 1972. *Soviet Criminal Law and Procedure,* 2d ed. Cambridge, Mass.: Harvard University Press.

Bialer, Seweryn, ed. 1981. *The Domestic Context of Soviet Foreign Policy*. Boulder, Colo.: Westview Press.

Brzezinski, Zbigniew K. 1967. *The Soviet Bloc: Unity and Conflict,* rev. ed. Cambridge, Mass: Harvard University Press.

Butler, W. E. 1983. *Soviet Law*. London: Butterworth.

Carrere d'Encausse, Helene. 1979. *Decline of an Empire: The Soviet Socialist Republics in Revolt*. New York: Newsweek Books.

DiMaio, Alfred John, Jr. 1974. *Soviet Urban Housing: Problems and Prospects*. New York: Holt, Rinehart and Winston.

Edmonds, Robin, 1983. *Soviet Foreign Policy: The Brezhnev Years*. New York: Oxford University Press.

Feifer, George. 1964. *Justice in Moscow*. New York: Simon and Schuster.

Feldbrugge, F. J. M., ed. 1973. *Encyclopedia of Soviet Law*. Leiden, Netherlands: A. W. Sijthoff.

Freedman, Robert O. 1978. *Soviet Policy Toward the Middle East Since 1970*, 2d ed. New York: Holt, Rinehart and Winston.

Goldman, Marshall I. 1987. *Gorbachev's Challenge: Economic Reform in the Age of High Technology*. New York: Norton.

Hoffmann, Erik P., and Frederick J. Fleron, Jr., eds. 1980. *The Conduct of Soviet Foreign Policy,* 2d ed. New York: Aldine.

Kirsch, Leonard. 1972. *Soviet Wages*. Cambridge, Mass.: MIT Press.

Lane, David, and Felicity O'Dell. 1978. *The Soviet Industrial Worker*. New York: St. Martin's Press.

Lapidus, Gail Warshofsky. 1978. *Women in Soviet Society: Equality, Development, and Social Change*. Berkeley, Calif.: University of California Press.

Matthews, Mervyn. 1978. *Privilege in the Soviet Union*. London: Allen & Unwin.

Nove, Alec. 1977. *The Soviet Economic System*. London: Allen & Unwin.

Rubinstein, Alvin Z. 1981. *Soviet Foreign Policy Since World War II: Imperial and Global*. Cambridge, Mass.: Winthrop Publishers.

Ruble, Blair A. 1981. *Soviet Trade Unions: Their Development in the 1970s*. Cambridge: Cambridge University Press.

Carol R. Saivetz, and Sylvia Woodby. 1985. *Soviet-Third World Relations*. Boulder, Colo.: Westview Press.

Smith, Gordon. 1978. *The Soviet Procuracy and the Supervision of Administration*. Alphen aan den Rijn, Netherlands: Sijthoff and Noordhoff.

Terry, Sarah Meiklejohn, ed. 1984. *Soviet Policy in Eastern Europe*. New Haven, Conn.: Yale University Press.

Ulam, Adam B. *Expansion and Coexistence: Soviet Foreign Policy, 1917–1973,* rev. ed. 1974. New York: Holt, Rinehart and Winston.

Volin, Lazar. 1970. *A Century of Russian Agriculture*. Cambridge, Mass.: Harvard University Press.

chapter *10*

Material Well-Being: Soviet Economic Performance

Improvement of the Soviet citizens' material well-being has been central to the professed objectives of the Soviet regime since its inception. The Party Program of 1919 committed the regime "to increase at all costs the quantity of products required by the population" and, in particular, to improve "the housing conditions of the toiling masses," the quality of their health care, and the conditions in which they worked. Seventy years later, the new version of the Third Party Program proclaims that "the basic programmatic goals of the CPSU are the rapid growth of the people's well-being, the all-round development of man, and the strengthening of our homeland's economic and defensive might."[1]

DEVELOPMENT OF THE COMMAND ECONOMY

The goal of material well-being for the toiling masses, in the official Soviet view, can be achieved only through rational utilization of the country's material resources by means of state planning. The building of this economic mechanism, the Soviet command economy,[2] constitutes the foundation of the Soviet strategy of economic development.

For reasons deep in the philosophical foundations of their system, the Soviets reject the marketplace and contend that a planned economy is a higher order of socioeconomic development. On the basis of Marx's analysis of capitalism, they argue that it is based on fallacious assumptions such as the myth that the marketplace produces optimal solutions to economic problems. They reject the individualistic and materialistic foundations of capitalism, arguing that it is unethical to base an economy on the principle that the highest good is achieved through maximization of individual wealth. And they reject what they see as the inevitable social consequences of capitalism, such as cycles of economic prosperity and depression, inequalities in income, and widespread unemployment. In contrast, they contend that a planned economy represents a step beyond the anarchy of the marketplace. Just as the discovery of the laws of physics has enabled man to harness the physical world, so the discovery of the laws of social development should permit the socioeconomic world to be harnessed for human progress. Production, consumption, prices, and wages all should be rationally planned.

Lenin's writing before the Bolshevik seizure of power added little to Marxist dogmas concerning economic management under socialism. Indeed, he did not begin to address this question until just months before the coup. His most comprehensive statement on the matter appeared in his pamphlet "The Impending Crisis and How To Combat It," published at the end of October 1917. In this he advocated

1. Amalgamation of all banks into a single bank, and state control over its operations, or nationalization of the banks.
2. Nationalization of the syndicates; i.e., the largest, monopolistic capitalistic associations (sugar, oil, coal, iron and steel, and other syndicates).
3. Abolition of commercial secrecy.
4. Compulsory syndication (i.e., compulsory amalgamation into associations) of industrialists, merchants, and employers generally.
5. Compulsory organization of the population into consumers' societies, or encouragement of such organization, and the exercise of control over it.[3]

Lenin's statement failed to answer two questions regarding the future Soviet economy that would prove to be central to the Soviet model of development: First, would the Soviet economy be elaborately planned? There is no mention of this in Lenin's pamphlet. And second, would nationalization extend only to banks and syndicates, as this statement appears to imply, or to all sectors of the economy? Lenin had responded to these two questions in varying ways in the preceding months. In *State and Revolution,* written in August of that same year, Lenin seemed to advocate comprehensive nationalization and planning by indicating that the economy would function much as the rest of the state bureaucracy, with the organization of "the *whole* economy on the lines of the postal service."[4] Yet in a pamphlet written one month later, "Can the Bolsheviks Retain State Power?", Lenin seems to argue against this: "The important thing will not be even the confiscation of the capitalists' property, but country-wide, all-embracing workers' control over the capitalists and their possible supporters. Confiscation alone leads nowhere. . . . Instead of confiscation, we could easily impose a *fair* tax." In this pamphlet, Lenin first appears to argue that the key to control is nationalization of the banks, and of the banks alone. Yet he then confuses this by advocating "the conversion of the bank, syndicate, commercial, etc., etc., rank-and-file employees into state employees," which seems to imply nationalization of a wide range of enterprises.[5] It was against this background of confused ideological directives that the Bolsheviks took control of the economy.

Whatever Lenin's original intentions, War Communism brought thoroughgoing nationalization and centralized control of both production and distribution.[6] The nationalization of all land was proclaimed immediately with the Land Decree of November 8, 1917. Before the end of 1917 the Soviet regime seized the State Bank and nationalized all private banks. The nationalization of railroads and the merchant marine followed. But in the first months after the Revolution most industry was still untouched, except for some factories nationalized by local soviets. It was the failure of the countryside to deliver foodstuffs to the cities, the runaway inflation resulting from the new regime's fiscal policies, the collapse of the market, and the closing of many factories that brought the large-scale intervention of the regime and nationalization of factories in order to restore the economy. The number of nationalized enterprises rose from 487 in June 1918 to approximately 3300 in September 1919 and 4500 in November 1920. By the last date all large-scale industry—and apparently many small shops as well—had been nationalized.

With this nationalization came the growth of a bureaucracy to oversee the economy. On December 15, 1917, the Supreme Council of National Economy (VSNKh or *Vesenkha*), an interdepartmental council attached to the Council of People's Commissars (*Sovnarkom*), began to oversee economic activity. With the aid of a network of regional councils, it carried out the nationalization of industry and administered the new state enterprises. To marshal economic resources for the war effort, direct production, and manage the rationing and distribution of production, VSNKh was supplemented by a growing bureaucracy. Whether this economic system under War Communism was motivated by the ideology of the Bolsheviks (and thus represents a model of the full-fledged communism that Lenin hoped to build) or whether it was a pragmatic and perhaps desperate response to the Civil War remains an issue of debate and considerable uncertainty in the West.

Although distinguished by its tolerance of private commerce, it was the NEP period that saw the creation of peacetime planning mechanism that would later permit the creation of a command economy. The Party in 1921 decided that the "commanding heights of the economy" (banking, foreign trade, and large-scale industry) would remain in the hands of the state, but that private entrepreneurs would be permitted to organize small-scale industrial enterprises with no more than 20 employees and that they could also lease small-scale enterprises from the state if already nationalized. Only in a few instances did the Party return nationalized industries outright to their former owners or permit private enterprises to employ more workers. Along with the growth of the private sector came decentralization in the state sector. Although the commanding heights of industry theoretically remained under the control of VSNKh or the regional councils, in many industries sectoral "trusts" actually enjoyed considerable independence. And planning during NEP did not mean operational control, but forecasting economic growth and developing guidelines for strategic investments.

It was the Stalinist Revolution that created the modern Soviet command economy. Private enterprise was suppressed in the last half of the 1920s through collectivization of agriculture, discriminatory taxes on the commerce of Nepmen, legal restrictions on private trade, and finally in 1930 the criminalization of private trade as "speculation." Thus, the contribution of the socialized sector of the economy to national income grew from less than half (45.9 percent) in 1925–1926 to 90.7 percent in 1932.

Operational authority over state enterprises was increasingly centralized as VSNKh asserted direct control. The combination of its additional responsibilities and the growth of the socialized sector of the economy quickly overburdened the council, and so on January 5, 1932, this method of control was replaced by a "ministerial system" of administration: Individual People's Commissariats (renamed Ministries in 1946) assumed responsibility for separate sectors of the economy. Principal enterprises came directly under the control of a Commissariat in Moscow, with the enterprise manager serving as administrative subordinate to the senior officials of the appropriate chief administration (*glavk*) within the Commissariat. Only enterprises of purely local significance fell under the control of a union-republic Commissariat or an administration of a local soviet.

Planning of the economy was intensified in 1927, when a Sovnarkom decree of June 8 called for "a united all-union plan." During the First Five-Year Plan, the planning of the economy was increasingly concentrated within Gosplan, which on February 3, 1931, was attached directly to the Sovnarkom. This role grew still further with the replacement of VSNKh by separate economic Commissariats, for now Gosplan alone was responsible for the coordination of plans throughout all sectors of industry. Under the direction of the Party leadership, Gosplan drew up a balance sheet for the whole economy for the plan period as well as operational plans for each enterprise. The detailed production and delivery plans that were developed by the branches within Gosplan were further elaborated by the appropriate Commissariats.

Organizing Production

With the establishment of a command economy, the Soviets came to face a major dilemma: While wanting to ensure that the economy would respond to the directives of the central leadership, they also sought to elicit maximum efficiency and initiative from individuals. Yet, they found that increased central control of the economy often comes at the expense of efficiency, and improved efficiency often requires decentralization.[7] How to balance the competing demands of control and efficiency?

The first attempt to answer this question came at a time when the Soviet leadership faced another dilemma, sometimes labelled the "Red versus Expert" controversy: The experts with managerial skills were often former members of the old regime's bourgeoisie, whom the Soviet leaders found ideologically untrustworthy, but the loyal Reds within the factories usually lacked suitable managerial experience, having been foremen or workers under the old order. The compromise settled upon by the new regime was to establish dual authority in management within each factory: A Red factory manager and his expert assistant manager or an expert manager with his Red assistant would share managerial authority. This management team was further checked by a triangular division of responsibility involving the trade union and the Party organizations in the factory, which would share decision-making authority in daily affairs. Such division of authority for the sake of control exacted a high price in efficiency.

Committed to rapid industrialization of Russia, Stalin found these costs too high and so introduced a threefold reform in the managerial structure of factories. Production efficiency was of paramount importance, and this required unified management (*edinonachalie*). Therefore, Stalin trimmed the power of the factory trade union and Party organizations. The trade union was not only to refrain from daily decision making, but in fact, was transformed into a vehicle for labor discipline to mobilize workers to meet production quotas. Similarly, the Party organizations were to cease meddling in daily decision making, and limit themselves to checking the fulfillment of the Plan and directives.

Second, Stalin replaced the dual management of experts and Reds with a new generation of Red experts. To support this, Stalin initiated a massive educational program to train loyal engineers and managers, who were brought into the factories in successive waves of purges and new appointments. While the first Red experts often had only primary or secondary education and so were soon purged, the second generation had specialized educations. A third wave of purges opened the way for the "Class of '38," with advanced engineering degrees.

Third, in place of the controls *within* management, Stalin maintained control *over* management by bracketing it with parallel hierarchies of control, creating institutionalized mutual suspicion. This system maintained institutionally separate but functionally overlapping ministerial, Plan, Party, and police controls.[8] The factory manager was, first of all, directly subordinate to a ministerial chain of command usually originating in Moscow, with the authority to direct production in the factory and to reward, impose sanctions upon, and even terminate the factory manager. (For more discussion of the organization of ministries see Chapter 6.)

The managers then and now are also controlled by the Plan, in that they are under legal obligation to produce according to its guidelines. The Plan involves a number of institutional actors in the development of quotas and supervision of managers' fulfillment of these. Central to the planning process is the State Planning Committee (*Gosplan*), which since 1965 has been responsible for both short-term and long-term plans. That is, Gosplan now drafts the annual operational plans, Five-Year Plans, and the occasional long-term plan such as the 15-Year Plan for 1986–2000.* (Prior to 1965 Gosplan shared these responsibilities with various agencies; e.g., *Gosekonomkomissiia* [1955–1957], *Gosekonomsovet* [1960–1962], and the All-Union *Sovnarkhoz* [1962–1965].) Gosplan comprises both summary departments and branch departments, under the di-

---

*A 1979 decree on "comprehensive planning" mandates longer-term planning across a wider range of balances. The 1981–1985 Plan introduced the target probram (*tsel' ovaia programma*) as the principal instrument to coordinate production across branches. It is unclear to what extent these changes will alter entrenched planning practices.

rection of its Chairman and his collegium. (See Figure 10.1.) The summary departments apparently maintain the balances in broad sectors of the economy, while it is the branch departments that develop plans for individual sectors of the economy.

Gosplan is responsible for developing four "balances," including one for material resources, another for finances, a third for labor resources, and a comprehensive plan for the overall economy. The critical balance is the first, for in the absence of a market it is the balance of supplies and production, not monetary transactions, that most concerns planners. The Plan developed by Gosplan balances highly aggregated figures—for example, there is only one entry for ball bearings even though the ministerial plans have approximately 750 specifications for them, and Gosplan's balances do not specify each individual supplier and recipient of production but rather broad sectors of the economy. Nonetheless, in 1973 Gosplan was reportedly responsible for nearly 2000 items, representing about 70 percent of all industrial production. In 1968 it reportedly allocated these among 120 economic entities. Most of the details of supplies, production, and sales for individual items and producers are worked out by the State Committee for Material and Technical Supply (*Gossnab*) and by the ministries—the former for about 18,000 items and the latter for another 40,000. Gosplan not only must account for output of some 2000 items, but also the resources required to produce them, many of which are the result of current production. Hypothetically, this yields a 2000 by 2000 matrix—with four million cells—to produce a resource balance of inputs and outputs. In a static economy, calculating the units of inputs such as steel, rubber, coal, and cement required to produce outputs such as tractors, homes, and steel would be a task of enormous proportions. But in an economy predicated on rapid economic growth this becomes a truly gargantuan problem. If tractor production is to increase, for example, not only must all the inputs to tractor production (e.g., steel, rubber) increase, but the inputs to these inputs must be increased, and then the inputs to these inputs . . . and so forth. To rebalance the economy requires considerable manpower and statistical ability.[9]

The development of a plan involves the initial generation of control figures by Gosplan and its respective departments, taking into consideration the previous period's production and the priorities handed down by the Party leadership. These are sent down to the ministries and through their respective glavki (chief administrations) to the enterprises. At each stage the figures are elaborated with more details. The comments and suggestions of enterprise managers on this proposal are passed up to the ministry and then, with the comments and suggestions of the ministerial officials, on to Gosplan, which must reconcile its original control figures with this input from below. The final plan is adopted as law by the Supreme Soviet; and then its appropriate parts are sent to individual ministries, which must develop operational plans for each of the factories under their control to enable the ministry as a whole to meet its quota.

The enterprise manager finally receives a *tekhpromfinplan* (an acronym for technical-industrial-financial plan) that spells out quotas for material output, levels of procurement, allotments for payroll and labor, and a financial plan that expresses gross production quotas in rubles. The manager is also given productivity

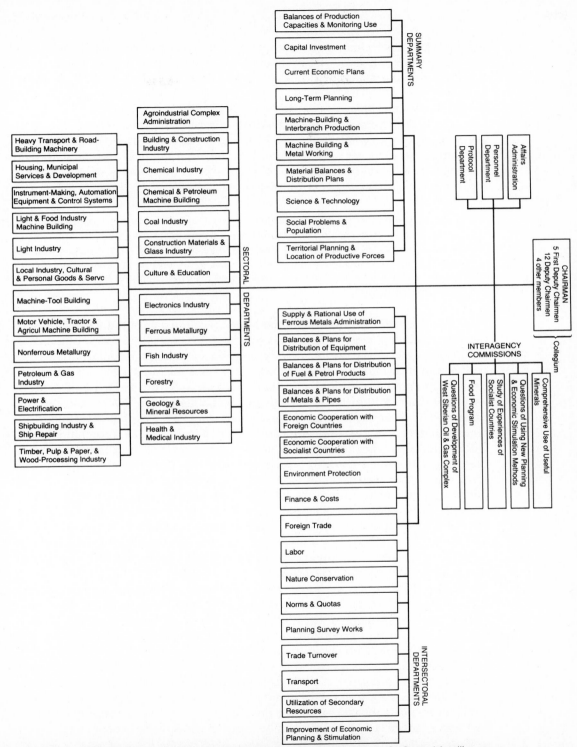

Figure 10.1 State Planning Committee (GOSPLAN). (*Source:* Data from U.S. Central Intelligence Agency, *Directory of Soviet Officials: National Organizations* [Washington, D.C.: CIA, 1986].)

targets, plans for technological innovation, and bonus and investment plans. The most important of these under Stalin—and so far even today despite some reforms—was the material output quota (usually specified in physical units such as tons of steel). This is usually an obligatory production minimum to be overfulfilled rather than a target to be approached.

In the Stalinist system, the supervisory control of the ministry over the enterprise manager who implements the Plan and of Gosplan over the ministry and the enterprise manager was reinforced by financial controls exercised through the Ministry of Finance and the state banks. The control functions of the Ministry of Finance, in the words of Merle Fainsod, include

> the preparation of government-wide budgets, the enforcement of budgetary discipline, and the investigation of dubious financial transactions on the part of administrative agencies. . . . [To support this] the ministry has its own control-inspection apparatus. Its inspectors may descend upon an enterprise or government department at any time and conduct inspections on the spot, with free access to all financial and other data.[10]

The State Budget drafted by the Ministry of Finance is the financial side of the Plan, including most expenditures relating to the socialized sector of the economy, such as defense, social security, communal services, administrative costs, and capital investment in the economy. Revenues are drawn principally from a turnover tax on items as they enter wholesale trade and from deductions from profits of individual enterprises. Through its accounting control over these expenditures and revenues (particularly through its control of capital investment and taxes on industry) the Ministry has a good picture of the economic activity within ministries and individual enterprises. It is assisted in this by a separate State Bank (*Gosbank*), which is "the recipient and reservoir of budget funds." Each enterprise must maintain an account in Gosbank. A Gosbank loan is "the only legal form of short-term credit" for an enterprise, and a Gosbank draft is the only legal medium of financial transactions between enterprises.[11] For long-term credit for capital construction, the enterprise manager must turn to the All-Union Bank for Financing Capital Investments (*Stroibank*). Thus, Gosbank, with the assistance of Stroibank, is in nearly constant surveillance of the economic activity within the enterprise.

Since the Plan has the force of law, an enterprise manager who violates the Plan is subject to legal sanctions. (These legal institutions are described more fully in the next chapter.) The Procuracy not only investigates such violations, but also prosecutes offenders before the courts. A factory manager who has padded accounts, bribed others to acquire supplies not allocated in the Plan, or pilfered state property for personal use is subject to prosecution. The Procuracy is assisted in its investigation of the legal transgressions of administrators and managers by the People's Control Committees. Enterprises that have failed to meet their contractual obligations under the Plan—such as not delivering goods or delivering goods of inferior quality—may be taken to commercial courts

(Gosarbitrazh) by other enterprises. If these proceedings turn up economic crimes by the manager, this matter may be referred to the Procuracy.

In addition to the scrutiny of Gosplan and the financial and legal agencies, specific aspects of Plan fulfillment and the production process bring a manager under the scrutiny of other state agencies, including the State Committee for Construction Affairs (*Gosstroi*), the State Committee for Labor and Social Problems (Goskomtrud), the State Committee on Prices (*Goskomtsen*), the State Committee for Science and Technology (*Gostekhnika*), and the State Committee for Supervision of Safe Working Practices in Industry and for Mine Inspection (*Gosgortekhnadzor*). All of these ministerial agencies (and others as well) in the course of their normal activities may oversee a part of the enterprise manager's fulfillment of the Plan, and as hierarchies that originate in Moscow may report managerial failures to their superiors.

In early 1987, as will be discussed below, Gorbachev proposed a series of reforms that would significantly reduce the Plan-related controls over individual enterprises. If implemented fully, these reforms would, of course, change the institutional dynamics described in the preceding paragraphs.

A third broad type of control to supplement ministerial and Plan control is Party supervision. Many departments of the all-union Secretariat parallel the major sectors of the economy, maintaining supervision of the respective ministries and state committees (see Chapter 8). The union-republic secretariat or the oblast committee maintains close watch over the enterprises within its territory through its right of control (*pravo kontrolia*). Any major enterprise will include at least one primary Party organization. And its secretary not only assists the manager in the fulfillment of the Plan, but as the lowest rung in the Party secretarial hierarchy ensures that the manager operates within the laws and the Plan, reporting regularly to superiors on enterprise affairs.

Lastly, police control has sought to combat economic crimes. (The police apparatus is described more fully in the next chapter.) Under Stalin, this control was implemented through the independent "Special Sections," particularly in larger factories, which maintained a network of informers. The head of the section was responsible for "checking on the political reliability of all employees, enforcing security regulations, and investigating and punishing cases of sabotage, industrial breakdowns, or other 'economic crimes' which impeded plan fulfillment or harmed state interests."[12] Since Stalin's death, with the trimming of the terror apparatus, much of the responsibility for combatting economic crimes has been given to the Ministry for Internal Affairs (MVD), although more serious crimes—particularly when involving national security, sabotage, or espionage—may involve the KGB (State Security Committee). But each now plays a less-invasive role in the factory.

In short, control under Stalin was institutionalized through parallel bureaucracies scrutinizing one another's behavior ensuring faithful implementation of the Plan and directives through mutual suspicion. Under the watchful eye of so many monitors, what factory manager would fail to follow scrupulously the dictates of Moscow?

The Dynamics of Planning and Implementation

Stalin's highly centralized system was designed to balance efficient, unified managerial control of the enterprise with central control over management. It sought to ensure faithful, but efficient, fulfillment of the Plan. It also produced a political process that led to new economic inefficiencies.

Because the institutionalization of mutual suspicion failed to function as designed (for the reasons discussed in Chapter 9), a political process of sorts emerged involving competition over the Plan both among parallel hierarchies and between superiors and subordinates. In fact, much of the "politics" among ministries and regions for special projects, described in the previous four chapters, is competition for scarce investment funds within the Plan. These interests apparently seek to influence the leadership's priorities prior to the drafting of a new Plan.

Once the planning process has begun, a more hierarchical political process commences. The final Plan is reportedly arrived at through a process that the Soviets describe as negotiated planning (*vstrechnoe planirovanie*), which is depicted in Figure 10.2. In the process of comment and consultation on the control figures of Gosplan, the input and output figures become a political issue. Shifting lines of conflict and alliance are manifest within the bureaucracy as the Plan moves along the action-channel (Gosplan–branch department–ministry–glavk–enterprise). For example, in the negotiations between Gosplan and its branch departments, the latter frequently find themselves in alliance with the ministries and enterprises below them, arguing against the superordinate planners for lower output quotas and higher supply allotments. But once the negotiations have moved along the action-channel to involve the branch departments and individual ministries, the former often find themselves in alliance with their Gosplan superiors. As this example suggests, not only alliances, but the positions of participants also shift as the process moves along its action-channel: At each negotiation point, participants closer to the superior-planner end of the action-channel try to convince participants below them to raise production and accept lower supply allocations. Those closer to the subordinate-production end attempt to convince participants above them to expand supply allocations and reduce production quotas. Against the authority of the planners and ministerial superiors the producer can bring to bear expertise and greater familiarity with the details of production in the enterprise, parrying their demands with arguments about their feasibility.[13]

The practice of seeking expanded allocations and lowered quotas is known in Soviet parlance as "insurance" or the "safety factor" (*strakhovka*).[14] Producers, particularly during Stalin's rule, have known that their performance is assessed, in the first instance, not on profitability (output relative to input), nor even simply on total output, but on percentage fulfillment or overfulfillment of the material output quota. Thus, producers have had an incentive to expand supply allocations but keep production quotas as low as possible. On the input side, managers seek a little extra in their supply allotment to ensure that there will be enough to meet the quota and to guard against irregularities in supplies that

NEGOTIATED PLANNING

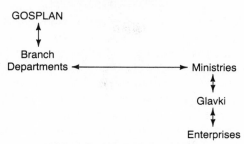

Figure 10.2 Negotiated Planning.

might slow the production process and jeopardize fulfillment of their plans. If the buffer stock is not used immediately, it can be hoarded as insurance for future production or even traded (illegally) for other supplies that are in short supply. On the output side, even if the managers know they can produce more, they frequently attempt to keep their quota low to ensure that they will have no difficulty fulfilling it and to guard against unforeseen contingencies.

The social consequence of *strakhovka* is serious economic inefficiency, over both the short and the long terms. The extra resources that the managers use in the production process are wasted and those that they hoard lie idle. Over the longer term *strakhovka* restricts growth due to what has been called the "ratchet principle." That is, a factory with a quota of 100 units in one year that produces 101 units has overfulfilled its quota by one percent and earned an appropriate bonus for this. The next year, however, the quota probably will be set at 101 or even higher, since the enterprise has demonstrated that this is within its capacity; and so, to earn a bonus the second year in a row the factory will have to be able to produce 102 units or higher. The restriction on growth comes when it is within the capacity of an enterprise to produce more than just the bare minimum needed to overfulfill its quota and earn its bonus. If the factory can produce 105 units the first year, the manager who takes a longer-term view of the production problem may still produce just 101, fearing that the second year's quota might be set at 105 units or even higher, jeopardizing the enterprise's ability to overfulfill the quota a second time. When many enterprise managers submit to this logic, imagine what happens to the whole economy! Quotas rise only incrementally, factories do not produce up to capacity, and so economic growth is retarded.

Even after the figures of a Plan are set in concrete (and they are actually always subject to change by the directives of the leadership), the politics do not end. In the implementation stage, planners and superiors are in the position of trying to ensure that production quotas are fulfilled, by means that do not violate the Plan or other laws. Producers and subordinates attempt to fulfill the production quotas by any means, and if unable to fulfill the quotas, to create the illusion that they have succeeded.

Perhaps the most common means to fulfill the Plan outside the strict bounds of law is *blat* (corruption).[15] Formally blat is the use of personal influence to obtain that to which one has no legal entitlement. It can mean bribery, but usually refers to trading favors. If a steel factory requires additional coal outside the Plan to meet its production quota or if it has not received the coal that it was promised under the Plan, how does the factory secure the needed supplies? Often the only answer is *blat*. And often blat requires the services of a *tolkach* ("pusher," "expediter," or "procurer"), who expedites delivery of Plan supplies or finds alternative sources outside the Plan. Since there is no legal provision for hiring a *tolkach,* the manager disguises the expediter with another title such as Senior Staff Researcher or Laboratory Technician and provides a fancy salary and plenty of money to travel and entertain. In a letter to the editor of *Izvestiia,* M. Zhebrak describes himself as "a supply manager by occupation and expeditor against his will." He writes,

> How often people write in your newspaper and in the press as a whole about expediters, about their unenviable role as superfluous people in the Soviet apparatus. They are depicted as sharp dealers, pushers, and contortionists who always manage to crawl back in through the window whenever they are pushed out the door. And it is true that our brother expeditors can be found in the corridors of chief administrations, plant offices, and the administration of railroads. We expedite strenuously, using all legitimate and illegitimate means to justify our existence and to push through the next shipment of materials that at times are desperately needed by the organization that sent us.[16]

The social consequence of blat is the diversion of resources from their intended purposes and labor that in the eyes of the planners is unproductive. It violates the Plan and yet may be indispensable to the success of the Plan.

What can managers do if even blat will not permit their enterprise to fulfill its quota? They may create the illusion of plan fulfillment by indulging in *ochkovtiratel'stvo* (dissimulation).[17] The term colloquially refers to cheating in cards by deception, but among factory managers has come to mean simulating success. If a factory produces just 99 percent of its quota, the manager may still earn a bonus by overstating the production—perhaps "borrowing" from the next month's output or claiming that the enterprise actually produced 101 percent, but unfortunately in the production process lost 2 percent that had to be written off the books as damaged items. Or, if the production period has not yet come to an end, a manager may change the planned assortment of items, deliberately lower the quality of output, or change the size. For example, if the quota is specified in tons of nails, larger nails will fill the quota more rapidly. So will substandard products. A complaint by Khrushchev illustrates this problem:

> It has become traditional to produce the heaviest chandeliers possible rather than just beautiful chandeliers to adorn homes. This is because the heavier the chandeliers manufactured, the more a factory gets since its output is figured in tons. So the plants produce chandeliers weighing hundreds of kilograms and fulfill the Plan. But who needs such a plan? . . .

> Furniture factories have Plans stated in rubles. Hence they find it best to make a massive armchair, since the heavier the chair the more expensive it is. Formally the Plan is fulfilled since the furniture makers add various details to the armchair and make it more expensive. But who needs such armchairs? . . . Everybody knows this. Everybody talks a great deal about this, but still the armchairs win.[18]

The social consequence of the armchairs' victory is wasted production.

The institutionalization of mutual suspicion should prevent such behavior, at least in theory. Yet, strakhovka, blat, and ochkovtiratel'stvo exist because mutual suspicion is subverted by and often supplanted by mutual guarantee (*krugovaia poruka*).[19] To cover up illegality and subversion of the Plan, managers rely upon alliances or "family circles" that tie them to the ministerial officials and Party secretaries who are supposed to exercise control over them. The latter may choose to overlook or even conspire in the managers' misdeeds, if these serve the purpose of meeting the gross output quotas in the Plan. They share common incentive structures, for all are rewarded for overfulfillment and all benefit from the managers' strakhovka, blat, and even ochkovtiratel'stvo, if they enable the managers to fulfill the Plan.

In short, the elaborate centralized mechanism that Stalin created produces its own political dynamic of center versus periphery and planners versus producers that has become one of the most important political processes within the Soviet Union. Its price is economic inefficiency that subverts the Plan and leads to unused productive capacity and wasted production. Since Stalin's day, the task facing the Soviet Union's leaders has been to design economic reforms that will change this political dynamic and eliminate these consequences.

Efforts To Reform the Economy After Stalin

While the Stalinist command economy enabled the political leadership to mobilize economic resources to meet their primary goals, it also divorced decision making from production by overcentralization; and this ultimately led to new inefficiences.[20] To cope with these inefficiencies, Stalin's heirs have experimented with reforms of both structures and incentives, but so far not a thoroughgoing transformation of the Stalinist economic system.

Khrushchev sought to bring decision making closer to the production process by introduction of his sovnarkhoz reform of 1957. This transferred much decision making from Moscow to the regional capitals of the sovnarkhozy. Yet Khrushchev was forced to retreat only a few years later as his reform fell victim to localism: Sovnarkhozy gave preference to local needs over national priorities, favoring the supply needs of local producers over others and diverting investment funds to local projects. The reform simply traded the evil of *vedomstvennost'* (departmentalism) for that of *mestnichestvo* (localism). Thus, a recentralization of decision making followed.

Upon coming to power, the Brezhnev-Kosygin leadership completed the process of recentralization, abolishing the sovnarkhozy and returning decision making to centralized ministries. To cope with the inefficiences of the command economy, they preferred to experiment with the incentive structures of managers and with the organization of the ministries themselves.

The initial reforms instituted after 1965 were in part the outcome of a debate that originated during the last years of Khrushchev over the decision-making authority and incentive structure of enterprise managers.[21] Reformers argued for decentralization of decision making to the enterprise level by simplification of the Plan, giving enterprise managers greater control over decisions about production, marketing, supplies, prices, wages, and hiring. The most prominent of these liberalizers in the early years of this debate was Evsei Liberman of Kharkov State University, for whom these proposals came to be known as the Liberman Reforms. In a series of articles that appeared in *Kommunist* and even *Pravda*, Liberman argued for Plan simplification. He contended that the Plan should eliminate gross physical output as the producers' chief success indicator and substitute return on assets (profit rate). Use of profitability as a success indicator, Liberman argued, would reduce the inefficiencies that attend strakhovka by discouraging managers from hoarding supplies and artificially restricting their production. Not surprisingly, the reformers encountered resistance from the entrenched, conservative planners who feared losing their powers to the managers.

The compromise that resulted from these debates was a modest reform in the incentive structure of enterprise managers. Announced by Alexei Kosygin in September 1965 as an experiment, the reform was initially applied to 430 factories before mid-1966, and then extended to 41,000 enterprises, representing 93 percent of industrial output, by early 1970. Henceforth, a simplified set of about eight targets would be given to individual managers. These would include targets for the volume of sales, key assortments of items to be produced, a wage fund, profit and profitability targets, a financial plan, an investment plan, an innovation plan, and a supply plan; but purportedly the chief success criterion would be profitability. Managers would be encouraged in this by a right to retain more of their profits; and these profits would support an enterprise's Material Incentive Fund to give bonuses, its Welfare Fund for collective incentives, and its Development Fund for modernizing the plant. Many of the decisions regarding the allocation of these funds were to be left to the managers.[22]

The implementation of this reform, however, did not fundamentally change economic practice: Bonuses were still given principally for plan fulfillment of quantitative targets; profits were frequently not left to the managers but transferred to the budget; and recurring shortages of inputs perpetuated strakhovka and blat. By December 1969, key provisions of the Kosygin Reforms had fallen into disfavor; and by the end of 1970, little remained of the autonomy supposedly granted enterprise managers by the reform. In fact, subsequent reforms, notably those introduced in July 1979, have had the effect of increasing the number of indicators handed down by ministries to enterprises once again—including new indicators for net output, delivery obligations, quality, and technological innovations.

The failure of the Kosygin Reforms can in part be attributed to organizational reforms introduced by the new leadership that worked at cross-purposes to these. The reestablishment of ministries and concentration of supplies allocation in Gossnab centralized decision making and re-created old patterns of subordination between glavki and enterprises. An organizational reform introduced in April 1973 sought to replace the ministerial glavki with industrial associations and to expand use of the enterprise group called the production association (*ob''edinenie*). The latter would amalgamate related enterprises, replacing them as the legal entity responsible for production, and would pool their research and development operations so as to promote research, prototype development, and actual production application of new technologies. The industrial association, which would maintain its own research and development units, would oversee the production associations and, like them, function on a cost-accounting (*khozraschet*) basis. In practice, the production association may have led to some further centralization of decision making, deciding even minor issues that should have been left to the factories, while many industrial associations are nothing more than glavki under a new label but not under new management. In this milieu, old hierarchical-ministerial patterns have reasserted themselves and seem to have subverted the earlier expansion of managerial autonomy.[23]

The Gorbachev leadership was at first less ambitious in its economic reforms. Reviewing the first year after Gorbachev's ascendancy to the General Secretaryship, one Western economist concluded, "In reality, the new General Secretary has so far undertaken no radical steps to revive the economy—which speaks tomes about both his acumen and possibly also his indecisiveness. [And despite the] florid phraseology . . . in all the rhetoric there is a startling lack of concreteness.[24] Gorbachev engineered important personnel changes in the economic administration of the Soviet Union: At the time of the 27th Party Congress, 35 of the members of the Council of Ministers responsible for administration of domestic economic affairs had been appointed since Gorbachev's ascendancy. He personally associated himself with a continuation of the discipline campaign inaugurated by Andropov, including new restrictions on alcohol sales and stiffer penalties on alcohol abuse. The investment priorities of the 12th Five-Year Plan (1986–1990) reflect a decision to increase investment at the expense of short-term consumption and to direct more of the investment rubles at modernizing existing enterprises, rather than building new productive capabilities. Gorbachev stressed the importance of computers and robotics to this modernization campaign. Yet, changes in the structure of economic administration and management were modest. The establishment of "superministries," such as the State Agroindustrial Committee that replaces several smaller ministries or the Bureau of Machine Building that coordinates existing ministries, further centralizes some decision making. The expanded use of profitability as a success indicator and the commitment to reducing unnecessary levels of authority between ministries and enterprises had expanded the discretion of the managers only slightly.

After 18 months as General Secretary, however, Gorbachev began to make more sweeping proposals. Under the theme of *perestroika* (restructuring), he pushed for fundamental changes in the Soviet command economy. His Report to the June 1987 Central Committee Plenum argues that these changes could no longer be delayed, but must be fully implemented in time for the 13th Five-Year Plan (1991–1996). Specifically, individual enterprises would be given greater autonomy in purchasing, production, and sales decisions. And wholesale and retail prices would no longer be set by governmental fiat, but by the market or by negotiations among individual buyers and sellers.

SOVIET ECONOMIC PERFORMANCE

Soviet economic organization was well suited to the problems that faced a country in the early stages of industrialization. It provided the Soviet Union with unusually high rates of economic growth in the early years of the Stalin revolutions, but as the Soviet economy has matured, it is no longer as successful in this regard. Indeed, not only has the Soviet economy failed to produce the same high levels of growth; it seems that as it matures it actually retards growth by exacting a high price in economic inefficiency.[25]

Soviet Economy in Crisis?

Central to the many issues faced by the Soviet leadership is this problem of rapidly declining growth rates. In the early years of the first Five-Year Plans the Soviet command economy achieved growth rates in gross national product (GNP) in excess of 11 percent a year. Even during the late Stalin and early Khrushchev years, these annual growth rates remained above 5 percent. Yet, in recent years, growth has slowed significantly, with annual growth in real GNP falling to 3.0 percent for 1971–1984 and to 2.5 percent in 1984.[26] (See Table 10.1.)

Table 10.1   ANNUAL GROWTH RATES IN SOVIET GNP/NMP, 1928–1984

	GNP (Bergson)	GNP (CIA)	NMP (Soviet)
1928–1937	11.9		
1937–1940	6.7		
1940–1944	−2.3		
1944–1950	6.6		
1951–1955	7.6	5.5	11.1
1956–1960		5.9	9.1
1961–1965		5.0	6.5
1966–1970		5.2	7.7
1971–1975		3.7	5.7
1976–1980		2.6	4.2
1981		1.9	
1982		2.6	
1983		3.7	
1984		2.5	

Sources: Bergson's estimate of gross national product appears in Abram Bergson, *The Real National Income of Soviet Russia Since 1928* (Cambridge, Mass.: Harvard University Press, 1961), 217. The CIA's estimates of GNP and the official Soviet figures for growth in net material product (NMP) appear in United States Congress, Joint Economic Committee, *USSR: Measures of Economic Growth and Development, 1950–1980* (Washington, D.C.: Government Printing Office, 1982), 20, 25; United States, Central Intelligence Agency, *Handbook of Economic Statistics, 1985* (Washington, D.C. 1985), 65; United States, Central Intelligence Agency, *The World Factbook, 1986* (Washington, D.C., 1986), 227.

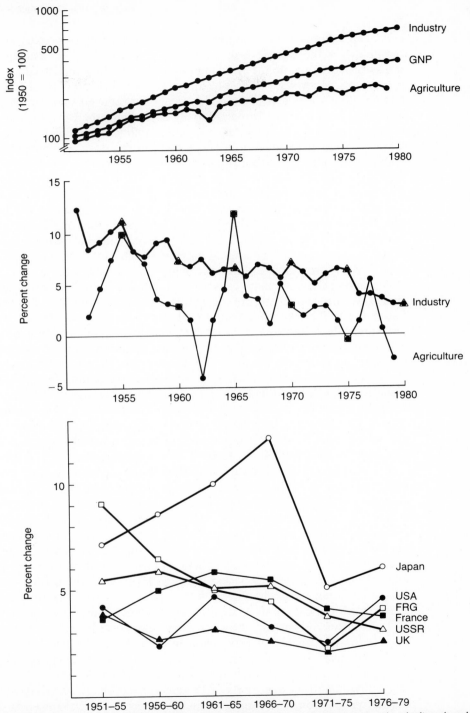

Figure 10.3 Soviet Economic Growth, 1950–1980. (top) Growth of industry and agriculture (moving 3-year average for agriculture); (middle) annual growth rate for industry and agriculture; (bottom) comparison with average annual growth rates of Western economies. (*Source:* Drawn from data in U.S. Congress, Joint Economic Committee, *USSR: Measures of Economic Growth and Development, 1950–80* [Washington, D.C., 1982].)

The command economy, as these growth rates show, is apparently most successful when the central task is mobilizing idle resources, usually in the early stages of modernization. For example, prior to Stalin's industrial and agricultural revolutions, labor was underutilized, particularly in the agrarian sector. By transferring labor to industry, the Soviet economy reduced underemployment. Even after this mobilization had been largely completed, the Soviet economy was able to maintain high growth rates due to its ability to mobilize a rapidly growing store of inputs to production. (This growth in the store of inputs came through a high growth rate in the labor force and through discoveries of new energy and mineral reserves.) Yet, as the Soviet economy has matured and there is no longer a large stock of idle resources and the absolute size of inputs to production has not continued to grow at its previous rates, the key to continued growth is less and less quantitative expansion of resources and more and more qualitative improvements in the factors of production. The command economy has proved less successful at developing more efficient uses of an increasingly static store of inputs to production; and so, growth rates have declined.[27] (See Figure 10.3.)

Among the immediate causes of this decline, one that has already been discussed is the inefficient use of inputs to production. The factory managers' search for strakhovka leads them to acquire the largest possible allocation of supplies and labor, knowing that this larger allocation will not diminish profits and will actually provide security against future irregularities in the supply cycle. For example, an enterprise manager has every reason to expand the supply of labor in his factory. A manager needs extra workers on hand, since he never knows when the Plan will suddenly be increased before the end of the year. Moreover, he realizes that some of his workers may be withdrawn during the year and sent either to a local farm to help with the harvest or to a high-priority construction project, so he must have a "buffer stock" of labor to protect his plant against such threats to its Plan fulfillment. Extra labor also protects the enterprise from the effects of storming (*shturmovshchina*). The monthly, quarterly, and annual production cycles place high demands on labor during peak production periods: For example, during the first third of each month the pace of production may be quite slow as the factory awaits supplies allocated for the month; and during the second third, once adequate supplies have arrived, production picks up. But during the last third of the month, after all the supplies are on hand and the deadline for fulfilling the monthly quota approaches, production picks up to a feverish pace. It is for this period of feverish production (storming), that the excess labor is necessary. Inefficient use of inputs has let to waste and even shortages in such critical inputs as hydroelectric power, energy, and iron ore.[28]

A second economic weakness that has contributed to declining growth rates is the low quality of production in both consumers' and producers' goods. In the extreme, low-quality production is simply waste—many products available to consumers are of such low quality that they remain unsold. In less extreme cases, low quality in the inputs to production reduces productivity, increases the costs of production, and results in final products that are themselves shoddy.

Third, lagging capital construction capacity has led to an imbalance between investment and construction. The Soviets have increased investment funds fairly rapidly to expand production, but construction capacity has not expanded to meet demand. As a consequence, there is a backlog of construction orders, and many projects, once started, remain uncompleted for long periods. In 1965, 69 percent of the construction plans for the year were not completed by year's end; by 1976 that figure had grown to 80 percent. Equipment placed in these half-completed factories stands idle and therefore wasted; and it begins to depreciate, particularly if exposed to the elements.[29]

A fourth economic problem that contributes to declining growth rates is the imbalance between incomes and the supply of consumer goods. Since Stalin's death, wages in the Soviet Union have risen substantially, but the supply of consumer goods has not kept pace. Expanded wages have been used as incentives to higher labor productivity; but with little to spend these on, offers of higher wages may not induce the desired worker response.

And, fifth, there is a low rate of technological innovation and technical change. Research and development often takes place, not in the factory, but in the Academy of Science or in a ministry far removed from the factory; and so, innovations are often inappropriate to actual production conditions. Moreover, there are few incentives for an enterprise manager to innovate. When a manager must decide whether to expand an existing production line or improve upon it, the prudent manager may simply expand the production line with existing technologies rather than stop production to replace the line with improved technologies, for the latter would risk not meeting the enterprise's quota. For these reasons, factories are slow to adopt modern technologies or other innovations and less efficient production techniques linger on well past their usefulness.[30]

Behind these immediate causes of declining growth are more fundamental, or structural, causes that help explain the presence of these weaknesses. Among these central structural flaws in the Soviet command economy is the continued divorce of decision making from production. (Phrased slightly differently, many of the dysfunctions in the Soviet economy result when hierarchical control interacts with nonhierarchical flows of real inputs and outputs.[31]) The centralization of key production and investment decisions in Moscow has meant that those who make key decisions cannot know the particularities of production in each factory affected by these decisions, and so must plan according to general rules of thumb. Yet, few enterprises conform to the average case, and so these rules of thumb, which become binding directives once included in a factory's Plan, usually result in inefficiencies. This has prompted the continued calls for, and experiments with, various decentralization schemes and simplified plans. Yet the old hierarchical-ministerial patterns always seem to reassert themselves.

A second root cause of recent economic difficulties is the structural security of producers. Factory managers who fail to innovate or to produce highest-quality goods bear little risk, since under the Plan their output is guaranteed buyers and their enterprises do not face competition. The absence of competition results from the insurmountable barriers to entry into the market; i.e., the difficulty of establishing new enterprises to produce new products with new techniques. In a market economy, efficient and innovative production is purportedly ensured by producers' fears that competitors will enter the market with new products or more-efficient production techniques, set up a factory, and start producing a better or cheaper product; an existing producer who does not keep up with such innovations will go bankrupt. In the Soviet economy this cannot happen. Similarly, labor security has retarded growth in labor productivity. The Soviets rightfully pride themselves in having minimized unemployment. Yet, because it is so difficult to dismiss an unproductive employee and because the laborer who has been released can easily find another job, major sanctions against labor inefficiency have been removed. One Soviet economist is quoted as saying, "The assurance of getting a job is the root cause of slack effort and low productivity."[32]

A third structural cause of Soviet economic ills is the large role of the military in the economy. High levels of military expenditure have not only taken money from personal consumption, but have also diverted funds from investment that could fund growth. According to CIA estimates, the Soviet Union in 1983 spent 14.0 percent of its GNP on defense (a percentage that has been relatively stable throughout the past decade) compared to 6.6 percent for the United States (up from 5.9 percent a decade earlier). Soviet expenditures have grown at an average of 4 percent per year since 1965, even in recent years as the Soviet economy itself has grown less rapidly. To illustrate the costs of this policy, researchers at the Centrally Planned Economies Project of Wharton Econometric Forecasting Associates have investigated the impact of alternative rates of growth in defense on overall Soviet economic performance. They conclude that in the period 1980–1985, an increase in the annual rate of growth for defense expenditures from 4.5 percent to 7.5 percent would reduce the rate of growth of GNP by 1 per cent. Conversely, a decrease in defense growth to 2.5 percent would raise GNP by 0.8 per cent per year.[33]

The fourth of these structural problems is the continued weakness of Soviet agriculture. But more about this later.

Strengths of the Soviet Economy

The Soviet command economy is not without certain natural strengths that may enable it to cope with these problems. Most importantly, the Soviet economy is still able to target resources to areas of high priority. In the period of high growth, the Soviets not only achieved high growth rates overall, but also achieved its highest growth rates in those sectors of the economy that would contribute to further growth. To quote British economist Raymond Hutchings:

> Development was concentrated on industry; within industry, on heavy industry; within heavy industry, on ferrous metals, machinery and engineering, and electric power; and generally on machinery rather than buildings. Emphasis was placed on economic development on a national scale rather than on private luxury; on economic rather than cultural development; and on multiplying productive objects rather than creating things of beauty.[34]

This pattern of emphasis should continue to be an asset even as the qualitative improvement in the factors of production replaces quantitative mobilization of resources as the prime economic problem. For example, the Academy of Sciences and Gostekhnika are empowered to supervise all research undertaken within the Soviet Union. The centralized evaluation of research and development, permitting planners to identify the most-promising innovations and target these with increased funding, can lead to efficient use of investment funds.

Second, the Soviet economy has been able to maintain high levels of investment. During the early Stalin years, investment accounted for a quarter to a third of national income and was targeted on fixed capital. In recent years, the return to investment has fallen (that is, the capital/output ratio has risen) as building construction and replacement of worn-out machinery consume a larger share of funds, but the level of investment is still high when compared to other, particularly Western industrial, societies. In 1984, investment consumed 30 percent of the Soviet GNP, but only 17 percent of the British and 15 percent of the American GNPs.[35]

A necessary concomitant of these first two assets—and a third strength of the Soviet command economy as it confronts its problems—is its ability to suppress nonproductive expenditures. For example, limitations on the quantity and variety of consumer goods, prohibitions on private purchases from overseas, and high obstacles to migration to major cities have meant that fewer scarce funds need be spent on expansion of production capacity in light industry, on foreign exchange, or on urban housing construction. The suppression of nonproductive expenditures has been made possible not only by the coercive powers of the Soviet regime, but also by its ability to instill in the population a sense of economic purpose that has justified these deprivations. This sense has flagged in recent years and consumer demand has risen, making it more difficult to resist nonproductive expenditures, but this capacity remains high compared to Western market economies and democracies. In 1984 consumption represented 60 percent of the end use of the British GNP and 65 percent of the American, but only 53 percent of the Soviet GNP.[36]

Fourth, the Soviets have developed a scientific community, particularly in the fields of applied science and engineering, to develop more-efficient productive techniques. The Soviets have specifically targeted engineering and science in higher education: One-half of all university degree recipients in the Soviet Union are graduated in math and science; and two-fifths of all higher education graduates have matriculated in engineering institutions.

And, fifth, the Soviet Union as a late developing society has been in a position to borrow foreign technology, such as hydroelectric generation or assembly line production, because the technologies to address many of the Soviet Union's economic problems have already been developed. Until recently the Soviets have not participated in international copyright or patent conventions, so that there have been few self-imposed restrictions on their use of such information. Conversely, the security concerns of Western industrialized nations, such as those who make up the Coordinating Committee for Multilateral Export Controls (CoCom), has led them to restrict access to some of the most sensitive technologies with military applications. Nonetheless, with some notable exceptions such as computers, much of the technology required by the Soviet economy is widely available. And in the late 1960s the Soviet Union began to expand its trade with the West, concentrating "on imports of equipment embodying a higher level of technology than that achieved in the Soviet economy."[37]

These strengths of the Soviet economy are real. Whether they are significant enough to permit it to overcome its structural weaknesses remains to be seen.

THE SPECIAL PROBLEMS OF SOVIET AGRICULTURE

Soviet agriculture has long been seen in the West as the most vulnerable side of the Soviet economy. Writing in 1951, a leading expert on the subject predicted, "The Soviet village is indeed the weakest point of the Soviet system, its Achilles heel. It will have a great part in the ultimate destruction of Soviet power."[38] The continued weakness of Soviet agriculture certainly remains a principal reason for the sluggish performance of the overall economy.

Like Soviet industry, agriculture is highly politicized and bureaucratized. The Stalinist agricultural revolution not only replaced the independent peasant farm with collective farms (the *kolkhoz*), state farms (the *sovkhoz*), Machine-Tractor Stations (MTS), and private plots, but made production on these subject to the direction of Gosplan and the People's Commissariats of Agriculture and State Farms in Moscow. The sovkhoz was created to operate as a factory in the field with wage labor. The Kolkhoz Charter or "model statute" of 1935 proclaimed the kolkhoz to be a voluntary cooperative, constituted on the basis of pooled means of production, that would elect its own chairman in a meeting of its members. In practice, the manager was appointed by the Party obkom and was subject to the directions of the Party raikom, the agricultural department of the raispolkom (operating under the authority of the People's Commissariat of Agriculture), and the local MTS administration.

The two decades following World War II were marked by disruptive tinkering with the administrative apparatus of agriculture without changing the hierarchical control over farms. The creation of the Council for Kolkhoz Affairs in 1946 and then its rapid demise, the division of the Ministry of Agriculture into separate Ministries for Food Crops, Industrial Crops, and Livestock in 1946 and its subsequent reunification in 1947, the strengthening of the MTS following Stalin's death and then their abolition in 1958, as well as the sovnarkhoz reform of 1957 and bifurcation of the Party in 1962, all affected agriculture adversely. Under Brezhnev and Kosygin, however, the old ministerial structure of control over agriculture was reinstated and greater organizational stability was ensured.

Today, much of the responsibility for agriculture has been concentrated in the State Agro-Industrial Committee (*Gosagroprom*), created in November 1985 to subsume the activities previously performed by the Ministries of Agriculture, Food Industry, Meat and Dairy Products, Fruits and Vegetables, and Rural Construction, and the State Committee for the Supply of Production Equipment to Agriculture. It is assisted by a new Ministry for Grain Products and a bevy of agencies that service the agricultural sector, including the Ministries of Fishing Industry, Land Reclamation and Water Resources, Machine Building for Animal Husbandry and Fodder Production, Mineral Fertilizer Production, and Tractor and Agricultural Machine Building.

Production was shared in 1985 among the sovkhozes with 53.5 percent of the sown land, kolkhozes with 43.8 percent, and private plots with 2.7 percent. Since their creation there has been a tendency toward the amalgamation of kolkhozes into larger enterprises, so that the average number of households in each kolkhoz has risen and the total number of kolkhozes has been cut. (See Table 10.2.) There has also been a tendency toward the conversion of kolkhozes into sovzhozes. The sovkhozes concentrate on extensive cultivation of grains (accounting for 56.5 percent of all Soviet soil sown to grain) and fodder (56.1 percent), but devote relatively little energy to more labor-intensive activities such as vegetable production (28.1 percent of the total). Just the opposite is true of the private plots, which concentrate on high-value, labor-intensive production, accounting for 45.4 percent of all Soviet soil dedicated to potatoes and other vegetables. Despite their small size, these plots also account for a significant part of Soviet animal husbandry, holding 30.8 percent of the cows, 17.9 percent of the pigs, and 78.5 percent of the goats in 1986.[39]

The production process that Stalin created resulted in a complex tangle of incentive structures that have not always been easily manipulated to effect optimal outcomes. The 1935 Kolkhoz Charter limited each peasant household to about an acre of individual land and up to "one cow and calves, one pig and piglets, four sheep and any number of rabbits and poultry.[40] The remainder of the kolkhoz land was worked collectively. From the produce of each kolkhoz were taken the compulsory deliveries to the state (for which the kolkhoz received a cash payment), payment in kind to the MTS for its heavy machinery services (sowing, harvesting, and so forth), and reserves for seed and fodder. From the cash revenues of the kolkhoz were deducted taxes, insurance, the capital fund, and the cost of administration and production. And from the produce of the private plots were taken compulsory deliveries to the state, and from its cash revenues were taken taxes. Thus, the income of a peasant household consisted of what was left after all these deductions: (1) a share of the produce retained by the kolkhoz and a share of its cash revenues after kolkhoz expenses, both of which were divided according to the relative number of workday units of each member (called the *trudoden'*) (2) the proceeds from its private plot, after compulsory deliveries and taxes, which could be consumed or sold; and (3) wages from auxiliary or seasonal employment for the local MTS, on state farms, or in factories.

The high levels of compulsory deliveries to the state and the low price paid for these resulted in low compensation for collective work relative to work on the private plots. Tensions between collective and private work were further exacerbated throughout the Stalin years by the growing gap between the low procurement price paid to the peasants for collective work and the high retail price they could earn in the markets for their private plot produce. This led to attempts by the kolkhozniki to evade collective work in order to work on their plots. Stalin responded in 1939 with legislation fixing *trudoden'* minima for all adult members

Table 10.2   THE CHANGING STRUCTURE OF SOVIET AGRICULTURE, 1928–1985

	1928	1940	1965	1970	1975	1980	1985
Kolkhoz							
Number (thousands)	33.3	236.9	36.9	33.6	29.0	26.3	26.7
Households (average)	13	79	426	435	473	492	479
Arable Land (thousand hectares, average)	0.1	1.4	6.1	6.1	6.4	6.6	6.4
Sovkhoz							
Number (thousands)	1.4	4.2	11.7	15.0	18.1	21.1	22.7
Arable Land (thousand hectares, average)	5.6	12.2	24.6	20.8	18.9	17.2	16.1

Source: Tsentral'noe statisticheskoe upravlenie, *Narodnoe Khoziaistvo SSSR 1922–1982: Iubileinyi statisticheskii ezhegodnik* (Moscow: Finansy i Statistika, 1982), 225–226; Tsentral'noe statisticheskoe upravlenie, *Narodnoe Khoziaistvo SSSR v 1985 g.* (Moscow: Finansy i Statistika, 1986), 179, 278, 287.

of kolkhozes. And heavy taxes were levied after World War II on the assets of private plots. But this led peasants to reduce their private livestock holdings and cut down fruit trees rather than pay the high taxes on these. Thus, Stalin's policies failed to boost agricultural output significantly.

Since Stalin's days, Soviet policies toward agriculture have undergone a reversal—from exploitation of agriculture to finance the industrialization of the Soviet Union to subsidization of agriculture at the expense of the urban sector. Initially, the effort to extract agricultural produce for industrial production and export led to high compulsory deliveries even when this produced shortages or famine in the countryside (as it did in 1932–1933 and, to a lesser extent, in 1936–1937). The low prices paid for this output kept peasant households in poverty: In 1935, the average household received an annual cash payment for collective work that was equivalent to the price of one pair of shoes, and in 1948, 20 days' work on collective land yielded only enough to buy a bottle of vodka. Concentration of investment funds on industry meant shortages of farm machinery, storage facilities, and transportation infrastructure in the countryside.

The Malenkov-Khrushchev leadership initiated significant changes in these policies—increasing the prices for compulsory-procurement and over-quota deliveries, reducing these quotas in many cases, cutting the taxes on private plots (and finally eliminating the compulsory deliveries from these in 1958), expanding investment in the rural sector, and raising production of farm machinery and fertilizers. Khrushchev also personally associated himself with—and staked his political future on—ambitious growing programs: The Virgin Lands Program inaugurated in 1954 would expand acreage by cultivating the fallow lands along the Kazakhstani-Siberian border and the corn (maize) program inaugurated in 1955 would expand fodder production. Other Khrushchevian policies, however, worked at cross-purposes to these, including the imposition of a heavier tax burden on private livestock, price imbalances that discouraged milk and meat production, intensified meddling of the Party apparatus, and disruptive reorganizations of agriculture.

The new Brezhnev-Kosygin leadership, identifying agriculture as a critical problem, announced an expansion in agricultural investment at a March 1965 Central Committee Plenum. It promised not only to increase the supply of farm machinery, but also to end the practices that had disrupted production, to eliminate restrictions on private livestock that had led to stagnation in meat and milk production, and to give greater attention to the previously neglected regions outside the black-earth zone. This has been matched in more recent years by public statements guaranteeing the long-term security of private plots and promising the implements and supplies essential to their success. Agriculture has become a net consumer of investment funds. Organizational reforms since 1965 have been modest, focusing on development of agro-industrial complexes (*agropromyshlennyi kompleks*) to coordinate production among farms and factories and on various experiments with work brigades on farms. At its May 1982 Plenum, the Central Committee adopted a much-heralded "Food Program" that would further increase investments in productive infrastructure (including transportation, storage, and social amenities), raise procurement prices, and expand experimentation with the agro-industrial complexes and small production brigades on kolkhozes.[3/8]

As Figure 10.4 shows, this change in policy has been reflected in a sustained increase in agricultural production. The destruction associated with the initial collectivization of agriculture and with World War II disrupted growth, but even in the period of post war reconstruction Soviet agriculture remained in a weak position, not surpassing its prewar peak until 1955. From the mid-50s, however, improvement has been sustained. From 1951 to 1975, the growth in total agricultural output averaged 3.5 percent a year, outpacing that in the United States (1.6 percent annually). In the Tenth Five-Year Plan period (1976–1980), grain production was up 68.7 percent over the Sixth Plan period (1956–1960), vegetable production up 74.2 percent, meat production up 87.3 percent, and egg production up 167.4 percent.[41] (Agricultural output in the Eleventh Plan period was poor, but rebounded in 1986.)

Nonetheless, Soviet agriculture has failed to meet the demands of the population and industry. Among the reasons commonly cited in the West for this failure, the nine problems listed below (inspired by the work of Alec Nove and James R. Millar) seem most important.[42] First, as in industry, excessive centralization removes decision making from the production process and leads to the multiplication of orders imposed on managers that may be inappropriate to local conditions. Second, and closely associated with the first, is the homogenization of plans. To quote the British economist Nove, "The enemy of agriculture is what the Russians call *shablon,* the imposition of some standardized decision or pattern on a vast variety of local conditions." Even in the absence of true decentralization, it would be a step forward if plans derived at the center were more responsive to the diversity of local conditions. Third, diseconomies of scale have resulted from excessive amalgamation of kolkhozes and sovkhozes, "which often have around 500 members or employees, scattered in several villages and engaged in a multitude of activities, cultivating numerous crops and keeping every kind of farm animal." Efficient management might result from division of these into smaller and more specialized farms. And fourth, the incentive structure of agriculturalists, like that of industrial producers, leads to the artificial suppression of production through *strakhovka.*[43]

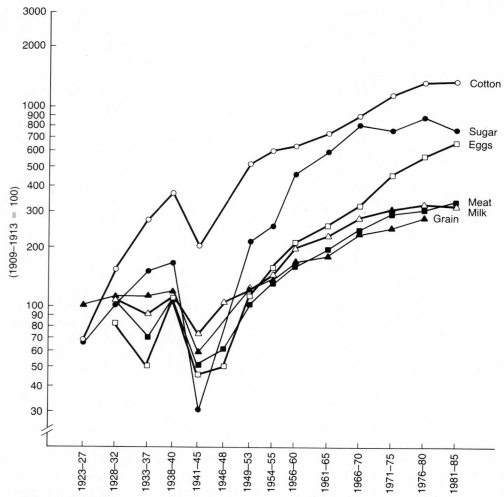

Figure 10.4 Average Annual Output, 1909–1985. (1909–1913 = 100.) (*Source*: Erich Strauss, *Soviet Agriculture in Perspective* [New York: Praeger, 1969]; Tsentralnoe Statisticheskoe Upravlenie, *Narodnoe khoziaistvo SSSR, 1922–1982* [Moscow: Finansy i Statistika, 1982], 227; "Osnovnye pokazateli ekonomichiskogo is sotsialnogo razvitiia SSSR za 1961–1985gg.," *Vestnik statistiki* No. 3 [March 1986],55.)

In addition, Soviet agriculture suffers shortages of the major inputs to production. Thus, a fifth problem is a shortage of skilled labor to operate and maintain modern farm machinery, a problem that is aggravated by the migration of skilled workers to the towns that can offer more amenities than the countryside. Sixth, there is a shortage of farm machinery, which reduces output and contributes to the labor shortages, particularly at peak production times. This is aggravated by "the absence of complementary equipment, which reduces the effectiveness of the available machines," and by shortages of small implements and spare parts. Seventh is a shortage of fodder for livestock. And eighth is the limitation of the transportation infrastructure, including unpaved roads that turn to mud in spring and autumn, shortages of storage facilities at railside, and a "lack of specialized forms of transport" for farm produce—all resulting in waste and spoilage as produce moves from farms to consumers.[44]

Lastly, the inability of Soviet agriculture to meet consumers' demands for more and higher-quality produce is aggravated by a pricing policy that has maintained the retail prices of staple foodstuffs virtually unchanged (there was no change for a decade and a half after 1962 and then only a 4 percent rise over the next five years) even as the procurement prices have risen substantially. Since wages rose by about 70 percent in the two decades after 1962, demand for (and consumption of) higher-quality agricultural produce has risen dramatically, outstripping supply.[45]

MATERIAL WELL-BEING OF SOVIET CITIZENS

Despite the many problems of the Soviet economy, the standard of living of the Soviet population has shown a substantial improvement since the death of Stalin, although the economic slowdown of the late 70s and early 80s has exacted a price in the rate of improvement. This improvement is reflected in the rise of Soviet wages, which in 1985 were reported to be 97.0 percent above their 1965 level, with agricultural wages showing one of the steepest increases at 142.8 percent. Other measures of living standards corroborate this trend. The Soviet diet has improved: Caloric intake rose over 8 percent between the mid-60s and 1980, and average protein consumption rose almost 11 percent. The availability of consumer durables has also risen: For example, the number of televisions in use per 1000 population rose 349 percent between 1965 and 1980.[46]

The movement in Soviet living standards prior to 1953 presents a less positive picture. Per capita consumption fell 3 percent between 1928 and 1937, and another 4 percent by 1940; by 1950 per capita consumption was only 11 percent above the 1928 level. It is important to an understanding of the Soviet model of economic development to note that this picture is slightly more positive if one includes consumption of communal services (free education, health care, and cultural services) in the measure of per capita consumption, for then this figure actually increased by 10 percent between 1928 and 1937 and by 27 percent between 1928 and 1950. Much of this growth was due to movement of rural populations into the industrial sector, however, which brought them a significant improvement in living standards by both improved incomes and greater access to communal services. For the urban population the Stalin years may have seen a substantial economic decline: The net average annual wage for nonagricultural wage earners and salaried employees actually fell 43 percent between 1928 and 1937, another 6 percent by 1940 and by 1950 had only recovered its 1937 level. The reality of daily life may have been even harsher than these aggregate numbers suggest. Nove, commenting on the early 1930s, notes, "The proper assessment of living standards at this time is rendered almost impossible not only by the existence of rationing, price differences, and shortages, but also of queues, decline in quality, neglect of consumer requirements."[47] Housing, as only one illustration, became scarce as the rush of rural populations to the urban centers outpaced Stalin's penurious investments: Urban housing space per capita fell 22 percent between 1928 and 1940. In short, during periods of most-rapid growth, the Soviet command economy exacted a high price in the living standards of its citizens, actually using this to finance economic growth.

In comparative terms, the present-day living standard of the Soviet people still lags behind that of Western industrialized nations. (See Table 10.3.) Per capita gross national product (GNP) shows the Soviet Union close behind the level of some Western industrial countries, ranging from 62.8 percent of the United States to 93.2 percent of the United Kingdom. Yet expenditures on investment and defense consume much higher shares of the Soviet GNP, so that comparisons of the portion of GNP available for consumption show the Soviet standard of living to lag significantly behind Western levels, ranging from about half the American level to four-fifths the British.[48]

Given the uniqueness of the Soviet strategy of economic development, it is important to compare not only the levels of consumption but also the patterns of consumption: In the necessities of life, such as food, Soviet consumption compares more favorably, with caloric intake and protein consumption about equal to that in major Western powers. In provision of social services and collective goods, such as urban transportation and public health care, the Soviet Union does as well as, or perhaps better than, these Western countries, in the *extent* of services—for example, making basic health care available to all citizens. It is in the *quality* of those services, such as the provision of specialized medical treatment, that the Soviet system falls behind. The figures for hospital beds and physicians per 10,000 population, which measure the former, place the Soviet Union well ahead of the West, but on various qualitative dimensions Soviet medicine lags. In the provision of noncollective goods in response to consumer demand beyond necessities, such as the provision of consumer durables, the Soviet living standard falls significantly behind Western economies, as the figures for televisions, radios, and passenger vehicles per capita show.[49]

Among the shortcomings in the Soviet standard of living today, housing still stands out. The Soviet regime has ensured that all citizens have a roof over their heads, meeting the basic needs of the population with the guarantee of housing that generally does not cost more than 4 percent of a tenant's income in rent. (Since the rent does not cover the cost of maintenance, let alone repayment of the construction costs, housing is heavily subsidized and administered as a social service.) Yet, beyond the "extensive" provision of this basic social guarantee, the Soviet system has been less successful; the quality of Soviet housing is often dismal. The average living space in Soviet housing units during the 1970s (513.4 square feet) was only 70.0 percent of Japanese and 51.8 percent of American housing units. The amenities in these Soviet units were sparse; even as late as 1985, an estimated 20 percent of Soviet urban families still lived in communal flats, with shared kitchen, toilet, and bath facilities. (The Party Program adopted in 1986 promises that communal housing will be eliminated by the end of the century.) In 1985, over a quarter of state-sector urban residences still lacked hot

Table 10.3   THE SOVIET LIVING STANDARD COMPARED, 1980–1984
(Soviet Levels as a Percent of Others)

	USA	UK	France	Germany	Japan
GNP per capita, 1984	62.8	93.2	80.1	66.7	69.8
Consumption per capita	51.2	81.9	66.3	62.8	62.7
Caloric intake, 1978–80	92.8	102.2	100.2	95.8	117.6
Protein consumption	94.1	110.0	95.6	111.1	113.6
Hospital beds per capita, 1980	213.7	159.3	102.5	108.8	108.8
Physicians per capita	205.7	266.4	217.2	165.6	285.0
Televisions per capita, 1981	48.5	74.5	84.8	—	55.5
Radios per capita	23.9	52.3	54.4	131.6	73.3
Passenger vehicles per capita	6.7	12.4	10.3	9.5	17.2

Source: United Nations, Department of International Economic and Statistical Affairs, Statistical Office, *Statistical Yearbook, 1982.* (New York: United Nations, 1985); United States, Central Intelligence Agency, *The World Factbook, 1986* (Washington, D.C., 1986).

water, over a fifth lacked gas, and over a tenth had no sewerage or central heating. Among rural homes the situation was even worse. Nonetheless, the housing picture has been improving since 1953. In the 11th Five-Year Plan (1981–1985), investment in housing construction was 183 percent higher than the level 25 years earlier. To ease the burden on state housing (usually constructed and administered by local soviets or enterprises), the state has encouraged construction of cooperative housing, in which citizens join in cooperative associations and become shareholders in the construction of an apartment building as well as private homes (except in the major urban centers, where this has been banned since 1962 to conserve land). In 1985, private ownership accounted for 22.8 percent of the urban housing space and 71.1 percent of the rural housing space. The amenities in housing have also improved, as the following disparate statistics illustrate: Per capita housing space increased 45.8 percent between 1958 and 1976, and another 9.0 percent between 1980 and 1985. And by 1980 the proportion of families living in communal flats had fallen to about a third of its 1960 level.[50]

Comparison of the present Soviet standard of living with its own previous levels and with levels in the West is complicated not only by the different stages of socioeconomic development and different patterns of distribution of resources available for personal consumption, but also by the heavy emphasis upon nondivisible, or collective, goods and upon less-tangible elements in the Soviet concept of "material well-being and cultural level of the people" (*material'noe blagosostoianie i kul'turnyi uroven' naroda*). The official Soviet figures on the well-being of the population include not only national income and retail sales, but also social program expenditures, housing stock, preschool enrollments, hospital beds, rest homes and sanitoria, subways, and sport facilities. Subsidies to the necessities of life such as food, housing, and urban transportation keep these within reach of all citizens and also make comparisons of incomes with earlier periods and across national lines misleading: One ruble in Moscow, roughly equivalent to $1.33 at official rates in the mid-80s, would buy about 10 pounds of bread or 4 quarts of milk in a state store, 20 rides on the subway or bus (with transfers), or theater tickets for two adults and two to five children. Social security programs, which include pensions, workmen's compensation, aid for dependent children, maternity leave, and health care, have been expanded; per capita expenditure on social programs, including education, rose 317 percent from 1960 to 1985. And the conditions of labor have improved as well, as illustrated by the decline in the average work week from 47.8 hours in a six-day week in 1955 to 40.5 hours in a five-day week in 1985. Retirement is set at the unusually generous ages of 60 for men and 55 for women. Although there are many flaws that one might point up in these Soviet programs, these figures underscore that Soviet progress in the standard of living of its population has been substantial and may fare far better when compared with Western societies than simple comparisons of personal income would suggest. The principal blemish on this record is the recent decline in life expectancy, particularly among Soviet males, which fell from a peak of 67.0 years in 1964 to 61.9 years in 1980. (Among Soviet women the drop was less pronounced—from 75.6 to 73.5 years over that period.) Much of this decline can be attributed to alchoholism and excessive use of abortion as a means of contraception (the latter leads to greater risks of infant mortality once a woman decides to carry a child full-term). Yet, as the ultimate summary statistic for the physical well-being of a population, this decline in life expectancy also signals continued deficiencies in the Soviet standard of living, such as diets high in saturated fats and deficient in vitamins, stressful working and living conditions, and poor public health and individual medical care.[51]

Well-Being and Economic Growth

Since Stalin's death, and particularly since the removal of Khrushchev, the effort to improve the material well-being of Soviet citizens has been closely tied to efforts to regain healthy growth rates in the economy. Increasingly the Soviet leadership has seen that a key to growth is increased worker productivity; and this requires improved incentives to workers. But raising living standards has proven to be a complex problem, one not easily solved. For example, as an incentive to more-efficient production, wages have been increased almost every year since 1968. While the average monthly wage was 96.5 rubles in 1965, it had risen to 190.1 rubles by 1985, or 97.0 percent in two decades.[52] Yet, wages have risen faster than the supply of consumer goods, vitiating incentive.

One consequence of this disparity between incomes and goods is an increase in savings. Between 1965 and 1985 savings climbed almost five times, rising to 91 billion rubles in 1975 and 221 billion rubles by 1985. The average size of savings accounts rose from 209 rubles in 1960 to 1293 rubles in 1985.[53] Since private funds are not used for investment in the Soviet economy (this is financed from State and enterprise revenues), savings do not have the same positive effect they do on a Western capitalist economy. The growth in savings defeats the purpose of increasing incomes as an incentive to greater worker productivity, since this money is not improving levels of consumption.

The discrepancy between incomes and goods also produces hidden inflation—that is, even though official retail prices have not risen or have risen only slightly, Soviet consumers must pay more for these same items.* With greater disposable incomes, customers give "gifts" to sales personnel to acquire items not ordinarily available. If this becomes common practice, the prices of these items have effectively risen. Inflation is very real and not at all hidden in the "private" markets. The difference between official and free-market prices of food grew from 37 percent in 1965 to 100 percent in 1978. Prices for foodstuffs in commission shops, which sell state produce at prices closer to the free market, in the early 1980s were reportedly two to three times the official state shop prices.[54]

The discrepancy between incomes and goods has also permitted the black market to flourish, for here customers with larger disposable incomes seek to buy items not currently available in the state stores. The imbalance between demand (wages) and supply (goods) has encouraged the theft of state property for private use, the resale of such stolen property, illicit production or provision of services using state property (such as a state vehicle to provide taxi service), and illegal private production.[55]

In addition to raising wages, the Party has sought to improve the citizen's lot and raise labor productivity by improving diet. An improved diet not only contributes to health and physical well-being among workers, but also serves as an incentive—something worthwhile for which to earn higher salaries. The March 1965 Central Committee decree to improve agriculture and the 1982 Food Program were in large part inspired by the regime's commitment to improve the quality of the Soviet diet. And the campaign has been successful: As Table 10.4 shows, Soviet citizens have increasingly substituted proteins for carbohydrates in their diets.

The effort to improve the Soviet diet is not without its unwanted consequences, however. One is a grain shortage. As consumption of meat rather than grain lengthens the food chain, it substantially increases the demand for grain and has led the Soviet Union to increase its grain imports. While Soviet grain production is adequate to feed the Soviet population with a high carbohydrate diet, it is inadequate to the needs of both people and cattle in a more balanced diet. A second unwanted consequence is the mounting government food subsidy that has become a drain on government revenues. A kilogram of beef in the late 1970s sold for about 2 rubles, but the government paid farmers 3.5 rubles; a kilogram of butter sold for 3.6 rubles, but the government paid farmers 5 rubles. The subsidy to food rose from about 3 percent of its cost in 1965 to about 16 percent in the mid-70s. In 1969 the total subsidy to agriculture cost the government about 7.9 billion rubles, but by 1980 about 30 billion rubles.[56]

A third response to the problem of worker well-being and labor productivity is an increase in the production of consumer goods, particularly the production of "big-ticket items" like automobiles to sop up savings. (See table 10.4) Yet, meeting consumer demand for such items has not been easy. As the Soviet population has become more affluent, it has become more concerned with the quality of these appliances and automobiles. But factory managers have had little incentive to respond to these demands, since the higher production costs of goods of

*Fyodor I. Kushnirsky argues that Soviet inflation may not be the significant problem for individual consumers or the state that it is sometime made out to be in Western analyses ("Inflation—Soviet Style," *Problems of Communism* 33 [January-February 1984], 48–53).

Table 10.4 CHANGING RUSSIAN—SOVIET CONSUMPTION PATTERNS, 1913–1985

	1913	1950	1960	1965	1970	1975	1980	1985
Food Consumption (kilograms consumed annually per capita)								
Meat	29	26	40	41	48	57	58	61
Vegetables	40	51	70	72	82	87	97	102
Grain products	200	172	164	156	149	141	138	133
Potatoes	114	241	143	142	130	120	109	104
Non-Foodstuff Consumption (per capita)								
Fabric (square meters)	13.4	16.5	26.1	26.5	30.4	32.5	34.7	37.1
Shoes (pairs)	0.4	1.1	1.9	2.4	3.0	3.2	3.2	3.2
Stock of Consumer Durables (items per 100 families)								
Radios	—	—	46	59	72	79	85	96
Televisions	—	—	8	24	51	74	85	97
Refrigerators	—	—	4	11	32	61	86	91
Washers	—	—	4	21	52	65	70	70
Vacuum cleaners	—	—	3	7	12	18	29	39

Source: Russia, Tsentral'noe statisticheskoe upravlenie, *Narodnoe Khoziaistvo SSSR v 1922–1972 gg.* (Moscow: Statistika, 1972), 372–373; *Narodnoe khoziaistvo SSSR, 1922–1982: Iubileinyi statisticheskii ezhegodnik* (Moscow: Finansy i Statistika, 1982), 448; *Narodnoe khoziaistvo SSSR v 1985 g.* (Moscow: Finansy i Statistika, 1986), 445–446.

higher quality are not entirely offset by higher sales prices. According to the State Quality Inspectorate, between 25 and 40 percent of basic household appliances are defective when they come off the production line. As the Soviet population has become more affluent, it has also become more conscious of style. In response, the regime has established the All-Union Scientific Research Institute of Consumer Demand and Market Conditions to study public demand for consumer goods and to undertake market studies. Yet, factory managers have as little incentive to alter production in response to change in tastes as they do to produce high-quality items, since they bear little of the responsibility for the sale of their goods.[57]

The increased production of consumer durables has resulted in some problems. More complaints about the quality of retail outlets and service have been aired in the media. Complaints have also been raised about the inadequacies of repair service. In response, the regime has periodically encouraged private activity in the area of consumer services—a right guaranteed under the 1977 Constitution (Article 17). Yet the shortage of spare parts (for no factories manufacture spare parts for sale to the public) feeds the black market, where one might purchase parts stolen from a factory.

In short, it will not be a simple matter for the Soviet Union to continue to raise the living standard of its population. If the growth of the Soviet economy depends significantly on increases in labor productivity, then, judging from the policies to improve the standard of living, growth may, indeed, be increasingly difficult to achieve.

THE FUTURE OF THE SOVIET ECONOMY

It is unclear in the late 1980s whether the Soviet economy will overcome its present problems or be overwhelmed by them.[58] Both the "Guidelines for the Economic and Social Development of the USSR for 1986–1990 and for the Period Ending in the Year 2000" and the new Party Program describe the Party's primary task as "accelerating the country's social and economic development." And indeed, "acceleration" is fundamental to the plans for Mikhail Gorbachev. Acceleration, the Party Program argues, requires that

> . . . every enterprise and branch will have to be reoriented toward full utilization of the qualitative factors of economic growth as a top priority. . . . By the end of the year 2000, the country's productive potential is to be doubled, and the fundamental qualitative renewal of this potential is to take place.[59]

How to achieve this acceleration is the issue on which much of Soviet politics currently turns. Whether formulas of the Party Program will be enough to solve the Soviet Union's economic ills and whether the Party can find the political consensus and the political will to make more substantial changes remain to be seen.

The options available to the Soviet leadership to combat its economic problems span the spectrum from doing nothing to radical reform.[60] At the one extreme, radical or "transformational" reforms that change the structure of the Soviet economic system would address the structural causes of Soviet economic problems. In the analysis of E. A. Hewitt of The Brookings Institution:

> [C]entral planners would abandon their attempts to control the daily operations of enterprises; the enterprises themselves would decide what to produce and how, from whom to buy inputs, and to whom to sell outputs. Prices—including exchange and interest rates—would be allowed to fluctuate . . . [These reforms would force] both enterprises and workers to worry about their ability to produce products that customers actually want.[61]

In Western analyses, the Hungarian "New Economic Mechanism" is frequently cited as a model for the Soviet future. This model would maintain state ownership of factories and an activist state that provides public goods such as health care, but would allow many of the production and sales decisions currently determined at the center to devolve upon producers and a quasimarket mechanism. In the estimation of many American specialists, this type of radical transformation is the only way in which Soviet economic problems can be solved. As Robert W. Campbell of Indiana University has argues, "Tinkering with details will not suffice . . . ."[62]

Such radical reforms have been discussed by Soviet economists for many years. Criticisms of the detailed involvement of planners and ministerial officials in the operations of enterprises are a recurring theme. Some reformers have even proposed "a major expansion of the private sector, including what might be dubbed 'privatization' of some consumer goods outputs"—perhaps by "leasing out small stores 'on a contract basis' "—and private "technology input firms." Some of these reforms have been the objects of experiments in Eastern Europe, and have received favorable comment in the Soviet press.[63]

Gorbachev has apparently listened to these reformers, some of whom, such as Abel G. Aganbegian, serve as his close advisors. The sphere for economic activity outside the state-owner sector has been widened. Legislation has legalized individual and family-owned economic undertakings, such as repair or taxi services, as long as these are spare-time activities; and it now permits establishment of cooperatives to provide some consumer and food services. But Gorbachev's proposals for change touch the very heart of the state-owned sector as well: To the June 1987 Central Committee Plenum he proposed that state enterprises be given greater autonomy and that prices be permitted to fluctuate with the market or interenterprise negotiations. The Central Committee adopted Gorbachev's major principles as guidelines for reform in its resolution "On the Tasks of the Party in the Fundamental Restructuring of Economic Administration." The adoption of the Law on State Enterprises at the June 1987 session of the Supreme Soviet appeared to be an important first step in the implementation of this reform. But Gorbachev seems to have in mind a still more radical expansion of enterprise autonomy (and risk). He seems to have embraced the proposals that the enterprises should lose their guaranteed market position and be permitted to go bankrupt when unprofitable and that enterprises should have control over their labor costs and be permitted to release unproductive workers. Against these threats of economic penalties Gorbachev's plans balance the incentive of higher incomes for enterprise managers and productive workers. Whether Gorbachev will be able to implement his plan by his target date of 1991—or at all—is still uncertain.

The obstacles to structural reform are high. Powerful vested interests within the ministerial apparatus and with direct access to the Politburo and Secretariat resist changes that would decrease their power. Central Committee Secretary Egor Ligachev has warned that reform of the Soviet economy must "take place within the framework of scientific socialism, without any shifts to a market economy or private property." Managers do not universally welcome the additional responsibility that would devolve upon them in such reforms. Many lack the managerial skills appropriate to a decentralized or market-oriented economy. And many Soviet leaders, who frequently appear to discount the value of long-term relative to short-term production, may find transformational change unattractive since it would probably lead to profound short-term dislocations and would disrupt production. Nor may they find the "costs" of a market orientation (such as unemployment) to be more acceptable than the costs of a command economy. Reflecting his frustration over such opposition, Gorbachev lamented to the June 1986 Central Committee Plenum that "inertia" was "still strong" in the economy and that it had been "naive to expect that the lags and shortcomings that had been accumulating for years could be overcome in only a few months."[64]

A likely outcome of compromise between the reforms and conservatives is a path that lies between the extremes of radical transformation and inaction–that is, moderate or "tinkering" reform that does not touch the structural causes of current economic problems but changes those policies that exacerbate them. The most modest of these would be personnel changes to find more efficient and innovative ministerial and managerial leaders. Thus, Gorbachev upon taking office replaced many ministers who had been accused of corruption or production failures. Equally modest is the recent exhortation for discipline and productivity and the campaign against alcohol abuse.[65] A slightly more ambitious reform would be tinkering with the success indicators of managers. For example, managers have recently been required to fulfill their plans for technological development or lose a quarter or more of their bonuses.[66] Reforms such as these, however, simply compound the number of indicators that burden the manager without changing the hierarchical structure that divorces decision making from production. More ambitious still are changes in the allocation of investment funds. Reallocation of the vast sums invested in military R&D and procurement to the civilian economy would dramatically expand the resources available to the latter. Expanded investment in consumer goods would raise labor productivity, as would investment in advanced technologies, such as Gorbachev's program of computerization. (Gorbachev's first Five-Year Plan [1986–1990], for example, proposes directing more investment funds toward replacement of decaying capital at the expense of new construction.) But these reallocations must come at the expense of vested interests that have so far had the power to resist major sacrifices. Most ambitious among these tinkering reforms are proposals for structural changes within the ministerial hierarchy. The production associations fall within this category, as do the recent experiment with "superministries" to coordinate among existing ministries and the plans to eliminate industrial associations. Limited experimentation with economic regionalization through territorial-production complexes of enterprise (and in some cases farms too) envisions a still more ambitious reorganization and transfer of decision-making authority bordering on structural reform. All of these reforms, however, seek to maintain growth without true structural changes in the centralized command economy.

Ironically, moderate reform of the Soviet economy may be doomed to failure. The University of California economist Gregory Grossman has argued persuasively that

> a command system is "locally stable" on a continuum from command to market institutions. Especially under taut resource commitments . . . the introduction of market-type arrangements at selected points will worsen, not improve, economic performance. . . . Thus, the central authorities, out of enlightened self-interest, must oppose the effect of limited decentralization and, in the end, the decentralization itself as well.[67]

Thus, moderate reform may only lead back to the status quo.

Continuation of the economic status quo may be a risky strategy for the Soviet leadership. Robert Campbell has argued that this path might permit the Soviet economy to "muddle through its most pressing problems. It may be, as Campbell argues, that an annual growth rate of 2 to 2.5 percent can be sustained without political repercussions. Yet if growth remains slow, the political conflict over trade-offs within a more nearly static store of investment funds may become more intense. And failure to continue to provide ever-higher living standards may be seen as a breach of Soviet regime's social contract with its people.[68] Leonid Brezhnev seemed to be aware of this when he told the 26th Party Congress in 1981,

The problem is to create a really modern sector producing consumer goods and services for the population which meet their demands. In concluding this point, I would like to consider it as more than a purely economic problem, and pose the question in broader terms. The things we are speaking of—food, consumer goods, services—are issues in the daily life of millions and millions of people. The store, the cafeteria, the laundry, the dry cleaners are places people visit every day. What can they buy? How are they treated? How are they spoken to? How much time do they spend on all kinds of daily cares? The people will judge our work in large measure by how these questions are solved. They will judge strictly, exactingly. And that, comrades, we must remember.[69]

If for a sizeable segment of the Soviet population the legitimacy of the Soviet regime rests on its ability to "deliver the goods," then the failure to do this may portend difficulties well beyond the narrow realm of economics.[70]

NOTES

1. *Pravda*, 7 March 1986.
2. On the development of Western research on Soviet-type economies, see Roger A. Clarke, "The Study of Soviet-Type Economies: Some Trends and Conclusions," *Soviet Studies* 35 (October 1983), 525–532. For an interesting discussion of nomenclature to describe the Soviet economy, see John Howard Wilhelm, "The Soviet Union Has an Administered, Not a Planned, Economy," *Soviet Studies* 37 (January 1985), 118–130.
3. V. I. Lenin, "Groziashchaia katastrofa i kak s nei borot'sia" ["The Impending Crisis and How to Combat It"], in *Polnoe sobranie sochinenii,* 5th ed. (Moscow: Politicheskaia Literatura, 1962), 34:161.
4. V. I. Lenin, *Gosudarstvo i revoliutsiia [State and Revolution],* in *Polnoe sobranie sochinenii,* 5th ed., (Moscow: Politicheskaia Literatura, 1962), 33:50.
5. V. I. Lenin, "Uderzhat' li Bol'sheviki gosudarstvennuiu vlast'?" ["Can the Bolsheviks Retain State Power?"], in *Polnoe sobranie sochinenii,* 5th ed. (Moscow: Politicheskaia Literatura, 1962), 34:306–308.
6. This description of the development of Soviet economic institutions and policies prior to 1928 draws heavily upon Alec Nove, *An Economic History of the U.S.S.R.,* rev. ed. (New York: Penguin Books, 1982), 68–82. Compare the analysis of Peter Wiles, *The Political Economy of Communism* (London: Blackwell, 1963). Other discussions of the development of the Soviet economy include Alexander Erlich, *The Soviet Industrialization Debate* (Cambridge, Mass.: Harvard University Press, 1960); and Maurice Dobb, *Soviet Economic Development Since 1917,* 3d ed. (London: Routledge and Kegan Paul, 1966). An important interpretation placing the Russian experience in perspective is Alexander Gerschenkron, *Economic Backwardness in Historical Perspective* (Cambridge, Mass.: Harvard University Press, 1962).
7. For a discussion of the development of controls over management, see Merle Fainsod, *How Russia Is Ruled,* rev. ed. (Cambridge, Mass.: Harvard University Press, 1967), 503–525. Also see Jeremy R. Azrael, *Managerial Power and Soviet Politics* (Cambridge, Mass.: Harvard University Press, 1967); David Granick, *The Red Executive* (New York: Doubleday, 1961); and Blair A. Ruble, *Soviet Trade Unions: Their Development in the 1970s* (Cambridge, England: Cambridge University Press, 1981).

8. Fainsod, 386–420.

9. Jerry F. Hough and Merle Fainsod, *How the Soviet Union Is Governed* (Cambridge, Mass.: Harvard University Press, 1979), 390; Raymond Hutchings, *Soviet Economic Development*, 2d ed. (New York: New York University Press, 1981), 149. See also Joseph S. Berliner, "Planning and Management" in Abram Bergson and Herbert S. Levine, eds., *The Soviet Economy: Toward the Year 2000* (London: Allen & Unwin, 1983), 358–360. On the implementation of the Party-state decree of July 12, 1979, see Morris Bornstein, "Improving the Soviet Economic Mechanism," *Soviet Studies* 37 (January 1985), 1–30.

10. Fainsod, 409, 415.

11. Hutchings, 161–162.

12. Fainsod, 507.

13. Hough and Fainsod, 390–391.

14. Joseph S. Berliner, *Factory and Manager in the USSR* (Cambridge, Mass.: Harvard University Press, 1957), 75–113.

15. Berliner, 182–230. *Blat* has been widely described in popular accounts of the Soviet Union such as Hedrick Smith, *The Russians,* rev. ed. (New York: Ballantine Books, 1984), 106–134; and Robert G. Kaiser, *Russia: The Power and the People,* rev. ed. (New York: Washington Square Press, 1984), 342–387.

16. Quoted in Fainsod, 513–514.

17. Berliner, 114–181.

18. *Pravda,* 2 July 1959.

19. Berliner, 243–247.

20. Michael Kaser, "Economic Policy," in Archie Brown and Michael Kaser, eds., *Soviet Policy for the 1980s* (Bloomington, Ind.: Indiana University Press, 1982), 187.

21. Abraham Katz, *The Politics of Economic Reform in the Soviet Union* (New York: Praeger, 1972); Moshe Lewin, *Political Undercurrents in Soviet Economic Debates: From Bukharin to the Modern Reformers* (Princeton, N.J.: Princeton University Press, 1974); Karl W. Ryavec, *Implementation of Soviet Economic Reforms: Political, Organizational, and Social Processes* (New York: Praeger, 1975).

22. Michael Kaser, "The Economy: A General Assessment," in Archie Brown and Michael Kaser, eds., *The Soviet Union Since the Fall of Khrushchev* (New York: Free Press, 1975), 198.

23. Gertrude E. Schroeder, "Soviet Economic 'Reform' Decrees: More Steps on the Treadmill," in Congress, Joint Economic Committee, *Soviet Economy in the 1980s* (Washington, D.C.: GPO, 1982), I:65–88; Gertrude E. Schroeder, "The Soviet Economy on a Treadmill of Reforms," U.S., Congress, Joint Economic Committee, *Soviet Economy in a Time of Change* (Washington, D.C.: GPO, 1979), I:312–340.

24. Borris Rumer, "Realities of Gorbachev's Economic Program," *Problems of Communism* 35 (May-June 1986), 22, 25. On the changes in economic policies under Andropov and Chernenko, see Fyodor I. Kushnirsky, "The Limits of Soviet Economic Reform," *Problems of Communism* 33 (July-August 1984), 33–43.

25. For an interesting counter-historical investigation that asks whether the Soviet economy would have performed better without the command economy, see Mischa Gisser and Paul Jonas, "Soviet Growth in Absence of Centralized Planning: A Hypothetical Alternative," *Journal of Political Economy* 82 (March-April 1974), 333–352.

26. Robert W. Campbell, "The Economy," in Robert F. Byrnes, ed., *After Brezhnev: Sources of Soviet Conduct in the 1980s* (Bloomington, Ind.: Indiana University Press, 1983), 70. See also Abram Bergson, "Soviet Economic Slowdown and the 1981—85 Plan," *Problems of Communism* 30 (May-June 1981), 24—36. Two very useful over-

views of current economic problems and policies are the collected essays in Bergson and Levine and those in U.S., Congress, Joint Economic Committee, *Soviet Economy in the 1980s.*

27. For a summary of the current debate over the causes of this decline, see Arthur W. Wright, "Soviet Economic Planning and Performance," in Stephen F. Cohen, Alexander Rabinowitz, and Robert Sharlet, eds.,*The Soviet Union Since Stalin* (Bloomington, Ind.: Indiana University Press, 1980), 125—129. Some recent, readable discussions of this matter include Jan Winiecki, "Are Soviet-Type Economies Entering an Era of Long-Term Decline?" *Soviet Studies* 38 (July 1986), 325–348; and Boris Rumer, "Structural Imbalance in the Soviet Economy" *Problems of Communism* 33 (July-August 1984), 24–32. On the problems of declining growth in the labor force and the reserves of energy, see Murray Feshbach, "Population and Labor Force," and Robert W. Campbell, "Energy," in Bergson and Levine, 79–111, 191–217.

28. For a report on a recent experiment permitting managers to economize on their labor force, see Henry Norr, "Shchekino: Another Look," *Soviet Studies* 38 (April 1986), 141–169.

29. Quoted in Karl W. Ryavec, "Economic Reform: Prospects and Possibilities," in Joseph L. Nogee, ed., *Soviet Politics: Russia After Brezhnev* (New York: Praeger, 1985), 190; George R. Feiwel, "Economic Performance and Reforms in the Soviet Union," in Donald R. Kelley, ed., *Soviet Politics in the Brezhnev Era* (New York: Praeger, 1980), 70–103. See also Boris Rumer, "Soviet Investment Policy: Unresolved Problems," *Problems of Communism* 31 (September-October 1982), 53.

30. On the problems of technological innovation, see Joseph S. Berliner, *The Innovation Decision in Soviet Industry* (Cambridge, Mass.: MIT Press, 1976); Ronald Amann and Julian Cooper, eds., *Industrial Innovation in the Soviet Union* (New Haven, Conn.: Yale University Press, 1982); and Bruce Parrott, *Politics and Technology in the Soviet Union* (Cambridge, Mass.: MIT Press, 1983). See also Alec Nove, *The Soviet Economy: An Introduction*, 2d rev. ed. (New York: Praeger, 1968), 183–184.

31. Robert W. Campbell, "On the Theory of Economic Administration," in Henry Rosovsky, ed., *Industrialization in Two Systems: Essays in Honor of Alexander Gerschenkron* (New York: Wiley, 1966), 186–203.

32. Andreas Tenson, "Obstacles to Scientific and Technical Progress in the USSR," *Radio Liberty Research Bulletin* 281/82 (July 12, 1982), 1.

33. U.S. Congress, Joint Economic Committee, *Soviet Military Economic Relations* (Washington, D.C.: GPO, 1983), 138–140, 190;U.S. Arms Control and Disarmament Agency, *World Military Expenditures and Arms Transfers, 1985* (Washington, D.C.: GPO, 1985), 81, 85.

34. Hutchings, 290.

35. U.S. Central Intelligence Agency, *The World Factbook, 1986* (Washington, D.C.: CIA, 1986), 227, 256, 258.

36. Central Intelligence Agency, 227, 256, 258.

37. Campbell, "Economy," 100–101.

38. Quoted in James R. Millar, "Post-Stalin Agriculture and Its Future," in Cohen, Rabinowitz, and Sharlet, eds., *Soviet Union Since Stalin,* 135.

39. U.S.S.R. Tsentral'noe Statisticheskoe Upravlenie (Ts.S.U.), *Narodnoe khoziaistvo SSSR 1922–1982: iubileinyi statisticheskii ezhegodnik* (Moscow: Finansy i Statistika, 1982), 225–226; Tsentral'noe Statisticheskoe Upravlenie (Ts.S.U.), *Narodnoe khoziaistvo SSSR v 1985 g.* (Moscow: Finansy i Statistika, 1986), 207, 236.

40. Nove, 242. Other useful surveys are Erich Strauss, *Soviet Agriculture in Perspective* (London: Allen & Unwin, 1969); and Lazar Volin, *A Century of Russian Agriculture* (Cambridge, Mass.: Harvard University Press, 1970). Also see the essays by D. Gale Johnson, "Agricultural Organization and Management," and Douglas B. Diamond, Lee W. Bettis, and Robert E. Ramsson, "Agricultural Production,", in Bergson and Levine, 112–177.

41. Millar, 143; Ts. S. U., *Narodnoe khoziaistvo, 1922–82,* 227.

42. Alec Nove, "Agriculture," in Brown and Kaser, eds., *Soviet Policy for the 1980s,* 170-185; Millar, 145–150.

43. Nove, "Agriculture," 173, 175, 178, 183.

44. Nove, "Agriculture," 175.

45. Campbell, "Economy," 112.

46. On consumer welfare, see Gertrude E. Schroeder, "Consumption," in Bergson and Levine, 311–349.

47. Nove, *Economic History,* 206; Janet G. Chapman, "Consumption," in Abram Bergson and Simon Kuznetz, eds., *Economic Trends in the Soviet Union* (Cambridge, Mass.: Harvard University Press, 1963), 236–240.

48. Central Intelligence Agency, 227, 256, 258.

49. United Nations, Department of International Economic and Statistical Affairs, Statistical Office, *Statistical Yearbook, 1982* (New York: United Nations, 1985); Carol R. Nechemias, "Welfare in the Soviet Union: Health Care, Housing, and Personal Consumption," in Gordon B. Smith, *Public Policy and Administration in the Soviet Union* (New York: Praeger, 1980), 181. On health care, see Aaron Trehub, "Quality of Soviet Health Care Under Attack," *Radio Liberty Research Bulletin* RL 289/86 (July 28, 1986); and David E. Powell, "The Emerging Health Crisis in the Soviet Union," *Current History* 84 (October 1985), 325.

50. Nechemias, 184–192; Ts. S. U., *Narodnoe khoziaistvo v 1985 g.,* 367, 426. On Soviet housing problems and policies, see Alfred J. DeMaio, Jr., *Soviet Urban Housing: Problems and Prospects* (New York: Holt, Rinehart and Winston, 1974); Warren Zimmerman, "Comparing the US and USSR on Social and Economic Issues," *Current Policy,* No. 905 (Washington, D.C.: U.S. Department of State, January 1987), 3.

51. Ts. S. U., *Narodnoe khoziaistvo v 1985 g.,* 399, 412. On Soviet welfare policies, see Bernice W. Madison, *Social Welfare in the Soviet Union* (Stanford, Calif: Stanford University Press, 1968); and for a comparative developmental approach, Gaston V. Rimlinger, *Welfare Policy and Industrialization in Europe, America, and Russia* (New York: Wiley, 1971). On life expectancy, see Murray Feshbach, "The Soviet Union: Population Trends and Dilemmas," *Population Bulletin* 37 (August 1982), 30–36.

52. Ts. S. U., *Narodnoe khoziaistvo v 1985 g.,* 397. For a speculative discussion of Gorbachev's policies regarding welfare and economic growth, see Walter D. Connor, "Social Policy Under Gorbachev," *Problems of Communism* 35 (July-August 1986), 31–46.

53. Ts. S. U., *Narodnoe khoziaistvo v 1985 g.,* 448. See also Jane P. Shapiro, "Soviet Consumer Policy in the 1970s: Plan and Performance," in Kelley, 104.

54. Nove, *Economic History,* 381; Kaser, "Economic Policy", 192.

55. Kaser, "Economic Policy," 190–191.

56. Shapiro, 115.

57. Shapiro, 115–116.

58. On alternative futures for the Soviet economy, see Mark M. Hopkins and Michael Kennedy, *Comparisons and Implications of Alternative Views of the Soviet Economy* (R-3075-NA) (Santa Monica, Calif.: Rand Corporation, 1984).

59. *Pravda,* 7 March 1986.
60. Joseph S. Berliner, "Managing the USSR Economy: Alternative Models," *Problems of Communism* 32 (January-February 1983), 40–56.; Ryavec, "Economic Reform"; Campbell, "The Economy", 112–121; Alec Nove, *Political Economy and Soviet Socialism* (London: Allen & Unwin, 1979), 156–157.
61. Ed. A. Hewett, "Economic Reform in the Soviet Union," *Brookings Review* 2 (Spring 1984), 11. See also Nove, *Political Economy,* 156–157; Feiwel, 96–101; and Ryavec, "Economic Reform," 184–185.
62. Campbell, "The Economy,"108, 110.
63. Ryavec, "Economic Reform," 194–199.
64. *Sovetskaia Rossiia,* 29 June 1985; *Izvestiia,* 22 June 1986. On the obstacles to reform, see Ronald Amann, "The Political and Social Implications of Economic Reform in the USSR," in Hans-Hermann Hohnmann, Alec Nove, and Heinrich Vogel, eds., *Economics and Politics in the USSR: Patterns of Interdependence* (Boulder, Colo.: Westview Press, 1986), 125–145; Ryavec, "Economic Reform," 197; Marshall I. Goldman, *Gorbachev's Challenge: Economic Reform in the Age of High Technology* (New York: Norton, 1987) 227–262.
65. For an assessment of the discipline campaign based on the experience of the Soviet railways, see Vladimir Kontorovich, "Discipline and Growth in the Soviet Economy," *Problems of Communism* 34 (November-December 1985), 18–31.
66. *Pravda,* 24 September 1983.
67. Wright, 122–123.
68. Campbell, "The Economy," 120, 187.
69. Quoted in Campbell, "The Economy," 74.
70. Stephen White, "Economic Performance and Communist Legitimacy," *World Politics* 38 (April 1986), 462–482; Seweryn Bialer, *Stalin's Successors: Leadership, Stability, and Change in the Soviet Union* (Cambridge, England: Cambridge University Press, 1980), 283–305

chapter 11

Justice and Injustices in the Soviet Legal System

Among the most important measures of the performance of a political system is justice. The American philosopher John Rawls has written of the *primacy* of justice: "Justice is the first virtue of social institutions, as truth is of systems of thought."[1] That is, political institutions should be evaluated first of all by the measure of justice they ensure. An inquiry into the justice of Soviet social institutions, while much needed, would go well beyond the limits of this book. And so the discussion here is far more circumscribed. Fundamental to modern notions of justice are the sometimes conflicting demands for procedural fairness and for equality of outcomes. Central to the first is justice in the legal proceedings of the state—justice in the colloquial sense. The second notion of justice is more likely to be concerned with distributive justice through equality among key ascriptive subgroups of society—between the sexes and among ethnic or racial groups. The Soviet model of development claims that it alone offers a certain path to the realization of these values in society. It is this claim that this and the next chapter will assess.

LAW AND THE TRANSFORMATION OF SOVIET SOCIETY

At the heart of Western legal procedures is law. But this most important element of justice in the Western conception does not play the same independent role in Soviet society.[2] Both Russian and Marxist legal traditions have conspired to give Soviet law a different role than it plays in most Western societies.

The Russian Empire adopted many of the superficial practices of Western justice, but only belatedly and without the principles that made those practices guarantees of justice. The codification of law began fairly late with the publication of Mikhail Speransky's 18-volume work in 1832. An independent court system was not established until 1864. And even then the Empire did not adopt the principle of a unified law or legal system for all classes. Instead, it initially excluded the majority of the population—the peasantry—from the codes of 1832 and later established separate judicial institutions for them with the creation in 1864 of the *volost'* courts and the imposition in 1889 of *zemskii nachal'nik* (land captain) control over the judicial functions of the village. Nor did it adopt the notion that the state itself was subordinate to fundamental principles of law. And the Empire tended to reject what it saw as the Western preoccupation with legalisms, declaring that concern with the minutiae of legal procedure often sacrificed justice.[3]

Marxist-Leninist ideology gave the Soviet leaders no reason to assign law a more exalted role. Early Marxists saw law as an attribute of class society, during the stage of development in which the state was an instrument of class domination. Friedrich Engels had written in *Anti-Duehring,* "The economic structure of society always forms the real basis from which, in the last analysis, is to be explained the whole superstructure of legal and political institutions. . . ."[4] In 1890, he described law as "the blunt, unmitigated, unaltered expression of the domination of a class."[5] When the state withers away and society assumes the responsibility for governing itself, there will be no need for law. As P. I. Stuchka, the first President of the USSR Supreme Court, wrote in 1927, "Communism means not the victory of socialist law, but the victory of socialism over any law, since with the abolition of classes with their antagonistic interest, law will die out altogether."[6] Thus, the early Bolsheviks viewed law neither as a permanent feature of human society nor as a limitation on all legitimate power, but as a transitory form by which a governing class constrains its enemies.

Nonetheless, law and the transformation of Soviet society since 1917 have been intimately intertwined. Law has become an instrument for remaking humankind and the socialist world in the transition to communism. The Soviets refer to this as the dynamic function of law. In particular, law must play an educational function (*vospitatel'naia rol'*), assisting the Party in the education of Soviet citizens to their obligations in a constantly changing society. According to one of the leading American specialists on Soviet law, Harvard Law School's Harold Berman,

> The subject of law, legal man, is treated less as an independent possessor of rights and duties, who knows what he wants, than as a dependent member of the collective group, a youth, whom the law must not only protect against the consequences of his own ignorance but must also guide and train and discipline. . . .
>
> The Soviet citizen is considered to be a member of a growing, unfinished, still immature society, which is moving toward a new and higher phase of development.[7]

Soviet legal procedure is designed to maximize the educational function of law. For example, court sessions do not necessarily take place in a courtroom, but may be held in factories or places of residence with the active participation of neighbors and co-workers. Judges are far less concerned with remaining neutral in these cases, and they may play an active role in lecturing, instructing, and cajoling the participants. According to Berman, "the judge plays the part of a parent or guardian; indeed, the whole legal system is parental."[8] George Feifer illustrates the educational role of judges in the proceedings of one court.

> The judge clears her throat, flips the pages of the record and finds her place with a stout finger. . . . "Have you been reprimanded for truancy at the factory?"
> "Yes"
> "Absent from work with no good reason—that is your attitude toward your work, toward your responsibilities. And rebukes for appearing drunk in the factory—did you get any of these?"
> He does not answer.
> "Did you?"
> "I think . . . well, yes."
> "How many?"
> "I don't know. I don't remember."
> "Four?"
> "Maybe. I didn't count. Sometimes it was on a holiday, when everybody was drunk."
> "Four reprimands! That's an unheard-of attitude toward work and life in our socialist society. Disgraceful! It started with disinterest in work; then drinking and hooliganism—and led from that to stealing; of course it led to stealing, naturally to stealing—do you understand that? Why were you repeatedly late? Why did you continue to violate work discipline in spite of your warnings? You ignored them. You drank on the job. You were truant. And then you stole. Logical."[9]

Such reprimands and the effort to reform the accused through lecturing are an important part of Soviet legal procedure. Its object is not simply the accused, but all those in attendance. Thus, the procedure encourages popular participation in the judicial process. This is enshrined in Article 162 of the Constitution of the USSR, which guarantees that "Representatives of public organizations and of work collectives may take part in civil and criminal proceedings." People's assessors sit alongside the judges so that citizens participate in the decision of the case and enforcement of the law. Social accusers and social defenders (citizens who know the accused and can speak to his or her vices and virtues) are brought in as well.

Due to its educational role, Soviet law tends to be more inclusive than law in Western societies. It is concerned with many features of personal life that in the West would be considered outside the realm of law. "Anti-parasite" laws, for example, proscribe individual avoidance of socially useful work. (Of course, Soviet law also is more inclusive because the economy is socialized.)

The use of law as an instrument of change has not been a constant in Soviet history. Indeed, Soviet law and its place in Soviet society have been affected profoundly by the transformations along the road to communism. Paradoxically, the importance of law, even though officially an instrument of change, has varied inversely with the pace of change. At the time of the Revolution, the new Bolshevik leadership eliminated the court system and legal profession of the *ancien régime.* Yet, the absence of a centralized legal system crippled the new regime's efforts to deal with crime, which jumped rapidly during the Civil War. (By 1918, robbery in Moscow had reached rates 10 to 15 times those in 1913.) Moreover, the fight against the opponents of the new regime demanded some mechanism to dispense "revolutionary justice." The new regime responded by reestablishing a court system, creating a two-track judicial system of People's Courts under the control of local soviets to adjudicate routine civil and criminal cases and of "revolutionary tribunals" to decide political cases on the basis of revolutionary consciousness. After the Civil War these were integrated in a common hierarchy of courts. The centralized legal system was initially a pragmatic response to pressing problems, not an expression of firm commitment to the principle that law and a court system are fundamental parts of a socialist state.

As the pace of change slowed, the New Economic Policy assigned law a slightly more exalted position. With the rejuvenation of the private sector, the need for law and judicial procedures became apparent. Thus, the New Economic Policy brought a new effort at codification beginning in 1922, with a Judiciary Act establishing the court system and with codes of criminal, land, labor, civil, and family law as well as civil and criminal procedure. Yet the Party still treated the legal system not as a permanent guarantee of individual rights or as a constraint on arbitrary government action, but as an instrument of state power and class rule in the transition period of the NEP.

In the early years of Stalin's rule (during the period of most rapid transformation), the role of law declined once again in both theory and practice. The transition to socialism, in the official theories of the day, was "a time of rapid changes which could not be crystallized in the form of a legal system but must be shaped by ever-shifting social-economic policy."[10] Even as the role of the state and as social control increased, law and the legal system declined in importance, for many of their functions were usurped by Party, police, and administrative organs.

Once the pace of Stalinist revolutions began to slow, however—and particularly as Stalin became increasingly concerned with preserving his system against reform—the role of law began to grow. In the second half of the 1930s a profound change took place in the official theories, and even some of the practices, of Soviet law. Since the death of Stalin, this "juridicization" of Soviet society has continued.

SOVIET LEGAL INSTITUTIONS AND PROCEDURES

In an important sense, justice in the Soviet Union is administered: Law is a series of regulations that are subordinate to policy. Courts, law schools, judges, and lawyers all function as parts of an integrated system of administrative hierarchies under the close scrutiny of the Communist Party.[11]

The Form of Soviet Law

The corpus of Soviet law or legal acts (*pravovyi akt*) is composed of constitutional law, statutes, and substatutory rules (see Table 11.1).[12] The constitutions of the USSR, the union republics, and the autonomous republics establish the institutions and set down the procedures of the state. According to its Article 173, the all-union Constitution has "supreme legal force. All laws and other acts of state bodies shall be promulgated on the basis of and in conformity with it."

Statutory law in the Soviet Union includes fundamentals of legislation, codes, and statutes. The fundamentals of legislation (*osnovy zakonodatel'stva*) enacted by the all-union Supreme Soviet establish guidelines for the legislative acts of all subordinate soviets. These include such acts as fundamentals for water law, marriage and family legislation, and criminal procedure. Codes (*svod zakonov*) are systematic bodies of law enacted by the union-republic supreme soviets to regulate social action in broad areas such as criminal law, civil law, and labor law. The statutes (*zakon*) of the supreme soviets of the USSR and union republics include both organic laws that regulate the procedures of state organs and ordinary legislation on current policy issues.[13]

More numerous than fundamental laws, codes, and statutes are the substatutory rules, including edicts, decrees or resolutions, and regulations. The all-union and union-republic presidia are empowered to issue edicts (*ukaz*). Normative edicts—that is, those issued by the Presidium exercising the legislative power of the Supreme Soviet—have the binding force of law until the next session of the Supreme Soviet, but must be enacted as statutes at that session. Non-normative edicts are the consequence of a Presidium exercising its exclusive powers; they do not change statutory law and so do not require later enactment by the Supreme Soviet. Resolutions (*postanovlenie*) of the Supreme Soviet and Presidium tend to regulate procedural matters. Decrees (*postanovlenie*) issued by the Council of Ministers regulate matters such as economic administration and cultural development within the overall laws passed by the Supreme Soviet. These decrees are, in fact, the most common of all-union enactments. Decrees issued by local soviets and their executive committees are formally "binding on all enterprises, institutions, and organizations as well as officials and citizens within the respective soviet's territorial jurisdiction." Lastly, administrative orders or regulations (*rasporiazhenie*) are issued by the all-union and union-republic Councils of Ministers and the executive committees of local soviets to guide their respective agencies in the implementation of the law.[14]

Court opinions play a minor role in the statutory authority of the Soviet legal system and normally are not considered part of Soviet law. The Supreme Court of the USSR may issue guiding explanations that direct lower courts in the application of a law to individual cases. Yet, there is no principle in the Soviet legal tradition of *stare decisis*—that previous decisions are binding in later cases. And there is no judicial review—no power of the courts to declare laws unconstitutional.

The content of these Soviet laws is distinguished by its homogeneity. Formally codes are enacted by the individual union republics. Georgia, for example, has adopted a law that protects the right to make wine at home—a right that does not exist in all republics. Nonetheless, these codes are actually quite uniform in their most important provisions, for they must conform to the guidelines set down in the respective all-union Fundamentals of Legislation.[15]

Table 11.1   LEGAL ACTS OF THE SOVIET STATE

	All-Union	Union-Republic	Local
Soviet	Osnovy zakonodatel'stva Zakon Postanovlenie	Zakon Postanovlenie	Postanovlenie
Presidium	Ukaz Postanovlenie	Ukaz Postanovlenie	
Council of Ministers (or Ispolkom)	Postanovlenie Rasporiazhenie	Postanovlenie Rasporiazhenie	Postanovlenie Rasporiazhenie

Source: "Law of the U.S.S.R. on the Basic Powers of the Krai and Oblast' Soviets of People's Deputies and the Autonomous Oblast' and Autonomous Okrug Soviets of People's Deputies," *Pravda*, 26 June 1980; A. I. Luk'ianov et al., *Sovety narodnykh deputatov: Spravochnik* (Moscow: Politicheskaia Literature, 1984), 135–160.

The Soviet Courts

At the heart of the Soviet legal system are the courts, which are organized as an appellate hierarchy stretching from the local people's courts (*narodnyi sud*) through the oblast' courts and then the supreme courts of the union republics, and finally to the Supreme Court of the USSR in Moscow. The court hierarchy parallels the basic territorial administrative structure of the Soviet state. (See Figure 11.1.)

At the base of this hierarchy is the people's court organized at the city, city-borough, or rural district level. Ninety percent of all cases originate here. The judge that oversees cases at this level is popularly elected for a five-year term. Legally, anyone 25 years of age or older can stand for election. Yet in light of the importance of law as an instrument of moral upbringing and the relative independence inherent in the work of judges, the Party exercises strict control over the nomination of candidates for judicial positions to ensure that those elected are loyal to the Party. In fact, some 95 percent of all judges in the early 1980s were members or candidate members of the Party or Komsomol in recent elections.[16]

There is no jury tradition in the Soviet system; instead the people's court judge is assisted by two people's assessors (*narodnyi zasedatel'*). The assessors are not professional judges, but citizens elected in open meetings of local labor and residential collectives for a term of two and a half years. During two weeks of each year of their term, assessors sit alongside the judge to participate in the decision of cases. Unlike American juries, these lay assessors are not limited to determination of the facts of a case, but may participate in all decisions concerning the case. Normally, however, these laymen appear to defer to the expertise of the judge.[17]

Immediately superior to the people's courts in union republics with oblasts are the oblast' courts or in all other republics the supreme court of the union republic. The judges at these levels are not elected by the citizenry, but by the oblast soviet or union-republic supreme soviet for five-year terms. These courts can be

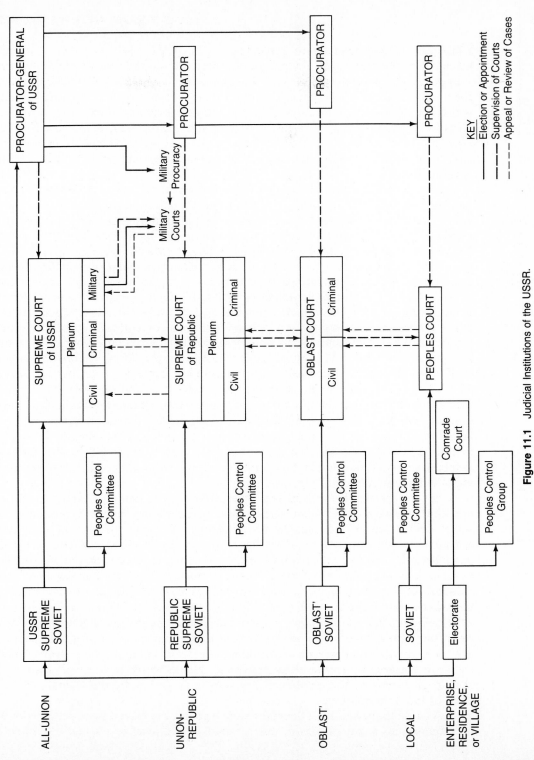

Figure 11.1 Judicial Institutions of the USSR.

KEY
———— Election or Appointment
– – – – Supervision of Courts
------- Appeal or Review of Cases

PROCURATOR-GENERAL of USSR

PROCURATOR

PROCURATOR

PROCURATOR

Military Procuracy

Military Courts

SUPREME COURT of USSR
Plenum
Civil   Criminal   Military

SUPREME COURT of Republic
Plenum
Civil   Criminal

OBLAST COURT
Civil   Criminal

PEOPLES COURT

Peoples Control Committee

Peoples Control Committee

Peoples Control Committee

Peoples Control Committee

Comrade Court

Peoples Control Group

USSR SUPREME SOVIET

REPUBLIC SUPREME SOVIET

OBLAST' SOVIET

SOVIET

Electorate

ALL-UNION

UNION-REPUBLIC

OBLAST'

LOCAL

ENTERPRISE, RESIDENCE, or VILLAGE

tribunals of first instance in important cases. Here also, people's assessors elected to five-year terms by the soviet may sit on the bench alongside the judges. More commonly, however, these courts hear cases on appeal from the people's courts (or from the oblast' court to the union-republic supreme court), which are decided by a three-judge panel without assessors. Each of these courts is divided into civil and criminal divisions, with a Presidium empowered to review the work of each. (In each union-republic court a plenum of the entire court also meets.) Decisions of the union-republic supreme courts are normally considered final.

The Supreme Court of the USSR, the only "federal" court in the regular Soviet legal system, according to Article 153 of the all-union Constitution is "the highest judicial body in the USSR and supervises the administration of justice by the courts of the USSR and Union Republics within the limits established by law." Its membership is elected by the Supreme Soviet to a five-year term and comprises a Chairman, a variable number of deputy chairmen and members, lay assessors, and, as ex officio members, the chairmen of the 15 union-republic supreme courts. (In early 1986 the membership included 2 deputy chairmen and 17 members, in addition to the Chairman, assessors, and ex officio members.) These are divided among civil, criminal, and military divisions, or collegia, for considering individual cases. The Court sits in plenary session to supervise the work of these divisions, review their decisions, or issue guiding interpretations (*rukovodiashchee raz''iasnenie*). It plays principally a supervisory and appellate role, but can serve as a court of first instance in unusually important cases that the Party leadership wants to publicize. (On the rare occasions that the Court exercises original jurisdiction, the presiding officer, or judge, is joined by people's assessors. Otherwise, appeals are heard by three-judge panels.) Appeals to this court cannot be made directly by private parties, but only on the "protest" of the USSR Procurator-General or the Chairman of the Supreme Court itself (although such protests may be made on behalf of a private party).[18]

Separate from this regular legal hierarchy are the comrade courts, arbitration courts, and military tribunals. The first, described in Chapter 5, normally resolve lesser cases of antisocial behavior through organs of popular self-administration in places of residence or work. Property and contract disputes between enterprises, organizations, or state organs are decided by the hierarchy of republic and local courts of arbitration under the supervision and guidance of the all-union *Gosarbitrazh*, which is appointed by and responsible to the Council of Ministers.[19] Military tribunals hear cases involving military personnel (including the KGB). They may also decide cases involving Soviet civilians when they are accused of espionage, acting as accomplices of uniformed personnel, or committing crimes in areas within the Soviet Union where martial law has been declared or areas outside the Soviet Union where Soviet troops are stationed. Decisions by these tribunals are subject to review by the Military Collegium of the Supreme Court.

Alongside, but outside, the court system stands the hierarchy of people's control committees at the all-union, union-republic, and local levels and of people's control groups in villages, enterprises, institutions, and public organizations. These are elected by the respective soviets or work collectives. The committees and groups are expected "to monitor fulfillment of state plans for economic and social development [and] combat violations of state discipline."[20] They play a quasi-judicial function in that they may inspect documents of economic and administrative agencies, order audits of their financial records, issue warnings, forward materials concerning violations to superior administrators or the Procuracy for action, and impose penalties or suspend officials.

The Procuracy

Paralleling the hierarchy of courts is the Procuracy (*Prokuratura*), which is roughly equivalent to an attorney general's office. The Procuracy, according to Article 164 of the Constitution, is invested with "the supreme power of supervision over the strict and uniform observance of laws" by all institutions, officials, and citizens.

The structure of the Procuracy is designed to ensure its independence from the all-union executive-administrative organs and from the union-republic and local organs. The Procurator-General of the USSR is appointed to a five-year term by the Supreme Soviet and is constitutionally responsible to that body, or its Presidium between sessions. This is an appointment in which the Party takes major interest. The Procurator-General then appoints the procurators at the union-republic and oblast' levels for five-year terms; and the union-republic procurators appoint the procurators at the city and raion level, also for five-year terms. This selection is supposed to ensure the appointees' independence and permit the Procuracy to serve as a check on the executive and legislative operations of the state. Each procurator, with assistance of a collegium, presides over the specialized departments that carry on the supervision and investigations within the competence of his or her office. (See Figure 11.2.) About one-eighth of the legal profession is employed by the Procuracy as procurators and another eighth are employed as investigators. Employment by the Procuracy is one of the highest paid of the legal professions and one of the positions most sought after by law students.[21]

Formally charged with guarding socialist legality, the Procuracy performs six major functions.[22]

1. *Prosecution.* It serves as a public prosecutor's office, undertaking the preliminary investigation of crimes and instituting criminal proceedings against those whom the investigations determine should be prosecuted. In the trial, the procurator prosecutes the case on behalf of the state.
2. *Supervision of Judicial Proceedings.* A closely related responsibility is supervising the legality of legal proceedings to ensure that uniform standards of judgment and sentencing are observed by the courts. A procurator who finds that the court has violated procedural norms or has misapplied the substance of law in deciding either a criminal or civil

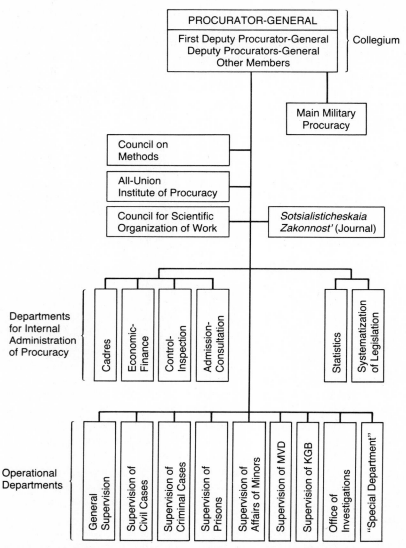

Figure 11.2 Procuracy of USSR. (*Source:* Data from U.S. Central Intelligence Agency, *Directory of Soviet Officials: National Organizations* [Washington, D.C: CIA, 1986].)

case may file a protest with the appellate court immediately superior to the court in question in order to force a review of the case.

3. *Supervision of Legislation.* The Procuracy ensures the conformity of the legislative acts of subordinate levels of government to the laws adopted by the all-union and union-republic governments. A procurator nor-

mally sits as consultant on the local soviet, advising that body on the legality of its draft acts and issuing protests to the soviet immediately superior to one that adopts an illegal decision.

4. *Supervision of Administration.* A closely related responsibility is supervision of the legality of administrative acts in the implementation of decisions. If an administrative organ, enterprise, social organization, or official is found to have engaged in an administrative transgression, the procurator may issue warnings to the transgressor or protests to a superior organ or official. If these go unheeded, the procurator may recommend administrative or criminal sanctions.

5. *Execution of Judicial Judgments.* The Procuracy is responsible for supervising places of detention, ensuring incarceration of those sentenced, overseeing conditions within the prisons, reviewing complaints of prisoners, deciding requests for parole, and supervising the release of prisoners.

6. *Supervision of Police.* The Procuracy supervises the police (both the MVD and KGB), reviewing citizen complaints and filing protests against illegal actions.

The Police

Alongside the courts and Procuracy are the two police organizations: the Ministry of Internal Affairs (the MVD) and the Committee on State Security (the KGB). The police apparatus has undergone important organizational as well as name changes since the creation of the Cheka. Its functions have changed also. During the relatively relaxed period of the NEP, the terror of the police was directed at the political opponents of the regime but spared the mass of the citizenry. With the initiation of the industrialization and collectivization campaigns, however, the targets grew to envelop Nepmen, kulaks, and the intelligentsia, reaching a peak during the Great Terror of the 1930s (see Chapter 3). In July 1934, the People's Commissariat of Internal Affairs (NKVD) was created with expanded responsibilites "for state security, all penal institutions, fire departments, police (militia), convoy troops, frontier guards, troops of internal security, highway administration, and civil registry offices (vital statistics)."[23] Most formal constraints on the NKVD, including the legal and procuratorial limitations, proved hollow. Beginning with World War II the police turned their terror against real and imagined Nazi collaborators in the German-occupied areas of the Soviet Union and against potential opponents to Soviet rule in the East European states occupied by the Red Army. In the second half of the war, the separation of the People's Commissariats (later Ministries) of Internal Affairs (NKVD, MVD) and State Security (NKGB, MGB) permitted the former to specialize in domestic public order and routine crime while the latter focused on political "crimes" and the growing foreign police operations.

Following Stalin's death the new leadership sought to contain the police, for they had good reasons to fear that the apparatus might still be turned against them. According to Merle Fainsod,

A wide-ranging series of reforms unfolded, involving among others, a curbing of the extrajudicial powers of the security police, the reassertion of Party control over the police, the dismantlement of the security police's economic empire, the release of hundreds of thousands of prisoners from the forced-labor camps, and the rationalization of the system of criminal justice.[24]

The MVD since 1954 has been responsible for the regular uniformed police, or *militsiia*. (From 1960 to 1966 the Ministry's functions devolved upon the union-republic ministries; and in the mid-60s it temporarily bore the name Ministry for the Protection of Public Order [MOOP].) As Figure 11.3 suggests, the MVD is responsible for maintaining public order through the *militsiia*, combatting and investigating crime, maintaining the prison system (with the exception of the places of special detention under the control of the KGB), and providing fire protection. More-specialized responsibilities include combatting economic crimes, providing security guards for transportation such as the railways, and maintaining troops to suppress domestic disorders.[25]

The KGB is responsible for both foreign and domestic operations. As shown in Figure 11.4, it combines within one organization responsibilities that in the United States are assumed by the Secret Service, the CIA, the FBI, the Coast Guard, the Border Patrol, and the National Security Agency, among others. The domestic operations of the KGB occupy the larger part of its resources

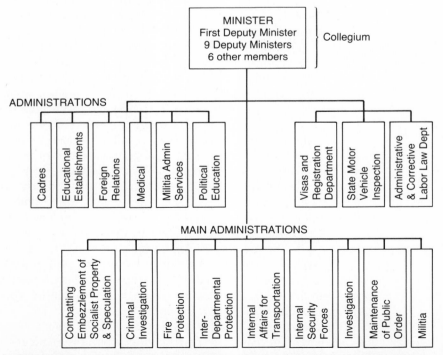

Figure 11.3 USSR Ministry of Internal Affairs. (*Source:* U.S. Central Intelligence Agency, *Directory of Soviet Officials: National Organizations* [Washington, D.C.: CIA, 1986].)

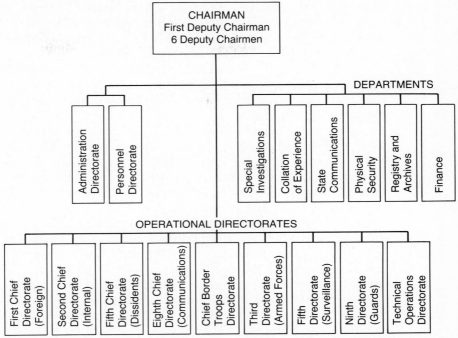

Figure 11.4 USSR Committee on State Security. (*Sources:* Data from U.S. Central Intelligence Agency, *Directory of Soviet Officials: National Organizations* [Washington, D.C.: CIA, 1986]; John Barron, KGB: *The Secret Work of Soviet Secret Agents* [New York: Readers Digest Press, 1974]; John Barron, *KGB Today: The Hidden Hand* [New York: Readers Digest Press, 1983].)

and manpower, involving well over 300,000 individuals. It maintains the border guards of the Soviet Union—militarized units of some 200,000 to 250,000 troops responsible for the defense of Soviet borders. (Many of the units involved in border skirmishes with the Chinese, for example, were not from the regular armed forces, but from the KGB.) The KGB provides the elite guard that protects the highest Soviet leaders. It is responsible for protecting state secrets through counterintelligence and security operations. It combats political "crimes" through its countersubversion operations, which have been construed to include activities against dissidents as well as oppositionists. Particularly important to these counterintelligence and countersubversion activities is the KGB's monitoring of the Soviet armed forces through its "special departments" within military units. And the KGB maintains the security of Soviet communications through its Government Signal Troops.[26]

The Legal Profession

The legal profession in the Soviet Union is a less-prominent segment of society than in the United States. In 1980 there were about 228,000 jurists with either a higher education or specialized secondary education, or only about a quarter as many on a per capita basis as in the United States.[27] Moreover, the Soviet legal community is not the high-status, independent profession found in the West, but a less-prestigious occupation that tends to be more hierarchical in its organization and more tightly controlled by the authorities.

A Soviet "jurist" earns his degree at one of 33 university law faculties (departments), one of 4 law institutes, or from the All-Union Institute of Soviet Law Teaching by Correspondence. While working on the degree, a student must decide on a specialized career.

Only about an eighth of the Soviet legal profession chooses the career of *advokat,* who defends clients in the courtroom and provides legal advice on such matters as divorce, wills, inheritance, legal recourse in civil disputes, and criminal defense. Although the closest of the Soviet legal professions to that of independent trial lawyers, the *advokat* does not "hang out a shingle" and begin a private practice, but, instead, must be hired by one of the regional colleges of advocates. These colleges are purportedly "voluntary organizations of persons engaged in advocacy," but membership is required by union-republic statutes in order to engage in advocacy. The college must convene a general meeting of its members (averaging 150, but as many as 1000 in Moscow) at least once a year, at which time it elects a governing body (Presidium) to a two-year term. The Presidium directs the work of the college, including the admission of members, assignment of members to bureaus or law offices (*iuristicheskaia konsul'tatsiia*) of approximately 20 jurists, and appointment of directors of these offices. The colleges of advocates themselves are under the close scrutiny of the USSR Ministry of Justice and the local soviets, which can reverse the decisions of a college's general meeting or Presidium.[28]

Almost a quarter of the legal profession chooses a career not as advocates but as jurisconsults (*iuriskonsul't*). These are legal advisers to state enterprises, institutions, and public organizations, working primarily in the fields of administrative law, civil law, and labor law, rather than criminal law.[29] The other two-fifths of Soviet jurists choose still other careers. About an eighth of the legal profession is employed in the Procuracy, and another fifth as legal consultants to the police (MVD and KGB). Another eighth of the legal profession chooses careers as judges.

Party Control of the Legal System

The Party leadership maintains keen interest in and close supervision over the legal system, for among other reasons, the legal profession, courts, and Procuracy are potential levers to begin loosening or even challenging Party control. To check this potential, the Party maintains high levels of membership saturation among jurists. In 1973, 82 percent of all procuratorial jurists were Party members. Among judges of the people's courts elected in the RSFSR in May 1977, 95 percent were members of the Party or Komsomol. Even 46.4 percent of the people's assessors elected in 1982 were Party members or candidates.[30]

Party control is reinforced by the institutionalization of mutual suspicion; the separate agencies of the legal system check one another, particularly by their overlapping and mutual monitoring. The Procuracy and KGB, for example, monitor each other as well as the other institutions of Soviet society. The separation of MVD and KGB was apparently designed to set each as a potential check on the other. The court system is not only under hierarchical control by the Supreme Court, but also under supervisory control by the Procuracy and Ministry of Justice.

The Ministry of Justice is specifically assigned the task of monitoring the work of the legal profession and the courts. It provides "general direction" and supervision over the activities of the colleges of advocates and may even expel advocates found "unsuitable."* It provides "organizational direction" to the courts and military tribunals, introducing proposals to the Supreme Court for guiding explanations that will direct the decisions of lower-court judges and ensure a more uniform application of the law throughout the court system.

The Party apparatus maintains direct supervision over the Ministry of Justice, courts, legal profession, Procuracy, and police through its Administrative Organs Department. This department supervises the activities of these legal agencies and, particularly through nomenklatura, controls key appointments.

Criminal Procedure

Soviet criminal procedure progresses through three distinct stages: pretrial investigation, trial, and appeal.[31] During the pretrial phase, the Procuracy appoints an investigator to inquire into the facts of the case, undertaking interrogation as well as independent accumulation of facts. The police can arrest the suspect during the pretrial phase, although they must normally secure the written authorization (warrant) of the Procuracy. According to Soviet law, a suspect can be detained by the police for up to 24 hours before the Procuracy is even informed and normally up to 72 hours (but as much as 10 days in extraordinary cases) before being apprised of the charges. After this, the suspect may be held for up to 9 months as the pretrial investigation proceeds. During the investigation, the suspect has no right to communicate with anyone on the outside, such as a telephone call to a lawyer, and so can be held incommunicado for the 9 months. Legal counsel for the suspect during the pretrial investigation has been permitted since 1970, but this is not required and is at the discretion of the procuratorial investigator. At the end of the investigation, the investigator, with the concurrence of his procurator, must decide whether to issue an indictment of the suspect or dismiss the case.

The trial itself is far less formal and takes place in far less-imposing surroundings than is common in the United States. Indeed, the Soviet courthouse is often a small building on a side street rather than the centerpiece of a city; and trials may even be held, during the so-called "visiting sessions," not in the courtroom but in factories or places of residence. During a trial, the courtroom will contain the judge and his people's assessors; the prosecutor form the Procuracy; the defen-

*The new law on the advokatura appears to give greater independence to the colleges of advokats on personnel matters; see Article 14, "Law on the Advokatura".

dant and his *advokat*; the witnesses, including the social accusers and social defenders; as well as onlookers from the community.

The trial itself is not an adversarial process in which the judge sits as an independent arbiter between prosecuting and defending attorneys, but an inquisitorial process in which the judge plays an active role in ferreting out the facts of the case. The judge is not bound by many procedural formalities, such as those that exclude evidence; biographical data about the accused, which in an American court might be ruled irrelevant to the case, can be brought forward to paint a complete picture of the accused. Social accusers and defenders not only testify before the court, but may question witnesses and comment upon points of law and the sentence. There are no grounds on which to refuse to testify, except for the counsel to the defendant and for the mentally ill.

The trial does not begin with a formal presumption of either the innocence or guilt of the accused. Nonetheless, the inquisitorial process, with its prolonged investigation of the crime before an official indictment, may bias the court toward the latter. Moreover, since Soviet judges, by their training, remuneration, social status, and personal prestige, are often overshadowed in the courtroom by the representatives of the Procuracy, they may defer to the prosecution and therefore bias the proceedings toward a presumption of guilt. The decision of the case is rendered by a majority vote among the judge and two people's assessors.

The appeal procedure in the Soviet Union is also far simpler than in the United States. Those found guilty may appeal only once—to the oblast' court from the people's court or to the union-republic supreme court from the oblast' court, but not to the USSR Supreme Court. An appellant takes the chance that the appellate court will find not that the accused was wrongly found guilty or punished excessively, but that the defendant was let off too leniently; and it can order a stiffer penalty. Appeals ("protests") can also be initiated by the Procuracy or by the Chairman of the appellate court. The Procuracy can appeal in the role of prosecutor, protesting on either substantive or procedural grounds; it may also appeal as part of its supervisory control over the courts, protesting an "improper decision."

ASSESSMENT OF SOVIET JUSTICE

Assessing the performance of a legal system raises issues at the very foundations of political science and philosophy, such as whether the proper standard of comparison should be some higher principle of natural rights or simply utilitarian considerations. Here (although the reader may legitimately protest) the assessment will be limited to the latter. Specifically, we ask whether the Soviet legal system minimizes the probability of erroneous prosecution, conviction, and punishment.

Central to this assessment, particularly in the absence of facts and figures, is the extent to which the Soviet Union has created a judicial process that guarantees court decisions based on a full and fair presentation of the relevant facts. Even an authoritarian regime has little interest in finding guilty those who are innocent of wrongdoing; and such a regime may normally have a strong interest in avoiding such pointless injustices lest these alienate its citizens.[32]

Since the death of Stalin, the trends in Soviet law have, on balance, favored the expansion of procedural guarantees, although some developments have run contrary to this. If the trends listed below continue into the future, they will provide a more secure guarantee of justice:[33]

- *"Juridicization" of Criminal Reponsibility.* Soviet justice has embraced the principle that criminal responsibility is limited to violations of existing, published laws. The Criminal Codes adopted since 1959 have established that "only a person . . . who intentionally or negligently commits a socially dangerous act *provided for by law* shall be subject to criminal responsibility and punishment."[34] Moreover, they establish that the law in question must be in force at the time of the act. This seemingly fundamental guarantee of justice has superseded the doctrine established in the 1926 Criminal Code that the social danger of an act even in the absence of a specific law proscribing it is a basis for punishment. Article 16 of that Code even provided, in what has been labelled the "doctrine of analogy," that "if any socially dangerous act is not directly provided for by the present Code, the basis and limits of responsibility for it shall be determined by application of those articles of the Code which provide for crimes most similar to it in nature."[35] The trend away from these earlier practices is part of the more general trend toward the "juridicization" of Soviet society–the expansion of the rule of law.
- *Codification of Law.* The establishment of law as the basis for criminal responsibility has required an effort to publish and codify the law. The three decades following adoption of the NEP Codes—despite the rapid transformation of society and rapid expansion in the definition of criminality—saw no new criminal or procedural codes. In December 1958, the Supreme Soviet adopted the Fundamental Principles for criminal legislation and criminal procedure, which were followed by corresponding codes in each union republic. Since then the codes have been routinely updated with the addition of new provisions and the removal of moribund ones. At the 25th Party Congress (1976), Brezhnev initiated a program to revise and update existing codes and to extend the codification of law through the compilation of laws and publication of these compilations. The subsequent revision of the RSFSR Criminal Code adopted in December 1982, for example, amended 133 of 246 articles.[36]
- *Rationalization of Substantive Norms.* The scope of the definition of criminality and its punishment have been made more precise (and in thousands of instances reduced), and punishments have increasingly been scaled to fit the crime. Some acts, such as abortions and resignation from a job without permission, have been decriminalized. The definition of other crimes has been made more precise and in this way narrowed; for example, intentional homicide has been distinguished from negligent manslaughter with a corresponding discrimination of sanctions. Complicity in a crime has been limited to intentional participation in a crime, while inadvertent participation has been decriminalized. Political crimes, such as divulgence of state secrets, have been defined more precisely and narrowly. The punishments for lesser crimes, such as "petty hooliganism" and first-offense petty theft of state or personal property, have been reduced. Indeed, the codes adopted from 1959 to 1961 mandated an across-the-board reduction in the maximum penalties, eliminating certain punishments altogether (e.g., being declared an enemy of the people), reducing the maximum

length allowable for other penalties (e.g., internal exile), and limiting the application of still other penalties (e.g., death penalty) to fewer crimes. (There has, however, been a tendency for penalties to creep upward since 1961, particularly for recidivists and for certain crimes such as economic and official crimes and crimes against the state, administration, or public security, as the Soviet regime has sought to combat some of its most pressing social problems through law.[37])

• *Expansion of Procedural Guarantees.* This has touched all phases of the legal process. In the all-important pretrial stage, which was so abused under Stalin, the maximum length of detention prior to presentation of an official accusation to the suspect has been reduced from 14 to 10 days. The power to confine the accused indefinitely during the pretrial investigation has been replaced by a 9-month limit on such confinement with the stipulation that normally the investigation should be concluded within 2 months. During the investigation the accused and witnesses must be apprised of their rights; they may not be interrogated at night; and the accused may not be compelled to give self-incriminating testimony. Since 1970, the accused may be permitted counsel during the preliminary investigation (and both minors and the handicapped have a *right* to counsel) rather than only after the indictment.

Trial procedure now offers a more certain opportunity for a full and fair presentation of arguments on behalf of the defendant, who now has a guarantee of defense counsel, the right to call witnesses, and the right to present oral arguments. Courts have observed stricter rules of evidence, limiting the role of hearsay, requiring that confessions be corroborated by other evidence, and expanding the role of experts. Throughout the legal proceedings, the Codes of Criminal Procedure seem to have inched closer to the principles—without explicitly adopting the terms—that the presumption at the beginning of a trial is on behalf of the innocence of the defendant and that the burden of proof rests with the prosecution. This is a reversal of earlier doctrines, particularly that enunciated under Stalin by Andrei Ia. Vyshinsky that in cases of counterrevolutionary crimes the burden of proof shifts to the accused.[38]

• *Systematization of Legal Institutions.* With the adoption of the Fundamental Principles of Judicial Organization of the USSR in 1958, corresponding union-republic Laws on Court Organization between 1959 and 1961, and all-union organic acts defining the responsibilities of specific legal agencies, the legal system has been increasingly institutionalized. The limits on various agencies, the supervisory control over each, and the rights of appeal from them are more clearly defined.

• *Limitations on the Role of the Police.* Simultaneously with the institutionalization of juridical agencies, the extraordinary agencies have been limited. The terror apparatus has been reduced in size with the dismantling of its economic empire, transfer of its production responsibilities to economic ministries, and reduction of the forced-labor camp population. Transferring responsibility for much of the pretrial investigation from the police to the Procuracy, except in cases involving state secrets, smuggling, or illegal currency transactions, has reduced the role of the police in this phase of the judicial process. Imposition of stricter Party and procuratorial control has limited the independence of the police and has forced more-scrupulous observance of procedural guarantees in most cases. (The late Brezhnev years apparently permitted corruption to grow in the police and Party control to flag. But in early 1987, the Gorbachev leadership took steps to purge corrupt officials in both the KGB and MVD and to reassert Party control.)

• *Limitation of Extraordinary Tribunals.* The Stalinist period had removed many cases from the courts and placed them under the jurisdiction of the Special Board of the NKVD and the military tribunals, often without the most basic procedural guarantees. Cases involving treason, espionage, terrorist acts, and sabotage were among those thus excluded. When the defendant was accused of terrorist acts, for example,

the investigation of such cases was to be concluded within a period of not more than ten days, the indictment . . . was to be handed to the accused twenty-four hours before trial, the case was to be heard without the participation of the defendant or his counsel, appeal from the judgment and submission of petitions for mercy were forbidden, and the death sentence was to be carried out immediately upon rendering of the judgment.[39]

In September 1953 the Special Board was abolished. The hearing of criminal cases is now restricted to the courts; the jurisdiction of the military tribunals over civilians is limited to espionage and complicity in the crimes of uniformed personnel; and the procedural guarantees of the codes have been extended to the military tribunals.

• *Expanded Popular Participation in the Judicial Process.* The routinization of popular participation through the posts of people's assessor, social accuser, and social defender as well as through visiting sessions may increase the chances for vigilantism. Yet, to the extent the broader public is involved, it may be more difficult than in the Stalin period for the authorities to engineer gross miscarriages of justice or to routinely abandon procedural guarantees and rules of evidence.

• *Professionalization of Jurists.* The rising levels of educational attainment and expertise, growing commitment to expanded standards of justice, and the new professional cohesion and activism among segments of the judicial community have improved the prospects for justice. For example, legal scholars played a critical role in winning expansion of the law governing governmental liability for personal injury and property damage resulting from administrative decisions or the acts of state agencies. In 1987, they have pressed for expanded guarantees during the preliminary investigation, for defendant rights in the courtroom, and for a more explicit presumption of innocence. To the extent this professionalization continues, jurists may increasingly observe the standards of justice in their own conduct, monitor the compliance of legal agencies with these standards, and demand still-higher standards in the future.[40]

• *Growing Ideological Accommodation of Law.* With the acceptance of the longevity of the state, if not its permanence, has come a recognition of the value of law. The Party Program adopted at the 27th Congress (1986) states:

> The strengthening of the legal basis of the state and public life, the unwavering observance of socialist legality and law and order, and the improvement of the work of the people's courts and other agencies of justice, procuratoral supervision, and the militsiia have been and remain a subject of constant concern for the Party.[41]

Legal propaganda reinforces this theme routinely. While far from the dignified status accorded it in the Anglo-American tradition, law is no longer the object of hostility or contempt in Party dogmas. To the extent the status of law continues to rise, it is more likely to ensure legal proceedings and even official actions that conform to the law.

All this is not to say that the Soviet legal system has achieved a level of justice that citizens of Western democracies would or should find acceptable, for the above are only trends in the post-Stalinist period, many of which, after 30 years, are still only in their nascence. Nor can we say that the continuation of these trends into the future is preordained.

Violations of procedural justice, although less common today, do continue. First of all, many cases that we might expect to find within the purview of the courts are excluded altogether from the procedural guarantees of Soviet law. Some are decided outside the court system without the procedures of the courts. Others decided within the courts are because of their "political" nature excluded from the same procedural guarantees as routine cases.

Soviet law places three categories of offenses outside the jurisdiction of the courts and so beyond the guarantees imposed on routine judicial proceedings.[42] Administrative offenses—that is, violations of administrative decrees or regulations—may bring fines, "correctional" tasks, confiscation of property, or arrest and detention. Minor traffic violations and driving while intoxicated are both treated as administrative violations with penalties ranging from a few rubles for the former up to suspension of one's driver's license for one to three years for the latter. Violations of customs or postal regulations, of the internal or external passport regulations, or of tax regulations are among the cases heard by administrative bodies. A second category of excluded cases is disciplinary offenses, in which administrative officials such as factory managers may impose penalties of censure, reprimand, fines, demotion, or dismissal on subordinates who have violated work rules by such infractions as absenteeism, drunkenness on the job, or damage to property. A third category is the cases of minor antisocial acts that are handled by the comrade courts.

A less-frequent but more-dramatic suspension of some procedural guarantees of Soviet law apparently takes place in the regular criminal procedure itself when the case is political, particularly in cases of individual dissidents accused of violating Articles 70, 190-1, or 190-3 of the RSFSR Criminal Code (see Chapter 5).[43] Dissidents have challenged the claim of the Soviet authorities that all procedural guarantees of the RSFSR Criminal Code and RSFSR Criminal Procedure Code have been observed. Allegedly, pretrial detention of some dissidents has extended beyond the 9-month limit, the limitations on the length of interrogation have been exceeded, depositions in the accused's own hand have been refused, unlawful searches and seizures have been conducted and witnesses for the accused have been intimidated. Court procedure has been stretched to the maximum benefit of the prosecution, apparently violating legal guarantees in some cases. The accused's relatives and friends have in a few cases been informed of the trial only six to seven hours before its opening and have even been prohibited from entering the courtroom or offering testimony. Courtroom spectators have been permitted to taunt the accused, and judges have interrupted defendants during their testimony to disrupt their arguments. The definition of state secrets has apparently been expanded in a few cases to permit trial of dissidents in closed sessions. Not all these alleged cases of violation of legal guarantees, however, go beyond the norms of Soviet criminal procedure; and, in many cases, even if all legal guarantees had been observed scrupulously by the authorities, the defendants probably could have been found guilty of violating the law against dissent and opposition. (That is, the injustice of these outcomes does not arise from the procedures of their investigation and trial.)

Still more damaging to justice is the use of psychiatric measures against political dissidents. In cases where the accused has been afflicted with mental illness, the procuratorial investigator or the court is empowered "to determine, on the basis of psychiatric opinion, whether such person should be relieved of criminal responsibility and whether he should be committed to a psychiatric hospital. . . . "[44] Where no crime has been committed, the decision to commit an individual to such an institution can be made by administrative means. In a perverse turnabout of the purported intent of these provisions, commitment to psychiatric hospitals has been used to detain and isolate dissidents without benefit of trial, simply removing dissidents from all procedural guarantees by declaring them mentally incompetent.

Gordon B. Smith, of the University of South Carolina, noted the exclusion of these cases from the full procedural guarantees of Soviet justice and argues that the Soviet Union today still maintains a dual legal system. One, little known in the West, routinely "maintains law and order, enacts and enforces the law, and adjudicates disputes that inevitably arise among citizens and institutions in modern societies." The other, about which we read more frequently, even though it may represent less than 1 percent of all cases, uses law and legal institutions "in an arbitrary and brutal manner to suppress political, national, and religious dissent."[45] In a sense, the two-track judicial system created at the beginning of Soviet power survives.

In addition to questions about the justice in cases excluded from procedural guarantees, Western analysts have asked whether the normal guarantees are themselves adequate.[46] During the pretrial investigation, the absense of counsel may be a greater problem in an inquisitorial than an adversarial justice system, for in this stage all facts that will be presented to the court are being assembled. An inquisitorial investigation may frequently predetermine the outcome of a trial, for the court may presume that the only cases that come before it are those in which the state feels certain of a conviction.

A second question about these procedural guarantees concerns the dual role of legal agencies. The Procuracy is responsible for defending the rights of citizens–ensuring that the procedural norms of socialist legality are observed by legal agencies. But it must also serve as prosecutor for the state and, more specifically, must carry forward the Party's transformational mission. It is unclear whether one agency can successfully carry out both missions, particularly when they come into conflict; the subordination of the Procuracy to the purposes of the Party and the state diminishes its ability to be an impartial defender of the procedural rights of the citizen. Similarly, the courts play a dual role, not only adjudicating cases, presumably impartially determining the guilt or innocence of the defendant, but also, on behalf of the Party, educating the accused, cajoling and lecturing him to help create the new Soviet man. The All-Union Fundamental Principles of Court Organization state:

> By all its activity the court shall educate citizens in the spirit of loyalty to the Motherland and to the cause of communism, and in the spirit of exact and undeviating execution of Soviet laws, of a protective attitude toward socialist property, of observance of labor discipline, of an honorable attitude toward state and social duty, and of respect for the rights, honor, and dignity of citizens and for rules of socialist communal life.[47]

Courts that play a parental role may be less effective in dispensing impartial justice; the subordination of the courts to the mission of the Party may undermine their independence as they attempt to weigh the competing claims of state prosecutor and defendant. Even the legal profession is expected to play the role of educator—to educate the accused about the citizen's responsibilities under Soviet law. But can an advokat who is assigned this educational role also actively defend the accused?

A third problem in the Soviet legal system is the lack of independence for the advokatura. According to Harold Berman:

> It is inaccurate to speak of the Soviet advocate as a "state employee": he is, indeed, subject to a large measure of control by administrative authorities, but both technically and substantially he is a member of an autonomous professional body that has its own traditions and is independent of the prosecutor's office (the Procuracy) as well as of the courts.[48]

Nonetheless, the right to practice depends upon continued employment by a college of advocates and, therefore, upon the concurrence of the local soviet and the all-union Ministry of Justice. Can an advokat so dependent on the state vigorously defend a client against the state prosecutor?

A fourth critical shortcoming in the guarantee of procedural justice is the absence of independent checks outside the legal agencies to spotlight violations of those norms. The Soviet press, for example, does not normally report court proceedings or outcomes and lacks the independence to bring injustices to public attention. Independent human rights groups that have attempted to play this role have been suppressed as dissidents. And, more fundamentally, the authorities appear to subscribe to few abstract notions of procedural justice that are in some way greater than the Party and state and, therefore, ultimately binding upon them. Even though the obstacles to a wholesale return to the juridicial practices of Stalinism appear to be very high, there may be no independent centers of power in Soviet society to prevent such backsliding if the Party leadership chooses to end its acquiesence in or acceptance of the trends toward greater procedural justice.

These are serious flaws in the procedural justice of the Soviet legal system. The future of socialist legality depends upon whether the trends toward juridicization will continue.

NOTES

1. John Rawls, *A Theory of Justice* (Cambridge, Mass.: Harvard University Press, 1971), 3.
2. An excellent survey of the issues is given in W. E. Butler, *Soviet Law* (London: Butterworths, 1983); for an alternative, very critical view of Soviet law, see Olympiad S. Ioffe, *Soviet Law and Soviet Reality* (Dordrecht, Netherlands: Martinus Nijhoff, 1985).
3. Harold J. Berman, *Justice in the U.S.S.R.,* rev. ed. (New York: Vintage Books, 1963), 187–225.
4. Friedrich Engels, *Anti-Duehring* (Moscow: Foreign Languages Publishing House, 1962), 41. On the interplay of ideology and legal policy, see R. W. Makepeace, *Marxist Ideology and Soviet Criminal Law* (London: Croom Helm, 1980).
5. Friedrich Engels, "Letter to Conrad Schmidt, 27 October 1980," in Karl Marx and Friedrich Engels, *Selected Works* (Moscow: Progress Publishers, 1983), 3:492.
6. Quoted in Berman, 26.
7. Berman, 283–284. On the role of Soviet law in the transformation of Soviet society, see Kazimierz Grzybowski, *Soviet Legal Institutions: Doctrines and Social Functions* (Ann Arbor, Mich.: University of Michigan Press, 1962); and John N. Hazard, *Managing Change in the U.S.S.R.: The Political-Legal Role of the Soviet Jurist* (Cambridge, England: Cambridge University Press, 1983).
8. Berman, 307.
9. George Feifer, *Justice in Moscow* (New York: Simon and Schuster, 1964), 29–30.
10. Berman, 41.
11. A useful reference volume on Soviet legal institutions is F. J. M. Feldbrugge, G. P. van den Berg, and William B. Simons, eds., *Encyclopedia of Soviet Law,* 2d. rev. ed. (Dordrecht, Netherlands: Martinus Nijhoff, 1985).
12. A useful collection of the most important laws of the Soviet Union can be found in Leo Hecht, *The Soviet Union Through its Laws* (New York: Praeger, 1983). More-complete collections are William E. Butler, *The Soviet Legal System* (Dobbs Ferry, N.Y.: Oceana Publications, 1978); and William B. Simons, *The Soviet Codes of Law* (Alphen aan den Rijn, Netherlands: Sijthoff and Noordhoff, 1980).
13. A. I. Luk'ianov, *Sovety narodnykh deputatov: spravochnik* (Moscow: Politicheskaia Literatura, 1984), 138, 144.
14. Articles 20, 22, "Regulations of the Supreme Soviet of the Union of Soviet Socialist Republics," *Pravda,* April 20, 1979; Article 1, "Law of the U.S.S.R. on the U.S.S.R. Council of Ministers," *Pravda,* 6 July 1978; Articles 29, 34, "Law of the U.S.S.R. on the Basic Powers of Krai and Oblast' Soviets of Peoples Deputies and of the Autonomous-Oblast' and Autonomous-Okrug Soviets of People's Deputies," *Pravda,* 26 June 1980.
15. Compare Harold J. Berman, *Soviet Criminal Law and Procedure: The RSFSR Codes,* 2d ed. (Cambridge, Mass.: Harvard University Press, 1972), 15.

16. *Pravda,* 27 June 1982.

17. John H. Minan and Grant H. Morris, "Unraveling an Enigma: An Introduction to Soviet Law and the Soviet Legal System," *The George Washington Journal of International Law and Economics,* 19 (1985), 14–15.

18. See "Law of the U.S.S.R. on the U.S.S.R. Supreme Court," *Pravda,* 2 December 1979; U. S. Central Intelligence Agency, *Directory of Soviet Officials: National Organizations* (Washington, D.C., 1986).

19. "Law of the U.S.S.R. on State Arbitrazh in the U.S.S.R.", *Pravda,* 3 December 1979.

20. "Law of the U.S.S.R. on People's Control in the U.S.S.R.", *Pravda,* 1 December 1979.

21. Gordon B. Smith, *The Soviet Procuracy and the Supervision of Administration* (Alphen aan den Rijn, Netherlands: Sijthoff and Noordhoff, 1978), 13–32.

22. Articles 22–45, "Law of the U.S.S.R. on the U.S.S.R. Procuracy", *Pravda,* 2 December 1979; Smith, 18–22, 29–32; Leon Boim and Glenn G. Morgan, *The Soviet Procuracy Protests, 1937–1973* (Alphen aan den Rijn, Netherlands: Sijthoff and Noordhoff, 1978).

23. Merle Fainsod, *How Russia Is Ruled,* rev. ed. (Cambridge, Mass.: Harvard University Press, 1967), 433.

24. Fainsod, 447.

25. Peter Deriabin and Frank Gibney, *The Secret World* (New York: Ballantine Books, 1982), 67–68, 106, 195, 200; U. S. Central Intelligence Agency.

26. Jeffrey T. Richelson, *Sword and Shield: Soviet Intelligence and Security Apparatus* (Cambridge, Mass.: Ballinger, 1986), 229–260; see also Harry Rositzke, *The KGB: The Eyes of Russia* (New York: Doubleday, 1981).

27. USSR Tsentral'noe Statisticheskoe Upravlenie, *Narodnoe khoziaistvo SSSR v 1980 g.* (Moscow: Finansy i Statistika, 1981), 368.

28. Zigurds L. Zile, "Soviet Advokatura Twenty-Five Years After Stalin," in Donald D. Barry, George Ginsburgs, and Peter B. Maggs, eds., *Soviet Law After Stalin* (Leyden, Netherlands: A. W. Sijthoff, 1977–1979), 3:207–237; "Law of the U.S.S.R. on the Advokatura in the U.S.S.R.", *Pravda,* 4 December 1979; Minan and Morris, 49.

29. Yuri Luryi, "Jurisconsults in the Soviet Economy," in Barry, Ginsburgs, and Maggs, 3:168–206.

30. Berman, *Soviet Criminal Law,* 93–93, 108–109; Smith, 25; John N. Hazard, *The Soviet System of Government,* 5th rev. ed. (Chicago: University of Chicago Press, 1980), 199; *Pravda,* 27 June 1982.

31. Much of the following discussion of criminal procedure is based on Berman, *Soviet Criminal Law.* See also Peter H. Juvelier, "Some Trends in Soviet Criminal Justice," in Barry, Ginsburgs, and Maggs, 3: 59–87. On civil procedure, see Dennis M. O'Connor, "Soviet Procedures in Civil Disputes: A Changing Balance Between Public and Civic Systems of Public Order," in Wayne R. LaFave, ed., *Law in the Soviet Society* (Urbana, Ill.: University of Illinois Press, 1965), 51–102.

32. Hazard, 207.

33. Compare Berman, *Justice,* 69–96.

34. Article 3, "Fundamentals of Criminal Legislation of the USSR."

35. Quoted in Berman, *Soviet Criminal Law,* 22.

36. Robert Sharlet, "Soviet Legal Policy under Andropov: Law and Discipline," in Joseph L. Nogee, ed., *Soviet Politics: Russia After Brezhnev* (New York: Praeger, 1985), 85–106; John N. Hazard, "Legal Trends," in Archie Brown and Michael Kaser, eds., *Soviet Policy for the 1980s* (Bloomington, Ind.: Indiana University Press, 1982), 98–117.

37. Berman, *Soviet Criminal Law,* 36–40, 43–44, 71–72; Sharlet, 93–100.

38. Yuri Luryi, "The Right to Counsel in Ordinary Criminal Cases in the U.S.S.R.," in Barry, Ginsburgs, and Maggs, 1:105–116; Berman, *Soviet Criminal Law,* 51–53, 56–62, 65–66, 85; Berman, *Justice,* 71; compare Hazard, *Soviet System,* 203–205.
39. Berman, *Soviet Criminal Law,* 51.
40. Donald D. Barry and Harold J. Berman, "The Jurists," in H. Gordon Skilling and Franklyn Griffiths, eds., *Interest Groups in Soviet Politics* (Princeton, N.J.: Princeton University Press, 1971), 324. See also Gordon B. Smith, "Socialist Legality and Legal Policy in the Soviet Union," in Gordon B. Smith, ed., *Public Policy and Administration in the Soviet Union* (New York: Praeger, 1980), 114–128; and Peter H. Juviler, *Revolutionary Law and Order: Politics and Social Change in the USSR* (New York: Free Press, 1976). For recent examples of legal scholars debating procedural guarantees, see *Literaturnaia gazeta,* 15 April 1987, and *Izvestiia,* 22 May 1987.
41. *Pravda,* 7 March 1986.
42. Berman, *Soviet Criminal Law,* 8–10.
43. Christopher Osakwe, "Due Process of Law and Civil Rights Cases in the Soviet Union," in Barry, Ginsburgs, and Maggs, 1:179–221; Vyacheslav Chornovil, ed., *The Chornovil Papers* (New York: McGraw-Hill, 1969).
44. Quoted in Berman, *Soviet Criminal Law,* 11.
45. Smith, "Socialist Legality," 189; Minan and Morris, 53–54.
46. Minan and Morris, 51–53; compare John Gorgone, "Soviet Criminal Procedure Legislation: A Dissenting Perspective," *American Journal of Comparative Law* 28 (Fall 1980), 577–613.
47. *Pravda,* 26 December 1958.
48. Berman, *Soviet Criminal Law,* 110.

chapter 12

Equality and Inequalities in Soviet Society

Continuing the discussion of justice begun in the previous chapter, we turn here to distributive justice. Specifically, has the Soviet model of development avoided the gross economic inequalities that so often accompany the transition to modernity? Has it eliminated the inequalities among ascriptive groups, such as nationalities and the sexes, that are said to characterize class-based societies?

For the leaders of the Bolshevik Revolution, equality among major social groups—economic, gender, and ethnic—was one of the highest of their professed goals. The Party's Program of March 1919, for example, committed the communists "to liberate women from all the burdens of antiquated methods of housekeeping" and to replace all national privileges with the fullest equality among nationalities. Yet, there is a significant limitation in the Soviet approach to engineering equality: To an important extent these inequalities are supposed to disappear as an inevitable consequence of the transition to communism—as distinctions among economic groups, such as those between peasants and industrial workers, are eliminated, as social differences between the sexes, particularly in the conditions of their labor, begin to converge, and as national distinctions disappear. Thus, the melioration of these inequalities is treated as subordinate to or derivative from the building of socialism. And, particularly in the case of economic and national differences, equality is to be achieved finally not so much through engineering equality among social groups as through the elimination of the social groups themselves.

CLASS AND ECONOMIC STRATIFICATION

Class distinctions, in the official Soviet view, are well on their way to extinction as the Soviet Union progresses toward communism. Class differences continue to exist, for "the working class and the co-operative peasantry differ in their relation to the means of production, this stemming from the existence of two forms of socialist property, that of the whole people, and collective-farm and co-operative property."[1] Still, exploiting classes who own the means of production have been eliminated. And those class differences that survive under mature socialism are nonantagonistic. With the completion of communist construction, even these class distinctions will be eliminated as well as the distinctions between urban and rural populations, manual and mental labor, executives and executors.[2]

Marxist critics of Soviet society have challenged this interpretation. The Yugoslav Milovan Djilas, for example, argues that a new class has, in fact, been established in Soviet society based not on private property but on state property: "The new class may be said to be made up of those who have special privileges and economic preference because of the administrative monopoly they hold . . . "[3] The British Marxist Tony Cliff argues that this new class, which he equates with the bureaucracy, has acquired many of the trappings of capitalist elites: "The state bureaucracy . . . possesses the state as private property. In a state which is the repository of the means of production the state bureaucracy— the ruling class—has forms of passing on its privileges. . . ."[4] Critiques such as these, however, do violence to Marx's definition of ownership and class.

Although classes in the narrow Marxist definition are probably on their way to extinction in the Soviet Union, stratification according to income and privilege is not. The official dogma that under socialism each will be rewarded "according to his work" would appear to legitimate such inequality; yet the Soviet regime remains very sensitive to the reality of disparities.

Stratification by income and wealth may be less extreme in the Soviet Union than in developed Western societies or less-developed Third World countries. The British Sovietologist Mervyn Matthews estimates that the top 0.2 percent of the Soviet labor force, which he labels the Soviet elite, earn monthly incomes (including salary and other benefits) at least 5 to 8 times the wage of the average Soviet worker. (By comparison, the top 0.2 percent of American income earners enjoy monthly after-tax incomes at least 12 times the average American wage.)[5] These income comparisons understate the relative economic inequalities in the United States, for the top of the pyramid in the United States reaches, in the Matthews's words, "an astounding peak" for which there is no Soviet equivalent. Gerhard Lenski of the University of North Carolina has estimated that in the Soviet Union the maximum income is 300 times the minimum income and 100 times the average, but in the United States the maximum is 11,000 times the minimum and 7000 times the average.[6] Moreover, the super-rich in the United States have amassed substantial wealth in stocks, bonds, and real estate, for which there is no equivalent among the Soviet elite.

The Soviet economic elite, according to Matthews's estimates, comprised in the early 1970s 227,000 income earners with monthly salaries above 450 rubles. Their composition broke down as follows:

36% High Party Officials

26% State, Komsomol, and trade union leaders

7% Leading enterprise managers

18% Intelligentsia (including senior academicians, doctors, jurists, journalists, and artists)

13% Diplomatic, military, and police officials

Reported basic monthly salaries of 500 rubles in the early 1970s might go to a well-known ballet dancer, the First Secretary of the Union of Cinematographic Workers, the director of a research institute, or a colonel; a salary around 600 rubles might go to an oblast first secretary or a major general; as much as 900 rubles a month was rumored to be the salary of the all-union General Secretary.

One's basic salary constitutes only a part of total monthly income in the Soviet Union, however, for these basic salaries can be supplemented in a number of ways. Supplements include second paid positions such as deputy to a Supreme Soviet (100 rubles a month honorarium plus travel and per diem during sessions for all-union deputies), "degree payments" for those with advanced academic credentials (100 rubles per month for holders of the Doctor of Science degree), honoraria and royalties for special performances, routine bonuses such as the "thirteenth month" (an extra month's pay), and second or "private" practices such as music lessons or medical treatment "after hours." And on top of these salaries, this elite enjoys certain nonmonetary benefits that have the effect of boosting their incomes. The system of closed shops or restricted distributors (such as grocers that cater to academicians or special cafeterias for members of the police) —a system that for historical reasons has been called the "Kremlin Ration" (*Kremlevskii paek*), academic ration, and so forth—not only ensures more-certain supplies of scarce items, but may also provide higher-quality items and at subsidized prices. The elite also enjoy substantially better housing, medical treatment, and holiday accommodations at about the same price as that charged average citizens for lesser benefits.[7]

Still, even when all this is taken into account, the wealthiest Soviet citizens, when compared to the American economic elite, were in Matthews's estimation "paupers indeed." The Soviet *elite* lifestyle may, in fact, be very close to that of *average* Americans earning a median income. In their diets, "the Soviet elite family may have approached average American levels in terms of quality and variety of food, with, however, a greater reliance on fish and tinned products."[8] An elite family of four might expect to rent a three- or four-room flat totalling 750 square feet, well below the average for median-income families in the early 70s in the United States, where a family owned (but mortgaged) a house of 5.2 rooms totalling 860 to 970 square feet. Although both typically owned a car, the Soviet family would pay at least five months' income, compared to less than three months' for the average American, for a much-smaller and less-reliable means of transportation.[9] Compared to the inequities commonly found in less-developed countries, and in light of the capacity of elites in such countries to extract an opulent lifestyle from the backs of their population, the relative modesty of the Soviet elite's lifestyle is remarkable.

Whether this modest inequality will continue into the future is unclear. On the one hand, some evidence points toward greater equalization. Income differentials appear to have declined since Stalin's death: The ratio between the top 10 percent of income earners and the bottom 10 percent fell from 7:1 under Stalin to 3:1 in 1970.[10] On the other hand, there is an apparent tendency for these inequalities to become increasingly hereditary. Among the older generations there were higher levels of mobility; a study of managers in a Leningrad factory found that only 16 percent were from families with higher education, and another study found that at least 70 percent of ministers and chairmen of state committees and over 50 percent of the directors of the largest industrial enterprises began their careers as laborers or peasants. Among younger generations, however, status appears to have become more hereditary. Studies suggest that the proportion of managers from white-collar backgrounds has increased since the 1950s and that managers from such backgrounds are more common among younger, second-tier managers than among their bosses. Studies of students enrolled in institutions of higher education (VUZ) or graduated as specialists show that they are drawn disproportionately from white-collar families.[11] Although the official Soviet dogmas may be able to justify the existing economic inequalities in the country, the tendency for these to become hereditary strikes at the very legitimacy of the Soviet system.

THE NATIONALITIES PROBLEM AND NATIONALITY POLICY

National inequalities within the Russian Empire created strong centrifugal pressures within the state inherited by the Bolsheviks. Indeed, the nationalities question has been among the most explosive problems the Soviets have faced since 1917. When the Bolsheviks took power, these nationalities were diverse in their cultures and levels of development, tended to be geographically concentrated in their homelands, and evinced strong desires for national autonomy. Thus, the effort to engineer equality among the ethnic groups of the Soviet Union has been intertwined with the effort to hold this diverse state together.

In the 1979 census, the Soviet people divided themselves among over 100 nationalities.[12] While many were very small in number, with as few as 500 members, 13 of these nationalities had populations over two million and 22 over one million. (See Table 12.1.) The vast majority of the Soviet population divides among five linguistic groups: the Indo-European, Ural-Altaic, Iberian, Circassian, and Paleo-Asiatic languages (See Figure 12.1.) Traditionally, this population also has divided into five principal religious communities: Christianity and Judaism in Europe, Islam in Central Asia, Buddhism in the Far East, and Animism in Siberia. The European Christians were divided among the Eastern Ortho-

Table 12.1 MAJOR NATIONALITIES OF THE USSR, 1979 (with populations over one million)

Nationality	Population	Percent of Total	Linguistic Group	Traditional Religion
Russian	137,397,089	52.4	Slavic	Orthodox
Ukrainian	42,347,387	16.2	Slavic	Orthodox
Uzbek	12,455,978	3.6	Turkic	Islam
Belorussian	9,462,715	3.6	Slavic	Orthodox
Kazakh	6,556,442	2.5	Turkic	Islam
Tatar	6,317,468	2.4	Turkic	Islam
Azeri	5,477,330	2.1	Turkic	Islam
Armenian	4,151,241	1.6	Indo-European	National Christian
Georgian	3,570,504	1.4	Iberian	Orthodox
Moldavian	2,968,224	1.1	Romance	Orthodox
Tadjik	2,897,697	1.1	Iranian	Islam
Lithuanian	2,850,905	1.1	Baltic	Roman Catholic
Turkmen	2,027,913	0.8	Turkic	Islam
German	1,936,214	0.7	Germanic	Lutheran
Kirgiz	1,906,271	0.7	Turkic	Islam
Jewish	1,810,875	0.7	Yiddish	Judaism
Chuvash	1,751,366	0.7	Turkic	Orthodox
Latvian	1,439,037	0.5	Baltic	Lutheran
Bashkir	1,371,452	0.5	Turkic	Islam
Mordvinian	1,191,765	0.5	Finnic	Orthodox
Polish	1,150,991	0.4	Slavic	Roman Catholic
Estonian	1,019,851	0.4	Finnic	Lutheran

Source: Tsentral'noe statisticheskoe upravlenie, *Chislennost' i sostav naseleniia SSSR po dannym vsesoiuznoi perepisi naseleniia 1979 goda* (Moscow: Finansy i Statistika, 1985), 71–73; Barbara A. Anderson and Brian D. Silver, "Estimating Russification of Ethnic Identity Among Non-Russians in the USSR," *Demography* 20 (November 1983), 466.

dox of Russia, the Ukraine, and the Caucasus; the Polish, Ukrainian, and Lithuanian Roman Catholics; and the Baltic Protestants.

Ideology and the Nationalities Question

After the Bolsheviks took power in 1917, they received scant guidance from Marxism on the nationality problem. Marx had said little that addressed the Soviets' immediate problems, for he had thought that nationalism was a passing phenomenon—as part of the superstructure of the capitalist socioeconomic formation, it would not survive the demise of capitalism. In the *Communist Manifesto* he wrote that working men have no country, and that national differences and antagonisms between peoples "are daily more and more vanishing, owing to the development of the bourgeoisie, to freedom of commerce, to the world market, to uniformity in the mode of production and in the conditions of life corresponding thereto."[13] Capitalism and the growing interdependence associated with advanced capitalism produced a decline in nationalism.

On practical problems of his day, such as independence for Poland and Ireland, Marx showed tactical flexibility, subordinating the question of nationalism to the larger issue of making proletarian revolution. For example, on the issue of Polish autonomy, Marx in 1870 argued for national self-determination, since

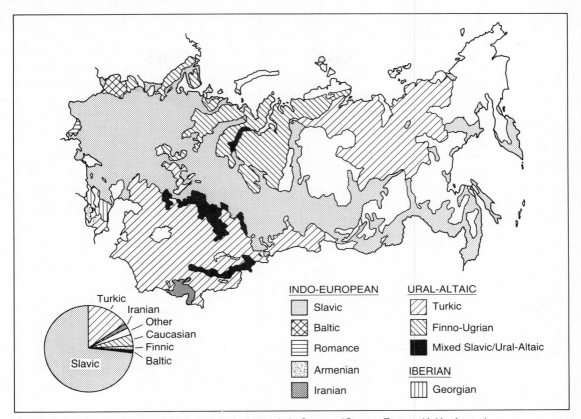

Figure 12.1 Geographic Distribution of Principal Linguistic Groups. (*Source:* Eugene K. Keefe et al., *Area Handbook for the Soviet Union* [Washington, D.C.: Government Printing Office, 1971].)

this would further the revolutionary cause. Seven years later, however, when it appeared that the Russian revolutionary movement was beginning to develop, he urged the Poles to remain within the Russian Empire. As Walker Connor has noted,

> Grand strategy was therefore to take precedence over ideological purity and consistency. Progressive national movements were to be supported only if consonant with the broader demands of the global movement. Alliances with otherwise unprogressive movements were condoned if strategically opportune. In any situation, national movements were not to be treated in isolation but viewed against this broader backdrop.[14]

The Bolsheviks' action program before 1917 showed the same tactical use of nationalism. The Party's First Program, adopted at the Second Congress of the Russian Social-Democratic Labor Party in 1903, set down two principles as the basis of the Party's nationalities policy: support for equal rights of nationalities within the Empire, including the right to use national languages in schools and in government; and support for the right of each nation to self-determination, including the right to secede from the Empire as an independent state. In subsequent clarifications of this policy, Lenin affirmed that the Party supported the *right* of national self-determination but did not advocate actual secession of nationalities. He used the metaphor of divorce—while affirming the right of divorce, he did not advocate it and would do everything in his power to urge people to reconcile. In particular, each request for secession should be reviewed from the perspective of the interests of the proletariat—does the secession promote the cause of the proletariat and socialist revolution or the cause of capitalist reaction? In practice, the Bolsheviks denied that right to most of the nationalities that attempted to secede during the Civil War.[15]

The Party currently maintains that a natural part of the transition phase leading to communism is the process of drawing together or fusion (*sblizhenie*) of nationalities and that a consequence of communism will be their merging (*sliianie*). Brezhnev, on the 50th anniversary of the founding of the USSR, reaffirmed this view:

> The further drawing together of the nations and nationalities of our country is an objective process. The Party is against forcing this process; at the same time the Party regards as impermissible any attempt whatsoever to hold back the process of the drawing together of nations—to obstruct it on any pretext or to artificially reinforce national isolation—because this would be at variance with the general direction of the development of our society and the interest of Communist construction.[16]

The ideology of the Soviet state treats national differences—and, therefore, the problems of national inequalities, ethnic animosities, and centrifugal nationalism—as legacies of the capitalist past that will be remedied as the Soviet Union progresses toward communism.

Soviet Nationality Policies

Until such time as the merging of nationalities is an accomplished fact, the Soviet regime must continue to cope with the diversity and centrifugal pressures of a multiethnic state. Soviet nationality policies have balanced accommodation to the ethnic diversity of the Soviet state with homogenizing pressures to speed along the fusion of nations. The former have included the creation of a federal institutional structure, indigenization, and the cultivation of national cultural forms. Among the latter are the reality of centralized political power, Sovietization, assimilation, and coercion. The importance of each of these policies and, hence, the balance between accommodation and assimilation has varied over time. Pressures for assimilation reached their peak in the last decade of Stalin's rule as the cumulative effects of homogenization under the Stalin revolutions, coercive deportation of whole nations, and forced Russification were felt. During the NEP and post-Stalinist periods, there has been greater balance between accommodation and assimilation, although the official pressure for homogenization over the longer term remains strong.

Federalism   Central to the Soviet political system since the creation of the Bolshevik state has been an institutional structure that could incorporate diverse nationalities and tie them together into a larger Soviet Union. Columbia University's Seweryn Bialer has argued:

> The freedoms afforded to non-Russian nations in the Soviet Union—territory, language, cultural heritage, symbols of statehood, indigenous elites— . . . however inadequate and imperfect, are very important to the everyday life of the non-Russian peoples. They are crucial as the safety valve for their rising and unfulfilled aspirations and as a basis for the containment of the national problem in the Soviet Union.[17]

This Soviet federalism is built upon the twin practices of indigenous administration and all-union co-optation. That is, the Constitution provides for 53 nationality-based territories, including 15 union republics, 20 autonomous republics, 8 autonomous oblasts, and 10 autonomous okrugs. It also provides for co-optation of representatives from these territories into the all-union state bodies, through the representation scheme in the Supreme Soviet's Council of Nationalities and through the ex officio memberships in the Supreme Soviet's Presidium, the Council of Ministers, and the Supreme Court. (Although the Party has not formalized such co-optation schemes, national representation in the all-union organs is conspicuous: Non-Slavic representation on the Politburo, for example, has fluctuated close to the proportion of these nationalities in the total population; in March 1986, 25 percent of the full members were non-Slavs, as close to proportionate representation as is mathematically possible given the limited size of that body.) The federalist structure accommodates the territorially-based sense of community that is often the foundation of modern nationalism, without sacrificing the unity of action demanded by the Party. Though the structure does not guarantee prudent policies, it provides a highly adaptable institutional framework within which such policies can be implemented.

Indigenization   Through indigenization (*korenizatsiia*) the Party has sought to ensure that the most visible leadership within each national unit is drawn from the indigenous population. As Clifford Geertz has observed, "a primordially based 'corporate feeling of oneness' remains for many the *fons et origio* of legitimate authority. . . . "[18]

In the 1920s the Soviet regime inaugurated the policy of placing national cadres in leading positions within each of the republics. As People's Commissar of Nationality Affairs Joseph Stalin announced: "It is . . . necessary that all Soviet organs in the border regions . . . should as far as possible be recruited from the local people. . . . Only in this way can Soviet power become comprehensible and dear to the laboring masses of the border regions."[19] Indigenization initially proved difficult, for there were few communists among these non-Russian nationalities. Thus, the Party inaugurated a program in 1921 to train national cadres.

The commitment of the Soviet regime to indigenization has vacillated over the decades. Stalin's purges hit the national cadres particularly hard, so that their proportionate share of posts—even in the nationality areas—apparently declined from the late 1920s through 1953. To reverse this policy after Stalin's death, the Party Presidium reportedly resolved to train a new generation of national cadres for service in minority areas and to replace incumbent officials in minority areas without command of the local language. Yet, even since 1953, the Party's indigenization policy has been torn between short-term accommodation to national desires and the longer-term objective of fostering the fusion of nationalities. The 1961 Party Program favored the latter, maintaining that "the growing scale of communist construction calls for the continuous exchange of trained personnel among nations," a policy that would appear to work at cross-purposes to indigenization. In contrast, the new version of this Program, consistent with its less-ambitious views of the achievement of communism, seems to balance these competing objectives, promising both "to develop inter-republic exchanges of cadres of workers and specialists and to expand and improve the training of skilled personnel from among citizens of all nations and nationalities living in a republic."[20]

The indigenization policy has resulted in expanded non-Russian Party membership and officeholding. The Party participation rate among the non-Russian nationalities—that is, the ratio of their percentage of the Party membership to their percentage of the total population, with 1.0 corresponding to equal representation—has risen from 0.74 in 1926 to 0.80 in 1961 and to 0.84 in 1982.[21] Still, while a few nationalities (most notably the Jews, Georgians, and Russians) have been consistently over represented in this statistical sense, most (and particularly the peoples of Central Asia) remain underincorporated. Co-optation of members of these nationalities into the key positions within the national territories has been most successful among the titular nationalities of the union republics. U.S. intelligence analysts Ellen Jones and Fred W. Grupp conclude:

> In 12 of the 14 republics, natives are over-represented among republic elites; in some cases, substantially so. Even in the area of internal security—traditionally thought of as a haven for Great Russian dominance in the provinces—native representation is significant. In 1979, for example, half of the republic KGB chairmen were "natives"; 62% of the Administrative Organs Department Chiefs (the agency within the Party that monitors military and internal control functionaries), and 85% of the republic level MVD chiefs were "natives."[22]

Of the 44 union-republic Party first secretaries between 1954 and 1976, 86.4 percent were drawn from the non-Russian nationalities. Indeed, in March 1986, all of these first secretaries were drawn from the titular nationalities of the respective republics. (In December 1986, this pattern was broken with appointment of an ethnic Russian as First Secretary in the Kazakh Republic.) Of 66 first secretaries of the autonomous republics, 57.6 percent were non-Russians between 1954 and 1976; and in March 1986, two-thirds of those whose nationality could be identified were indigenous. This indigenization appears to have contributed to the cohesion of the multiethnic Soviet state, particularly by tying indigenous elites to the Soviet system through the mobility opportunities offered them.[23]

National Cultural Forms   Following the Revolution, the Soviet state began a rigorous program to develop indigenous cultural forms, creating written languages, preserving traditional dances and literary forms, and restoring architectural monuments. Thus, the poems of Suleiman Stalsky, an illiterate Daghestani living in a Caucasian mountain village whom Maxim Gorky described as the "Homer of the Twentieth Century," were transcribed as he recited them and subsequently published widely. The improvised songs of the Kazakh bard Dzhambul Dzhabaev were similarly preserved.[24] These forms were not cultivated simply for their own cultural value, but because they were the most-effective vehicle for bringing the message of socialism; requiring the minorities to learn Russian ways before they could comprehend the socialist message would not only have made the process of Sovietization protracted, but also would have made it seem more alien.

The Bolsheviks insisted that each nationality have its own written language, but this created some complex problems. Some nationalities did not have a unique language. It is not at all clear whether the language spoken by most Belorussians, for example, was distinct from—or simply a dialect of—Russian in 1917. The Bolsheviks, nonetheless, decided to promote usage of an officially distinct Belorussian language as the basis of this nationality. In Central Asia the lingua franca Chagatai, a common language written in Arabic script used among the local intelligentsia, was gaining currency in most major cities. The Soviets chose to suppress this and develop separate Uzbek, Kazakh, Turkmen, and Kirgiz written languages. Among many nationalities the indigenous languages had not yet been committed to writing; so the regime sent linguists around the Soviet Union to develop written languages for many groups, some of which, such as the Selkupi in the Tomsk area and the Ude in the Far East, "had no prospect of developing a culture of their own." These programs were coupled with the national campaign to promote literacy as a vehicle for Sovietization.[25]

The consequences of these policies are difficult to discern. It is unclear to what extent Soviet policies permit all languages an equal opportunity to develop as distinctive cultural forms. While the titular nationalities of the union republics have the opportunity to receive a complete education through the university level in the native tongue, the less-populous nationalities may receive instruction only through the primary or secondary grades, if at all. Conversely, complete instruction in Russian is available almost everywhere. Similarly, the production of printed material for the minority languages may not place these on an equal footing with Russian: Although 41.4 percent of the Soviet people considered their native tongue to be something other than Russian, only 23.2 percent of the titles and 16.1 percent of the total runs of books and brochures in 1983 were in these other languages.[26] Nonetheless,

> some 127 different languages are still spoken in the country, 18 of them by at least a million people each. Radio programs are broadcast in 67 languages, school textbooks are printed in 52 and journals in 42, theaters give performances in 47, and works of fiction are reportedly printed in 76 different languages.[27]

Among all 15 of the titular nationalities of the union republics, the percentage that considers the indigenous language its mother tongue has remained relatively constant, not changing more than five percentage points in the five decades from

1926 to 1979. And among all but 2 of these nationalities this figure was still above 90 percent in the latter year. (See Table 12.2.) This continued use of indigenous languages may possibly be due to official policies.

Centralization   Underpinning the homogenizing policies of the Soviet Union is the reality of centralized power. Although the state is organized on federal lines, the Party is not. The Second Party Program, adopted in 1919, made this explicit. Even at a time when the Soviet republics were formally independent, the Eighth Congress decreed: "The Central Committees of the Ukrainian, Latvian, Lithuanian Communists enjoy the status of regional committees of the Party, and are wholly subordinated to the Central Committee of the RKP."[28] Democratic centralism in both the state and Party leads to the subordination of nationality-based territories to Moscow. The scope of all-union plans and policies strips subordinate authorities of much decision-making responsibility.

In addition to the normal controls over subordinate authorities, the Party's second Secretaries in the non-Russian areas perform a special role that might be labelled the Russian-Prefect, the "nationality administrator," or the "controller and watchdog"—the representative on the scene from Moscow to keep a watch on the minority leaders. Thus, 65.8 percent of union-republic and 56.6 percent of autonomous-republic second secretaries between 1954 and 1976 were Russians or Russified Slavs. The second secretaries are assisted by Russians throughout the Party apparatus in minority areas. As Bialer cautions, these Russians may play only a limited role: "It is wrong to assert that these Russian officials are actually the managers of the republics, behind-the-scenes substitutes for native figureheads."[29] Nonetheless, they are critical to maintaining Moscow's control over the national territories.

Sovietization   An essential part of the homogenization of the Soviet peoples results from the regime's efforts to infuse national forms with a socialist content— the so-called Sovietization of peoples. The national forms cultivated by the new regime were not to be a vehicle for perpetuating distinct heritages, but for purveying a common unifying message: socialism. Thus, the themes of Dzhambul Dzhabaev's songs, which were originally devoted to "the wide pastures of Kazakhstan and the lives of the nomadic cattle breeders," changed under the pressures of Stalinism to "the collectivization of agriculture, the five-year plans, the Stakhanovite movement, the adoption of the Soviet constitution, and attacks on bourgeois nationalists and kulaks."[30]

The efforts to make these diverse traditions "national in form but socialist in content" inevitably came at the expense of some national forms themselves: The effort to make all nationalities socialist has meant imposing a uniform Soviet institutional structure. Party, state, industrial enterprises, and collective farms, invariant throughout the Soviet Union, have replaced traditional institutions and have made the people more alike. Creation of a unified political structure undermined the influence of the chieftains and religious leaders who had led the more traditional cultures. Land reform and sedentarization meant an at-

Table 12.2 LINGUISTIC AUTONOMY AND GEOGRAPHICAL INTEGRITY OF MAJOR SOVIET NATIONALITIES, 1979 (with populations over one million) (Percentages)

Nationality	Linguistic Autonomy			Geographical Integrity	
	Native Is First Language	Fluent In Russian	Not Fluent In Native	Percent In Homeland	Percent of Homeland
Slavic					
Russian	99.8	—	0.0	82.6	82.6
Ukrainian	82.8	66.9	10.4	86.2	73.6
Belorussian	74.2	82.4	15.2	80.0	79.4
Caucasian					
Armenian	90.7	47.1	6.9	65.6	89.7
Georgian	98.3	28.4	1.3	96.1	68.8
Baltic					
Lithuanian	97.9	53.8	1.5	95.1	80.0
Latvian	95.0	61.5	3.4	93.4	53.7
Estonian	95.3	28.8	3.2	92.9	64.7
Other European					
Moldavian	93.2	53.3	4.7	85.1	63.9
German	57.0	94.3	43.0	—	—
Jewish	14.2	97.0	80.4	0.6	5.4
Chuvash	81.7	82.9	14.0	50.7	68.4
Mordvinian	72.6	92.9	20.1	28.4	34.2
Polish	29.1	70.9	70.9	—	—
Central Asian					
Uzbek	98.5	49.9	1.2	84.9	68.7
Kazakh	97.5	54.3	2.0	80.7	36.0
Tadjik	97.8	30.4	1.9	77.2	58.8
Turkmen	98.7	26.3	1.1	93.3	68.4
Kirgiz	97.9	29.8	2.0	88.5	47.9
Other Turkic					
Tatar	85.9	82.1	10.5	26.0	47.6
Azeri	97.8	31.2	1.5	86.0	78.1
Bashkir	67.0	72.0	31.5	68.2	24.3

Source: Tsentral'noe statisticheskoe upravlenie, *Chislennost' i sostav naseleniia SSSR po dannym vsesoiuznoi perepisi naseleniia 1979 goda* (Moscow: Finansy i Statistika, 1985), 71–73.

tack on the foundations of their traditional ways of life. Development of a unified educational system meant sacrificing traditional religious schools in Central Asia. All literature and art had to conform to the tenets of socialist realism; and all Soviet writers, artists, architects, and performers, regardless of nationality, had to submit to the discipline of their respective unions.

Assimilation   Homogenization is not simply the inevitable consequence of Sovietization, the building of a new "international" culture that transcends particular cultures, but also the result of programs to induce the minority cultures to assimilate through Russianization, Russification, and attacks on the indigenous cultures. Russianization is the policy of promoting literacy in the Russian language among the non-Russian nationalities. A decree of March 13, 1938, mandates that all secondary school students, regardless of nationality, must study the Russian language. In the 1950s this requirement was extended down to the first grade. The incentives to learn Russian well are compelling, for access to the leading institutions and posts requires a firm command of this language. Instruction in the best universities is in Russian; the daily affairs of the all-union institutions at the pinnacle of Soviet society are also conducted in Russian.

Russianization among the minority populations has apparently succeeded in making nearly half (49.1 percent in 1979) fluent in Russian as a second language, and the growth in this figure in recent years appears to be quite substantial—up almost a third (from 37.1 percent) in the nine years since the 1970 census. It is not entirely clear, however, whether acquisition of Russian as a second language contributes to abandonment of one's native tongue. The proportion of non-Russians who considered Russian their first language stood at only 13.1 percent in 1979, up only 1.5 percentage points since 1970 and less than doubled (up from 7 percent) in the half century since the 1926 census. Brian Silver finds in his analysis that "policies designed to increase the knowledge of Russian as a second language need not lead to loss of the traditional national languages as mother tongues."[31]

Russification is the policy of forcing non-Russians to abandon elements of their own cultures for those that are Russian. Central to these efforts has been the official policy to promote linguistic fusion—to make the minority languages more like Russian. For example, Stalin in the late 1930s forced the non-Russian languages of the Soviet Union to adopt the Cyrillic alphabet. (Linguists sent to Siberia and Central Asia during the previous decade to develop national written languages for the Turkic and Mongol peoples had relied upon the Latin alphabet, for at the time this was purported to be the most modern, universal, and "proletarian" alphabet. Between 1936 and 1940, however, nearly all of the minority alphabets were replaced by Cyrillic.) At the end of World War II, after annexing the eastern portions of Romania, even the Moldavians speaking a dialect of Romanian, a Romance language distantly related to Italian, were forced to transliterate their language into Cyrillic. Thus, 60 of the 66 written Soviet languages currently use this alphabet. Among the titular nationalities of the union republics only five—the Armenians, Georgians, Estonians, Latvians, and Lithuanians—do not employ it; and even these, particularly the Baltic peoples, have experienced periodic pressures to change.[32]

The transliteration of non-Russian languages into Cyrillic set the stage for further Russification by making it easier to adopt Russian loan words. Indigenous languages among nationalities at earlier stages of socioeconomic development often lack vocabularies appropriate to modern institutions. Words for new concepts such as automobile, dialectical materialism, or nuclear fusion must be either created from archaisms and neologisms or borrowed from other languages. To increase the assimilative consequences of this process, Soviet nationalities have been required to adopt Russian terms for such concepts and to employ the Russian orthography. Increasingly, therefore, the political, scientific, and technological vocabularies of many languages are Russian. A study of Kazakh-language newspapers over two decades ago found that between 20 and 30 percent of the words employed were Russian. And in the Yakut-language press, about 30 percent of the vocabulary was Russian. Linguistic fusion has not been universally successful, however: In Moldavia, for example, there has been "a dramatic exodus of Slavic-origin words from Moldavian publications since the late 1940s."[33] And at present, the "new terms that are being coined in Moldavia are Romance-based."[34]

Assimilation has also meant an attack on the traditions of non-Russian nationalities. This reached its peak under Stalin after the Second World War. "From 1948–1953, the Mongol national epic *Geser* was attacked as a symbol of feudalism, Pan-Mongolism, and religious prejudice."[35] Similarly, the Azerbaidjani national epic *Dede Korkut,* the Turkmen *Korkut Ata,* the Kazakh *Koblandy-Batyr,* and the Uzbek *Alpamysh* were all banned. Only the Kirgiz national epic *Manas* was not condemned in its entirety in these years, but even this was highly censored to remove "reactionary" passages, so that the published work contained fewer than 10 percent of its original lines.[36] Even now, minority writers who express too much affection for their native lands or peoples have been routinely condemned as bourgeois nationalists.

The attack on the traditions of the non-Russians has also involved rewriting history to attempt to alter national memories. In his study of Soviet historiographical treatment of the non-Russian nationalities, Lowell Tillett of Wake Forest University argues that Soviet historians support official policies "not only by touting the accomplishments of the Soviet period, but by rewriting the history of the Russian Empire in such a way as to reduce friction and violence among its peoples to a minimum, and to emphasize the positive results of Russian empire-building."[37] The Tsarist conquest of the non-Russian nationalities is portrayed as a progressive step bringing political stability, a higher standard of living, and a more-advanced civilization. National resistance leaders, who have traditionally been the focus of national identity among many of these minorities, are either ignored, portrayed as reactionaries, or recast as friends of the Empire. The Russians are extolled as the leading element in Russia—as the elder brother (*starshii brat*) to be emulated by other nationalities. The history of the Soviet period portrays the Soviet Union as "the first to show the whole world a splendid example of Marxist-Leninist resolution of the complex nationalities problem, welding peoples together in a single fraternal family."[38] As an instrument of socialization, the alteration of history can sometimes not only blunt or erase memories, but also "create" new ones.

The success of this Russification effort is unclear. The rate of ethnic reidentification among non-Russians varies widely: According to one estimate, the titular nationalities of union republics experience much lower rates of assimilation than the numerically smaller nationalities such as the Karelians and Mordvinians. Indeed, for 11 of the titular nationalities of union republics, the "halving time"—the hypothetical number of years before half of those between the ages 0 and 38 would change their ethnic identification—was in excess of 500 years, reaching a high of 2954 years for the Uzbeks. And among 5 of these (Georgians, Armenians, Lithuanians, Kazakhs, and Belorussians), the combination of low Russification rates among their members and high rates of assimilation to their nationality by other, smaller nationalities has produced virtually no net loss or, in the case of the Georgians, an actual gain in members as measured by the hypothetical "halving time."[39]

Soviet policies may actually have had the unintended consequence of heightening rather than erasing national identification and consciousness. According to Carleton University's Teresa Rakowska-Harmstone,

> The failure of government policies to achieve the goal of equality may well have contributed to a resurgence and intensification of national feelings based on perceptions of real or imagined discrimination in development policies and on the urge to press particular demands on the central authorities. The merging of such attitudes with traditional ethnic antagonisms and the desire to preserve distinct cultural heritages seems to be providing the basis for the growth of a qualitatively new form of nationalism.

The emergence of this new nationalism she attributes to the development of indigenous modern elites concerned for the welfare of their respective national communities, the federal system that permits minority elites to develop contacts with the mass of co-nationals and to pursue policies to reinforce national identification, and continued hegemony and "national chauvinism" by the Great Russians.[40]

Coercion   The ultimate sanction behind these homogenizing policies has been coercion. The Soviet leadership has made it clear that it will move swiftly against those who are too nationalistic. The policy of indigenization in the 1920s brought to power national cadres who sometimes subverted the policies of Moscow. When Stalin inaugurated his campaign to eliminate the kulaks and bourgeoisie, leaders of Belorussia argued that since their republic had never developed an indigenous bourgeoisie, it could be spared the worst of the intensified class struggle. Similarly, national leaders in Central Asia resisted complete integration of their economies within the five-year plans. Stalin responded with purges to eliminate these leaders; indeed, the indigenous minority leadership was among the hardest hit by the Stalin Purges. The post-Stalinist leadership has made it clear that excessive enthusiasm for national autonomy will still bring retribution. In 1962, the Chairman of the Council of Ministers of the Kazakh Republic was removed after expressing while intoxicated sentiments that were considered just a little too nationalistic. Four years later, the First Secretary of the Armenian Party was removed for failing to take adequate steps to curb disturbances in the Armenian capital of Erevan on the 50th anniversary of the Turkish massacre of Armenians. In 1973, both the Ukrainian Party First Secretary Petr Shelest and the Georgian Party First Secretary V. P. Mzhavanadze were removed from the Politburo, with criticisms of their "national narrow-mindedness" and overzealous promotion of local interests. And in December 1986, the Kazakh First Secretary

Dinmukhamed Kunaev was removed and the Kazakh Party apparatus purged under similar charges.

The use of coercion took on its most extreme forms during World War II with the assault on whole nationalities. In 1941, because of fears that the Germans would exploit the loyalties of the Volga Germans, approximately 380,000—the entire population—were moved from the Volga River to Central Asia and southern Siberia. In 1943–44, as the Soviet Armies began to reclaim Nazi-occupied regions, Stalin ordered the forcible removal of those nationalities he accused of collaborating with the Nazis. In the Daghestan region approximately 408,000 Chechen, 92,000 Ingush, 76,000 Karachai, 43,000 Balkars, and 134,000 Kalmyks were removed to Central Asia and southern Siberia. On the Crimea more than 200,000 Crimean Tatars were removed. It is said that Stalin entertained the notion of deporting the entire Ukrainian population, but lacked the boxcars needed to move millions. Most of these deported nationalities have since 1957 been rehabilitated and resettled in their homelands. The exceptions are the Volga Germans and Crimean Tatars, who have been rehabilitated but not permitted to return to the Volga or Crimea.

Assessment of Soviet Nationality Policies

The integration of Soviet society is closely tied to the engineering of equality among nationalities. Ellen Jones and Fred W. Grupp describe Soviet nationality policy as "an attempt to integrate the minority nationalities into modern Soviet society by equalizing ethnic socioeconomic levels and political participation rates."[41] Western assessments of the success of this policy are mixed: Rakowska-Harmstone, for example, finds "little real change in the relative standing of national groups."[42] Studies of inequalities among republics in the distribution of socioeconomic benefits, which are frequently used as indirect measures of inequalities among national groups, appear to support this conclusion. Jones and Grupp, however, find that more direct statistical measures of national socioeconomic and political participation by the various nationalities "point unambiguously to convergence [among them]. . . . As a result, many of the differences in rates of economic and political participation between minority groups have been reduced."[43] (See Figure 12.2.) This has been accomplished through such policies as "affirmative action" programs of quotas and remedial education "to promote fuller minority representation in higher education" and recruitment campaigns to expand minority participation in the Party and in state posts.[44]

Jones and Grupp add, however, some important qualifications to the finding of reduced differences among minorities. First, equalization has had winners and losers: Late modernizing nationalities, particularly among the Islamic peoples, have improved their relative standing as they "caught up" with the Russians. But those nationalities such as the Jews, Armenians, and Georgians who had "historically led the Slavs in the modernization process or in access to high status roles [suffered] a gradual erosion of their relative advantage." Second, the gains for the winners have not been constant over time. "Some equalization policy . . . has been most successful in promoting rapid declines in ethnic and regional disparities during periods of prosperity [such as the 1960s]. It has been less successful in sustaining this progress during periods of contracting economic growth [such as the 1970s]."[45] And even though the overall trend appears to be toward greater equalization among nationalities, substantial inequalities remain: The proportion of Central Asian Turks who have completed a higher education ranges from under one-half to less than two-thirds of the educational attainment rate among Russians; and the CPSU membership rate among Latvians, Lithuanians, Uzbeks, Tadjiks, and Turkmen remains below two-thirds that of the Russians.[46]

Demographic Transition and Future Nationality Problems

In recent years, substantial attention has been focused on the future of the national problem in the Soviet Union and whether these Soviet policies will continue to cope with this successfully. In particular, the unequal levels of socioeconomic development among the peoples of the Soviet Union has complicated the nationality issue with a problem frequently called the *demographic transition*. As the Soviet Union has modernized and so become more urbanized, population growth rates have fallen. But because the pace of modernization and urbanization has not been equal among the different nationalities, differential growth rates have resulted. (Urbanization itself ranged in 1979 from 70.5 percent in the RSFSR and Estonia down to 40.2 percent in Uzbekistan and below 40 percent in Kirgizia and Tadjikistan.) In particular, while the annual growth rates in recent years have been below 1.0 percent for many of the European nationalities, it has been above 3.0 percent for much of the Asian population. (See Table 12.3.) If this disparity continues through the end of the century, the titular nationalities of the Asian union republics will rise from 12.0 percent of the total Soviet population in 1979 to 18.5 percent in 2000. In short, a growing proportion of the population is Turkic, a phenomenon known colloquially in the Soviet Union (and this is something of a slur) as "the yellowing" (*ozheltenie*) of the Soviet Union.[47]

This demographic trend has attracted attention at the very top of the Soviet state, leading Brezhnev to call for development of a demographic policy for the Soviet Union. Many of the resulting programs have sought to give European women an incentive to bear children or at least remove some of the obstacles to bearing more than one child in urban and industrial regions. These have included paid leave for working mothers to spend the early years with their children, increased monthly payments to single mothers, expanded provisions for birth grants and monthly child allowances, and guarantees of housing for couples with children. More recently, it has been suggested that Central Asian women should be encouraged to limit the number of births. The problems produced by the demographic transition, however, particularly as they bear on inequities among the nationalities, are complex and cannot be resolved so simply.[48]

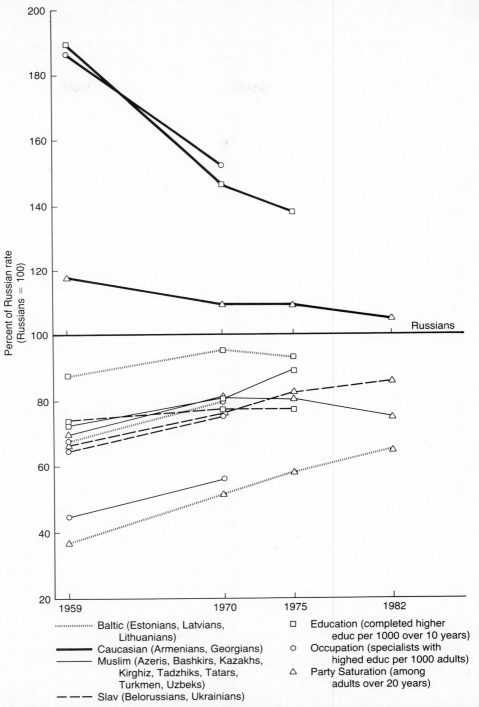

Figure 12.2 Convergence/Equalization among Soviet Nationalities, 1959–1982. (*Source:* From data in Ellen Jones and Fred W. Grupp, "Modernization and Ethnic Equalization," *Soviet Studies* 36 [April 1984], 159–184.)

Table 12.3   GROWTH RATES FOR THE MAJOR SOVIET NATIONALITIES, 1959–2000

Nationality	Annual Growth Rate		Percent of Population			
	1959–70	1970–79	1959	1970	1979	2000*
European Nationalities						
Armenians	2.25	1.73	1.3	1.5	1.6	1.9
Moldavians	1.81	1.07	1.1	1.1	1.1	1.2
Georgians	1.71	1.07	1.3	1.3	1.4	1.4
Lithuanians	1.24	0.75	1.1	1.1	1.1	1.1
Russians	1.12	0.70	54.6	53.4	52.4	50.3
Germans	1.19	0.53	0.8	0.8	0.7	0.7
Belorussians	1.23	0.49	3.8	3.7	3.6	3.3
Ukrainians	0.82	0.43	17.8	16.9	16.2	14.6
Chuvash	1.30	0.37	0.7	0.7	0.7	0.6
Estonians	0.16	0.14	0.5	0.4	0.4	0.3
Latvians	0.19	0.07	0.7	0.6	0.5	0.5
Poles	−1.31	−0.15	0.7	0.5	0.4	0.4
Mordvinians	−0.15	−0.61	0.6	0.5	0.5	0.3
Jews	−0.46	−1.64	1.1	0.9	0.7	0.3
Asian Nationalities						
Tadjiks	3.94	3.45	0.7	0.9	1.1	1.9
Uzbeks	3.93	3.43	2.9	3.8	4.8	8.0
Turkmen	3.89	3.22	0.5	0.6	0.8	1.2
Kirgiz	3.75	3.07	0.5	0.6	0.7	1.1
Azeri	3.69	2.52	1.4	1.8	2.1	2.9
Kazakhs	3.52	2.39	1.7	2.2	2.5	3.4
Bashkirs	2.08	1.13	0.5	0.5	0.5	0.5
Tatars	1.62	0.70	2.4	2.5	2.4	2.3

*Straight-line projection based on 1970–1979 annual growth rate.

Source: Tsentral'noe statisticheskoe upravlenie, *Naselenie SSSR; Chislennost', sostav, i dvizhenie naseleniia* (Moscow: Statistika, 1975), 37–39; Tsentral'noe statisticheskoe upravlenie, *Chislennost' is sostav naseleniia SSSR po dannym vsesoiuznoi perepisi naseleniia 1979 goda* (Moscow: Finansy i Statistika, 1985), 71–73.

One aspect of the demographic problem is economic. The uneven growth rates among nationalities is associated with uneven regional growth. During the 1970s, the average annual population growth rate for the RSFSR was 1.3 percent, while for Central Asia it was 3.6 percent. In the former, the birth rate by 1970 had fallen below the level necessary simply to replace the parent population.[49] Thus, the growth in population in the industrial centers of the Russian Republic is not keeping pace with the demand for labor, but in the less-industrialized regions of Central Asia it is outstripping the available jobs. How to bring together labor and industry?

One possible solution might be to use the European population more intensively, perhaps by raising the retirement age. But any program that would seriously erode the quality of life among citizens is likely to encounter stiff resistance. Another might be to reduce significantly the number of males conscripted each year, releasing them for the labor force. This is unlikely to meet with approval from the military or even a Party leadership concerned with its effect upon Soviet military power. A third alternative is to reduce the years of compulsory schooling. But the demands for a modern industrial labor force with skills appropriate to advanced technology require more, not less, education. And the trend in recent Soviet policies has been toward raising the number of years of schooling that must be completed.

Rather than using the European population close to the industrial centers more intensively, the Soviet leaders may attempt to use the Asian, and particularly the Turkic, populations more extensively. Involving the latter more fully in the modern industrial economy of the Soviet Union may prove difficult, however. Much of the Turkic population appears to have few of the skills needed for modern industry. For example, their levels of educational attainment tend to be lower than for the European population. Moreover, the bulk of the Turkic population is located far from the industrial centers. Bringing the labor force and jobs together by relocating industry would be very costly and not particularly "rational" from the perspective of producers since both supplies of raw materials and finished products for markets would have to be shipped over great distances. Labor and industry might be brought together by encouraging migration from the "labor-surplus" regions to the industrial centers. Yet, according to Ann Helgeson, "interregional migration, far from alleviating some of the regional labor imbalances in the country, has tended to exacerbate the problems." The net redistribution of population appears to be from the "frost-belt" of the RSFSR toward the "sun-belt" of the northern Caucasus and southern Ukraine, where there is a relative labor surplus. The Turkic population, in particular, appears to be unwilling to move to the industrial centers of the frost belt. Many prefer to live in the countryside. And since they tend to have larger families, they find the housing in the northern urban areas inadequate. Moreover, when ethnic tensions have risen, some Turks have found the Russians in these northern cities as inhospitable as their climate.[50]

A second consequence of the demographic transition is a decline in the draft-age population. At its peak in the late 1970s, the Soviet military manpower system guaranteed an annual cohort of about 2.6 million 18-year-old males from which the armed services could draft. This had fallen below 2.0 million a year by 1985, while Soviet military manpower needs have remained at an estimated 1.3 to 1.6 million a year.[51] As the draft must take a larger share of the eligible cohort, it must reach further down into the manpower pool in order to meet its numerical needs, with obvious implications for the quality of the Soviet armed forces.

An additional consequence of this diminishing cohort—one that is aggravated by the unevenness of the demographic transition among nationalities—is the growing proportion of recruits drawn from the Asian populations. In the late 1980s, between a fifth and a quarter of the draft-age population is drawn from the Turkic nationalities, and by the end of the century, Turkic draftees will rise to about two-fifths of the total. The Turkic recruits tend to have fewer modern skills essential to handling sophisticated equipment. And they tend to be less fluent in the Russian language. Peter Zwick of Louisiana State University cites evidence that "the ability of army recruits (particularly those from Central Asia and Transcaucasia) to use basic Russian remains very poor. . . . [For example,] these recruits cannot comprehend even the most basic commands in Russian. . . . " The Kirgiz Party First Secretary reported in 1983 that conscripts who did not know enough Russian were sent to special courses to prepare them for military service, but implied that even after this, 30 percent of the conscripts were unqualified for service in combat areas and special units.[52]

To compound these problems, the Soviet leadership apparently fears that armed forces composed of non-Slavic troops, particularly when committed to action against fellow nationals, may prove unreliable. Following the initial invasion of Afghanistan, the French Sovietologist Alexandre Bennigsen noted, "Soviet Muslims fraternized with their Afghan co-religionists and, instead of teaching them the beauties of Marxism-Leninism, were taught Islam."[53] Indeed, according to Rand Corporation analysts Alexander Alexiev and S. Enders Wimbush, to limit potential dangers, "the most prominent stationing principle is that of extraterritoriality—the stationing of soldiers away from their own ethnic regions of the USSR."[54]

To deal with the military effects of the demographic trends, the Turkic recruits have frequently been placed in low-priority units, such as construction or farming detachments, rather than in the more advanced services such as the Strategic Rocket Forces, which has led to a form of de facto segregation in the military. Alexiev and Wimbush estimate combat units to be 80 percent or more Slavic and noncombat units to be 70 to 90 percent non-Slavic. This segregation is aggravated by the ethnic differences between conscripts and officers, for the latter are disproportionately drawn from the Russian and European populations. Ninety-one percent of the generals appointed between 1940 and 1970 were Slavs; and 60 percent of these officers were Russian. Of the 42 generals listed in the press between 1974 and 1975, 40 were Slavs, 1 an Armenian, and another a Volga German. A stratified military of elite European units and inferior Asian detachments—and within the latter European officers and Asian conscripts—can create serious problems of command and control, discipline, and morale.[55]

A third problem associated with the demographic transition is political. Will the Asian populations continue to accept Slavic and Russian dominance? Underrepresentation in the Party, in positions of managerial or administrative authority, and in the centers of decision-making power may become harder to justify as these Asian populations claim a larger share of the total population. And with this, their demands for a larger share in Soviet power may become more insistent. This trend has been manifest in recent Supreme Soviet sessions, when Central Asian representatives have cited their "leading role" in Soviet population growth as a justification for special attention in the allocation of scarce funds. Resentment over the continued centralization of decision-making power in Moscow appears to be growing.[56]

Whether the Soviet Union will continue to cope with these problems successfully—at least keeping them below the point of social turmoil—is unclear. Typical of the more pessimistic view (one that is widespread in the United States) a recent article in *Fortune* magazine predicts, "The new minority status of ethnic Russians . . . could well trigger a series of internal explosions powerful enough to fracture the Soviet state itself."[57] Bialer has argued that "the multinational character of the Soviet Union poses potentially the most serious threat to the legitimacy of the Soviet state and to the stability of the Soviet regime."[58]

Those who predict catastrophe, however, often overlook the many complexities of demographic change in the Soviet Union, such as falling growth rates among the minorities and growing assimilation. Moreover, they tend to underestimate the capacity of the Soviet regime to "muddle through" or, failing that, to marshal immense coercive resources to keep problems of its multinational population from reaching an open crisis.[59]

THE STATUS OF SOVIET WOMEN

Inequality between the sexes occupies a special place in the official Soviet view. Unlike equality among classes and nationalities, equality between the sexes is not to be achieved by elimination of the categories themselves nor even by elimination of the differences between them. Rather, in this view, women for immutable biological reasons play a distinctive role in the socioeconomic life of society at all stages of development—even into communism. In this view, "the mistake made by feminists in the United States . . . is that they take equality of the sexes to mean that men and women become more alike. A more realistic socialist notion of equality . . . takes immutable differences between the sexes as a given point of departure . . . "[60] Thus, equality of the sexes appears to mean equality of opportunity, not equality of outcomes. Yet with the premise of the immutable uniqueness of women, it is unclear whether even the former can actually be accomplished.

The Soviet model of development has had a complex, and not entirely consistent, impact on the status of women. While the young Bolshevik regime came to power with a commitment to the liberation of women and accomplished much in this regard, the pressures of forced-draft modernization led to their oppression with a unique "double burden." The young regime extended legal equality in its early acts, including the extension of full citizenship to women, removal of restrictions on the movement of married women, and legislation of equal pay for equal work. Along with these reforms came the liberalization of various Tsarist policies on issues frequently identified as "women's issues," including legalization of abortion, simplification of divorce, and maternity pay for working women. At the end of the second year of Soviet power, Lenin could proclaim: "In one of the most backward countries in Europe, more has been done to emancipate woman, to make her the equal of the 'strong sex', than has been done during the past 130 years by all the advanced, enlightened, 'democratic' republics of the world taken together."[61] Throughout the 1920s the Party's *Zhenotdel* (*Zhenskii otdel*), or Women's Department, mobilized Soviet women into the public life of the new society and agitated for their liberation—for example, convincing women in the Muslim regions to throw off their veils.

The economic revolutions of the Stalinist period, in one sense, contributed to the further equalization of the sexes by encouraging "a massive influx of women into industry, with women constituting some 82 percent of all newly employed workers between 1932 and 1937."[62] But this increase in employment was not matched by a corresponding decline in their other responsibilities, particularly their household responsibilities, and this led to the "double shift" or "double burden" of Soviet women. As Gail Warshofsky Lapidus of the University of California has argued:

> Except in the area of child care, and possibly communal dining, the Soviet household was obliged to provide for itself a large share of goods and services supplied by the market in other societies at comparable levels of development. . . . The economic role of the household in Soviet development had direct consequences for the position of women. In the absence of a radical change in the sexual division of labor, the burden of household responsibilities fell largely on their shoulders.[63]

In addition, the pronatalist policies of this period had the effect of actually increasing the household burden of women and forcing a retreat from the liberal policies on divorce and abortion. The subordination of women's issues to the economic goals of the day was marked by the dissolution of the Zhenotdel in 1930 and the audacious claim that the "woman question" had been solved and therefore was a closed issue.

The post-Stalinist period, particularly since 1960, has been marked by growing awareness that the "woman question" has not been solved under "mature socialism" and that full gender equality remains a goal, perhaps one to be achieved only under communism. Policies affecting the status of Soviet women, however, still seem to be shaped primarily not by concerns for their status but by other, principally economic objectives. Pronatalist policies, particularly among the European nationalities, have come to have a new urgency; and these have tended to reinforce traditional differences between gender roles. These policies "attempt to reduce the female work shift outside the home to allow women more time to perform their duties inside the home. . . . " By subordinating its policy on the "woman question" to its efforts to create the largest labor force for both the short and the long run, the Soviet Union has largely ignored many of the complex questions of gender equality, such as burden sharing within the household. Moreover, the pronatalist policies may actually have the consequence of reinforcing inequalities in the work force by encouraging the concentration of women in low-paying jobs and by interrupting their careers with extended leaves that hinder their promotion to higher-status positions.[64]

Despite these substantial limitations, Soviet policies have achieved some important successes in equalizing the life chances of the sexes—most dramatically in education, somewhat less so in employment, and only modestly in politics. In all these areas there is a pattern of expanding female participation, but persistent inequalities between women and men. "In the eyes of the new leaders, education was an essential means of liberating women from ignorance and superstition, of preparing them for active working lives, and of reducing inequality between the sexes." Thus, the literacy rate among women rose rapidly, equalling that among men by the time of the 1979 census: This stood at 32.3 percent (25.3 points behind men) in 1920; 81.6 percent (11.9 points behind) in 1939; and 99.8 percent in 1979. Women's share of enrollment in higher education rose from under one-fifth before the Revolution to almost a third in the late 1920s, and exactly half in 1974. These aggregate indicators, it is worth noting, may hide some significant inequalities; although admitted to higher-education institutions in equal numbers, female applicants may outnumber male applicants for some institutions by a factor of two to one, suggesting the existence of discriminatory quotas.[65]

The rapid expansion of female participation in the labor force under Soviet rule is reflected in the fact that women throughout the 1970s and 1980s have constituted 51 percent of all workers. Even though Soviet women have entered all segments of the economy, inequalities between the sexes tend to linger through sectoral and vertical segregation and through assignment of women to positions below their abilities. Women tend to be concentrated in those sectors and in those positions within each sector that bring lower status and less financial reward. The emphasis upon heavy industry in Soviet development, for example, has led to higher salaries and benefits in this sector, but women are less fully represented in positions here. Moreover, "Soviet women remain badly underrepresented in top-level and managerial posts, in relation to their participation in the work force as a whole." The inequities implied by this sectoral and vertical segregation are compounded by the tendency to assign women to positions below their qualifications. As a consequence, Soviet women tend to earn only two-thirds to three-quarters as much as men.[66]

The political role of Soviet women shows a similar, but more pronounced, pattern of expanding participation and persistent inequalities. The early years of Soviet rule brought a rapid expansion in political participation by Soviet women: The proportion voting rose from around one-third in 1926 to over four-fifths in 1934; the proportion of women deputies in local soviets rose from about one-eighth in the former year to about three-tenths in the latter. This has continued to expand, so that in 1987 virtually all women vote and they hold more than half of the seats on local soviets. Yet women are largely excluded from the centers of power. Although women have constituted more than half of the Komsomol membership in recent years, they account for only about one in four Party members. In the Central Committee, fewer than 4 percent of all deputies elected since its creation have been women.[67] And only two women have ever been elected to the highest Party organs: E. A. Furtseva to the Politburo (1957–1961) and Secretariat (1957–1960) and A. P. Biriukova to the Secretariat (1986–). While women participate widely in the political life of the Soviet Union, in many ways on an equal footing with men, they do not share political power in any way that can be construed as equal.

As in the case of economic and ethnic inequalities, the progress of the Soviet system in guaranteeing gender equality has been substantial. And some comparative statistics suggest that it may fare very well when compared to Western societies, particularly when compared against similar stages of socioeconomic modernization. Nonetheless, the remaining inequalities in Soviet society are very real and it is not preordained that the Soviet path of development will be able to erase them in the future.

NOTES

1. A. M. Rumiantsev, *Dictionary of Scientific Socialism* (Moscow: Progress Publishers, 1984), 232.
2. Rumiantsev, *232*.
3. Milovan Djilas, *The New Class: An Analysis of the Communist System* (New York: Praeger, 1957), 39.
4. Tony Cliff, *Russia: A Marxist Analysis* (London: International Socialism, 1964), 122.
5. Mervyn Matthews, *Privilege in the Soviet Union: A Study of Elite Life-Styles Under Communism* (London: Allen & Unwin, 1978), 180.
6. Gerhard E. Lenski, *Power and Privilege: A Theory of Social Stratification* (New York: McGraw-Hill, 1966), 311–313.
7. Matthews, 23, 31, 38.
8. Matthews, 176, 177, 179.
9. Matthews, 176, 177.
10. Alec Nove, *The Soviet Economic System* (London: Allen & Unwin, 1977), 209.
11. Matthews, 157–159.
12. USSR Tsentral'noe Statisticheskoe Upravlenie, *Chislennost' i sostav naseleniia SSSR po dannym vsesoiuznoi perepisi naseleniia 1979 goda* (Moscow: Finansy i Statistika, 1985), 71–73. Descriptive introductions to the diverse nationalities include Zev Katz, Rosemarie Rogers, and Frederic Harned, eds., *Handbook of Major Soviet Nationalities* (New York: Free Press, 1975); and Shirin Akiner, *Islamic Peoples of the Soviet Union* (London: Kegan Paul International, 1975).
13. Karl Marx and Friedrich Engels, *Manifesto of the Communist Party* in Karl Marx and Friedrich Engels, *Selected Works* (Moscow: Progress Publishers, 1969), 1:124–125.
14. Walker Connor, *The National Question in Marxist-Leninist Theory and Strategy* (Princeton, N.J.: Princeton University Press, 1984), 14. Compare Robert Conquest, *Soviet Nationalities Policy in Practice* (New York: Praeger, 1967), 7.
15. V. I. Lenin, "Sotsialisticheskaia revoliutsiia i pravo natsii na samoopredelenie" ["Socialist Revolution and the Right of Nations to Self-Determination"], in *Polnoe sobranie sochinenii*, 5th ed. (Moscow: Politicheskaia Literatura, 1962), 27:255–256.
16. *Pravda,* 22 December 1972.
17. Seweryn Bialer, *Stalin's Successors: Leadership, Stability, and Change in the Soviet Union* (Cambridge, England: Cambridge University Press, 1980). See also John N. Hazard, "Statutory Recognition of Nationality Differences in the USSR," in Edward Allworth, ed., *Soviet Nationality Problems* (New York: Columbia University Press, 1971), 83–116.
18. Clifford Geertz, "The Integrative Revolution: Primordial Sentiments and Civil Relations in the New States," in Clifford Geertz, ed., *Old Societies and New States: The Quest for Modernity in Asia and Africa* (New York: Free Press, 1963), 120.
19. Quoted in Conquest, 50.
20. Connor, 281; *Program of the Communist Party of the Soviet Union* (New York: International Publishers, 1963), 118; *Pravda,* 7 March 1986.
21. Calculated from data in USSR Tsentral'noe Statisticheskoe Upravlenie (Ts.S.U.), *Narodnoe khoziaistvo SSSR, 1922-1982: Iubileinyi statisticheskii ezhegodnik* (Moscow: Finansy i Statistika, 1982), 33, 49; and Paul S. Shoup, *The East European and Soviet Data Handbook* (New York: Columbia University Press, 1981), 130, 140.
22. Ellen Jones and Fred W. Grupp, "Modernization and Ethnic Equalization in the USSR," *Soviet Studies* 36 (April 1984), 174; Bialer, 213–214.
23. Helene Carrere d'Encausse, *Decline of an Empire: The Soviet Socialist Republics in Revolt* (New York: Newsweek Books, 1979), 143; Bialer, 216.

24. Conquest, 64.
25. Eugene K. Keefe et al. *Area Handbook for the Soviet Union* (Washington, D.C.: Government Printing Office, 1971), 196.
26. Carrere d'Encausse, 175–182; USSR Tsentral'noe statisticheskoe upravlenie, *Narodnoe khoziaistvo SSSR v 1983g.* (Moscow: Finansy i Statistika, 1983), 521–523, 532–533.
27. Murray Feshbach, "The Soviet Union: Population Trends and Dilemmas," *Population Bulletin* 37 (August 1982), 9.
28. Quoted in Conquest, 27.
29. Bialer, 214–215; John Miller, "Cadres Policy in Nationalities Areas," *Soviet Studies* 29 (January 1977), 3–36.
30. Conquest, 64.
31. Ts. S. U., *Chislennost' i sostav naseleniia,* 71: Brian D. Silver, "Language Policy and the Linguistic Russification of Soviet Nationalities," in Jeremy R. Azrael, ed., *Soviet Nationality Policies and Practices* (New York: Praeger, 1978), 301.
32. Jonathan Pool, "Soviet Language Planning: Goals, Results, Options," in Azrael, 227.
33. Conquest, 76.
34. Pool, 235.
35. Conquest, 66.
36. Conquest, 66-69.
37. Lowell Tillet, *The Great Friendship: Soviet Historians on the Non-Russian Nationalities* (Chapel Hill, N.C.: University of North Carolina Press, 1969), 1.
38. V. A. Golikov, comp., *Sovetskii Soiuz: Politiko-ekonomicheskii spravochnik* (Moscow: Politizdat, 1975), 88.
39. Barbara A. Anderson and Brian D. Silver, "Estimating Russification of Ethnic Identity Among Non-Russians in the USSR," *Demography* 20 (November 1983), 461–489.
40. Teresa Rakowska-Harmstone, "The Dialectics of Nationalism in the USSR," *Problems of Communism* 23 (May-June 1974), 9–10. Also see Zvi Gitelman, "Are Nations Merging in the USSR?" *Problems of Communism* 32 (September-October 1983), 35–44.
41. Jones and Grupp, 159.
42. Rakowska-Harmstone, 12.
43. Jones and Grupp, 178-179.
44. Peter R. Zwick, "Soviet Nationality Policy: Social, Economic, and Political Aspects," in Gordon B. Smith, *Public Policy and Administration in the Soviet Union* (New York: Praeger, 1980), 159.
45. Jones and Grupp, 159, 179.
46. Jones and Grupp, 164, 171, 173.
47. Feshbach, 19–26. The best overview of this problem is Jeremy R. Azrael, "Emergent Nationality Problems in the USSR," in Azrael, ed., 363–390.
48. Ann Helgeson, "Demographic Policy," in Archie Brown and Michael Kaser, eds., *Soviet Policy for the 1980s* (Bloomington, Ind.: Indiana University Press, 1982), 133–139.
49. Helgeson, 123.
50. Helgeson, 128–129. On recent problems attending interregional migration, see Ann Sheehy, "Racial Disturbances in Yakutsk," *Radio Liberty Research Bulletin* RL 251/86 (July 1, 1986). See also Ann Sheehy, "Central Asian Republics Under Pressure To Improve Use of Labor Resources," *Radio Liberty Research Bulletin* RL 287/86 (July 25, 1986).

51. Harriet Fast Scott and William F. Scott, *The Armed Forces of the USSR,* 2d ed. (Boulder, Colo.: Westview Press, 1981), 304; Herbert Goldhamer, *The Soviet Soldier: Soviet Military Management at the Troop Level* (New York: Crane, Russak and Company, 1975), 7; Azrael, 372.

52. Zwick, 154. See also Ann Sheehy, "Concern About the Preparedness of Central Asians for Military Service," *Radio Liberty Research Bulletin* RL 213/86 (May 30, 1986); Dan N. Jacobs and Theresa M. Hill, "Soviet Ethnic Policy in the 1980s: Theoretical Consistency and Political Reality," in Joseph L. Nogee, ed., *Soviet Politics: Russia After Brezhnev* (New York: Praeger, 1985), 171.

53. Alexandre Bennigsen, "Soviet Muslims and the Muslim World," in S. Enders Wimbush, *Soviet Nationalities in Strategic Perspective* (London: Croom Helm, 1985), 220.

54. Alexander Alexiev and S. Enders Wimbush, "The Ethnic Factor in the Soviet Armed Forces" (Report R-1930/1) (Santa Monica, Calif.: Rand Corporation, 1983), 7. See also Alexander R. Alexiev, "Soviet Nationalities Under Attack: The World War II Experience," in Wimbush, 61–74.

55. Alexiev and Wimbush, 8; Carrere d'Encausse, 162.

56. Feshbach, 20; Bialer, 207.

57. Herbert E. Meyer, "The Coming Soviet Ethnic Crisis," *Fortune* 98 (August 14, 1978), 156.

58. Bialer, 212.

59. Gail W. Lapidus, "Ethnonationalism and Political Stability: The Soviet Case," *World Politics* 36 (1984), 555–580; Gail W. Lapidus, "The Nationality Question and the Soviet System," *Proceedings of the Academy of Political Science* 35 (1984), 98–112.

60. Mary Buckley, "Soviet Interpretations of the Woman Question," in Barbara Holland, ed. *Soviet Sisterhood: British Feminists on Women in the USSR* (London: Fourth Estate, 1985), 43–44.

61. Quoted in Gail Warshofsky Lapidus, "Sexual Equality in Soviet Policy: A Developmental Perspective," in Dorothy Atkinson, Alexander Dallin, and Gail Warshofsky Lapidus, eds., *Women in Russian* (Stanford, Calif.: Stanford University Press, 1977), 119.

62. Lapidus, "Sexual Equality", 125.

63. Lapidus, "Sexual Equality," 128.

64. Lapidus, "Sexual Equality", 136–138; Buckley, 42, 49–50.

65. Richard B. Dobson, "Educational Policies and Attainment,' in Atkinson, Dallin, and Lapidus, 267–269, 284, 287; Ts. S. U., *Narodnoe khoziaistvo SSSR, 1922–1982,* 41.

66. Gail Warshofsky Lapidus, *Women in Soviet Society: Equality, Development, and Social Change* (Berkeley, Calif.: University of California Press, 1978), 162, 194–198, Ts. S.U. *Narodnoe khoziaistvo SSSR, 1922–1982,* 403; Jo Peers, "Workers by Hand and Womb—Soviet Women and the Demographic Crisis," in Barbara Holland, ed., *Soviet Sisterhood: British Feminists on Women in the USSR* (London: Fourth Estate, 1985), 121–122.

67. Lapidus, *Women in Soviet Society,* 198–231; Bohdan Harasymiw, "Have Women's Chance for Political Recruitment in the USSR Really Improved?" in Tova Yedlin, ed., *Women in Eastern Europe and the Soviet Union* (New York: Praeger, 1980), 140–184.

chapter *13*

Soviet National Security Policies

Among the functions of governments, none is more central than the defense of national security. Richard Smoke has written, "The axiom of *the primacy of national security* among the responsibilities of government cannot be escaped." As Smoke also observes, "[I]t seems to be a fundamental attribute of human affairs that governments will accept national security as . . . a goal to which, if it seems necessary, almost every other social and national goal will be sacrificed."[1] Quite ironically, the Bolshevik leaders who took power in 1917 were least prepared, either by their previous training or by their ideology, for the demands of foreign policy. They tended to assume that traditional international relations would soon be a thing of the past. But foreign policy matters actually became a primary concern of the new regime as it dealt with the German and later British, French, Japanese, and American occupation of its soil. In the years since, particularly during the Second World War and early Cold War, these concerns have at times been preeminent, leading to the sacrifice of other goals.

The Bolshevik Revolution of 1917 brought to power a regime with a split international personality, for it was both a sovereign state and an international revolutionary movement.* This "schizophrenic" nature created a tension in the regime's foreign policy, a tension that runs throughout the seven decades of Soviet power. On the one hand, as a sovereign state in the international community, the Soviet Union must seek national security, which has oftentimes meant

---

*Soviet historians dispute the contention that world revolution was one of the objectives of the young soviet regime. See, for example, Nikolai Sivachev and Nikolai N. Yakovlev, *Russia and the United States: U.S.-Soviet Relations from the Soviet Point of View* (Chicago: University of Chicago Press, 1979), 34.

coming to an accommodation with the powers of the existing international order and even at times seeking to stabilize the status quo. On the other hand, as leader of an international revolutionary movement, the Soviet Union has sought to overturn the status quo and the very governments with which it has sought accommodation. These two goals are often incompatible; the second subverts the first. And so, the gains of diplomacy have more than once been lost to revolutionary excesses. With time the Soviet Union has more and more subordinated the second of these to the first, taking a more pragmatic view of revolution and international affairs. Nonetheless, even as late as the 1970s, there appear to have been instances when revolutionary adventures (such as the jump to support socialist Ethiopia in 1977) have led to significant diplomatic losses.

THE SOVIET WORLD VIEW

Marxist-Leninist theory provides the Soviet leadership only the broadest of guidelines in the field of foreign policy. The most important doctrinal statement on international affairs prior to 1917 appears in Lenin's *Imperialism: The Highest Stage of Capitalism,* which he wrote while in Zurich in 1916. In this tract Lenin argues that 20th-century capitalism is profoundly different from that of the 19th century, replacing competitive industrial capitalism with monopolistic finance capitalism. The latter flourishes by exporting capital and goods and importing raw materials, for only through these international transactions can it maintain high profits. In the late 19th century, with the growing internationalization of individual capitalist economies, the major capitalist powers divided the Third World into colonies, as each sought exclusive control of markets and materials within an empire. But once this scramble for empire had divided up the entirety of the Third World, it brought the imperialist powers into conflict with one another, for imperialist economies could continue to expand only by preying on other capitalist countries. Lenin argued that up to 1900 capitalism had been a progressive force, bringing down the feudal order, but after the turn of the century, once imperialism had become dominant, it began to decay. The sign of that decay was World War I, a war in which the major imperialist powers turned on each other.[2]

Lenin's theory of imperialism provided not only a broad theoretical perspective on the 20th century, but also more specific conclusions about contemporary events. First, the theory explained the new lease on life enjoyed by capitalism in the late 19th and early 20th centuries. Capitalism had not fallen from its own internal limitations, because it could exploit the backward countries of the world; and with the proceeds of that exploitation it had created a labor aristocracy at home and co-opted it into the bourgeois order. Second, the theory of imperialism explained the new contradictions that had emerged within the capitalist world—contradictions that would ultimately cause its downfall. Specifically, imperialism had globalized the class conflict, transforming the class struggle within individual societies into a world-wide confrontation between the bourgeoisie and an alliance of proletarians with the backward countries' toiling masses. Third, the theory points to the intensification of uneven development among capitalist countries as a source of new international conflict, creating antagonistic contradictions among them as some benefit from imperialism and others lag behind. And fourth, as a consequence of imperialist predacity and the deepening contradictions within the international capitalist system, war among capitalist countries is an ever-present danger.

From these philosophical foundations, the Soviets have derived more specific propositions that complete the doctrinal component of ideology as it bears upon Soviet foreign policy. The propositions are definitional or axiomatic and provide the conceptual building blocks from which the Soviet world view is apparently constructed. The first of these is that all foreign policy is class-based, reflecting the class nature of the regimes that make it. Thus, the foreign policy of the Soviet Union, by definition, is a proletarian foreign policy. In the words of the current Party program:

> The CPSU's international policy stems from the humane nature of socialist society, which is free of exploitation and oppression and has no classes or social groups with an interest in unleashing wars. It is indissolubly linked with the Party's fundamental, strategic tasks within the country, and it expresses the Soviet people's uniform desire—to engage in constructive labor and to live in peace with all peoples.[3]

Conversely, the international policy of capitalist states is bourgeois foreign policy: "What bourgeois governments present as national state interests is usually a far cry from genuine national interests . . . and prove to be merely the class interests of these governments themselves and of the monopoly-capital groups they represent."[4]

A second axiom derived from the Leninist theory of imperialism is that the policy of the proletariat is peace while that of the capitalist states is aggression. The foreign policy of imperialist states is inevitably expansionary, seeking to add new territories, peoples, and markets in order to preserve capitalism at home. Conversely, Soviet foreign policy by definition opposes aggression and war. The proletariat's interest is in domestic, socioeconomic and cultural development, which requires peace: "*The inner laws of socialist society* make the socialist states an irreconcilable adversary of aggression and conquest, of encroachment on peace, on the security and independence of nations. Socialist foreign policy aims to curb aggressors and to ensure peace and the independence of peoples."[5]

A third doctrinal proposition is that conflict is an inevitable feature of world politics—as long as antagonistic class differences persist. Under Lenin this was contained in the proposition that war among the imperialist powers was inevitable. He was more ambiguous on the question of the inevitability of war between capitalist and socialist states. During the Allied Intervention against his regime he predicted that war was likely. In his report to the Eighth Party Congress in 1919, Lenin argues: " . . . the existence of the Soviet Republic side by side with imperialist states for a long time is unthinkable. One or the other must triumph in the end. And before that end supervenes, a series of frightful collisions between the Soviet Republic and the bourgeois states will be inevitable."[6]

In the more peaceful times of the New Economic Policy, as Lenin attempted to build stable ties with the West and in particular to gain access to Western technology to rebuild the Soviet economy, he then talked increasingly of the possibility of peaceful coexistence. Under Khrushchev, the latter became a dominant theme and the doctrine of inevitability of capitalist-socialist war was put to rest. In his report to the 20th Party Congress in 1956, Khrushchev declared,

> There is, of course, a Marxist-Leninist precept that wars are inevitable as long as imperialism exists. This precept was evolved at a time when (1) imperialism was an all-embracing world system and (2) the social and political forces which did not want war were weak, poorly organized, and hence unable to compel the imperialists to renounce war. . . .
>
> In that period this precept was absolutely correct. At the present time, however, the situation has changed radically. . . .
>
> In these [present] circumstances certainly the Leninist precept that so long as imperialism exists, the economic basis giving rise to wars will also be preserved, remains in force. That is why we must display the greatest vigilance. As long as capitalism survives in the world, the reactionary forces representing the interests of the capitalist monopolies will continue their drive towards military gambles and aggression, and may try to unleash war. But war is not fatalistically inevitable. . . . [7]

Indeed, in recent years Party pronouncements have stressed the need to avoid war: According to the current Party Program, "The most critical problem facing mankind today is the problem of war and peace." The growing power of the socialist camp makes it possible to deter imperialist aggression and war, and the rise of nuclear technology makes "the peaceful coexistence of states with different social systems" a necessity.[8] This does not mean, however, that class struggle has come to an end. Rather, the means have changed from war to a peaceful struggle—a struggle of ideologies.

A fourth proposition derived from the Leninist theory of imperialism is that Soviet support for national liberation is a required part of *socialist internationalism*. The international communist movement, as the vanguard of the larger workers' movement, stands in the lead of a global progressive movement struggling against imperialism and war and for social progress. As the leader of socialism in its global struggle with capitalism, it is incumbent on the Soviet Union to aid these "progressive forces." In its relations with Third World states that have pursued "the path of socialist-orientation" in their development, the Party Program promises support in such areas as economic and cultural development, training national cadres, and building defensive capabilities. More generally, in its relations with the Third World, "the CPSU favors the development of ties with all national-progressive parties that take anti-imperialist and patriotic positions."[9]

Fifth, the spread of socialism brings a new form of international relations—*proletarian internationalism*. Because there are no antagonistic class interests among proletarian societies, harmony and cooperation are inevitable. The Party Program claims,

Socialism has brought into existence a new and unprecedented type of international relations, those that have taken shape among the socialist states. Their firm foundation is made up of Marxist-Leninist ideology; class solidarity; friendship, cooperation, and mutual assistance in accomplishing the tasks of the construction and defense of the new society; and equality of every state and respect for its independence and sovereignty.[10]

Even as the imperialists try to divide the states of the socialist commonwealth by nationalist subversion, "the CPSU proceeds from the premise that the durable unity and class solidarity of the socialist countries is of especially great importance in these conditions." In pursuit of this goal, the Soviet action program calls for improvement of the Warsaw Pact as "an instrument of collective defense against the aggressive aspirations of imperialism," for "further deepening of socialist economic integration as the material basis of the cohesion of the socialist countries," and for cooperation in the development of Marxist-Leninist theory.[11]

And lastly, it is axiomatic in the Soviet world view that the evolution of the international system favors the growth of the socialist community, at the same time that capitalism declines. According to the Party Program, capitalism "is still strong and dangerous, but it is already past its zenith. . . . Its sphere of domination is shrinking inescapably, and its historical doom is becoming increasingly obvious." [12] This is an historical process that cannot be forced by the Soviet Union, but should not be retarded by the imperialists either.

Soviet Communists are convinced that the future belongs to socialism. Every person deserves to live in a society free of social and national oppression, in a society of true equality and true democracy. . . . Revolution is the logical result of social development and the class struggle in a given country. The CPSU has always considered and continues to consider the "export" of revolution, its imposition on anyone from outside, to be fundamentally unacceptable. But all forms of the "export" of counterrevolution are also a very flagrant encroachment on the free will of the peoples, on their right to independently choose their path of development. The Soviet Union resolutely opposes attempts to forcibly halt and turn back the course of history.[13]

THE EVOLUTION OF SOVIET FOREIGN POLICY

Although the principal axioms of the Soviet world view have been relatively constant since 1917, Soviet foreign policy itself has seen significant shifts in the major problems and objectives of the Soviet state.[14] Behind those shifts is the rise of the Soviet Union first to great power status, reclaiming the postion held by the Russian Empire before 1917, and then to superpower status—a unique role for it.

1917–1921: Civil War and Isolation

The foreign policy experiences of the Soviet regime during its first four years continued to influence Soviet foreign policy well after the Civil War.[15] The Bolsheviks learned that world politics are a source of immediate threat to the survival of their regime, reinforcing their perceptions of the bourgeois states as hostile. But they also saw that they must learn the arts of traditional statecraft—as well as those of revolution—if they hoped to survive.

The initial domestic tasks of the new regime (consolidating its control over the former Empire) were hopelessly intertwined with global politics, including the negotiation of an armistice with Germany and the withdrawal of the interventionist armies. The Civil War left the new Soviet regime isolated from the international community, reinforced by an economic boycott and embargo imposed by the Western powers.

In these years, the regime built the institutions to implement its foreign policy, which in addition to the Red Army and Cheka included the People's Commissariat of Foreign Affairs (*Narkomindel*) and the Third, or Communist, International (*Comintern*). Much of the credit for the creation of the professional diplomatic corps within the Narkomindel belongs to Georgi Chicherin, who served as Commissar, following Trotsky's resignation in 1918, until 1930. The Comintern, created in March 1919, was not officially an organ of the Soviet state, but an international movement uniting Leninist parties from around the world. This division of Narkomindel and Comintern institutionalized the dual nature of Soviet foreign policy.

1922–1933: Reentering the World Community

As the Soviet Union began its postwar reconstruction, it discovered that it required access to Western technology and, hence, peace and stability in its international relations; and so it sought to reenter the world community.[16] In March 1921, the Soviet Union scored its first significant success by gaining de facto recognition from the British government. The successes culminated, in November 1933, in the American decision to recognize the Soviet regime and establish diplomatic ties. The Soviet entry into the community of nations was a protracted process, hindered by a reservoir of Western hostility dating from the Treaty of Brest-Litovsk and the Civil War, by the calls for revolution issuing from the Moscow-based Comintern, and by the unresolved issues of debts of the previous Russian governments and property confiscated from Western owners that the Soviet regime refused to recompense. The most important early success in circumventing the embargo and *cordone sanitaire* erected by the Western powers came in Soviet relations with Germany—also a pariah in the international community. The treaty of Rapallo (April 1922) with Germany not only established full diplomatic relations between the Weimar and Soviet governments, but also close cooperation through trade, German military facilities on Soviet soil, and German technological assistance.

These years also witnessed growing institutionalization and compartmentalization of the world revolutionary movement and its subordination to the state interests of the Soviet Union. The Second Comintern Congress reinforced discipline within the Comintern when in July 1920 it adopted the "21 Conditions" for admission of parties to the organization. These Conditions included requirements that all member-parties support the Soviet republic and follow the Soviet path to power and socialism. Moscow's control over the organization was further strengthened at the Fifth Comintern Congress (June–July 1924), which empowered the Soviet-dominated Executive Committee of the Comintern to issue orders binding on all member parties and to expel individual members of foreign Communist parties or even whole parties. That the Soviet Union harnessed the Comintern to its state interests is not to say that the Soviet Union had abandoned its interest in world revolution. Indeed, the Soviet Union still engaged in revolutionary adventures that jeopardized the gains of its diplomacy, including conspiracy in a German coup attempt in 1923 and support for the British general strike of 1926. (The latter led the British government to break diplomatic relations with the Soviet Union until 1929.)

1934–1941: The Threat of War and Efforts To Avert It

After a decade of peace, the Soviet regime once again faced a threat to its security from foreign powers and the possibility of another war.[17] For the Soviet Union the greatest threat was that of continued isolation in the global community as the predatory powers that surrounded the Soviet Union turned against it. In the East, Japan invaded Manchuria in 1931, and by March 1932 established the puppet state of Manchukuo along the Soviet border. In the following years, the Japanese turned their eyes westward—first toward the Chinese provinces of Jehol and Chahar, then toward the Mongolian People's Republic, and finally on Sinkiang. Hitler's rise to power in 1933, on an anticommunist platform, seemed to threaten aggression from the West as well. The Soviet foreign policy that took shape in the mid- to late 30s combined attempts to avert war with efforts to turn any aggression by Japan or Germany away from the Soviet Union. This placed a premium on traditional diplomacy; and so, throughout this period, the Soviet Union increasingly subordinated its support of revolution to the security needs of the state. To reinforce the status quo, it joined the League of Nations in 1934, and began to press for an alliance system in Europe with France and the East European states and in Asia with China. It repeatedly urged the Western powers as well as its neighbors in Eastern Europe and China to take joint action against Germany and Japan—notably in the Abyssinian Crisis (1934–1935), Rhineland Crisis (1936), Spanish Civil War (1936–1939), and Czech Crisis (1938–1939). Yet, its efforts failed. The Soviet Union's neighbors feared the Bolshevik regime and any alliance that might legitimate Soviet aggression against them. The Western powers continued to be suspicious of communist subversion and doubted Soviet sincerity; after all, its military capabilities had been decimated by the Purges and the costs of the actions that the Soviet Union urged would be borne by the West alone. Having failed to avoid war, the Soviet Union in 1939 turned its efforts to deflecting war from the Soviet Union through an accommodation with Germany. In August it signed the Nazi-Soviet Pact, which created a tense peace with Germany on the foundation of a territorial division of Eastern Europe. Yet, even this failed to keep war from Soviet soil, and on June 22, 1941, Germany invaded.

1941–1945: The Second World War

For discussion of Soviet foreign policy during World War II, see Chapter 3.[18]

1945–1953: Reemergence as a Great Power

The Soviet Union emerged from the World War II as a great power, regaining the status it had held before 1914 but lost in the destruction of the Revolution and Civil War. The Soviet rise to power came both from Soviet domestic policies to build its industrial and military might and from the collapse or exhaustion of the great powers that had dominated Europe and Asia before the War—Germany, Japan, France and Great Britain. The political vacuum that resulted from the collapse of the Axis and Western empires permitted the Soviet Union to expand its influence through conquest and revolution. The Soviet Union directly annexed border regions in East Europe and northeast Asia. Beyond these territories it added satellite regimes: While prior to World War II, Mongolia was the sole Soviet satellite, after 1945 this was joined by Soviet-imposed regimes in East Germany, Poland, Czechoslovakia, Hungary, Bulgaria, Romania, and Northern Korea. Indigenous communist revolutions brought allied regimes to power in China, Yugoslavia, and Albania.

As before World I, Russia remained a continental or regional power without the global reach enjoyed by the Western colonial powers or the United States. Its army was a continental force unable to project power great distances from Soviet territory; and its navy was still limited to a coastal mission unable to project Soviet power onto the high seas. Its economy was too small to provide financial and trade levers to influence other states. Moreover, Soviet influence was limited by the highly ideological tone of its policies in these years. These limitations permitted the United States and its European allies to build a string of alliances (e.g., NATO, Baghdad Pact, SEATO, ANZUS) surrounding the Soviet Union and containing its expansion.

The confrontation between expanding Soviet influence and that of the United States, labelled the "Cold War," reached crisis proportions in Berlin (1948), with the Soviet-imposed blockade of the western portions of the city, and over Korea (1950–1953). The reasons for this confrontation are the objects of one of the most important debates in contemporary historiography. The orthodox interpretation sees Soviet aggression at the root of the Cold War. The revisionist interpretation challenges this, in many cases arguing that America's forceful response or overreaction to Soviet security concerns was responsible for the Cold War.[19]

1953–1964: Rise to Superpower Status

Stalin's death brought a new course not only in domestic policies but in foreign policy as well.[20] The consequence of these new policies was the emergence of the Soviet Union as a global power for the first time in Russian history. Indeed, by

1962 the Soviet Union was operating off the very shores of the United States in Cuba.

The collective leadership recognized that they could not maintain Stalin's policies, which had created tensions with China, an explosive situation in Eastern Europe, a hostile response from the West, and the containment of Soviet influence in the Third World. They thus sought to stabilize their relations with the West, facilitating negotiated settlements to the key East-West issues that remained from the Stalin era—in the Korean Armistice (1953), the Geneva Agreements on Indochina (June 1954), and the Austrian State Treaty (May 1955). Accommodation evaded the Soviet Union in Germany and Berlin, however. The new leadership sought to satisfy China by renegotiating the unequal alliance Stalin had imposed on it in 1950, liquidating the commercial concessions exacted from China as part of that treaty, and expanding Soviet economic aid to Chinese industry. In Eastern Europe, the Soviets sought a new basis for bloc unity. Despite the setback to unity that came in 1956 with the Polish reform movement, the Hungarian Revolution, and the Soviet suppression of the latter, the Soviet Union cultivated an institutional basis for bloc unity in the revived Council for Mutual Economic Assistance (CMEA or COMECON) and the new Warsaw Treaty Organization (WTO). The most dramatic change in Soviet foreign policy during this period was the rise of Soviet power in the Third World. Rather than reject the new nonaligned states as lackeys of imperialism, the Soviets welcomed them as potential friends. In 1955 they initiated the relationship with Egypt and India that would be central to their Third World policies over the next decade and a half. The Soviet regime also turned its attention to national liberation movements in the Third World, hoping to find in these the seeds of radical revolutions that would bring to power pro-Soviet, if not communist, regimes.

The foreign policies of the late Khrushchev years, however, presented the Soviet Union with some of its greatest setbacks and most dangerous crises of the postwar period. Its relationship with China deteriorated, for the Soviets were unwilling to give in to Chinese pressures for forceful opposition to imperialism and shared leadership within the international communist movement; and they gave only tepid support to China in its confrontations with Taiwan, the United States, and India. This conflict came out into the open in 1960 with the Chinese attack on revisionism in the *Red Flag* article "Long Live Leninism!" (April) and at the Moscow Conference of 81 Communist parties in November. By 1964, Mao Tse-tung had raised the issue of China's territories lost to the Russian Empire through "unequal treaties." Relations with the West turned from rapprochement in 1959, marked by Khrushchev's visit to the United States in September, to deepening confrontation, initiated in May 1960 with the U-2 incident and the failure of the Paris Summit. Tensions mounted in 1961 with the showdown in Vienna between Khrushchev and John F. Kennedy, the resumption of Soviet atmospheric nuclear testing, and the Berlin Crisis; they peaked in October 1962 over the Cuban Missile Crisis—perhaps the most dangerous confrontation between the two superpowers since 1945. Nonetheless, the following year saw the beginnings of the détente that would grow in the late 1960s, initiated with the hot line agreement (June 1963) and the atmospheric test ban treaty (July 1963).

1965–1987: The Rise to Parity

Having accused Khrushchev of a "voluntaristic and unrealistic approach to the . . . events of international life" that gave rise to "either smug overconfidence or weakness in the face of the military threat from imperialism," the collective leadership set out in 1965 on a policy that scaled Soviet ends to its available means. At the same time, they continued to build up those means for the future. The resulting policy in the first post-Khrushchevian years sought to reverse the erosion of relations with China and maintain unity in the international communist movement, to find a more enduring basis for Soviet predominance in Eastern Europe, to stabilize relations with the West, and to explore opportunities for expanded Soviet influence in the Third World.

These goals were not actually accomplished during this first period. Instead, relations with China deteriorated, so that by March 1969, military skirmishes over Damansky Island (Chen Pao) in the Ussuri River resulted in the death of 31 Soviet border guards. The Soviet hold over Eastern Europe slipped, as Rumania asserted its independence and Czechoslovakia instituted liberalizing reforms. To reassert its control, Moscow resorted to armed force once more—this time in Czechoslovakia (August 20-21, 1968), restating the limitations on East European sovereignty in the so-called "Brezhnev Doctrine." In relations with the West, the independent foreign policy of Charles DeGaulle and the new *Ostpolitik* of the West German coalition government offered the Soviet Union new opportunities to engage Western European governments directly. Yet, the Vietnam War and Soviet invasion of Czechoslovakia created new obstacles to improved relations with the United States and so prevented a fuller accommodation in Europe.

Brezhnev's consolidation of his authority in the area of foreign policy by 1969 is associated with the flowering of détente with the West.[21] The primary Soviet objective appears to have been resolution of the outstanding territorial issues of World War II. Five agreements were signed in quick succession: the Treaty of Moscow (August 1970) with the Federal Republic of Germany, the Treaty of Warsaw (December 1970) between the FRG and Poland, the Quadripartite Agreement on Berlin (1971) to secure the rights of the occupying powers, the treaty between the FRG and the German Democratic Republic (1972), and the Final Agreement of the European Conference on Security and Cooperation (1975). These agreements committed the signatories to respect the existing division of Eastern Europe, a legacy of World War II imposed by occupying Soviet armies. A second objective appears to have been arms control. Talks with the United States that opened in November 1969 produced the ABM Treaty and Interim Agreement on the Limitation of Strategic Offensive Weapons (SALT I) in 1972 and a Threshold Test Ban Treaty limiting underground tests to less than 150 kilotons in 1974. And a third objective was expanded economic ties with the West, particularly to gain access to advanced Western technology. Beginning in the late 1960s, agreements with Britain, France, Italy, and West Germany led to the construction of new factories in the Soviet Union; and the grain agreement of 1972 expanded trade with the United States.

Even the heyday of détente in the early 1970s encountered obstacles. The growing cooperation between the United States and China, highlighted by Richard Nixon's visit to Beijing in February 1972 and Soviet pressure on Poland to crush a strike in Poznan in 1970 served as causes for suspicion and complaint on both sides. Soviet limitations on human rights at home and American insistence that wider respect for these rights was a precondition for expanded détente were another obstacle. And the détente relationship suffered repeated blows from a series of crises in the Third World, including the Cienfuegos crisis of 1970 in which the United States accused the Soviets of violating the 1962 agreement over Soviet military facilities in Cuba, the Indo-Pakistani War of 1970-1971 in which the superpowers supported opposite sides, and the Yom Kippur War (October 1973) that brought both superpowers close to intervention against one another.

It was, in fact, crises in the Third World that played a large part in the decline of détente in the second half of the 1970s. Soviet support for the MPLA-dominated government of Angola after November 1975, against the Western-backed movements that had been forced out of a coalition government and into armed opposition, contributed to the deterioration of East-West relations. Provision not only of arms and advisors to the Angolan government, but also troop transport for some 17,000 Cuban troops, caused particular consternation in Washington. Soviet support for the Marxist regime of Lt. Col Haile-Meriam Mengistu in Ethiopia, beginning in 1977, was also underwritten with arms, advisors, and about 16,000 Cuban troops. The rapid spread of communism throughout Indochina in 1975 further poisoned relations between the superpowers, but it was Soviet support for Vietnam as it invaded Cambodia in December 1978 and replaced the Khmer Rouge goverment of Pol Pot with a pro-Vietnamese regime in January 1979 that brought this to the crisis stage: The triangular relationship between Moscow, Washington, and Beijing threatened to explode as China invaded Vietnam, the Soviet Union appeared to threaten retaliatory action against China, and the United States considered action on China's behalf. The final blow to détente came in December 1979 as the Soviet Union invaded Afghanistan.

The invasion of Afghanistan was an important catalyst—but not the sole cause—in the deterioration of East-West relations after 1979. Indeed, the action was the most visible cause and symbol of growing Soviet isolation and the seeming ineffectiveness of Soviet foreign policy during the last years of Brezhnev, the Andropov-Chernenko interregnum, and the first years of Gorbachev. The war itself appeared to mire over 100,000 Soviet troops in an inconclusive and interminable bloodletting with Muslim tribesmen, in which Soviet control appeared to be limited to strategic cities. The diplomatic opposition to the Soviet intervention was expressed in stinging rebukes at the United Nations General Assembly, where votes calling for Soviet withdrawal passed 104 to 18 in January 1980, 116 to 23 in November 1981, and 122 to 19 in November 1985.

Relations with the West, and with the United States in particular, visibly hardened. Arms control and the arms build-up on each side continued to occupy much of the attention of the superpowers and the world. The SALT II Agreement, although observed in its broad outlines by each superpower, was never ratified. The modernization and growth of Soviet and American Eurostrategic missiles led to a flurry of proposals to reduce or eliminate these systems, a Soviet propaganda campaign encouraging peace demonstrations in Europe, and on November 23, 1983, a Soviet walk-out from the INF (Intermediate-Range Nuclear Forces) Talks in Geneva. The American commitment to its Strategic Defense Initiative and Soviet insistence that this must be abandoned or curtailed stalled strategic arms negotiations as well.

Tensions were exacerbated by developments in the Soviet bloc. The Solidarity crisis in Poland that began with strikes in the summer of 1980 culminated in the assumption of power by General Wojciech Jaruzelski in October 1981, the imposition of martial law from December 1981 to December 1982, and an American embargo of Poland in that period. Soviet warnings to the Poles in March, April, June, and August 1981 to clamp down on Solidarity fed the suspicion that the Soviet Union had masterminded the martial law—declaring that "the Soviet Union bears a heavy and direct responsibility for the repression in Poland," the President of the United States imposed trade sanctions against the Soviet Union on December 29. The Soviet downing of KAL-007 in 1983 heightened hostility on both sides. Soviet human rights violations and American insistence that these are inextricably linked to an improvement of East-West relations seemed to place an insurmountable obstacle in the way of any such improvement.

The deterioration was highlighted by a score of petty incidents such as the American boycott of the 1980 Moscow Olympics, the counterboycott by the Soviet Union of the 1984 Los Angeles Olympics, American accusations that the Soviets had used "spydust" to track American diplomats in the USSR, Soviet charges that its KGB officer Vitaly Yurchenko was the victim of U.S. "kidnapping and terrorism," and the arrests of the Soviet United Nations employee Gennady Zakharov and the American journalist Nicholas Daniloff as spies. The willingness to air and then blow out of proportion these lesser issues suggests the depths to which relations had sunk. The meetings between President Reagan and General Secretary Gorbachev in Geneva (December 1985) and in Reykjavik (October 1986) seemed exceptions to the general tone of relations, but had little enduring meliorative effect.

Soviet diplomacy since 1980 has produced few successes in the Third World. Negotiations with China foundered over Chinese demands that the Soviet Union withhold assistance to Vietnam, withdraw its forces from Afghanistan, and reduce its troop strength along the Sino-Soviet border. The growing military cooperation between the United States and China made this a more threatening relationship for the Soviet Union. In the Middle East the Soviet Union found itself excluded from the Arab-Israeli peace process and made few gains from the American expulsion from Iran. Support for Iraq in its war with Iran did win the Soviet Union favor in certain (but not all) Arab nations, paving the way for expanded diplomatic ties. Perhaps due to its limited successes in other parts of the Third World, the Soviet Union seemed to strengthen its ties with the radical or Marxist regimes of the region.

The rise to superpower status and extension of Soviet influence around the world have come at a heavy price to the Soviet Union's limited resources. By the early 1980s, subsidies to Eastern Europe cost an estimated $20 billion a year and to Cuba another $3.5 billion, while the war in Afghanistan cost over $2.5 billion. Total foreign operations may have drained $30 billion each year from the already hard-pressed Soviet economy.

THE INSTRUMENTS OF SOVIET POWER TODAY

Among the most important changes in the second half of the 20th century have been the growth of Soviet power and the rise of the Soviet Union to superpower status. Power, as used here, denotes the ability of the Soviet Union to get other states to act in ways desired by the Soviet Union. This includes military power, by which the Soviet Union seeks to achieve its objectives through *force majeure* (e.g., Czechoslovakia, 1968), but more commonly political power, by which it seeks to achieve these objectives by inducing others to give them to it (e.g., Berlin, 1959). Like other major countries, it exercises political power through the instruments of diplomacy, force, propaganda, and economic rewards or punishments.

Diplomacy

The key purpose of diplomacy as an instrument of power is to explain a state's goals abroad in order to persuade others to adjust their policies to conform to those objectives. The chief instrumentality of Soviet diplomacy is the Ministry of Foreign Affairs. As Figure 13.1 shows, the Ministry has a familiar organization, with geographical and functional departments performing many of the operational responsibilities of the agency. The Ministry shares some elements of Soviet diplomacy with departments of the Party Central Committee: Specifically, the Department for Liaison with Communist and Workers Parties in Socialist Countries (DLCWPSC) is operationally responsible for party-to-party relations with other communist countries, and the International Department (ID) is responsible for these relations with nonruling communist parties.[22]

In foreign countries the operational agency of Soviet diplomacy is the Soviet Mission Abroad, which is formally responsible to the Ministry of Foreign Affairs through the ambassadors.[23] But operating within the Mission are typically a military attaché reporting to the Ministry of Defense, a trade mission responsible to the Ministry of Foreign Trade, possibly an economic assistance mission reporting to the State Committee for Foreign Economic Relations, and, of course, intelligence officers under various covers reporting to the KGB or to military intelligence. Outside the embassy will be various independent trade, tourism, and press agencies that are responsible to their parent organizations (e.g., Intourist, TASS) in Moscow.

The diplomatic agencies of any state have always made an indirect contribution to its power by providing intelligence information and even framing options essential to skillful policy. In this the Ministry of Foreign Affairs has been assisted by the relevant institutes of the Academy of Sciences, including the World Economics and International Relations Institute (*IMEMO*) and five area institutes

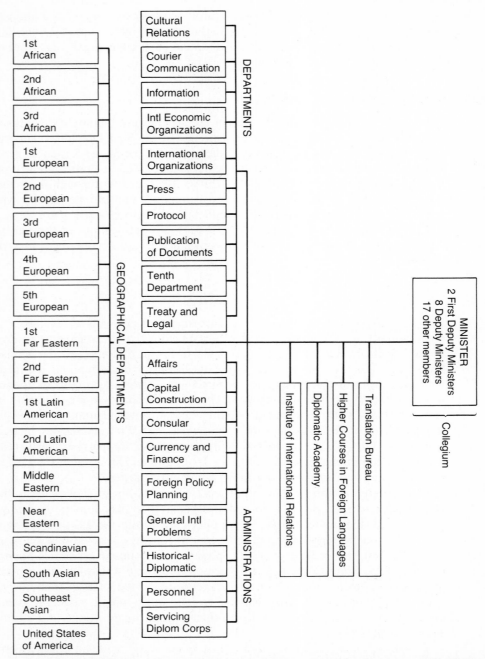

Figure 13.1 USSR Ministry of Foreign Affairs (*Source:* From data in U.S. Central Intelligence Agency, *Directory of Soviet Officials: National Organizations* [Washington, D.C.: CIA, 1986].)

such as the Africa Institute or the United States of America and Canada Institute. The activity of the KGB and military intelligence directorate (GRU) in the collection of foreign intelligence has attracted growing attention in recent years. The KGB's First Directorate is apparently responsible for coordinating most such activities, although the Ministry of Defense's Chief Intelligence Directorate (GRU) is formally charged with military espionage.[24]

The diplomatic agencies of the Soviet Union are under tight Party scrutiny. In addition to their operational responsibilities, the DLCWPSC and ID maintain surveillance over the diplomatic agencies in the countries for which they are responsible. And the Cadres Abroad Department supervises Soviet citizens serving outside the Soviet Union.

Soviet diplomatic "style" has often been characterized as unique or idiosyncratic. American diplomats with considerable experience in negotiations with Soviet representatives under Stalin presented a picture of a diplomatic style essentially different in premises and means from that of the United States. At the root of this difference was the Soviet premise that other states are essentially hostile. In such a fundamentally antagonistic milieu, compromise is not a desirable objective, and concessions to reach compromises will be seen as a sign of weakness. Philip Moseley in 1951 presented a view that is often heard nearly four decades later:

> One of the difficulties of Soviet-Russian vocabulary is that the word "compromise" is not of native origin and carries with it no favorable empathy. . . . "Compromise for the sake of getting on with the job" . . . is alien to the Bolshevist way of thinking and to the discipline which the Communist Party has striven to inculcate in its members.[25]

As a consequence, Soviet negotiating style was said to use a number of unconstructive techniques such as the "red herring" and public pronouncement to bind their reputation to a negotiating position.

More-recent studies of Soviet negotiating behavior have thrown some doubt on these earlier conclusions, or at least their continued relevance after four decades. Soviet perceptions of the West, and of the United States most notably, seem more complex and sophisticated than earlier, evincing an understanding of the diversity of American points of view on international security issues. Soviet diplomats have stressed the importance of compromise. And Soviet behavior (in arms negotiations, for example) suggests a willingness to make concessions to reach such compromises. These later findings by and large do not support the contention that the Soviets employ unique techniques in their negotiating style.[26]

The available evidence is not sufficient to permit us to discern why Western analysts have come forward with such disparate views of Soviet diplomatic style. One answer is that one or the other of the assessments is simply wrong, biased by the xenophobia of the early Cold War or the wishful thinking of détente. Another is that both views are accurate, but describe rapidly changing Soviet diplomatic behavior at different points in time. And a third is that both are pictures of parts of a larger Soviet style and that the changing nature of superpower and global politics brings forth different aspects of that style.

Force

Force can be used as an instrument of either military or political power. In the words of the Harvard University economist Thomas C. Schelling, "A country can repel and expel, penetrate and occupy, seize, exterminate, disarm and disable, confine, deny access, and directly frustrate intrusion or attack." This is force employed as an instrument of military power. But "there is something else . . . that force can do. . . . [M]ilitary force can be used *to hurt*. . . . [I]t can *destroy* value. . . . [I]t can cause an enemy plain suffering. . . . The power to hurt is bargaining power. To exploit it is diplomacy. . . . "[27] The Soviets have developed military capabilities for both purposes.

The Council of Defense, as best we can ascertain, is responsible for coordination of defense policies (see Chapter 6), with the Ministry of Defense operating under its direction. The Ministry's kollegium, the Main Military Council, undertakes the strategic direction of the armed forces in peacetime. (See Figure 13.2.) Its decision-making responsibility, however, appears limited to supervising implementation of decisions made at higher levels. Immediately below this the General Staff, under the direction of the Chief of the General Staff, operates as the executive arm of these bodies. Subordinate to the General Staff are the five military services—the Ground Forces, Navy, Air Forces, Strategic Rocket Forces, and Troops of National Air Defense (*PVO Strany*)—as well as various special troop formations.[28]

The Soviet Union's military alliance with Eastern Europe, the Warsaw Treaty Organization (WTO), serves as the principal institutional foundation for Soviet predominance over its Western neighbors. (Of course, in the final analysis, Soviet predominance in the region does not rest on international institutions.) The WTO ties the Soviet Union to the German Democratic Republic, Poland, Czechoslovakia, Hungary, Romania, and Bulgaria. The alliance makes a direct contribution to Soviet security by guaranteeing a buffer zone that keeps hostile forces at arm's length, by securing a forward position should war come to the center of Europe, and by providing an increment of forces (East European troops). It also provides a mechanism to maintain control over the military establishments of its European allies. By marshalling support for Soviet foreign policies (for example, through declarations of the organization's Political Consultative Committee), the WTO can place a ratifying, and in the eyes of many a legitimating, imprimatur on those policies. And through the exchange of information and views among states, it provides a mechanism for alliance management that may remedy disintegrative problems short of a showdown of force.[29]

In his comprehensive study of Soviet military diplomacy, Stephen S. Kaplan of the Brookings Institution finds that the Soviet military was used in 190 incidents between June 1944 and August 1979. (As a benchmark, it is useful to note that the Soviet Union used its armed forces less than three-fourths as frequently as the United States.) He finds that these incidents break down as follows:

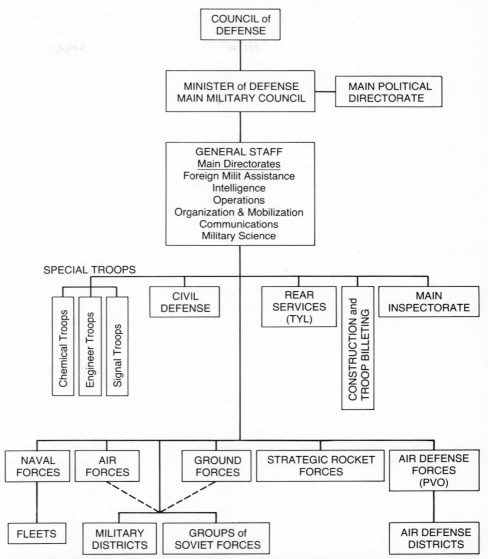

Figure 13.2 USSR Ministry of Defense (*Source:* Data from U.S. Central Intelligence Agency, *Directory of Soviet Officials: National Organizations* [Washington, D.C.: CIA, 1986].)

14 percent to expand Soviet territory or assert Soviet authority over neighbor-
    ing territories (most before the end of 1945);

27 percent to coerce loyalty in an unorthodox communist regime or to de-
    fend it against domestic or foreign opposition;

34 percent to respond to hostile actions by neighboring or NATO states or
    to weaken or intimidate any of these states ;

24 percent to intervene in Third World affairs.[30]

The Soviet military instrument is, of course, not used solely in coercive ways. Soviet naval port calls, for example, have supported diplomatic efforts to improve relations with other states. Soviet military sales and assistance constitute the most common form of cooperative military diplomacy. Between 1975 and 1985 these totalled an estimated $126.5 billion (constant 1983 U.S. dollars), compared to $103.5 billion in sales by the United States.[31]

Kaplan's study of Soviet military diplomacy finds that it has been characterized by prudence, avoiding resort to open violence in most instances and coupling coercive diplomacy with negotiations to resolve events short of a contest in violence. In particular, the Soviet Union appears to have sought to avoid uses of its military forces that would bring direct confrontation with U.S. forces or that might threaten use of nuclear forces. Perhaps as a consequence of these self-imposed limitations, Soviet coercive diplomacy appears to have had only limited success.[32]

Propaganda

Propaganda has been defined as the attempt by state agencies to form or alter attitudes of another people by use of instruments of communication so as to elicit desired reactions to subsequent events. From the tactics for building a mass movement in Tsarist society the Soviets have adapted propaganda to an international audience with the most advanced techniques of mass communication. Radio Moscow's worldwide broadcasts outside the Soviet Union in 1985 were reported to average 1680 program hours per week in 64 languages (compared to 1306 hours in 42 languages for Voice of America). The Soviet Union maintains an active publishing program for foreign audiences. TASS, the official Soviet news agency, maintains bureaus and correspondents in about 100 countries, and Novosti (APN), the "unofficial" agency, reportedly maintains information exchanges with over 100 international and national news agencies and more than 7000 newspapers and magazines. Face-to-face contacts with foreign nationals—in a sense an expansion of the agitation techniques used to make revolution, but now through cultural exchanges and friendship societies—also carry the propaganda message. Soviet-controlled international front organizations such as the World Peace Council and spectacles such as the World Youth Festival in Moscow can offer forums to propound and "second" Soviet positions. The Party's International Department apparently orchestrates these activities.[33]

Soviet propaganda since the 1950s has grown remarkably more sophisticated. The overt use of ideologically charged jargon such as "imperialist hyenas" or "the blood-suckers of the people" has declined. Its themes are less often appeals to narrow partisan objectives such as class struggle and increasingly those with wide appeal such as peace and disarmament. There is greater tolerance and even active use of themes that may not be ideologically "pure" but are nonetheless complementary to Soviet interests, such as nonalignment. And, correspondingly, the target audience has been expanded to include all "progressive" peoples.

Among the active measures that have attracted considerable attention in recent years is so-called "disinformation" (from the Russian word *dezinformatsiia* or misinformation). This term has at times become all-encompassing in Western usage, including virtually all Soviet propaganda activities and more [34] Here the term is used in a narrower sense (in the hope of giving it greater analytic precision) to mean the covert dissemination of deliberately falsified information to form or alter attitudes of another people—a subset of propaganda. This can include planting a false news story for rebroadcast or republication in foreign media or the covert circulation of forged documents (either altered or completely fabricated) in foreign countries.

Whether Soviet propaganda and disinformation have been effective is a difficult question to answer. Studies of American overt propaganda suggest that it may have only a limited effect on events around the world. Most importantly, Soviet propaganda may not convert members of its audience so much as reinforce existing attitudes. It may sometimes create new attitudes where none previously existed, but only as long as these are consistent with previously held beliefs. Similarly, disinformation may have only limited utility. The Soviet forgeries that have come to light have apparently had little more than nuisance effect, as one would expect from isolated and incongruent documents in the context of multifaceted relations. Whether undiscovered forgeries have had a more significant pernicious effect is, of course, impossible to know; yet, isolated documents may at most serve as catalysts and, if incongruent with other information, may be dismissed or readily exposed.[35]

Economic Relations

As instruments of power, economic relations are used to induce desired behavior in other states by offering rewards and threatening sanctions. Normally the economic inducements used are trade and aid. The administration of these in the Soviet Union is the responsibility of the Ministry of Foreign Trade (*Minvneshtorg*) and the State Committee for Foreign Economic Relations (*GKES*). The former administers the state's monopoly of foreign trade, overseeing specialized foreign trade associations that conduct actual exports and imports. (Reforms in the late 1980s may give individual industrial ministries greater autonomy in their foreign trade operations, although the extent to which this reform will actually be implemented remains to be seen.) The GKES administers the Soviet development assistance program, overseeing the work of specialized technical assistance associations that actually construct the projects in recipient countries.

Trade can be used as an instrument of power through manipulation of tariffs and quotas or imposition of boycotts and embargos that promise financial benefits or threaten economic harm to other societies. The less-developed state of the Soviet economy and the legacy of Stalinist autarky have deprived the Soviet Union of much of the economic leverage enjoyed by the United States and even many lesser powers in the West. Total Soviet trade in 1984, totalling $171.8 billion at official exchange rates, was only 29 percent of U.S. volume and lagged behind that of West Germany, Japan, France, and the United Kingdom.[36] Thus, the Soviet Union has had fewer trade levers with which to coerce or reward foreign powers. Nonetheless, this has attracted considerable Western concern, particularly as the Soviet Union has come to supply a larger share of the market for certain strategic resources such as natural gas in Western Europe.

The principal exception to this pattern of limited economic leverage is the Soviet economic predominance in Eastern Europe. The Soviet Union accounts for about two-fifths of the total trade of its East European allies in the WTO, ranging from about one-fifth of Romania's trade to about three-fifths of Bulgaria's. To provide an institutional basis for this trade integration and dependence, the Council for Mutual Economic Assistance (CMEA) has grown from a hollow shell in 1949 to a complex international organization in the 1980s. Its 10 members, including the 7 WTO states plus Mongolia, Vietnam, and Cuba, have committed themselves, with varying degrees of enthusiasm, to the elaboration of an "international socialist division of labor." This is to include product specialization based on comparative advantage, expanded trade interdependence, and coordination of economies through either supranational or coordinated planning. The CMEA's progress in these areas has been slowed or even stalled by nationalistic opposition and the limitations of the individual economies of members.[37]

Credits and loans, in the form of development assistance or trade facilitation, can be used as instruments of power as offers are made to induce or reinforce desired behavior or threats of withdrawal are made to deter or reverse undesired actions. Soviet economic assistance to the non-Communist states, which between 1954 and 1984 totalled an estimated $30.0 billion in commitments, but only $14.1 billion in actual deliveries, has drawn considerable attention in the West. Yet, this program has been limited, with all actual deliveries of aid in 1984 totalling only $1.4 billion, or 12.7 percent of the American, 14.9 percent of the Japanese, and 27.6 percent of the French totals. The Soviet effort pales even further when one notes that there are no private flows of investment funds or export credits from the Soviet Union to the less-developed countries, while these flows from the West have been substantial, surpassing the level of official credits.[38]

The actual consequences of Soviet international economic policies appear to be modest. Empirical studies of the relationship between economic assistance, trade dependence, and political compliance of recipients with the Soviet Union suggest some causal interconnectedness among these. Yet with the small volume of both trade and aid, the political payoffs have been limited.[39]

Measuring Soviet Power

Among the most contentious issues in Western assessments of the Soviet position in the world are the many alternative estimates of Soviet power: Certainly the growth of Soviet power since World War II has been substantial, but has the Soviet Union achieved superiority or only parity relative to the United States? Is it possible that the Soviet Union is still only a distant second among the world's powers? Much of this disagreement is an inevitable consequence of the ambiguities of power—what is it, and how is it measured? Even if one posits a definition of power, as was done at the beginning of this section, its measurement remains an uncertain matter.

In attempts to estimate Soviet power, there has been a preference for more-concrete but indirect measures of power in the form of statistics on the power resources (e.g., troop strength) of the Soviet Union rather than more-direct but necessarily less-tangible estimates of the relationships of influence and control that are power itself. Within the former there has been a tendency to focus solely upon measures of military strength, which may be the sole area in which the Soviet Union excels, while ignoring the other constituents of power, such as economic levers, in which the Soviet Union trails hopelessly. The reasons for this focus include not only the uncertainties of aggregating such disparate elements of power, but also the tendency to focus on extreme (but unlikely) scenarios of East-West military showdowns rather than the daily jockeying for influence around the world.

Soviet military power has, in fact, made substantial gains in the years since 1945, rising from a regional great power to superpower status on par with the United States. Soviet active manpower has grown from a level 46 percent above U.S. levels in 1960 to one 125 percent above these levels 25 years later, or a total of 4.8 million on January 1, 1985. Total Soviet ground forces and naval infantry strength is currently over 3.0 million, or 224 percent above the total troop strength of the U.S. Army and Marine Corps. Soviet materiel shows similar strength, with the number of tanks deployed to ground forces and naval infantry units growing 50.9 percent in the 25 years following 1960, reaching 52,810 on January 1, 1985, or 296 percent more than were deployed to the U.S. Army and Marine Corps units. In naval forces the investment in Soviet power has yielded 638 major naval combatants (aircraft carriers, battleships, cruisers, destroyers, frigates, and submarines), or 74.3 percent more than in the U.S. Navy.[40]

But estimating Soviet military power (not to mention its total power) from such statistics alone is a problematic undertaking. These figures hide important differences between Soviet and American forces that make the figures incommensurable and that affect the power potential of each side. For example, Soviet active military manpower figures, even if one excludes internal security forces (which the U.S. Department of Defense estimates do not always exclude), include a number of noncombat troops that may not belong in the troop comparisons: Congressman Les Aspin argues that, even after internal security troops are removed from the estimates, 22 percent of the Soviet forces (based on 1975 figures) perform tasks assigned to civilians in the U.S. military-industrial establishment (e.g., construction, agriculture, civil defense). Another 17 percent are "excess" manpower that, due to Soviet inefficiences, add nothing more to Soviet combat capabilities than the smaller American force contributes to U.S. capabilities. It may be that one must subtract at least two-fifths of the Soviet manpower total to come up with a number that can be compared with U.S. troop strength in any meaningful way. But we may even yet be left with an inflated picture of Soviet military power, for the "quality" of Soviet manpower may not be equal to that of American personnel, reducing the power potential of its armed forces: In estimates of manpower costs in Soviet health and education, for example, the CIA normally makes a 20 percent quality discount on Soviet personnel, since levels of educational attainment and technical sophistication are much lower than in the United States. In light of the growing importance of high technology in military practice, should we make such a "quality" adjustment in comparisons of military personnel?[41]

Similar problems of counting can be found in comparisons of materiel. First, what does one count? This problem is illustrated by the comparisons of Soviet and American strategic weapons (see Table 13.1): A frequently cited comparison is the number of delivery vehicles: ballistic missiles (ICBMs and SLBMs), in which the Soviet Union has a 44.5 percent edge, and long-range bombers, in which the United States has a 39.3 percent advantage. Taken as a whole this comparison of strategic forces shows the Soviet Union with a 25 percent advantage in missiles and bombers. It is not the delivery vehicles that destroy targets, though, but the warheads and bombs they carry; and since not all delivery vehicles are created equal perhaps we should count the warheads directly rather than the delivery vehicles they ride. In this the United States has a 25.9 percent advantage in ballistic missile warheads and a 213.3 percent advantage in bombs. Likewise, not all warheads and bombers are created equal either; this comparison does not account for the Soviet advantage in yields (megatonnage) or the American advantages in accuracies and reliability. Should our measures of power take into account all these considerations as well? Even these "improved" estimates do not account for all quality differences in the weaponry of each side. Since the United States has chosen to substitute quality for quantity in many parts of its force posture, this would be an important oversight. In 1986 the U.S. Department of Defense estimated that in 24 major deployed military systems, the United States surpassed Soviet technological levels in over half and matched Soviet levels in over a quarter; the Soviets surpassed American technology in only a sixth of these deployed systems. And while all Soviet military technology currently deployed lies within American capabilities, as much as 30 percent of America's technology is currently beyond the reach of the Soviet Union. Should estimates of Soviet military capabilities, then, include a "quality" discount?[42]

Doubts about the utility of such measures of power resources as surrogates for more direct measures of Soviet power have led to considerable skepticism about the former, but few efforts to estimate the latter. One such effort undertaken by researchers at the Center for Defense Information paints a very different picture of the trends in Soviet power. They found that the number of Soviet-influenced regimes expanded from 7 in 1945 to 18 in 1986, but that this did not keep pace with the explosion in new nations. As a consequence, the percentage of independent states that were Soviet-influenced rose from 9 percent in 1945 to a peak of 14 percent in 1958 and then declined to 11 percent by 1986. Moreover, since pro-Soviet regimes have tended to be among the poorer states in this world, the power that has accrued to Soviet Union through this influence is less than one might first imagine. The percent of world GNP produced by these states peaked at only 9 percent in 1958 and fell to 6 percent in 1986. Comparing the cumulative power of regimes, the researchers estimate that the power of the

Table 13.1   THE U.S.-SOVIET STRATEGIC BALANCE (January 1, 1985)

	USA		USSR	
	Delivery Vehicles	Warheads/ Bombs	Delivery Vehicles	Warheads Bombs
ICBM	1054	7242	1398	5754
SLBM	656		988	
Bombers	316	3296	145	1052

Source: John M. Collins, *U.S.-Soviet Military Balance, 1980–1985* (Washington, D.C.: Pergamon-Brassey's, 1985).

United States and its allies was over two and half times that of the Soviet Union and its clients, and that if one includes pro-Western countries not in formal alliance with the United States this rose to over three times and with China to over three and a half times the power of the pro-Soviet states. In sharp contrast to the measures of military power resources, analysis of influence presents a picture of essentially static Soviet power since 1960 and marked inferiority in comparisons with the United States.[43]

All this debate points up the considerable uncertainty in our estimation of Soviet power. In the opinion of this author, much work remains to be done on this issue. The student of Soviet affairs should not throw up his or her hands in despair or resignation in the face of this ambiguity. Rather, this should be seen as a challenge to improve our analysis of this all-important question—one that simply won't go away.

EXPLAINING SOVIET INTERNATIONAL BEHAVIOR

It is not only analysis of the means of Soviet foreign policy (that is, Soviet power) that has caused disagreement and uncertainty among Western scholars. It is also the search for the origins and objectives of Soviet policies that has divided and befuddled us. In their attempts to explain Soviet foreign policy—to find its objectives and motive forces—scholars have divided among at least seven schools of thought. Each is distinctive in that it looks at a different attribute of the Soviet Union to find these objectives and causes. And, as presented here, each looks progressively more deeply into Soviet society for these explanations. (See Table 13.2.)

Strategic Theories

Strategic theories share the common assumption that Soviet behavior can be explained in terms of national interests. Strategic theories argue that Soviet leaders seek to defend and promote the power interests of the state and that any leadership atop a state with similar capabilities and in a similar international milieu would act much the same. Robert Strausz-Hupe, for example, has explained So-

Table 13.2   THEORIES OF FOREIGN POLICY: SEVEN SCHOOLS OF THOUGHT

School of Thought	Principal Explanatory Variable
(1) Strategic Theories	Capabilities and International Milieu
Perceptual Theories	Leadership and Perceptions
(2) Psychological Theories	
(3) Ideological Theories	
Systemic Theories	Political System
(4) Constitutional Theories	
(5) Political Theories	
Social Theories	Social System
(6) Cultural Theories	
(7) Developmental Theories	

viet expansion in Eastern Europe by what he sees as the two immutable security objectives of the Russian state: to protect the major demographic and industrial centers of European Russia and to block future invasion from the West.[44] Soviet foreign policy is not significantly affected by the identity of its leaders nor by their ideology nor even their nationality. The primary variables that distinguish Soviet foreign policy from the policies of other states and explain changes in Soviet policy over time are shifts in the international environment that present new threats or opportunities to the national interest and changes in the capabilities or power of the Russian-Soviet state.

Strategic theories, in fact, provide the most-common explanations for Soviet international behavior, such as those encountered in newspapers that attempt to explain events by reference to the national security objectives of the Soviet Union. Models of the arms race like the action-reaction model, which explains Soviet deployments as a strategic response to those of the United States, are predicated on a strategic theory of Soviet international behavior. And so are those American military doctrines that seek to convince the Soviet Union that a first strike would be unprofitable due to the American capacity to inflict unacceptable damage in a retaliatory strike.

Within the strategic theories school of thought one prominent analytic approach tends to emphasize geographical constraints on foreign policy. In the form of geopolitics this verges on geographical determinism. Some see in Soviet foreign policy the perennial Russian search for secure borders; others see in it the search for warm-water ports. Interestingly, this was recently an important argument in those circles that attributed the Soviet invasion of Afghanistan to an age-old Russian drive to the Indian Ocean.

Strategic theories beg the question whether analysis can safely ignore other attributes of states that affect their foreign policies. Is it true that the United States, for example, would behave as the Soviet Union if placed in similar circumstances? Can our analytic models safely ignore changes in the internal attributes of the Soviet Union (for example, a change in leadership as occurred in 1953) in attempting to explain its foreign policy? It is these questions that have led other theorists to look more deeply into the Soviet Union to explain its international behavior.

Perceptual Theories

Perceptual theories argue that the motivations and objectives of Soviet international behavior must be found within the leaders who hold power over the Soviet Union and, in particular, within their perceptions. These may be conditioned by the unique psychology of the leaders or their Marxist-Leninist ideology. Thus, the Soviet Union does not act just like any other state in similar circumstances with similar capabilities, but has a unique style.

Psychological theories emphasize the role of personalities: Specifically, Soviet leaders respond to international events as psychological threats and opportunities to act out their inner drives. Psychological approaches have produced studies of individual Soviet leaders that purport to explain foreign policy. In 1945 Charles Prince produced one of the first psychoanalytic studies of Stalin, arguing that he "behaved somewhat like the paranoic." He traces this to Stalin's early experiences: Growing up in a tyrannical household, Stalin at an early age rebelled against authority and developed delusions of grandeur as he imagined that he defended his mother from his father; and for this rebellion and his feelings toward his mother he developed feelings of guilt and repressed desires. This volatile psychological mixture was reinforced by his later confrontation with authorities of his theological seminary and the Tsarist government. The consequence, according to Prince was ruthless destructiveness and an urge to dominate. Arguing that "Stalin is Russia, and vice versa," Prince contends that one can explain Soviet foreign policy before 1953 by these attributes of Stalin's personality.[45]

Nathan Leites of the Rand Corporation has argued that one cannot explain Soviet foreign policy through the psychology of a single leader but rather must examine the psychology of the entire Soviet leadership. In his view, the Bolshevik movement from its inception has tended to attract and promote a specific character-type that is unique in history. This "Bolshevik character" is a "reaction-formation" to unconscious drives—specifically, fears of annihilation and fears of their own latent homosexual tendencies. These deep, unsuspected psychological drives are the roots of the Bolshevik conception of politics and political strategy that Leites labels "the operational code of the Politburo." In this view, politics is conflict summarized as *"kto-kogo"* (who-whom)—who will dominate whom, who will annihilate whom. In such a world there can be no neutrals or compromise; one must push to the limit. This leads to a foreign policy characterized by destructive expansionism—expansion and destruction to protect themselves from being controlled and annihilated, expansion to protect themselves from their own fears of being passive and submitting.[46]

To most in the West, *ideological theories* are probably the most familiar perceptual theories. These contend that the Soviet Union is driven by the prescriptions of Marxist-Leninist ideology. The brief for ideology as a principal motive force in Soviet foreign policy notes that the Bolsheviks came to power as professedly ideological movement and that all who have risen to power have done so within a bureaucracy in which orthodoxy is a vital criterion for promotion. The Bolshevik ideological view of the world thus gives rise to a unique foreign policy, which John Mackintosh has characterized in the following terms: "There have been two themes in Soviet foreign policy since the revolution in 1917, the drive for the revolutionary conquest of the world, and the protection of the heartland of communism."[47]

Systemic Theories

According to *systemic theories,* in order to understand Soviet foreign policy one must look beyond the changing Soviet leadership to the nature of the political system over which they preside. *Constitutional theories* argue that it is the nature of the Soviet regime—its "constitution" in the larger sense—that accounts for its foreign policy. For example, totalitarian theories argue that the totalitarian nature of the Soviet regime drives it to an expansionistic foreign policy. Indeed, Carl J. Friedrich and Zbigniew K. Brzezinski see revolutionary expansionism as an inextricable part of the totalitarian syndrome.[48] A variant of this argument contends that it is the demands of regime maintenance in totalitarian society, particularly the need to legitimate repression and deprivation at home, that lead to an expansionary foreign policy. According to Harvard University's Adam B. Ulam, "Influence and power outside their own country are seen by the Soviet leaders as a necessary condition for the preservation of their regime in its full autocratic rigor."[49] And in a similar vein, Peter Meyer has argued, "Soviet imperialism is motivated neither by the interests of the 'Russian nation' nor by the interests of 'international communism'. Its driving force is the interest of the Soviet bureaucratic regime."[50]

Political theories approach Soviet foreign policy as policy—as the outcome of domestic political processes—and they proceed from the axiom that one can only understand policies by examining the processes by which they emerge. Unlike the other theories, which treat the Soviet Union as a unified actor, political theories assert that the analyst must treat it as a plural actor, even in international affairs. Soviet foreign policy is not necessarily the unfolding of a coherent Soviet plan, but the result of temporary and shifting political compromises at home.[51]

Political theories point up that decision making is constrained by the bureaucratic organizations that present information and options to decision makers and that implement their decisions. The inputs to decision are only an imperfect reflection of reality, often limited by the parochial perceptions of the bureaucracies that generated them. Similarly, the implementation of a decision by these bureaucracies may only imperfectly reflect the actual decision, as standard operating procedures mold implementation into set routines. Moreover, the decision itself is the consequence of pulling and hauling at the center among the decision makers. There are multiple actors in the decision itself, differing among themselves over goals and means. In accord with political theories, the conflict school's analysis of foreign policy focuses on the impact of leadership politics, and the political interests school concentrates on the "pulling and hauling" among interests like the military and police.

Social Theories

Lastly, social theories claim that one must look still more deeply into Soviet society—beyond the changing politics of Russia—to find the forces that drive Soviet foreign policy. *Cultural theories* find the driving force in the enduring features of Russian culture. Soviet leaders in this view are, first and foremost, Russians and are subject to the inescapable formative pressures of Russian culture. Cultural theorists argue that it does not matter that the ideology of the Soviet leaders is different from that of previous Russian leaders or that the regime that currently rules Russia appears to have changed—Russian leaders act as Russians. Pitrim Sorokin wrote during World War II, "Since the middle of the thirties the foreign policy of Stalin has been merely a continuation of the foreign policy pursued by the Czarist regime during the years of its vigor."[52] The British historian Arnold J. Toynbee has argued that Russian leaders whether Soviet or Tsarist share a common world view that is shaped by the influences of Byzantine civilization and Russia's role as heir to Byzantium.[53] They share a common view that their historical mission is to bring salvation to a sacrilegious world, a common fear and hatred of the West as a source of heresy and corruption, and a common sense of infallibility. The anthropologist Geoffrey Gorer has even claimed that one can explain important features of Soviet foreign policy by examining Russian child-rearing techniques—in particular, by the practice of tightly swaddling Russian children.[54]

Developmental theorists argue that the explanation for Soviet foreign policy lies in the socioeconomic structure of that society, and specifically in its stage of socioeconomic development. The official Soviet explanation for its foreign policy is, of course, just such a theory: What distinguishes Soviet foreign policy from that of the United States or even that of the Tsarist regime is its development beyond imperialism to socialism.

The theories contained in these diverse schools of thought not only purport to explain the motive force and objectives of Soviet foreign policy, but also imply what changes would be necessary to bring about a shift in Soviet policies. Strategic theories see changes coming from growing (or declining) Soviet power and new threats or opportunities in the international environment. Perceptual theories argue that changes in the personnel leading the Soviet state or at least reeducation of existing leaders would be necessary. Systemic theories see political change—either reform of processes within existing institutions or transformation of the entire political system—as the only hope for change in Soviet foreign policies. And social theories find this possibility only in a profound cultural or socioeconomic revolution.

In more recent years, there has been a tendency to avoid such explicit theorizing about Soviet foreign policy. Yet, the theories presented above have considerable intellectual appeal in that they provide the basis for a more rigorous study of foreign policy. They can complement empirical Sovietology as they provide those qualities that we seek in social science analysis.[55] The avoidance of explicit theory building does not mean we have escaped the hold of these theories. As attested by the frequency with which these explanations recur, the avoidance of overt theory-building may only make us the unconscious captives of some unexamined assumptions and may lead to sloppy reasoning and dubious conclusions.

The assumptions contained in these theories have immense practical importance. As the examples cited in the introduction to this text underscore, our analysis of Soviet foreign policy is shaped by our accepted theories. For example, political theories that see the Soviet Union as a plural actor would interpret Khrushchev's letters during the Cuban missile crisis or the motives behind the shooting of KAL-007 or the Soviet view of thermonuclear war very differently than would a monolithic view of the Soviet Union. Similarly, the assumption that ideology sets the objectives of Soviet foreign policy would lead to very different interpretations of each of these three cases than would the assumption of a value-optimizing strategic pursuit of the national interest.

NOTES

1. Richard Smoke, "National Security Affairs," in Fred I. Greenstein and Nelson W. Polsby, eds., *International Politics* (Reading, Mass.: Addison-Wesley, 1975), 248.

2. V. I. Lenin, *Imperializm, kak vysshaia stadiia kapitalizma [Imperialism as the Highest Stage of Capitalism]* in *Polnoe sobranie sochinenii*, 5th ed. (Moscow: Politicheskaia Literatura, 1962), 27:386.

3. *Pravda,* 7 March 1986.

4. V. Gartman, "Class Nature of Present-Day International Relations," *International Affairs* No. 9 (September 1969), 56.

5. B. Ponomaryov, A. Gromyko, and V. Khvostov, eds., *History of Soviet Foreign Policy, 1917–1945* (Moscow: Progress Publishers, 1969), 10.

6. Quoted in Joseph L. Nogee and Robert H. Donaldson, *Soviet Foreign Policy Since World War II* (New York: Praeger, 1981), 22.

7. Quoted in G. F. Hudson, Richard Lowenthal, and Roderick MacFarquhar, eds. *The Sino-Soviet Dispute* (New York: Praeger, 1961), 43–44.

8. *Pravda,* 7 March 1986.

9. *Pravda,* 7 March 1986.

10. *Pravda,* 7 March 1986.

11. *Pravda,* 7 March 1986.

12. *Pravda,* 7 March 1986.

13. *Pravda,* 7 March 1986.

14. Perhaps the most readable survey of the history of Soviet foreign policy is Adam B. Ulam, *Expansion and Coexistence: Soviet Foreign Policy, 1917–1973,* 2d ed. (New York: Praeger, 1974).

15. Noteworthy histories of early Soviet diplomacy include Richard K. Debo, *Revolution and Survival: The Foreign Policy of Soviet Russia, 1917–1918* (Toronto, Canada: University of Toronto Press, 1979); Olga H. Gankin and Harold H. Fisher, *The Bolsheviks and the World War: The Origin of the Third International* (Stanford, Calif.: Stanford University Press, 1940); James W. Hulse, *The Forming of the Communist International* (Stanford, Calif.: Stanford University Press, 1964); John M. Thompson, *Russia, Bolshevism, and the Versailles Peace* (Princeton, N.J.: Princeton University Press, 1967); Richard H. Ullman, *Anglo-Soviet Relations, 1917–1921*, 2 vols. (Princeton, N.J.: Princeton University Press, 1961–1968); Piotr S. Wandycz, *Soviet-Polish Relations 1917–1921* (Cambridge, Mass.: Harvard University Press, 1970); John W.

Wheeler-Bennett, *The Forgotten Peace: Brest-Litovsk, March 1918* (New York: Morrow, 1939); and Allen S. Whiting, *Soviet Policies in China, 1917–1924* (New York: Columbia University Press, 1954).

16. Among the monographs on this period are Franz Borkenau, *World Communism* (Ann Arbor, Mich.: University of Michigan Press, 1962); Conrad Brandt, *Stalin's Failure in China, 1924–1927* (Cambridge, Mass.: Harvard University Press, 1958); Robert P. Browder, *The Origins of Soviet-American Diplomacy* (Princeton, N.J.: Princeton University Press, 1953); Harvey L. Dyck, *Weimar Germany and Soviet Russia 1926–1933* (New York: Columbia University Press, 1966); Gabriel Gorodetsky, *The Precarious Truce: Anglo-Soviet Relations 1924–1927* (London: Cambridge University Press, 1977); George A. Lensen, *Japanese Recognition of the USSR: Soviet-Japanese Relations, 1921–1930* (Tallahassee, Fla.: Diplomatic Press, 1970); Sow-Theng Leong, *Sino-Soviet Diplomatic Relations, 1917–1926* (Honolulu, Hawaii: University of Hawaii Press, 1976); Kurt Rosenbaum, *Community of Fate: German-Soviet Diplomatic Relations, 1922–1923* (New York: Syracuse University Press, 1965); and Richard C. Thornton, *The Comintern and the Chinese Communists, 1928–1931* (Seattle, Wash.: University of Washington Press, 1969).

17. On the events leading up to World War II, see Max Beloff, *The Foreign Policy of Soviet Russia, 1929–1941,* 2 vols. (New York: Oxford University Press, 1947–1949); Louis Fischer, *The Soviets in World Affairs,* 2 vols. (New York: Vintage, 1960); Louis Fisher, *Russia's Road from Peace to War, 1917–1941* (New York: Harper and Row, 1969); Kermit E. McKenzie, *Comintern and World Revolution, 1928–1943* (New York: Columbia University Press, 1964); Robert C. North, *Moscow and Chinese Communists* (Stanford, Calif.: Stanford University Press, 1953); William Evans Scott, *Alliance Against Hitler: The Origins of the Franco-Soviet Pact* (Durham, N.C.: Duke University Press, 1962); Edward H. Carr, *Twilight of the Comintern, 1930–1935* (New York: Pantheon, 1983); and Dan H. Jacobs, *Borodin: Stalin's Man in China* (Cambridge, Mass.: Harvard University Press, 1981).

18. On the diplomacy of World War II, see Robert Beitzell, *The Uneasy Alliance: America, Britain, and Russia, 1941–1943* (New York: Knopf, 1973); Alan Clark, *Barbarossa: The Russian-German Conflict, 1941–1945* (New York: Morrow, 1964); Alexander Dallin, *German Rule in Russia, 1941–1945: A Study of Occupation Policies* (New York: St. Martin's Press, 1957); John R. Deane, *The Strange Alliance: The Story of Our Efforts at Wartime Cooperation with Russia* (New York: Viking, 1947); John Erickson, *The Road to Stalingrad: Stalin's War with Germany* (New York: Harper and Row, 1975); Herbert Feis, *Churchill-Roosevelt-Stalin* (Princeton, N.J.: Princeton University Press, 1957); George C. Herring, Jr., *Aid to Russia, 1941–1946: Strategy, Diplomacy, and the Origins of the Cold War, 1941–1947* (New York: Columbia University Press, 1973); Leon C. Martel, *Lend-Lease, Loans, and the Coming of the Cold War* (Boulder, Colo.: Westview Press, 1979); William H. McNeill, *America, Britain, and Russia: Their Cooperation and Conflict, 1941–1946* (New York: Oxford University Press, 1954); Edward Rozek, Jr., *Allied Wartime Diplomacy: A Pattern in Poland* (New York: Wiley, 1958); Albert Seaton, *The Russo-German War, 1941–1945* (New York: Praeger, 1971); and Barton Whaley, *Codeword Barbarossa* (Cambridge, Mass.: MIT Press, 1973).

19. On the beginnings of the Cold War, see Diane S. Clemens, *Yalta* (New York: Oxford University Press, 1970); Herbert Feis, *Between War and Peace: The Potsdam Conference* (Princeton, N.J.: Princeton University Press, 1960); D. F. Fleming, *The Cold War and Its Origins, 1917–1960,* 2 vols. (New York: Doubleday, 1961); Martin F. Herz, *Beginnings of the Cold War* (Bloomington, Ind.: Indiana University Press,

1966); Vojtech Mastny, *Russia's Road to the Cold War* (New York: Columbia University Press, 1979); William O. McCagg, Jr., *Stalin Embattled, 1943–1948* (Detroit, Mich.: Wayne State University Press, 1978); Martin McCauley, ed., *Communist Power in Europe, 1944–1949* (New York: Barnes and Noble, 1977); Thomas G. Patterson, *Soviet-American Confrontation: Postwar Reconstruction and the Origins of the Cold War* (Baltimore, Md.: Johns Hopkins University Press, 1973); and Daniel Yergin, *Shattered Peace* (Boston: Houghton Mifflin, 1977). On the early Cold War see Hamilton Armstrong, *Tito and Goliath* (New York: Macmillan, 1951); William B. Bader, *Austria Between East and West, 1945–1955* (Stanford, Calif.: Stanford University Press, 1966); Max Beloff, *Soviet Policy in the Far East, 1944–1955 (New York: Oxford University Press, 1953); W. Phillips Davison, The Berlin Blockade: A Study of Cold War Politics* (Princeton, N.J.: Princeton University Press, 1958); Vladimir Dedijer, *The Battle Stalin Lost: Memoirs of Yugoslavia, 1948–1953* (New York: Viking, 1971); Josef Korbel, *The Communist Subversion of Czechoslovakia* (Princeton, N.J.: Princeton University Press, 1959); Charles MacVicker, *Titoism: Pattern for International Communism* (New York: St. Martin's Press, 1957); J. P. Nettl, *Eastern Zone and Soviet Policy in Germany* (New York: Oxford University Press, 1951); Marshall D. Shulman, *Stalin's Foreign Policy Reappraised* (Cambridge, Mass.: Harvard University Press, 1963); Robert R. Simmons, *The Strained Alliance: Peking, Pyongyang, Moscow and the Politics of the Korean Civil War* (New York: Free Press, 1975); and Adam B. Ulam, *Titoism and the Cominform* (Cambridge, Mass.: Harvard University Press, 1963).

20. General surveys of foreign policy in the Khrushchev era include David J. Dallin, *Soviet Foreign Policy After Stalin* (Philadelphia: Lippincott, 1961); Arnold L. Horelick and Myron Rush, *Strategic Power and Soviet Foreign Policy* (Chicago: University of Chicago Press, 1966); Thomas W. Wolfe, *Soviet Power and Europe, 1945–1970* (Baltimore, Md.: Johns Hopkins University Press, 1970); and William Zimmerman, *Soviet Perspectives of International Relations 1956–1967*. On relations with Eastern Europe see Kazimierz Grzybowski, *The Socialist Commonwealth of Nations* (New Haven, Conn.: Yale University Press, 1964); Ghita Ionescu, *The Breakup of the Soviet Empire in Eastern Europe* (Baltimore, Md.: Penguin, 1965); Richard Lowenthal, *World Communism: Disintegration of a Secular Faith* (New York: Oxford University Press, 1964); Ferenc Vali, *Rift and Revolt in Hungary* (Cambridge, Mass.: Harvard University Press, 1961); and Paul Zinner, *Revolution in Hungary* (New York: Columbia University Press, 1962). On the Sino-Soviet dispute, see O. B. Borisov and B. T. Koloskov, *Soviet-Chinese Relations 1945–1970* (Bloomington, Ind.: Indiana University Press, 1975): William E. Griffith, *Albania and the Sino-Soviet Rift* (Cambridge, Mass.: MIT Press, 1963); William E. Griffith, *The Sino-Soviet Rift* (Cambridge, Mass.: MIT Press, 1964); and Donald S. Zagoria, *The Sino-Soviet Conflict, 1956–1961* (Princeton, N.J.: Princeton University Press, 1962).

21. Soviet foreign policy in the Brezhnev period is surveyed in Robin Edmonds, *Soviet Foreign Policy: the Brezhnev Years* (New York: Oxford University Press, 1983). Soviet relations with Eastern Europe are discussed in Robert Littell, ed. *The Czech Black Book* (New York: Praeger, 1969); Robin A. Remington, ed., *Winter in Prague: Documents on Czechoslovak Communism in Crisis* (Cambridge, Mass.: MIT Press, 1969); Peter F. Sugar and Ivo J. Lederer, eds., *Nationalism in Eastern Europe* (Seattle, Wash.: University of Washington Press, 1969); Jiri Valenta, *Soviet Intervention in Czechoslovakia, 1968* (Baltimore, Md.: Johns Hopkins University Press, 1979); and Gerhard Wettig, *Community and Conflict in the Socialist Camp: The Soviet Union, East Germany, and the German Problem, 1965–1972* (New York: St. Martin's Press, 1975).

On relations with the West, see Karl E. Birnbaum, *The Soviet Union and the Two German States: East-West Negotiations in Europe, 1970–1972* (Lexington, Mass.: Lexington Books, 1973); Anton W. DePorte, *Europe Between the Superpowers: The Enduring Balance* (New Haven, Conn.: Yale University Press, 1979); Josef Korbel, *Détente in Europe: Real or Imaginary?* (Princeton, N.J.: Princeton University Press, 1972); Thomas B. Larson, *Soviet-American Rivalry* (New York: Norton, 1978); John Newhouse, *Cold Dawn: The Story of SALT* (New York: Holt, Rinehart, and Winston, 1973); Morton Schwartz, *Soviet Perceptions of the United States* (Berkeley, Calif.: University of California Press, 1978); Strobe Talbott, *Endgame: The Inside Story of SALT II* (New York: Harper and Row, 1979); Adam B. Ulam, *Dangerous Relations: The Soviet Union in World Politics, 1970–1982* (New York: Oxford University Press, 1983); and Thomas W. Wolfe, *The SALT Experience* (Cambridge, Mass.: Ballinger, 1979). On Sino-Soviet relations, see Tai Sung An, *The Sino-Soviet Territorial Dispute* (Philadelphia: Westminster Press, 1973); and O. Edmund Clubb, *China and Russia: The "Great Game"* (New York: Columbia University Press, 1971). On relations with the Third World, see David E. Albright, ed., *Communism in Africa* (Bloomington, Ind.: Indiana University Press, 1980); Helen D. Cohn, *Soviet Policy Toward Black Africa: The Focus on National Integration* (New York: Praeger, 1972); M. Confino and S. Shamir, eds., *The U.S.S.R. and the Middle East* (New York: Wiley, 1973): Karen Dawisha, *Soviet Foreign Policy Towards Egypt* (London: Macmillan, 1979); Robert H. Donaldson, *Soviet Policy Toward India: Ideology and Strategy* (Cambridge, Mass.: Harvard University Press, 1974); Robert H. Donaldson, ed., *The Soviet Union in the Third World: Successes and Failures* (Boulder, Colo.: Westview Press, 1980); W. Raymond Duncan, ed., *Soviet Policy in Developing Countries* (Waltham, Mass.: Ginn-Blaisdell, 1970); Robert O. Freedman, *Soviet Policy Towards the Middle East since 1970,* 2d ed. (New York: Praeger, 1978); Galia Golan, *Yom Kippur and After: The Soviet Union and the Middle East Crisis* (Cambridge, England: Cambridge University Press, 1976); Galia Golan, *The Soviet Union and the Palestine Liberation Organization* (New York: Praeger, 1980); Bhabani Sen Gupta, *Soviet-Asian Relations in the 1970s and Beyond* (New York: Praeger, 1976); Mohamed Heikal, *The Sphinx and the Commissar: The Rise and Fall of Soviet Influence in the Middle East* (New York: Harper and Row, 1978); Geoffrey Jukes, *The Soviet Union in Asia* (Berkeley, Calif.: University of California Press, 1973); Roger Kanet, ed., *The Soviet Union and the Developing Nations* (Baltimore, Md.: Johns Hopkins University Press, 1974); Arthur Jay Klinghoffer, *The Soviet Union and International Oil Politics* (New York: Columbia University Press, 1977); Robert Legvold, *Soviet Policy in West Africa* (Cambridge, Mass.: Harvard University Press, 1970); Jacques Levesque, *The USSR and the Cuban Revolution: Soviet Ideological and Strategic Perspectives, 1959–1977* (New York: Praeger, 1978); Alvin Z. Rubinstein, *Red Star on the Nile: The Soviet-Egyptian Influence Relationship Since the June War* (Princeton, N.J.: Princeton University Press, 1977); Alvin Z. Rubinstein, *Soviet and Chinese Influence in the Third World* (New York: Praeger, 1975); and Christopher Stevens, *The Soviet Union and Black Africa* (New York: Holmes and Meier, 1976).

22. K. J. Holsti, *International Politics: A Framework for Analysis,* 3d ed. (Englewood Cliffs, N.J.: Prentice-Hall, 1977), 183–184; Robert W. Kitrios, "International Department of the CPSU," *Problems of Communism* 33 (September-October 1984), 47–75.

23. Aleksandr Kaznacheev, *Inside a Soviet Embassy* (Philadelphia: Lippincott, 1962).

24. In addition to the sources on the KGB cited in Chapter 11, see U.S. Department of State, *Expulsion of Soviets World Wide, 1985* (Foreign Affairs Note) (Washington, D.C.: Government Printing Office, January 1986).

25. Philip E. Moseley, *The Kremlin and World Politics* (New York: Vintage, 1960), 32. See also S. D. Kertesz, "American and Soviet Negotiating Behavior" in S. D. Kertesz and M. A. Fitzsimons, eds., *Diplomacy in a Changing World* (Notre Dame, Ind.: University of Notre Dame Press, 1959), 141; Christer Jonsson, *Soviet Bargaining Behavior: The Nuclear Test Ban Case* (New York: Columbia University Press, 1979), 46–54.

26. Jonsson, 55–78.

27. Thomas C. Schelling, *Arms and Influence* (New Haven, Conn.: Yale University Press, 1966), 1–2.

28. The best introduction to the organization of the Soviet military is Harriet Fast Scott and William F. Scott, *The Armed Forces of the USSR,* 3rd ed. (Boulder, Colo.: Westview Press, 1984).

29. Christopher D. Jones, *Soviet Influence in Eastern Europe: Political Autonomy and the Warsaw Pact* (New York: Praeger, 1981); Robin A. Remington, *The Warsaw Pact* (Cambridge, Mass.: MIT Press, 1972).

30. Stephen S. Kaplan, *Diplomacy of Power: Soviet Armed Forces as a Political Instrument* (Washington, D.C.: Brookings Institution, 1981), 27–60. See also Bradford Dismukes and James McDonnell, eds., *Soviet Naval Diplomacy* (New York: Pergamon Press, 1979); and Bruce D. Porter, *The USSR in Third World Conflicts: Soviet Arms and Diplomacy in Local Wars, 1945–1980* (Cambridge, England: Cambridge University Press, 1984). On other aspects of Soviet military policy, see Ken Booth, *The Military Instrument in Soviet Foreign Policy, 1917–1972* (London: Royal United Services Institute, 1973); Herbert S. Dinerstein, *War and the Soviet Union,* 2d ed. (New York: Praeger, 1962); Raymond L. Garthoff, *Soviet Military Policy: A Historical Analysis* (New York: Praeger, 1966); Robert W. Herrick, *Soviet Naval Strategy: Fifty Years of Theory and Practice* (Annapolis, Md.: United States Naval Institute, 1968); Derek Leebaert, ed., *Soviet Military Thinking* (London: Allen & Unwin, 1980); Michael MccGwire, Ken Booth, and James McDonnell, eds., *Soviet Naval Policy: Objectives and Constraints* (New York: Praeger, 1975); and Michael MccGwire and James McDonnell, eds., *Soviet Naval Influence: Domestic and Foreign Dimensions* (New York: Praeger, 1977).

31. On Soviet arms transfers, see Jon D. Glassman, *Arms for the Arabs: The Soviet Union and War in the Middle East* (Baltimore, Md.: Johns Hopkins University Press, 1975); Wynfred Joshua and Stephen P. Gibert, *Arms for the Third World: Soviet Military Aid Diplomacy* (Baltimore, Md.: Johns Hopkins University Press, 1969); and John F. Copper and Daniel S. Papp, eds., *Communist Nations' Military Assistance* (Boulder, Colo.: Westview Press, 1983).

32. Kaplan, 641–686.

33. Terence H. Qualter, *Propaganda and Psychological Warfare* (New York: Random House, 1982), 27; Kitrios, 47–75.

34. John Barron, *KGB: The Secret Work of Soviet Secret Agents* (New York: Bantam Books, 1974), 32. See also Richard H. Shultz and Roy Godson, *Dezinformatsia: Active Measures in Soviet Strategy* (New York: Pergamon Press, 1984).

35. Holsti, 221–226. On Soviet propaganda, see Frederick C. Barghoorn, *The Soviet Cultural Offensive* (Princeton, N.J.: Princeton University Press, 1960); Frederick C. Barghoorn, *Soviet Foreign Propaganda* (Princeton, N.J.: Princeton University Press, 1964); and Edward Taborsky, *Communist Penetration of the Third World* (New York: Speller, 1973).

36. U.S. Central Intelligence Agency, *Handbook of Economic Statistics, 1985* (Washington, D.C.: Central Intelligence Agency, 1985), 76, 78, 96.

37. On the institutional bases of East European integration, see Zbigniew K. Brzezinski, *The Soviet Bloc: Unity and Conflict,* rev. ed. (Cambridge, Mass.: Harvard University Press, 1967); Michael Kaser, *COMECON* (London: Oxford University Press, 1967); Henry Wilcox Schaeffer, *COMECON and the Politics of Integration* (New York: Praeger, 1972); and Richard Szawlowski, *The System of the International Organizations of the Communist Countries* (Leyden, Netherlands: Sijthoff, 1976).

38. C.I.A., 109, 114–115.

39. Philip G. Roeder, "The Ties That Bind: Aid, Trade, and Political Compliance in Soviet-Third World Relations," *International Studies Quarterly* 29 (June 1985), 191–216.

40. John M. Collins, *U.S.-Soviet Military Balance, 1980–1985* (New York: Pergamon-Brassey's, 1985), 5. On Soviet military capabilities, see Robert P. Berman, *Soviet Air Power in Transition* (Washington, D.C.: Brookings Institution, 1978); Robert P. Berman and John C. Baker, *Soviet Strategic Forces: Requirements and Responses* (Washington, D.C.: Brookings Institution, 1982); Barry M. Blechman et al., *The Soviet Military Buildup and U.S. Defense Spending* (Washington, D.C.: Brookings Institution, 1977); and Jeffrey Record, *Sizing Up the Soviet Army* (Washington, D.C.: Brookings Institution, 1975).

41. Les Aspin, "Are the Russians Really Coming?" (Washington, D.C.: Council on National Priorities and Resources, 1976); Les Aspin, "How to Look at the Soviet-American Balance," *Foreign Policy* 22 (Spring 1976), 96–106; Franklyn D. Holzman, "Are the Soviets Really Outspending the U. S. on Defense?" *International Security* 4 (Spring 1980), 94–95.

42. Collins, 5; Holzman, 93–94, 95–97; U.S. Department of Defense, *The FY 1987 Department of Defense Program for Research and Development,* Statement by the Undersecretary of Defense, Research and Engineering to the 99th Congress, 2d sess., 1986 (Washington, D.C.: February 1986).

43. "Soviet Geopolitical Momentum: Myth or Menace?" *Defense Monitor* 9 (1980), 1–24; "Soviet Geopolitical Momentum: Myth or Menace?" *Defense Monitor* 15 (1986), 1–32.

44. Robert Strausz-Hupe, "The Western Frontiers of Russia," in Hans W. Weigert et al., eds., *New Compass of the World* (New York: Macmillan, 1949), 155.

45. Charles Prince, "A Psychological Study of Stalin," *The Journal of Social Psychology* 22 (November 1945), 120–129.

46. Nathan Leites, *A Study of Bolshevism* (Glencoe, Ill.: Free Press of Glencoe, 1954); Nathan Leites, *The Operational Code of the Politburo* (New York: McGraw-Hill, 1951).

47. Gerhart Niemeyer and John S. Reshetar, Jr., *An Inquiry into Soviet Mentality* (London: Atlantic Pres, 1956), 49–50; J. M. Mackintosh, *Strategy and Tactics of Soviet Foreign Policy* (New York: Oxford University Press, 1963), 1.

48. Carl J. Friedrich and Zbigniew K. Brzezinski, *Totalitarian Dictatorship and Autocracy* (Cambridge, Mass.: Harvard University Press, 1965), 353.

49. Adam B. Ulam, "The Soviet Union and the Rules of the International Game," in Kurt London, ed., *The Soviet Impact on World Politics* (New York: Hawthorn Books, 1974), 43; Richard Pipes, *Survival Is Not Enough* (New York: Simon and Schuster, 1984).

50. Peter Meyer, "The Driving Force Behind Soviet Imperialism," *Commentary* (March 1952), 217.

51. Graham T. Allison, *Essence of Decision: Explaining the Cuban Missile Crisis* (Boston: Little, Brown and Company, 1971); Graham T. Allison and Frederic A. Morris, *What Determines Military Force Posture: A Preliminary Review of Case Studies and Hypotheses* (Discussion paper No. 34D) (Cambridge, Mass.: Harvard University, Ken-

nedy School of Government, 1975); Arthur J. Alexander, *R&D in Soviet Aviation* (R-589-PR) (Santa Monica, Calif.: Rand Corporation, 1970); Karl F. Spielmann, *Analyzing Soviet Strategic Arms Decisions* (Boulder, Colo.: Westview Press, 1978).

52. Pitrim A. Sorokin, *Russia and the United States* (New York: Dutton, 1944), 196.
53. Arnold J. Toynbee, *A Study of History, 2d ed.* (London: Oxford University Press, 1948), II:79–81, 154–158, 175–177; III:278–284, 364–365; V:177–187, 311–318.
54. Geoffrey Gorer, *The People of Great Russia* (London: Cresset Press, 1949), 93–194.
55. Johan Galtung, *Theory and Methods of Social Research* (New York: Columbia University Press, 1967), 465.

five
CONCLUSION

"Let the name and deeds of the great Lenin live for ages"

chapter 14

The Soviet Model and Its Future

On November 7, 1987, the Soviet regime entered upon its eighth decade. On this date, the Soviet leaders could celebrate not only their success in holding onto power—sometimes against heavy odds as in the Civil War and Second World War—but also the transformation of the Soviet Union from an impoverished peasant society to a modern, or modernizing, industrial society. They succeeded where the *ancien régime* had failed by addressing Russia's most pressing social problems. And in resolving or meliorating these, they had transformed their state into the world's second superpower.

PULLING THE PIECES TOGETHER: MODELS AND METAPHORS

The means by which the Soviet regime accomplished this feat constitute a different path of development than followed by the societies that preceded it; and this path has come to be seen as a distinctive Soviet or Leninist model. How to explain this Soviet experience and the nature of the society it created remain questions of considerable disagreement and uncertainty. The Soviets themselves, as explained throughout the preceding chapters, see their society as a transitional socialist socio-economic formation, now labelled "mature socialism," on its way to communism. Western analysts have tended to dismiss this. In their efforts to pull together all the pieces of the Soviet experiment they have put forward a number of alternative models and metaphors, which tend to fall into four analytic approaches, here called developmental, structural, ideological, and cultural (see Table 14.1). All these analytical approaches are alike in that they attempt to bring order to our perceptions of the Soviet Union—not just of Soviet politics,

Table 14.1 MODELS OF THE SOVIET SYSTEM

Analytic Approach	Model
Developmental	Communist
	Non-Soviet Marxist
	Non-Marxist
Structural	Totalitarian
	Bureaucratic
	Quasipluralistic
Ideological	Ideological
Cultural	Cultural

but of Soviet society and economics as well—and to help us understand its true nature. They differ in that each focuses on a different aspect of the Soviet experience to define what is central and what peripheral to that experience, to explain the parallels and differences between the Soviet experience and that of other societies, and to predict its future.

Developmental approaches, like the official Soviet interpretation of their experience, see Soviet society as a stage in the social, economic, and political development of society. The model of *state capitalism* argues that the Soviet Union, despite its professed socialism, has developed into a unique form of capitalism. Some Western Marxists who subscribe to this view argue that the premature revolution in Russia–before the Empire had completed the building of capitalism and before the emergence of a numerous proletariat—doomed the Soviet Union's ambitions to build socialism. The laws of history require the development of capitalism, continuation of the state, and class-based rule in the Soviet Union, even though the dominating class is now based on state rather than private property.[1]

Decades earlier Leon Trotsky had put forward a different Marxian developmental model, one that might be labelled the model of *arrested socialist development*, arguing that the Soviet Union is a "contradictory society, halfway between capitalism and socialism." The nationalization of property under Soviet rule has precluded the reintroduction of capitalism—even state capitalism. Nonetheless, Russia's poverty and low level of technological development have given rise to a bureaucratic dictatorship under the Party and placed socialism beyond attainment. To complete the transition to socialism may require a second revolution.[2]

Not all developmental models of Soviet society are Marxist. Seeing communism as a "disease of the transition," Walt W. Rostow of the University of Texas has described Soviet communism as a means to supply effective modern state organization so that a society can consolidate the preconditions to modernization, launch a takeoff, and drive a society to technological maturity. Communism provides the

political organization capable of launching and sustaining the growth process in societies where the preconditions period did not yield a substantial and enterprising commercial middle class and an adequate political consensus among the leaders of the society. It is a kind of disease which can befall a transitional society if it fails to organize effectively those elements within it which are prepared to get on with the job of modernization.[3]

Like all the developmental models, Rostow's analysis implies that with further development, the present Soviet system will be rendered obsolete—if it has not been already.

Impressed by the immense power of what Philip Selznick has called the "organizational weapon" in the Bolshevik seizure of power, *structural* analytical approaches initially stressed the centrality of hierarchical organization to Soviet society. Models of *totalitarianism,* for example, argue that the atomization of society and substitution of Party-controlled institutions for private associations permit the domination of all society through organization. Harry Eckstein and David A. Apter have written:

> The essence of totalitarianism, then, is that it annihilates all boundaries between the state and the groupings of society, even the state and individual personality. . . . No doubt there are "islands of separateness" in any actual totalitarian society; but the whole thrust of the system is directed at the integration of these "islands" into the flat homogeneity, the totality, of totalitarian life. . . . Certainly no other social order . . . has tried to integrate so many aspects of human existence: family life, friendship, courtship, education, work, leisure, production, exchange, worship, status, art, manners, travel, dress—even that final assertion of human privacy, death.[4]

With growing dissatisfaction over the totalitarian model, extensions, revisions, and criticisms of it have led to a series of alternative hierarchical, or *bureaucratic,* models and, in particular, to a search for metaphors that capture the essence of Soviet society. Allen Kassof argues that liberalization of Stalinist totalitarianism has led to "totalism without terror." Nonetheless, the Soviet regime is still impelled by "the drive . . . to establish a highly organized and totally coordinated society. . . . " The society that emerges from this Kassof labels "administered society".[5] Arguing against the utility of the totalitarian model, Alfred G. Meyer of the University of Michigan presents yet another metaphor:

> The USSR is best understood as a large, complex bureaucracy comparable in its structure and functioning to giant corporations, armies, government agencies, and similar institutions—some people might wish to add various churches—in the West. It shares with such bureaucracies many principles of organization and patterns of management.[6]

Comparing the Soviet Union to a company town, which he calls "USSR Incorporated," Meyer defines "the Soviet system as total bureaucratization": "All organized life—political, economic, cultural—goes on within the framework of institutions created and managed by the party; and the leaders have striven to destroy all organized life not so dominated."[7] In much the same vein, the Australian Sovietologist T. H. Rigby calls the Soviet Union a "command society" based on command-obedience relationships and "the running of a large nation as a single organization."[8]

The criticisms of these monolithic models have given rise to *quasipluralistic* models that at least imply a different view of the structure of Soviet society, even though on their face they are concerned principally with the political realm. These are predicated on the argument that interests and institutions in the Soviet society are not entirely hierarchically controlled, but have enough autonomy to initiate some independent action, including political activity. If it is true that the Soviet system is characterized by the politicization of all society, or at least by the "fusion" of politics and other spheres of society, then such models as corporatism imply a model for all Soviet society.[9]

Ideological analytical approaches stress the centrality of Marxism-Leninism to Soviet practice and development. Arguing that communist ideology functions as "the theology of the ruling group," the British economist Peter J. D. Wiles claims that "the essence of Lenin and his successors is simply this, that they are the executors of the prophet Marx." Wiles disputes his critics' claim that "Marx provided no blueprint": "The common Western view, that 'Marx said nothing about socialism', is simply false." Among the "specific legacies" of Marxism, Wiles lists nationalization, agricultural cooperation or collectivization, equality of pay, planning, increased production and productivity as keys to progress, worship of capital, mysticism about labor, eschewal of rent on land and interest on capital, and precedence to heavy over light industry. Wiles summarizes "the whole tremendous movement towards Full Communism" as "an immense economic revolution. Its objects are purely ideological, and it is surely impossible for the most purblind empiricist to deny the importance of ideology now that this movement is becoming a practical program."[10]

Stressing the continuity of Soviet practice with the Tsarist past, *cultural* approaches emphasize the roots of the contemporary regime in Russian traditions. Sir John Maynard, writing during World War II, argued that "Russia is in flux; but it is the same Russia, though with a new and important psychological addition made by the Revolution." To illustrate this he cites the following examples:

> All Russian regimes have been sudden and arbitrary: and, in their dealings with the land, in particular, have been entirely free from scruples regarding the sacredness of property. . . .
>   Old Russia was always rough, with its Siberian exiles, its judicial floggings, and its free use of the knout. . . .
>   Planning, . . . a characteristic feature of the new regime, is not as new as at first glimpse it looks to be. Minute regulation of human activities on some sort of traditional plan was, in fact, normal to mediaeval Europe. . . .
>   Even the "Party"—that unique misnomer of the vocation of leadership—is not really new: but rather a new application of an ancient institution: the priesthood. Think of it as a lay Church: beside which all rivals are but heretics. . . . [11]

Similarly, anthropological studies of Soviet attitudes toward authority and of the Great Russian national character have tended to stress the fundamental immutability of Russian-Soviet society.

As in the study of decision making or foreign policy, there is no commonly accepted model of the Soviet system *in toto*, but unlike the study of decision making, Western scholars have shied away from all-encompassing models in recent years. As George Breslauer of the University of California has noted, "Western frustration with the short-comings of the 'totalitarian model' has led to a backlash against the use of labels per se. . . . "[12] This also reflects a shift within the field toward a more empirical Sovietology that has been preoccupied with studies of the parts that make up the whole, but may have ignored the whole. It also reflects a tendency among those who do not eschew such models to prefer models developed in comparative studies outside Sovietology. These models typically point out the parallels and dissimilarities between Soviet and other societies through the variables they identify rather than treating Soviet society as *sui generis*.[13]

THE SOVIET FUTURE

The successes of the Soviet model of development in addressing the problems inherited from the old order have not been complete. The present Soviet regime faces a number of pressing problems—some new, others not—that contain within them the seeds of further transformation in the Soviet system. The most commonly noted of these vulnerabilities is the Soviet economy. The economy has slowed to the point that in some years it has produced nearly zero growth. The traditional solutions are no longer as fruitful; the Soviets cannot simply mobilize an idle labor force and undeveloped resources for growth. These problems take on particular importance because the Soviet regime has made continued growth in the economy and in the living standard of its people a basis of its legitimacy. It has continued to deliver on this promise through food imports and subsidies to food and basic services, but in the future it may not be able to keep up with the rise of citizen expectations.

Is this the basis for crisis? Marshall I. Goldman of Wellesley College, predicting that Soviet living standards may actually decline in the future, warns that "the growing rumbling of the Soviet political and economic system would serve as a strong indicator that the Soviet Union is ripe, if not overdue, for a change." Nonetheless, he cautions against apocalyptic predictions:

> By most standards the Soviet Union should have crashed at least five decades ago and at least once a decade since then. But the U.S.S.R. has survived. This should constitute a lesson in humility for anyone tempted to conclude that the Soviet Union is on the verge of collapse. Yet, the fact does remain that, in one way or other, the Soviet system has some enormous problems to overcome and that it will have to adapt and reform if it is to make it intact to the year 2000.[14]

These economic problems are aggravated by the closed nature of Soviet society and, in particular, its continued isolation from what is sometimes called the "information revolution." The pace of scientific and technological innovation in the

West has accelerated dramatically with breakthroughs in such disparate fields as medicine, agriculture, and electronics. Continued modernization—that is, keeping up with this rapid technological innovation—requires open and frequent participation in international conferences, exchanges of scholars, unfettered access to the scientific literature of other nations, teleconferencing with colleagues in one's own nation and around the world, and nationwide and transnational computer networks to exchange information. It particularly requires removal of obstacles to the exchange of ideas at home. But the Soviet Union still restricts access to the most fundamental information, such as statistics on infant mortality or economic production, and to the technology of information, such as photocopying machines. In borrowing from the West, the Soviets have sought to avoid the infection of the West's political ideas. In restricting access to Western ideas, however, they increasingly run the risk of falling farther behind technologically. Loren Graham of MIT has offered this prediction: "The question is not whether the Soviets will accept communication technology—they will. External competition will force them to. [They cannot] join the computer revolution with their own rules. In a few years they will be forced to face the fact that they have to loosen controls or lose the race".[15] Whether they join the information revolution or not, it threatens to force changes in the Soviet system.

A third problem is the rise of divisive nationalism. Some of this is the expression of old nationalisms and some is entirely new. The success of the Soviet regime and its association with the Russian nation has given rise to revived Russian nationalism both outside the Party and within it. Russian Party secretaries are reported to be increasingly resentful of the demands placed on the system by the non-Russian nationalities. Among average Russians, as the Russian population gets closer to losing its majority status within the Soviet Union, increasingly defensive and xenophobic feelings toward the other nationalities have been noted. Paralleling this is the persistence of non-Russian nationalisms that are increasingly resentful of Russian predominance. The French Sovietologist Helene Carrere d'Encausse concludes her analysis of the contemporary Soviet nationalities problems with the pessimistic observation: " . . . of all the problems facing Moscow, the most urgent and the most stubborn is the one raised by the national minorities. And like the Empire that it succeeded, the Soviet State seems incapable of extricating itself from the nationality impasse."[16] If it does not extricate itself from this problem, the Soviet state may find its present tranquility threatened.

Growing demands for expanded civil liberties expressed at times through public dissent represent yet another vulnerability of the Soviet system. The soviet dissident Andrei Amalrik has offered an apocalyptic vision of this movement's future:

> . . . as the regime becomes progressively weaker and more self-destructive it is bound to clash . . . with two forces which are already undermining it: the constructive "middle class" (rather weak) and the destructive movement of the "lower classes", which will take the form of extremely damaging, violent, and irresponsible action once its members realize their relative immunity from punishment.[17]

Whether violent or not, the withdrawal of support from a regime that has required active citizen involvement in public life may threaten that regime.

A fifth vulnerability is the incomplete institutionalization of the political succession. Ironically, the greatest strength of the Soviet model of development—its organizational capacity—also contains one of its greatest weaknesses. Each change from one leader to the next has been a critical point in Soviet politics, a time when the potential for system transformation has been at its highest.

And last are the many vulnerabilities created by the Soviet regime's national security problems. The regime's definition of security needs places an immense burden on the Soviet economy. Foreign contacts with other societies, whether Leninist or not, threaten to infect its population with dangerous ideas about the good life. In the extreme, war or even protracted international crisis might be the catalyst that produces the simultaneity of crises in economics, technological backwardness, national disintegration, popular discontent, and political succession that might overburden the Soviet regime's problem-solving capabilities.[18]

It is in these vulnerabilities that the seeds for further transformation in the Soviet system can be found. This is not to say that such a change is likely. The Soviet system will probably be able to address each of these problems as long as it faces them one at a time. And if it is permitted this luxury, the solutions to these problems will probably not effect profound changes in the Soviet Union. But if these vulnerabilities reach the crisis stage simultaneously they may overload the Soviet system's problem-solving capabilities and lead to its transformation.

Students of Soviet affairs have drawn radically different conclusions about the ability of the Soviet regime to manage these vulnerabilities and, therefore, about the future of Soviet development. One of the first efforts to formulate a prediction or scenario for the Soviet future (aside from the official Soviet scenario of full communism) was the theory of convergence. This predicts that the future development of the Soviet Union and of Western societies will make them more alike. This view tends to emphasize that modernization is an homogenizing experience. Convergence theorists have noted the similarities between the communist vision of the Soviet Union's own future "and the widely accepted idealization of the American way of life—affluent, depoliticized, classless, and conflictless." They have pointed out the parallels that already exist between East and West in their social problems (e.g., alcoholism, pollution, and urban congestion), in their popular cultures (materialistic and sterile), in their achievement-orientation (e.g., careerism, conformism, and accomplishment), and in the functional similarity of their institutions. These theorists divide among themselves, however, in their vision of the point toward which they believe East and West are converging. Those who foresee evolution of both East and West toward some midpoint predict a form of democratic socialism: "The Soviet Union will liberalize, the United States will socialize; and 'only one thing seems certain, the convergence of the evolution of East and West toward democratic socialism'." Others see the imperatives of industrialization and modernization leading the Soviet Union toward the Western model of competitive and participatory politics, "freedom of thought and creativity," and "a civic culture of mutual accommodation." A more pessimistic view of modernity predicts movement of Western societies toward a more authoritarian model, due to the tendency of industrialism to promote "the bureaucratic organization of the total society." Critics of convergence theory have characterized certain strains as "pacifist moralizing, wishful thinking, or sheer impatience with the Cold War." Much of it rests on a crude economic determinism. Convergence theories underestimate the independence, persistence, and importance of ideological, institutional, and cultural differences, even in the face of socioeconomic convergence. [19]

Recent efforts to project Soviet developments into the future have been more skeptical about the prospects for convergence and have tended to stress attributes of the Soviet model that will continue to distinguish its future development from that of the West. These efforts have resulted in at least five alternative views of the Soviet future: continuation of the present system, a Stalinist reaction, moderate liberalization, radical reform, and instability.

The most likely scenario is a continuation of current Soviet trends that Breslauer has labelled "welfare-state authoritarianism." In this, the future would be characterized by continued growth of institutional pluralism and political participation by the representatives of the chief Soviet institutions. It would find fairly widespread popular support based on its continued ability to improve the material well-being and physical security of the Soviet citizenry. Critics of this view argue that it makes heroic assumptions about the future stability of the Soviet model of development: Specifically, the political leadership will respond to the most pressing domestic problems rather than continuing to postpone reforms. The population will tolerate exclusion from the major decisions that affect their daily lives and can be bought off with material incentives. Functional elites will be satisfied with consultation and eschew open political contest. And the Soviet system will face no sharp shocks such as war or economic collapse. All these vulnerabilities are the opening for substantial change.[20]

Andrei Amalrik and Alexander Yanov have warned that one possibility is a sharp turn to the right in a neo-Stalinist reaction, developing what Breslauer has called a "Russian fundamentalist" state. Zbigniew K. Brzezinski warned in the late 1960s that continued stagnation might bring "a reactionary palace coup" with "a more assertive ideological-nationalist reaction, resting on a coalition of secret police, the military, and the heavy industry-ideological complex. . . ."[21] The combination of more-assertive Great Russian nationalism, prolonged economic crisis, and intensified foreign pressures such as a Sino-American military alliance might force a showdown among Soviet interests. Since it would no longer be possible to "muddle through" by buying off all interests, hard trade-offs would have to be faced. And this might create the condition for a Stalinist reaction.

Amalrik argues that there is a strong political base for this neo-Stalinist state within the Soviet Union. Many regional Party secretaries within the RSFSR purportedly subscribe to a combination of Stalinist political values and Great Russian nationalism. They are likely to find allies in the ideological apparatus of the trade unions, the Komsomol, and KGB and within the military-industrial complex. This coalition could appeal to the Russian nationalist intelligentsia that aspires to resurrect traditional values and to the *lumpenproletariat*—the unskilled Russian peasantry and working class who would welcome better conditions at the expense of the non-Russian nationalities. The regime would reassert totalitarian and chauvinistic values.[22]

Many of the proposals for structural reform of the Soviet system, such as those economic reforms discussed in Chapter 10, hold out the hope that a more promising possibility for the future is a turn, not to the right, but toward further liberalization of the Soviet system. Current trends toward consultation with affected interests, especially within the technocratic elite, and growing co-optation of members of that elite into central policy-making bodies might lay the foundations for a more participatory polity, albeit one still limited to the elite segments of Soviet society. Such a regime might give precedence to economic modernization and efficiency. In the pursuit of these ends, the technocratic elite might be forced to break the Party's implicit "social contract" with the Soviet people by sacrificing many of the egalitarian values that have led to inefficiencies, such as job security and the food subsidies. They might even legislate greater wage differentials as an incentive to productivity. Thus, this "liberalization" might come at the expense of the mass of the population at the lower end of the socioeconomic ladder.[23]

The dissident Soviet historian Roy Medvedev has argued for a still more thorough-going liberalization of the Soviet Union toward what he has labelled "socialist democracy." Medvedev argues that further expansion of participation, within the context of the institutions of a one-party state and an economy based on public ownership of the means of production, could lead to demands for open political competition through elections and for true accountability of elected officials to electors. The occasion for such a transformation might be a crisis that points up the costs of the Soviets' closed society; if the costs of the information revolution, for example, were to become acute and the Soviet Union lagged even further behind the West, the Party might bow to the necessity of opening Soviet society to a wider exchange of views at home and to broader infusion of views from the outside.[24]

Robert Conquest and Zbigniew K. Brzezinski have criticized all the foregoing views for their assumption that the Soviet system will master its vulnerabilities, manage change, and achieve some steady-state equilibrium in the future. If the multiple vulnerabilities accumulate, simultaneously reaching crisis proportions, and the Soviets respond by simply attempting tinkering reforms, a protracted period of instability may follow, marked by constantly shifting policies as the Soviet regime searches for solutions. At the root of this problem, according to Brzezinski, is the institutionalization of political participation—initially a major success of the Bolshevik regime. This has not kept pace with subsequent social developments, so that the political system has not continued to incorporate the ever-expanding circle of politically relevant groups. This last scenario, however, underestimates the ability of the Soviet leaders to anticipate these problems and manage them. It also rests on the small probability that if these vulnerabilities reach crisis proportions they will do so not individually, but simultaneously.[25]

Critics of these scenarios of reaction, reform, transformation, and instability have argued that each overlooks the ability of the current leadership to muddle through—to cope with existing problems incrementally, keeping them below the crisis stage. Moreover, they tend to overestimate the cohesion and strength of the alliance that would engineer the change, be it neo-Stalinists, technocrats, or social democrats. In fact, each hypothetical coalition appears to be too weak and too remote from the centers of power to replace the existing political leadership at the center. None of the imagined coalitions of interests, as best we can tell, constitutes a unified or cohesive alternative, for each appears to be deeply divided within itself by cross-cutting cleavages. And each of these scenarios underestimates the costs of change and the resulting strength of its opponents. A Stalinist reaction, for example, would cost the Soviet Union and the Party dearly; and "liberalization" that violates the implicit social contract with its people would seriously erode the legitimacy of Party rule.

In short, of these alternative futures, continuation of the present system with only tinkering reform may be the most likely. As Arthur Schlesinger, Jr. argues,

> The great bureaucracies of history, if permitted sufficient time, have often displayed a capacity for lumbering adaptation. Given a world without major war, given a Soviet economy without major crisis, given the imperative of a scientific age, a muddling evolution would seem more likely to this historian than stark confrontation and upheaval.[26]

Samuel P. Huntington has questioned the extent to which the vulnerabilities of the contemporary Soviet system pose serious threats to its stability: "None of the challenges which are identified for the future . . . appear to be qualitatively different from the challenges which the Soviet system has demonstrated the ability to deal with effectively in the past."[27] Seweryn Bialer also finds stability in the Soviet future. The sources of this stability, he argues, can be found in the performance of the Soviet regime as measured by the rise in living standards, in rising popular expectations that have tended to be material and modest, in the successful institutionalization of both popular political participation concerned with "low politics" and professional participation concerned with "high politics," and in the openness of social and political recruitment into elites and subelites that leads to high social and political mobility among social strata. All this underpins the legitimacy of the Soviet regime. The proponents of change are handicapped not only by this legitimacy but also, because change threatens instability, by the "fear of disorder and attachment to orderly society" among both elites and the broader populace. In this success of the Soviet regime and the weaknesses of its domestic opponents lies its long-term stability.[28]

NOTES

1. See David Lane, *Politics and Society in the USSR,* 2d ed. (London: Martin Robertson, 1978), 171–183. See also the debate in *The Soviet Union: Socialist or Social-Imperialist?* compiled by the editors of *The Communist* (Chicago: RCP Publications, 1983). For the Chinese variant of the theory of state capitalism, see Richard

Lowenthal, "The Degeneration of an Ideological Dispute," in Douglas T. Stuart and William T. Tow, eds., *China, the Soviet Union, and the West: Strategic and Political Dimensions in the 1980s* (Boulder, Colo.: Westview Press, 1982), 68.

2. Leon Trotsky, *The Revolution Betrayed* (London: Plough Press, 1957), 248–252. See also the discussion in David W. Lovell, *Trotsky's Analysis of Soviet Bureaucratization* (London: Croom Helm, 1985).

3. Walt W. Rostow, *The Stages of Economic Growth: A Non-Communist Manifesto* (Cambridge, England: Cambridge University Press, 1964), 164.

4. Harry Eckstein and David E. Apter, "Totalitarianism and Autocracy–Introduction," in Harry Eckstein and David E. Apter, eds., *Comparative Politics: A Reader* (New York: Free Press, 1963), 434.

5. Allen Kassof, "The Administered Society: Totalitarianism Without Terror," *World Politics* 16 (July 1964), 558, 562, 572.

6. Alfred G. Meyer, *The Soviet Political System: An Interpretation* (New York: Random House, 1965), 467.

7. Alfred G. Meyer, "USSR, Incorporated," in Donald W. Treadgold, ed., *The Development of the USSR: An Exchange of Views* (Seattle, Wash: University of Washington Press, 1964), 23.

8. T. H. Rigby, "Traditional, Market, and Organizational Societies and the USSR," *World Politics* 16 (July 1964), 544.

9. See, for example, Valerie Bunce, "The Political Economy of the Brezhnev Era: The Rise and Fall of Corporatism," *British Journal of Political Science* 13 (1983), 159–179.

10. P. J. D. Wiles, *The Political Economy of Communism* (Cambridge, Mass.: Harvard University Press, 1962), 48–49, 56–57, 63.

11. John Maynard, *The Russian Peasant and Other Studies* (New York: Collier Books, 1962), 11–12, 24–28.

12. George W. Breslauer, *Five Images of the Soviet Future: A Critical View and Synthesis* (Berkeley, Calif.: Institute of International Studies, University of California, 1978), 6.

13. On the attributes of models, see Karl W. Deutsch, *The Nerves of Government: Models of Political Communication and Control* (New York: Free Press, 1966), 8.

14. Marshall I. Goldman, *USSR in Crisis: The Failure of an Economic System* (New York: Norton, 1983), 181.

15. Quoted in "Moscow Faces the New Age", *Newsweek* 108 (August 18, 1986), 20.

16. Helene Carrere d'Encausse, *Decline of an Empire: The Soviet Socialist Republics in Revolt* (New York: Newsweek Books, 1979), 274.

17. Andrei Amalrik, *Will the Soviet Union Survive Until 1984?*, rev. ed. (New York: Harper and Row, 1980), 43. For a more modest view of the destabilizing potential of dissent, see Ludmilla Alexeyeva, *Soviet Dissent: Contemporary Movements for National, Religious, and Human Rights* (Middletown, Conn: Wesleyan University Press, 1985), 453, 455, 457.

18. See Amalrik's discussion of the impact of war with China in *Will the Soviet Union Survive Until 1984?*, 45–63.

19. Alfred G. Meyer, "Theories of Convergence," in Chalmers Johnson, ed., *Change in Communist Systems* (Stanford, Calif.: Stanford University Press, 1970), 313–341. See also Zbigniew K. Brzezinski and Samuel P. Huntington, *Political Power: USA/USSR* (New York: Viking Press, 1964), 419–436. A comparison of convergence and Marxism-Leninism appears in Jeffrey W. Hahn, "Is Developed Socialism a Soviet Version of Convergence?" in Jim Seroka and Maurice D. Simon, eds., *Developed Socialism in the Soviet Bloc: Political Theory and Political Reality* (Boulder, Colo.: Westview Press, 1982), 21–36.

20. Breslauer, 4; Merle Fainsod, "Roads to the Future," in Zbigniew K. Brzezinski, ed., *Dilemmas of Change in Soviet Politics* (New York: Columbia University Press, 1969), 134.

21. Zbigniew K. Brzezinski, "Concluding Remarks," in Brzezinski, ed., 154; Alexander Yanov, *Détente After Brezhnev* (Berkeley, Calif.: Institute of International Studies, 1977), chapters 3–4.

22. Amalrik, "Ideologies in Soviet Society," in Amalrik, 180–181.

23. Timothy J. Colton, *The Dilemma of Reform in the Soviet Union* (New York: Council on Foreign Relations, 1984).

24. Roy A. Medvedev, *On Socialist Democracy* (New York: Knopf, 1975).

25. Robert Conquest, "Immobilism and Decay", in Brzezinski, 71–72; Zbigniew K. Brzezinski, "The Soviet Political System: Transformation or Degeneration," in Brzezinski, ed., 30.

26. Arthur Schlesinger, Jr., "A Muddling Evolution," in Brzezinski, ed., 47–48.

27. Samuel P. Huntington, "Remarks on the Meanings of Stability in the Modern Era," in Seweryn Bialer and S. Sluzar, eds., *Radicalism in the Contemporary Age* (Boulder, Colo.: Westview Press, 1977), 3:277.

28. Seweryn Bialer, *Stalin's Successors: Leadership, Stability, and Change in the Soviet Union* (Cambridge, England: Cambridge University Press, 1980), 146, 148, 205.

Index